MICROSOFT®
OFFICE
EXPERT SOLUTIONS

MICROSOFT®
OFFICE
EXPERT SOLUTIONS

Conrad Carlberg, Ph.D.

with

Terry Allen	John Lacher	Sharon Podlin
Susan Daffron	Toni Messer	Brian Reilly
Shane Devenshire	Sue Mosher	Heidi Sullivan-Liscomb
Kathy Ivens	Susann Novalis	Diane Tinney
	Donna Payne	

Microsoft Office Expert Solutions

Library of Congress Catalog No.: 96-67569

ISBN: 0-7897-0391-2

98 97 96   6 5 4 3 2 1

Interpretation of the printing code: the rightmost double-digit number is the year of the book's printing; the rightmost single-digit number, the number of the book's printing. For example, a printing code of 96-1 shows that the first printing of the book occurred in 1996.

Credits

President
Roland Elgey

Vice President and Publisher
Marie Butler-Knight

Publishing Director
Brad R. Koch

Editorial Services Director
Elizabeth Keaffaber

Managing Editor
Michael Cunningham

Director of Marketing
Lynn E. Zingraf

Assistant Product Marketing Manager
Kim Margolius

Senior Series Editor
Chris Nelson

Acquisitions Editor
Deborah F. Abshier

Product Directors
Joyce J. Nielsen
Lorna Gentry

Production Editor
Lori A. Lyons

Editors
Lisa M. Gebken
Theresa Mathias
Rebecca Mounts
Lynn Northrup
Christine Prakel
Linda Seifert

Technical Editors
Kyle Bryant
Karl Hilsmann
Brad Lindaas

Technical Specialist
Nadeem Muhammed

Acquisitions Coordinator
Tracy Williams

Operations Coordinator
Patty Brooks

Editorial Assistant
Carmen Krikorian

Book Designer
Barbara Kordesh

Cover Designer
Barbara Kordesh

Production Team
Jason Carr
Chad Dressler
Joan Evan
Trey Frank
Amy Gornik
Jason Hand
Sonja Hart
Damon Jordan
Daryl Kessler
Clint Lahnen
Stephanie Layton
Laura Robbins
Bobbi Satterfield
Kelly Warner

Indexer
Brad Herriman

Composed in *Stone Serif* and *MCPdigital* by Que Corporation.

For Toni. With love.

—Conrad

Acknowledgments

I would like to acknowledge with thanks:

The staff and consultants at Que, who worked so hard to create this book in an unreasonable time frame—particularly Debbie Abshier, Joyce Nielsen, Lori Lyons, and Tom Barich.

My MVP comrades, the Microsoft Product Support Staff, and the participants on the Office online forums, for teaching me so much about these applications over the years.

The authors who contributed to this book, tolerated my occasional acerbity, and did not strangle me.

About the Authors

Conrad Carlberg is president of Network Control Systems, Inc., a software development and consulting firm that specializes in the statistical forecasting of data network usage. He holds a Ph.D. in statistics from the University of Colorado and is a three-time recipient of the Microsoft Excel Most Valuable Professional award.

Terry Allen has been in the computer industry for 16 years, and his previous clients have included Shell, Rolls-Royce, and NCR. Terry's work has encompassed traditional computer programming and writing technical publications and European R&D projects. He has developed a number of systems using WordBasic and has a special interest in all types of hypertext systems.

Terry now works for Communication Arts, based in Surrey, England, and specializes in constructing sophisticated Web sites on the Internet, primarily for clients in the media industry. The company develops systems based on PCs and Silicon Graphics hardware. He is also a Microsoft Word MVP and regularly contributes to the Microsoft forums on CompuServe. Terry has a degree in Mathematics and an MBA. He lives in Lindfield, a village in Sussex, England, with his veterinarian wife, two small children, and a very black dog.

He can be contacted via CompuServe, **#100031,3056**, or via the Internet at **terry@comarts.co.uk**. Terry looks after the Communication Arts Web site on **http://www.comarts.co.uk**.

Susan Daffron is a Word MVP and has been doing desktop publishing-related work since 1987. Susan and her husband own Logical Expressions, a company that specializes in technical writing, editing, design, and custom programming. Before starting her business, she worked in technical publications departments in the electronics, manufacturing, and publishing industries. Susan has a degree in English from Mount Holyoke College and writes on a variety of topics for desktop publishing magazines. She and her husband live in Carlsbad, California, with two cats who provide moral support during deadlines and computer-related crises. She can be reached at **74452.3616@compuserve.com**.

Shane Devenshire is an independent consultant specializing in project management, databases, graphics packages, and the scientific and business application of spreadsheets. He is a founding partner of the MAR&SHA Corporation, a computer consulting company providing application development, programming, and training in both the mainframe and personal computer areas. He has written over 240 computer-related articles for twenty journals here and abroad. He has been a guest editor for *PC World* magazine in 1994 and 1995 and has been on the product review board of *INFO World*. He has three years experience in the bio-tech arena, five years in business management, and 13 in computer-related industries. He coauthored *Excel Professional Techniques*, *Using 1-2-3 Release 4 for DOS*, and *Making Microsoft Office Work*.

Kathy Ivens has been a computer consultant since 1984, and teaches diverse computer courses at a variety of institutions. She has authored and coauthored a number of books on computer subjects. She is a frequent contributor to national magazines, writing articles and reviewing software.

Before becoming an expert in computing, Ms. Ivens spent many years as a television producer, where she had fun producing sports programs and was moderately amused producing news and entertainment programs. Preceding that career, she worked as a community organizer for social agencies in the Philadelphia, Pennsylvania area. She still doesn't know what she wants to be when she grows up.

She has three wonderful daughters and is married to a terrific (and lucky) man; none of them has ever figured out precisely what she does for a living.

John Lacher MBA, CPA, is a winner of the Microsoft Excel Most Valuable Professional award. He is the lead author of *VBA Database Solutions* from Que and is a contributing author to *Building Integrated Office Applications*. John is an independent consultant who provides Excel and Office training and development services to clients around the world via E-Mail and Data Conferencing. He has over 20 years experience as a developer of computer applications and as a manager in both technical and executive functions. He can be reached on CompuServe at **73447,2431** or over the Internet at **73447.2431@compuserve.com**.

Toni Messer is an independent consultant with over 20 years experience in the computer and telecommunications industries. As a salesperson, sales trainer, and manager, she delivered hundreds of presentations to business groups and individuals. She holds a Bachelor of Arts degree in English and is working toward a degree in Graphic Design and Illustration.

Sue Mosher is an independent Windows consultant in Arlington, Virginia, just outside Washington, DC. She was named a Microsoft MVP in 1994 in recognition of her technical expertise and ability to help people make the most of Windows. Her company, Slipstick Systems, provides a variety of Windows-related services, including database analysis and development, Windows networking, and Windows Help file authoring. She is also a contributing editor of the *Inside Windows: Networking Edition* newsletter. Before starting her own business, she was a broadcast journalist and software developer for The Associated Press for 15 years. She also played rock 'n' roll on the radio as a disc jockey in her younger days.

Susann Novalis, Ph.D., is a Professor of Mathematics and Associate Dean of the College of Science and Engineering at San Francisco State University. With degrees in mechanical engineering and aeronautical science, she has more than 20 years experience teaching applied mathematics at all university levels. Her administrative work has provided a dozen years experience with computer database management systems. The release of Microsoft Access at the end of 1992 was the beginning of intense involvement in application development and computer training with Access. While maintaining a full-time administrative position, Dr. Novalis teaches and creates training materials for Access classes at the university and has published articles in *Access/Visual Basic Advisor*. She is the author of *Automating Access Databases With Macros*, Sybex, Inc. 1996, and is a contributing author of Que's *Special Edition Using Access for Windows 95*, by Roger Jennings. You may contract her via CompuServe, **73312,3437**, or the Internet, **novalis@sfsu.edu**.

Donna Payne is a computer consultant based in Seattle, Washington. She is a Microsoft Excel MVP on CompuServe and is a Microsoft Certified Excel and Visual Basic for Applications Trainer. Donna has developed custom applications for international technology-based firms and has performed consulting services to Microsoft and Northern Telecom. She is the originator of a networking group for women programmers. Donna can be reached via CompuServe at **73573.500@compuserve.com**.

Sharon Podlin is a graduate of the University of Texas and is president of PTSI, a consulting firm specializing in the development and presentation of computer training courses. Sharon has over 15 years in the industry and has worked primarily with Fortune 100 companies, including J. C. Penney, Hyatt International Hotels, and United Airlines. She actively participates in the Microsoft Certified Professional program as well as being a Microsoft Certified Trainer for a wide range of products, including Microsoft SQL Server, Excel, Visual Basic for Applications, and Window NT. She can be reached via CompuServe at **76350,1424**.

Brian Reilly is a partner in Singer and Reilly Enterprise in New York City, which is a company that designs custom applications for corporate communication management. His background in consumer products management has convinced him of the need to be able to suppress unwanted information and graphically show only actionable information with instantly understandable graphics. Brian holds a BA in Communications from Fordham and an MBA from Columbia. An avid sailor of the Northeastern waters, he appreciates the difference between a datasheet and a spinnaker sheet. He can be reached on CompuServe at **75663,3456**.

Heidi Sullivan-Liscomb is a consulting technical writer who got her start working as an intern for MapInfo Corporation in Troy, New York. During her time there, she was fortunate enough to participate in writing the documentation for both their Macintosh and Windows products. Heidi graduated Magna Cum Laude with a degree in English Literature and intends to continue writing.

Diane Tinney is proprietor of The Software Professional, a business that provides education, development support, and consulting on a variety of Windows 3.x, Windows 95, and Windows NT applications. Diane specializes in the integration of Windows products, specifically, database design and implementation. Diane is the author of Que's *Paradox for Windows Programming By Example,* and is a contributing author to Que's *Killer dBase 5.0 for Windows, Using Microsoft Office for Windows, Using Paradox for Windows, Using Microsoft Office 95,* and *Installing and Configuring Windows 95.* You can reach Diane via Internet at **Dtinney@warwick.net**.

We'd Like to Hear from You!

As part of our continuing effort to produce books of the highest possible quality, Que would like to hear your comments. To stay competitive, we *really* want you, as a computer book reader and user, to let us know what you like or dislike most about this book or other Que products.

You can mail comments, ideas, or suggestions for improving future editions to the address below, or send us a fax at (317) 581-4663. For the online inclined, Macmillan Computer Publishing has a forum on CompuServe (type **GO QUEBOOKS** at any prompt) through which our staff and authors are available for questions and comments. The address of our Internet site is **http://www.mcp.com** (World Wide Web).

In addition to exploring our forum, please feel free to contact me personally to discuss your opinions of this book: I'm **75703,3251** on CompuServe, and I'm **lgentry@que.mcp.com** on the Internet.

Thanks in advance—your comments will help us to continue publishing the best books available on computer topics in today's market.

Lorna Gentry
Product Director
Que Corporation
201 W. 103rd Street
Indianapolis, Indiana 46290
USA

Contents at a Glance

Contents

3   Advanced Array Formulas   55

4   User-Defined Functions   75

8   Word Macros   185

9   Word Styles   221

15   Customizing PowerPoint   381

IV   Access   399

16   Critical Skills in Access   401

17   Understanding Relational Databases   443

18   Advanced Queries   475

19 Understanding the Data Languages in Access 517

20 Getting Started with Access Programming 555

V Schedule+   601

21 Critical Skills in Schedule+   603

22 Exchanging Information Using Schedule+   637

VI Exchange   697

25 Installing and Configuring Exchange   699

VII Integration   817

28 Critical Skills for Integrating Applications   819

Introduction

Welcome to *Microsoft Office Expert Solutions*! This book is intended as a follow-up and extension to *Special Edition Using Microsoft Office for Windows 95*, also from Que. If you have read that book—or, if you already know the basics and want to take your knowledge of the Microsoft Office suite to the next level—*Microsoft Office Expert Solutions* is your source.

No one person has the time or work experience to develop the degree of in-depth knowledge of all the Office programs needed for a book of this sort. Therefore, Que has assembled a team of working professionals to write about the Office suite. Each contributor has extensive background in one or more of these Windows 95 applications:

- ▶ *Excel*, the spreadsheet program
- ▶ *Word*, the word processor
- ▶ *PowerPoint*, the presentation manager
- ▶ *Access*, the database management system
- ▶ *Schedule+*, the personal information and task manager

As a bonus, *Microsoft Office Expert Solutions* also contains a section on Exchange, the Windows 95 application that helps you manage electronic mail, faxes, and file transfers.

You can find information about each contributor's credentials in *About the Authors*, in the front matter of this book.

How This Book Is Organized

Microsoft Office Expert Solutions is structured around these applications, with several chapters devoted to each one. In addition, you'll find several chapters that show you advanced techniques to integrate the capabilities of the programs. For example, Chapter 30, "Integrating Excel and Access," gives you the tools and concepts you need to take advantage of Data Access Objects, and use them to streamline the flow of information between Excel and Access.

▶ Part I, "Excel," covers advanced charting techniques, advanced array formulas, writing user-defined functions, creating customized applications, and optimizing VBA code.

▶ Part II, "Word," shows you how to create and use macros in Word, how to speed up your work with style sheets, how to customize your workspace, and how to use new Word Version 7 capabilities to do desktop publishing.

▶ Part III, "PowerPoint," discusses the considerations involved in moving a presentation across electronic networks to other users, printers, and service bureaus. Part III also includes how to create electronic presentations and customize PowerPoint so that it works most efficiently for you.

▶ Part IV, "Access," introduces you to the power of relational databases, shows you how to create advanced database queries, gets you going in Structured Query Language (SQL), and demonstrates how to use VBA to create your own Access applications.

▶ Part V, "Schedule+," covers managing Schedule+ files, converting your data from other personal information managers, permitting other users to access your schedule, and maintaining security when you have given those permissions to other users.

▶ Part VI, "Exchange," solves the mysteries of configuring Exchange and its different services, and shows you how to manage faxes and e-mail most efficiently.

▶ Part VII, "Integration," gives you the techniques needed to make the Office applications work together. Excel and Word, Excel and Access, Excel and PowerPoint, Word and Access, Word and PowerPoint, and Schedule+ and Exchange are covered here.

The Companion CD

Microsoft Office Expert Solutions comes with a companion CD that contains all the data files and coding examples used in the book. You can find the documents shown in nearly all the book's figures on the CD (the exceptions are figures that show such items as built-in dialog boxes and help windows).

In addition, the companion CD contains Coding Gems and other software that extend the capabilities of the applications in the Office Suite. For example, you'll find the function calls (and their arguments) included in the Windows 32-bit Applications Programming Interface (API) on the CD.

You can find more information about the contents of the CD, including installation instructions, in the appendix.

Getting Up to Speed

Microsoft Office Expert Solutions is written for people who have some, but perhaps not extensive, knowledge of the applications in the Office suite. Therefore, this book assumes that the reader has mastered the basics of each one. Certain skills are necessary, however, to get the most benefit from each section in the book—skills that you might not have acquired as yet or that bear some review.

Each section begins with a chapter on the critical skills involved in each application. The skills discussed in these chapters are not first-time-user basic, but provide information about techniques you will need in order to master the subject matter in subsequent chapters. For example, Chapter 1, "Critical Skills in Excel," discusses topics such as the Excel model as it applies to Visual Basic for Applications (VBA). You need some familiarity with the interplay of objects, methods, and properties in order to benefit from the chapters on advanced charting techniques, writing your own custom functions, and optimizing your VBA code.

Most of the Critical Skills chapters focus on techniques for using the application itself. There is one exception: Chapter 12, "Critical Skills for Presentations," focuses on preparing and delivering a presentation. If you are to deliver a presentation to an audience, you need to appreciate that you—not your slides—are the star of the show. Although PowerPoint is an exceptionally strong tool for creating your slides and overheads, it can't control such critical elements as the organization of your presentation, your demeanor, your vocal style, and the way you arrange information on the slides. But these are the elements that make or break your presentation, and you will find useful suggestions about them in Chapter 12.

Conventions Used in This Book

Microsoft Office Expert Solutions uses a few conventions to make its instructions clearer.

Something that you are intended to type is shown in **boldface**. For example: "Enter the formula **=SUM(IF(A1:A20="Northwest",B1:B20,0))** in cell D1."

VBA code statements are shown in a slightly smaller, monospace typeface. For example:

```
Function CubeRoot(InputNumber As Double) As Double
```

Keywords and variable names from VBA statements that are discussed further in the text are shown in monospace italic. For example, "*InputNumber* is passed to the function when you enter **=CubeRoot(8)** on the worksheet."

Special terms, when they are first introduced, are shown in italic. For example: "The term *template* may be familiar if you've used desktop publishing (DTP) applications before."

All Microsoft Office applications have menus and menu items. Each menu and each menu item has a "hot key," or "accelerator," associated with it. And most Office dialog boxes have hot keys associated with their buttons and boxes. *Microsoft Office Expert Solutions* indicates a hot key in this way:

Choose <u>T</u>ools, <u>O</u>ptions, and check the Tip Wi<u>z</u>ard check box to disable it.

Brief tips that help you use an application more quickly or efficiently are set off like this:

 Tip

You can use hot keys to speed up your interaction with an application—they're often faster than using the mouse pointer. And, if your mouse suddenly quits working, you'll need them. To use a hot key, press and hold down the Alt key, and then press the hot key.

Additional information that helps you make a decision appears like this:

 Note

If you want to use two hot keys in a row (as in <u>F</u>ile, <u>O</u>pen), release the Alt key after you press F, and then press O. Or, you can continue to hold down the Alt key after you press F and as you press O. If your sequence is Alt+F, then Alt+O, the application switches from the <u>F</u>ile menu to the F<u>o</u>rmat menu.

If an action or a sequence is likely to result in an undesirable outcome, you'll see a warning shown like this:

 Caution

Although it's convenient, Datasheet view in Access can lead to problems in the long run. A field's data type will be wrong if the data you initially enter isn't a good example of the information you need to store in the field.

Enough introductory material. Let's move on to the good stuff, starting with Excel.

Excel

Critical Skills in Excel

by Conrad Carlberg

In this chapter

◆ **Using Array Formulas**
Learn how to enter array formulas, when to use them, and how to edit them.

◆ **Recording and Editing Macros**
Use the macro recorder to give you a head start with your VBA code.

◆ **Using Objects, Methods, and Properties**
Distinguish among objects, methods, and properties, and get help on which elements go with which.

◆ **Making VBA Declarations**
Learn the ins and outs of declaring subroutines, functions, variables, and arrays.

You might use Excel productively for a long time—months, even years—without encountering some of the features that can make your work faster and easier. Three of those features are charting techniques, array formulas, and Visual Basic for Applications (VBA). The first section of *Microsoft Office Expert Solutions*, covering Chapters 1 through 6, goes into detail about these tasks:

▶ Applying special charting techniques

▶ Using Excel's array formulas to your best advantage

▶ Getting VBA to do the repetitive work, freeing you to do the creative work

If you have read Que's *Special Edition Using Microsoft Office for Windows 95*, you have learned how to create charts in Excel, how to enter an array formula, and how to record and write some basic VBA code. Chapters 2 through 6 of *Microsoft Office Expert Solutions* go into much greater depth on these topics. This chapter discusses several skills and concepts you need to know to take advantage of the material in Chapters 2 through 6.

Using Array Formulas

As you may know, an *array* is a set of values arranged in a particular way. An array could consist of values arranged in a row, in a column, or in rows and columns. Although it is often useful to think of an array in terms of rows and columns, it's important to realize that an array does not necessarily exist in a worksheet range. An array might exist only in your computer's memory, if you're processing it with VBA. An array can also exist in a single cell on a worksheet, even though you can't see it directly.

In Excel, an *array formula* is a worksheet formula that contains an array. In many cases, you begin by selecting several contiguous worksheet cells. Then you type *one* formula. Finally, instead of pressing Enter, you press the key combination Ctrl+Shift+Enter. When you take these steps, you *array-enter* a formula.

After you have made your entry, your formula appears in the formula bar surrounded by curly braces, like this example:

    {=TRANSPOSE(A1:B10)}

The TRANSPOSE() worksheet function reorients a range of data by 90 degrees. In figure 1.1, notice that the values in cells A12:J13 are, although reoriented, the same as those in A1:B10.

Fig. 1.1

Array formulas often occupy a range of worksheet cells.

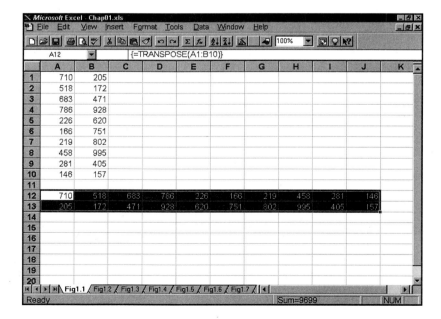

> **Note**
>
> As with virtually all the figures in *Microsoft Office Expert Solutions*, you can find the worksheet illustrated in figure 1.1 on the companion CD. Open the file named CHAP01.XLS and select the worksheet named Fig1.1.

To enter an array formula, you do *not* type the curly braces yourself. If you do, Excel interprets the formula as a text entry rather than as a formula. The key combination Ctrl+Shift+Enter causes the curly braces to appear.

Understanding Why You Use Array Formulas

Array formulas often are entered in a single cell (see fig. 1.2).

Fig. 1.2

You can use array formulas to display arrays and to summarize them.

	A	B	C	D	E
1	Product	Units Sold	Unit Price	Product Revenue	
2	A	5	$1	$5	
3	B	10	$2	$20	
4	C	1	$5	$5	
5	D	20	$2	$40	
6					
7			Total	$70	
8					
9				$5	
10				$20	
11				$5	
12				$40	
13					
14				$70	

*D14 = {=SUM(B2:B5*C2:C5)}*

In figure 1.2, cell D2 contains the formula =B2*C2, D3 contains =B3*C3, and so on. You can obtain the same results by selecting cells D9:D12 and array-entering this formula:

```
=B2:B5*C2:C5
```

(From now on, the array formulas shown in the text will omit the curly braces, to avoid suggesting that you should type them yourself.)

This array formula returns the product of two ranges—B2:B5 and C2:C5. This technique is handy because you need to enter the formula only one time, rather than four times as in D2:D5.

You can do better yet. Cell D14 contains this array formula:

```
=SUM(B2:B5*C2:C5)
```

This formula encloses the result of the multiplication of the original two ranges within the SUM() function. The result, of course, is the total of the product of Unit Price and Units Sold.

Now consider this array formula:

```
=SUM(IF(A1:A20="Northwest",B1:B20,0))
```

This array formula creates a conditional sum. Wherever the value "Northwest" appears in A1:A20, the array formula adds the corresponding value in B1:B20. If some other value is in A1:A20, the array formula adds zero. See figure 1.3, which shows the result of this array formula in cell D1.

Fig. 1.3

Array formulas enable you to get results that would otherwise require a macro.

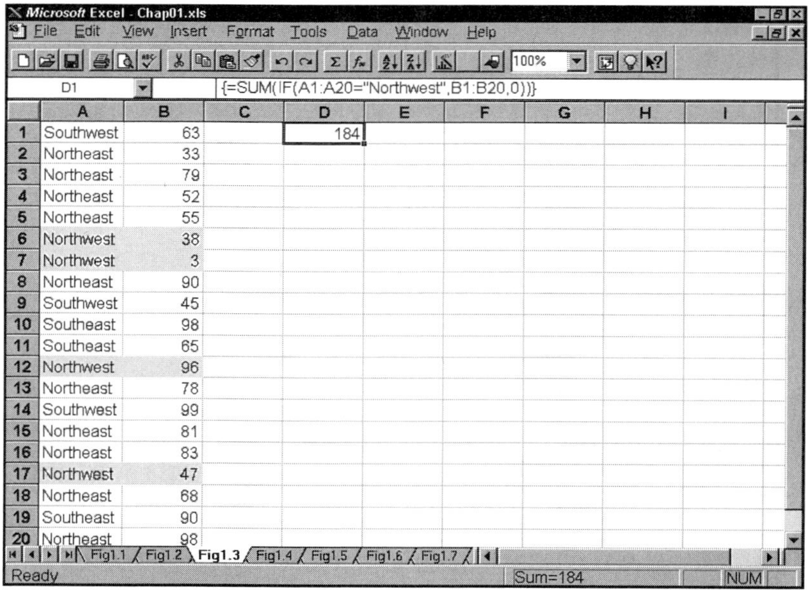

	A	B	C	D	E	F	G	H	I
1	Southwest	63		184					
2	Northeast	33							
3	Northeast	79							
4	Northeast	52							
5	Northeast	55							
6	Northwest	38							
7	Northwest	3							
8	Northeast	90							
9	Southwest	45							
10	Southeast	98							
11	Southeast	65							
12	Northwest	96							
13	Northeast	78							
14	Southwest	99							
15	Northeast	81							
16	Northeast	83							
17	Northwest	47							
18	Northeast	68							
19	Southeast	90							
20	Northeast	98							

D1 {=SUM(IF(A1:A20="Northwest",B1:B20,0))}

If Excel did not offer the array formula capability, you would need to write a macro to look at the values in A1:A20, one by one, and total the values in B1:B20 when the logical condition is met. By using the array formula, you don't need a macro. As a bonus, the array formula's result automatically recalculates if you change any of the pertinent values in A1:B20, just as a standard, single-value formula does.

Editing and Deleting Array Formulas

Several of Excel's built-in functions *require* that you enter them as array formulas. For example, the FREQUENCY() function counts the number of values in one range that fall between values in another range (see fig. 1.4).

Fig. 1.4

To see all the results of the FREQUENCY() *function, you must first select a range of cells and array-enter the function.*

	A	B	C	D	E	F	G	H	I
1	Student	Grade	Bin		Range	Frequency			
2	1	95	60		0-60	1			
3	2	81	70		61-70	7			
4	3	74	80		71-80	4			
5	4	63	90		81-90	3			
6	5	69	100		91-100	5			
7	6	78							
8	7	84							
9	8	94							
10	9	100							
11	10	64							
12	11	75							
13	12	95							
14	13	67							
15	14	68							
16	15	70							
17	16	60							
18	17	88							
19	18	94							
20	19	71							
21	20	68							

F2 `{=FREQUENCY(B2:B21,C2:C6)}`

The FREQUENCY() function shown in figure 1.4 is array-entered in cells F2:F6. For the results to appear in each of the five cells, you must begin by selecting the full range, F2:F6. Similarly, to delete the array formula, you must select the full range before pressing the Delete key. Otherwise, Excel returns the error message Cannot change part of an array.

> **Tip**
> To select the full range of cells occupied by an array formula, begin by selecting one of the cells. Then press Ctrl+/.

Although you first must select the entire array formula range to delete it, you do not need to do so in order to edit the formula. Suppose that you want to change the array formula in cells F2:F6 of figure 1.4 so that its first argument is B2:B20 rather than B2:B21:

=FREQUENCY(B2:B20,C2:C6)

Select any cell in F2:F6. In the formula bar, change the reference from B21 to B20. Then press Ctrl+Shift+Enter, just as you do when you originally enter the array formula. Excel makes the change you entered in all cells occupied by the array formula.

α Note

You receive the `Cannot change part of an array` message if you try to enter a value or formula in one cell that's already part of a multiple-cell array formula. This problem is easy enough to avoid when you enter information on a single worksheet. If you enter a formula in a 3D range, however, you may not immediately see what has happened.

Suppose that you have an array formula on Sheet2 in cells A1:C1. With Sheet1 active, you Shift+click Sheet4's tab, thus selecting Sheet1:Sheet4. You then enter the value 6 in cell B1 on Sheet1, which attempts to overwrite the array formula in A1:C1 on Sheet2. You receive the `Cannot change part of an array` message.

The topics covered in this section—the rationale for array formulas and entering, deleting, and editing them—are the basis for the material you will find in Chapter 3, "Advanced Array Formulas." You also learn how to write functions that return arrays to the worksheet in Chapter 4, "User-Defined Functions."

Recording and Editing Macros

Perhaps the best way to become familiar with VBA is to use the macro recorder. After starting the recorder, you carry out an action, or sequence of actions, in any workbook sheet. Subsequently, you can examine the VBA code that Excel creates and infer how the code is related to the actions you took.

Automating Repetitive Tasks

The macro recorder is a useful way to create the basis for a macro that you expect to use repeatedly. In practice, the recorder can usually create only the basis for such a tool. Suppose that you want a macro that will automatically assign a Currency format to a range of cells, color the cells light blue, and put a border around the range. You start the recorder, carry out the actions, stop the recorder, and examine the VBA code. You find that the VBA code refers specifically to the range that was selected when you applied the formatting (see figs. 1.5 and 1.6).

Fig. 1.5
Cells A1:A10 are formatted as Currency, light blue, and bordered.

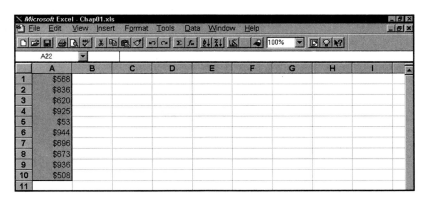

Fig. 1.6
The macro recorder created this code when the formatting in figure 1.5 was applied.

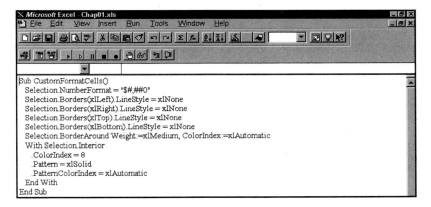

As it stands, this macro has very limited value because it sets the format characteristics of only the cells that are selected when the macro runs. To make the macro more general, so you can format any range of cells, you need to make some changes to it. This process is discussed in the following section, "Generalizing Specific Statements."

To create the macro shown in figure 1.6, follow these steps:

1. On a worksheet, select cells A1:A10.

2. Choose Tools, Record Macro, Record New Macro.

3. In the Record New Macro dialog box, type **CustomFormatCells** in the Macro Name edit box. Then choose OK.

4. Choose Format, Cells. On the Number tab, choose the Currency format and set the Decimal Places to zero.

5. Click the Patterns tab. In the Color box, choose the light blue color at the far right end of the first row.

6. Click the Border tab. Click the <u>O</u>utline box and click the third Style box in the left column. Then choose OK.

7. Choose <u>T</u>ools, <u>R</u>ecord Macro, <u>S</u>top Recording (or click the Stop Recorder button, which appears in its own toolbar when you start the recorder).

If you want to verify that the macro works as expected, select a range of cells. Choose <u>T</u>ools, <u>M</u>acro, and select CustomFormatCells in the <u>M</u>acro Name/Reference list box. Then choose <u>R</u>un. The cells you selected have the same formatting characteristics as the A1:A10 range.

Generalizing Specific Statements

Suppose that you record a macro as just described. When you run the macro, it carries out exactly the same actions you took when you recorded it. Although this procedure is helpful in a learning sense, you cannot use the macro in even a slightly different context without editing it.

For example, you create a chart with one data series. You then select the data series and record a macro that formats the data series according to your specifications. If you subsequently want to use that macro to format *more than one* data series on a given chart, you must either run the macro once for each series on the chart, or modify the macro to format all the data series.

Furthermore, when you carry out the actions recorded by the macro, you often select different objects in your workbook and then make changes to them. For example, when you format a data series in a chart, you first select the data series and then apply the formats you want.

VBA enables you to change properties or apply methods to workbook objects without selecting them. Therefore, you may not need to cause the macro code to select an object and then modify it—this step just slows down the execution of the code. You frequently want to modify the recorded code to take action on an object directly, without actually selecting it first.

 Tip

If you have used the Excel 4 macro language extensively but don't yet have experience with VBA, you are probably in the habit of selecting objects before modifying them. Keep in mind that this Excel 4 requirement does not hold in VBA.

Suppose that you have entered the data shown in A1:B6 of figure 1.7.

Fig. 1.7

A VBA macro is a convenient way to enter formulas and to format cells C2:C6.

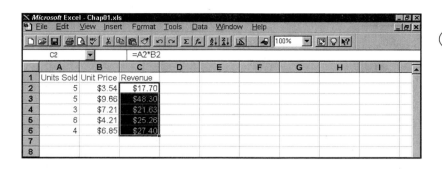

You now start the macro recorder and take the following actions:

1. In C2, enter the formula **=A1*B1**.

2. Select C2, and using the cell's fill handle (the small box in the cell's lower right corner), drag it down through C3:C6.

3. With C2:C6 still selected, choose Format, Cells. Click the Number tab, choose the Currency format, and choose OK.

4. Stop the macro recorder.

Here's the code that the macro recorder creates:

```
Sub CalculateRevenue()
    Range("C2").Select
    ActiveCell.FormulaR1C1 = "=RC[-2]*RC[-1]"
    Range("C2").Select
    Selection.AutoFill Destination:=Range("C2:C6"), Type:=xlFillDefault
    Range("C2:C6").Select
    Selection.NumberFormat = "$#,##0.00"
End Sub
```

Now you want to revise this code so it doesn't select particular cells. In other words, you want to generalize the code so the action it takes depends on whatever cell is active when you run the code. Also, you want to speed up the macro so it doesn't select three different ranges as it executes (C2 twice and C2:C6 once).

Suppose that you want to make the first numeric cell in the Unit Price column active, and then run the macro so it fills the five cells to the right and below the active cell. In other words, if cell C11 is active when you start the macro, it fills cells D11:D15. You can change the macro as follows:

```
Sub RevisedCalculateRevenue()
    Selection.Offset(0, 1).Resize(5, 1).FormulaR1C1 = "=RC[-2]*RC[-1]"
    Selection.Offset(0, 1).Resize(5, 1).NumberFormat = "$#,##0.00"
End Sub
```

The important revision is the replacement of the several Select statements by two statements that depend on the active cell. The active cell is identified by the Selection object.

That active cell—regardless of its actual location on the worksheet—has an Offset range. In this example, the Offset is zero rows below and one column to the right of the active cell. So if C11 is the active selection, the Offset returns cell D11 (zero rows below, one column to the right).

You can expand the reference to cell D11, the Offset, by using the Resize method. In this example, the arguments to the Resize method specify that VBA should expand the range D11 to a range reference five rows high and one column wide. The offset and resized reference is now D11:D15.

Finally, you enter a formula that employs relative references in D11:D15. The formula returns the product of the value two columns to the left (and in the same row) times the value one column to the left (and in the same row). In the case of D11, the formula placed in the cell is

```
=B11*C11
```

Notice that you accomplish two enhancements by revising the macro recorder's code:

▶ *The macro is generalized*, so it acts on a range that's defined by the active cell, instead of acting only on cell C2 and the range C2:C6.

▶ *The macro is made more efficient*. VBA doesn't need to select any cells before placing the formulas and setting the formats.

Using Objects, Methods, and Properties

Before you can take full advantage of VBA, you need to have a feel for three aspects of Excel: objects, methods, and properties. You use VBA to manipulate objects by calling their methods and changing their properties. For example:

▶ A worksheet is an object.

▶ When you activate a worksheet, you do so by calling its Activate method.

▶ When you change the worksheet's name—the label that appears on its sheet tab—you do so by setting the worksheet's Name property.

An object such as a worksheet has a variety of methods and a variety of properties associated with it. The easiest way to determine the methods you can use on an object, and the properties you can set, is to use Excel's online help.

In practice, you seldom want a laundry list of the methods or properties that apply to a given object. More often, you know that you want to set a property of the object or call a method of the object. In that case, you need to know the property's name or the method's name.

Suppose that you want to learn how to use VBA to set a dialog box button's *hot key*—the key that, combined with the Alt key, substitutes for clicking the button. Take these steps:

1. Choose <u>H</u>elp, Microsoft Excel <u>H</u>elp Topics.

2. Click the Help dialog box's Index tab. In the first edit box, type **Button object** and choose <u>D</u>isplay.

 Tip

Another way to get help on an object, property, or method, is to type a word such as **Button** on a module sheet, highlight it, and press F1.

---

3. The help window shown in figure 1.8 appears. Notice the Properties and Methods items near the top of the window.

4. Click Properties to see a list box of properties associated with the button object, and click Methods to see a list box of associated methods.

Fig. 1.8

Online help for an object gives you access to its associated properties and methods.

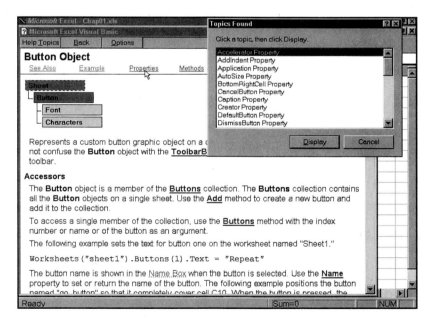

In the Properties list box, you find an Accelerator property, and you infer (correctly) that this is the property for the button's hot key. If you want to make sure of the Accelerator property's syntax, you can select it in the list box and choose <u>D</u>isplay.

Many objects in Excel belong to *collections*. Suppose that you have 16 worksheets in a workbook. Each worksheet belongs to the collection of Worksheets. When you want to use VBA to activate a particular worksheet, you must tell VBA which worksheet you want to activate. Do so by specifying the worksheet's index number or a text string with the worksheet's name. For example:

```
Worksheets(1).Activate
```

or

```
Worksheets("Sheet1").Activate
```

If Sheet1 is the first worksheet in the workbook, the first statement makes Sheet1 the active sheet. The second statement would make Sheet1 active regardless of its location in the workbook.

Be aware of a few special properties of the Application object. (Excel is itself an object; when you run VBA from within Excel, Excel is the Application object.) You can use Excel's ActiveWorkbook property to refer to the workbook that is active when the statement executes:

```
WorkbookToSave = ActiveWorkbook.Name
```

This statement places the name of the active workbook in the variable *WorkbookToSave*.

At times, you may need to refer to the workbook that contains your VBA code when another workbook is active. For example, you may need to disable an option button on a dialog sheet in the workbook that contains your VBA code, but BOOK1.XLS is the active workbook. In that case, use the ThisWorkbook property:

```
ThisWorkbook.DialogSheets("Dialog1").OptionButtons(1).Enabled = False
```

Using the Object Browser

As you gain experience using VBA, you will learn what methods and properties are associated with a particular object. In addition to using online help, a good way to look up those methods and properties is with the Object Browser.

Suppose that you have created a dialog box and want to initialize the value of the first edit box to 95. You begin by using this statement:

```
ThisWorkbook.DialogSheets("Dialog1").EditBoxes(1).Value = 95
```

But when you run the code, it terminates with an error at this statement. The error message states that EditBox does not have Value property.

What do you do? If an edit box doesn't have that property, how can you set its value? Start with the Object Browser. Choose View, Object Browser or click the Object Browser button on the Visual Basic toolbar. The Object Browser appears, as shown in figure 1.9. Select Excel in the Libraries/Workbooks drop-down.

Fig. 1.9
*Use the Object Browser
to find out what
properties and methods
apply to a given object.*

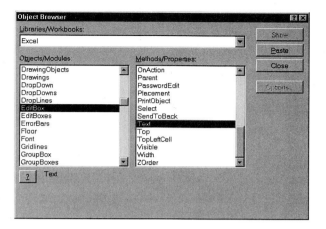

When you look up the EditBox object in the Object Browser, you find that the closest
you can come to a Value property for the object is Text. So you modify your VBA statement this way:

```
ThisWorkbook.DialogSheets("Dialog1").EditBoxes(1).Text = 95
```

As it happens, this statement works.

The Object Browser is also a good tool for finding methods and properties that belong
not to Excel, but to VBA. For example, Excel has a square root function:

```
=SQRT(9)
```

In most cases, you can call an Excel worksheet function in your VBA code by referencing
the Application object (remember, when you're running VBA in Excel, Excel itself is the
Application object). For example:

```
Result = Application.Odd(4)
```

This statement would store the value 5 in Result: the Odd function returns the next higher
odd integer. But now consider this example:

```
Result = Application.Sqrt(9)
```

If you use this statement, you get the error message Object doesn't support this property
or method.

Why? VBA supplies its own square root function, Sqr, and doesn't recognize the
worksheet function SQRT(). Instead of trying to use Application.Sqrt, use this statement:

```
Result = Sqr(9)
```

You can find this information by starting the Object Browser and selecting VBA in the
Libraries/Workbooks drop-down, as shown in figure 1.10.

Fig. 1.10
*The Object Browser
also shows you what
methods and properties
are available from
VBA.*

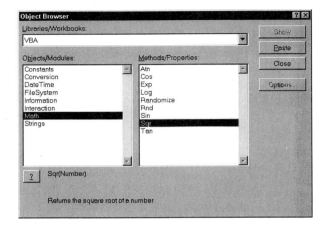

 Tip

You can use the Object Browser to go quickly to a VBA procedure you have written. With the workbook containing the subroutine open (but not necessarily active), start the Object Browser. Select your workbook in the Libraries/Workbooks drop-down, your module in the Objects/Modules list box, and the subroutine in the Methods/Properties list box. Then choose Show to go directly to the procedure.

Looping through Objects in a Collection: The *For* Loop

If you have done any programming in a language such as BASIC, Pascal, FORTRAN, or C, you have come across the concept of loops. A *loop* is a structure in a program that executes repeatedly until some condition is met.

VBA supports loops of various kinds. Here's an example of a For...Next loop:

```
Total = 0
For i = 1 to 10
   Total = Total + Cells(i,1)
Next i
```

This snippet of code begins by assigning a value of zero to the variable *Total*. The code then adds to *Total* the value in each cell from A1 to A10. (The loop increases the value of the variable *i* from 1 to 2, then from 2 to 3, 3 to 4, and so on until the value reaches 10). When *i* equals 1, this expression evaluates to Cells(1,1), or cell A1:

```
Cells(i,1)
```

When *i* equals 2, `Cells(i,1)` evaluates as `Cells(2,1)`, or cell A2. The tenth time through the loop, *i* reaches the limit specified by the `For` statement, so the loop terminates. The variable `Total` now contains the sum of the values in A1:A10.

Another type of loop in VBA is called a `For Each` loop, which often is used to cycle through all the objects that belong to a parent object.

For example, suppose that you suspect that a workbook contains some VBA modules hidden from your view. Assuming that the workbook's structure is not password protected, you could use this code to make all its sheets—worksheets, charts, dialogs or modules—visible:

```
Sub ShowHiddenSheets
Dim SheetCount As Integer
Dim i as Integer
SheetCount = ActiveWorkbook.Sheets.Count
For i = 1 to SheetCount
    ActiveWorkbook.Sheets(i).Visible = True
Next i
End Sub
```

By using a `For Each` loop, you can simplify the code a little:

```
Sub ShowHiddenSheets
Dim SheetInBook As Variant
For Each SheetInBook In ActiveWorkbook.Sheets
    SheetInBook.Visible = True
Next SheetInBook
End Sub
```

When VBA encounters this `For Each` statement, it looks to the collection of sheets in the active workbook. VBA then causes the *Variant* variable `SheetInBook` to represent each of the sheets in turn. Within the `For Each` loop, the Visible property of the current sheet is set to True. (See "Declaring Variables" later in this chapter for information about *Variant* variables.)

This loop relieves you of the responsibility of counting the number of sheets in the active workbook and using that number as the ending value in a standard `For...Next` loop. You also can use the *Variant* variable to stand in for the object in question—here, sheets—and thus to take on any properties such as Visible that belong to the object.

Usually, when you assign an object to a variable, you have declared that variable as the object's type. But when you use a `For Each` loop, you must declare its control variable as *Variant*.

Of course, the applicability of `For Each` is not limited to sheets in workbooks. You can use `For Each` to cycle through the data series in a chart:

```
Dim SeriesInChart As Variant
For Each SeriesInChart In ActiveChart.SeriesCollection
   SeriesInChart.Border.Weight = xlThin
Next SeriesInChart
```

You also can use For Each to cycle through each edit box in a dialog sheet:

```
Dim EB As Variant
For Each EB In ThisWorkbook.DialogSheets("Dialog1").EditBoxes
   EB.Text = ""
Next EB
```

More generally, you can use a For Each loop to cycle through any set of objects in a collection.

Making VBA Declarations

As with most programming languages, your code must *declare* certain structures before you can use them. To declare a structure is to inform VBA of its existence, its name, and its important characteristics.

For example, you might write a VBA subroutine that automates the creation of a pivot table. The first statement in the subroutine declares the structure. The declaration can be (and frequently is) as simple as this:

```
Sub MakePivotTable()
```

The first word, Sub, tells VBA that the statement is declaring a subroutine. The next word, MakePivotTable, is the subroutine's name. The empty parentheses indicate that the subroutine receives no arguments. (VBA adds the parentheses on your behalf if you don't want to type them.) If the subroutine were to receive arguments, their names would appear within the parentheses. See the following section, "Declaring Subroutines and Functions," for more information on declaring these structures.

You are not required to declare any single-value variables used in your code, but you should. If you don't, you have a harder time debugging and otherwise maintaining your code, and the variables default to certain, possibly inefficient, characteristics. See "Specifying Option Explicit" later in this chapter for more information.

You do need to declare most of the arrays your code uses, because VBA has no other way to know how many dimensions the arrays have, or how large the arrays' dimensions should be. See "Using ReDim" later in this chapter.

Declaring Subroutines and Functions

You have already seen this example of a subroutine declaration:

```
Sub MakePivotTable()
```

You have several ways to execute, or *call*, this subroutine. For example, you could assign the subroutine to a toolbar button, a worksheet button, a menu item, or an element in a dialog box. Or, the user could choose Tools, Macro to choose and run the subroutine.

Suppose that MakePivotTable is executed, not directly by the user, but by another subroutine:

```
Sub MainDriver()
MakePivotTable
```

When VBA executes MainDriver, the first thing it does is transfer control to the subroutine MakePivotTable. MakePivotTable executes and then returns control to MainDriver.

It's often useful for MainDriver to provide information to MakePivotTable. You may want MakePivotTable to put the new pivot table on a new worksheet and to give that worksheet the name OutputSheet. To perform this task, you pass the string OutputSheet to MakePivotTable:

```
Sub MainDriver()
MakePivotTable "OutputSheet"
```

By including "OutputSheet" on the line that calls MakePivotTable, you make that string available to MakePivotTable, which can then use the string to name the new worksheet. In that case, you need to declare the subroutine MakePivotTable so it knows what's coming:

```
Sub MakePivotTable(OutputSheetName As String)
```

By declaring the subroutine with an argument in the parentheses, you specify that the subroutine is to receive information from whatever calls it. The subroutine will put the information into a variable named OutputSheetName, and that variable is a string variable.

The presence of this argument in the parentheses has two implications:

▶ You cannot call MakePivotTable without passing the information as part of the calling statement.

▶ You cannot pass information that is not a string value to MakePivotTable.

That is, after you have declared MakePivotTable with the argument OutputSheetName and specified that OutputSheetName is to contain a string, this call from MainDriver would not work:

```
MakePivotTable
```

VBA would stop with a Wrong number of arguments error message. This statement would not work either:

```
MakePivotTable 3.1416
```

VBA would stop with a Type mismatch error message.

A subroutine is one of two types of procedures you can use in VBA. The other type of procedure is a *function*. What's the difference? A VBA subroutine can make changes to workbooks, but you cannot execute it by typing its name in a worksheet cell. A VBA function cannot make changes to workbooks, but you can execute it by typing its name in a worksheet cell.

For example, with the proper code, `MakePivotTable` could insert a new worksheet in a workbook and place a pivot table on the worksheet. These are changes to a workbook. But if you declared the procedure in one of these two ways, the procedure could neither add the worksheet nor place a pivot table on it:

```
Function MakePivotTable()
```

or

```
Function MakePivotTable(OutputSheetName As String)
```

In contrast, suppose that you write this function:

```
Function CubeRoot(InputNumber As Double)
CubeRoot = InputNumber ^ (1/3)
End Function
```

By declaring the procedure as a function rather than a sub, you are able to make this entry in a worksheet cell:

=CubeRoot(8)

The number 2 would appear in the cell. However, if you declared the procedure this way:

```
Sub CubeRoot(InputNumber As Double)
```

and made this entry in a worksheet cell:

=CubeRoot(8)

Excel would display the error message `That name is not valid`. Excel expects a function named `CubeRoot`, not a subroutine.

As part of a function's declaration, you often specify the type of data you want it to return, as this example shows:

```
Function CubeRoot(InputNumber As Double) As Double
```

By including `As Double` at the end of the declaration, you specify that `CubeRoot` is to return a double-precision value.

Declaring Variables

Unlike subroutines and functions, you're not required to declare single-value variables explicitly in VBA. Nevertheless, declaring them is a good idea.

When you declare a variable, you identify several different aspects:

- ▶ The variable's name
- ▶ The variable's scope
- ▶ What sort of data the variable can contain—for example, integers, floating-point numbers, and strings
- ▶ Whether the variable is an array of values and (optionally) the dimensions and size of the array

You usually declare a variable by means of the keyword Dim (short for *dimension*), as in this example:

```
Dim RowCount As Integer
```

The variable's name, of course, is RowCount. The variable is declared as an integer variable, so you cannot assign a string to it. In other words, this statement, subsequent to the declaration, would work:

```
RowCount = 10
```

But this statement wouldn't work:

```
RowCount = "Ten"
```

If you assign a floating-point number to RowCount, it will be truncated:

```
RowCount = 3.1416
```

If RowCount is declared as an integer, it will contain the value 3 after 3.1416 is assigned to it.

RowCount can contain a single value only. If you want RowCount to be an array, which can contain more than one value, you need to declare it differently. For example:

```
Dim InputData (10) As Integer
```

The parentheses following the variable's name indicate to VBA that the InputData variable is an array. In this example, InputData can store up to ten different integer values.

What procedures can use a variable depend on where the variable is declared. Consider the RowCount declaration:

- ▶ If RowCount is declared at the module level—before any functions or subroutines have been declared—it is available to all functions or subroutines in the module.
- ▶ If RowCount is declared at the procedure level—between a Sub or Function statement and the associated End Sub or End Function statement—then RowCount is directly available only to the procedure where it is declared. (But you can pass it to another procedure; see Chapter 6, "Optimizing VBA Code," for more information.)

You also can declare a variable using the `Private` or `Public` keywords. If you do so, you must declare the variable at the module level, before you declare any procedures. For example:

```
Private RowCount As Integer
Public ColumnCount As Integer
```

RowCount is declared as `Private` and is available to all procedures in the module, but to no procedure in another module. Declaring a variable as `Private` is the same as declaring it with the `Dim` keyword at the module level.

In contrast, *ColumnCount* is available to any procedure in any other module (in fact, it's available to a VBA module in another application such as Access).

What if you don't specify the type of data that a variable can contain? In that case, the variable can contain any type of data:

```
Dim ScratchData
```

VBA assigns the `Variant` type to `ScratchData`, because the `Dim` statement doesn't specify a type such as `Integer` or `String`. A `Variant` type can contain integers, strings, Boolean values (True and False), even an object such as a worksheet range.

`Variants` sound convenient, but you pay for your convenience. `Variants` require more memory to store and more time to process than do other variable types. Furthermore, you cannot constrain `Variants` to a particular type of information.

Suppose that you made a logical mistake in your code (I know, you and I wouldn't, but it happens a lot to other people). The variable `ScratchData` is supposed to contain a numeric value such as the number of worksheets in a given workbook. Coding late at night, you write these statements:

```
ScratchData = ActiveSheet.Name
MsgBox ScratchData
```

This code is just temporary; you want to verify that the sheet you expect to be active really is active, so you arrange to display a message box with the name of the active sheet. After verifying your expectation, you intend to remove that code...but you forget.

If `ScratchData` is a `Variant`, anything can happen; the code may run just fine, or it might terminate with a runtime error. However, if you declared `ScratchData` as an `Integer` variable, you get an error message when VBA examines your code for syntax errors. This message serves as a warning and reminder, and you can revise and subsequently remove the statement before it causes any damage.

The moral is: Declare variables as specific data types. Don't declare variables as `Variant`, and don't let them default to `Variant`, unless you have good reason to do so.

Using *ReDim*

One extremely handy way to declare a variable as an array uses empty parentheses:

```
Dim InputData () As Integer
```

This statement informs VBA that InputData is an array that will contain integer values, but it defers until later any information about how many values InputData can contain. You would declare InputData in this fashion if you needed to take some steps before specifying the size of the array. The parentheses in the declaration indicate that InputData is an array.

 Note

Don't confuse the parentheses in the declaration of a variable with the parentheses in the declaration of a subroutine or a function. If you're declaring a variable, the parentheses mean that the variable is an array. If you're declaring a subroutine or function, the parentheses surround any arguments that the subroutine or function might take.

Suppose that you want the array InputData to contain the values the user has highlighted on the worksheet. You don't know beforehand the range that the user will highlight; yet, you need to declare InputData at the start of the procedure. In that case, use ReDim:

```
Sub GetInputData()
Dim InputData () As Integer
Dim RowCount As Integer
Dim ColumnCount As Integer
RowCount =  Selection.Rows.Count
ColumnCount = Selection.Columns.Count
ReDim InputData (RowCount, ColumnCount) As Integer
```

You can defer specifying the number of dimensions in the array (here, two dimensions) as well as their sizes until you know how many you need the array to have.

Why not do it this way:

```
Sub GetInputData()
Dim RowCount As Integer
Dim ColumnCount As Integer
RowCount =  Selection.Rows.Count
ColumnCount = Selection.Columns.Count
Dim InputData (RowCount, ColumnCount) As Integer
```

This procedure doesn't work. You cannot use other variables in a Dim statement.

You also cannot use properties or methods in a Dim statement, as this example shows:

```
Dim InputData (Selection.Rows.Count, Selection.Columns.Count) As Integer
```

If you're going to specify an array's dimensions and size in a `Dim` statement, you need to use actual values:

```
Dim InputData (10, 20) As Integer
```

The array `InputData` now has 10 rows and 20 columns.

Declaring and Setting Object Variables

A special kind of variable in VBA is an *object* variable. An object variable in your code stands for an object in a workbook. You declare an object variable just as you do any other, but you specify its type as the type of object you want the variable to represent. Some examples:

```
Dim InputRange as Range
Dim OutputSheet As Worksheet
Dim Btn As Button
```

After you have declared the object variable, you need to assign a particular object to it. The assignment statement takes a different form than it does for an ordinary variable assignment. For example, if `OutputSheet` has been declared as the `Worksheet` type, you might assign `OutputSheet` to represent Sheet1 in the active workbook:

```
Set OutputSheet = ActiveWorkbook.Sheets("Sheet1")
```

Notice the use of the keyword `Set`. When you assign an object to an object variable, you must use this keyword. If, instead, you use this line, the statement will fail:

```
OutputSheet = ActiveWorkbook.Sheets("Sheet1")
```

If you declare `OutputSheet` as type `Worksheet`, you cannot assign another object type to it. For example:

```
Dim OutputSheet As Worksheet
Set OutputSheet = ActiveWorkbook.Sheets(1)
```

If the first sheet in the active workbook is a worksheet, then the `Set` statement works fine. But if the first sheet is a chart sheet, a dialog sheet, or a module, then the `Set` statement fails. The type of the `OutputSheet` variable does not match the type of the active workbook's first sheet.

You also can declare an object variable as type `Object`:

```
Dim OutputSheet As Object
Set OutputSheet = ActiveWorkbook.Sheets(1)
```

An `Object` type can be any sort of workbook object: a worksheet, a chart sheet, a button, and so on. Declared as `Object`, `OutputSheet` can refer to any sort of workbook sheet, so the `Set` statement works regardless of whether the workbook's first sheet is a worksheet, a module, a dialog sheet, or a chart sheet.

As is the case with ordinary variables, though, it's best to declare an object variable as the specific type you want it to represent throughout your code.

As you see in Chapter 6, "Optimizing VBA Code," declaring object variables to represent workbook objects can make your code much more efficient. But object variables have other uses. For example, you can place a workbook object, such as a range of cells, into a Variant variable:

```
Dim InputValues As Variant
InputValues = ActiveWorkbook.Sheets(1).Range(Cells(1,1),Cells(5,5))
```

Tip

The Cells expression is one good way to specify a particular worksheet cell. Its syntax is Cells*(row number, column number)*. Use Cells twice in a Range expression to identify a worksheet range; the first instance identifies the range's upper-left corner, and the second instance identifies the range's lower-right corner.

The two preceding lines of code declare InputValues as a Variant variable. The assignment statement does *not* mean that InputValues represents cells A1:E5. The statement assigns the values in those 25 cells to InputValues, which then (automatically) becomes a VBA array. For this reason, the Set keyword is not needed in the assignment statement; InputValues is a Variant variable, not an Object variable.

One problem exists. Suppose that cells A1:E5 are formatted as Currency, with two decimal places shown. But the values may have more than two significant digits to the right of the decimal point. For example, the value 9.74549153030812 may be in A1, and because it's formatted as Currency, the value appears on the worksheet as $9.75.

However, consider this statement:

```
InputValues = ActiveWorkbook.Sheets(1).Range(Cells(1,1),Cells(5,5))
```

After this assignment statement has executed, the value in the (new) array InputValues is not 9.74549153030812, not 9.75, but 9.7455. The process of assigning the values in A1:A5 to InputValues drops some significant digits.

Therefore, your results will be more accurate if you use this code:

```
Dim InputValues As Range
Set InputValues = ActiveWorkbook.Sheets(1).Range(Cells(1,1),Cells(5,5))
```

Now, the value returned by InputValues(1,1) is 9.74549153030812.

Specifying *Option Explicit*

Using this statement at the beginning of a module sheet is a good idea:

```
Option Explicit
```

If you place this statement at the beginning of a module sheet—that is, prior to declaring any subroutine or function—you specify that any variable used in that module must be explicitly declared.

If you don't use `Option Explicit`, VBA enables you to declare variables on the fly. That is, in the middle of a subroutine, you can suddenly include this statement, and VBA doesn't complain:

```
TempVar = Selection.Rows.Count
```

A new variable, `TempVar`, is created and assigned the number of rows in the current selection on the active worksheet. Handy, but dangerous.

What if, later in the module, you use this statement:

```
TempVar = ActiveSheet.Name
```

This statement is legal, because when you declare a variable implicitly in this fashion, VBA gives it the `Variant` data type. (What else can VBA do?) But when you're debugging your code or maintaining it at some later date, do you really want to worry about whether `TempVar` contains some number of rows or the name of a sheet?

What if you mistype the name `TempVar`? Suppose that `TempVar` contains some integer that you want to decrease by 1:

```
TmpVar = TempVar - 1
```

Notice that `TempVar` is misspelled on the left side of the assignment statement. Instead of decreasing `TempVar`'s value by 1, this statement creates a new variable named `TmpVar`, which contains the value in `TempVar`, minus 1. In a lengthy subroutine, this error could take you considerable time to track down.

But if you use `Option Explicit`, you are required to declare `TempVar` with a `Dim`, `Private`, or `Public` statement:

```
Option Explicit
Dim TempVar As Variant
```

By requiring that variables such as `TempVar` be explicitly declared, you prevent the problems that typos can induce. Now, if VBA encounters this statement, it complains that `TmpVar` hasn't been declared:

```
TmpVar = TempVar - 1
```

This complaint signals that you may have misspelled a name or that you have forgotten to declare a variable you're trying to use.

1

`Option Explicit` acts as a reminder that you may want to avoid using the same variable for radically different purposes. For example:

```
Option Explicit
Sub GetSelectionData()
Dim TempVar1 As Integer, TempVar2 As String
TempVar1 = Selection.Rows.Count
TempVar2 = ActiveSheet.Name
```

This code is much easier to trace and debug than code that uses one variable indiscriminately at different points. Even better would be to give the variables descriptive names such as `RowCount` and `SheetName`.

 Tip

You can cause every new module sheet that you insert into a workbook to include `Option Explicit` automatically. Choose Tools, Options and click the Module General tab. Select the Require Variable Declaration check box and choose OK.

Specifying *Option Base 1*

When you declare an array in VBA, by default its first element is element number 0. You may find this default arrangement inconvenient, but you can change it with the `Option Base 1` statement. This statement usually goes at the top of a module sheet; you can place the statement with your `Option Explicit` statement. For example, suppose that your module contains this code:

```
Option Explicit
Sub GetSelectionData
Dim DataArray() As Integer, i As Integer, DataRegion As Range
```

Without `Option Base 1`, `DataArray` is indexed starting at 0; you refer to its first element as `DataArray(0)`. This `Dim` statement tells VBA *how many* elements are in `DataArray`, not how those elements are indexed. So if you want to move information from the active worksheet selection into `DataArray`, you need to use this code, or something very similar:

```
Set DataRegion = Selection
ReDim DataArray(DataRegion.Rows.Count)
For i = 0 to DataRegion.Rows.Count
    DataArray(i) = DataRegion(i + 1, 1)
Next i
End Sub
```

Notice the assignment statement in the `For...Next` loop. `DataArray` is filled by referring to the 0th, 1st, 2nd... elements. But the assignment statement also refers to the 1st, 2nd, 3rd... elements of the object variable `DataRegion`. Not only is this code slightly less efficient in terms of execution speed, but it can induce a headache when you need to debug or modify the code.

If you use `Option Base 1`, the code may look like this:

```
Option Explicit
Option Base 1
Sub GetSelectionData
Dim DataArray() As Integer, i As Integer, DataRegion As Range
Set DataRegion = Selection
ReDim DataArray(DataRegion.Rows.Count)
For i = 1 to DataRegion.Rows.Count
   DataArray(i) = DataRegion(i , 1)
Next i
End Sub
```

This code can help you keep your indexes straight when you are working with VBA arrays. Whether or not you use `Option Base 1`, the index used by collections of Excel objects begins at 1: Sheet1, Button1, Cells(1,1), and so on. Using `Option Base 1` makes VBA arrays conform to the same convention.

 Note

You can override the effect of *omitting* `Option Base 1` by specifying the 1 subscript in the array's declaration. For example:

```
Dim DataArray(1 To 20) As Integer
```

This declaration sets the stage for an error in the following statement, even if you omitted `Option Base 1` from your module:

```
DataArray(0) = 10
```

 Tip

When you use Data Access Objects (DAO) in your VBA code, avoid using `Option Base 1`. DAOs are indexed starting with 0 rather than 1. See Chapter 30, "Integrating Excel and Access," for more information.

Unlike `Option Explicit`, no option is available to automatically place `Option Base 1` into a new module sheet. If you want to arrange for each new module to contain `Option Base 1`, follow these steps:

1. Open a new workbook and choose <u>I</u>nsert, <u>M</u>acro, <u>M</u>odule. When you have a new module sheet, type **Option Base 1** at the top of the sheet.

2. Delete any other sheets in the workbook so it contains only the sheet Module1.

3. Choose File, Save As. Navigate to the Templates folder in the MSOffice folder, so that Templates is in the Save In drop-down box. In the File Name edit box, name the workbook **Module**. In the Save as Type drop-down box, choose Template(*.xlt). Choose Save.

4. When you want to insert a new module in a workbook, right-click the sheet tab that you want to follow the new module. From the shortcut menu, choose Insert. Select MODULE.XLT from the General tab of the Insert dialog box and choose OK.

Note

You cannot insert a new module sheet based on a template by choosing Insert, Macro, Module.

Summary

This chapter discussed several skills that you will need in order to make full use of the information about Excel in Chapters 2 through 6.

You have learned the basics of entering and using array formulas. You'll make use of this information in Chapter 3, "Advanced Array Formulas," and Chapter 4, "User-Defined Functions." These chapters describe how you can solve otherwise perplexing problems in data analysis and reporting.

You have also learned some of the fundamentals of using VBA. You've seen how the macro recorder can give you a jump start at writing VBA code. You've been introduced to the Excel object model—its objects, methods, and properties—and to some of the specifics of VBA declarations. You'll put these skills to use in Chapters 5 and 6, which explain how to create and optimize your own customized applications. You'll also use this information in Chapter 30, where you learn how to integrate Excel with Access.

The next chapter, "Special Charting Techniques in Excel," also makes use of VBA to help you increase the value of the charts you create in Excel.

chapter 2

Special Charting Techniques in Excel

2

by Conrad Carlberg

In this chapter

◆ **Putting data labels on charts**
Provide more information about the data series by showing its values next to its points.

◆ **Managing the chart axes**
Learn how the horizontal and vertical axes differ, and how to add a secondary vertical axis.

◆ **Managing the data series**
Manipulate the data series within the chart, and make it respond automatically to new data.

C harts are an underused capability in Excel. Although many useful methods exist for displaying data on worksheets—pivot tables, outlines, and data filters, for example—these methods just don't have the visual impact of charts.

Suppose that you want to make a point with an audience or with readers about the increase in a product's revenues over time. You can make your point much more powerfully with a chart than you can with a display of worksheet cells.

Or suppose that you are snooping through a large data set, looking for trends in the data. You can identify trends much more easily by viewing them on a chart than by peering at individual data points.

Charts also can help you avoid serious errors. Suppose that you use Excel's CORREL( ) function to get the correlation between two variables, and the function returns 0.85. That's a good, strong relationship. But if you don't chart the data as well, you may not realize that most of that correlation is due to one extreme point. Without that one point, the correlation may be only .05. You probably would avoid that trap if you put the data into an XY chart before reaching any conclusions.

Granted that charts add impact and help you identify patterns and avoid errors, how can you make your charts more useful? Start by learning to manage charts more effectively. This chapter shows you how.

Putting Data Labels on Charts

Excel has loads of ways to put labels on charts. You can label the chart itself. You can label the y-axis and the x-axis. You can stick floating text anywhere on the chart. You can label the data points themselves.

Why would you want to label individual data points?

▶ By themselves, charts don't show specific values. When you want to show particular values on a chart, putting the number on the chart is useful, along with the bar, column, or point that represents that number.

▶ You may be more interested in certain records than others. By labeling the records of greatest interest, you can draw attention to them or make them easier to find.

▶ You may want to label individual data points with information not on the chart itself.

See figure 2.1 for examples of these three approaches.

Distinguishing Between Data Values and Data Labels

When you enter data labels on a chart, you can enter either the numeric value of a point (for example, $6,635,820 in fig. 2.1) or a text label (Highest in fig. 2.1). The data label is usually, but not necessarily, a data point's value on the y-axis or its label on the x-axis. Whether a numeric value or a text label, the data label shows up in the chart as text. Perhaps confusingly, Excel terms either type, numeric or text, as a data label.

To enter data labels on an existing chart, take these steps:

1. Open the chart for editing by switching to a chart sheet or by double-clicking an embedded chart.

2. Click the chart's data series to select it.

3. Choose Insert, Data Labels or click the right mouse button and choose Insert Data Labels from the shortcut menu. The Data Labels dialog box appears (see fig. 2.2).

4. Click Show Value or Show Label, and choose OK.

Specific values

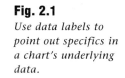

Fig. 2.1
*Use data labels to
point out specifics in
a chart's underlying
data.*

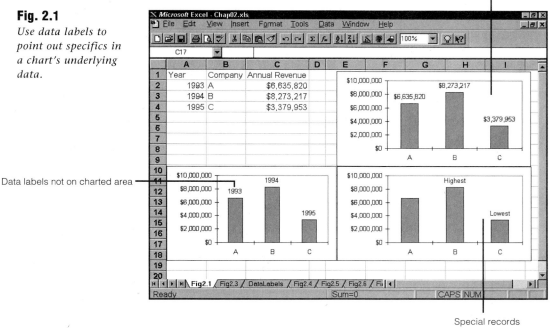

Data labels not on charted area

Special records

Fig. 2.2
*Using the Data Labels
dialog box, you can
place labels on any
chart type.*

If you choose Show Value, Excel places the value used by the chart's y-axis near each
data point. If you choose Show Label, Excel places the value used by the chart's x-axis
near each data point. Figure 2.3 illustrates this distinction.

 Tip

You sometimes may have difficulty selecting a data series by clicking it. For example, the minimum value for the y-axis may be set too high so that you cannot
see the data series. In that case, select any chart object (such as the plot area)
and press the down-arrow key until the data series is selected.

Fig. 2.3

Whether they contain the x-axis or the y-axis value, chart data labels are just text elements. You can edit label contents in the formula bar.

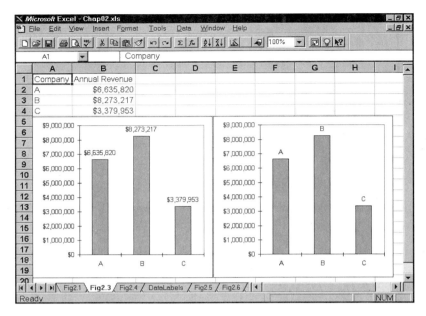

Labeling Data Points with VBA

Users who switch to Excel from Lotus 1-2-3 are often disconcerted by the absence of a 1-2-3 feature in Excel. In 1-2-3, the user can specify a range on a sheet and cause the values in that range to appear on the chart as data labels. Excel does not have this capability. The closest approximation is to use a Visual Basic for Applications (VBA) macro. An example of how you might code the macro is in a module named DataLabels, in the file named CHAP02.XLS on the companion CD.

Suppose that you have on a worksheet the names, tenure, and salary of several employees. As part of a headcount analysis, you want to examine the relationship between tenure in years and salary. You decide to create an XY chart, with salary as the y-axis and tenure as the x-axis. You want to label any data points with the name of the employee under the following circumstances:

▶ The employee's tenure is below the average tenure, and the employee's salary is above the average salary. These employees are being paid more than you might expect, given the length of time they have been on staff.

▶ The employee's tenure is above the average tenure, and the employee's salary is below the average salary. These employees are being paid less than you might expect.

The following macro creates the chart and its data labels. It is the one found in the DataLabels module in the CHAP02.XLS file on the companion CD:

```
Option Explicit
Option Base 1
Sub LabelTheData()
Dim Labels As Range, Years As Range, Salary As Range, InputData As Range
Dim Count As Integer, i As Integer, AverageYears As Single, _
    AverageSalary As Single
Dim NameArray() As String
```

The initial portion of this macro requires that all variables be explicitly declared and that the first element of all arrays be element number 1. The first part also declares the variables used in the macro.

```
Selection.CurrentRegion.Select
Set InputData = Selection
```

The first of the preceding two statements selects the entire region that contains the currently selected cell, much as Excel selects the entire region surrounding a single cell when you choose <u>D</u>ata, <u>S</u>ort (see fig. 2.4). The second statement then assigns the object variable *InputData* to represent that selection.

> ⚛ **Tip**
> You can select the current region using the keyboard by selecting a cell within the region and pressing Ctrl+* (asterisk).

Fig. 2.4

If the active cell is in the range A1:C17, the CurrentRegion.Select *method makes the entire range active.*

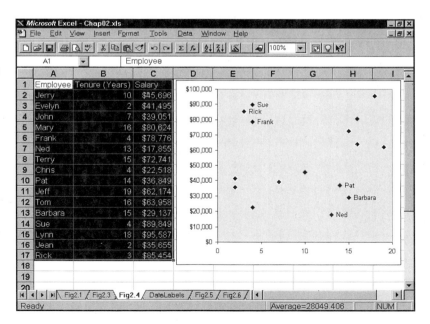

```
Count = InputData.Rows.Count - 1
ReDim NameArray(Count)
```

The code then counts the number of rows in the selection (subtracting 1 for the header row), to assign the number of observations on the worksheet to the variable Count. In figure 2.4, this number is 16. Count is then used to establish the number of elements in the variable NameArray.

```
Set Labels = InputData.Offset(1, 0).Resize(Count, 1)
Set Years = InputData.Offset(1, 1).Resize(Count, 1)
Set Salary = InputData.Offset(1, 2).Resize(Count, 1)
```

Given the data layout shown in figure 2.4, the preceding three statements assign the second through seventeenth rows of columns A, B, and C to the object variables Labels, Years, and Salary, respectively. For example, the Offset method causes Labels to represent the range that is offset by one row and zero columns from the InputData range; so Labels initially represents A2:A18. Then, the Resize method changes the number of rows in Labels from 17 to 16 (the value of Count). So Labels represents A2:A17.

The Years object is defined in the same way, except that it is offset by one column from InputData. Similarly, Salary is offset by two columns from InputData.

```
ActiveWorkbook.Names.Add Name:=ActiveSheet.Name & "!Years", _
    RefersToR1C1:=Years
ActiveWorkbook.Names.Add Name:=ActiveSheet.Name & "!Salary", _
    RefersToR1C1:=Salary
```

Two names, Fig2.4!Years and Fig2.4!Salary, are added to the worksheet. Because the active sheet's name, in this case, is Fig2.4, the names are made local to that worksheet.

```
AverageYears = Application.Average(Years)
AverageSalary = Application.Average(Salary)
```

The variables AverageYears and AverageSalary are assigned by taking the averages of the two ranges.

```
For i = 1 To Count
  If (Salary(i, 1) > AverageSalary And Years(i, 1) < AverageYears) Or _
    (Salary(i, 1) < AverageSalary And Years(i, 1) > AverageYears) Then
    NameArray(i) = Labels(i, 1)
  End If
Next i
```

The preceding For...Next loop checks each record on the worksheet and assigns a value in the Labels range (A2:A17) to the array NameArray according to the criteria you have established; the salary is either higher or lower than expected, given the employee's tenure. In these cases, NameArray contains that employee's name.

```
ActiveSheet.ChartObjects.Add(179.4, 3.6, 270, 228).Select
ActiveChart.ChartWizard _
    Source:=Sheets(ActiveSheet.Name).Range("Years, Salary"), _
    Gallery:=xlXYScatter, Format:=1, PlotBy:=xlColumns, _
    CategoryLabels:=1, SeriesLabels:=0, HasLegend:=2, Title:="", _
    CategoryTitle:="", ValueTitle:="", ExtraTitle:=""
```

Now, a new chart object is embedded in the worksheet and selected. The Chart Wizard is invoked and supplied with the range names (Years and Salary) that are used as the x-axis and y-axis values, respectively.

```
ActiveChart.SeriesCollection(1).ApplyDataLabels _
    Type:=xlShowLabel, LegendKey:=False
```

The preceding command just establishes data label objects on the chart.

```
For i = 1 To Count(NameArray)
    ActiveChart.SeriesCollection(1).Points(i).DataLabel _
        .Characters.Text = NameArray(i)
Next i
End Sub
```

Finally, a For...Next loop places all the values in NameArray into the data labels on the chart. If an element in NameArray has been assigned a value from A2:A17 on the worksheet—that is, if the employee's salary is unexpectedly large or small—that name is placed in the associated data label. Otherwise, the element in NameArray is empty, and nothing is written to the data label.

 Tip

After you have selected a chart's data series, you can select specific points in the series using the right and left keyboard arrows.

Managing the Chart's Axes

The difference between a chart's x-axis (usually the horizontal dimension on a chart) and its y-axis (usually the chart's vertical dimension) causes Excel users untold amounts of grief. Resolving problems caused by misunderstanding the nature of the axes is a common issue for Microsoft's support staff. You can save yourself some headaches by understanding the axes' differences, and the implications of those differences, before you start charting.

Note

The x-axis of a Line, Area, XY, or Column chart is its horizontal dimension. The x-axis of a Bar chart is its vertical dimension (a Bar chart is just a Column chart rotated 90 degrees).

Understanding the X-Axis

In most cases, the chart's x-axis is a category axis. This means that the axis scale treats each x-value as a different category.

Suppose that you are charting the annual revenue for three different companies, using the Column Chart format. In most cases, you have no special reason for wanting the chart to place the columns for companies A and B one-half inch apart, and to place Company C's column another two inches away on the x-axis.

In contrast, suppose that you are charting the annual revenue for 1990, 1991, and 1995 for a single company. You may find it useful for the chart to separate 1990's column from 1991's column by an inch, and to separate 1995's column from 1991 by four inches. Doing so emphasizes the actual numeric difference between 1991 and 1995 (see fig. 2.5).

Fig. 2.5

The x-axis of an XY chart separates x-values by their magnitude.

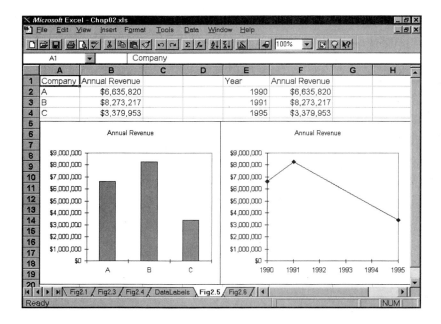

All chart types except for XY, Pie, and Doughnut charts provide an equal separation among different x-axis values. Pie and Doughnut charts separate their x-axis values by the numeric magnitude of the y-values.

The simple example in figure 2.5 points out only the cosmetic aspect of the choice between equal-spacing and value-spacing the x-axis. The choice becomes more important when you are analyzing the relationship between two numeric variables—say, the square footage of a store and its annual revenue (see fig. 2.6).

Fig. 2.6

Using an XY chart format is best when you insert trendlines into a chart.

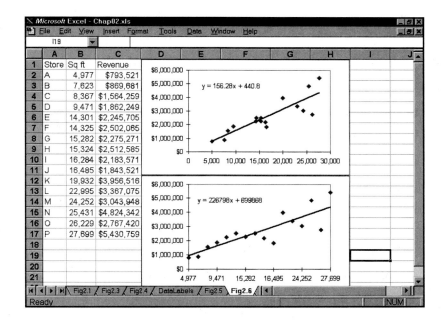

Notice that the trendlines in the two charts have slightly different slopes, and that the spread of the actual data values differs. More important, consider the difference between the two trendline equations. In the XY chart, the trendline equation is

$$y = 156.28x + 440.8$$

In the Line chart, the trendline is

$$y = 226798x + 699868$$

Quite a difference. In the XY chart's equation, you multiply 156.28 times the store's square footage, and add 440.8. In the Line chart's equation, you multiply 226798 times the *numeric order* of the store, and add 699868. So for store 1, the predicted revenue would be 226798×1+699868.

This difference in equations is consistent with the difference in chart types. The Line chart creates an x-axis that displays categories: Store 1, Store 2, and so on. The XY chart creates an x-axis that displays values: square footage for Store 1, square footage for Store 2, and so forth.

You probably would not want to predict a store's revenue based on where it appears in a list of data (although in time-forecasting applications, this method can sometimes be correct). But many users tie themselves into knots by displaying trendlines and trendline equations using a chart type, and thus an x-axis, that makes no sense to the kind of analysis they're trying to carry out.

Unless you know for sure why you're choosing a chart that uses categories rather than values for its x-axis, don't use anything other than an XY chart if you intend to plot trendlines and use trendline equations.

Using Secondary Y-Axes

A common application in charting is to show some worksheet ranges as a column chart and another worksheet range as a line chart. A simple example, used in quality control, is the Pareto chart (see fig. 2.7).

Fig. 2.7

*The Pareto chart—
a sorted histogram—
shows the rate of
occurrence of quality
violations in columns
and the cumulative
rate of violations as
a line.*

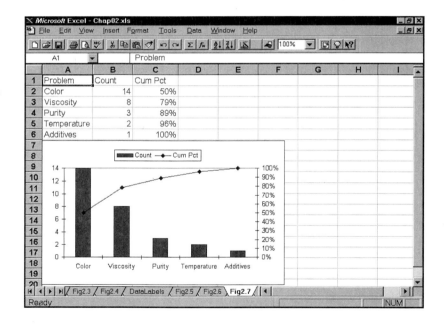

To get a Pareto chart, you select the Combination chart type in the Chart Wizard. This chart type, by default, uses two y-axis scales: one at the left and one at the right edge of the chart. The left y-axis scale pertains to the columns, and the right y-axis scale pertains to the line.

Another example is an expense and income chart, where things get a little more complicated because you generally have several expense classifications to chart and only one income classification. One way of charting such data appears in figure 2.8.

Fig. 2.8

This stacked-column and line chart is not drawn automatically; you must arrange the chart's custom format.

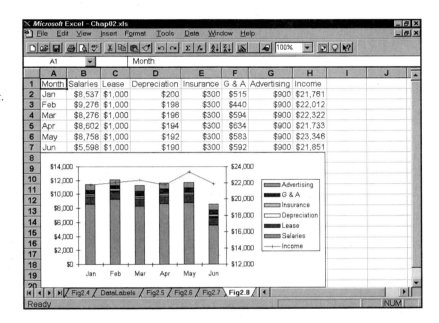

The difficulty lies in the fact that when you select several columns before creating a Combination chart, Excel has no way of knowing how many worksheet ranges to treat as chart columns and how many ranges to treat as chart lines. For example, if you start with eight worksheet ranges—one for the x-axis and seven for the data series—a Combination chart shows four series as columns and three as lines.

To create the chart as shown in figure 2.8, follow these steps:

1. Open the file named CHAP02.XLS on the companion disk. Activate the Fig2.8 tab, select A1:H8, and start the Chart Wizard.

2. In Step 2 of the Wizard, select a Column chart.

3. In Step 3 of the Wizard, select a Stacked Column chart (subtype 3).

4. In Step 4, make sure to click the Data Series in <u>C</u>olumns option button. Set <u>U</u>se First Column(s) for Category (X) Axis Labels to 1, and set U<u>s</u>e First Row(s) for Legend Text to 1.

5. Finish the Chart Wizard. Then open the chart for editing and click the uppermost series in one of the columns. You should see *S7* in the Name Box, indicating that Series 7 has been selected. This is the Income series, which you want to show as a Line rather than part of a stacked column.

6. Choose F<u>o</u>rmat, Chart <u>T</u>ype. Make sure that the <u>S</u>elected Series option button is chosen, select the Line chart type, and choose OK.

7. Double-click the Income series (or single-click it and choose F<u>o</u>rmat, S<u>e</u>lected Data Series). Select the Axis tab and click the <u>S</u>econdary Axis option button. Choose OK.

Your chart should now appear as shown in figure 2.8.

Using this technique, you can add an extra y-axis to your chart, determine which data series should be plotted against which y-axis, and format each series in your chart as the type you want (Column, Line, XY, and so on).

Managing a Chart's Data Series

The two principal methods to manage a chart's data series are by means of the Format menu and by editing the chart's reference to the data series. By editing the reference, you can cause the chart to react automatically to changes in the worksheet.

The Format menu gives you access to many options beyond simply altering the appearance of the data series. Select the data series by double-clicking an embedded chart or by switching to a chart sheet. Click the series to select it and then choose F<u>o</u>rmat, S<u>e</u>lected Data Series (or just double-click the data series).

All chart types, other than the 3D Surface chart, offer these formatting tabs:

▶ A Name and Values tab, where you can change the name of the y-axis values and its reference. Often, a quicker way to make these changes is by editing the chart's data series reference; see the next section for a description of how to do this.

▶ An X Values tab, where you can change the reference to the x-axis values. Again, editing the chart's data series reference is usually quicker.

▶ A Data Labels tab, where you can choose to display on the chart the labels for different data points. You can display either the point's x-axis value or its y-axis value as its label.

▶ A Patterns tab, where you can specify the color, pattern, and weight of data points, and where appropriate, the lines connecting them.

> **α Note**
>
> Formatting the data series of a 3D Surface chart offers only a Patterns tab. To manage the patterns on this type of chart, you need to use a special sequence to access the dialog box. After the chart is accessible for editing, you do not click the series itself. Instead, first click the legend box and then double-click one of the legend keys in the legend box. The Patterns dialog box appears; use it to change the data series border and area settings.

For two-dimensional XY, Column, Bar, Line, and Area charts, a formatting tab also is available for Y Error Bars, where you can choose to display the amount of error associated with different observations. You have probably come across the concept of error bars in the results of opinion polls, which often report that their results have a margin of error of plus and minus some percentage. You also can specify X Error Bars for an XY chart, which has a numeric x-axis as well as a numeric y-axis.

Finally, all two-dimensional charts offer an Axis tab, where you can specify that the selected data series is to refer to a secondary chart axis. To use this option, the chart must have at least two data series. 3D charts do not offer this formatting tab.

Editing a Chart's Data Series

Although you can change the characteristics of a data series on a chart by means of Format, Selected Data Series, you often can do so more quickly by editing the data series itself. The key to changing what a data series represents is in understanding the syntax of the SERIES function. You cannot find this function in the online help topics, nor can you enter it in a worksheet. The only place the function shows up is in the formula bar when you select a data series in a chart.

For example, suppose that you open the chart shown in figure 2.9 and select the data series by clicking it. You see this line in the formula bar:

```
=SERIES(Fig2.9!$C$1,Fig2.9!$B$2:$B$17,Fig2.9!$C$2:$C$17,1)
```

The function has four arguments:

▶ The first argument, *Fig2.9!$C$1*, defines the location of the series name on the worksheet, if a name exists. Often, this name is the column header in a list. In figure 2.9, the name is the text value Salary. By default, Excel uses that name for the chart title.

▶ The second argument, *Fig2.9!$B$2:$B$17*, defines the worksheet location of the x-axis values.

▶ The third argument, *Fig2.9!$C$2:$C$17*, defines the worksheet location of the y-axis values.

▶ The fourth argument, *1*, is the index number of the series on the chart. If the chart showed two data series, the second series would have *2* as the fourth argument to the SERIES function.

Fig. 2.9

The formula bar displays the full reference to the selected data series.

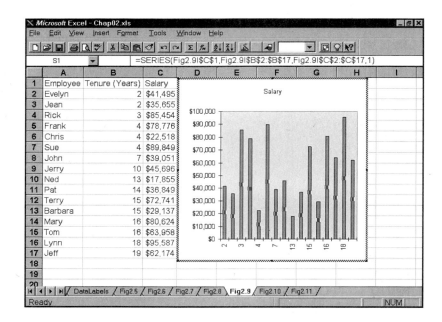

After you have the SERIES function showing in the formula bar, you can edit it just as you edit a worksheet function. You can switch the worksheet references to turn an XY chart by 90 degrees, or you can modify the references to show an entirely different set of x- or y-values. You can delete the chart title by removing the first argument. Or you can change the worksheet references to defined names. These options are discussed in the next three sections.

Using Dynamic Data Series

Suppose that you have a chart you want to update as new information becomes available. This situation tends to occur when you are charting time-sensitive information. For example, you might be tracking quarterly revenue for a business enterprise, or average weekly rainfall amounts, or your monthly utility expenses.

In cases such as these, you probably don't want to recreate your chart every time you enter new data on the worksheet. You also can save time if you don't need to edit the chart data series to capture new values (although you *can* do so).

The solution is to use a dynamic data series, which causes the chart's data series to refer to a name, rather than to a reference to a specific worksheet range. Consider this name reference, which defines the name RevenueRange:

```
=OFFSET(Sheet1!$A:$A,0,0,COUNTA(Sheet1!$A:$A),1)
```

Recall that the OFFSET() function returns a worksheet range, so RevenueRange refers ultimately to that range. Here, the basis for the offset is column A on Sheet1: Sheet1!$A:$A. RevenueRange is offset from its basis by zero rows and zero columns—so the range it refers to begins in A1.

RevenueRange has as many rows as are returned by COUNTA(Sheet1!$A:$A). This function, of course, returns a count of the number of values in its reference argument. If values are in A1:A5 only, RevenueRange has five rows. RevenueRange has one column, because the final argument in the OFFSET() function is 1.

Each time you enter a new value in column A, RevenueRange is redefined to have an additional row, because the value returned by the COUNTA portion of the definition changes. (Of course, if you use Tools, Options to set the worksheet calculation to Manual, you need to press F9 before COUNTA() recalculates.)

Now, if your chart uses RevenueRange as an argument to its data series, Excel recalculates the chart to encompass the new definition of RevenueRange. For example, you might edit the chart's data series by replacing a worksheet address with the name RevenueRange:

```
=SERIES(,,Sheet1!RevenueRange,1)
```

In that case, when RevenueRange is redefined, the data series also is redefined, and the chart is redrawn to capture the new entry in column A. See figure 2.10 for an example.

α Note

Be careful with dynamic range names. If you somehow get a stray entry in the range that's returned by the OFFSET() function in the range definition, the range will be one row too large. Consider this definition:

```
=OFFSET(Sheet1!$A:$A,0,0,COUNTA(Sheet1!$A:$A),1)
```

If your intended values are in A1:A12 and you somehow get a value in A500, the OFFSET() range includes 13 rows rather than 12 because COUNTA picks up the vagrant value in A500.

Fig. 2.10

The chart updates automatically as you add new values in column A.

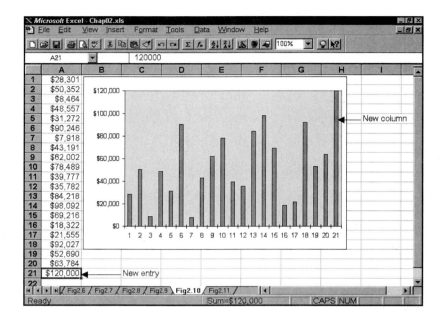

Understanding Relative Range Names

Worksheet names are often recommended as a way to avoid problems associated with relative references. For example, consider this formula:

```
=SUM(A1:A10)
```

If you copy the preceding formula one cell to the right, it looks like this:

```
=SUM(B1:B10)
```

But this formula may not be your intention. You could, of course, use this formula:

```
=SUM($A$1:$A$10)
```

But that can be inconvenient if other formulas reference the same 10 cells. So, from different sources, you learn to define a name such as MyRange as referring to $A$1:$A$10, and use the name as an argument in place of the worksheet addresses.

Therefore, you come to associate the notion of a range name with that of absolute references. This association is reinforced by the fact that Excel, by default, inserts the dollar signs into the worksheet reference when you define or create a new name.

Range names need not refer to absolute worksheet references. They also can refer to relative ranges, and you can use this capability to bring about some handy charting effects.

Try this effect first:

1. Open a new workbook.
2. With cell A1 still active, choose Insert, Name, Define.
3. In the Names in Workbook edit box, enter a name such as RelativeRange.
4. In the Refers To edit box, enter this reference:

   =Sheet1!B2

   If you decide to click cell B2 instead of typing the reference, be sure to remove the dollar signs from the reference.
5. Choose OK.

You have defined RelativeRange as referring to the cell that's one column to the right and one row below the cell that was active when you defined the name. A1 was active when you defined RelativeRange as referring to B2.

Using the Name Box, go to RelativeRange. B2 is now the active cell. Use the Name Box again to go to RelativeRange. C3 is now the active cell. The reference to RelativeRange is always one column right and one row below the active cell.

When you entered the address in the Refers To edit box, you made it a purely relative reference; that is, RelativeRange's row *and* column depend on the active cell. You can make the address a mixed reference, in which either the row or the cell is anchored. You also can make the address a reference to more than just one cell, as this example shows:

1. Select cell A1.
2. Choose Insert, Name, Define.
3. Click RelativeRange in the Names in Workbook list box.
4. In the Refers To box, change the reference of RelativeRange to

   =Sheet1!A$1:A$5

5. Choose OK.

The effect of defining the reference in this way is to make RelativeRange depend on the column, and only on the column, of the active cell. RelativeRange always refers to rows 1 through 5 of the active cell's column. If you select, say, cell F20 and use the Name Box to go to RelativeRange, F1:F5 is activated.

Using Relative Ranges in Charts

How can you use this effect for charting purposes? Consider figure 2.11.

Fig. 2.11

The chart updates when you move the active cell and press F9.

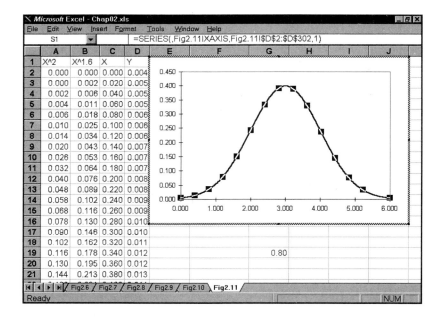

The chart in figure 2.11 depicts a normal, or *bell*, distribution, the basis for statistical tests in various sciences. This example is an XY chart, with the format of the data series set to suppress markers and to show the line. The chart's y-values are located in $D$2:$D$302. Because the chart is an XY chart, the spacing of its x-axis values is based on their magnitude, as is the spacing of its y-axis values.

Notice in the formula bar shown in figure 2.11 that the x-values use the reference Fig2.11!XAXIS. The sheet-level name Fig2.11!XAXIS was defined by selecting a cell in column C and defining its reference as

```
=Fig2.11!C$2:C$302
```

Columns A and B contain the values in column C raised, respectively, to the power of 2 and to the power of 1.6. These values enable the user to transform the chart's x-values, resulting in the curve skewing to the right (the right tail of the distribution stretches out). The ability to display different degrees of skews is useful for understanding the effect of data transformations on normally distributed data. This feature also is useful for choosing a transformation to normalize skewed data (see fig. 2.12).

Fig. 2.12

The effect of squaring the original x-values is to skew the distribution to the right.

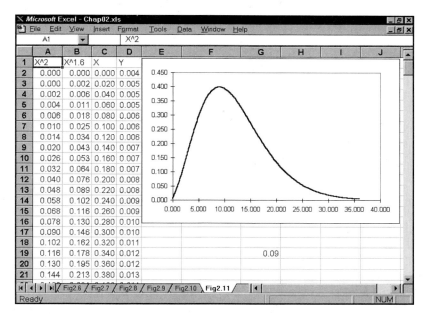

To obtain the distribution shown in figure 2.12, you select any cell in column A and press F9. The range named XAXIS adjusts according to your selection of a cell in column A, making the name refer to cells A$1:A$302. Then, when you press F9, the chart recalculates according to the x-axis values it finds in column A. You also can view a less extreme degree of skew by choosing a cell in column B and pressing F9.

Another item is needed to bring about this effect, in addition to the data set, the chart, and the relative range name. The act of selecting a different cell to change the reference of the range name is not enough by itself to cause the chart to recalculate. You must press F9. But pressing F9 is not enough by itself to recalculate the chart. F9 just recalculates a worksheet if a volatile function is somewhere on the sheet. Therefore, you also need to put a formula such as this somewhere on the worksheet:

    =NOW()

or

    =RAND()

In figure 2.12, RAND() is found in cell G19, but you can hide it behind the chart if you don't want to display it. The existence of a volatile function causes Excel to recalculate the entire worksheet, including the chart. If you used a nonvolatile function instead, such as the following, it would cause a sheet recalculation only if one of its arguments changed:

    =SUM(A1:A10)

In the discussion of dynamic range names in the preceding section, the use of COUNTA in the range definition causes the recalculation when you include an additional value in the range's worksheet region.

This technique is very useful in different situations:

▶ You have recurring data that you want to chart separately. For example, you might want to display monthly revenue for different years. Each column could contain revenue by month for each year in your data set.

▶ You are using Excel to deliver an electronic presentation. Changing the chart's appearance on the presentation screen according to the location of the active cell may be more convenient than scrolling from chart to chart.

▶ You want to focus visually on possibly minor deviations in the appearance of the chart, without the distraction of attending to the worksheet and keyboard to change a data series' reference.

Summary

This chapter has discussed some ways you can change the nature of a chart to make it more informative and efficient. You have learned how to insert data labels into a chart, both manually and by means of VBA. Creating data labels manually using the Insert menu gives you the greatest amount of control over the contents and appearance of the data labels. However, you can use VBA to execute your instructions about which data points should have labels, as well as what those labels should display.

You have learned about the difference between y-axis and x-axis operation, and the way Excel interprets your x-axis values. This chapter also has described how to customize a combination chart so that one or more series refers to the chart's primary left y-axis, and another series refers to the chart's secondary right y-axis.

You have learned how to edit the arguments to a chart's data series, making it sensitive to the number of values in a worksheet's range. Then Excel can automatically update the points in the chart and you don't need to recreate the chart as more data enters your worksheet.

Finally, you have learned how to use relative ranges to make the data series displayed in a chart sensitive to the location of the worksheet's active cell. Then you can easily redraw a chart based on a cell you choose, again speeding up the visual analysis of your data.

chapter 3

Advanced Array Formulas

3

by Conrad Carlberg

In this chapter

◆ **Understanding when array formulas are necessary**
Some functions require array formulas, and some results can't be obtained otherwise.

◆ **Creating arrays in your formulas**
You can use array formulas to put an entire analysis into a single cell.

◆ **Using worksheet functions in array formulas**
Extend the reach of your formulas by including worksheet functions.

Array formulas are an enormously useful means of obtaining results from Excel that may not be available directly from worksheet functions. With some study, you will find that you can use array formulas instead of writing a macro, and instead of painstaking visual examination of your data. Furthermore, you may enter some worksheet functions as array formulas. Unless you understand how array functions work, you cannot take full advantage of Excel's functionality.

Understanding When Array Formulas Are Necessary

Some conditions exist in which you must array-enter a formula. An example is a function that returns its results in more than one cell. In that case, you must begin by selecting a range that can accommodate all the function's results, and then type the formula and enter it with Ctrl+Shift+Enter.

Tip

The Function Wizard does not enter functions as array formulas. To array-enter a function with the Function Wizard, select a range of the necessary dimensions and then use the Wizard. After the Wizard has finished, click in the formula bar and press Ctrl+Shift+Enter.

Using Arrays That Aren't on the Sheet

Even when a formula occupies only one cell, you may need to array-enter it. The basic rule of thumb is that if the formula uses an array, and that array is not on the worksheet, you should array-enter the formula.

For example, this formula uses an array (the values in A1:A5):

```
=SUM(A1:A5)
```

However, the array A1:A5 is on the worksheet and is directly accessible to the SUM() function. You do not need to array-enter the formula.

In contrast, consider this formula:

```
=SUM(ROW(A1:A5))
```

This formula returns the sum of the row numbers occupied by the range A1:A5 (that is, 1+2+3+4+5). These row numbers are not on the worksheet, and to get the sum of 15 you must array-enter the formula. Entered as a simple formula, it returns 1—the first value only in the array of row numbers.

Similarly, you must array-enter this formula:

```
=SUM(A1:A5*B1:B5)
```

Although the arrays of values in A1:A5 and in B1:B5 are on the worksheet, the array that represents their products (A1*B1, A2*B2, and so on) is not on the worksheet. Array-enter the formula by using Ctrl+Shift+Enter.

Using the Worksheet Array Functions

Excel has several worksheet functions that *require* you to enter them as array formulas. As you might expect, these functions return arrays to the worksheet.

For example, suppose that you have data on the percent of sales quota that each of several sales staff has achieved. You want to find out how many staff fall within 70%–79%, 80%–89%, 90%–100%, and so on. You do so in Excel by using the FREQUENCY() function (see fig. 3.1).

Fig. 3.1

FREQUENCY() *takes
arrays as arguments
and returns an array
as its result.*

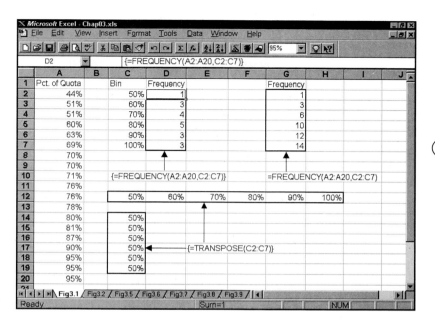

3

In the figure, cells D2:D7 contain the FREQUENCY() function, entered as an array formula. Notice, in the label pointing to D2:D7, that the formula is surrounded by curly braces. The braces are an indicator that Excel has accepted the entry as an array formula.

 Note

Recall from Chapter 1 that when you have array-entered a formula with Ctrl+Shift+Enter, Excel indicates that it has accepted the entry as an array formula by surrounding it with curly braces.

Cells G2:G7 contain the same function, but entered as a multiple-selection (the range G2:G7 is highlighted, and the formula is typed and then entered with Ctrl+Enter rather than Ctrl+Shift+Enter). Notice the absence of the curly braces in the label that points to G2:G7. Because the braces are missing, you can tell that the formula was not array-entered by means of Ctrl+Shift+Enter.

All the cells occupied by the array formula in D2:D7 refer to the same addresses: A2:A20 and C2:C7. If you open the file named CHAP03.XLS from the companion CD, you will find that the formula in cell G2 refers to A2:A20 and C2:C7, in G3 to A3:A21 and C3:C8, and so on. The pattern is as though you had entered the formula in G2 and then dragged it down through G3:G7, with the cell references adjusting accordingly.

Only the array-entered version of the formula (D2:D7) returns the results you're after—the number of entries in the list that fall within each bin in C2:C7.

To return the proper results, several worksheet functions must be array-entered, and array-entered in the proper location. For example:

▶ TRANSPOSE() changes the orientation of its argument. This function is entered as an array formula in C12:H12 in figure 3.1, where C2:C7 is transposed from a column to a row. The function also is entered, incorrectly, in C14:C19, where it displays only the first value in its range argument.

▶ Various statistical and matrix functions return arrays, and you need to know the dimensions of the range to highlight before you array-enter the formula. The statistical functions include LINEST(), TREND(), LOGEST(), GROWTH(). The matrix functions include MINVERSE() and MMULT(). In addition, the matrix function MDETERM() requires that you array-enter it, even though it occupies one cell only.

▶ COLUMN() and ROW() return arrays when their arguments are ranges, and they must be array-entered to return the full scope of the columns or rows in the range argument.

Creating Arrays in Your Formulas

When you enter an array formula, one or more arrays often are hidden within it. Whatever function or operators you use in the formula act on the hidden arrays to return the result. If you know how to enter, examine, and manipulate those arrays, you can achieve some extremely useful results.

Displaying and Evaluating Array Fragments

Consider the quick-and-dirty sales analysis shown in figure 3.2. Within the array formulas in cells D2 and D5 are arrays. You can display them by taking these steps:

1. Open the file named CHAP03.XLS from the companion CD, and select the worksheet named Fig3.2.

2. Select cell D2. The array formula appears in the formula bar.

3. With your mouse pointer, highlight the fragment A2:A20="West". (When you move the pointer into the formula bar, it changes to an I-bar. Place the I-bar just to the left of the fragment, hold down the mouse button, and drag right.)

4. With the fragment highlighted, press F9. The formula's appearance changes, as shown in figure 3.3.

5. Click the Cancel box, or press Esc, to leave the formula bar. If you press Enter or click the Enter box, the formula keeps the array rather than the logical expression.

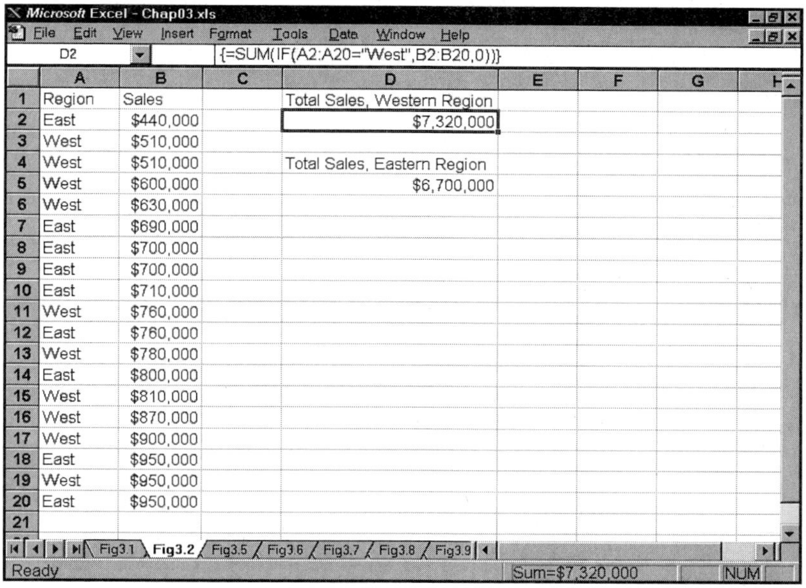

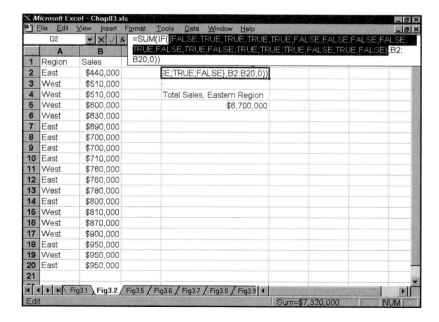

Fig. 3.2

The SUM(IF(...)) *syntax has broad applicability in Excel.*

Fig. 3.3

By calculating a fragment within a formula, you evaluate its contents.

Tip

In Excel, the F9 key means "calculate." With a worksheet active, pressing F9 calculates the worksheet's contents; with a portion of a formula highlighted, pressing F9 calculates that portion.

You have highlighted a logical expression and calculated it. The result is an array of TRUE and FALSE values, depending on whether an individual entry in A2:A20 equals "West".

If you highlight the fragment B2:B20 and press F9, you see an array that contains the values in that range.

Now, highlight the entire fragment IF(A2:A20="West",B2:B20,0) and press F9. You see that Excel has combined the two arrays (a TRUE/FALSE array and the array of values in B2:B20) into one array. For the list items that meet the logical condition, the array contains the corresponding value in B2:B20. For those items that fail the logical condition, the array contains zero—as specified by the IF statement.

Finally, the SUM() function adds up the values in the full array and returns the total of the values in B2:B20 if, and only if, the corresponding value in A2:A20 equals "West" (see fig. 3.4).

Fig. 3.4

After Excel has evaluated the component arrays, the result is the set of values that SUM() totals.

	A	B		
	Region	Sales	Total Sales, Western Region	
1				
2	East	$440,000	870000;900000;0;950000;0})	
3	West	$510,000		
4	West	$510,000	Total Sales, Eastern Region	
5	West	$600,000	$6,700,000	
6	West	$630,000		
7	East	$690,000		
8	East	$700,000		
9	East	$700,000		
10	East	$710,000		
11	West	$760,000		
12	East	$760,000		
13	West	$780,000		
14	East	$800,000		
15	West	$810,000		
16	West	$870,000		
17	West	$900,000		
18	East	$950,000		
19	West	$950,000		
20	East	$950,000		
21				

Microsoft Excel - Chap03.xls

File Edit View Insert Format Tools Data Window Help

D2 `=SUM({0,510000;510000;600000;630000;0;0;0;0;760000;0;780000;0;810000;870000;900000;0;950000;0})`

Fig3.1 \ **Fig3.2** \ Fig3.5 \ Fig3.6 \ Fig3.7 \ Fig3.8 \ Fig3.9

Edit   Sum=$7,320,000   NUM

Building Up Array Formulas

When you are working with very complicated array formulas, it is a good idea to build the fragments directly on the worksheet before trying to combine them into one formula. Figure 3.5 provides a slightly more complex example.

Fig. 3.5

Creating the array formula's components individually, and only then combining them, can help you keep the elements straight.

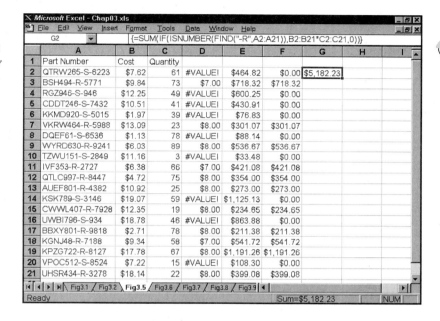

Column A in figure 3.5 contains the part numbers of equipment that you have in your inventory. Some of the parts are held for resale: they have an R somewhere in the number. Other parts are service stock: you use them to replace defective equipment for customers who have maintenance contracts.

Column B contains your unit cost for each equipment part, and Column C contains the quantity of each that you have on hand. You want to know the total cost of the equipment you have for resale, as opposed to service spares.

You need to find those part numbers that have the string "-R" in them. Because an unknown number of letters and numbers can precede this string in a part number, you must use Excel's FIND() function to locate an instance of "-R".

When the string exists in the part number, you want to multiply the part's unit cost by the quantity on hand. Finally, you total the result of the multiplication.

You have a lot to keep in mind as you're creating a single array formula, so you put the individual components explicitly on the worksheet. After you have each component working as you want, you can combine the components into a single formula this way:

1. In cells D2:D21, array-enter this formula:

   =FIND("-R",A2:A21)

   The formula returns #VALUE! if the string "-R" is not found in a part number, and otherwise returns the point where the string begins.

2. In cells E2:E21, array-enter this formula:

   =B2:B21*C2:C21

   This formula is the product of each part's unit cost and its quantity in your inventory.

3. In cells F2:F21, array-enter this formula:

   =IF(ISNUMBER(D2:D21),E2:E21,0)

   This formula looks to the values in D2:D21. If the value is a number—that is, if Excel is able to find the string "-R" in the part number—then the formula returns the part's cost times its quantity in E2:E21. Otherwise, the formula returns a zero value.

4. Now you're in a position to begin building a single-cell array formula. In G2, array-enter this formula:

   =SUM(F2:F21)

5. Select any cell in the range F2:F21. The cell's formula appears in the formula bar. Highlight the entire formula *except the equals sign* by dragging across it. You should have this portion highlighted:

   `IF(ISNUMBER(D2:D21),E2:E21,0)`

6. Choose Edit, Copy (or press Ctrl+C). Click the Cancel box or press Esc.

7. Select cell G2 and highlight the reference to F2:F21 in its formula. Choose Edit, Paste (or press Ctrl+V). Press Ctrl+Shift+Enter to reenter the formula as an array formula. It should now appear as

   `{=SUM(IF(ISNUMBER(D2:D21),E2:E21,0))}`

8. Select any cell in E2:E21 and highlight its formula—again, omitting the equals sign. Choose Edit, Copy and click the Cancel box.

9. Highlight the reference to E2:E21 in G2 and choose Edit, Paste. Reenter the formula as an array formula. The formula in G2 should now appear as

   `{=SUM(IF(ISNUMBER(D2:D21),B2:B21*C2:C21,0))}`

10. Select any cell in D2:D21 and again copy the formula, omitting the equals sign. Click the Cancel box, select G2, highlight the reference to D2:D21, and choose Edit, Paste. Reenter the formula with Ctrl+Shift+Enter. The formula in G2 should now appear as

```
{=SUM(IF(ISNUMBER(FIND("-R",A2:A21)),B2:B21*C2:C21,0))}
```

You now have a single-cell array formula that returns the total cost of all parts in your inventory that are intended for resale. You can delete the intermediate formulas you entered in D2:F21, because G2 now refers only to the data in A2:C21.

As you gain more experience with array formulas, you may be able to envision the full array formula and just type it into a cell or range. Until you have that facility, though, build the formula in staged fragments as described above, and then combine the fragments into a single formula. In very complex situations, even experienced users rely on this step-by-step technique.

Combining Logical Expressions in Array Formulas

In the preceding section, you learned how to assemble simple array fragments into a more complicated single-cell formula. This method is not the only way to combine array fragments.

Suppose that you have a more complicated logical condition to evaluate (see fig. 3.6).

Fig. 3.6

You can use an array formula to test more than one condition, like Region and Group in this example.

	X Microsoft Excel - Chap03.xls				_|&|X
	File Edit View Insert Format Tools Data Window Help				_|&|X
	E4 ▼		{=SUM((Region="West")+(Group="Sales"))-SUM((Region="West")*(Group="Sales"))}		
	A	**B**			
1	SSN	Region	Group	0	
2	433-19-1495	North	Executive	4	
3	866-54-7929	West	Sales	19	
4	424-96-3230	West	Sales	15	
5	593-31-3194	West	Sales		
6	414-28-3410	North	Administration		
7	286-58-7625	South	Sales		
8	155-73-9293	East	Technical		
9	765-14-1293	South	Administration		
10	300-79-9374	North	Administration		
11	584-43-2231	North	Administration		
12	446-45-5027	North	Technical		
13	160-34-2340	South	Executive		
14	894-07-5336	West	Sales		
15	359-62-5205	North	Sales		
16	624-60-1718	East	Technical		
17	946-41-3675	South	Technical		
18	816-71-4512	North	Sales		
19	722-60-3012	East	Technical		
20	498-39-9672	West	Technical		
21	601-27-3904	South	Administration		
	Fig3.1 / Fig3.2 / Fig3.5 \ **Fig3.6** / Fig3.7 / Fig3.8 / Fig3.9				
	Ready			Sum=15	NUM

Figure 3.6 shows employees' Social Security numbers, Regions, and Groups in the organization to which the employees belong. Each worksheet range is named: SSN, Region, and Group.

Suppose that you want to determine the number of employees in the North region who are in Sales. Your first thought may be to use this array formula:

```
=SUM(IF(AND(Region="North",Group="Sales"),1,0))
```

You may expect the AND fragment to return an array of TRUE and FALSE values, depending on whether a record in the list contains North in the Region range, and Sales in the Group range. The IF() function would convert that TRUE/FALSE array to 1s and 0s. Finally, the SUM() function would total the 1s to return the number of employees who meet both criteria.

Intuitively, that approach is fine. In fact, it doesn't work.

The formula is used in cell E1 of figure 3.6, and it returns a zero value. The problem is that when you introduce the AND function into an array formula, the formula does not create the usual "hidden" array of TRUE and FALSE values. You can demonstrate this point to yourself. Open the file named CHAP03.XLS on the companion disk, activate the worksheet named Fig3.6, and select cell E1. The cell contains this array formula:

```
{=SUM(IF(AND(Region="North",Group="Sales"),1,0))}
```

In the usual way, highlight this fragment:

```
AND(Region="North",Group="Sales")
```

Press F9 to evaluate the fragment. Instead of displaying an array of TRUE and FALSE values, depending on whether both criteria are met, the fragment evaluates to one FALSE value. The logical operator AND does not return an array. Furthermore, unless all records in the worksheet ranges satisfy the two criteria, AND returns FALSE.

Of course, a workaround is available. Use the multiplication operator, ×, rather than AND, in this fashion:

```
=SUM((Region="West")×(Group="Sales"))
```

This formula is used in cell E2 of figure 3.6. Notice that the formula returns 4, which is, in fact, the number of records in the list that meet both criteria.

When you apply a mathematical operation to a logical array, Excel converts the values to 1s and 0s. Try evaluating the fragment (Region="West") by highlighting it and pressing F9. You see an array of TRUE and FALSE values. You obtain the same result if you evaluate the fragment (Group="Sales"). If you evaluate the fragment (Region="West")×(Group="Sales") you see an array of 1s and 0s.

When you multiply the two arrays together, Excel converts the result as follows:

- ▶ TRUE×TRUE = 1
- ▶ TRUE×FALSE = 0
- ▶ FALSE×TRUE = 0
- ▶ FALSE×FALSE = 0

With the array of 1s and 0s, you do not need to use the IF() function or the AND operator. You simply sum the result of the multiplication of the two logical arrays.

But what if you wanted not to count the number of employees in the North region who are in Sales, but rather the number of employees who are either in the North region or in Sales. Start by using the + operator rather than the × operator:

```
=SUM((Region="West")+(Group="Sales"))
```

The result of this array formula is 19, as shown in cell E3 of figure 3.6. When you add the two logical arrays together, Excel converts the results as follows:

- ▶ TRUE+TRUE = 2
- ▶ TRUE+FALSE = 1
- ▶ FALSE+TRUE = 1
- ▶ FALSE+FALSE = 0

A TRUE evaluates to 1 and a FALSE to 0. Therefore, the array formula results in an overcount because some employees are in both the West region and in the Sales group; they cause the value 2 in the summed array. To correct for that overcount, use this array formula:

```
{=SUM((Region="West")+(Group="Sales"))-SUM((Region="West")×(Group="Sales"))}
```

Subtracting the number of employees in Sales in the West corrects the overcount, as shown in cell E4 of figure 3.6.

Using Worksheet Functions in Array Formulas

So far, this chapter has discussed the use of two different worksheet functions in array formulas: SUM() and IF(). Although these functions are two of the most useful components of array formulas, they by no means exhaust the list.

This section describes the use of other worksheet functions in array formulas, including FREQUENCY(), MATCH(), and FIND(). You also learn how to use the INDIRECT() function in a way that was not originally intended by the designers—to build an address by concatenating text values.

Checking for Duplicates in Lists

Users frequently ask for a way to determine whether a list contains duplicate records. You have a couple of ways to make this determination using worksheet commands. One way is to sort the list and then either scan it visually for duplicates or use a formula like this in, say, cell B2:

```
=IF(A2=A1,"Duplicate","")
```

Another way is to use the Advanced Filter to copy only unique records from a list to another location. If the number of unique records returned by the Advanced Filter equals the number of records in the original list, then no duplicates exist.

However, both these approaches are time consuming and clumsy. A quicker and more elegant method is by way of an array formula (see fig. 3.7).

Fig. 3.7

The MATCH() *and* FREQUENCY() *functions are often handy components in array formulas used to analyze lists.*

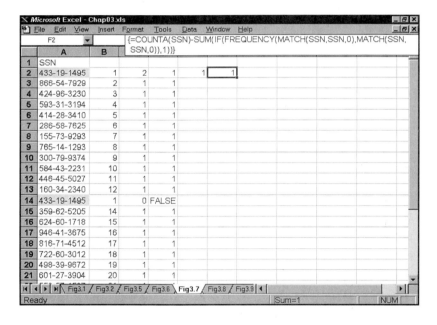

Suppose that you have a list of social security numbers, as shown in column A of figure 3.7 (this list extends through row 30 of column A). The range is named SSN. You want to make certain that the list contains no duplicates. Begin by array-entering, in B2:B30, this formula:

```
=MATCH(SSN,SSN,0)
```

As shown in figure 3.7, this formula returns the first position in SSN where each of SSN's values exists. Duplicate SSNs exist (rows 2 and 14 in figure 3.7), so MATCH() returns the value 1 in both B2 and B14. The social security number 433-19-1495 appears in both A2 and A14, and MATCH() returns the first instance of that social security number in both cases.

Now, in C2:C30, array-enter the FREQUENCY() function, as follows:

```
=FREQUENCY(B2:B30,B2:B30)
```

The FREQUENCY() function returns a count of the number of instances in one list for each range of numbers in another list. Here, the function compares the numbers in B2:B30 with themselves. Because the MATCH() function in column B returns two instances of the value 1, FREQUENCY() counts two instances, as shown in cell C2. Notice also that in cell C14, FREQUENCY() returns zero (the corresponding value of 1 in B14 has already been counted in cell C2).

Next, array-enter in D2:D30 this IF() function:

```
=IF(C2:C30,1)
```

Where's the logical expression you're used to seeing in an IF() function? It's there; it's just lurking. Recall that when you perform an arithmetic operation on a logical expression, Excel converts TRUE to 1 and FALSE to 0. Similarly, when you use numbers in place of a logical expression, Excel treats zeros as FALSE and other numbers as TRUE.

Here, the IF() function in D2:D30 evaluates the numbers in C2:C30. When it encounters a zero, the function returns FALSE. In other cases, it returns 1, the value if TRUE.

In cell E2, enter this formula:

```
=COUNTA(SSN)-SUM(D2:D30)
```

This formula simply subtracts the number of *nonduplicate* records from the total number of records in SSN. Because D2:D30 contains a 1 if a record is not a duplicate, and a 0 if it is a duplicate, the total of the 1s in D2:D30 is the number of unique records. The difference between the number of records in SSN and the number of unique records is the number of duplicates.

Finally, you can assemble these different formulas into a single-cell array formula as shown in cell F2 of figure 3.7:

```
=COUNTA(SSN)-SUM(IF(FREQUENCY(MATCH(SSN,SSN,0),MATCH(SSN,SSN,0)),1))
```

Again, as you gain facility using array formulas, you may find it less and less necessary to build their components in separate ranges and then combine them into a single cell.

Breaking the String

As you just saw in "Building Up Array Formulas," the data often has a pattern you can use as an anchor point for a formula—whether or not it's an array formula. The preceding discussion focused on finding a particular string, "-R", in a text value. You often can generalize the concept of working with a pattern to less-defined situations.

For example, suppose that you have a list of people's names. The list, which occupies one column, contains first and last names, and possibly one or more middle initials or names as well. You want to extract the last name from each cell in the column (see fig. 3.8).

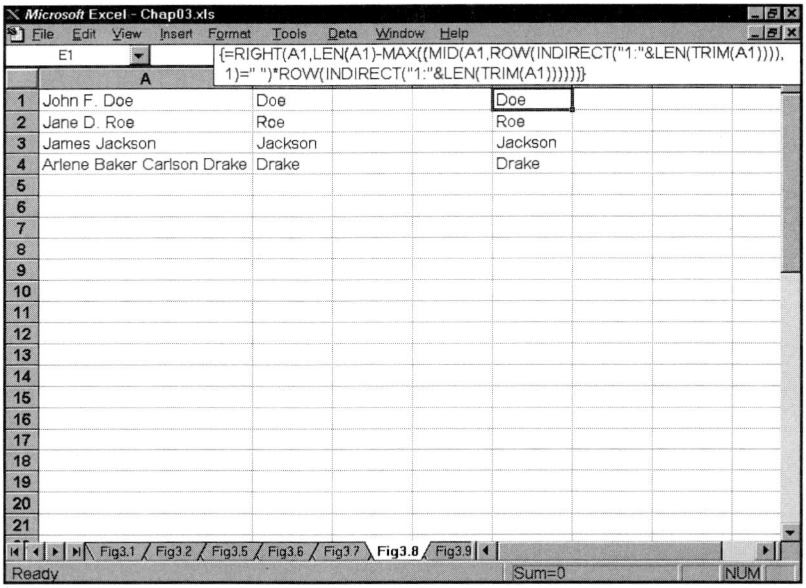

Fig. 3.8

The ROW() *function is a convenient way to put a series of integers into an array formula.*

In this case, the pattern is more vague than the existence of an "-R" in the text that's being analyzed. To extract the last name from any of the values in A1:A4 of figure 3.8, the task is to find the final blank space in the value that is followed by other characters. Those characters after the final blank are the person's last name.

You don't know how many blanks the value may have. It will have one blank with just a first and last name, two blanks with a middle initial or middle name, and three blanks with two middle names. The value may even have a leading blank or a trailing blank.

Here's the array formula that extracts the last name, shown in B1:B4 of figure 3.8:

```
{=RIGHT(A1,LEN(A1)-FIND(" ",A1,MAX(IF(ISNUMBER(FIND(" ",TRIM(A1),
    ROW($A$1:$A$50))),FIND(" ",TRIM(A1),ROW($A$1:$A$50)))))))}
```

The formula looks formidable, but it's not that bad. Instead of building up the formula from individual worksheet arrays, as was done in the prior section, try breaking it down into its components.

The core of the formula is

```
TRIM(A1)
```

The TRIM() function strips any leading and trailing blanks from the value in cell A1. Then you don't need to worry about extra blank characters that may have entered the value through mistyping.

The array formula also makes use of this expression:

```
=ROW($A$1:$A$50)
```

When used as part of an array formula, the expression returns an array that consists of the row numbers of the range in its argument: $A$1:$A$50. The row numbers of that range, in array form, are {1;2;3;...;49;50}.

3

 Tip

In Excel arrays, values in different rows of the array are separated by semicolons. Values in different columns are separated by commas, in this fashion: {1,2,3,...,49,50}.

The TRIM() and the ROW() functions work together as arguments to the FIND() function. FIND() returns the starting position of one string within another string. The basic syntax of FIND() is

```
=FIND(string to find, string to examine, place to start)
```

So, FIND("A","DATA",1) returns 2. Starting at position 1 of "DATA", which is "D", FIND() looks for the next instance of "A". The function finds "A" in the second position within "DATA", and so returns 2. FIND("A","DATA",3) returns 4, because it starts the search at the third position in "DATA".

So, consider this fragment of the array formula:

```
FIND(" ",TRIM(A1),ROW($A$1:$A$50))
```

The fragment returns this array:

```
{5;5;5;5;5;8;8;8;#VALUE!;#VALUE!;#VALUE!;...;#VALUE!}
```

Starting the search at position 1 (the first value returned by the ROW() function), FIND() locates a blank (" ") at position 5 in "John F. Doe". Starting at position 2, the second value returned by the ROW() function, FIND() also locates a blank in position 5. Not until FIND() starts at position 6, where it has bypassed the first blank, does the function begin to return the value 8. This value is the position of the second blank in "John F. Doe".

When ROW($A$1:$A$50) begins to return a value greater than 8, the starting point for the search is beyond the final instance of a blank in "John F. Doe". So FIND() begins to return #VALUE! because it cannot find a blank after position 8 in the string.

This array of numbers and #VALUE!s is placed in an IF() function:

```
IF(ISNUMBER({5;5;5;5;5;8;8;8;#VALUE!;...;#VALUE!}),{5;5;5;5;5;8;8;8;
    #VALUE!;...;#VALUE!})
```

The IF() specifies that in case a value in the array is a number, return that number. Otherwise, return nothing. The formula results in this array:

```
{5;5;5;5;5;8;8;8}
```

Now, surround that array with the MAX() function:

```
MAX({5;5;5;5;5;8;8;8})
```

MAX() returns the largest value in the array, or 8. Not coincidentally, 8 is the position of the final blank in "John F. Doe".

Before finishing this analysis, review these points:

1. The formula started by stripping any leading or trailing blanks from the value in A1.

2. The FIND() function specified " " as the value to locate, the value in A1 as the string to be searched, and the array {1;2;3;…;49;50} as the positions in A1 to start the searches.

3. The result of the FIND() function was an array consisting of numbers—positions where a blank was found—and #VALUE! errors—positions beyond which a blank was not found.

4. The array of numbers and #VALUE!s was evaluated by ISNUMBER(), inside an IF() function. If a value in the array was a number, that number was returned; otherwise, nothing was returned.

5. The maximum value in the array found in step 4 was obtained. This value is the numerically largest position in "John F. Doe" that contains a blank: 8.

Substituting that value, 8, into the full array formula results in this expression:

```
{=RIGHT(A1,LEN(A1)-8)}
```

In words, this expression means to take the length of the value in A1, returned by the LEN() function, and subtract 8 from it. The length of "John F. Doe" is 11, and 11–8 is 3. Then, the RIGHT() function returns the rightmost three characters from cell A1, or "Doe".

In summary, the array formula takes a string of indeterminate length, with an indeterminate number of blanks in it, and returns a string containing the characters following the final blank. Exactly the same formula, changing only the address of the person's full name, returns "Roe" in A2, "Jackson" in A3, and "Drake" in A4.

A minor problem may arise, though. What if the person's name is much longer than 50 characters? The result of ROW($A$1:$A$50) looks for a final blank no farther than 50 characters into the full name. And what if the full name is fairly short? Trying to peer 50 characters into "Al Smith" is wasteful. This problem is handled in the next section.

 Note

You may wonder, by the way, why you cannot get the last name by using <u>D</u>ata, T<u>e</u>xt to Columns. In some cases, that approach may be correct. But if new names are brought into the worksheet, possibly overwriting existing names, you need to repeat the Text to Columns process. And when some people use two names and others use three or more, the last names end up in different columns. The use of the array formula avoids these problems.

The point of this section has been to direct your attention to the possibility of dealing with strings on a character-by-character basis. Often, you can perform this task by combining a function that returns a sequence of numbers (in this example, ROW() was used) with a text function that uses the sequence as an argument to specify locations within the base string.

Verifying Data Accuracy

Many communications technologies depend on verifying that the bits sent from the transmitting equipment (like a modem or channel service unit) are acquired properly by the receiving equipment at the other end of the communication link. These technologies use complicated algorithms to ensure that the signal is received properly. A very simple version of this sort of verification is to take the sum of the individual digits in a number, and send that sum along with the number itself.

For example, suppose that you send the number 1358. To determine that it's received properly, you also send the number 17: 1+3+5+8. At the receiving end, the equipment adds the individual digits. If the receiver gets the same sum (17) that you sent, then it's long odds that both numbers were sent correctly.

Figure 3.9 shows an example of how you can use an array formula to emulate this process, in a slightly different context.

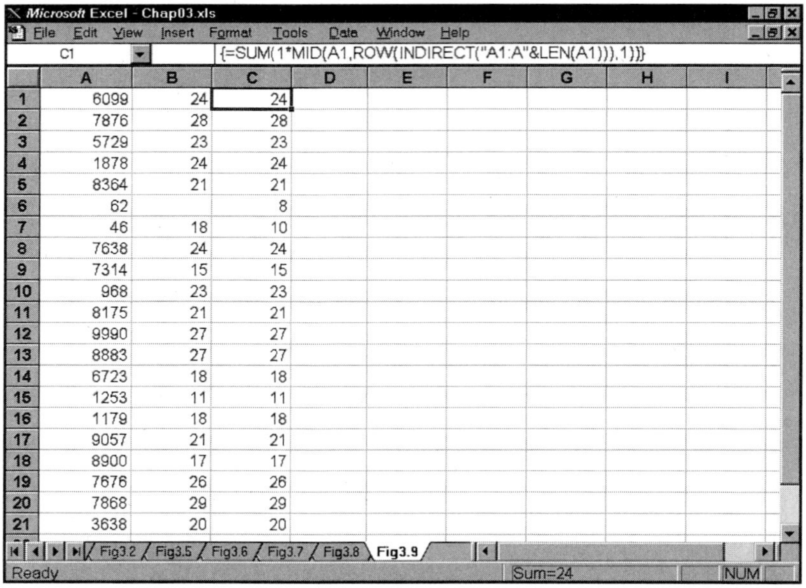

Fig. 3.9

An error, due to a stray carriage return character, has caused the value 6246 to occupy two cells rather than one.

When you use Excel to open a text file, the Text Wizard usually starts. You are given an opportunity to specify the boundaries between columns in the file. At times, gremlins such as nonprinting characters interfere with the accuracy of the import process, especially if the text file's columns are intended to be a fixed width. For example, if a carriage return character has found its way into the text file where it does not belong, your data can be taken out of sync.

Figure 3.9 shows how to provide for data verification in a way that's similar to data verification in communications. Column A contains the desired data, and column B contains a checksum for each row in column A: the sum of the individual digits. Both columns A and B were imported into an Excel worksheet from a text file.

Cell C1 uses this array formula to recalculate the checksum for the number in cell A1:

```
{=SUM(1*MID(A1,ROW(INDIRECT("A1:A"&LEN(A1))),1))}
```

The interesting part of this formula is its use of the INDIRECT() function:

```
INDIRECT("A1:A"&LEN(A1))
```

The fragment LEN(A1) just returns the number of characters in cell A1—in this case, 4. After LEN() is evaluated, the INDIRECT() function becomes

```
INDIRECT("A1:A4")
```

The normal use of INDIRECT() is to obtain the value of a cell specified in the argument. Although INDIRECT() displays cell contents, it actually returns the reference of the cell or range of the argument. In this example, however, the function is used because it accepts a text string as an address—that is, `"A1:A4"`. By specifying `LEN(A1)` as the final portion of `INDIRECT()`'s argument, the reference is allowed to vary as a function of the number of characters in A1, A2, or whatever cell is used as an argument to `LEN()`.

Surrounding the `INDIRECT()` function by the `ROW()` function gives

```
=ROW(INDIRECT("A1:A4"))
```

When array-entered, this expression returns the array {1;2;3;4}. This array contains the row number of each row in A1:A4.

Continuing to peel the onion, the `MID()` function becomes

```
MID(A1,{1;2;3;4},1)
```

The `MID()` function returns characters from its first argument (here, A1), starting at each position in its second argument (here, {1;2;3;4}), and as many characters as specified in its third argument (here, 1). Therefore, the `MID()` function, when used on cell A1, evaluates to this array:

```
{"6","0","9","9"}
```

Multiplying each element of the array by 1 converts the elements from text to numeric values, and the `SUM()` function totals them. This result provides the required checksum to compare with the checksum read from the text file, in column B: 6+0+9+9 = 24.

Summary

In this chapter, you have learned some ways to determine when a formula must be array-entered. In particular, you must array-enter a formula that uses a function that returns an array itself, and a formula that employs arrays not found directly on the worksheet.

You have learned how to evaluate portions of array formulas by means of the F9 (Calculate) key, and how to use that facility to peer inside the formula to examine the arrays it returns—arrays that may not be visible on the worksheet.

This chapter has also described how to enter the components of a complicated array formula directly on the worksheet, and subsequently how to combine those components into a single formula. You have seen how to multiply and add logical arrays in formulas to emulate the effect of logical ANDs and ORs.

You saw three examples of using array formulas to return otherwise inaccessible results: checking for duplicate values in a list, verifying that data has entered the worksheet correctly, and extracting the final name from a cell that contains a first, middle, and last name.

Sometimes, of course, even an array formula cannot return the results you are after. In these cases, you usually need to resort to creating your own, user-defined functions. Using VBA, you can create new functions that the user can enter directly on the worksheet, just as though they were built-in functions such as SUM() and IF(). You also can arrange to create user-defined array functions. The next chapter explores this topic in detail.

chapter 4

User-Defined Functions

4

by Conrad Carlberg

In this chapter

◆ **Distinguishing between subroutines and functions**
You use subroutines and functions for different purposes.

◆ **Writing a user-defined function**
This section describes a user-defined function's elements, its scope, and its use in the Function Wizard.

◆ **Writing a user-defined array function**
Learn how to write a function that returns an array, and use it to increase your code's speed.

Excel supplies over 300 built-in functions, ranging from the simple SUM() to the esoteric WEIBULL(). You also can find many additional functions in the Analysis ToolPak, which contains user-defined functions supplied by Microsoft. These functions extend the reach of the built-in functions so you can, for example, obtain imaginary numbers.

Excel cannot anticipate *all* the needs you may have, though, and it offers you the ability to write your own custom functions. The custom functions you write act just like those found in the Analysis ToolPak. You can enter the functions directly on the worksheet, or you can use them in other VBA code to smooth out your subroutines.

Distinguishing Between Subroutines and Functions

Two basic structures occupy VBA modules: subroutines and functions. You can create a block of VBA code that begins with a statement like this (where Sub is short for *subroutine*):

```
Sub ShowUnlockedCells()
```

Or code that begins like this:

```
Function TruncateRandom()
```

One major difference exists between a sub and a function:

- ▶ Subs can make changes to objects in your workbook.
- ▶ Functions can't.

On the other hand:

- ▶ If you enter the name of a sub in a worksheet cell, it cannot return a value.
- ▶ Functions can.

Think of the distinction in these terms: When you want to do something to a workbook, such as change the number format of a range of cells, delete a column, save a workbook, or display a toolbar, you use Excel's main menu. If you want to do something with VBA that you may also do from a menu, write a sub.

However, when you want to calculate something, such as a sum or an imaginary number, you enter a formula on the worksheet (perhaps including the name of a function, and perhaps some arguments). If you want to do something with VBA that you might also do by entering a formula in a worksheet cell, write a function.

When you write a function in VBA, it's called a *user-defined function*, or *UDF*. As usual, all the VBA UDFs and subroutines described in this chapter are in the file named CHAP04.XLS on the companion CD.

Changing Objects

Writing a subroutine in VBA often is easier than writing a function because you can make use of the macro recorder to give you a head start. For example, suppose that you want to write a subroutine to flag each cell in the worksheet's used range if the cell is unlocked. You take these steps:

1. Choose Tools, Record Macro, Record New Macro.
2. In the Macro Name edit box, type **ShowUnlockedCells** and choose OK.
3. Select cell A1.
4. Choose Format, Cells and click the Patterns tab.
5. Select the red cell in the Color box and choose OK.
6. Click the Stop Recording button or choose Tools, Record Macro, Stop Recording.

When you click the new sheet tab that appears (usually named *Module1*, unless a numbered module sheet is already in your workbook), it should look like this:

```
Sub ShowUnlockedCells()
    Range("A1").Select
    With Selection.Interior
        .ColorIndex = 3
        .Pattern = xlSolid
        .PatternColorIndex = xlAutomatic
    End With
End Sub
```

Now, if you've had a little practice in writing VBA code, you can edit the macro so it looks like this:

```
Sub ShowUnlockedCells()
Dim SheetCell As Variant
For Each SheetCell In ActiveSheet.UsedRange
    If SheetCell.Locked = False Then
        With SheetCell.Interior
            .ColorIndex = 3
            .Pattern = xlSolid
            .PatternColorIndex = xlAutomatic
        End With
    End If
Next SheetCell
End Sub
```

The main result of the editing is to cause the subroutine to examine all cells in the worksheet's used range, not just cell A1. If you write this macro, if E10 is unlocked, and if G15 is the worksheet's last cell, your worksheet will look like figure 4.1 when you run the macro.

Fig. 4.1

The subroutine can modify the characteristics of workbook objects.

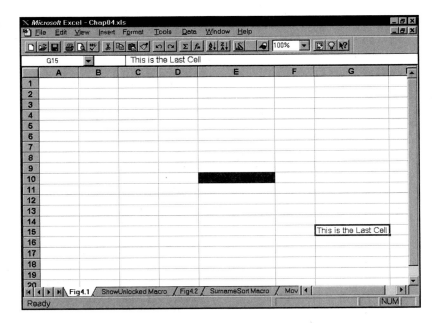

Making these modifications is due to knowing these things:

▶ How to create a For Each...Next loop.

▶ The control variable of a For Each...Next loop must be declared as a Variant.

▶ The range to the left and above the Last Cell of a worksheet is its UsedRange.

▶ The locked vs. unlocked status of a cell is its Locked property.

You do not need to know that you change a cell's pattern by referring to its Interior, that a cell's color is controlled by its ColorIndex, that 3 means *Red*, that a cell's Interior has a Pattern and a PatternColorIndex property, and so on.

The macro recorder can be a huge time-saver when you're creating VBA code that manipulates workbook objects. You just turn on the recorder, do something similar to what you want your code to do, stop the recorder, and then modify the code to give it a broader effect.

The same is not true of writing a UDF. If you use the macro recorder to emulate the action of entering a formula, all you get is a subroutine that enters that exact formula in the active cell. You need to be much more creative, and rely on your own knowledge and ingenuity, to write a UDF.

Returning Results

People who are new to VBA sometimes get the impression that you can create a macro using the macro recorder, and then cause the macro to execute by entering its name in a worksheet cell, just as you do with a built-in function or a UDF. That, of course, isn't possible.

For example, suppose that you have the subroutine ShowUnlockedCells, given earlier, in a module of the active workbook. You cannot enter =ShowUnlockedCells() in some worksheet cell and thereby cause the macro to run. Instead, you need to choose Tools, Macro, select ShowUnlockedCells from the list box, and choose Run.

You also cannot replace the keyword Sub in the procedure definition and replace it with Function. If you then enter =ShowUnlockedCells() on the worksheet, the function merely returns the #VALUE! error value. If a function attempts to modify an object, as does ShowUnlockedCells, it returns #VALUE!.

Furthermore (yes, this is getting tiresome, but people try these things, so we want you to know about them), you cannot call a subroutine from a function and expect that subroutine to modify a workbook object. Calling a subroutine from a function is entirely possible, but if that subroutine attempts to change an object, then the function itself fails.

On the other hand, calling a function from a subroutine is typical. The function usually returns a value that the subroutine needs, and the subroutine uses the value to complete its work. This event occurs most frequently when a subroutine needs to recalculate a value repeatedly. Instead of using the same calculation code over and over in the subroutine, you just call the function from the subroutine each time you need a new value.

For example, suppose that you have a list of names consisting of first, middle, and last, in cells A1:A100 of a worksheet. You want to sort the list by *last* name (see fig. 4.2).

Fig. 4.2

Sorting this list by last name requires that you separate the surname from the first and middle names.

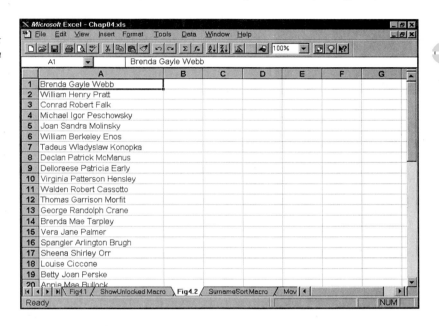

Using <u>D</u>ata, <u>S</u>ort on this list doesn't work because Excel would sort it on the basis of first name. One alternative is to write VBA code that strips the surnames from the strings in column A, writes them to column B, and then sorts the columns using column B as the sort key. This procedure implies a subroutine, because you need to change objects. The subroutine might look like this:

```
Option Explicit
Option Base 1
Sub SortBySurname()
Dim CountNames As Integer, i As Integer, CurrentSurname As String
Dim NameRange As Range
Selection.CurrentRegion.Select
Set NameRange = Selection
CountNames = NameRange.Rows.Count
```

Through this point in the subroutine, some variables have been declared and their values set. The meat of the routine is in this loop:

```
For i = 1 To CountNames
    CurrentSurname = GetLastName(NameRange(i, 1))
    NameRange.Offset(i - 1, 1).Resize(1, 1) = CurrentSurname
Next i
```

In the loop, the name of the *i*th person in NameRange—the worksheet range that contains the full names—is passed to the UDF named GetLastName. The UDF returns the *i*th person's surname, and the subroutine writes that surname in the corresponding row of column B.

The subroutine finishes by selecting the data in both columns A and B and sorting that range on column B:

```
Selection.CurrentRegion.Select
Selection.Sort Key1:=NameRange.Offset(i - 1, 1).Resize(1, 1), _
    Order1:=xlAscending, Header:= xlNo, OrderCustom:=1, _
    MatchCase:=False, Orientation:=xlTopToBottom
End Sub
```

The UDF, GetLastName, may be coded like this:

```
Function GetLastName(FullName)
Dim LetterCounter As Integer
Dim WhichCharacter As Integer
FullName = RTrim(FullName)
LetterCounter = Len(FullName)
```

Again, the preceding five statements declare the function and its variables, and make two preliminary assignments. FullName is replaced by the value of FullName, with trailing blanks trimmed off. LetterCounter is given the value of the length of the right-trimmed full name.

Then, this loop finds the location of the final blank character in the full name:

```
Do While InStr(LetterCounter, FullName, " ", 1) = 0
    LetterCounter = LetterCounter - 1
Loop
```

The control variable LetterCounter tells the InStr() function where to look in FullName for a blank character. Because LetterCounter was initialized to the number of characters in FullName, InStr() begins by examining FullName's final character. If that character is *not* a blank, InStr() returns a zero value. Then, LetterCounter is decremented by 1. The next time the loop executes, InStr() examines the next-to-last character in FullName.

The loop progresses until InStr returns a number other than zero, which means the final blank character in FullName has been found. Then, the function itself is assigned the value that it is to return:

```
GetLastName = Right(FullName, Len(FullName) - LetterCounter)
End Function
```

The UDF itself is assigned the rightmost characters in FullName—those following the final blank character. The UDF returns this value to the main subroutine: the current surname.

After control returns to the main subroutine for the final time, the sub completes the work of putting the surnames on the worksheet and performing the sort (see fig. 4.3).

Fig. 4.3

The surnames are copied from the full names into column B, and the data in columns A and B is sorted using the surnames as the sort key.

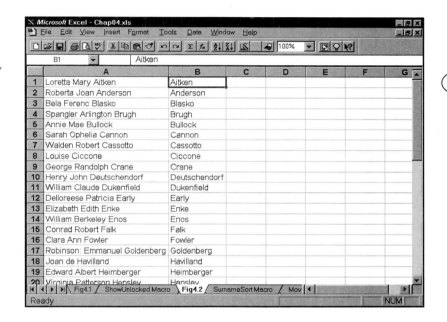

Yes, this code could be placed in the body of the SortBySurname subroutine, eliminating the need for a UDF entirely. But several reasons exist for making the code a separate function:

▶ You may want to do things with the surname other than sorting the list of full names. If the code is separated as a function, you can use the function in other contexts without having to rewrite the code.

▶ Interpreting the subroutine's purpose is easier if the code that gets the surname is separate. You don't need to pore over the function's code to trace the subroutine's actions.

▶ In general, working with smaller chunks of code is easier than working with lengthier ones. When you're writing your VBA code, try to make each subroutine or function no longer than a screenful of code. That way, you don't need to scroll around as much to keep track of what's going on.

Writing a User-Defined Function

With Excel, you not only can write your own UDF, but you can make it look just like a built-in function. You can make the UDF accessible to other workbooks so the module that contains the UDF need not be in the active workbook.

You also can make the UDF accessible to the Function Wizard and assign it to a function category such as Math and Trig, Text, Date, and so on. You can even include a custom Help topic so a user can obtain context-sensitive information on how to use your UDF. This section describes how to make these things happen.

Identifying the Elements

Most UDFs have these elements:

▶ A name, so you can enter that name in a worksheet cell. The name is specified in the first statement of the function itself, which is called the *function declaration*.

▶ Arguments that you supply to the function when you call it. These arguments can be worksheet ranges or actual values. The names and types of the arguments are given in the function declaration statement.

▶ Code that calculates the value the function should return.

▶ Code that makes the function itself equal to the value it calculates.

Suppose that you want to write a function to return a moving average—the average, perhaps, of your utility costs for the three prior months, whenever those months actually occur. Here's one way to write the function:

```
Function MovingAverage(PriorThree As Object)
Dim TemporaryValue As Double, i As Integer
TemporaryValue = 0
For i = 1 To 3
    TemporaryValue = TemporaryValue + PriorThree(i, 1)
Next i
MovingAverage = TemporaryValue / 3
End Function
```

The UDF's first statement, the function declaration, defines the name of the function and the arguments it takes. PriorThree is defined as an object and refers to the monthly utility costs that are passed to the function. For example, suppose that you entered this line on the worksheet:

```
=MovingAverage(A1:A3)
```

PriorThree refers to the worksheet range A1:A3.

Then, two additional variables are declared. TemporaryValue holds the result of the UDF's intermediate calculations, and i is a control variable for the For...Next loop.

The loop cycles through the three values in the range named `PriorThree`, each time adding the current value to `TemporaryValue`. After the loop is complete, `TemporaryValue` is divided by 3, and the result is assigned to the function `MovingAverage`. That value is the value of the cell where you enter this line (see fig. 4.4):

```
=MovingAverage(A1:A3)
```

Fig. 4.4

The UDF behaves exactly like a built-in function when you enter it on the worksheet.

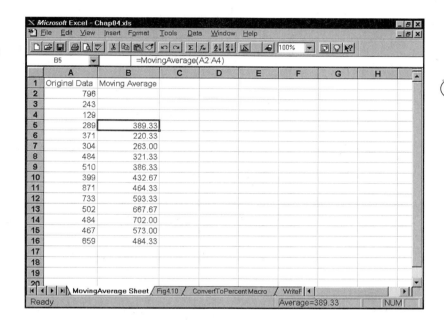

Notice that the UDF contains each of the four basic elements:

- ▶ A name (`MovingAverage`)
- ▶ Arguments that you can supply to the function (`PriorThree`)
- ▶ Code that calculates the value the function should return (the `For...Next` loop)
- ▶ Code that makes the function itself equal to the value it calculates (setting `MovingAverage` equal to `TemporaryValue / 3`)

Notice also that `PriorThree` is defined as an Object type in the function declaration. The Object type is a generic type, which can stand for any valid object: a range, a cell, a worksheet, a button, and so on. Usually, when you declare an object variable, you can and should declare it as the specific object it is meant to represent, as these two examples show:

```
Dim InputRange As Range
```

or

```
Dim OutputCell As Cell
```

However, when you declare a UDF that is to accept an object as an argument, you should declare the argument as Object, not as Range or Cell. Specifically, this syntax works:

```
Function MovingAverage(PriorThree As Object)
```

But this syntax does not work:

```
Function MovingAverage(PriorThree As Range)
```

If you declared PriorThree as Range, the UDF would return the #NAME? error value.

One further point: the TemporaryValue variable is not needed. It was included in this example for clarity. Instead, you can use this version:

```
Function MovingAverage(PriorThree As Object)
Dim i As Integer
MovingAverage = 0
For i = 1 To 3
   MovingAverage = MovingAverage + PriorThree(i, 1)
Next i
MovingAverage = MovingAverage / 3
End Function
```

 Tip

If you want your function to recalculate automatically whenever a calculation occurs anywhere on the worksheet (like NOW() or RAND()), use Application.Volatile as the first statement after your function declaration.

Defining the Arguments

A function's *arguments* are the values you pass to it, as in this simple example:

```
=SUM(1,1,2,4,8,16,32)
```

The numbers 1,1,2,...,32 are the function's arguments. Consider this example:

```
=SUM(A1:A10)
```

The values in the range A1:A10 are the arguments to the SUM() function. When you write a UDF, you must supply information that defines the names of the arguments and their data types.

You need to define the names of the arguments so your code can refer to them as the function does its work. The MovingAverage function described earlier is declared in this way:

```
Function MovingAverage(PriorThree As Object)
```

The argument `PriorThree` is defined in the declaration so the function has something to work with. The argument is defined as the Object type because the intent is to pass a worksheet range to the function.

Suppose instead that you write a UDF that returns 1 divided by the product of two arguments, and the arguments can be floating-point numbers. In that case, you can declare the UDF in this way:

```
Function Reciprocal(FirstNumber As Double, SecondNumber As Double)
```

Both `MovingAverage()` and `Reciprocal()` also can be declared this way:

```
Function MovingAverage(PriorThree)
Function MovingAverage(PriorThree As Variant)
Function Reciprocal(FirstNumber, SecondNumber)
Function Reciprocal(FirstNumber As Variant, SecondNumber As Variant)
```

The first two declarations are equivalent, as are the second two. When you do not supply a data type for a function's arguments, VBA treats them as variants. Therefore, the user can supply anything when entering this function:

```
=MovingAverage("Paul")
```

```
=Reciprocal(TRUE,FALSE)
```

The functions do not work as intended, but the values `"Paul"`, `TRUE`, and `FALSE` are accepted by the functions because their arguments were defined as Variant.

It's usually best to define arguments explicitly (as Double, or as Object, or as String, and so on) for a couple reasons:

▶ Variants occupy more memory than other variable types, and processing Variants takes slightly more time than processing a more basic data type.

▶ Documenting and debugging your code is easier when you have defined arguments explicitly.

You may be familiar with built-in functions such as `MATCH()` or `LINEST()` that enable you to omit certain arguments if you want, as this example shows:

```
=MATCH(4,A1:A200,1)
```

The preceding formula is equivalent to this formula:

```
=MATCH(4,A1:A200)
```

The third argument, 1 in the first example, is optional and defaults to 1 if it's omitted.

You can specify that an argument or arguments in your UDF are optional by using the Optional keyword in the UDF's list of arguments. For example, suppose that you want to create random integers, and that you want—optionally—to specify the order of magnitude of the integers as well as a minimum value. On the worksheet, you can enter this line:

```
=TRUNC(RAND()×100)+100
```

This formula returns a random integer between 100 and 199. If this requirement is frequent, you may want to write a UDF along these lines:

```
Function IRand(Optional Magnitude As Variant,
   Optional Lowest As Variant)
If IsMissing(Magnitude) Then
   Magnitude = 10
End If
If IsMissing(Lowest) Then
   Lowest = 1
End If
IRand = Int(Rnd() * Magnitude + Lowest)
End Function
```

All you need to enter is the following formula to return a random integer between 1 and 10, because you have defined the arguments as optional:

```
=IRAND()
```

The preceding formula is equivalent to entering this:

```
=TRUNC(RAND()×10) + 10
```

Or you can enter this formula to return a random integer between 100 and 200:

```
=IRAND(100,100)
```

To arrange for one or more arguments to be optional, you must follow a couple of rules:

▶ After you have specified that an argument is optional, all subsequent arguments also must be optional. That is, this declaration is legal:

```
Function IRand(Optional Magnitude As Variant, Optional Lowest As Variant)
```

So is this declaration:

```
Function IRand(Magnitude As Variant, Optional Lowest As Variant)
```

But this one isn't:

```
Function IRand(Optional Magnitude As Variant, Lowest As Variant)
```

▶ You must declare an optional argument as Variant.

In the IRAND function, notice the use of the If statements. They check to see if an argument is missing. If it is, the If statements assign default values to the arguments.

Note

The IRAND code uses the VBA Int() function. Although this function is available in VBA and is described in the online Help for VBA, it does not appear in the list of Math functions in the Object Browser. Keep in mind that Int() is available if you ever need to truncate a value to an integer when you're using VBA.

Extending the Function's Scope

When you create a UDF, it's available initially only to the workbook that contains its module. That is, if you open another workbook and use the UDF, the new workbook is unable to find it, and Excel returns the #NAME? error value. The best way to extend the UDF's scope—to make it available to other workbooks—is to store it in an add-in.

Add-ins have several advantages:

▶ They can be made available to Excel automatically when you start it, and because they're available to Excel, they're also available to any workbook, new or existing, that you open.

▶ Add-ins are precompiled. Excel has already checked the code's syntax for errors, so it need not check again. This step saves a little time when you invoke add-in functions or subroutines.

▶ Add-ins are not visible to the user, so they aren't in the way of other workbooks that you have open.

▶ Because add-ins are invisible, the user cannot edit any special code you place in the add-in. (Yes, there are ways to open, display, and edit an add-in, even one created in Excel version 7. To keep our Good Citizenship award, we're not disclosing them.)

 Note

Add-ins are not truly "compiled" in the traditional sense; that is, they are not files that can be directly executed outside the context of Excel. However, the term "compiled" has been extended to add-ins through informal usage.

To save your UDFs in an add-in, take these steps:

1. Combine all your UDFs into one module or into several modules in one workbook.

2. Delete any worksheets and dialog sheets from the workbook. This step is not a requirement, but it saves disk space and it's nearly always feasible to omit such sheets from add-ins that contain only UDFs.

3. Choose Tools, Ma_k_e Add-In. The Save File dialog box appears.

4. Navigate to a folder where you want to store the add-in. The location is unimportant; Excel saves information about the path for you.

5. Choose OK.

To arrange access to the UDFs stored in the add-in, take these steps:

1. Choose Tools, Add-Ins. The dialog box shown in figure 4.5 appears.

2. Mark the check box that corresponds to your add-in.

3. Choose OK.

Now, any time you start Excel, your UDFs are available to any workbook you have open. This availability continues until you use Tools, Add-Ins and clear your add-in's check box.

Fig. 4.5

Checked add-ins are available to Excel. Add-ins are not necessarily installed until you require them.

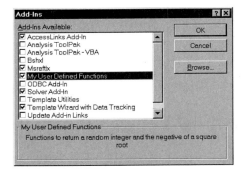

Notice in figure 4.5 that the selected add-in has, in the comment box, a title and comments that describe its functionality. To specify a title and comments, follow these steps:

1. Choose File, Properties.

2. Click the Summary tab. The dialog box shown in figure 4.6 appears.

3. Enter a brief title in the Title edit box.

4. Enter a brief comment in the Comments box. The comment typed in the Summary tab can be longer, but only the first 112 characters appear as a description below the Add-ins Available list box.

5. Choose OK.

Fig. 4.6

You can define a title and comments for your add-in by using File, Properties.

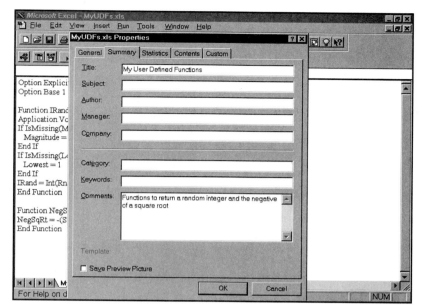

4

Putting a UDF in the Function Wizard

You can arrange for your UDF to appear in the Function Wizard. To do so, take these steps:

1. With the module that contains the UDF active, choose View, Object Browser, or click the Object Browser button. The Object Browser dialog box appears (see fig. 4.7).

2. Select the workbook that contains the module in the Libraries/Workbooks drop-down box.

3. Select the name of its module in the Objects/Modules list box.

4. Select the UDF's name in the Methods/Properties list box. Click Options. The Macro Options dialog box appears (see fig. 4.8).

5. Type a description for your UDF in the Description edit box. This text appears in the Function Wizard's dialog box when you select the UDF.

6. Choose a category for your UDF in the Function Category drop-down box.

7. Choose OK to close the Macro Options dialog box, and choose Close in the Object Browser dialog box.

Fig. 4.7

Use the Object Browser
to make your UDF
available to the
Function Wizard.

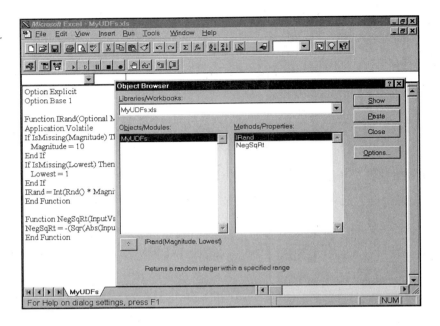

Fig. 4.8

Set the options for your
UDF as it will appear
in the Function
Wizard by using the
Macro Options dialog
box.

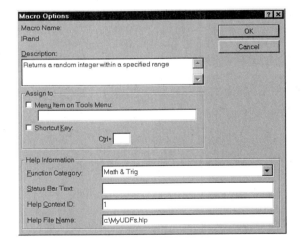

Do you see why you do not assign a menu item or an accelerator (shortcut) key in the Macro Options dialog box when you are using it to specify options for a UDF? Remember, you cannot modify an object by means of a VBA function—you can use it only to return values. If you placed a new menu item in the Tools menu that represented the UDF, what would that item do when selected?

A menu item cannot actually enter the function in the worksheet. That action would constitute changing an object. Because a function cannot change an object, the function would calculate a value but the value wouldn't appear anywhere. Your user must enter the UDF from the keyboard or from the Function Wizard.

You use the Menu Item on Tools Menu and the Shortcut Key check boxes only if you are setting the options for a subroutine—perhaps one that entered the UDF on the worksheet for you, much like the Sum button on Excel's Standard toolbar. You then can start the subroutine from the Tools menu or by way of a keyboard shortcut. The subroutine can modify an object, and you can actually see its result.

After you have set the options for your UDF, it appears in the Function Wizard, as shown in figure 4.9.

Fig. 4.9

The Description and Function Category that you assign to the UDF in the Macro Options dialog box take effect in the Function Wizard.

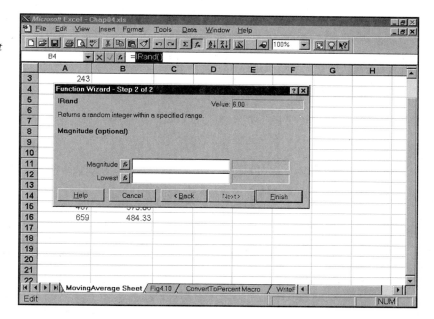

Providing Custom Help

You can provide custom help on the use of your UDF. This help information is displayed when the user clicks the Help button in the Function Wizard, after selecting the UDF from the list of available functions.

Arranging to display custom help involves several steps:

1. Decide what information you should show.

2. Optionally, decide to make several help topics available in the same file. You might do this if, for example, you place several UDFs in the Function Wizard and include help information about each UDF in one help file.

3. Place the information in a text file.

4. Run a conversion utility on the text file.

5. Specify to Excel that the help file exists and where it exists.

At a minimum, your help file should contain this information:

▶ The name of the function

▶ A description of what the function does

▶ A listing of the function's arguments

▶ An example of the usage of the function, with specific arguments and the return value for those arguments

Suppose that you want to provide a help file for two functions: IRAND() and NegSqRt(). (Both these functions are in the module named MYUDFS in MYUDFS.XLS on the companion CD.) You begin by creating a text file that contains this text:

*1

IRAND( ) function

The IRAND( ) function returns a random integer. It takes two arguments:

Magnitude is the order of magnitude of the random number.

Lowest is the smallest value that IRAND returns.

Both Magnitude and Lowest are optional. If you omit Magnitude, it defaults to 10. If you omit Lowest, it defaults to 1.

Examples:

=IRAND(100,200) returns a random integer between 200 and 300.

=IRAND( ) returns a random integer between 1 and 10.

*2

NegSqRt( ) function

The NegSqRt( ) function returns the negative of a number's square root. It takes one argument:

InputValue is a number that you supply. InputValue is not optional. If InputValue is itself negative, NegSqRt returns the negative of the square root of the absolute value of InputValue.

Examples:

=NegSqRt(9) returns –3.

=NegSqRt(–49) returns –7.

(This text is in MYUDFS.TXT on the companion CD.) Note the use of asterisks before the numbers in the preceding text. You use asterisks to set off one topic from another, and to identify a topic with a particular topic number.

You can create the text file using an application such as Notepad or the Windows Write accessory. You also can use Word. If you use a program such as Word to create the file, be sure to save it as a text file, not as a Word document. In Word, you use File, Save As, and choose Text Only (*.TXT) in the Save File as Type drop-down box.

After you have saved the file, you need to convert it to the proper help file format using conversion utilities such as HELPCONV.EXE and HC.EXE. These utilities accept your text file as input and convert it to a format that's compatible with the Windows help facility.

For example, if you use HELPCONV.EXE, you exit to DOS and go to a directory that contains both HELPCONV.EXE and your text file. Suppose that your text file is named MYUDFS.TXT. At the DOS prompt, you type this line:

HELPCONV MyUDFs.txt

Press Enter. HELPCONV.EXE performs some preliminary conversions on your text file and hands it off to HC.EXE. The latter utility finishes the conversion process. When the process is finished, two files are in place of the original MYUDFS.TXT. The original version of your text file is in the directory, but now it is named MYUDFS.BAK. The converted version of the file, named MYUDFS.TXT, also is in the directory, even though the file is no longer a pure text file. MYUDFS.TXT is now the help file itself.

The final step is to specify to Excel that the help file exists and where to find it. Take these steps:

1. From Excel, open the file named MYUDFS.XLS.

2. With the module sheet active, choose View, Object Browser or click the Object Browser button.

 Tip

A quicker way to get to the Macro Options dialog box is to place your cursor on the function's declaration line, choose Tools, Macro, and click the Options button.

---

3. Select MYUDFS.WKS in the Libraries/Workbooks drop-down box.

4. Select the MyUDFs module in the Objects/Modules list box. This module contains your UDFs.

5. Select IRAND in the Methods/Properties list box. Click Options. The Macro Options dialog box appears (again see fig. 4.8).

6. The help information for the IRAND function is topic 1, identified by the characters *1, in the custom help file. Therefore, type **1** in the Help Context ID box.

7. Suppose that you have stored the custom help file in C:\MSOFFICE\EXCEL. In that case, type this line in the Help File Name text box:

   C:\MSOFFICE\EXCEL\MyUDFs.txt

8. Choose OK to close the Macro Options dialog box.

9. Repeat steps 5 through 7, but define the options for the NegSqRt function rather than the IRAND function. In step 6, type **2** in the Help Context ID box.

10. Choose OK in the Macro Options dialog box, and choose Close in the Object Browser dialog box.

You now can use Tools, Make Add-In to convert MYUDFS.XLS to MYUDFS.XLA. The information about the help file and its topics are stored with the add-in version. When you use the Function Wizard to enter the function, and you click the Help button in any of the Function Wizard's steps, help information appears, as shown in figure 4.10.

Fig. 4.10

A topic in your custom help file appears when the user chooses Help from the Function Wizard.

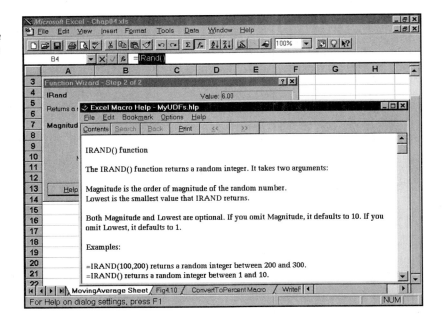

You also can use the preceding steps to create a help file that's associated with a Help button on a custom dialog box. You create the help file itself in the same fashion—

by creating a text file, possibly with numbered topics, and converting it using HELPCONV.EXE. But instead of using the Macro Options dialog box to assign the help file to a particular function, you take these steps:

1. Select or create a Help button on your dialog sheet.

2. Click the Edit Code button on the Forms toolbar. This step creates a new subroutine on the module sheet, which executes when the user clicks the Help button.

3. In the new subroutine, type this line of VBA code:

```
Application.Help "C:\MSOFFICE\EXCEL\MySubs.txt", 2
```

(This line assumes that your help file is named MYSUBS.TXT, is located in the C:\MSOFFICE\EXCEL subdirectory, and that the help topic you want to display is topic 2 in MYSUBS.TXT.)

Now, when your user wants help information about using your custom dialog box, clicking the Help button in the dialog box displays the text you placed in the custom help file.

Writing a User-Defined Array Function

The UDFs that this chapter has discussed so far have all returned single values. You also can write UDFs that return arrays—much like built-in functions can return arrays.

For example, the built-in FREQUENCY() function returns the number of numeric values in one range that fall between the limits defined in another range (the "bin" range). To obtain the full output, you must first make a worksheet selection consisting of several cells, and then array-enter the FREQUENCY() function and its arguments.

You can write UDFs that operate in the same fashion. If the user starts by selecting several cells, and then array-enters your UDF and its arguments, the UDF returns an array of values.

Declaring an Array

Two major differences exist between a UDF that returns a value in a single cell and a UDF that returns an array:

▶ The statement that assigns values to the name of the UDF sets the UDF equal to an *array*.

▶ The function itself must be declared as *Variant*, or declared with no particular data type—which defaults to Variant.

Here's an example of a UDF that returns its arguments as percentages:

```
Option Explicit
Option Base 1
Function ConvertToPercent(InputArray As Object) As Variant
Dim TempArray As Variant
Dim RowCount As Integer, ColumnCount As Integer
Dim i As Integer, j As Integer, Total As Double
RowCount = InputArray.Rows.Count
ColumnCount = InputArray.Columns.Count
ReDim TempArray(RowCount, ColumnCount)
For i = 1 To RowCount
   For j = 1 To ColumnCount
      Total = Total + InputArray(i, j)
   Next j
Next i
For i = 1 To RowCount
   For j = 1 To ColumnCount
      TempArray(i, j) = InputArray(i, j) / Total
   Next j
Next i
ConvertToPercent = TempArray
End Function
```

Notice that the function is declared as a Variant. This declaration is necessary because the next-to-last statement assigns the values in TempArray to ConvertToPercent. Because the function itself is declared as Variant, VBA is able to dimension the function to the same dimensions as TempArray, and to populate the function's values with those in TempArray.

The user can enter ConvertToPercent on the worksheet by highlighting a range of the same dimensions as another range, and array-entering, say, =ConvertToPercent(A1:C10). The result is shown in figure 4.11. The Percent format used in cells E1:G10 has been set by hand—not, of course, by the UDF.

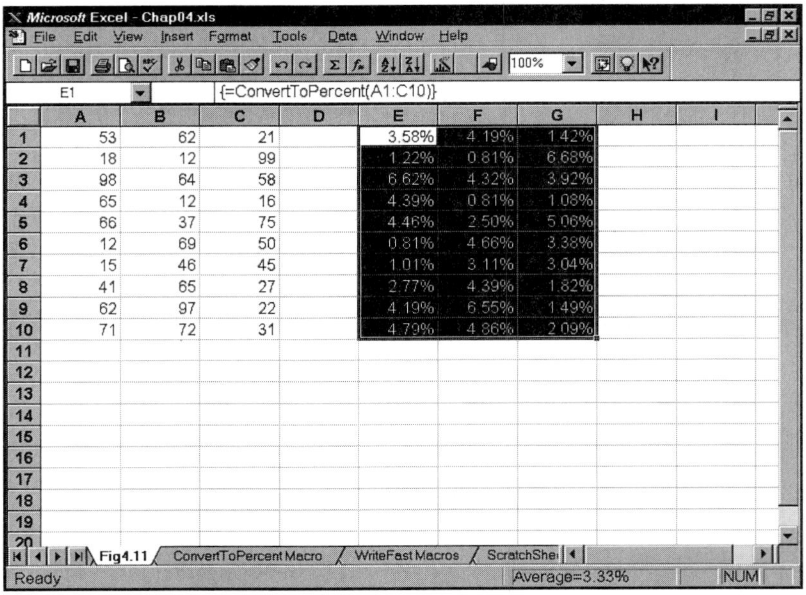

Fig. 4.11

The user array-enters a UDF that returns an array, just as you enter a built-in array formula.

Increasing Speed with a User-Defined Array Function

A unique way to use a UDF is as a means of quickly writing the results of a VBA subroutine to a worksheet.

You can write output to a worksheet using three broad methods:

▶ *Cell by cell.* For example:

```
For i = 1 to 50
    For j = 1 to 50
        Cells(i,j) = OutputArray(i,j)
    Next j
Next i
```

Here, OutputArray contains the values that the subroutine has calculated, and each of 2500 values (50 × 50) is written, one by one, to a cell on the active worksheet. This technique is the slowest of the three methods.

▶ *Range assignment.* For example:

```
Range("A1:AX50") = OutputArray
```

Here, OutputArray is written, *en masse*, to the 50-row-by-50-column worksheet range. This method is faster than the cell-by-cell method, but it is not the fastest way.

▶ *Array formula assignment.* For example:

```
Function WriteFast()
WriteFast = OutputArray
End Function
Sub Output
Range("A1:AX50").FormulaArray = "=WriteFast()"
End Sub
```

This version is the fastest of the three methods. It fills the worksheet range with the array formula {=WriteFast()}. Because the UDF WriteFast() sets itself equal to OutputArray, the worksheet range displays the contents of OutputArray.

If you use this approach to put a VBA array on a worksheet, you probably want to replace the array formula with its values. You can, of course, select the range and then use Edit, Copy and Edit, Paste Special, Values. But you also can do it with your VBA code:

```
OutputRange.FormulaArray = "=WriteFast()"
OutputRange.Copy
OutputRange.PasteSpecial Paste:=xlValues, _
    Operation:=xlNone, SkipBlanks:=False, Transpose:=False
```

The first statement fills OutputRange with the array formula. The second copies OutputRange, and the third pastes the values back into OutputRange.

Even including the time needed to copy and paste the values, the array formula method is faster than the cell-by-cell and range-assignment alternatives. The times required to perform each method are shown in figure 4.12. Notice that the larger the array to be output, the greater the advantage to using the array formula method.

You can find the VBA code used to obtain the data for figure 4.12 in the module named WriteFast Macros, in CHAP04.XLS.

Fig. 4.12

The array formula method is the fastest means of writing a VBA array to a worksheet.

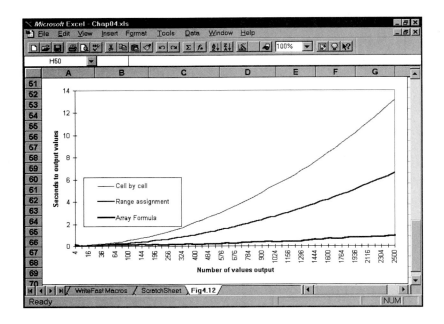

Summary

In this chapter, you learned what a UDF can do, in contrast to what a subroutine can do. You use a UDF to return values; you use a subroutine to modify objects.

This chapter also discussed the elements of a UDF—its declaration, its arguments, its calculations—and setting the UDF equal to the result of its calculations.

You learned how to extend the scope of a UDF by placing it in an add-in, how to make a UDF available to the Function Wizard, and how to supply context-sensitive help to the user.

Finally, the chapter explained how to write a user-defined array function and how it can speed the output of values to the worksheet.

The next chapter, "Customized Applications," gives you more information about using VBA to automate routine tasks, to extend the reach of Excel's analysis and reporting capabilities, and to give a workbook a customized look and feel.

chapter 5

Customized Applications

5

by Conrad Carlberg

In this chapter

◆ **Customizing menus**
Learn how to add a menu, a menu item, a submenu, or a menu item on a shortcut menu.

◆ **Creating a dispatcher**
This section describes how to structure more effectively the code that accompanies your custom menu items.

◆ **Providing demos**
Learn how to construct a demonstration version of your application, to help the inexperienced user understand how to run it.

By using VBA, you can develop a complete application that takes advantage of Excel's capabilities—easy data entry, dialog boxes, charting options, and so on—to offer the user a tailor-made analysis and reporting tool.

Consider the Analysis ToolPak (ATP), for example. The ATP is a collection of customized applications that turn a worksheet program into a platform for basic-to-intermediate statistical analysis and engineering functions. ATP automates the mind-numbing routine of mathematical transformations; it looks up values in reference distributions, creates standard reports, and provides charts that give the user deeper insight into the nature of the worksheet data.

The advantages of a customized application go well beyond these, of course. For example, when Microsoft was getting ready to publish Windows 95, thousands of software developers were faced with the task of revising their Windows 3.x programs for compatibility with the new operating system. If you create an application in VBA, however, it's unlikely that changes to the operating system will have any major effect on the way your code runs.

Furthermore, VBA gives you the opportunity to integrate custom Excel applications with custom applications for other programs such as Access.

If speed of execution is of primary importance to you, then you should consider writing something such as a DLL, or a compiled EXE file that will run outside the context of Excel. But if the *longevity* of your application is of primary importance, and if you want to take advantage of Excel's built-in capabilities, then a custom VBA application is a strong choice.

When you build a custom application using VBA, you must supply the code that brings about the result. This code varies from situation to situation. One group of subroutines and functions is needed to help a contractor choose among financial and technical proposals from suppliers. Another set is needed to perform a sophisticated statistical analysis. Another set is needed to help a stockbroker speed the order-entering process.

Regardless of the intent of the custom application, however, you can employ several techniques to make it easier to use. These techniques are covered in this chapter.

Customizing Menus

A custom menu is almost indispensable to a custom application. A custom menu enables users to run the application in the same way they perform such actions as saving a file, creating a chart, or formatting cells. The similarity of the user interface provides a comfort level that encourages the user to run your code.

First, a few terms:

▶ The *menu bar* is the set of menus at the top of the Excel window. Excel has different menu bars; the one you see depends on what sort of sheet is active.

▶ The menu bar contains *menus*. For example, if a worksheet is active, the menu bar contains a File, Edit, View, Insert, Format, Tools, Data, Window, and Help menu.

▶ The menu contains *menu items*. For example, the View menu contains these items: Formula Bar, Status Bar, Toolbars, Full Screen, and Zoom.

▶ A menu item might have a *submenu* (also known as a *cascading menu*). An example of a submenu is the menu that pops out when you choose Edit, Clear.

You can customize any of these menu structures to support your application, and the Auto Open subroutine is usually the place to begin the process.

Starting with the *Auto_Open* Subroutine

If your code has an Auto_Open subroutine, Excel executes the Auto_Open code immediately when the user opens the file that contains the code. Execution may occur in these cases:

▶ The user opens an XLS file by using File, Open.

▶ The user starts Excel, when your code has been stored in an XLA file that was installed with Tools, Add-Ins.

▶ Another VBA subroutine opens the XLS file or installs the add-in.

The Auto_Open subroutine is the place to put commands that you want to take effect before the user even begins to interact with your application. Examples include these actions:

▶ Putting custom commands in the menu system or custom buttons on the toolbars. Also, if you want to limit the user's options for commands such as File, Save As, Auto_Open is the place to take care of that.

▶ Looking for and possibly opening any necessary supporting files. These files may include data files and custom help files.

▶ Setting any necessary workspace, workbook, or worksheet options.

▶ Displaying a dialog box for the user to enter a password.

▶ Setting any required global variables, such as a path name in which to save files created by the code, or other variables that represent names you find convenient (for example, ThisBook for ActiveWorkbook.Name).

Establishing an Auto_Open subroutine is easy. Simply create a subroutine with the name Auto_Open. Any code that you include is automatically executed when the file opens.

 Tip
To prevent an Auto_Open subroutine from running when its workbook is opened, press the Shift key just before opening it and continue to hold the key as the file opens.

Establishing a New Menu Item

The Auto_Open subroutine shown in this section installs a new menu item, Summarize, in the user's Data menu. The sub performs these actions:

▶ Checks to see if Data Summary is already in the Data menu. If not, the sub adds the menu item to the Data menu and assigns another subroutine to it.

▶ If Summarize is already in the Data menu, the sub checks to see if Summarize is already associated with the proper subroutine, named DataSummary. If it isn't, the sub displays a warning message and stops processing.

▶ If Summarize is already in the Data menu and is associated with the DataSummary, the sub closes the workbook. This action may occur if the user opened the workbook twice in succession. You don't want Summarize to appear twice in the Data menu.

You can find this subroutine in the file named CHAP05.XLS on the companion CD:

```
Sub Auto_Open()
Dim Item As Variant, MenuIndex As Integer, _
    OnActionName As String, MenuProblem As Boolean
MenuProblem = False
OnActionName = "'" & ThisWorkbook.Path & "\" _
    & ThisWorkbook.Name & "'!DataSummary"
```

The first few statements in the subroutine declare several necessary variables and assign a couple of values. The MenuProblem variable starts as False, but is set to True if the sub finds a problem in the Data menu. The OnActionName variable is set to the value of the workbook's path, the workbook's name, and the name of the macro that should execute when the menu item is chosen. For example, OnActionName might take this value:

'C:\MSOffice\Excel\Book1'!DataSummary

A With block is established so subsequent statements can refer to the Data menu's objects without having to fully qualify those objects:

```
With MenuBars(xlWorksheet).Menus("Data")
```

The Auto_Open subroutine uses a For Each...Next loop to look through the menu items that already exist in the Data menu:

```
For Each Item In .MenuItems
    If Item.Caption = "S&ummarize" Then
        MenuIndex = Item.Index
        MenuProblem = True
    End If
Next Item
```

If an item's caption (the label in the drop-down box that you see when you choose Data) already exists in the Data menu, then the variable MenuIndex is set to the number—the Index property—of that item. This step makes it easier to find that item later in the Auto_Open subroutine. Also, the Boolean variable MenuProblem is set to True.

If MenuProblem is still False when the For Each...Next loop finishes, then Summarize has not been found in the Data menu. In that case, establish a new With block that refers to the collection of MenuItems:

```
If Not MenuProblem Then
    With .MenuItems
        .Add Caption:="-"
        .Add Caption:="S&ummarize", OnAction:="DataSummary"
    End With
```

In the `With` block, add a separator to the Data menu. The separator is the horizontal line that you find between groups of related items in a menu, and it's created by adding the caption "-". Then, add the menu item itself; give it the caption "S&ummarize" and associate it with the subroutine named `DataSummary`. Adding the separator and the menu item is the normal, expected action for `Auto_Open` to take.

 Tip

The & symbol in the caption "S&ummarize" establishes a shortcut key for the menu item. Because the symbol precedes the letter *u*, the shortcut key for the menu item is u̲.

The following code executes if `MenuProblem` is `True`; that is, a menu item with the caption "S&ummarize" already exists:

```
ElseIf .MenuItems(MenuIndex).OnAction <> OnActionName Then
    MsgBox "Something is wrong with the Summarize item in " _
        & "your Data menu. Cannot begin processing."
    End
```

In this case, the OnAction property of that menu item is tested. If the OnAction property does not equal `OnActionName` (already set, near the start of the `Auto_Open` subroutine as described earlier), then something's wrong.

At some earlier time, the menu item was left in the Data menu, but somehow became disassociated with the proper subroutine. This situation may occur, for example, if Excel crashed before an `Auto_Close` subroutine removed the menu item, and the file that contains the `OnAction` subroutine was moved or renamed. In that event, Excel cannot do much more. So, display a warning and return control to the user by ending the `Auto_Open` subroutine.

The final possibility is covered by the following code:

```
Else
    ThisWorkbook.Close (False)
End If
```

This code executes under two conditions: `MenuProblem` is `True`, and the menu item's OnAction equals `OnActionName`. In other words, the menu item's "S&ummarize" caption has been found in the Data menu and is associated with the `DataSummary` subroutine. So, just close the workbook without saving changes.

You prevent changes to a workbook from being saved by specifying `False` as the first argument to the `Close` method. (From the user's perspective, you prevent Excel from asking whether changes should be saved.) The reason you close the workbook is that the menu item is already in the Data menu, and `DataSummary`'s functionality is already available in Excel. Therefore, you have no need to keep the workbook open.

5

Finally, close the main With block and end the Auto_Open subroutine:

```
End With
End Sub
```

Establishing New Submenus and Shortcut Menu Items

The following code establishes a submenu in the Data menu:

```
With MenuBars(xlWorksheet).Menus("Data")
    .MenuItems.Add Caption:="-"
    .MenuItems.AddMenu Caption:="S&ummarize"
    With .MenuItems("Summarize")
        .MenuItems.Add Caption:="By Columns", OnAction:="ColumnSummary"
        .MenuItems.Add Caption:="By Rows", OnAction:="RowSummary"
    End With
End With
```

You place this With block in your Auto_Open subroutine, just as you do in the example on adding the Summarize menu item. Inside the outer With block, you add a separator, and then you add a submenu named Summarize to the Data menu. The submenu is added by means of the AddMenu method.

The inner With block treats the new submenu as a menu item. The MenuItem object can itself have menu items, which are the individual options in the submenu. You add these options inside the inner With block. When this code is executed and the submenu is selected, the Data menu appears as shown in figure 5.1.

Fig. 5.1

Use the AddMenu method to establish a new submenu, or cascading menu, on an existing menu.

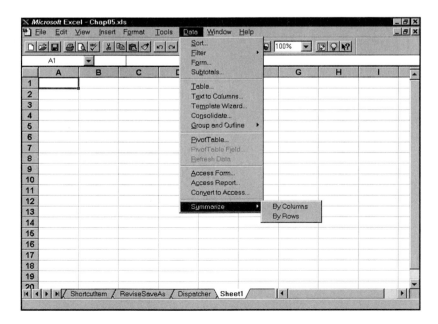

You can even add a new item to a shortcut menu (the menu that appears when you click the right rather than the left mouse button). However, you cannot add or delete a shortcut menu. Use the following code to add an option to the shortcut menu that appears when you right-click a worksheet cell:

```
ShortcutMenus(xlWorksheetCell).MenuItems.Add _
    Caption:="Summarize", OnAction:="DataSummary"
```

Replacing Built-In Menu Items

At times, you may want to restrict the user's capability to make use of different options on Excel's main menu. For example, when the user saves a new workbook by means of File, Save As, you might want to make sure that the file is saved in a particular subdirectory. In that case, you can use VBA code in the Auto_Open sub to redefine the effect of choosing File, Save As. Your Auto_Open sub might be as simple as this:

```
Sub Auto_Open()
SetCustomMenus
End Sub
```

Suppose that you want to make sure the user saves a file in the folder C:\MSOffice\Excel. The general approach is as follows:

1. Replace the built-in Save As command in the File menu with a custom Save As command.

2. When the user chooses the Save As command, display the built-in Save As dialog box.

3. The user specifies a path and a file name in the Save As dialog box. Get the file name from the dialog box.

4. Replace the path specified by the user with C:\MSOffice\Excel, and save the file there.

You cannot directly redefine the actions taken when the user chooses a built-in command from Excel's main menu. You can, though, delete the built-in command and replace it with one of your own, as this example shows:

```
Sub SetCustomMenus()
With MenuBars(xlWorksheet).Menus("File")
    .MenuItems("Save As...").Delete
    .MenuItems.Add Caption:="Save &As...", OnAction:="CustomSaveAs", Before:=6
End With
End Sub
```

The SetCustomMenus subroutine first removes the built-in Save As command from the File menu by means of the Delete method, and then adds a new Save As command. The subroutine assigns the CustomSaveAs subroutine to the new Save As command and specifies that the new Save As command is to appear before the sixth item in the File menu.

Note

Horizontal separators in a menu are counted as menu items. For example, the fourth menu item in the default File menu is the separator between <u>C</u>lose and <u>S</u>ave.

After the built-in Save As command is deleted from the File menu, the menu's sixth item is Save Workspace. The new, custom Save As command is to appear before that menu item, which places the command in the same location normally occupied by the built-in version of the File, Save As command. This placement is specified by setting the Before argument to 6.

This code executes when the user chooses <u>F</u>ile, Save <u>A</u>s:

```
Sub CustomSaveAs()
Dim FileSaveName As String
Dim FindLastBackSlash As Integer
```

You need two variables. `FileSaveName` is the name the saved file will have, *including its path*. `FindLastBackSlash` locates the file name itself, *exclusive of the path*.

The Excel application has a method named `GetSaveAsFileName`:

```
FileSaveName = Application.GetSaveAsFilename()
```

This method displays the built-in Save As dialog box and returns the path and name the user wants to use for the file to be saved. However, the method does not actually save the file—it just returns the path and name the user specifies. So when this statement executes, the `FileSaveName` variable contains that path and name.

If the user cancels the dialog box, the method returns `False`. The following code executes if the user chooses to save the file instead of canceling the dialog box:

```
If FileSaveName <> False Then
   FindLastBackSlash = Len(FileSaveName)
```

The variable `FindLastBackSlash` is initially set to the length of the path and name the user has specified. Suppose that `FileSaveName` is C:\MyDocu~1\NewFile.xls. Then, `FindLastBackSlash` is set to 23, the number of characters in `FileSaveName`.

You use the VBA function `Instr` to find the final backslash in `FileSaveName`. Any characters that follow the final backslash constitute the file name itself, exclusive of its path. A `Do` loop searches for that final backslash, beginning at the end of `FileSaveName`. As long as `Instr` returns zero, a backslash has not yet been found:

```
Do While InStr(FindLastBackSlash, FileSaveName, "\") = 0
   FindLastBackSlash = FindLastBackSlash - 1
Loop
```

The Do loop terminates when InStr returns a non-zero value, indicating that the loop has found the last backslash in FileSaveName. It remains to attach a new path to the file name, save the file there, and notify the user:

```
    FileSaveName = "C:\MSOffice\Excel\" _
        & Right(FileSaveName, Len(FileSaveName) - FindLastBackSlash)
    ActiveWorkbook.SaveAs (FileSaveName)
    MsgBox "File has been saved as " & FileSaveName
End If
End Sub
```

Regardless of where the user attempted to save the file, the custom File, Save As command causes it to be saved in C:\MSOffice\Excel.

Setting Options with *SendKeys*

When someone is testing your VBA code to help you find unexpected problems, you want to select the Break on All Errors check box (on the Module General tab of the Tools, Options dialog box). VBA code does not automatically fail when it encounters certain errors, such as a type mismatch, unless this check box is selected.

However, no VBA property or method exists to set this option. If you want to set the option in your Auto Open subroutine, you must resort to the SendKeys method:

```
    Application.SendKeys("%TOVM%B+~")
```

This example sends the keystrokes shown within the double-quotes to the key buffer. The method emulates what happens if you use the keyboard shortcut keys to set the Break on All Errors option. The % symbol stands for the use of the Alt key. The sequence %TO emulates pressing Alt+T+O, which displays the Options dialog box.

Unfortunately, two Ms appear in the Options dialog box: Module General and Module Format. The preceding SendKeys example starts by selecting the View tab by means of the V key. Then the sequence sends an M; choosing M when the View tab is active always selects the Module General tab next.

Finally, the %B+ keys select the Break on All Errors check box, and the ~ key emulates pressing Enter.

You can use this technique to set other options in the Module General and Module Format tabs of the Options dialog box. Use the same %TOVM sequence to choose the Module General tab, but change the B to D, for example, to Display Syntax Errors. To choose the Module Format tab, use %TOVMM rather than %TOVM.

Note

Where possible, avoid using the SendKeys method in your code. Use object, methods and properties instead. A string of letters and symbols is hard to debug and maintain.

Cleaning Up after Yourself: The *Auto_Close* Subroutine

You should normally undo any custom settings you established with an Auto_Open subroutine when the user decides to close the workbook. Just as you use an Auto_Open subroutine to establish the settings, you use an Auto_Close subroutine to undo them.

Suppose that your Auto_Open subroutine places a Summarize item on the Data menu, preceded by a horizontal separator line. When the user chooses the Summarize item, its OnAction property causes a subroutine named DataSummary to execute. Because the DataSummary subroutine is normally found in the workbook that contains the Auto_Open subroutine, closing the workbook usually makes DataSummary unavailable. Therefore, you should remove from the Data menu the menu item that calls DataSummary. This subroutine performs that task:

```
Sub Auto_Close()
Dim i As Integer, MenuItemIndex As Integer, MenuItemCount As Integer
With MenuBars(xlWorksheet).Menus("Data")
   MenuItemCount = .MenuItems.Count
   MenuItemIndex = 0
```

As usual, the first few lines of the subroutine declare it, define some necessary variables, establish a With block for convenience, and assign initial values to some variables. In this case, MenuItemCount is assigned the number of menu items in the Data menu. MenuItemIndex is initialized to zero (principally for clarity).

Then, a For...Next loop is used to find the Summarize menu item. You're pretty sure that Summarize is somewhere in the Data menu, because your Auto_Open subroutine should have placed it there. But what if the user bypassed the Auto_Open subroutine when opening the workbook by holding down the Shift key? In that case, the menu item doesn't exist, and a statement such as the following fails with a run-time error, because VBA cannot find the menu item to delete it:

```
MenuBars(xlWorksheet).Menus("Data").MenuItems("S&ummarize").Delete
```

Therefore, it's wise to look for Summarize before trying to delete it. This For...Next loop tries to find the menu item:

```
For i = 1 To MenuItemCount
   If .MenuItems(i).Caption = "S&ummarize" Then
      MenuItemIndex = .MenuItems(i).Index
   End If
Next I
```

If the loop finds the menu item, it sets the value of MenuItemIndex from zero (its initial value) to the value of the menu item's index. This value is then used to decide whether to try to delete the menu item:

```
If MenuItemIndex <> 0 Then
   .MenuItems(MenuItemIndex - 1).Delete
   .MenuItems(MenuItemIndex - 1).Delete
End If
```

If MenuItemIndex doesn't equal zero, Summarize was found in the Data menu. Therefore, first delete the menu item that immediately precedes MenuItemIndex, which is MenuItemIndex - 1. This menu item is the horizontal separator that the Auto_Open subroutine put into the Data menu. Taking this step changes the index of the Summarize menu item itself—if its index was 19, removing the separator makes its index 18. Therefore, the second statement in the If block removes the Summarize menu item itself.

Finally, end the With block, and end the subroutine:

```
End With
End Sub
```

Recall that to redefine the meaning of a built-in menu item, you begin by deleting the item from the menu. Then you add an item with the same caption that is associated with your own code. The process of deleting your custom item is identical to the process just described (and you use a similar approach to remove a custom submenu or a custom item on a shortcut menu). However, you also need to reestablish the built-in menu item:

```
MenuBars(xlWorksheet).Menus("File").MenuItems.Add _
   Caption:="Save As...", Restore:=True, Before:=6
```

After you have deleted your custom Save As menu item, you use this line of code to put the built-in version back in. The use of the Restore keyword indicates that Excel is to restore the original, default action associated with the Save As menu item. The use of the Before keyword ensures that the menu item is placed properly in the menu. In this case, Before is set to 6, because the Save As item should be the sixth item in the File menu. Placing Save As before the current sixth item makes Save As item number 6. If you do not specify a Before argument, the item is placed at the end of the menu—an inconsiderate way to return the File menu to the user.

Finally, to clear a check box in either the Module General or the Module Format tab on the Options dialog box, just change the + symbol to a – symbol in the SendKeys statement:

```
Application.SendKeys("%TOVM%B-~")
```

Where the sequence B+~ fills the check box, the sequence B–~ clears it.

Creating a Dispatcher

When you write your own code—whether in VBA or in another language such as C or Pascal—you often strive to make the code as *structured* as possible. The term *structured* has many meanings and implications, but one is that a structured program is characterized by small chunks of code. Each chunk is a procedure that is more easily managed, debugged, and maintained than a long, convoluted procedure.

On your screen, you can view an entire subroutine or function that contains 10 or 20 lines of code. You're scrolling back and forth constantly if it contains 100 lines. Furthermore, if you're passing arguments to the procedure, managing many arguments becomes difficult. Other things being equal, shorter procedures use fewer arguments than long procedures.

If your program has choice points, you may find that you can reuse a smaller chunk of code in different circumstances, instead of rewriting that code wherever it's needed. For example, suppose that you place two custom menu items in the File menu: one that enables the user to end the application without saving any changes to workbooks, and one that does save the changes. You use this structure:

▶ The first menu item calls ExitNoSave, a subroutine that loops through all open workbooks, setting their Saved properties to True even though changes have been made. The final step in the loop is to close the workbook. Because its Saved property is True, Excel does not ask the user whether it should save the changes when it closes the book.

▶ The second menu item calls SaveAndExit, a subroutine that loops through all open workbooks, saving and closing them.

The problem with this structure is that the code that closes the workbooks exists twice: once in the ExitNoSave subroutine and once in the SaveAndExit subroutine. Here's a better structure:

▶ The first menu item first calls SavedIsTrue, a subroutine that loops through open workbooks and sets their Saved property to True. Then the menu item calls CloseAllWorkbooks, which closes all workbooks.

▶ The second menu item first calls SaveBooks, which saves changes made to the workbooks. Then the menu item calls CloseAllWorkbooks, which closes all workbooks.

The difference is that the second structure uses `CloseAllWorkbooks` twice, which means you have less code to write and less code to maintain. Suppose that at some point you need to make a change to the VBA code that closes the workbooks. In the first structure, you need to remember to make that change in two places: once in `ExitNoSave` and once in `SaveAndExit`. In the second structure, you need to make the change only in `CloseAllWorkbooks`.

Granted, changes to the VBA code may not be a big deal in this example. But the example is a simple one. When you get into more complex situations, keeping your procedures short and modular becomes more important.

However, a problem exists. You assign a subroutine to a custom menu item by means of the item's OnAction property, as this example shows:

```
MenuBars(xlWorksheet).Menus("File").MenuItems.Add _
    Caption:="Exit, No Saves", OnAction:="SavedIsTrue"
```

You cannot assign more than one subroutine to a menu item with its OnAction property. One solution is to assign a different subroutine to each custom menu item that itself calls the required subroutines. This technique gets messy. A better way is available.

Suppose that you have five custom menu items, each assigned to the same menu (the menu may be a built-in menu such as File or Data, or a custom menu that you have attached to the main menu bar). Set the OnAction property of *each* menu item to a subroutine named, for example, `Dispatcher`, using this code:

```
Sub AddMenu()
With MenuBars(xlWorksheet)
.Menus.Add Caption:="Custom"
   With .Menus("Custom").MenuItems
       .Add Caption:="Exit, Don't Save", OnAction:="Dispatcher"
       .Add Caption:="Exit, Save", OnAction:="Dispatcher"
       .Add Caption:="Open Workbooks", OnAction:="Dispatcher"
       .Add Caption:="Process Workbooks", OnAction:="Dispatcher"
       .Add Caption:="About this Program", OnAction:="Dispatcher"
   End With
End With
End Sub
```

The result of this code is shown in figure 5.2.

The `Dispatcher` subroutine might look like this:

```
Sub Dispatcher()
Dim Action As Variant
Dim WorkbookPath As String
WorkbookPath = ActiveWorkbook.Path & "\"
Action = Application.Caller
```

5

Fig. 5.2

Each menu item in the Custom menu sends program control to the Dispatcher *subroutine.*

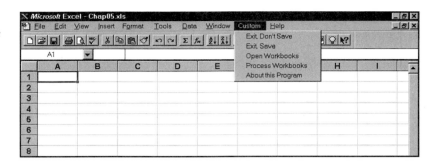

The first few statements in the Dispatcher subroutine define necessary variables and assign their values. The WorkbookPath variable is needed by two subroutines (SaveBooks and OpenWorkbooks). WorkbookPath is defined and assigned within the Dispatcher subroutine because a menu item cannot pass a variable argument to its associated subroutine.

The Action variable is defined as a Variant. It holds the results of the call to the Caller function. Caller returns an array (which is why Action is defined as a Variant) with these ordered elements:

1. The number of the chosen menu item in the menu
2. The number of the menu in the menu bar
3. The number of the menu bar

So, if the user chooses the first menu item in the menu, Caller(1) returns 1. If the user chooses the second menu item, Caller(1) returns 2, and so on. This result enables you to determine what action to take when the user chooses a menu item from a custom menu.

You can implement the proper action by means of the Select Case statement:

```
Select Case Action(1)
Case 1
   SavedIsTrue
   CloseAllWorkbooks
```

These four lines of code specify that VBA should look at the value in Action(1). In case that value is 1, VBA executes two subroutines: SavedIsTrue and then CloseAllWorkbooks.

For the following three lines of code, the Select Case statement is still in effect:

```
Case 2
   SaveBooks (WorkbookPath)
   CloseAllWorkbooks
```

In case Action(1) equals 2, VBA executes the SaveBooks subroutine, using WorkbookPath as an argument. Then, VBA executes CloseAllWorkbooks.

The remaining code in Dispatcher works similarly. The Select Case statement passes control to a particular Case, depending on the value of Action(1). Each Case causes control to pass to a different subroutine, depending on which menu item the user chose:

```
Case 3
    OpenWorkbooks (WorkbookPath)
Case 4
    ProcessWorkbooks
    CreateSummary
Case 5
    AboutThisProgram
End Select
End Sub
```

By using this approach, you accomplish several objectives:

▶ You enable an individual menu item to cause the execution of more than one subroutine.

▶ Because an individual menu item can now cause more than one subroutine to execute, you can make those subroutines shorter, easier to manage, and reusable.

▶ Because each menu item executes the Dispatcher subroutine, you do not need to revise the OnAction properties of the different menu items when changes to the VBA code are needed. Instead, you modify the Dispatcher subroutine.

▶ When several different actions require the same argument (in the preceding example, that argument is WorkbookPath) you can define and assign it in one place, rather than in several different subroutines.

Providing Demos

If your application is at all complex, supplying the user with a demonstration version is a good idea. A good demo usually contains these items:

▶ A button that displays a general explanation of what happens when the user runs the demo

▶ A button that steps the user through the application, with pauses at appropriate places to explain different choices or points of interest

▶ A way out, in case the user wants to end the demonstration before its normal stopping point

The creation and use of these items are discussed in the following sections.

Giving the User an Overview

Figure 5.3 shows the initial worksheet that appears when the user opens the file named SPCDEMO.XLS (found on the companion CD).

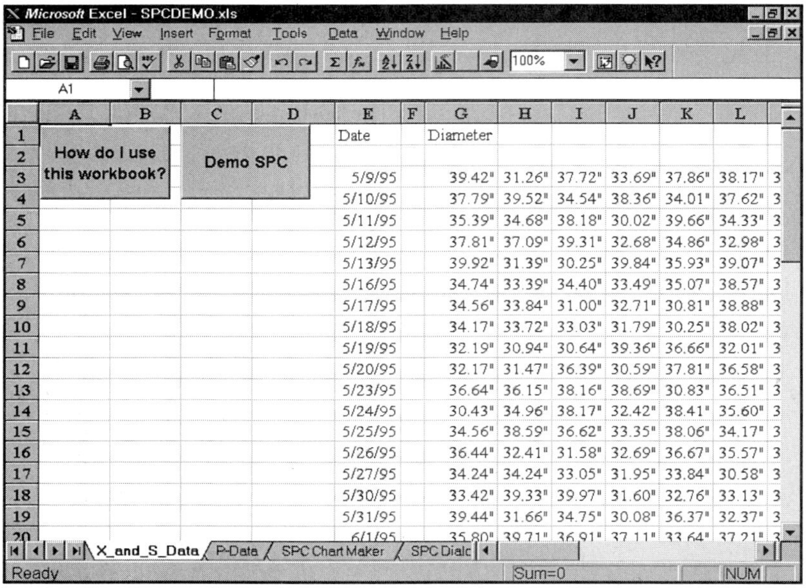

Fig. 5.3

The How do I use this workbook? *button shows an overview; the Demo SPC button steps the user through a demo.*

When the worksheet shown in figure 5.3 was prepared, the macro named ShowHelp1 was assigned to the How do I use this workbook? button. That macro is shown here:

```
Sub ShowHelp1()
Application.ScreenUpdating = False
ActiveSheet.Buttons("Demo Button").Enabled = False
ActiveSheet.TextBoxes.Add(4.8, 57.6, 165.6, 107.4).Select
```

At the beginning of the subroutine, the screen is frozen to make the code run faster and to avoid distracting the user by irrelevant screen actions. The button that runs the demo is disabled to avoid conflicts between the routines assigned to the two buttons. A text box is placed on the active worksheet at the coordinates specified by the Add method. The text box is selected.

Then the selected text box is assigned to the module-level object variable BoxName:

```
Set BoxName = Selection
Range("A1").Select
With BoxName.Interior
    .Pattern = xlSolid
    .ColorIndex = 36
End With
```

`BoxName` is declared at the top of the module, outside of any subroutine, to make it available to any subroutine in the module. Cell A1 is selected, to keep the sheet's appearance clean. The interior properties of the text box are set by making its pattern solid and its color set to yellow. (This color was chosen to make the text box appear as a yellow sticky note.)

The characters to appear in the text box are assigned:

```
BoxName.Characters.Text = "To run SPC, choose the SPC" _
    & " Chart option from the Data menu. You will" _
    & " see a dialog box where you can enter a worksheet" _
    & " range of dates or times for your observations," _
    & " and where you can enter another range that contains your" _
    & " measurements. Click More now."
```

The font for the text box characters is set:

```
BoxName.Font.Name = "Arial"
BoxName.Characters(start:=243, length:=4).Font.ColorIndex = 3
BoxName.Characters(start:=243, length:=4).Font.FontStyle = "Bold"
```

The font is set to Arial. Four characters, starting at the 243rd, are to appear in red (`ColorIndex` = 3) and in boldface. These characters are the word *More* at the end of the text.

In the following code, the `How do I use this workbook?` button is given the label `More`, its characters are set to red, and a new macro is assigned to it:

```
With ActiveSheet.DrawingObjects("Help Text Button")
    .Characters.Text = "More"
    .Characters.Font.ColorIndex = 3
    .OnAction = "ShowHelp2"
End With
```

Next, the screen is unfrozen, and the subroutine ends. Figure 5.4 shows the appearance of the worksheet at the end of `ShowHelp1`:

```
Application.ScreenUpdating = True
End Sub 'ShowHelp1
```

The following subroutine `ShowHelp2` is very similar to `ShowHelp1`. `ShowHelp2` replaces the characters in the text box, makes the word *Finish* red and boldface, and makes the words *Demo SPC* bold. The subroutine assigns the macro `ShowHelp3` to the button that's currently labeled *More*, changes its text to *Finish*, and keeps its color index red:

```
Sub ShowHelp2()

Application.ScreenUpdating = False
BoxName.Characters.Text = "You can also choose to create X-and-S" _
    & " charts or a P-chart. You can run SPC from any workbook," _
    & " not just this one, because the SPC Chart option stays in" _
    & " the Data menu until you close this workbook." _
    & " Click Finish, then click the Demo SPC button for a demo."
```

```
BoxName.Characters(start:=205, length:=6).Font.ColorIndex = 3
BoxName.Characters(start:=205, length:=6).Font.FontStyle = "Bold"
BoxName.Characters(start:=228, length:=8).Font.FontStyle = "Bold"
BoxName.Font.Name = "Arial"
With ActiveSheet.DrawingObjects("Help Text Button")
    .OnAction = "ShowHelp3"
    .Characters.Text = "Finish"
    .Characters.Font.ColorIndex = 3
End With
Application.ScreenUpdating = True
End Sub 'ShowHelp2
```

The worksheet now appears as shown in figure 5.5.

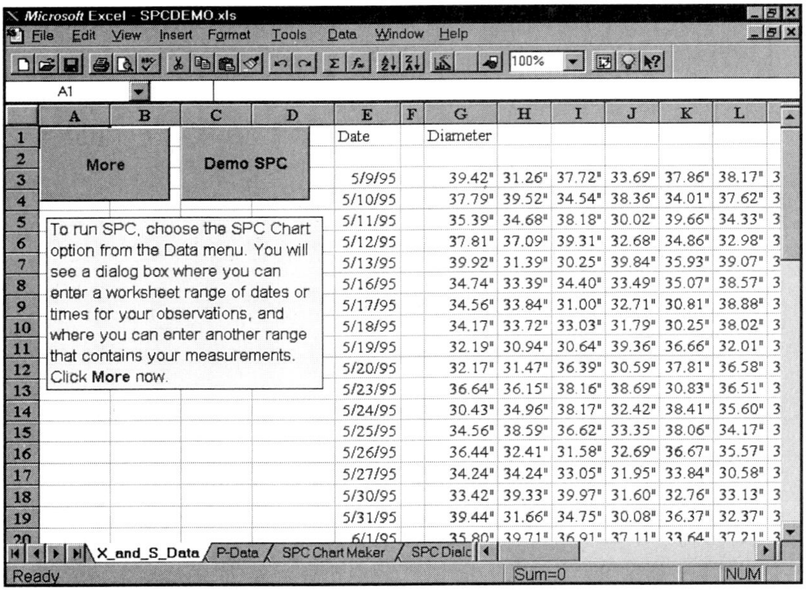

Fig. 5.4

After the user clicks the How do I use this workbook? *button, the worksheet contains an explanatory text box, the button is relabeled, and the button is assigned a new macro.*

When the user clicks Finish, ShowHelp3 executes, returning the worksheet to its original appearance:

```
Sub ShowHelp3()
Application.ScreenUpdating = False
BoxName.Delete
ActiveSheet.Buttons("Demo Button").Enabled = True
With ActiveSheet.DrawingObjects("Help Text Button")
    .OnAction = "ShowHelp1"
    .Characters.Text = "How do I use this workbook?"
    .Characters.Font.ColorIndex = xlAutomatic
End With
Application.ScreenUpdating = True
End Sub 'Sub ShowHelp3
```

Fig. 5.5

After the user clicks the More button, the information in the text box changes, the button is relabeled, and the button is assigned the final macro, ShowHelp3.

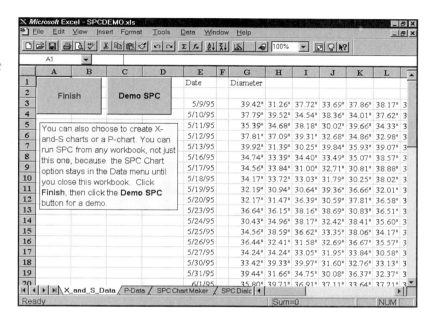

The text box named BoxName is deleted, the Demo Button is reenabled, and the Help Text Button is restored to its original macro, caption, and color index.

Stepping the User through the Application

The code associated with a Demo button is concerned primarily with three objectives:

▶ Emulating the run-time usage of the application

▶ Explaining what the user should do at different points in the application

▶ Preventing the user from taking actions that may cause problems in the demo

When the user opens SPCDEMO.XLS, the Demo SPC button on the X_And_S_Data worksheet has the subroutine HelpXChart1 assigned to it:

```
Sub HelpXChart1()
Dim WhichItem As Integer
ActiveSheet.Buttons("Help Text Button").Enabled = False

WhichItem = MenuBars(xlWorksheet).Menus("Data").MenuItems("SPC Chart").Index
MenuBars(xlWorksheet).Menus("Data").MenuItems(WhichItem).Delete

MenuBars(xlWorksheet).Menus("Data").MenuItems.Add Caption:="SP&C Chart"
```

The preceding three statements exist to avoid a conflict. The workbook's Auto_Open subroutine places an SPC Chart item in the Data menu and assigns the item to a subroutine named SPCChart. Because the main intent of the demo is to step the user through the program and explain what to do at different points, the SPC Chart menu item should not have any action associated with it. The user cannot enter the program by choosing the menu item.

The remainder of the subroutine is analogous to the actions taken when the user clicks the `How do I use this workbook?` button. A text box is established, the text is placed in the box, the Demo SPC button is recaptioned, and another macro is assigned to the button:

```
Application.ScreenUpdating = False
ActiveSheet.Buttons("Help Text Button").Enabled = False
ActiveSheet.TextBoxes.Add(4.8, 57.6, 194.4, 132.2).Select

Set BoxName = Selection
Range("E3").Select

BoxName.Characters.Text = _
    "1. Click the Data menu." & Chr(10) & "2. Click the SPC Chart menu item." _
    & Chr(10) & "3. Click the Demo SPC button to continue." & Chr(10) & Chr(10) _
    & "You will see a dialog box. _
    & Drag its title bar to move it around the worksheet."
```

To emphasize the shortcut keys associated with the Data menu and its custom SPC Chart menu item, the letter D and the letter C are underlined in the text box:

```
BoxName.Characters(start:=14, length:=1).Font.Underline = xlSingle
BoxName.Characters(start:=40, length:=1).Font.Underline = xlSingle
BoxName.Characters(start:=72, length:=8).Font.ColorIndex = 3
BoxName.Characters(start:=72, length:=8).Font.FontStyle = "Bold"
BoxName.Font.Name = "Arial"
With BoxName.Interior
    .Pattern = xlSolid
    .ColorIndex = 36
End With
With ActiveSheet.DrawingObjects("Demo Button")
    .Font.ColorIndex = 3
    .OnAction = "HelpXChart2"
End With
Application.ScreenUpdating = True

End Sub 'HelpXChart1()
```

 Tip

Characters in a text box normally wrap to the next line at a space between words. To force a carriage return at the end of a sentence or paragraph, use VBA's `Chr` function with 10 as its argument.

After the subroutine `HelpXChart1` has run, the worksheet appears as in figure 5.6.

Fig. 5.6

Although the menu item SPC Chart is disabled, the text box advises the user to select it. This instruction merely shows the user how to initiate the program outside the context of the demo.

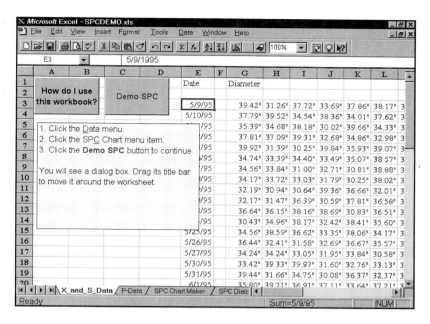

When the user clicks the Demo SPC button again, in response to the text box's third instruction, the subroutine named HelpXChart2 executes:

```
Sub HelpXChart2()
Application.ScreenUpdating = False
BoxName.Characters.Text = _
    "1. Highlight E3:E22." & Chr(10) _
    & "2. Click in the Measures box." & Chr(10) _
    & "3. Highlight G3:N22." & Chr(10) _
    & "4. Click the X-and-S Charts button." & Chr(10) _
    & "5. Type a label in the Chart label box." & Chr(10) _
    & "6. Click OK."
```

The text box is filled with specific instructions to the user. In the preceding example, the text box tells the user how to use the program's dialog box. By following the directions, the user fills in the dialog box's edit boxes and option buttons properly.

Again, the shortcut keys associated with the edit boxes and option buttons in the dialog box are underlined in the text box:

```
BoxName.Characters(start:=38, length:=1).Font.Underline = xlSingle
BoxName.Characters(start:=86, length:=1).Font.Underline = xlSingle
BoxName.Characters(start:=138, length:=1).Font.Underline = xlSingle
BoxName.Font.Name = "Arial"
```

This step is the last one in the demonstration, so the Demo SPC button returns to its original color index and its original macro assignment:

```
With ActiveSheet.DrawingObjects("Demo Button")
    .Font.ColorIndex = xlAutomatic
    .OnAction = "HelpXChart1"
End With
```

The SPC Chart menu item, which has no action associated with it, is deleted and replaced with an item that executes the main SPCChart procedure when the user selects it:

```
With MenuBars(xlWorksheet).Menus("Data")
    .MenuItems("SPC Chart").Delete
    .MenuItems.Add Caption:="SP&C Chart", OnAction:="SPCChart"
End With
Application.ScreenUpdating = True
SPCChart
```

The application executes when the statement SPCChart is encountered. Early on, SPCChart displays its dialog box, and the user makes the entries in the dialog box per the instructions in the text box (see fig. 5.7).

Fig. 5.7

By following the instructions in the text box, the user presents the proper information to the program by way of the dialog box.

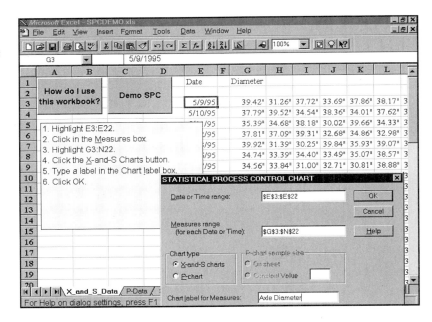

When the SPCChart application has finished running, control returns to the demo code in HelpXChart2. A subroutine named CleanUp is called, which takes certain actions depending on whether its argument is True or False; these actions should not be taken during the normal completion of the demo. Finally, the Help Text Button, which was disabled earlier, is reenabled, and the demo terminates:

```
Application.ScreenUpdating = False
Call CleanUp(False)
ActiveSheet.Buttons("Help Text Button").Enabled = True

End Sub 'HelpXChart2
```

Providing the user with a way out of a demonstration is important. In this case, an early-out is managed by way of the dialog box's Cancel button. That button is assigned this subroutine:

```
Sub Button3_Click() 'User chooses Cancel
If ActiveSheet.TextBoxes.Count > 0 Then
    BoxName.Delete
End If
```

The code looks for a text box on the active worksheet, deleting the text box if it exists. This text box, of course, is what displays instructions to the user.

Because the user can run the demo from either of two worksheets, the worksheet buttons are enabled on both worksheets:

```
With Worksheets("X_and_S_Data")
    .Buttons("Help Text Button").Enabled = True
    .Buttons("Demo Button").Enabled = True
End With
With Worksheets("P-Data")
    .Buttons("Help Text Button").Enabled = True
    .Buttons("Demo Button").Enabled = True
End With
```

Then the screen is unfrozen and the code terminates:

```
Application.ScreenUpdating = True
End
End Sub 'Sub Button3_Click()
```

Summary

In this chapter, you have learned how to customize Excel menus and menu items to support a custom application. In particular, you have learned how to modify menus by adding menu items and submenus, and how to modify shortcut menus. These modifications mean little unless you have subroutines associated with them. This chapter has described how to assign actions either directly or via a dispatcher that uses Caller. Finally, you have seen how to put these techniques together to provide a demonstration of your application to the user.

These techniques, when used properly, make your application's user interface more intuitive, attractive, and efficient. In the next chapter, you learn more about optimizing the VBA code that supports the custom application itself.

chapter 6

Optimizing VBA Code

by Conrad Carlberg

In this chapter

◆ **Referencing objects, properties, and methods**
How to make your code clearer and increase its speed of execution.

◆ **Passing arguments**
Why you should make variables local to their procedures, and how to make them available elsewhere.

◆ **Enhancing your code with API calls**
Using API to position dialog boxes on the screen and to manipulate the application Control menu.

The word *optimizing* can take on various meanings in the context of programming. It can mean any of the following:

▶ Increasing the speed of execution

▶ Using available memory efficiently

▶ Making the code more structured, so it's easier to write, debug, and maintain

▶ Employing pre-written code to bring about results you can't accomplish otherwise

At first, it might seem that the most important task is to increase an application's execution speed. Although that's certainly important to the end user, it's arguable that improving the code's structure saves even more time. Several weeks, or even several days, after you've written some VBA code, you can find that it's difficult to determine why you wrote the code as you did. Comments are helpful here, of course, but using sensible names for variables, writing code in small, modular chunks, and employing structures such as With…End With blocks are also critical.

Fortunately, the different aspects of optimization are seldom mutually exclusive. The next section discusses ways to optimize your VBA code that make it more structured and increase its execution speed.

Referencing Objects, Properties, and Methods

In Chapters 1–5, you've seen examples of ways to reference different items in the Excel model. Those examples followed three referencing styles:

▶ The dot operator

▶ The With structure

▶ Assignment of a variable to an object

These three styles have different uses, and they execute at different speeds. To make your VBA code execute optimally, you need to attend to these differences—make use of the most efficient style when the circumstances call for it.

Using the Dot Operator

The dot operator is the symbol that connects an object, property, or method in the Excel model to its parent object. For example, suppose you're assigning a value to a data label in an Excel chart. Your statement might look like this:

```
Application.Workbooks(2).Charts(1).SeriesCollection(1) _
    .Points(5).DataLabel.Characters.Text = 4
```

Here, the statement begins by referring to the first chart in the second workbook in the application. The chart belongs to the workbook, which belongs to Excel.

 Tip
You can continue one VBA statement from one line to another by using a space and an underscore at the end of the first line.

The statement takes you down the Excel object hierarchy. Reading from left to right, it starts with the topmost object in the hierarchy, the Application object. This refers to Excel itself. The next object is the Workbook object—in this case, the second workbook that's open at the time the statement executes. The next object is the first chart in the collection of charts that belong to the second workbook. The statement continues until, at last, it reaches the Text property and assigns the number 4 to that property.

As written, the statement acts like a trail of bread crumbs for VBA to follow as it locates the item to which you want to assign the number 4. It directs VBA's attention first to the application (Excel), then to the second workbook in Excel, then to the first chart in that workbook, then to the first data series in that chart, then to the fifth data point in that series, then to the fifth point's data label, to the data label's characters, and then to the text that the characters should contain. That text should be the number 4.

This is overkill. To switch metaphors, suppose you're driving a car in San Francisco, and you're looking for 157 Market Street. You could start by taking a road atlas of the United States from your glove compartment, opening it, then finding the page that shows California, then finding the inset that shows San Francisco, then finding Market Street, and looking for the block numbers.

But you don't do that. You would usually have the road atlas on the passenger seat and open at the right page, so when you reach a stoplight you can glance at the inset and decide whether to turn left or right. To start by taking the atlas from the glove box every time you had to make a decision takes too much time.

It's the same way in VBA. When you present VBA with a statement like the one shown earlier, it's like getting to the map inset by starting with the glove compartment. Instead, you should rely on VBA knowing the context that's current when it encounters the statement. A more efficient way to write the statement that assigns a data label is:

```
ActiveChart.SeriesCollection(1).Points(5).DataLabel.Characters.Text = 4
```

By using the application's ActiveChart property, you get VBA to jump right to the chart you're interested in—the one that's active—rather than forcing VBA to start by opening the glove compartment. You avoid referring to the Application object, finding the second workbook in the collection of open workbooks and the first chart in that workbook.

α **Note**

The Excel Application has several properties that you find convenient when you need to refer to particular objects. ActiveChart, for example, refers to the active chart, no matter how many workbooks or charts are open. The ActiveWorkbook and ActiveSheet properties work similarly.

The ThisWorkbook property always refers to the workbook that holds the VBA code that's executing, regardless of which workbook is active. This is particularly useful when you need to make a change to a dialog sheet in the workbook that contains the VBA code.

Sure, you might need to go through the whole rigmarole in some circumstances. If some workbook other than the one you're interested in happens to be active at the time the statement executes, then you need to direct VBA's attention to the proper chart in the proper workbook. Typically, though, the chart you want to modify is active and in the active workbook when you execute the statement.

So, keep the current context in mind as you write your VBA code. Doing so can help you reduce the number of characters you must type and the amount of time that VBA requires to execute the code.

Using the *With* Structure

There are many situations in which you must access several objects, which belong to another object higher up in the hierarchy. For example:

```
ActiveChart.Axes(xlCategory).TickLabels.Font.Name = "Times New Roman"
ActiveChart.Axes(xlCategory).TickLabels.Font.FontStyle = "Regular"
ActiveChart.Axes(xlCategory).TickLabels.Font.Size = 10
ActiveChart.Axes(xlCategory).TickLabels.Font.ColorIndex = 1
ActiveChart.Axes(xlCategory).TickLabels.Font.Background = xlAutomatic
```

These five statements set various properties that belong to the font of the tick labels on the category axis of the active chart. The font is set to Times New Roman, its style is set to Regular (instead of, say, Bold Italic), and so on.

Notice, though, that each statement supplies a map that describes how to get to the font: "from the active chart, go to the category axis, then go to its tick labels, then set the tick label font name. Then, from the active chart, go to the category axis, to its tick labels, then set the tick labels' font's style. Then,…"

This is useless. After you describe how to get to the font you want to manipulate, it's not necessary to describe that route again. Use the With structure instead:

```
With ActiveChart.Axes(xlCategory).TickLabels.Font
    .Name = "Times New Roman"
    .FontStyle = "Regular"
    .Size = 10
    .ColorIndex = 1
    .Background = xlAutomatic
End With
```

The With statement specifies that all subsequent statements, up to the End With statement, refer to items that belong in the same context. The name, the style, the size, the color index, and the background all belong to the tick label font on the category axis of the active chart. By using the With structure, you save VBA the time of starting with the ActiveChart object each time it sets a property. You also save yourself keystrokes and typing errors.

Note

You can also *nest* one `With` inside another. Here's a simple example:

```
With Workbooks(1).Worksheets(1)
    .Select
    With .Range("OutputRange")
        .ClearContents
        .NumberFormat = "$#,##0.00"
    End With
End With
```

The basis for the second `With` is a range. The range belongs to Worksheets(1), which is the basis for the first `With`. So this code is redundant, even though it has fewer statements:

```
Workbooks(1).Worksheets(1).Select
With Workbooks(1).Worksheets(1).Range("OutputRange")
    .ClearContents
    .NumberFormat = "$#,##0.00"
End With
```

6

When you perform an action on properties—or use methods or access objects—that belong in the same context, use the `With` structure to minimize the route that VBA must traverse to get where it's going.

These don't have to be different properties or methods to gain from the `With` structure. Suppose you're working with a collection of objects, setting the same property for each one. You might use a loop combined with a `With`:

```
With ActiveChart.SeriesCollection(1)
    PointCount = .Points.Count
    For i = 1 To PointCount
        If LabelArray(i) <> 0 Then
            .Points(i).DataLabel.Characters.Text = LabelArray(i)
        Else
            .Points(i).DataLabel.Characters.Text = ""
        End If
    Next i
End With
```

Here, you're looping through each point in a data series. The basic context is the first data series in the active chart. All objects and properties inside the `With` belong to that data series.

Inside the `With`, the `For...Next` loop begins. This statement:

```
.Points(i).DataLabel.Characters.Text = LabelArray(i)
```

must be inside the loop because the control variable, i, identifies the data point whose data label is to be assigned.

Particularly when you're working with pivot tables, the `With` structure can make things easier on you. Consider this block of code:

```
With Sheets("Sheet1").PivotTables(1).PivotFields(1)
   For i = 1 to .PivotItems.Count
      .PivotItems(i).Name = LabelArray(i)
      .PivotItems(i).ShowDetail=True
   Next i
End With
```

It happens that some properties, such as the ShowDetail property of an item in a pivot table, take more time to change than to read. Therefore, unless you know that the property must in all cases be changed, it's more efficient to test the property first, and change it if necessary. The following code does that:

```
With Sheets("Sheet1").PivotTables(1).PivotFields(1)
   For i = 1 To .PivotItems.Count
      With .PivotItems(i)
         If .Name <> LabelArray(i) Then .Name = LabelArray(i)
         If Not .ShowDetail Then .ShowDetail=True
      End With
   Next i
End With
```

(Notice the use of the nested `With` structures in the prior example.) In the absence of the `With` structure, you have to use this code:

```
For i = 1 To Sheets("Sheet1").PivotTables(1).PivotFields(1).PivotItems.Count
   If Sheets("Sheet1").PivotTables(1).PivotFields(1) _
      .PivotItems(i).Name <> LabelArray(i) Then
         Sheets("Sheet1").PivotTables(1).PivotFields(1) _
            .PivotItems(i).Name = LabelArray(i)
   End If
   If Not Sheets("Sheet1").PivotTables(1).PivotFields(1) _
      .PivotItems(i).ShowDetail Then
         Sheets("Sheet1").PivotTables(1).PivotFields(1) _
            .PivotItems(i).ShowDetail=True
   End If
Next i
```

Notice how much easier it is to read and understand what's going on when the `With` structure is in use. (Thanks to Robert Affleck for the tip about testing a property before changing it.)

The principal benefits to using the `With` approach instead of the dot operator approach are to improve the structure of your code and reduce the amount of typing you do. Although there is an increase in execution speed, the amount of that increase is quite small. This issue is discussed in more detail in the next section.

Using an Object Variable

You obtain a greater increase in speed if you create an object variable that stands in for an object you're modifying. For example, this code

```
Dim WhichCell As Range
Set WhichCell = ThisWorkbook.ActiveSheet.Cells(1, 1)
For i = 1 To 1000
    WhichCell = i
Next i
```

executes three times faster than does this code, which uses the full dot operator approach:

```
For i = 1 To 1000
    ThisWorkbook.ActiveSheet.Cells(1, 1) = i
Next i
```

But this code

```
With ThisWorkbook.ActiveSheet
    For i = 1 To 1000
        .Cells(1, 1) = i
    Next i
End With
```

executes only about 20 percent faster than does the full dot operator approach.

To obtain a meaningful speed advantage from the use of an object variable, instead of referring to the object itself by means of a sequence of dot operators, you would need to access the object many times. Notice that the loops in the previous three examples each execute 1,000 times. Benchmarked on a 486DX-33 running Windows 95, the execution times for each loop were:

▶ Fully-qualified dot operator: 8.7 seconds

▶ With...End With: 6.8 seconds

▶ Object variable: 2.9 seconds

A 5.8 second increase in speed (8.7–2.9) is a useful benefit. Remember, though, that this increase occurs over 1,000 instances of the reference. If your code accesses an object only a few times, then the advantage would be measured in 1,000th of a second—probably not enough to bother with.

Nevertheless, the With approach and the object variable approach have other advantages. A With...End With block makes your code more structured and easier to trace. An object variable can be useful when you want to pass it from one subroutine to another.

Speaking of passing an object variable, let's move on to the issue of procedure arguments.

Passing Arguments

When you create a VBA application of any complexity, you usually find that you need several subroutines and functions in the code. These procedures often require access to the same variables. For example, Sub GetInputData() might read values from a worksheet into a VBA array named DataArray. Sub ProcessData() might make changes to the values in DataArray, and Sub WriteData() might output DataArray to a new worksheet. Each of these three subroutines needs access to DataArray.

One way to provide that access is to declare DataArray as a module-level array, above and outside any subroutines in the module. For example:

```
Option Explicit
Option Base 1
Dim DataArray() As Double

Sub GetInputData()
.
.
.
End Sub

Sub ProcessData()
.
.
.
End Sub

Sub WriteData()
.
.
.
End Sub

Sub Main()
GetInputData
ProcessData
WriteData
End Sub
```

In this example, all subroutines in the module have access to DataArray. This is a convenient way to make the array available, at least at the outset, but it can cause problems later.

Suppose that you declare a module-level variable named Temp. Six months after writing your code, you decide to make some minor changes to it and find that you have also declared another variable named Temp *within* subroutine ProcessData. Although VBA has rules about how to interpret the name Temp (within ProcessData, Temp refers to the variable declared there; elsewhere, Temp refers to the module-level variable), you won't find it easy to keep the references straight.

Or suppose that you declare Temp at the module level, and several—but not all—of the subroutines in the module use it. You find a problem in the module's output results, and suspect that the problem is in how a subroutine modifies Temp. You will have to go through the code line by line, first to determine which subroutines refer to Temp, then to determine the order in which they modify Temp.

Or, suppose you write a subroutine or function that you find very useful in other modules or workbooks. If it's expecting to have access to a module-level variable named Temp, you'll have to declare Temp at the module level in the other modules, and it will have to have the characteristics (for example, data type) that were intended when you first wrote the subroutine.

The solution is to declare variables at the module level only when necessary, and to declare other variables at the procedure level. In many cases, you can make procedure-level variables available to other procedures by passing them as arguments to the procedure. In the previous example, this might work as follows:

```
Option Explicit
Option Base 1

Sub GetInputData (DataArray)
.
.
.
End Sub

Sub ProcessData (DataArray)
.
.
.
End Sub

Sub WriteData (DataArray)
.
.
.
End Sub

Sub Main()
Dim DataArray() As Double
GetInputData DataArray
ProcessData DataArray
WriteData DataArray
End Sub
```

Here, DataArray is declared within the subroutine named Main. As Main calls the other three subroutines, it passes DataArray to each one, thus making the array available to them for reading values from the worksheet, processing the values and writing them back to a worksheet.

Notice the advantages of this structure:

▶ The statement that declares each subroutine includes its argument—in this case, each subroutine other than Main takes DataArray as an argument. Should you want to declare another variable with any of those subroutines, it's immediately obvious that it's already using a variable named DataArray. This is a red flag that you shouldn't try to declare another variable named DataArray in the same subroutine.

▶ You can immediately tell which subroutines have access to DataArray, and in which order they work with it. In this example, DataArray is available to all of them. But if Main called other subroutines without passing DataArray to them, it would be obvious to you that they don't have access to the array. If there's a problem associated with the array, you can eliminate them as potential culprits.

▶ It's not necessary that the subroutine that receives the array use the same name in its argument list as is used by the calling subroutine. That is, this code is legal:

```
Sub GetInputData (Values)
.
.
.
End Sub

Sub Main()
Dim DataArray() As Double
GetInputData DataArray
ProcessData DataArray
WriteData DataArray
End Sub
```

Although Main passes DataArray to GetInputData, GetInputData will refer to the array as Values. This means you can use GetInputData in another module without worrying about name conflicts. It doesn't matter what name the calling subroutine uses—GetInputData always refers to it as Values.

There are two ways in which a calling subroutine can pass an argument to another subroutine: by reference and by value. These methods are discussed in the following two sections.

Passing by Reference

When you pass a variable as an argument to a procedure by *reference*, you pass the variable itself. If the called procedure, whether a subroutine or a function, modifies the value of the variable (or a value in an array) then that variable has the new value in any procedure that has access to it. This is the default situation in VBA.

Here's an example:

```
Sub GetInputData()
Dim InputArray As Variant, LogInputArray As Variant
InputArray = Range(Cells(1, 1), Cells(3, 3))
ConvertToLogs InputArray
Range(Cells(9, 1), Cells(11, 3)) = InputArray
End Sub

Sub ConvertToLogs(ByRef ValueArray As Variant)
Dim i As Integer, j As Integer
For i = 1 To UBound(ValueArray, 1)
   For j = 1 To UBound(ValueArray, 2)
      ValueArray(i, j) = Log(ValueArray(i, j))
   Next j
Next i
Range(Cells(5, 1), Cells(7, 3)) = ValueArray
End Sub
```

Notice the ByRef keyword in the declaration of the subroutine ConvertToLogs. It is there for clarity only: this is the default condition. The declaration could also have been:

```
Sub ConvertToLogs (ValueArray As Variant)
```

and the effect would have been the same. Notice also that both subroutines write the array to the worksheet. Although the two subroutines refer to the array using different names, it is really the same array. Figure 6.1 shows what happens when you pass arguments by reference.

Fig. 6.1

Using ByRef *in* ConvertToLogs *changes the values in the variable itself.*

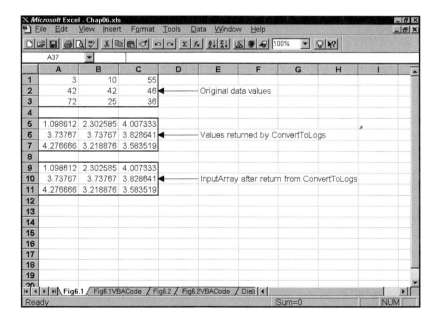

Cells A1:C3 contain the original data values as they are read into InputArray
by GetInputData. Cells A5:C7 contain the logarithms of those values, as written by
ConvertToLogs. And cells A9:C11 contain the values in InputArray, output by GetInputData,
after ConvertToLogs has done its work. The values in A5:C7 are identical to those in
A9:C11, demonstrating that the changes made to the array by ConvertToLogs are in effect
after control has returned to GetInputData.

Passing by Value

In contrast to the effect of ByRef, the ByVal keyword passes not the variable itself but its
value to the called procedure. If the called procedure modifies the value, that modification is not reflected in the variable: the *value* was used, not the variable.

See how this works in GetInputData and ConvertToLogs:

```
Sub GetInputData()
Dim InputArray As Variant, LogInputArray As Variant
InputArray = Range(Cells(1, 1), Cells(3, 3))
ConvertToLogs InputArray
Range(Cells(9, 1), Cells(11, 3)) = InputArray
End Sub

Sub ConvertToLogs(ByVal ValueArray As Variant)
Dim i As Integer, j As Integer
For i = 1 To UBound(ValueArray, 1)
   For j = 1 To UBound(ValueArray, 2)
      ValueArray(i, j) = Log(ValueArray(i, j))
   Next j
Next i
Range(Cells(5, 1), Cells(7, 3)) = ValueArray
End Sub
```

Notice the keyword ByVal in Sub ConvertToLogs. The values in InputArray, not InputArray
itself, are passed to ConvertToLogs. Figure 6.2 shows the result. Compare it to figure 6.1.

In figure 6.2, it is A1:C3 and A9:C11 that are identical, not A5:C7 and A9:C11. This is
because when control returns to GetInputData, ConvertToLogs has not changed the values
in the array: rather, it has changed the values that were passed to it.

If you want to use ByVal, you must specify it to override the default ByRef condition.
When would you want to use ByVal? Among other situations, you want to use it in these
cases:

▶ When you repeatedly use the same procedure to change values, but in a different
way each time. You can convert a variable or an array repeatedly without modifying its original values.

▶ When the receiving procedure requires you to use ByVal. This is often the case in
API calls. See the following section, "Enhancing Your Code with API Calls," for
more information.

Fig. 6.2

Using ByVal *in* ConvertToLogs *leaves the values in* InputArray *unchanged.*

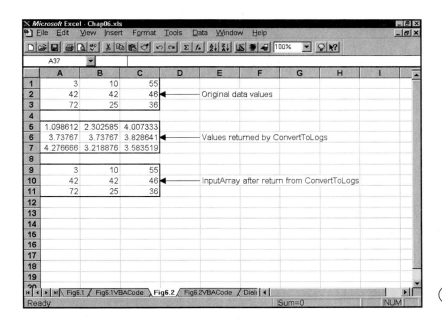

▶ In some cases, you might need to pass an argument by value because there is a conflict between the data type of the argument and the type of the called procedure. For example:

```
Sub OutputValue(Part As Long, Whole As Long)
Dim PartPercent As Single
PartPercent = GetPercent (Part, Whole)
  .
  .
  .
End Sub

Function GetPercent(FirstVal As Integer, SecondVal As Integer) As Single
GetPercent = FirstVal / SecondVal
End Function
```

As this code is written, it fails because Part and Whole are declared as long integers, whereas GetPercent expects integers. But if GetPercent receives values, instead of variables, the code works:

```
Sub OutputValue(Part As Long, Whole As Long)
Dim PartPercent As Single
PartPercent = GetPercent (Part, Whole)
  .
  .
  .
End Sub
```

```
Function GetPercent(ByVal FirstVal As Integer, _
    ByVal SecondVal As Integer) As Single
GetPercent = FirstVal / SecondVal
End Function
```

Why not just change the declarations of FirstVal and SecondVal to Long? You could, of course, but what if GetPercent were a much more complicated procedure that you are recycling from another module? Or, what if different procedures call GetPercent, and the arguments that they pass might be Single, Double, Variant, and so on? If you can't predict the variable type that the procedure will receive, ByVal is a useful option.

ByVal is slightly less efficient in memory and speed than ByRef. Arguments passed by reference require four bytes (because only the memory address of the variable is passed). Arguments passed by value require between two and 16 bytes, depending on the argument's data type: an integer requires the least memory and a variant requires the most (an array passed by value could, of course, require much more memory). The more memory required to pass the argument, the longer it takes to pass it.

Enhancing Your Code with API Calls

There are some aspects of Excel that you simply cannot control by means of its menu structure, its INI file, or VBA. For example, when Excel displays a dialog box—whether custom or built-in—the dialog box position depends on the position of the previous dialog box that was displayed. Many developers want to position a dialog box at a particular screen location, often in the center. Occasionally, you might want to display two dialog boxes simultaneously; then, even though only one is active, it can be useful to ensure that the dialog boxes don't overlap.

Or, you might want to limit the options available to the user for closing, resizing, or minimizing a document window. Suppose you wrote an Auto_Close subroutine that arranges an orderly shutdown, but its functionality requires that certain conditions have been met. To ensure the proper context for a shutdown, you have replaced the Close and Exit items in the File menu with your own custom commands. But these will not operate properly if the user chooses the Close button in the application window. You want to disable that button, but neither Excel nor VBA offers a way to do that.

The solution is to use an API call in your VBA code. *API* stands for *Applications Programming Interface*. It is a generic term that refers to the way you can access certain tools provided by Microsoft or by a third party who has distributed compiled code. Among the tools Microsoft provides are functions in files named USER32.EXE, KERNEL32.EXE, and GDI32.DLL. KERNEL32.EXE has code that helps with tasks such as memory management, and USER32.EXE contains functions that enable you to exert greater control over items such as windows and menus. GDI32.DLL contains functions that pertain to graphic output from an application, such as to the screen or an output file.

> **Tip**
>
> Prior to Windows 95, the library files lacked the 32 in their names. You can still use old API calls in Windows 95 if you run them from a 16-bit application, such as Excel 5, and if you still have the old library files on your disk.

Understanding the Basics of API Calls

To make an API call from your VBA code, you first need to *declare* the function that you want to use. Here's an example:

```
Declare Function DeleteMenu Lib "USER32" _
    (ByVal Menu As Long, ByVal Pos As Long, ByVal Flags As Long) As Long
```

The declaration looks intimidating, but it's not too bad. The Declare statement is used at the module level to specify several of the function's components:

▶ The name of the function that will be called. Here, its name is DeleteMenu.

▶ The Lib keyword, which indicates that the next part of the declaration identifies the library where the function is found. Here, the function DeleteMenu is found in USER32. (You don't need the EXE extension for USER32, KERNEL32, or the DLL extension for GDI32, because they are standard libraries. For other libraries, such as those you create yourself, you should use their extensions.)

▶ A list of arguments to the function. The functions in the libraries usually require that their arguments be passed by value. The DeleteMenu function takes three arguments, each of which is a Long integer. Here, the arguments are named Menu (the number identifying the menu to be processed), Pos (the item in the menu that the function will delete), and Flags (a number that uniquely identifies certain options that the function will apply).

▶ An As clause following the list of arguments, which specifies the data type that the function returns. Here, the data type is a Long integer.

Inside the function itself, the arguments have different names. Just as when you call a procedure that's written in VBA from another VBA procedure, the arguments in the calling statement do not need to have the same names as the arguments in the called procedure.

Any VBA procedure that calls the function must have access to the function's declaration. Because the declaration is placed at the module level, all procedures on that module have access to it. You can place the Public keyword just before the Declare keyword to make the function available to procedures located on other module sheets.

6

At some point, you need to call the function. Here's how you might call `DeleteMenu`:

```
Call DeleteMenu(260,0,1024)
```

The use of this function, as well as the identification of the values to pass to it in the argument list, is discussed in the later section "Deleting Control Menu Items."

Tip

32-bit API calls differ from 16-bit API calls in several ways. The function names, for example, are now case-sensitive, and some names have changed (functions that receive string arguments now have an "A" appended to their names). You can examine the names, arguments and types by opening WIN32API.TXT, found on this book's companion CD.

Positioning Dialog Boxes

The following code allows you to position a custom dialog box on the screen. You can find the code in the file named CHAP06.XLS on the companion CD. The code begins by declaring a couple of functions:

```
Declare Function SetWindowPos Lib "USER32" _
   (ByVal hWnd As Integer, ByVal hWndAfter As Integer, _
   ByVal x As Integer, ByVal y As Integer, ByVal cx As Integer, _
   ByVal cy As Integer, ByVal flags As Integer) As Integer

Declare Function FindWindowA Lib "USER32" _
   (ByVal szClass As String, ByVal szTitle As String) As Integer
```

These two functions, `SetWindowPos` and `FindWindowA`, exist in the file named USER32 (note the "A" in `FindWindowA`, which takes string arguments). `SetWindowPos` takes several arguments: `hWnd`, `hWndAfter`, `x`, and so on. These values are passed to the function by value, not by reference. As you gain more experience with API, you will find that many of its functions require that their arguments be passed by value.

The arguments to `SetWindowPos` that you're interested in for present purposes are `hWnd` (the window's handle), `x` (its horizontal coordinate), and `y` (its vertical coordinate). The other arguments pertain to the window's order on the screen—whether it's on top of or under other windows.

Tip

Another difference between 16-bit and 32-bit API calls is that some arguments and functions have changed data types—for example, from Integer to Long. Again, check WIN32API.TXT for the proper type declarations in your calls.

The following VBA subroutine calls the API functions and passes the proper values to them:

```
Sub ShowDialogBoxByPos(ByVal HorizontalPosition As Integer, _
    ByVal VerticalPosition As Integer)
```

The subroutine is declared, and it receives two arguments by value: the horizontal and vertical positions on the screen that are desired for the custom dialog box.

```
Dim DialogWindowHandle As Integer
    DialogWindowHandle = FindWindowA("bosa_sdm_XL", S
        ActiveDialog.DialogFrame.Text)
```

The first function call is to `FindWindowA`. A window class (`"bosa_sdm_XL"`) is passed to it, as is the text name of the dialog frame. The function returns the dialog window's handle, which is an integer that uniquely identifies the window. Now the code has access to that number.

Next, an `If` statement is used to ensure that a legitimate handle has been returned—that is, the integer returned by `FindWindowA` is not a zero value. If the integer is not zero, the second function is called with, among other arguments, the window's handle:

```
    If DialogWindowHandle <> 0 Then
        SetWindowPos DialogWindowHandle, 0, HorizontalPosition,
            VerticalPosition, 0, 0, 21
    End If
End Sub
```

The call to `SetWindowPos` passes the dialog window's handle, along with the desired horizontal and vertical coordinates and some other required arguments.

```
Sub PrepareDialogBox()
    ShowDialogBoxByPos 300, 400
End Sub
```

The subroutine named `PrepareDialogBox` calls the subroutine named `ShowDialogBoxByPos`, with 300 as the horizontal coordinate and 400 as the vertical coordinate. `PrepareDialogBox` is assigned to the dialog box's dialog frame, so when the frame appears on-screen, it is re-positioned by the VBA code and the API calls to the 300, 400 placement. Finally, this subroutine

```
Sub ShowTheBox()
    ThisWorkbook.DialogSheets("Dialog1").Show
End Sub
```

begins the entire process by invoking the dialog box.

It's easy to lose sight of the flow by examining the code line by line. Here it is again, in the order that it actually occurs:

6

1. The subroutine ShowTheBox begins to put the dialog box on the screen.

2. When the dialog frame appears, the subroutine PrepareDialogBox—which is assigned to the dialog box frame—executes.

3. PrepareDialogBox calls ShowDialogBoxByPos with the horizontal and vertical coordinates as arguments.

4. ShowDialogBoxByPos first calls the API function FindWindowA, which obtains the handle associated with the dialog box window.

5. ShowDialogBoxByPos then calls the API function SetWindowPos, with the proper handle and with the horizontal and vertical coordinates.

6. SetWindowPos positions the dialog box frame according to the specified coordinates, control returns from ShowDialogBoxByPos to PrepareDialogBox, and from there to ShowTheBox.

Figures 6.3 and 6.4 show the effect of running this VBA code with different arguments for the horizontal and vertical coordinates.

Fig. 6.3

The horizontal and vertical coordinates are 100 and 100.

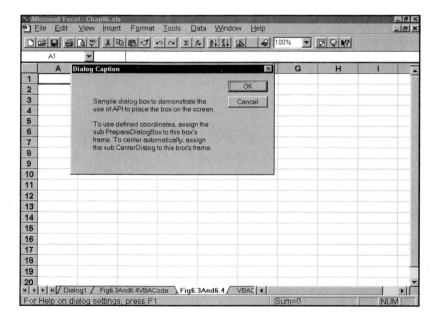

It's not necessary to use both the PrepareDialogBox and the ShowDialogByPos subroutines, because PrepareDialogBox does nothing more than call ShowDialogByPos. You could instead establish the coordinates in ShowDialogByPos, assign it to the dialog frame, and have ShowTheBox call ShowDialogByPos.

Fig. 6.4

The horizontal and vertical coordinates are 300 and 400.

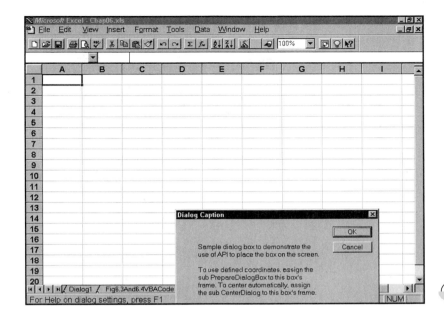

However, it's useful to keep two separate procedures. You might want to perform other actions in PrepareDialogBox, such as setting the dialog box's focus on the basis of the results of an error-trapping routine. In that case, and from the point of view of structuring your code, it's useful to keep PrepareDialogBox for housekeeping tasks and ShowDialogByPos specifically for the task of positioning the dialog box.

Centering Dialog Boxes

What if you don't want to specify the particular screen coordinates for the dialog box? This can happen if your application might run on a computer with a different monitor size than yours: for example, the user's screen might have a different aspect ratio. In such cases, it's useful to let VBA center the dialog box on the screen by using API calls.

The code to do this isn't too different from the code in the previous section. A couple of extra procedures are needed. In the following code, those procedures are GetWindowRect and GetSystemMetrics. The SetWindowPos and FindWindowA functions are also needed, as before:

```
Declare Function SetWindowPos Lib "USER32" _
    (ByVal hWnd As Integer, ByVal hWndAfter As Integer, _
ByVal x As Integer, ByVal y As Integer, _
    ByVal cx As Integer, ByVal cy As Integer, S
    ByVal flags As Integer) As Integer

Declare Function FindWindowA Lib "USER32" S
    (ByVal szClass$, ByVal szTitle$) As Integer
```

```
Declare Sub GetWindowRect Lib "USER32" _
   (ByVal DialogWindowHandle As Long, _
   ByRef StartPos As DialogBoxPlacement)
```

The subroutine `GetWindowRect` returns the coordinates of the dialog box window—the initial screen coordinates of its left, top, right, and bottom sides. These coordinates are returned by the `StartPos` argument.

```
Declare Function GetSystemMetrics Lib "USER32" (ByVal iOption As Long) As Long
```

The function `GetSystemMetrics` returns information about the number of points on the full screen. Depending on the value of its argument, `iOption`, it returns either the height or the width of the full screen.

```
Type DialogBoxPlacement
   Left As Long
   Top As Long
   Right As Long
   Bottom As Long
End Type
```

A user-defined data type is also needed. Notice, in the declaration of `GetWindowRect`, the argument `StartPos` is defined as the `DialogBoxPlacement` type. This user-defined data type calls for a variable based on it to have four elements: the coordinates of the left, top, right, and bottom sides of the dialog box as it initially appears on the screen.

Finally, `CenterDialog` is the subroutine that places the dialog box in the screen's center. It could be assigned directly to the dialog box frame, or it could be called by another subroutine assigned to the frame and that might carry out other housekeeping tasks.

```
Sub CenterDialog()
Dim DialogWindowHandle As Long
Dim HorizontalPosition As Long, VerticalPosition As Long
Dim DialogBoxWidth As Long, DialogBoxHeight As Long
Dim Box As DialogBoxPlacement
```

Several additional variables are needed. `DialogBoxWidth` and `DialogBoxHeight` are calculated to find how much screen is left after allowing for the width and the height of the dialog box. The `Box` variable is typed as `DialogBoxPlacement`, the custom type established earlier, so it has a Left, a Top, a Right, and a Bottom element. These elements again define the screen coordinates of each side of the dialog box.

```
DialogWindowHandle = FindWindowA("bosa_sdm_XL", ActiveDialog.DialogFrame.Text)
If DialogWindowHandle <> 0 Then
   GetWindowRect DialogWindowHandle, Box
```

The dialog box's handle is passed to the API function GetWindowRect. Because the argument Box is passed by reference (see the declaration of GetWindowRect), it returns the initial dialog box coordinates to CenterDialog.

```
DialogBoxWidth = Box.Right - Box.Left
DialogBoxHeight = Box.Bottom - Box.Top
```

The number of points occupied by the dialog box's width and height are calculated. These are, of course, independent of its screen placement. Then, the width and height are used to find the vertical point and horizontal point that will place the dialog box in the center of the screen:

```
HorizontalPosition = (GetSystemMetrics(0) - DialogBoxWidth) / 2
VerticalPosition = (GetSystemMetrics(1) - DialogBoxHeight) / 2
```

The call to GetSystemMetrics, with an argument of zero, returns the screen width in points. Subtracting the width of the dialog box from the screen width results in the number of horizontal points available on the screen outside of the dialog box. Dividing that result by two gives the horizontal point that will center the dialog box left to right.

Similarly, passing the number 1 as an argument to GetSystemMetrics returns the screen height in points. Another formula determines the vertical point needed to center the dialog box from top to bottom. Finally, these points are used, as before, to center the dialog box:

```
Call SetWindowPos(DialogWindowHandle, 0, _
    HorizontalPosition, VerticalPosition, 0, 0, 21)
End If
End Sub
```

By using this code, you have fewer worries about displaying a dialog box on other monitors. It takes care of the issue of the screen's aspect ratio on your behalf. You need not worry about the user's screen resolution (for example, VGA versus SVGA). It also relieves you of the responsibility of assigning the horizontal and vertical positions without any information about the screen that will display the dialog box.

Deleting Control Menu Items

The Control menu and its associated buttons are not directly under the control of VBA. There is a Control menu, and associated buttons, for the Excel window and for the active document window (see fig. 6.5).

Fig. 6.5

The Control menu lets the user quickly perform different actions on its associated window.

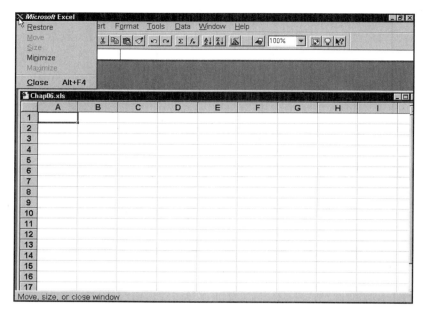

Suppose you want to limit the user's options in using the Control menu. Perhaps you need to arrange for an orderly shutdown of your application, or need to ensure that the Excel window occupies a particular portion of the screen. For *document* windows, you can remove the user's options—maximizing, minimizing, sizing, closing, moving, and restoring the window—in two ways: by choosing Tools, Protection, Protect Workbook, and selecting the Windows check box, or programmatically by means of this VBA statement:

```
ActiveWorkbook.Protect Structure:=True, Windows:=True
```

In contrast to a document window's Control menu, you cannot use VBA alone to do the same for the Excel window's Control menu. For that, you need to make an API call. Here's the code that disables the Excel window's Control menu:

```
Declare Function GetActiveWindow Lib "User32" () As Long

Declare Function GetSystemMenu Lib "User32" _
   (ByVal WindowHandle As Long, ByVal Revert As Long) As Long

Declare Function DeleteMenu Lib "User32" _
   (ByVal Menu As Long, ByVal Pos As Long, ByVal Flags As Long) As Long

Sub DeleteControls()
   Dim X As Integer
   For X = 1 To 7
      Call DeleteMenu(GetSystemMenu(GetActiveWindow, False), 0, 1024)
   Next X
End Sub
```

There are seven items in the Control menu: Restore, Move, Size, Minimize, Maximize, Close, and the horizontal separator between Maximize and Close. The DisableControl subroutine calls the USER.EXE function DeleteMenu seven times, one for each item in the Control menu.

The third argument in the DeleteMenu function specifies which menu item to delete. The menu items are indexed beginning with item number zero. Each time the For...Next loop executes, the 0th item in the menu is deleted. When the loop finishes, the Control menu and the associated buttons are disabled.

 Tip

Most collections in the Excel object model are indexed starting with the number 1. The Excel window's Control menu items do not belong to the Excel object model, and are indexed starting at zero.

When DeleteControls has finished, the Control menu does not appear when you click the Excel icon in the upper-left corner of its window, and the Minimize, Restore (Maximize), and Close buttons in the upper-right corner of the menu have no effect.

This is the code to restore the menu to its fully operating status:

```
Sub RestoreControls()
    Call GetSystemMenu(GetActiveWindow(), 1)
End Sub
```

Because DeleteMenu allows you to specify individual menu items, you can use it to selectively limit user options. Suppose you want the user to be able to move and resize the Excel window, but not to close the application by means of the Control menu. In that case, you would want to remove the Close option, and (for appearance's sake) the horizontal separator immediately above the Close option. You could use the code in DeleteCloseControl:

```
Sub DeleteCloseControl()
    Call DeleteMenu(GetSystemMenu(GetActiveWindow, False), 6, 1024)
    Call DeleteMenu(GetSystemMenu(GetActiveWindow, False), 5, 1024)
End Sub
```

Figure 6.7 shows the menu's appearance after you run DisableControlClose.

In DeleteCloseControl, notice the order in which the third argument is passed to DeleteMenu: first the seventh, then the sixth item is deleted (remember the Control menu's indexing starts at zero). The reason is that if the order were reversed—first the sixth, then the seventh—there would be no seventh item after the sixth is deleted.

6

An alternative, but one that might confuse you some time after you put the subroutine into your code, is:

```
Sub DeleteCloseControl()
    Call DeleteMenu(GetSystemMenu(GetActiveWindow, False), 5, 1024)
    Call DeleteMenu(GetSystemMenu(GetActiveWindow, False), 5, 1024)
End Sub
```

This code would first delete the horizontal separator, which is the sixth item in the menu (again, remember that the items are indexed beginning with zero) so the index 5 refers to the sixth item. After the separator is gone, the Close option is the sixth item in the menu, and indexed as 5. And the second time that DeleteMenu is called, it deletes the Close option.

Fig. 6.7

The menu's Close option is absent, and the application's Close button is deleted.

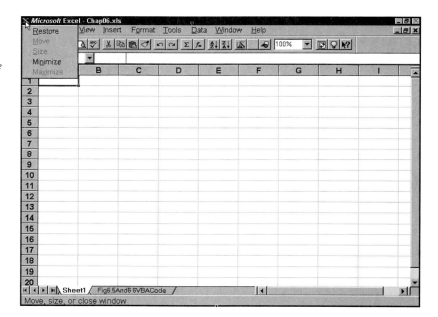

Summary

In this chapter, you learned some techniques to improve your VBA code. Using the With...End With approach to referencing objects, methods, and properties makes your code more structured, and can slightly increase its execution speed. Pairing the With approach and a test for a property can increase execution speed dramatically. The use of object variables in particular can bring about major increases in execution speed.

You also learned more about passing arguments to other procedures. Doing so is less convenient than using module-level or public declarations when you first create your code. But it pays dividends when it's time to modify or otherwise maintain the code: it's much easier to trace what happens to a variable at runtime.

API functions let you do more in Excel than is possible using VBA alone. They give you access to more objects and methods than are directly available in VBA. You saw examples of how to use API to position a custom dialog box and to delete items in the Excel Control menu.

Don't assume that API calls are available for Excel only. Other Office applications that support VBA, including Access, can also use them. For example, when VBA is implemented for Word, only minor modifications would be needed to adapt the Control menu code to the Word environment.

Speaking of Word, the next chapter begins *Microsoft Office Expert Solution's* discussion on Word with an overview of critical skills.

PART II

Word

chapter 7

Critical Skills in Word

7

by Susan Daffron

In this chapter

◆ **Automatic Text Functions**
Enter text quickly using AutoCorrect, AutoFormat, and the Spike.

◆ **Complex Documents**
Learn how to use outlining, sections, headers and footers, and field codes to ease the creation of complex documents in Word.

◆ **Tables**
Add tables to your documents and learn how to format columns, rows, and individual cells.

Microsoft Word is huge. The program can handle everything from a one-page letter or memo to massive book-length tomes with indexes and hundreds of cross references. You first encounter Word's weighty nature when you install the program. A full installation hogs up vast amounts of hard disk space, and the program requires a great deal of memory to run. Huge also means powerful in this case. Using Word, you can do things with a word processor that no one even imagined a few years ago. Formerly far-fetched ideas like automatic text formatting and correction, wizards, mail merges, and desktop publishing features are all commonplace now—if you can figure them out, of course.

All this hugeness comes at a price. Word can be intimidating, confusing, and downright aggravating at times. If you are buying an *Expert Solutions* book like this one, you probably have already experienced some tense moments with Word. Anyone trying to learn word processing for the first time has been there. Anyone switching to Word from another word processing application has been there. I've been there. And so have many other people. You are not alone.

The goal of the Word section of this book is to give you the information you need to become a Word expert. After you know how Word constructs a document and how the application itself is put together, you start to get a feel for how Word "thinks" about things. Then you are well on your way to expert status. Keep in mind that if you don't like an aspect of Word, you probably can change it. Once you realize that you can customize almost every Word function, the possibilities loom large. Realizing the power you have over the application itself makes it much less intimidating.

Although this chapter is titled "Critical Skills in Word," it assumes that you already know certain basic skills that are undeniably critical to working with Word, such as typing and formatting text, and opening and saving documents. In Word, many of these simple tasks are intuitive and work the same way they do in virtually every other Windows program.

Instead of focusing on basic functions, this chapter focuses on ways to get Word to work for you, not against you. Other decidedly critical elements of Word are described in other chapters, so they are not discussed here. Styles, for example, are integral to working efficiently in Word. In fact, styles are so important that they rate their own chapter (Chapter 9, "Word Styles"). Customizing the Word interface so it works the way you do is another big step you can take toward getting more work done in less time. That topic is discussed extensively in Chapter 10, "Customizing the Workspace."

This chapter focuses on avoiding some of the problems people encounter when they create voluminous quantities of text. In Word, people often run into problems when they create documents longer than one or two pages. The way you approach the construction of a short letter is different than the way you approach a long document. This chapter tells you how to avoid those problems before they happen and explains a few Word features that can help you create documents more quickly and efficiently.

Creating Text Quickly

Word has several features you can use to improve your productivity. No one can deny that typing repetitive documents is boring, but you can use some of Word's automatic features to remove some of the drudgery. Many people never bother to try these functions, which is a shame because they are easy to use and can save you hours of time.

Knowing about Word's automatic formatting tools also is important because you may want to turn some of them off. When you install Word, it turns on several automatic text formatting options by default. However, many people find these automatic functions confusing, and you may become extremely disconcerted watching your computer change something you typed. If strange things seem to be afoot, one of the automatic formatting options may be the culprit.

Using Automatic Formatting

Word 95 includes a great deal of automation. If you have spent any time with the online help, you have noticed that unlike previous versions where you quietly read the help file, the new Answer Wizard eerily walks you through the processes. You may find this feature disconcerting. In a similar manner, you can set up Word so it changes things automatically as you type. You may need to get used to this arrangement. If you like to be in total control of your word processing environment, you may never get used to this feature. Like most functions, however, you can configure these options so Word works exactly the way you want.

AutoCorrect

AutoCorrect is great for those of us who cannot type the word *the*. My fingers' personal favorite is *teh*, for example. When the office is really cold, I start lapsing into *hte* as well. You can use AutoCorrect to fix common typos like these.

You add AutoCorrect entries by choosing Tools, AutoCorrect. You see a huge list of words with the incorrect spellings on the left and the correct spellings on the right (see fig. 7.1). Type the incorrect and correct spelling of a word in the Replace and With boxes. Make sure that a check mark appears next to Replace Text as You Type. If you want to delete some of the words out of the list, highlight the entry and choose the Delete button.

Fig. 7.1

Add your favorite typos and other words you misspell frequently to the AutoCorrect list.

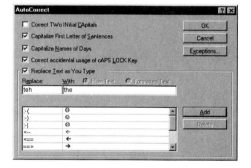

You can add AutoCorrect entries when you do a spell check. As you spell check the document, click the AutoCorrect button in the Spelling dialog box to add the word to the list.

Another less obvious way to use AutoCorrect is to expand abbreviations or shortcuts for long phrases. For example, if you work for a large law firm with a convoluted name, such as Schneider, Goodrich, Lowell and Thompson, you can create an AutoCorrect entry called *sglt* that magically changes this acronym into the full company name.

Note

Make sure when you add AutoCorrect entries that you don't add an abbreviation that is actually a word. For example, if your company name is Acme Towing, and you create an AutoCorrect entry called *at*, you will find the words *Acme Towing* in many more places than you expected (or wanted).

You can use AutoCorrect in a slightly different way to store both text and formatting. If you highlight a piece of text and then choose <u>T</u>ools, <u>A</u>utoCorrect, the highlighted text is placed in the <u>W</u>ith box. Using this approach, you can actually store formatted text such as fields, symbols, paragraph marks, imported graphics, or other non-text objects. If you choose the <u>F</u>ormatted Text option button, Word saves the entry with its original formatting. If the selection contains only text or you choose the <u>P</u>lain Text option button, Word stores the text without formatting.

For example, if you need to add a number of index entries, you can define an AutoCorrect entry called *xe* that actually inserts an XE field. Instead of typing the keyboard shortcuts for an index entry, you can type **xe** and edit the field directly. Similarly, if the law firm of Schneider, Goodrich, Lowell and Thompson always needs to appear in imposing bold type, you can highlight the name and save it as an AutoCorrect entry complete with its official formatting. Now whenever you type **sglt**, the full company name appears in commanding bold type (see fig. 7.2).

Fig. 7.2

By using AutoCorrect, you can add shortcuts for long phrases or text that you need to type frequently, such as company names.

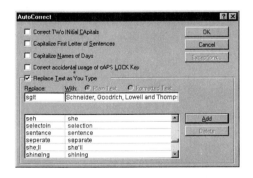

 Tip

When you type an AutoCorrect entry into your document and nothing seems to happen, make sure that you precede the AutoCorrect name with a space and follow it with a space or a punctuation mark. Often, just pressing the spacebar makes an ornery AutoCorrect problem go away.

The AutoCorrect dialog box has several other options with varying degrees of usefulness, depending on the type of text you usually write. You may want to experiment with these settings:

▶ *Correct TWo INitial CApitals*. This option corrects words that have the first two letters capitalized. Word changes the second capital letter to a lowercase letter. If you use computer company names or acronyms with strange capitalization, you may encounter problems. For example, a company called PCwarehouse automatically would be changed to Pcwarehouse, and INet would become Inet. Although this option has been vastly improved in Word for Windows 95, you may need to set up exception lists as described here.

▶ *Capitalize First Letter of Sentences*. This option capitalizes the first letter of the first word in a new sentence. This option can be a pain in the neck because Word gets confused if abbreviations with periods are used in the middle of a sentence (such as Inc. or Co.). Periods appear in the middle of sentences more often than you might expect, and having magic capital letters appear all over your document can be quite vexing.

▶ *Capitalize Names of Days*. This option capitalizes the first letter in the day of the week. For most people, this option can remain on without causing any undue consternation.

▶ *Correct accidental usage of cAPS LOCK Key*. This option corrects your typing if you accidentally hit the CAPS LOCK key. Word switches the case of the letters and turns off CAPS LOCK. The option works only if you fumble at the beginning of a sentence, however. Any all-cap text left in the preceding sentence (before the period) remains uppercase. In other words, say you press CAPS LOCK HERE. Word only fixes the text in this sentence (for example, the text that appears after the period). In this case, the word "here" is still left in uppercase letters.

You can create exception lists for these options. If you like the feature and you run into only a few terms that you don't want Word to correct, choose Tools, AutoCorrect. Choose the Exceptions button and add your text. If your exception lists start getting really long or you find you are adding exceptions constantly, turning off the option or creating AutoCorrect entries for the terms may make more sense. For example, you can create an AutoCorrect entry called *pc* that changes every instance of *pc* to *PC*.

AutoText

AutoText works almost like AutoCorrect. In fact, AutoCorrect is just a type of AutoText. However, AutoText has a couple of aspects that make it more flexible than AutoCorrect.

The most important difference between the two is that you can save AutoText entries to different templates. AutoCorrect entries are always saved into the NORMAL.DOT template, so they are available no matter what document you are working on. Conversely, you can save your AutoText entries to a specific template or copy AutoText entries between templates (see fig. 7.3). If you use a number of templates, this ability to organize your AutoText can be quite handy.

Fig. 7.3

Saving AutoText entries to a specific template makes them available to only those documents that use the template.

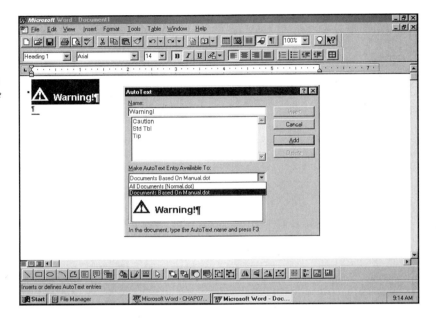

Another important difference between AutoCorrect and AutoText is that AutoText does not replace *every* instance of a certain set of keystrokes with a block of text. You need to type the F3 key to activate an AutoText entry. In other words, you could make *at* the AutoText name for Acme Towing, but AutoText would not replace it every time you type the word *at*. If you set up the keystroke as an AutoText entry rather than an AutoCorrect entry, you must press F3 after you type the AutoText name to activate the AutoText function. In the example, pressing F3 forces *at* to expand to *Acme Towing*.

When you insert an AutoText entry, you can type just the first few letters (enough to uniquely identify the name) to insert it. For example, if you have AutoText entries named *fred* and *food*, you can type *fr* and press the F3 key to insert the *fred* AutoText entry.

 Tip

If you use an AutoText entry often, you may want to add it to a toolbar button or create a keyboard shortcut for it as described in Chapter 10, "Customizing the Workspace."

To create an AutoText entry, follow these steps:

1. Highlight the text or graphics you want to store. If you want to include the paragraph formatting in the entry, make sure you include the paragraph mark in your selection. (To see paragraph marks, choose Tools, Options, click the View tab, and select Paragraph Marks.)

2. Choose Edit, AutoText.

3. Type a name for the entry in the Name box. Word suggests a name, but you can enter your own name by typing over the selection. AutoText names can be up to 32 characters long and can include spaces (see fig 7.4).

4. If necessary, change the Make AutoText Entry Available To drop-down box to a different template. The default setting is All Documents, which saves the entry into the Normal template, but you can save an AutoText entry to any template you want.

5. Click the Add button.

Fig. 7.4

If you use a symbol repeatedly throughout a document, such as the Caution icon shown here, you should turn it into an AutoText entry.

Spike

The Spike is like an invisible clipboard on steroids. Even though almost nobody (except Microsoft) seems to know about it, the Spike can be useful in situations when you need to move a large amount of text. The big difference between the Spike and the regular Clipboard is that you can cut multiple items with the Spike. When you use the regular Windows Clipboard, as soon as you cut or copy an item, anything in the Clipboard is replaced with the new item. If you want to cut various pieces of documents and put them into another document, you need to keep going back and forth, cutting and pasting between the two documents. When you add things to the Spike, it keeps the new material with whatever was already in there until you clear the Spike. You can think of the Spike as one of those desk spikes that people use to store old phone messages. As new messages come in, they are impaled on the desk spike, so newer messages are at the top and older ones are beneath. When you clear off a desk spike, the messages fall on the desk in the order they were placed.

You can use Word Spike for moving chunks of a document around. The key to using the Spike is to remember that you are removing (for example, *cutting*, not copying) text and graphics from a document. You can put the items somewhere else (such as another document), but you must cut an item first. If you don't want to damage the original documents, make sure you close the documents without saving the changes when you are finished. After your artifacts are placed in the Spike, you can insert them into another document or the same document.

To use the Spike, follow these steps:

1. Highlight the text or graphics you want to put in the Spike and press Ctrl+F3.
2. Keep adding text into the Spike until you have all the text you need stored in the Spike.
3. Place your cursor where you want to insert the contents of the Spike. Make sure to place your cursor so it is at the beginning of a line or surrounded by spaces.
4. To insert the contents of the Spike and clear the Spike, press Ctrl+Shift+F3. If you do not want to clear the Spike, you can type **spike** and press F3.

   Basically, the Spike is a special type of AutoText, so this technique works the same way you add other AutoText entries. Because the contents remain stored in the Spike, you can add the same text multiple times by typing **spike** and pressing F3.

α **Note**

When you insert the contents of the Spike, you insert everything stored in the Spike in the same order you cut it. In other words, suppose you cut three text blocks: text 1, text 2, and text 3, into the Spike. When you insert the contents, the text blocks appear in the order they were cut: text 1, text 2, text 3. You cannot restore partial contents of the Spike.

If you forget what you've put in the Spike, you can open the Spike by checking out its AutoText entry. Choose Edit, AutoText and select Spike from the Names list. You see a preview of the text that is currently in the Spike.

AutoFormat

AutoFormat is another tool you can use to quickly reformat text. You find AutoFormat in two places. You can choose it from the Format menu or you can choose Tools, Options and click the AutoFormat tab. Two settings are in the AutoFormat tab: AutoFormat and

AutoFormat as You Type. The AutoFormat controls set the options for the Format, AutoFormat command. However, you need to watch out for AutoFormat as You Type. If you don't know that these options are turned on, your life with Word may be filled with unexplainable oddities.

When you change the option button to AutoFormat as You Type, you see a whole slew of options. For example, if you have Automatic Numbered Lists enabled and you begin a paragraph with A. Smith, Word tries to number the paragraph automatically after you press Enter.

With most of the AutoFormat options, Word frequently has a hard time figuring out what you want to do. Often, turning these options off is better for your mental health. Every situation is different, so experiment and see which options work for you.

You use the Format, AutoFormat command to have Word quickly format a document. Unfortunately, Word often gets confused if you let it apply all the possible options. For example, Word cannot possibly figure out what constitutes a heading every time. Consequently, Word often screws up the job. And fixing Word's mistakes can take longer than just cleaning up the file by hand.

Choosing the Options button is always a good idea before you let Word go wild on a file. Afterwards, you can review the changes and see what Word did. AutoFormat works better on some files than others. If you run AutoFormat and the results are hopeless, you can choose Edit, Undo or click the Undo button on the toolbar to put the file back the way it was. Then you can run AutoFormat again with fewer options selected (see fig. 7.5).

Fig. 7.5

Setting just a few AutoFormat options increases the likelihood that Word will reformat your document the way you want it.

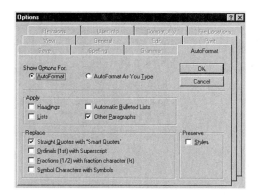

One convenient way to use the AutoFormat function is by using just a few options to format raw ASCII text, so the text word-wraps correctly. For example, text files that you download from the Internet are often filled with blank paragraphs and extra hard returns. Cleaning up these files by hand is tedious at best. Using AutoFormat is much easier. Selecting just the Other Paragraphs and Smart Quotes options removes the blank paragraphs and hard returns and changes all the straight quotes to typographic quotes. Then you can add your styles as you see fit.

Using Find and Replace

The Find and Replace functions are underutilized by many Word users. Many people laboriously scroll through a document to fix formatting or codes. For repetitive tasks, you often can use the Find and Replace functions to dramatically speed up your work. The trick to using Find or Replace is to use it to find unusual things like tab characters, field codes, formatting, styles, or even spaces. For example, if you tend to type two spaces rather than one after a period, you can use Replace to quickly replace two spaces with one space.

To use either of these functions, choose Edit, Find or Edit, Replace. To search for special characters, choose the Special button and select an item. You also can type codes directly into the Find What box. Note that the codes are case-sensitive. For example, to search for paragraphs, you must enter a carat character (^) and a lowercase p. An uppercase P doesn't work.

If you prefer, you can copy text from the document (Ctrl+C) and paste it into the Find What box (Ctrl+V).

The codes for the special characters you can find and replace are shown in table 7.1.

Table 7.1   Special Character Codes

Character	Code
Paragraph mark	^p
Tab character	^t
Annotation mark	^a
ANSI or ASCII characters	^0+3-digit character code number
Any character	^?
Any digit	^#
Any letter	^$
Caret character	^^
The contents of the Clipboard	^c
The contents of the Find What box	^&

Character	Code
Endnote mark	^e
Field	^d
Footnote mark	^f
Graphic	^g
Column break	^n
Manual line break	^l
Manual page break	^m
Section break	^b
Em dash	^+
En dash	^=
Nonbreaking space	^s
Nonbreaking hyphen	^~
Optional hyphen	^-
White space	^w

For example, to remove extra paragraph returns from a document, you can find three paragraphs (^p^p^p) and replace them with two (^p^p). Similarly, if a file has a table embedded in the text that is formatted with spaces rather than tabs, you can find and replace multiple spaces with a tab (^t). Then you can go back and highlight the tabbed text and choose Table, Convert Text to Table to create a perfectly formatted Word table.

 Tip

You can repeat your last Find by pressing Shift+F4. For example, if you want to examine all the hard page breaks you entered into a document, you can type **^m** in the Find What box and then press Shift+F4 to step through all the page breaks in a document.

You also can use Find and Replace for styles. If you have formatted your document with styles, you can search for every instance of Heading 1, for example. Or if you want to change the formatting of all the text formatted in one style to another, don't go through the tedious task of reapplying styles—just do a Replace All.

Creating Complex Documents

Creating short documents in Word is undeniably easy. You type the text, format it, and print it. But not all documents are short. More and more people are using Word in place of desktop publishing applications to create long, complex documents with headers, footers, graphics, indexes, and tables of contents. Suddenly, the same program that seemed so easy for a letter gets much more complicated. Microsoft has added these features to Word, but many of the ways you work with them are not intuitive. If you plan to create long documents, you need to learn about some of Word's advanced features. Of course, learning these features can help you with much more than just long documents, so your time is well spent.

Working in Outline View

When you create long documents, you can get so wrapped up in writing and formatting that you lose the "big picture." Using Word's Outline view can give you a good overview of a document's structure. In Outline view, you can rearrange your headings and text, change the hierarchy of your document, and easily move to a particular location in the document. You can switch back and forth between Outline view and Normal or Page Layout view any time you need to get a different perspective.

Managing Heading Levels

To use Outline view effectively on an existing document, you need to set up your document using the built-in heading styles. (Working with styles is described in detail in Chapter 9, "Word Styles.") By setting up the document using the heading styles, you create a text hierarchy that organizes your document.

To switch to Outline view, choose <u>V</u>iew, <u>O</u>utline. Word adds an extra toolbar filled with numbers and arrows. All your document text is indented to indicate its level in the hierarchy. You click the numbers and symbols on the toolbar to hide and display the different levels of your outline (see fig. 7.6).

You use the following tools to work with text in Outline view:

- ▶ Left-arrow button (or Alt+Shift+left arrow) promotes headings.
- ▶ Right-arrow button (or Alt+Shift+right arrow) demotes headings.
- ▶ Double-arrow button (or Alt+Shift+5 on the numeric keypad) changes a heading to body text.
- ▶ Up-arrow button (or Alt+Shift+up arrow) moves the outline element before the previous element in the document.

▶ Down-arrow button (or Alt+Shift+down arrow) moves the outline element after the following element in the document.

▶ Plus-sign button (or Alt+Shift+plus key) expands the text for the outline element you select.

▶ Minus-sign button (or Alt+Shift+minus key) collapses the text for the outline element you select.

Fig. 7.6

Double-clicking the plus sign in the margin expands an outline element.

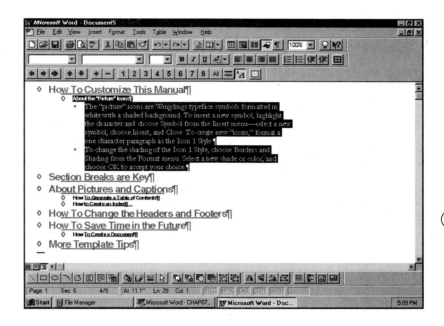

If you promote or demote headings, the subheads below it in the hierarchy stay the same unless you select the plus sign with the heading. In that case, you are selecting the text as a group, so the whole group of text is promoted or demoted.

If you like to create an outline before you write, writing directly into Outline view helps organize your headings and formats them with the heading styles automatically. Working in Outline view takes some getting used to, but after you have promoted and demoted a few headings, it all starts to make more sense.

Adding Numbering

After you have your outline the way you want it, you can have Word add automatic numbering to your headings. Choose Format, Heading Numbering. You can choose from the six built-in numbering formats or you can set up your own.

To set up your own custom numbering scheme, click the Modify button (see fig. 7.7). You can change the numbering, font, and alignment for each level. For example, if you want to add text before the number, such as the word *Section*, you type it in the Text Before box. You can modify the formatting for the different heading levels by moving the scroll bar in the Level box to change the heading level.

Fig. 7.7

You set formatting options for your numbering in the Modify Heading Numbering dialog box.

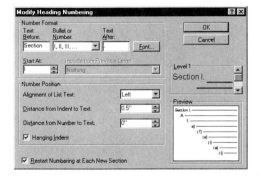

Automatic heading numbering has a few advantages, but quite a few limitations as well. If you cannot get the automatic heading numbering to work the way you want, you can use fields to number text in Word (described later in this section).

The advantage of automatic heading numbering is its automatic link to the cross-referencing function. When you use the Insert/Cross Reference dialog box, your numbers reference correctly. With automatic heading numbering, although you can include numbers from one level to another, you cannot change the numeric formatting. For example, you cannot have Roman numerals at the top level carry them down as Arabic numerals in the sublevels. In addition, if you include text in one level as described earlier (the word *Section*, for example), you cannot carry down just the number to the next level without also carrying down the text.

A couple of other issues relate to formatting. Every time you access the Heading Numbering dialog box, Word resets all the indents for your heading styles. Repeatedly fixing your indents is extremely annoying if you decide to change your numbering down the road. In addition, you cannot easily skip numbering levels. For example, if you want to number your headings 1.1, 2.1, 4.1, you must put in an extra paragraph (3.1) and format it as hidden text to simulate a skipped level.

Finally, heading numbering is saved in the document, not in the paragraph as part of a style. When you apply a template by choosing File, Templates, your numbering is lost if you have the Automatically Update Styles box checked in the Templates and Add-ins dialog box. As a style is reapplied from the template, it wipes out the numbering. This limitation makes it difficult to ensure consistency across documents. The differences between document-level formatting versus the paragraph-level formatting stored in styles is explained in detail in Chapter 9, "Word Styles."

Working with Long Documents

When you are working with a great deal of text, organizing it can be an onerous task. Long documents often require cross references, graphics, tables of contents, and indexes, so readers can find the information they need. However, when you work with long documents, you need to consider the trade-off between file size and stability.

With any software program, the larger your file sizes become, the more likely your system is to crumple under the load. This risk is true of image-editing applications, desktop publishing applications, and unfortunately, word processing applications like Word. Anyone who has not experienced the pain of losing all or part of a large, critical file hasn't been using computers very long—or is very lucky. When you create large documents, try to keep your file sizes as small as possible.

For that reason, this chapter does not explain the Master Document function. If you do a search in the Word online help for long documents, you see many references to this feature. The Master Document function creates an enormous, memory- and resource-intensive document, which greatly increases your odds of crashing Word. In fact, the Word 6 implementation of Master Document didn't work at all. Under Word 95, unless you have a very fast system with lots of RAM, the process is painfully slow and potentially unstable.

Instead of struggling to tame the Master Document function, break up your long document into multiple files (and take the time you would have spent toiling with your master document to learn about sections, fields, and bookmarks).

Using Sections

If you have an enormous 250-page document, you should make each chapter (or other logical section) a separate document. Divide your document so that each chapter is less than 50 pages long. However, for medium-sized documents of fewer than 50 pages, you can use section breaks to divide your document into chapters. Breaking your document into sections lets you format each section differently, almost as if each section were its own document. You can change such formatting as headers, footers, numbering, and columns for each section.

Working with Breaks

Every document starts as one big section. To insert a new section into your document, choose Insert, Break and click one of the choices in the Break dialog box (see fig. 7.8).

Fig. 7.8

When you add section breaks, you can choose from several different types.

You have four types of section breaks:

▶ *Next Page*. Begins the new section at the top of the next page.

▶ *Continuous*. Begins the new section without inserting a page break. The break occurs at the insertion point. You often use continuous section breaks when you work with columns (as described in Chapter 11, "Desktop Publishing with Word") or when you need to protect part of a document, such as a form.

▶ *Even Page*. Begins the new section on the next even-numbered page (usually the left-hand page in a book). If you insert the break on an even-numbered page, the next odd-numbered page is left blank.

▶ *Odd Page*. Begins the new section on the next odd-numbered page (usually the right-hand page in a book). If you insert the break on an odd-numbered page, the next even-numbered page is left blank.

By using Insert, Break, you also can insert page breaks and column breaks. These functions can be useful if you need to force your text to end in a certain place. In Normal view, a page break appears as a dotted line with the words *Page Break* to distinguish it from the soft page breaks that Word inserts automatically at the end of every page.

Creating Headers and Footers

Most long documents contain headers and footers to help readers navigate through the document. Headers and footers are the repeating text that is printed at the top and bottom (respectively) of every page in a document. For example, many books are set up with the book or chapter name in the header and the page number in the footer.

Headers and footers are intimately involved with the settings in the Page Setup dialog box. Before you start adding headers and footers, think about whether you want your document to have different headers and footers on the odd and even pages or a different header or footer on the first page. If so, you need to choose File, Page Setup and click the Layout tab. Make sure that you have a check mark next to Different Odd and Even pages or Different First Page.

Depending on how you set up your document, you can type different information in the headers and footers on the first page or on the odd and even pages in a section. (Remember that Word considers a document one big section until you add section breaks.) If you create multiple sections in your document, you can link your headers and footers to previous sections.

For example, if you want the footers to be the same on all the even pages in the sections of a document, you can link them together. Then when you change the text or formatting in the even-page footer in the first section, the even-page footers in the following sections change as well. Conversely, you can have the header or footer information be different in each section by breaking the link to the previous section. Unlinking the header or footer from the previous one forces it to live in its own little world, unaware of the contents of the headers or footers in the other sections.

To create a header or footer, follow these steps:

1. Choose View, Header and Footer.

2. Using the Header and Footer toolbar, click the Switch Between Header and Footer button to move your cursor into the header or footer area. The buttons are small, so you may want to turn on ToolTips to remind you what each button does (see fig. 7.9).

Fig. 7.9

If you cannot remember the button functions in Header and Footer view, turn on ToolTips. You can show ToolTips by enabling the option in View, Toolbars.

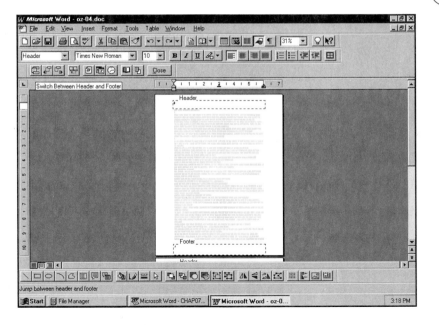

3. Enter the text or graphics you want into the area within the dashed line. You also can click the page number, date, or time buttons to add this information automatically.

4. You can use the Same as Previous button to link the header or footer to the previous section. If you have different first, odd, or even pages set up or multiple sections, you can use the Show Previous and Show Next buttons to view the other headers and footers in the document.

5. Click the Close button.

 Note

When you are in Header and Footer view, you cannot edit the text in the main body of the document.

Headers and footers are more flexible than they may seem at first glance. Virtually anything you can do to regular text, you can do to headers and footers. You can insert graphics, change fonts, add tabs, add tables, and add frames to name just a few things. See Chapter 11, "Desktop Publishing with Word," for more information about adding graphics and tables in headers and footers.

 Tip

When you are in Page Layout view, you can jump directly to Header and Footer view by double-clicking in the grayed header or footer area. Similarly, double-clicking in the grayed document area takes you out of Header and Footer view.

Formatting Page Numbers

Most long documents have page numbers in the header or footer. Although you can easily click the little number button in Header and Footer view to add a page number, changing the format of the page number is less intuitive. For example, in a large document, you may want to begin a section with a number other than 1 or change the type of numbering from Arabic to Roman numerals.

To format an existing page number, highlight the page number and choose Insert, Page Numbers. Choose the Format button and change the options. For example, to have the section start at a number other than 1, change the number in the Start At box (see fig. 7.10). If you unlink headers or footers with page numbers in them, yet you still want the numbering to be continuous across sections, choose the Continue from Previous Section option button.

Fig. 7.10

If you want your page numbering to start with a number other than 1, you need to reformat using the Page Number Format dialog box.

Using Fields

Fields are the key to creating long documents. Basically, a *field* is a hidden code that you insert to tell Word to do something. For example, the page number you insert into a footer is actually a {PAGE} field. Normally, you just see the result of the field—the page number—rather than the field code. To see the field codes in a document, choose Tools, Options and click the View tab. Place a check mark next to Field Codes. Certain fields are also formatted as hidden text, so you may need to place a check mark next to Hidden Text to see particular field codes, such as TOC.

Word has more than 60 field codes you can use. To get a glimpse of the world of fields, choose Insert, Field and click All. You may never use many of these fields, but it's good to know they are exist just in case. When you work with fields, the first thing you discover is that many fields have *switches*. A switch is a backward slash character (\) that you use as an optional instruction to customize a field result in some way.

These fields are most important for working with long documents:

▶ *XE*. Adds an index entry. The text you enter in an XE field is included in the index when you generate it using an INDEX field.

▶ *INDEX*. Creates an index. The INDEX field goes through and reads all the index entries you add with XE (Index Entry) fields and collates them into an index. You can insert an INDEX field by choosing Insert, Index and Tables.

▶ *TOC*. Creates a table of contents. The TOC field collects entries for a table of contents using the built-in Heading 1-9 styles, styles you specify, or entries you specify using TC (Table of Contents entry) fields. You can insert a TOC field by choosing Insert, Index and Tables.

▶ *TC*. Adds a Table of Contents entry. You use the TC field if you do not want to generate a table of contents using the built-in heading styles. You also can use the TC field to add entries for other lists, such as a table of figures.

▶ *RD* (Referenced Document). Used to temporarily retrieve files into a separate document such as a table of contents, so you can compile an index or table of contents using a TOC or INDEX field. When you use RD fields, you need to set the starting page numbers or sequence fields in the documents referenced by the RD field before you update the table of contents or index.

▶ *SEQ*. Used to sequentially number items in a document such as chapters, tables, or figures. SEQ fields enable you to move text around (which changes the numerical sequence) and reorder the numbers just by updating the fields.

▶ *PAGEREF* and *REF*. Used for cross references. PAGEREF inserts the page number of a bookmark's location for a cross reference. REF inserts the contents of the bookmark.

▶ *IncludePicture*. Used to insert a graphic. Whenever you choose Insert, Picture, Word actually puts in an IncludePicture field. Adding the \d switch links the graphic to the original file, which reduces file size.

▶ *IncludeText*. Used to insert all or part of a document (using a bookmark) into another document. You can use the IncludeText field in conjunction with the REF or PAGEREF fields to create cross references across documents.

The most important tool for working with fields is the online help. Word comes with exhaustive documentation on each of its field codes. After you select a field and it appears in the Field Code box, you can press the F1 key to go directly to the help topic for that field (see fig. 7.11). Every field code help topic provides the correct field syntax and descriptions of the optional switches you can add to a field.

Fig. 7.11

Getting to know the online help is a good idea if you plan to work with fields.

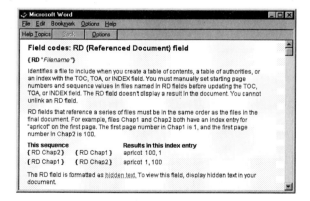

Several keyboard shortcuts are handy for working with fields. All shortcuts include the F9 key, so they are easy to remember:

▶ *F9*: Updates selected fields. To update all fields in a document, press Ctrl+A (Select All) and then press F9.

- ▸ *Shift+F9*: Switches selected fields between the field codes and the results.
- ▸ *Ctrl+F9*: Inserts field code brackets { }, so you can type in a field code directly instead of using the Field dialog box.
- ▸ *Ctrl+Shift+F9*: Unlinks a field. Unlinking permanently replaces a field with its result.

Word enters some fields when you use a certain dialog box. For example, the Insert Index Entry dialog box inserts an XE field, and the Index and Tables dialog box inserts an INDEX or table of contents (TOC) field. Other fields are accessible only by using Insert, Field or by typing them in directly using Ctrl+F9. Most fields don't update automatically. If you have performed any actions that may affect the result of a field, make sure to update the fields.

Using SEQ Fields for Numbering Chapters

SEQ fields are useful for numbering repeating elements in a large document. You can format these fields in many ways and use them to reset the starting number. For example, if your document has a numbering scheme set up with the chapter number and then the page number (1-1, 2-1, 3-1, and so on), you can use an SEQ field to set the chapter number. You assign a name to each numbering sequence you want to set up. For example, this code starts a numbering sequence called *chapter*:

```
{ SEQ chapter \r 3 }
```

The \r switch resets the chapter number sequence so it starts at 3. Another handy switch is the \c switch, which looks for the closest prior instance of that sequence and repeats the result. You may use this switch for inserting chapter numbers in headers or footers. For example:

```
Page { SEQ chapter \c } - { PAGE }
```

If you place this text in the footer of Chapter 3, the result is *Page 3-1* when the document is printed.

Another feature of SEQ fields is that you can use switches to change the type of numbering. When you are in the Insert Field dialog box, you can click the Options button to see the optional field switches for a field (see fig. 7.12). The SEQ field has options that let you set numbers to appear as ordinal text, cardinal text, roman numerals, all caps, or initial caps just by using a different switch. For example, if your appendixes use letters rather than numbers for the chapter headings, this code numbers the chapter *A*:

```
{ SEQ Chapter \r 1 \*Alphabetic }
```

The *Alphabetic switch converts the numeric value 1 to a letter value (A). You need to begin the word *Alphabetic* with an uppercase A if you want an uppercase result. If the *a* is lowercase, your chapter is numbered with a lowercase *a*.

Fig. 7.12

The Field Options dialog box contains descriptions of the switches you can add to a field. Clicking the Add button adds the switch to the code.

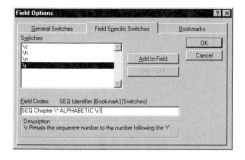

You can use SEQ fields as an alternative to Word's built-in numbering functions. As discussed earlier, the built-in heading numbering has some limitations. Although using fields for numbering isn't as convenient as using Word's built-in numbering, fields offer more control. For example, you can use a different sequence name for each level of heading, so that the first instance of the following code results in 3.1.1 (assuming you are still in Chapter 3):

```
{SEQ Chapter \c}.{SEQ Heading2}.{SEQ Heading3}
```

Similarly, you can use SEQ fields to number figures or tables. For example, you can use this code to number a figure followed by a caption:

```
Figure {SEQ Chapter \c}-{SEQ Figure}. The Field Dialog Box.
```

Because this caption is composed of SEQ fields, you can move the caption anywhere in the file or to another file. When you update fields, the SEQ field causes the figure to be renumbered, reflecting its new location.

Like other fields, SEQ fields can appear anywhere in the document, but they don't automatically show updated results, so you need to update the fields. Be sure to update all the fields in all your documents with the F9 key before you generate a table of contents or index.

Inserting Index Entries

The Index Entry (XE) field is another field often used in large documents. Inserting index entries is an arduous task, but readers love indexes, so including an index is often mandatory for large documents.

To mark the text you want to incorporate into the index, follow these steps:

1. Select a word or words you want to add as an index entry. If you prefer, you can enter different text by placing the insertion point where you want the XE code to appear.

2. Press Alt+Shift+X. The Mark Index Entry dialog box appears (see fig. 7.13).

3. If you highlighted text, it appears in the Main Entry box. Otherwise, type your first-level index entry text. You also can type a second-level entry in the Subentry box. If you need a three-level index, you can follow the subentry text with a colon and type the third-level entry text.

4. Choose Mark. The Mark Index Entry dialog box stays open, so you can continue to add entries. You can mark every occurrence of the entry text by choosing Mark All. Note that Mark All marks the first occurrence in each paragraph of matching text. Use this option carefully, however, or you may end up with an index that is unwieldy and difficult to use.

Fig. 7.13

The Mark Index Entry dialog box remains open until you click the Close button.

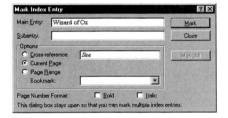

After you have all your index entries defined, you are ready to create an index. If your document is short, you can just add the INDEX field at the end of your document or in its own section. If you have a very large document, you may want to make the index a separate document and use RD fields, as described in the next section.

Using RD Fields

When you are ready to create a table of contents or index for a large document consisting of multiple files, you can use RD (Referenced Document) fields. RD fields briefly retrieve your chapters, just long enough for Word to compile the document. RD fields are formatted as hidden text. You can work with these fields more easily if you place a check mark next to Hidden Text in the View tab under Tools, Options.

When you add RD fields, you must place them in the order the chapters should appear in the final document. For example, the RD code for Chapter 1 of your document must be listed before the RD code for Chapter 2, or the page numbers appear out of order in the index or table of contents.

If the files you reference with an RD field are not located in the same directory as your table of contents or index file, you need to use double backslashes in the path name. For example, if you display hidden text and field codes, your table of contents file looks like this:

```
{ RD C:\\DOCS\\MANUAL\\CHAPTER1.DOC }
{ RD C:\\DOCS\\MANUAL\\CHAPTER2.DOC }
{ RD C:\\DOCS\\MANUAL\\CHAPTER3.DOC }
{ TOC }
```

You can place all your RD codes on one line and format them in small type, so they don't greatly affect the layout of the table of contents. If you prefer, you can create a new section and place the RD codes on a blank page after the TOC code.

You can choose Insert, Index and Tables to insert the Index or TOC code; or use Insert, Field to insert the code directly. Note that the Index and Tables dialog box has numerous formatting options that enable you to create a custom table of contents or index. You can select one of the built-in styles (Classic, Modern, Fancy, and so on). Or if you have your own ideas about how you want your TOC to look, click From Template and click the Modify button to format the TOC 1–9 styles the way you like (see fig. 7.14).

Fig. 7.14

You can modify the TOC 1–9 styles to create your own look for the table of contents.

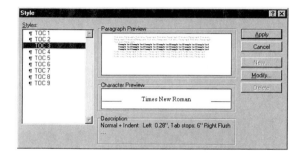

The easiest way to create a table of contents is by using the built-in heading styles (Heading 1–Heading 9). If you prefer, you can click the Options button in the Table of Contents tab to assign different styles to specific TOC levels. You also can generate a table of contents from TC codes you have inserted in the document or from a combination of headings and TC codes. If you intend to do anything this tricky, however, refer to the online help for more information about the TOC field code switches. Typing your own TOC field gives you more control. For example, this code tells Word which heading levels and sequence numbers to include:

```
{TOC \o "1-3" \s chapter }
```

The \o switch tells Word to use the built-in Heading levels 1 through 3. The \s switch says to include the chapter numbers from the sequence defined in the chapter SEQ fields. This TOC code results in a three-level table of contents with a chapter-page (1-1, 2-1, 3-1) number format.

By intentionally applying the built-in heading styles to certain elements in your document, you can later generate a listing of just those elements. For example, if you need to create a list of figures, you can apply the Heading 9 style to all your figure captions. Using the field code {TOC \o "9-9" } generates a table of contents that includes just the Heading 9 styles.

Creating Cross References

Cross references are another characteristic of long documents that require some work. In Word, you create cross references using bookmarks in conjunction with the PAGEREF field. You use bookmarks to mark a location in a document. You use a bookmark to name a place. Later, you can use a cross reference to point to the bookmark.

Adding Bookmarks

A bookmark acts as a marker that tells Word where to get the information you need. A bookmark can be a specific location in the text, or you can highlight text and wrap a bookmark around that piece of text. You can later reference the text enclosed in the bookmark or place it somewhere else.

To define a bookmark, follow these steps:

1. Select the text, item, or location you want to mark.

2. Choose Edit, Bookmark.

3. In the Bookmark Name box, type a name for the bookmark (see fig. 7.15). A bookmark name must begin with a letter. The name can contain letters, numbers, and underscore characters. It cannot be more than 40 characters long, and it may not include spaces.

4. Choose Add. The new bookmark name is added to the list.

Fig. 7.15

A bookmark identifies a place in your text that you can reference later using a cross reference.

Cross Referencing Text in the Same File

After you have added bookmarks, you can create a cross reference to tell your readers where to find certain information. If you want to cross reference information within the same file, you choose Insert, Cross-Reference to add the reference. You can cross reference more than just bookmarks, however. A cross reference can refer to a bookmark, footnote, endnote, caption, or text formatted with the built-in heading styles. If you have a long document, however, inserting references to the heading names can sometimes get unwieldy and even buggy.

To create a cross reference within the same document, follow these steps:

1. Choose Insert, Cross-Reference (see fig. 7.16).

2. Select the type of reference (Heading, Bookmark, Footnote, Endnote, Equation, Figure, Table) from the Reference Type box.

3. Select the type of information you want to insert into the document (such as a bookmark text or page number). These options vary depending on the type of reference you select.

4. Select the item for which you want to create a reference. For example, if you select Bookmark from the Reference Type box, you see a list of all your bookmark names in the For Which Bookmark box.

5. Click the Insert button. The Cross-Reference dialog box stays open so you can continue adding references.

6. When you are done, click Cancel.

Fig. 7.16

You add cross refer-
ences within the same
file using the Cross-
Reference dialog box.

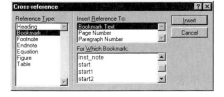

Cross Referencing Text in Other Files

Creating a cross reference to a place in another file is a little more difficult than cross referencing in one file. You cannot use Word's Insert, Cross-Reference function to cross reference an item in another file. Instead, you must use the IncludeText field and pass it the bookmark name in the other file. The IncludeText field brings in just the text marked by a bookmark. If you are referencing normal text that does not contain any fields, you can use the IncludeText field and pass it the name of the file and the bookmark name:

```
{INCLUDETEXT C:\\DOCS\\MANUAL\\CHAPTER1.DOC mybookmark1}
```

Again, note that you use double backslashes (\\) to indicate the path name.

If you have used SEQ, PAGE, or other numbering fields, you need to be a little more crafty when you reference these items. Because these numbers are created from fields themselves, the numbers will update when IncludeText brings them into the new location. For example, a field that was 2.1 in the original file may end up as 3.2 after the fields update in the file with the cross reference. However, you can prevent this problem by adding the \! switch to the field:

```
{ INCLUDETEXT C:\\DOCS\\MANUAL\\CHAPTER1.DOC mybookmark1 \! }
```

The \! field prevents the field results from being updated unless they are updated in the original file.

Referencing Page Numbers in Other Files

If you create a large document made up of multiple files, and you want contiguous page numbers, it can be a nuisance going into each document and updating the page number using the Format Page Number dialog box. Repagination and editing in a large document can cause the page count to change frequently. Using fields, you can update the page number across documents automatically. Basically, you create a bookmark at the end of the first file. In the second file, you place a reference to the bookmark in the first file and use a SUM field to add the page number in the first file to the number in the second.

Although the steps may seem cumbersome, you need to go through the process only once. In a huge document that repaginates often, the initial effort is worthwhile. Follow these steps:

1. Open the first document. Select the last paragraph mark in the file and create a bookmark. For example, name this bookmark **end_of_file**.

2. Place your cursor to the left of the last paragraph mark. Press Ctrl+F9 to insert a set of field code braces. Within the braces, type **PAGEREF end_of_file**.

3. Select your new PAGEREF field and create another bookmark. For example, type a bookmark named **chapter1**. Press F9 to update the field. The last page number of the document should appear. If you don't want the page number to be visible in this document, format it as hidden text by highlighting it, choosing F̲ormat, F̲ont, and placing a check mark next to H̲idden.

4. Open your second document and place your cursor where you want the starting page number to appear. You are going to create a *nested* field, which is a field within another field. Press Ctrl+F9 to insert a pair of braces. Inside the braces type **=sum(**.

5. Press Ctrl+F9 again to insert another pair of braces. In this pair, type this line:

   INCLUDETEXT C:\\DOCS\\MANUAL\\CHAPTER1.DOC chapter1 \\ *ARABIC \!

   The path name should point to the first document, and *chapter1* is the name of the bookmark you created in step 3. The field should look like this:

   ```
   {=SUM({INCLUDETEXT C:\\DOCS\\MANUAL\\CHAPTER1.DOC chapter1 \*ARABIC \!}
   ```

6. Place your cursor between the two closing braces and type a comma. Press Ctrl+F9 to insert yet another pair of braces. Inside the braces, type **PAGE**. Move your cursor between the last two right closing braces and type **)**. The final nested field should look like this:

```
{=SUM({INCLUDETEXT C:\\DOCS\\MANUAL\\
➥CHAPTER1.DOC chapter1 \*ARABIC \!},{PAGE})}
```

7. Select the SUM field and press F9 to update the field. The SUM field should add the last page number of the first document to the current page number of the second document. If you want to continue the page numbers to other documents, repeat the process by inserting bookmarks at the end of the second document and placing the SUM field in the third, and so on throughout the rest of the chapters.

When you edit the documents enough to alter the pagination, you must update the fields in your documents. Otherwise, Word displays obnoxious error messages, such as Bookmark does not exist, rather than the correct field result. If this situation becomes a problem, you may want to add a command to your AutoOpen or AutoClose macros to update all the fields in the document. The automatic macros are described in Chapter 10, "Customizing the Workspace."

Tips for Reducing Document File Size

The key to working with large documents is to keep your file sizes as small as possible. If you have a slow computer, keeping file size down is especially important for your mental health. (If you have ever spent valuable time watching Word painfully repaint and repaginate, you know what I mean.) The more tables, graphics, and other spiffy features you include in your document, the more likely you are to experience problems as your files bloat.

The following tips can help reduce Word pain:

▶ If you are working on a slow PC, try to keep your files fewer than 50 pages. If you have numerous complex graphics and tables, you may want to make your chapters even shorter. The fewer complicated features you use, the longer your document can be before you begin experiencing problems.

▶ Use SEQ fields to automatically number your sections and make your table of contents and indexes separate documents. In your table of contents or index, use RD (Referenced Document) fields to pull in the component parts of your document.

▶ Use Insert, Picture to add your graphics. Linking graphics to the original files on your disk decreases the Word file size. Make sure a check mark appears next to Link to File when you insert pictures. Also make sure that no check mark appears next to Save with Document. When you turn on field codes, you should see a code that looks like the following:

```
{ INCLUDEPICTURE C:\\DOCS\\MANUAL\\FIG22.BMP \d *\MERGEFORMAT }
```

The \d switch tells Word to link the graphic to the original file and not embed it in the document.

▶ Select the Picture Placeholders box in the View tab under Tools, Options (see fig. 7.17). Word shows each picture as a box, which is much faster than displaying the actual picture. The box is the same size as the picture, which keeps the document pagination in tact.

▶ Turn off background repagination. This option is available only when you work in Normal view. Some of us oldsters remember that Word 2 had a command called Repaginate Now on the Tools menu, which let you control when Word repaginated. You can add that command (called ToolsRepaginate in Word command lingo) back into your Tools menu. Adding commands to menus is described in Chapter 10, "Customizing the Workspace."

Fig. 7.17

Selecting Picture Place-holders in the View tab of the Options dialog box can speed up screen redraw immensely.

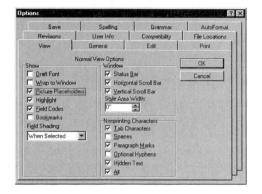

Working with Tables

Word has more uses for tables than you might expect. Used for more than just boring tabular data, tables frequently take the place of complicated tab settings because you can tell what's going on more easily in a table. You can use tables for everything from a sheet of labels to forms to side-by-side text. Anytime you find yourself struggling with tabs, you probably should switch that text to a table.

Word tables employ many of the same concepts used in Excel. Like an Excel spreadsheet, a Word table is a grid made up of columns and rows. The box created by the intersection of a column and row is called a *cell*. When you format a table, you can apply formatting to the whole table, a column, a row, or an individual cell.

You can insert tables in a number of ways. You can use the toolbar, a wizard, or the menus, depending on how you like to work. The toolbar is the most graphical way to insert a table, and the wizard is the slowest.

For the most control in creating a table, use the menu commands and follow these steps:

1. Before you do anything, make sure that the table gridlines are turned on. (Many people "lose" their tables because they cannot see them.) Choose Table, Gridlines, so a check mark appears next to the word Gridlines in the menu.

2. Now you can create your table and see it too. Choose Table, Insert Table. The Insert Table dialog box appears.

3. Type the number of columns you want in your table in the Number of Columns box.

4. Type the number of rows into the Number of Rows box (see fig. 7.18). Bear in mind that you can easily add or delete rows later, so if you're not sure how many rows you want, just guess.

5. If you like wizards, you can choose the Wizard option and let it walk you through the rest of the table construction. If you want to try a preformatted table style, choose AutoFormat.

6. When you're done, click OK. Word inserts a new table into your document.

Fig. 7.18

To insert a table, you first need to decide how many rows and columns you want.

After you have created your table, you find the cursor sitting in the first cell of the table (the first row of the first column). Now you can start typing. The text wraps within the confines of the cell, and the entire row grows to accommodate the height of the tallest cell in the row.

Much to the surprise of many users, certain keys work differently when you work with tables. For example, the Tab key does not insert a tab character; it moves you to the next cell. To actually put a tab character within a cell, you need to type Ctrl+Tab.

Use these key combinations to move around within a table:

▶ *Tab.* Moves the cursor one cell to the right.

▶ *Shift+Tab.* Moves the cursor one cell to the left.

▶ *Left- and right-arrow keys.* Move the cursor through the cells character by character.

▶ *Up- and down-arrow keys.* Move the cursor up and down through the table rows and the text rows within the cells.

▶ *Alt+Home.* Moves the cursor to the first cell in the row. (Pressing the Home key by itself moves the cursor to the left edge of the cell.)

> *Alt+End*. Moves the cursor to the last cell in the row. (Pressing the End key by itself moves the cursor to the right edge of the cell.)

> *Alt+Page Up*. Moves the cursor to the first cell at the top of the column.

> *Alt+Page Down*. Moves the cursor to the last cell at the bottom of the column.

If you are typing along and you get to the end of the table, but you need another row, press the Tab key to create a new row of cells. Your cursor appears in the first cell of the new row.

Formatting Tables

Most people don't get their tables just right when they first create them. You easily can spend hours twiddling around with table formatting. You can add borders and shading, merge cells, split cells, and format the paragraphs within the cells using most of formatting commands you can apply to paragraphs anywhere else. You can adjust the paragraph line spacing to make your cells taller; you can sort and calculate your tables. The mind reels. Most of these formatting options are intuitive. For example, splitting and merging cells does just what you would think it does. Arguably, the most difficult aspect of formatting tables is selecting just the cells you want to work with.

When you edit tables, a good idea is to turn paragraph marks on by choosing <u>T</u>ools, <u>O</u>ptions, View and adding a check mark next to Paragraph <u>M</u>arks. When paragraph marks are off, you may have difficulty telling whether you have selected the cell itself or just the text in the cell. When paragraph marks are turned on, you can tell the entire cell is highlighted because the little square paragraph indicator is highlighted as well.

You can use these shortcut keys to highlight parts of your table:

> *Shift+arrow keys*. Selects text character by character. If you continue the selection to the next cell, the entire adjacent cell is selected.

> *F8+arrow keys*. Selects text in the current cell and extends the selection as you continue to press the arrow keys. Pressing the Esc key ends the selection.

> *Alt+5 on the numeric keypad*. Selects the entire table. NumLock must be off for this shortcut to work.

 Tip

The easiest way to select an entire row is by clicking the mouse in the left margin. Be sure that the final paragraph marker on the right side is highlighted.

If you select Auto as the column width when you create a table, Word creates a table with equally sized columns that fill the space between the left and right margins. You can very easily change column width later if you want.

When your cursor goes over a column border, it changes to a special cursor that looks like a double bar with arrows sticking out of it. You can change the column width by holding your cursor over the column you want to adjust, then clicking and holding the mouse button. Drag the column marker to the left or right to adjust the column (see fig. 7.19).

Fig. 7.19

You adjust a table column by dragging the border to the new width.

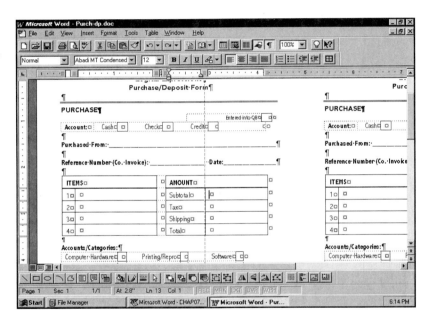

The gridlines you see around tables do not print. These guides help you tell which cell you are working in. To add real borders (that *do* print) to your table, select a cell, multiple cells, a row, a column, or the whole table. Choose Format, Borders and Shading. The Cell Borders and Shading dialog box appears. You can format your cells using the same options as the standard Borders and Shading dialog box that you use for text. See Chapter 11, "Desktop Publishing with Word," for more information on adding lines, borders, and shading.

Adjusting Cell Height and Width

As you get used to creating tables, you may get more ambitious in your formatting. To create forms or other complicated derivations of a table such as labels, you need to adjust your rows and columns to precise widths and height.

You cannot use the mouse to make the cells in your tables a precise height and width. You need to choose Table, Cell Height and <u>W</u>idth. You can change the row height from Auto to a specific setting by changing the H<u>e</u>ight of Rows drop-down box to Exactly and typing a value in the <u>A</u>t box (see fig. 7.20). You enter the value in inches ("), points (pt), or lines (li) by typing the abbreviation after the number.

Fig. 7.20

You can set the rows of your table to an exact height by changing the Height of Rows drop-down box to Exactly and typing a specific value.

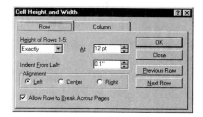

Similarly, you can set the column width and change the space between columns by entering values in the Column tab. Click the Column tab and click the Next and Previous buttons to scroll through the columns. Enter the values in the boxes for each column.

Summary

⑦

Because Word is such a large program, it can be used in vastly different ways by different people. Depending on how you use Word, different elements of the program may be critical to you. Some people use Word strictly to write documents, others use it to lay out unformatted text or tables, and others use it to create complex forms. All of these people have different aspects of Word that they deem critical.

You can use this chapter as a starting point for learning more about the features of Word that are critical to you in your work. For example, another way to create lots of text quickly is by using macros. If you use Word to create repetitive documents, you should refer to Chapter 8, "Macros" for information on how you can automate the tasks in your work.

If you create documents with complex formatting, you should refer to Chapter 9, "Word Styles," and Chapter 11, "Desktop Publishing with Word." The chapters describe what you can and cannot do with Word's desktop publishing features.

For those of you who need to create fill-in forms, your first step is to get to know the field reference in the online help. If you want to create more advanced forms, you should refer to a programming reference book, such as the *Word Developer's Kit* (Microsoft Press), that discusses Word's macro language, WordBasic.

chapter 8

Word Macros

by Terry Allen

8

In this chapter

▶ **Introduction to Macros**
Learn what macros are and how you can use them to automate your work.

▶ **Macro Recording**
Record your keystrokes into a macro and assign the macro to a keyboard key shortcut.

▶ **Macro Editing**
Learn how to edit macros in Word's macro editing window.

▶ **The WordBasic Language**
Learn the syntax of the WordBasic language and get acquainted with the Dialog Editor.

▶ **The Auto Macros**
Start Word and automatically run your macros.

I f you regularly do the same tasks over and over again, you should learn about Word macros. Writing a macro saves you time and ensures accurate results when you perform repetitive tasks. You can use Word effectively without ever programming a macro, but you can be far more efficient and avoid the tedium of repetitive tasks by harnessing one the most powerful aspects of Word for Windows. When you create macros, you have almost complete control over Word.

What Is a Macro?

A *macro* is a series of statements that tell Word to do something. To create these statements, Word uses a macro language called *WordBasic*. You can think of the WordBasic language as a dialect of the popular Basic programming language. Originally based on Microsoft QuickBasic, WordBasic uses many of the instructions of Basic in conjunction with Word-specific statements and functions. By using WordBasic, you can format text, draw pictures, perform calculations, and do many other functions.

All macros are implemented using WordBasic. Even those macros that you record using the macro recorder are saved as WordBasic code. The macro recorder is a great way to learn how to use WordBasic—just record what you want to do and then look at the WordBasic code in the macro editing window.

Almost anything you can do with the mouse and keyboard can be performed using WordBasic commands. If you don't know a particular command name, think about how you'd perform the task manually. For example, if you want to know which command to use for changing text color, think about how to do it using the menus. To change the text color, you would choose F<u>o</u>rmat, <u>F</u>ont, and select the appropriate color from the Font dialog box that appears. The WordBasic command to achieve the same effect is called `FormatFont`. Similarly, to insert a table, choose T<u>a</u>ble, <u>I</u>nsert Table. Joining these commands results in `TableInsertTable`, which also happens to be the WordBasic command you use to insert a table from within a macro.

 Note

The WordBasic language is used only in Word. In the next release, WordBasic will probably be replaced with Visual Basic for Applications (VBA). VBA is more flexible than WordBasic and is currently being used in other Microsoft applications, such as Excel and Project.

Creating Your First Macro

You can create macros in two ways: using the macro recorder or using the macro editor. No matter how you create a macro, Word stores the WordBasic macro code in a template. If you want your new macro to be accessible every time you use Word, you must store it in a global template such as NORMAL.DOT. If your macro performs actions that are specific to a certain task , you may want to create a separate template just for that purpose and store the macro inside it.

The easiest way to start building a macro is by using the macro recorder. For example, suppose you always need to change certain text to red. Normally, to do this you have to choose F<u>o</u>rmat, <u>F</u>ont and change the color. This task isn't particularly difficult, but if you need to change the text color 15 times on every page, you may want to automate the process.

Recording a Macro

When you record a macro, Word keeps track of every action you perform. Word continues recording your actions until you tell it to stop. A more detailed explanation with a description of how you create a specific macro follows this quick overview.

To record a macro, do the following:

1. Choose Tools, Macro. The Macro dialog box appears (see fig. 8.1).

Fig. 8.1

Name your macro using the Macro dialog box. The PresentIt, or other macros, may appear in the list because they are stored in the Normal template.

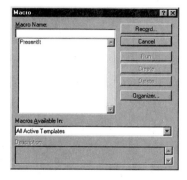

2. Type in the name of the macro and a description (see fig. 8.2). The description is there to remind you what the macro does.

Fig. 8.2

You can assign your macro to a toolbar button, menu item, or keyboard shortcut in the Record Macro dialog box.

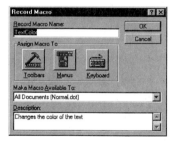

3. Click the Record button. The Record Macro dialog box appears.

4. Optionally, click the Toolbars button to assign the macro to a toolbar, the Menus button to assign it to a menu, or the Keyboard button to assign a keyboard shortcut. The Customize dialog box appears with the appropriate tab selected. Assign the macro and click OK. (Note that you can assign the macro to a toolbar, menu, or shortcut later if you want.)

The Macro Recorder toolbar appears on-screen, and your cursor changes to a tape cassette pointer (see fig. 8.3).

Fig. 8.3

During a macro recording session, you see the Macro toolbar, which has buttons that let you stop or pause macro recording.

Stop

Pause

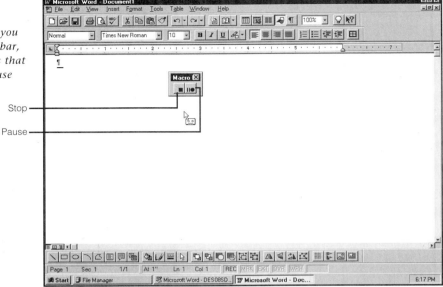

5. Begin performing the actions that you want included in your macro.

6. When you are finished, click the Stop button.

Now that you've experimented a little with the macro recorder, these instructions take you step-by-step through the recording process to create a macro called `TextColor`.

Choose <u>T</u>ools, <u>M</u>acro to bring up the Macro dialog box (refer to fig. 8.1). Name the macro **TextColor** and give your new macro a description such as **Changes the color of text**. As soon as you type in the name, four buttons are enabled:

▶ *Recd*. Activates the macro recorder.

▶ *Cancel*. Cancels the current dialog box. Press this button when you've brought up the dialog box by mistake.

▶ *Crete*. Opens up a WordBasic editing window.

▶ *Organizer*. Displays the Organizer dialog box, which allows you to choose where your macros are stored.

Click the Recd button; the Record Macro dialog box appears (refer to fig. 8.2). This dialog box enables you to change the name and description of the macro you're about to record, locate the macro in any of the open templates, and assign the macro to a toolbar, menu, or keyboard shortcut. In this example, you assign the macro a keyboard shortcut. Later you can change the keyboard assignment or add the macro to a toolbar or menu. Chapter 10, "Customizing the Workspace" describes the process in detail.

In the Record Macro dialog box, click the <u>K</u>eyboard button to assign a keyboard shortcut. The Customize dialog box appears (see fig. 8.4).

Fig. 8.4

You can add a keyboard shortcut to your new macro using the Customize dialog box.

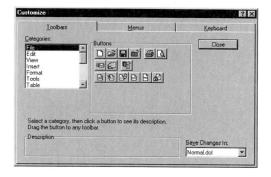

Follow these steps to assign a shortcut:

1. Place your cursor in the Press <u>N</u>ew Shortcut Key box and type a keyboard combination. You need to use a letter in conjunction with one or more of the Alt, Shift, and Ctrl keys. If the shortcut combination you press is already assigned to another function, a message appears.

2. Use the Save Changes In drop-down box to select the template that will contain the new shortcut. Select NORMAL.DOT if you want the settings to be global.

3. Click the <u>A</u>ssign button, and your keyboard shortcut appears in the C<u>u</u>rrent Keys box.

4. Click Close.

The Macro toolbar appears as a floating toolbar (refer to fig. 8.3). The cursor changes to include a cassette tape icon to remind you that whatever happens from now on is being recorded. You also see that the REC box in the status bar changes from gray to black to indicate that you're recording the macro.

 Tip

You can start the macro recorder by double-clicking the REC box in the status bar. Also, if you're currently recording, you can stop recording by double-clicking the REC box.

Before you start recording your actions, click the Pause button and type some text onto the page. It should all appear as black text. The Pause button on the Macro toolbar lets you temporarily turn off the recording in case you want to do something in the middle of a long recording.

Click the Pause button again to stop pausing so your actions can be recorded. Now perform the actions that you want to record in the TextColor macro. Change the text color to red by choosing F_ormat, _Font. Choose Red from the _Color drop-down box. Stop the recording, in one of three ways:

▶ Click the Stop button on the Macro toolbar.

▶ Double-click the REC area on the status bar.

▶ Choose _Macro, _Tools. Notice that the Record button has changed to a Stop Recording button.

Running the Macro

If you don't attach the macro to a toolbar, menu, or keystroke, you can run macros using menu commands. Select some black text in the main document. Choose _Tools, _Macro, and you see the familiar Macro dialog box with the Run button enabled. Select the TextColor macro from the list and click Run. Remember that the macro changes the text to red, so be sure to test it on text that is not already red.

Because you applied a shortcut key to the example TextColor macro, you also can use the shortcut key to activate the macro.

Editing Macros

Recording macros is a good way to begin working with macros, but if you want to do anything elaborate, you have to venture into the realm of programming. If you don't consider yourself a programmer, you may want to start by opening up your TextColor macro in the macro editing window. Doing so gives you your first glimpse of WordBasic, Word's macro language.

Before you start editing macros, you should make sure you installed the WordBasic help files. WordBasic Help is not installed by default in the typical Office 95 setup. If you don't have the WordBasic help files installed, you should install them as soon as possible. You need the online help to research how each command works. Look in Explorer and check in the WINWORD folder to see if you have a file called WRDBASIC.HLP. If you don't find the file, you have to run the Office 95 setup again. Choose a Custom setup and install just the WordBasic help files. You also should install the Word Dialog Editor application.

To open your TextColor macro, follow these steps:

1. Choose _Tools, _Macro.

2. Select the TextColor macro from the dialog box.

3. Click the Edit button. A macro editing window opens with the contents of the TextColor macro displayed. An additional toolbar—the Macro toolbar—appears as shown in figure 8.5.

Fig. 8.5

When a macro editing window is open, you see the Macro editing toolbar, in addition to the Standard and Formatting toolbars.

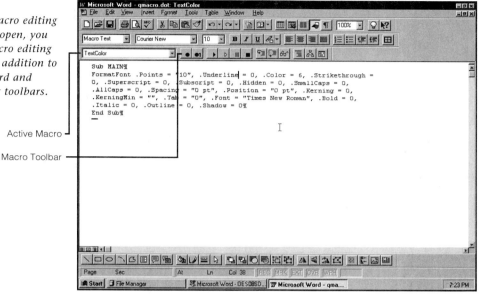

Active Macro

Macro Toolbar

8

In a macro editing window, notice that there are several unfamiliar buttons on the Macro toolbar. These button functions are described in table 8.1, sequentially from left to right. The drop-down list box lists all the available macros. You can move among several different macros by selecting a different name in this box.

Table 8.1   Macro Editing Toolbar Buttons

Button	Description
Active Macro	The name of the macro that runs if you click the Run button. (This name is not necessarily the macro you are currently editing.)
Record	Starts recording the macro.
Record Next Command	Records only the next command.
Start	Starts the macro displayed in the Active Macro list box.
Trace	Starts the active macro in Trace mode. Each line of the macro is highlighted as it is processed.

continues

Table 8.1   Continued

Button	Description
Continue	Toggles between Pause and Continue. This button either pauses the execution of the macro or restarts the macro after a pause.
Stop	Stops a macro that is currently running.
Step	Steps through the macro, pausing after each line. Click this button to move onto the next line. This button is useful when you are debugging macro code.
Step Subs	Steps through the macro, pausing after each line. However, subroutines are run in their entirety rather than being stepped through.
Show Variables	Shows variables at any given point in the execution of the macro.
Add/Remove REM	Adds or removes REM statements to the start of each selected line of code. (Any statement preceded by REM is ignored by WordBasic. These REM statements, or comments, allow you to add text that describes what the code is doing.)
Macro	Brings up the macro window.
Dialog Editor	Brings up the Word Dialog Editor application.

The text that appears in the window is the WordBasic code that makes up the TextColor macro. Here's what you should see:

```
Sub MAIN
FormatFont .Points = "10", .Underline = 0, .Color = 6, .Strikethrough =
0, .Superscript = 0, .Subscript = 0, .Hidden = 0, .SmallCaps = 0,
 .AllCaps = 0, .Spacing = "0 pt", .Position = "0 pt", .Kerning = 0,
 .KerningMin = "", .Tab = "0", .Font = "Times New Roman", .Bold = 0,
 .Italic = 0, .Outline = 0, .Shadow = 0
End Sub
```

Anatomy of a Macro

Every macro starts off with Sub MAIN and normally finishes with End Sub. All the text that appears between these two lines are commands that tell WordBasic what to do.

In this case, you have a single command, `FormatFont`, that is spread over five lines. The `FormatFont` command itself is followed by a number of named parameters that tell the command how to work. A *named parameter* takes the form of *.name=value*. You can think of parameters as instructions to the command that tell it how to operate. For details of the `FormatFont` command, do a search in the WordBasic online help.

> **Tip**
>
> For information about WordBasic commands and their parameters, position the cursor on the command and press the F1 key.

For example, the named parameter `.Points="10"` tells the `FormatFont` command to set the point size of the font to 10 points. The period before the name is important; it indicates that what follows is a named parameter. Each named parameter and its value are separated from the other parameters by a comma.

Editing Command Parameters

When you use the macro recording feature to generate code, notice that it tends to add every possible parameter. In this example, the macro recorder inserted all 19 parameters for the `FormatFont` command, even though all you really needed to do was set the value of the `.Color` parameter.

In this case, you should remove the extra parameters because you don't want the macro to change those values. When you remove the parameters, the macro looks like this:

```
Sub MAIN
FormatFont .Color = 6
End Sub
```

> **Note**
>
> You don't always want to remove the extra parameters from the macro statements you record. For example, when you use the `EditFind` command, Word remembers the settings from the last time you ran the `EditFind` command. Those settings are used by the `EditFind` command in your macro as the default settings, which may not be appropriate for the macro task. Be sure to include all the parameter settings your macro needs to run properly.

After you remove the extra parameters, choose File, Close. Word prompts you to save the changes to the macro. Click OK, and you are returned to the document.

If you bring up the help page for FormatFont, you see that the explanation of the .Color parameter refers you to the CharColor function (see fig. 8.6). Click the CharColor page to see the list of values for the .Color parameter, as shown in table 8.2.

Fig. 8.6

Use the WordBasic help to get information about command parameters.

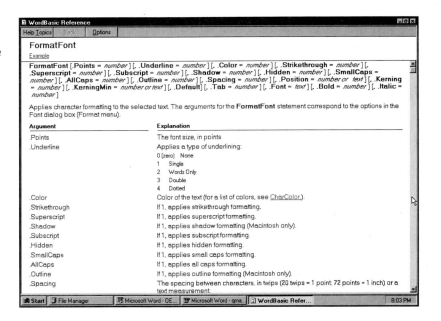

Table 8.2 Numeric Values for the *Color* Parameter

Value	Color
0	Auto
1	Black
2	Blue
3	Cyan
4	Green
5	Magenta
6	Red
7	Yellow
8	White
9	Dark Blue
10	Dark Cyan

Value	Color
11	Dark Green
12	Dark Magenta
13	Dark Red
14	Dark Yellow
15	Dark Gray
16	Light Gray

The command `FormatFont .Color=6` means "Format the font's color as red." As you can see in the online help, you also can use the `CharColor` command to change font color. In WordBasic, you can choose from a number of commands to perform a task.

You can change the command to format the text to some other color by changing the parameter value. For example, `FormatFont .Color=2` changes the selected text to blue.

You can test your changes to the macro by opening a new document based on the template your macro is stored in. While you are still in the macro editor, choose File, New and select your macro template. A blank document opens with the Macro toolbar showing. Make sure your macro name appears in the Active Macro drop-down list box. Select the text and click the Start button on the Macro toolbar. You can switch back to the macro editor by selecting it from the Window menu or pressing Ctrl+F6.

When you are satisfied with your editing changes, close the macro by choosing File, Close. Answer Yes to the prompt when Word asks if you want to save the macro.

Using WordBasic

WordBasic is based on the Basic programming language and includes a large number of commands especially designed to let you perform actions specific to word processing in Word. Like any other language, WordBasic has syntax rules. You can think of this syntax as the "grammar" of WordBasic.

This section provides an overview of WordBasic grammar and how to use it in conjunction with the Word functions and commands.

WordBasic Architecture

The TextColor macro you created earlier consisted of just one WordBasic instruction. However, Word macros can be far more complex. As soon as you begin adding decision-making capabilities to your macros, you enter the world of programming.

A WordBasic macro is made up of the following components:

▶ *Word statements*. Instructions that tell Word to do something. For example, `FormatFont` is a statement that tells Word to change the attributes of a font.

▶ *Word functions*. Commands that return information you can use in the macro. For example, `CharColor()` returns the color value of the selected text. You can then use this value in your macro.

▶ *Variables*. Named locations in memory where a macro stores information that it needs to use later.

▶ *Control structures*. Looping or conditional statements that enable you to repeat a series of instructions or control which part of the macro code is executed under certain circumstances.

▶ *User-defined subroutines and functions*. Commands can be collected into units called *subroutines* or *functions*. These units group all the commands that perform a certain task, so that task can be performed more than once by a macro or used by other macros.

▶ *Comments*. Text that appears after a REM statement or a single apostrophe. You use comments to provide additional information about what the code does. Comment text may appear on the same line as a command if it is preceded by an apostrophe; a REM statement must appear on its own line.

The next sections go into detail about the components of the WordBasic architecture.

Using Variables

A *variable* is the term used for an area of memory that WordBasic can read from and write to. You can define two types of variables in WordBasic: numeric variables and text variables.

You use variables to store information that you need later. For example, you can save the value returned by the `CharColor()` function in a variable called `SaveColor`, like this:

```
SaveColor = CharColor()
```

If the color is black, the value 1 is stored in the `SaveColor` variable. By creating a variable, your macro can remember the original color of the text. The macro can then change the color of the text, but still keep track of the original text color.

```
Sub MAIN
SaveColor = CharColor()
FormatFont .Color = 6
Insert "This text is red"
FormatFont .Color = SaveColor
End Sub
```

This small macro stores the current text color in a variable called SaveColor. The FormatFont command then changes the font color to red (6). The next line inserts red text that says This text is red. The second FormatFont command returns the text color to the color saved in the SaveColor variable.

When you name your variables, you must follow certain rules:

▶ Text variable names end with a $ to differentiate them from numeric variable names.

▶ You can only use numbers, letters, or an underscore (_) when choosing names. For example, "My_document$" is a valid name, while "My document" is not valid because it has a space in the name.

▶ The name cannot begin with a number.

▶ The name cannot be more than 40 characters long.

▶ The name must not be a reserved word. *Reserved words* are words that WordBasic recognizes as having a special meaning. Examples include IF, THEN, WHILE, and ENDSUB. Reserved words are probably not words you'd want to use anyway, but if you're not sure about a word, try searching the online help for that word. If it's in the online help, it's probably a reserved word.

Numeric Variables

A *numeric variable* is one that contains only numeric data. If you want to perform arithmetic on variables, they have to be numeric variables. For example, you could use a numeric variable called DayOfMonth to hold the day of the month, or you could have an InvoiceValue variable to hold the value of an invoice. To set a numeric variable, you use an equal sign:

```
DayOfMonth = 25
```

You can use the standard arithmetic operators +, – , / (divide) and * (multiply) on numeric variables. For example, if you store your invoice total in a variable called InvoiceValue, you can calculate a 7 percent tax amount using the following statement:

```
InvoiceTax = InvoiceValue * .07
```

The tax amount is stored in a numeric variable called InvoiceTax.

You can compare numeric variables using *relational operators*. Operators *operate* on variables. They are called *relational* operators because they determine the relationship between two variables. A list of these relational operators is shown in table 8.3.

8

Table 8.3   Relational Operators Used in WordBasic

Operator	Meaning
=	Equal to
<>	Not equal to
>	Greater than
>=	Greater than or equal to
<	Less than
<=	Less than or equal to

For example, to check that the numeric variable InvoiceValue doesn't exceed the numeric variable CreditLimit, you would write:

```
If InvoiceValue <= CreditLimit Then
```

Relational operators work with conditional control structures such as If...Then and While...Wend statements to perform comparisons. Conditional control statements are described later in this chapter in "Controlling the Flow of the Macro."

Text Variables

Text variables are sometimes called *string variables* because they are used to hold a string of characters. A *character string* is any sequence of text within a set of quotation marks. "Monday", "123", and "Microsoft Word for Windows" are all valid text strings.

Notice that "123" is a text string made up of the characters 1, 2, and 3. It's not the same as the number 123. You cannot perform arithmetic functions on the "123" text string without first converting it to a numeric variable. (Do a search for the Val() function in the online help for more information on converting string values to numeric values.)

You set text variables in the same way as numeric variables, for example:

```
DayOfWeek$ = "Wednesday"
```

You can join text strings together using the + operator. For example,

```
Insert "Today is " + DayOfWeek$
```

inserts the text Today is Wednesday into the active document (assuming DayOfWeek$ had previously been set to Wednesday).

You can also compare text variables in the same way you can compare numeric variables. The relational operators (=, <>, >, >=, <, <=) perform alphabetic comparisons instead of numeric comparisons. Alphabetic comparisons are always made from left to right. In an alphabetic comparison, the leftmost character of the first string is compared to the left-most character of the second string.

For example, alphabetically, the text string "Ant" is less than the text string "Beetle" because A is less than B. In ASCII, lowercase letters are higher in the alphabet than uppercase letters, so "Ant" is less than "ant" because "A" comes before "a." Similarly, the text string "199" is less than "20" because "1" comes before "2."

Arrays

An *array* is similar to a table in which each cell is a variable. Once you've defined an array, you can refer to a particular element within the array using an index into the array. An *index* is like a cell address for a table; it indicates the location of a cell within the table.

Like a table, an array may have more than one dimension. A one-dimensional array is similar to a single-column table. A two-dimensional array is similar to a two-column table. Unlike tables, arrays are not limited to two dimensions, however. A three-dimensional array can be compared to a cube that is broken into cells in three-dimensional space. As you can imagine, multidimensional arrays become very confusing very quickly. Most Word macros never use arrays with more than one or two dimensions.

Returning to a simple one-dimensional array, the index of the first element of any array is zero, the second is one, the third is two, and so on. You create an array of numbers by using the Dim (which stands for Dimension) keyword before the variable name and the last index number in parentheses after the name. For example,

```
Dim Color$(16)
```

creates an array of 17 string variables that can be referred to as Color$(0), Color$(1), Color$(2), and so on. You could then write some WordBasic code to set these array elements as follows:

```
Color$(0) = "Auto"
Color$(1) = "Black"
Color$(2) = "Blue"
Color$(3) = "Cyan"
Color$(4) = "Green"
Color$(5) = "Magenta"
Color$(6) = "Red"
Color$(7) = "Yellow"
Color$(8) = "White"
Color$(9) = "Dark blue"
Color$(10) = "Dark cyan"
Color$(11) = "Dark green"
Color$(12) = "Dark magenta"
Color$(13) = "Dark red"
Color$(14) = "Dark yellow"
Color$(15) = "Dark gray"
Color$(16) = "Light gray"
```

Arrays are very useful when you don't know in advance which element you want to use. Using the text color example, you can use an array to provide the choices in a list box.

8

Users of your macro can choose the text color in a document from any one of the colors in the array. In the previous example, each of the font color values are mapped to a descriptive text string using the array. The user sees the names (rather than the values) in the dialog box in the macro.

Working with Dialog Records

Dialog records are a special type of variable that store the settings describing the dialog boxes that appear on the Word screen. You can retrieve or set values used in the predefined dialog boxes that are included in Word. You can also build your own sophisticated dialog boxes using WordBasic and the Dialog Editor.

To use your own dialog boxes, first describe what the dialog box looks like. Next, create a dialog box record, and then activate the dialog box. If you're using one of Word's built-in dialog boxes, you don't need to describe the dialog box, but you still must create a dialog box record and activate the dialog box.

As with arrays, use a `Dim` statement to define a dialog record. The dialog record needs a name and a pointer to the dialog box it's referring to, so the syntax of the command appears like this:

```
Dim DialogRecord As DialogBoxName
```

You can use any name for `DialogRecord` as long as it's not one of Word's reserved words. (Do a search in the online help, if you're not sure whether a word is reserved or not.) `DialogBoxName` can be any Word command name. As mentioned earlier, some Word commands are a composite of their menu command sequence, such as `FileSaveAs`. However, Word has other commands that do not correspond to the menu commands. To see a list of Word's commands, choose Tools, Macro and change the Macros Available In drop-down box to Word Commands (see fig. 8.7). Once you know the command name, you can do a search in the online help to find out what it does.

Fig. 8.7

In the Macro dialog box, you can see a list of Word command names by switching the Macros Available In drop-down list box to Word Commands.

Accessing Word's Built-In Dialog Boxes

Once you have defined a dialog record, you can get information about the dialog box. For example, if you want to access the settings of a dialog box without opening the dialog itself, you can find out what the current settings are. For example,

```
Dim dlgFont As FormatFont
```

creates a dialog record called dlgFont for the FormatFont dialog box.

Once you define the dialog record, you can retrieve the current values using the GetCurValues statement. You can then change the settings stored in the dialog by changing the parameters. If you put this value into a variable, you can use it later on in the macro. This macro retrieves the current font from the FormatFont dialog box and stores that value in a variable called CurrentFont:

```
Dim dlgFont As FormatFont
GetCurValues dlgFont
CurrentFont = dlgFont.Font
```

Many people like to change the default file list that is displayed in the File Open dialog box. If you create a macro with the same name as a Word command, Word uses your command instead of its built-in command. The FileOpen command uses a dialog box description that is also called FileOpen.

To change the default file list, you create a new macro called FileOpen. Within your new command, the first thing you do is define a dialog record called dlg that refers to Word's FileOpen dialog box like this:

```
Dim dlg As FileOpen
```

Once you define the dialog record, you can change it to suit your own needs. By default, the FileOpen dialog box shows you a list of all the files ending in a DOC extension. But, what if you want to see all files instead of just those with a DOC extension? The technique is simple, as you can see in the following code:

```
Sub MAIN
Dim dlg As FileOpen
GetCurValues dlg
dlg.Name = "*.*"
If Dialog(dlg) Then
    FileOpen dlg
EndIf
End Sub
```

The Dim line defines a dialog record called dlg that will hold the same information as the FileOpen dialog box. The GetCurValues command retrieves the settings of the Word FileOpen dialog box and stores the settings in your dlg record.

8

Now you can access these settings using named parameters in the dlg dialog record. If you do a search in the online help for FileOpen, you discover it has a parameter called Name in the FileOpen dialog box. The dlg.Name = "*.*" statement sets the value of Name to *.* so that the FileOpen dialog box displays all files instead of just DOC files. (If you want to display a different type of extension, such as XYZ, you would change *.* to ***.XYZ**).

Once you change the settings of the dialog record, you then display the dialog box using the Dialog() command. The standard FileOpen dialog box appears with the new file filter in place.

Creating Dialog Boxes

By using WordBasic, you can do more than just access Word dialog boxes. You can create your own dialog boxes as well. The macro code for dialog boxes can become rather complex, so the easiest way to create your own dialog boxes is to use Word's built-in Dialog Editor.

Adding Message Boxes and Input Boxes

If you only need to display simple statements or receive a small amount of input from the user, the simplest dialog boxes in WordBasic are MsgBox and InputBox. Word uses MsgBox to display simple messages and InputBox to get simple user input. Adding these user-defined dialog boxes is a good way to get started creating user-defined dialogs and puts a professional gloss on any macro you write.

You can use the MsgBox statement to display a brief message in a small dialog box. Adding a simple message box dialog to your macro only requires one statement. Just place your message text after the MsgBox command enclosed in quotation marks, like this:

```
MsgBox "I have no response to that."
```

The message text must be fewer than 255 characters. You can override the default dialog box title, "Microsoft Word," by passing a new title to the MsgBox command. The title of this dialog box

```
MsgBox "I have no response to that.", "My New Macro"
```

is My New Macro.

Like MsgBox, the InputBox statement displays a dialog box. However, InputBox also prompts the user to enter information into a text field. The statement returns the text entered by user to the macro when the user clicks OK. If a user clicks Cancel, an error occurs. You can use the On Error statement to trap the error, if desired. This InputBox statement prompts a user to enter the secret password in the text field. The text the user enters is returned to the macro in the Password$ string variable.

```
Password$ = InputBox$("What's the secret password?")
```

Defining Dialog Boxes

Defining a dialog box by hand involves a lot of error-prone typing, so you should get to know Word's Dialog Editor if you plan to create any complex dialog boxes. Using the Dialog Editor can be fun because instead of indicating the placement of dialog box items using numbers, you position items graphically. For example, the following example is the definition of the dialog box shown in figure 8.8. This assumes that the text array Color$() has been defined and filled with the 17 different colors supported by Word.

```
Begin Dialog UserDialog 360, 215, "TextColor"
    Text 20, 15, 77, 13, "Text color", .Text1
    ListBox 20, 30, 140, 110, Color$(), .ForeColor
    Text 200, 15, 135, 13, "Background color", .Text2
    ListBox 200, 30, 140, 110, Color$(), .BackColor
    OKButton 252, 155, 88, 21
    CancelButton 252, 180, 88, 21
End Dialog
```

Fig. 8.8

This is how the dialog box defined in the TextColor *macro looks to the user.*

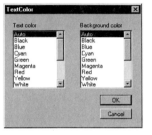

The definition of the dialog box comes between a Begin Dialog line and an End Dialog line. Each line starts with an item identifier. For example, the first line after the Begin Dialog line starts with the word Text. This means that this line is defining some text that appears in the dialog box; in this case the text is Text color. The numbers you see are the position (20,15) and size (77,13) of the text in the dialog box using measurements from the top-left of the dialog box.

The numbers represent X,Y coordinates, which are measured relative to the top-left of the dialog box. The horizontal (X) value represents the distance from the left side of the dialog box to the element. This distance is measured in units, which equal 1/8 the size of the system font. The *system font* is the font that is used for displaying text in dialog boxes. The vertical (Y) value represents the distance from the top of the dialog box. This distance is measured in units that equal 1/12 the size of the system font.

The second line starts with the keyword ListBox. This means that a list box is to be created of the specified size and location, and it should be filled with the contents of the text array Color$(). The .ForeColor is a name you can use to refer to the list box from within the WordBasic code that processes the user input to the dialog box. When a selection is made from the list box, the .ForeColor variable is set to the index into the list box,

8

so if the user selects Blue (the third entry), the value 2 is stored in `.ForeColor`. When you are processing the results of the dialog box, you refer to the value using the dialog record name followed by the variable name, so in this case you'd use `TextColor.ForeColor`.

The next two lines are very similar to the first two lines. They define the text and list box for the background color.

The last two lines in the dialog box definition define the OK and Cancel buttons.

Other elements that could appear on a user-defined dialog box, but don't in the example, are check boxes, combo boxes, drop-down list boxes, file previews, group boxes, option buttons, and groups, pictures, and push buttons. For a more detailed discussion of user-defined dialog boxes, refer to New Rider's *Inside Word for Windows 95* or the online help.

Using the Dialog Editor

Luckily, Word comes with a Dialog Editor that allows you to design the dialog boxes graphically rather than by entering the code into the macro by hand. The Dialog Editor is a separate application that's used to create a dialog box that you can then cut and paste directly into your macro code. You can also copy a dialog box definition from a macro and paste it into the Dialog Editor to edit the definition graphically.

Basically, when you use the Dialog Editor, you design a dialog box by inserting controls onto the screen. Once you have finished adding controls, you select them and copy them to the Clipboard. Then you switch back to the macro editing window and paste the dialog in the correct location. The graphical representation of the dialog box you created is converted into WordBasic macro code when you paste it into the macro.

To create a dialog box using the Dialog Editor, follow these steps:

1. Click the Dialog Editor button on the Macro toolbar. The Dialog Editor opens with an empty dialog box in the window.

2. Select the controls you want to add by choosing the control from the Item menu. You can add the following controls:

   Buttons. Includes buttons used in most Windows applications. You can add the standard OK and Cancel buttons or push buttons that allow you to add your own text to the button. You also can add option buttons that allow users to choose one item from a list, and check boxes for yes or no choices to be made.

   Text. Appears on the background of the dialog box. You normally use text items to explain how the dialog box should be used.

   Text boxes. Used to receive user input into the dialog box. They appear as white boxes.

Group boxes. Appear as thin boxes with a title. These boxes are used to group elements within the dialog box.

List boxes. Include the three types of list boxes used by most Windows applications. You can add a standard list box, a vertically scrolling list the user can select from. The combo list box is a combination of a standard list box and a text box that allows users to choose an item from a list or type in a value. The drop-down list box expands to its full size only when a user clicks it, so it takes up less room in the dialog box.

Pictures. Add pictures from a file, autotext entry, bookmark, or the Clipboard. For example, you can create a logo using Paint, store it as a BMP file, and add it to your dialog box.

Fig. 8.9

Insert button controls into your new dialog box by choosing Insert, Button. You can select from this list of button types shown in the New Button dialog box.

3. After you insert a control and it is selected, you can drag the item with the mouse. When you position your mouse over the item, the cursor changes to a four-headed arrow to indicate that you can move the item. If you want to change the size of an item, hold the mouse over an item's border, so that the cursor changes to a left-right arrow or an up-down arrow. Drag the mouse to change the size of an object. Holding down the Shift key constrains the sizing to just one direction.

4. Once you have an item roughly positioned where you want it, use the Information dialog box to view the exact position and size of an item (see fig. 8.10). Select an item and choose Edit, Info or double-click the item to display the Information dialog box. By using the Information dialog box, you can precisely align items by typing in the coordinates of the items.

Fig. 8.10

Use the Information dialog box to enter placement values and change item labels and identifiers.

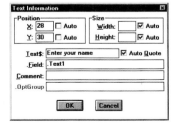

5. When you insert an item, Word adds a label. You can change this default label by selecting the item and typing in the text you want directly on-screen. You can also change the label text in the Information dialog box, if you prefer.

6. In many dialog boxes, the items on the screen return a value to the macro. These values are stored in *identifiers*. When you create an item, the Dialog Editor assigns default identifiers such as .TextBox1 or .ListBox1. Changing these default identifiers can make your code easier to understand. Use the .Field box in the Information dialog box to change an item's identifier in the .Field box to a term that is more meaningful to you.

7. When you are finished with your dialog box, select the dialog box in the Dialog Editor and copy it. To select the entire dialog, click its title bar or choose Edit, Select Dialog.

8. Choose Edit, Copy to copy the dialog box. Close the Dialog Editor or switch to the macro editing window. Choose Edit, Paste to paste the dialog box definition where you want it to appear in the macro. Your graphic representation is converted into a set of instructions that begin with a Begin Dialog statement and conclude with an End Dialog statement.

After you've designed your dialog box and copied it into the macro, you still need to tell WordBasic to activate the dialog box. First, you have to declare a name for the dialog box using the Dim keyword. This tells WordBasic to set aside a location in memory for the dialog box. You then issue the Dialog command to display the dialog box, and finally, you process the results.

Creating a Dialog Box

This section guides you through the process of creating the dialog box used for the TextColor macro. While you are creating the dialog box, you can double-click any element of the dialog box at any time to bring up the Information dialog box for the element.

You change the dialog box title by typing a new title into the Text$ area. The new title replaces the default title of Microsoft Word. You usually type the macro name (TextColor, in this case) into the title field. Leave the Auto Quote check box next to the Text$ box checked. If you do not select Auto Quote, you must explicitly enter double quotes around any text you enter into the field.

Leave the Position values set to Auto. With this setting, Word automatically places the dialog box in the center of the screen. If you prefer, you can enter your own values by deselecting Auto and dragging the dialog box to a new position. The new values are placed in the Position fields. The TextColor dialog box must be at least 360×215 units, although you can make it larger if you want.

Now you need to place some text, buttons, and list boxes within the dialog box. To create a list box that looks like the one in figure 8.8, set the attributes of each item to those shown in each step. Remember that you must double-click the item to bring up the Information dialog box so you can alter the settings.

To alter the settings, follow these steps:

1. Choose Item, Text. The word Text appears in the top-left corner of the dialog box. Set the attributes as follows:

Position	X=20, Y=15
Size	X=Auto, Y=Auto
Text$	Text color
.Field	.Text1

2. Choose Item, List Box; the New List Box dialog box appears. Select Standard and click OK. The list box appears in the dialog box below the text.

   When you display the Information dialog box, it shows an Array$ value. The Array$ value is the name of a text array that is loaded into the list box when the dialog box is activated. In the TextColor macro, the Color$() array contains a list of the possible colors. This array is loaded into the foreground color list box and the background color list box in step 3. The macro determines the foreground color the user selects, so this item is given a field name of .ForeColor. Set the attributes as follows:

Position	X=20, Y=30
Size	X=140, Y=110
Array$	Color$()
.Field	.ForeColor

3. Add another text item by choosing Item, Text. Set the attributes as follows:

Position	X=200, Y=15
Size	X=Auto, Y=Auto
Text$	Background color
.Field	.Text2

4. Add another standard list box by choosing Item, List Box. Set the attributes as follows:

Position	X=200, Y=30
Size	X=140, Y=110

8

A̲rray$	Color$()
.F̲ield	.BackColor

5. Choose I̲tem, B̲utton; the New Button dialog box appears. Select the OK button type and click OK. An OK button appears on the dialog box. Set the attributes as follows:

Position	X̲=252, Y̲=155
Size	X̲=88, Y̲=21 (auto)
T̲ext$	OK (you can't change it)
.F̲ield	(blank)

6. Add a Cancel button the same way you added the OK button. Set the attributes as follows:

Position	X̲=252, Y̲=180
Size	X̲=88, Y̲=21 (auto)
T̲ext$	Cancel (you can't change it)
.F̲ield	(blank)

7. Select the entire dialog box by choosing E̲dit, S̲elect Dialog.

8. Copy the dialog box to the Clipboard by choosing E̲dit, C̲opy, or by pressing Ctrl+C (see fig. 8.11.)

9. Switch back to the macro editing window within Word and paste the dialog box into the code. The graphical design now gets inserted into the macro as WordBasic code.

Fig. 8.11

Select the entire dialog box by choosing E̲dit, S̲elect Dialog.

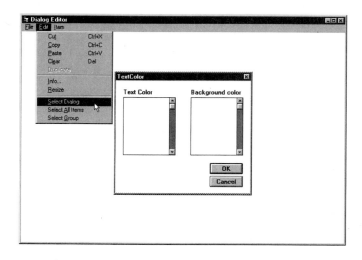

The following WordBasic code shows the TextColor dialog box in its entirety. Users select text and background colors from the dialog box. If the user presses the OK button to exit the dialog box, the choices are to set the colors accordingly. The macro uses the FormatFont command to color the text, and the HighlightColor command to set the highlighting (background) color.

```
Sub MAIN
'-----------------------------------------------------------------
' This macro uses a dialog box to get the text and background colors
' from the user. It then sets the text and background colors using
' the FormatFont and HighlightColor commands
'-----------------------------------------------------------------
Dim Color$(16)                          ' Holds the colors known to Word
Color$(0) = "Auto"
Color$(1) = "Black"
Color$(2) = "Blue"
Color$(3) = "Cyan"
Color$(4) = "Green"
Color$(5) = "Magenta"
Color$(6) = "Red"
Color$(7) = "Yellow"
Color$(8) = "White"
Color$(9) = "Dark blue"
Color$(10) = "Dark cyan"
Color$(11) = "Dark green"
Color$(12) = "Dark magenta"
Color$(13) = "Dark red"
Color$(14) = "Dark yellow"
Color$(15) = "Dark gray"
Color$(16) = "Light gray"

' Now define a user dialog that presents the user with a choice of
' text and background colors
Begin Dialog UserDialog 360, 215, "TextColor"
     Text 20, 15, 77, 13, "Text color", .Text1
     ListBox 20, 30, 140, 110, Color$(), .ForeColor
     Text 200, 15, 135, 13, "Background color", .Text2
     ListBox 200, 30, 140, 110, Color$(), .BackColor
     OKButton 252, 155, 88, 21
     CancelButton 252, 180, 88, 21
End Dialog

' Tell Word to set aside a chunk of memory called TextColorDialog for
' use with the user-defined dialog defined above
Dim TextColorDialog As UserDialog

' Display the dialog and place the return value in ButtonPressed
ButtonPressed = Dialog(TextColorDialog)

' If the OK button was used (dialog returns -1) set the chosen colors
' otherwise show a message saying the macro was aborted
If ButtonPressed = - 1 Then
     FormatFont .Color = TextColorDialog.ForeColor
     HighlightColor TextColorDialog.BackColor
Else
     MsgBox "Cancel pressed - TextColor aborted", "TextColor"
EndIf

End Sub
```

8

Controlling the Flow of the Macro

Before editing the macro any further, you need to explore some of the ways of controlling the flow of a macro. At its simplest, a macro is a list of commands to be carried out one after the other; but in practice, a useful macro frequently has to make decisions about when to perform certain actions. WordBasic provides several statements called *control structures* that you can use to control when specific statements of your macro are executed.

If...Then...ElseIf...Else...End If

Use an If...Then...ElseIf...Else...End If control structure (commonly known as an *If structure*) when you want your macro to run a block of statements only under specific circumstances. For instance, you might want your macro to say, "If the text is red, then make it black; otherwise, make it red." So how do you write code to do this?

Translating this statement into a WordBasic If structure results in

```
If the text is red Then
    Make the text black
Else
    Make the text red
Endif
```

This translation is the first step toward creating valid WordBasic code. Next you need to convert the condition (the text is red) and commands (Make the text black and Make the text red) into proper WordBasic syntax as well.

From the earlier macro, you already know that Make the text red can be written as **FormatFont .Color = 6**. If you look up the value of Black in the CharColor help page or in table 8.2, you can see that Make the text black equates to **FormatFont .Color = 1**. Now you just need to figure out how to check whether the text is red in the first place. You may have noticed in the online help for CharColor that the CharColor() function gives you the color of the selected text. So now you can change the macro to be

```
If CharColor() = 6 Then
    FormatFont .Color = 1
Else
    FormatFont .Color = 6
End If
```

This macro changes red text to black text, and it changes text of any other color to red text.

You can include IF structures within IF structures to perform more complicated processing. If structures in this arrangement are said to be *nested*. For example, you might not want to change the color of the text if it is anything other than black or red. You can add this new condition to your macro by coding the following:

```
CurrentColor = CharColor()
If CurrentColor = 6 Then
    FormatFont .Color = 1
Else
    If CurrentColor = 1 Then
        FormatFont .Color = 6
    End If
End If
```

The macro now reads, "If the color is red, make it black. If the color is black, make it red." If the color is anything other than black or red, the macro does nothing.

The new macro stores the value returned by the CharColor function in a numeric variable named CurrentColor. The macro then checks the value of CurrentColor with the If structure. This approach is more efficient than calling the CharColor() function repeatedly. You can also use this approach when you want to make sure that your If structure is always testing the original text color, regardless of any color changes that might be caused by other statements in the macro.

Notice that the nested If structure does not use an Else. The Else is optional, and in this case, unnecessary, because this new macro is not supposed to do anything if the text isn't black or red.

 Tip

The statements that belong to each part of the If structure shown in this section are indented. Each nesting level introduces another indention level. You are not required to indent your code, but doing so improves the code's readability.

8

You can write the code for the previous macro in a different way by using the ElseIf keyword. An ElseIf keyword is essentially an Else and an If joined together. The same example using ElseIf would look like

```
CurrentColor = CharColor()
If CurrentColor = 6 Then
    FormatFont .Color = 1
ElseIf CurrentColor = 1 Then
    FormatFont .Color = 6
End If
```

ElseIf helps you avoid deeply nested If structures. Suppose, for example, that you want your macro to perform a different action for each of the 17 possible values returned by CharColor. Coding the macro with a nested If structure results in deeply indented code that would be very difficult to read. By using ElseIf, the code does the same work and is much easier to read.

ElseIf is most appropriate in situations where you need to test a series of related but mutually exclusive conditions. In the previous example, the text color conditions are obviously related, and they are also mutually exclusive: text can be only one color at a time.

Select...Case...End Select

The Select...Case...End Select structure (commonly known as a *Select structure* or a *Case structure*) is very similar to an If structure with many ElseIf components. The difference is that the conditions of the Case structure always refer to the same variable or function.

The TextColor macro is a good example of a situation where you might want to use a Case structure. Converting the If structure to a Case structure yields the following code:

```
CurrentColor = CharColor()
Select Case CurrentColor
    Case 6
        FormatFont .Color = 1
    Case 1
        FormatFont .Color = 6
    Case Else
End Select
```

In this macro, the Select Case statement identifies the variable to be tested (CurrentColor). Each of the Case statements that follow define one of the possible values for CurrentColor (with the exception of Case Else). The first Case statement checks for CurrentColor that is equal to 6 (red), and the second Case statement checks for 1 (black). The appropriate FormatFont commands go under their corresponding Case statement.

When you run the sample macro, Word compares the value of CurrentColor to the value of each Case statement until it finds a match. Once a matching Case statement is found, Word runs the commands under that Case statement. The macro then continues with the first statement that follows End Select.

You can use the Case Else statement to provide the commands that Word should execute if none of the preceding Case statements were triggered. The TextColor macro does not have any commands to perform for Case Else, so the next statement is End Select, which ends the Case structure. The Case Else statement is coded into the macro because Word displays an error message if none of the Case statements are triggered (for example, if the color is anything other than black or red) and no Case Else is found.

The online help for the Select Case statement discusses more tasks you can do with Case structures that are beyond the scope of this chapter.

On Error

The On Error statement is used for handling errors in the macro. It enables you to define a chunk of code that takes over the processing when an error occurs. If you don't use an

On Error statement and an error does occur, Word displays an error message and the macro quits. A full discussion of error handling is beyond the scope of a single chapter, but you can use this brief introduction to error handling to get started. To learn more about error handling, refer to New Rider's *Inside Word for Windows 95* or consult the online help under the keywords **On Error**.

There are two main types of error that can occur when running a macro: Standard Word errors, and errors that are specific to WordBasic.

 Note

Whether you include any form of error handling depends on who is going to be using the macro. If you are the only person ever likely to use the macro and you're happy with it occasionally failing abruptly, you may never need to use error handling. However, if you're fussy or you produce macros that other people use, you should add error handling.

The three variants of the On Error statement are discussed in the following sections.

On Error Goto label

The On Error Goto *label* statement must be placed before any code that might cause an error. If an error does occur, the macro jumps to the label and continues processing from there. A *label* is just a line that consists of a label name followed by a colon.

In the following example, the user is asked to type in the name of a document. The document is then printed, and if printing is successful, a series of other commands are carried out. If an error occurs, the macro jumps to the MissingFile label and exits the subroutine.

```
Sub MAIN
On Error Goto MissingFile
FileToPrint$ = InputBox$("Full filename of document to print")
FilePrint .FileName = FileToPrint$
...commands to be carried out if printing was successful...
MissingFile:
End Sub
```

In the previous example, the error handling consists of just jumping over the commands that are carried out when printing is successful. If there are alternate commands that you want to perform when an error *does* occur, you need to add another label and another Goto statement.

The following example extends the previous example to include a message that appears when printing fails. It includes another label—EndOfSub—which allows the non-error code to jump over the error code with a Goto statement.

8

```
Sub MAIN
On Error Goto MissingFile
FileToPrint$ = InputBox$("Full filename of document to print")
FilePrint .FileName = FileToPrint$
…commands to be carried out if printing was successful…
Goto EndOfSub

MissingFile:
MsgBox "Document " + FileToPrint$ + " was not printed"

EndofSub:
End Sub
```

If an error does occur, Word stores an error code in a variable called Err. You can use this variable to determine exactly what error occurred. For example, if the user cancels the print job, an error occurs (Word treats Cancel as an error), and Err is set to code 102. The following code extends the example to skip the message box if the user presses Cancel:

```
Sub MAIN
On Error Goto MissingFile
FileToPrint$ = InputBox$("Full filename of document to print")
FilePrint .FileName = FileToPrint$
…number of commands to be carried out if printing was successful…
Goto EndOfSub

MissingFile:
If Err = 102 Then Goto EndOfSub
MsgBox "Document " + FileToPrint$ + " was not printed"

EndofSub:
End Sub
```

On Error Resume Next

The On Error Resume Next statement lets you trap errors and ignore them. Use this statement before commands that can generate errors that do not affect the operation of your macro. If an error does occur, your macro continues running at the command following the one that generated the error.

On Error Goto 0

Use the On Error Goto 0 statement to cancel any previous error handling in your macro. On Error Goto 0 ensures that Word will halt the macro and display an error message if an error occurs.

Loops

It's often useful to repeatedly perform the same set of instructions. For example, you might want to search a document for a particular phrase and mark the locations in some way. You could do this by positioning yourself at the start of the document and then repeatedly issuing a find command to search for the next occurrence of the phrase. You stop searching when you reach the end of the document.

In programming, this sort of repeated activity is known as a *loop*. There are two forms of loops in WordBasic: the For loop, which loops for a predefined number of times, and the While loop, which repeats until a specific condition is met.

For Loops

You use a For loop to perform the same set of commands a specific number of times. A For loop is controlled by a variable that is set to a starting value before the first iteration of the loop. After each iteration of the loop, the control variable is incremented and compared to an ending value. The loop terminates when the control variable is incremented beyond the ending value. The following simple example sets each element of an array to 100:

```
Dim MyArray(9)              ' Array of ten values
For Index = 0 To 9 Step 1
    MyArray(Index) = 100    ' Set the initial value
Next Index
```

The For loop in the previous example uses a control variable named Index. Before the loop begins, Index is set to 0 (Index = 0). The Next statement marks the end of the For loop (Next Index). The command between the For statement and the Next statement (MyArray(Index) = 100) is performed with each iteration of the loop. Also, Index is incremented by 1 (Step 1) with each iteration of the loop. As soon as Index exceeds 9 (To 9), the loop terminates, and the macro continues at the command that follows the Next statement.

The Step clause is optional. If you do not provide a Step clause, then Step 1 is assumed. The sample macro includes it to demonstrate the full syntax of the For loop structure. You can specify a positive or a negative number for Step. If you use a negative number, the control variable is decremented instead of incremented.

Putting the name of the control variable on the Next statement line is optional, but you should include it for clarity. Doing so becomes particularly important if you nest For loops or have several commands within the loop.

While Loops

The other form of loop construct is the While loop. A While loop continues while a condition is true. You start a While loop by specifying the condition that must be true in order for the loop to continue. The line that ends the While loop is the keyword Wend.

The following macro repeatedly asks the user for a secret password until the user enters the words **Open sesame** or clicks the Cancel button:

```
Sub MAIN
    On Error Goto EndOfSub
While Attempt$ <> "Open sesame"
        Attempt$ = InputBox$("What's the secret password?")
    Wend
EndOfSub:End Sub
```

8

This macro uses an `On Error` statement (described earlier in this chapter) to trap the error that occurs if the user clicks the Cancel button in the InputBox dialog.

Modular Programming

As you get into serious macro programming, you'll soon discover that your code becomes unwieldy unless you break it up into smaller modules. You'll also discover that you occasionally need to use the same set of statements at different points in your macro. You can create subroutines and functions to deal with these situations.

Subroutines

A *subroutine* is a collection of commands that can be used as often as you need them. All WordBasic macros contain at least one subroutine—MAIN—so you've already seen the structure of a simple subroutine. It starts with a Sub MAIN name line and ends with an `End Sub` line:

```
Sub MAIN
    Subroutine code goes here...
End Sub
```

The following macro uses a subroutine to print out the same name and telephone number three times:

```
Sub MAIN
    InsertNameAndNumber
    InsertNameAndNumber
    InsertNameAndNumber
End Sub

Sub InsertNameAndNumber
    Insert "Father Christmas"        'Insert the name
    InsertPara                       'Insert a paragraph marker
    Insert "+99 123 456 789"         'Insert the phone number
    InsertPara : InsertPara          'Insert two paragraph marker
End Sub
```

The InsertNameAndNumber subroutine is in the same macro as the MAIN subroutine. Once you have created a subroutine, you can call it using its name just as if it were one of the built-in WordBasic commands. If you prefer, you can put the option keyword Call in front of the subroutine name to help you distinguish references to your subroutines from references to built-in commands.

You can pass variables into subroutines to customize their behavior. Just include a list of variable names after the subroutine name on the Sub line. The following amended version of the InsertNameAndNumber subroutine lets you specify the name and number when you call the subroutine:

```
Sub MAIN
    InsertNameAndNumber("Father Christmas", "123 456 789")
    InsertNameAndNumber("Rudolf the reindeer", "123 555 777")
    InsertNameAndNumber("Sledge mechanics", "234 556 665")
End Sub

Sub InsertNameAndNumber(Name$, PhoneNumber$)
    Insert Name$                      'Insert the name
    InsertPara                        'Insert a paragraph marker
    Insert PhoneNumber$               'Insert the phone number
    InsertPara : InsertPara           'Insert two paragraph marker
End Sub
```

Functions

A *function* is like a subroutine, except that it returns a value. You can write a function
that returns a numeric value or a text value. A function that returns a text value has a
$ as the last character of the function name to indicate that the return value is a text
string. A function definition starts with the keyword Function followed by its name and
ends with an End Function line. Whereas a subroutine runs until it hits the End Sub line,
a function must return a value, so you must include at least one line where the name of
the function is set to a value.

Like subroutines, functions can be written to do just about anything. The following example function returns a numeric value that is the largest of two passed values:

```
Function Largest(A, B)
    If A > B Then
        Largest = A
    Else
        Largest = B
    EndIf
End Function
```

To return a value from a function, set the name of the function to a value. In this example, the Largest function returns the value of A (Largest = A) if A is larger than B, and
it returns B (Largest = B) if A is not larger than B. Generally, you set the return value near
the end of the function, but you don't have to. The function continues to run even after
you set the return value.

The following example is a text function that returns the text Same if two passed strings
are identical, and Different otherwise:

```
Function Compare$(A$, B$)
    If A$ = B$  Then
        Compare$ = "Same"
    Else
        Compare$ = "Different"
    EndIf
End Function
```

The Auto Macros

You can give a macro any name you choose. If you give your macro a name that's the same as one of Word's built-in commands, such as FileOpen or FormatFont, your macro overrides the built-in Word command. Similarly, if you create a macro with a special name, you can run it automatically when you start Word or open a document. These five command names are reserved for Word's auto macros. If you name your macro one of these names, Word automatically executes a macro at a certain time. These *auto macros* are described in table 8.4.

Table 8.4   The Auto Macros

Macro Name	Automatically Runs When
AutoExec	You start Word.
AutoNew	You create a new document.
AutoOpen	You open an existing document.
AutoClose	You close a document.
AutoExit	You quit Word.

You can use the auto macros when you want Word to perform the same set of actions automatically. For example, you might create an AutoOpen macro that logs accesses to a particular file, or an AutoClose macro to tidy up some temporary files.

For more information about auto macros and examples of their use, refer to Chapter 10, "Customizing the Workspace," and the Word online help. Do a search using the keywords **auto macros**.

Where to Get More Information

There are a number of sources for extra information about WordBasic. The most accessible source is the online help. When you're entering WordBasic code, you can quickly jump to the relevant help topic by highlighting a word and pressing the F1 function key. Note that the WordBasic online help is *not* installed in a typical Office installation. You have to perform a full installation or specifically choose to install the online help during a custom installation.

Inside Word for Windows 95, published by New Riders, includes a comprehensive introduction to WordBasic, and a substantial command reference index.

If you have questions about Word or macros, you can ask Microsoft via two CompuServe forums: **MSWORD** and **PROGMSA**. The MSWORD forum has sections devoted to general questions about Word. Although there is a section in the MSWORD forum devoted to macros, for answers to advanced macro questions you should head for the PROGMSA forum.

If you are developing lots of macros, you may also want to subscribe to Microsoft's TechNet CD subscription service. TechNet is a complete reference to all Microsoft products and includes the contents of the Microsoft Knowledge Base in addition to an online version of the *Microsoft Word Developer's Kit*. The Knowledge Base is a compendium of all reported bugs in Microsoft products and is an invaluable resource if you are working extensively in Word. Because TechNet is a CD-ROM, you can search the contents by keyword. For more information about TechNet, on CompuServe type **GO TECHNET**. You can also get information over the Internet from Microsoft's home page at **http://www.microsoft.com**.

Summary

In this chapter, you learned how to use macros to automate your work. You learned how to record frequently used keystrokes into a macro and assign the macro to a keyboard key combination. You learned how to edit macros in word's editing window.

In addition, this chapter showed you the syntax for the WordBasic language and how to use the Dialog Editor. You also learned how to run your macros automatically.

8

chapter 9

Word Styles

by Susan Daffron

9

In this chapter

◆ **Working with Styles**
Automate your documents using character and paragraph styles and style controls such as Based On and Style for Following.

◆ **Using Templates**
Uncover the power of templates by learning how to attach templates to documents, copy styles between templates, and work with the Style Gallery.

◆ **Using Wizards**
Learn to use wizards to create complex documents and find out how to create your own custom wizard.

U sing Word without taking advantage of styles is like riding a bike with training wheels: you can get where you want to go, but you can't get there very quickly. If you only create the occasional single-page document, you might prefer to format it directly using the menu and toolbar commands. You might decide that you never need to learn about styles. Life is uncomplicated and serene.

But most of us don't have that luxury. For example, suppose your company's critical 50-page proposal has to be sent out in the next hour. After taking three long hours to review the document, the boss comes back and says the font Arial looks "wrong" and maybe "we" should change the headings from 10- to 12-point type, so the proposal looks longer and more impressive.

If you set up the document using styles, rather than scanning through all 50 pages and laboriously changing each heading one by one (and missing the deadline), you only need to make one change in one dialog box that instantly ripples through the document. You reprint the proposal and give it to the courier as everyone in the office applauds your efficiency.

You can amaze and astound your coworkers this way if you use styles to format your document. A style lets you save all the formatting attributes of a particular type of text, such as a heading as a name. When you need to change the formatting, rather than changing it in every paragraph you have formatted as a heading, you change the style called Heading. Any paragraphs you have applied the Heading style to change automatically when you change the style.

Working with Styles

Whether you've ever consciously applied a style, styles lurk in the background of every document. That lone paragraph mark you see when you open a blank document has a style called Normal applied to it (assuming you have Paragraph Marks turned on—which you should if you plan to format with styles). All styles, including Normal, are stored in templates. When you load a blank document, you are really loading the Normal template, NORMAL.DOT. Every document that uses the NORMAL.DOT template contains the Normal, Heading 1, Heading 2, and Heading 3 styles. You always see these three styles, although other built-in styles hide in the background until you use them for special documents such as indexes and tables of contents. You can see the complete list of all the styles in the template in the Style drop-down box on the Formatting toolbar by holding down the Shift key when you click the arrow. Another way to inspect the styles is by looking in the Style dialog box. Choose Format, Style and change the List drop-down box to All Styles. The Style dialog box also gives you a detailed summary of the formatting saved in each of your styles in the Description box.

 Tip

If you add a Style Area in Tools, Options, View, in Normal view, your style names appear listed on the left side of the document. You can double-click a style name displayed in the Style Area to display the Style dialog box (see fig. 9.1).

Fig. 9.1
Double-clicking on a style in the Style Area lets you quickly jump to the Style dialog box.

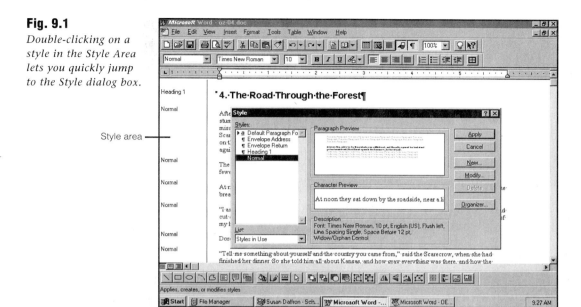

Style area

Using the Built-In Styles

The easiest way to start using styles is by applying one of the built-in styles. Most documents require headings, so the next time you format a big bold Arial heading, try applying a style instead. Place your cursor anywhere in the heading paragraph, and select Heading 1 from the Style list box on the Formatting toolbar (see fig. 9.2). Your text magically sports a new Arial bold look.

Alternatively, if you prefer keyboard shortcuts, you can press Ctrl+Shift+S to place your cursor in the Style list box on the Formatting toolbar. The field is highlighted so that you can type in the style name. When you press the Enter key, Word applies the style to the paragraph.

Notice that when you apply a paragraph style, the formatting affects the entire paragraph, whether the paragraph is one line or 50 lines long. Style and formatting information is actually stored in the paragraph marker itself (which is why you should turn on Paragraph Marks when you work with styles).

Storing the formatting information in the paragraph marker sounds logical, but it can be confusing. And when your text unexpectedly reformats, it can be downright annoying. For example, if you copy a section of text and you don't copy the paragraph marker with it, you lose all the formatting (or style) that was stored in that paragraph marker when you paste it in its new location.

9

Fig. 9.2

You can try out the built-in heading styles by selecting them from the Formatting toolbar.

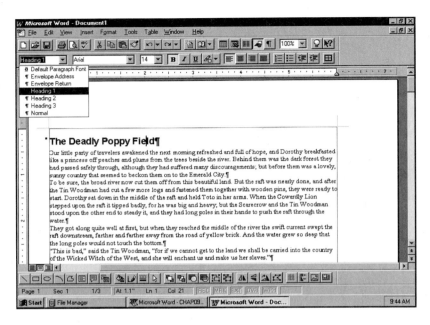

Similarly, as you type, you can end up with some extra paragraph markers or paragraphs you want to delete from the middle of the document. Because the formatting information is stored in the paragraph marker, when you delete these unwanted paragraphs, the text that remains takes on the style or formatting of the following paragraph. If you use a lot of styles, sometimes you might unintentionally format paragraphs incorrectly if you don't notice which style is applied to the paragraph after you paste the text.

Knowing about the built-in styles is important in Word because the built-in heading styles are reserved for special tasks. For example, if you intend to use some of Word's automatic features, you need to set up your document with the built-in heading styles. The Heading 1 through Heading 9 styles are used by Word for the outlining feature, the display in the Style Gallery, and optionally in the creation of tables of contents.

Creating Styles

When the thrill of applying heading styles wears off, you'll probably want to begin creating your own styles. After all, you can only get so far with Arial bold and, let's face it, the built-in styles in the Normal template are ugly. Adding new styles to your style list is easy. Getting your styles to stick to the template is less easy. Some of the most powerful aspects of using styles hinge on whether you select one little check box in a dialog box. In Word, seemingly trivial things like this check box can trip you up, so mouse ahead carefully. If you plan to add a lot of styles, it's a good idea to create a new template so you can experiment freely without worrying about destroying the default NORMAL.DOT template. The section later in this chapter, "Working with Templates," discusses templates in detail.

There are two ways to add styles: the right-brained approach and the left-brained approach. If you are a visually oriented person (right-brained), you might prefer creating styles "by example." By example means you select a paragraph and start formatting it the old-fashioned way using the formatting commands in the toolbars and menus. In other words, you create an "example" for Word to base the new style on. You tweak and twiddle your settings until you find true beauty. Then, with your cursor still in this enchanting new paragraph, you type a new name in the Style list box on the Formatting toolbar (see fig. 9.3).

Fig. 9.3

Creating a style by example is easy, but it has some limitations.

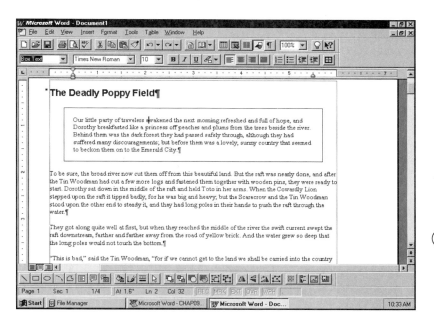

Now, here's the catch. If you create a style by example, the style won't be saved in the template. Any new documents you create based on the template will not automatically contain your new carefully crafted style. Word is supposed to work this way, but that makes it no less annoying when you discover after all that work that none of your styles were saved into the template.

A little check mark is the culprit. If you want your new style to be saved in the template, place your cursor in the paragraph with the new style. Choose F_ormat, S_tyle. Your new style is highlighted in the style list. Click _Modify and then select the _Add to Template check box.

When you save a document, unless you go through the New Style or Modify Style dialog box and select the Add to Template check box, your new style stays with that one document. The template doesn't know about your style until you tell it by adding a check mark in the dialog box.

Now that you know the limitation of the right-brained approach, you can probably guess the left-brained approach to creating styles. You can set up a style directly just by going to the Style dialog box and following these steps:

1. Select Format, Style. The Style dialog box appears.

2. In the Style dialog box, click the New button. The New Style dialog box appears.

3. Type a new style name into the Name box.

4. Click the Format button and start changing the settings. Before you close the New Style dialog box, make sure the Add to Template check box is selected if you want to include your new style in the template (see fig. 9.4).

Fig. 9.4

When you add a new style using the New Style dialog box, you can ensure that the style is saved in the template.

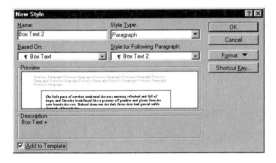

  Tip

If you add styles to the NORMAL.DOT template frequently, you might want a reminder to alert you to what you've done. Choose Tools, Options and click the Save tab. Select the Prompt to Save Normal Template check box. When you select this option, Word asks if you want to save the changes you made to the default settings in NORMAL.DOT.

Modifying styles works the same way as creating a new style. Again, you can use the left- or right-brained approach. You can modify the style "by example," by highlighting text in the paragraph, changing it, and selecting the style name from the list. Word asks you if you want to redefine the style or reapply the style (see fig. 9.5). To modify the style, you select Redefine.

Fig. 9.5

When you change an attribute and apply the same style, Word asks if you want to reapply or redefine the style.

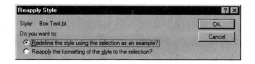

This method does not store the changes in the template unless you choose F<u>o</u>rmat, <u>S</u>tyle, click <u>M</u>odify, and select the <u>A</u>dd to Template check box. If you want to be sure all your style modifications are saved into the template, it's safer to modify them directly in the first place.

As you start creating styles, devise a descriptive naming scheme so you can tell the styles apart and remember why you created them. However, when you create a lot of styles, it's easy to end up with a lot of long style names. Adding a shorter name, called an *alias*, lets you use the short name in place of the long one when you apply styles. If you use the keyboard to apply styles—by pressing Ctrl+Shift+S to put your cursor in the Style list box and typing the style name directly—all you have to do is type the alias name, and press Enter to apply your style. You can add aliases when you create new styles or when you go back and modify styles later.

To add an alias, when you type the style name in the Name box in the Modify Style or New Style dialog box, add a comma after the name and type your alias name. For example, if you have a long style name such as Numbered Text Level 2, you could add an alias called NT2. In the Style list box on the toolbar, the entry looks like: Numbered Text Level 2,NT2. When you apply the style, all you need to type is NT2.

 Tip

If you click the Help button on the Standard toolbar and then click text in your document, Word gives you style and formatting information about the text.

Character versus Paragraph Styles

Until now, the discussion of styles has been referring to paragraph styles. But Word actually has two types of styles: paragraph styles and character styles. Although character styles are not used as often as paragraph styles, they can be just as useful. You use a character style in situations where you want to format a section of text without formatting the whole paragraph. For example, you could use character styles in a software manual or computer reference book to indicate the keyboard shortcuts, such as Ctrl+S, if you want them to stand out from the surrounding text. Character styles are great for situations in which you want to be sure your formatting is consistent for a specific type of word or phrase.

To apply a character style, you just highlight the text and select the style from the Style list box on the Formatting toolbar. Character styles display in the style list with an underlined *a* (a) next to them; the paragraph styles show a paragraph marker next to them. If you switch the List drop-down box in the Style dialog box to All Styles and scroll through the Style list, you'll notice that certain common formatting characteristics such as page numbers, footnotes, and annotations are actually character styles.

Creating a character style is very similar to creating a paragraph style. Choose Format, Style, click New, and choose Character from the Style Type list box (the default is Paragraph). Make your modifications and select the Add to Template check box if you want the style to be available the next time you use the template. Not surprisingly, when you create a character style, the only options you can change when you click the Format button are Font and Language. The Paragraph, Tabs, Border, Frame, and Numbering options are grayed (see fig. 9.6).

Fig. 9.6

As the name implies, you only can save font and language formats in a character style. The other options in the Format menu are grayed.

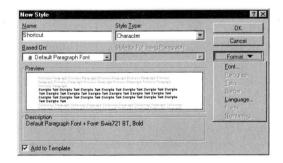

Powerful Style Controls

You can use two powerful style controls in the New Style or Modify Style dialog box to automate your documents. The Based On and Style for Following Paragraph controls are more powerful than they may seem at first glance. If you set up your document carefully, you can use the power of these two commands to save yourself a lot of time. Note that you can only access these attributes by going through the Style dialog box. If you prefer to create your styles "by example," you have to go back in and edit these settings later by choosing Format, Style.

Based On

You can base any one of your styles on any other style. If you have a document with a Normal style set to Times 10 point, another style based on the Normal style also will be set to Times 10 point unless you specifically change the font. If you redefine the Normal style to a different font, the other styles in the document based on Normal change as well.

For example, if you change the font in Normal from Times to Arial, Word changes the font for all the styles based on Normal (see fig. 9.7). This change affects all the styles you set up, and other built-in character styles, such as footnotes, headers, footers, and page numbers. If you don't want these character styles to change when you change the Normal style, choose Format, Style, switch the List drop-down box in the Style dialog box to All Styles, and select the character style (such as Page from the list of styles). Change the Based On list box in the Modify Style dialog box to no style.

Fig. 9.7

You can set up your document so that one Heading style inherits formatting from another heading.

Using the Based On feature, you can create an inheritance hierarchy by creating one style that is based on another style, which in turn is based on another style, and so on (up to nine levels). Changing a style in the hierarchy causes a ripple effect on the styles following it in the hierarchy. For example, suppose you create a style called Body Text that is 11 point Times. Next, you create a style based on Body Text called Body Text Italic. This style has all the attributes of Body Text plus italic. Now, you create a style based on Body Text Italic. You add right justification and call this style Body Text Italic Right. It has the attributes of Body Text and Body Text Italic plus right justification. If you change the font of the original Body Text style to Garamond, the font changes in Body Text Italic (which is now Garamond Italic) and in Body Text Italic Right (which is now right-justified Garamond Italic text).

Based On is a powerful feature and can take some getting used to. If you forget that you based styles on others and accidentally cause a tidal wave of ripple effects through your document, just remember that Word has multiple levels of undo. If you completely screw up, click the Undo button on the Standard toolbar and return to your preceding styles.

9

Style for Following Paragraph

A similar and equally powerful feature is the Style for Following Paragraph. In the New Style or Modify Style dialog box, you can set the style that follows the style you are creating or modifying. The default following style always shows the style name of the style you are creating or editing. But you can set this name to any name in the style list. If your initial response is, "so what?" think about how your document is constructed. For example, in most documents a heading is followed by normal body text, or a caption always follows a photograph. Just as in the Based On option, you can set up a hierarchy. If you are creating a document with multiple levels of indention, you could create different forms of normal text to follow the different heading levels, so that Heading 1 is followed by Normal 1, Heading 2 is followed by Normal 2, and so on.

Removing Formatting

Sometimes when you work with styles, it can be difficult to tell what formatting has been applied by the style and what has been applied by you using the formatting commands. If you set the font directly using the commands in the Format menu, they override the style settings. So, you can easily end up with an atypical Heading 1 style that doesn't look like other Heading 1 styles. When this happens, you can remove all local font formatting by highlighting the paragraph and pressing Ctrl+spacebar. This removes the Language setting and all the settings in the Format, Font, and Format Character Spacing tabs, including bold, underline, italic, superscript, subscript, spacing, and position.

More subtle changes can occur in your document if you adjust the paragraph spacing manually. If certain paragraphs look out of whack, you can restore the settings stored in the style by highlighting the paragraph and pressing Ctrl+Q.

Exporting Styles

Many desktop publishing applications can bring in Word styles and convert them to their own format. However, you might find that there is a lag in the version of Word that your DTP application can import. Historically, both QuarkXPress and PageMaker have been one or two versions behind in developing import filters for Word. You can always find the latest import filters online on the vendor forums on CompuServe or the Internet. Even if you can't import the latest version of Word, you can do a Save As and save your file as an earlier version of Word (such as Word 2) that your DTP application can import.

Many books and magazines are formatted in QuarkXPress, and these users import Word style sheets all the time. If you apply style sheets in Word that have the same names as the style sheets in a QuarkXPress document, when the text is imported, QuarkXPress applies its own style definitions to the paragraphs that have those style names. The document formats automatically and is ready to go. Although this process sounds automated and streamlined, you need to watch out for a few potential problems.

The Word styles and the QuarkXPress style names must match *exactly*. Even though the names have to match, the style definitions do not. As long as you have not strayed away from the styles in Word, QuarkXPress brings in the file with the styles already applied and uses the QuarkXPress style sheets with the same name to add formatting.

Certain formatting carries over into QuarkXPress nicely, but you also can do things in Word that make a mess for the desktop publisher to clean up. For example, making one word bold by applying local formatting is okay—QuarkXPress makes the single word bold in whatever font it has defined in its style sheet. However, using local formatting in Word to change line spacing or indents causes big problems. Adding specialized features in Word (such as drop caps) is equally disastrous. QuarkXPress can't interpret this information, so it adds strange formatting to the document. Removing this formatting can take hours for the person doing the desktop publishing. So, if you are bringing styles into QuarkXPress, think about how QuarkXPress would handle it *before* you apply local formatting in Word.

Because the style names must match exactly between Word and QuarkXPress, it can be handy to print out your document with the style names next to the paragraphs. That way, you can verify that you haven't applied any styles that QuarkXPress won't recognize. You can use the following macro to add the style name enclosed in brackets to the left of each paragraph:

```
Sub MAIN
StartOfDocument
Insert "<" + StyleName$() + "> "
EditFind "^p", .Direction = 0, .PatternMatch = 0          'Searches for next paragraph
CharRight
While EditFindFound() And Not AtEndOfDocument()
    Insert "<" + StyleName$() + "> "'Inserts the Stylename enclosed in <>
    EditFind "^p", .Direction = 0, .PatternMatch = 0     'Finds next Para
    CharRight
Wend
End Sub
```

After you've printed out your document, you can remove the style names by running this macro:

```
Sub MAIN
StartOfDocument
    EditReplace .Find = "\<*\> ", .Replace = "", .Direction = 0,  .MatchCase = 0,
    .WholeWord = 0, .PatternMatch = 1, .SoundsLike = 0,  .ReplaceAll, .Format = 0,
    .Wrap = 1
End Sub
```

Tip

You can also use the preceding macro code to remove HTML tags from Web page text.

Working with Templates

All the styles in a document are stored in a template. You use templates to store common information such as styles, layout information, and text for a certain type of document. The term *template* might be familiar if you've used desktop publishing (DTP) applications before. In general, Word treats its styles and templates differently than those programs do, however. This change can be confusing at first. You need to switch your mind-set to how Word "thinks" about a document. If you spend a lot of time tweaking your formatting settings and styles, it can be very frustrating to discover that your carefully crafted styles were not saved or carried over to another document the way you expected.

Like DTP applications, every document in Word is based on a template. Even if you never set up a template of your own, every document is based on the Normal template. A primary difference between Word templates and templates in other applications, however, is that in Word, if you change the template later, your changes are *not* reflected in your original document unless you specifically tell Word to reapply the changed template to the document. This concept is important. You can end up with a slew of documents all based on the same template that don't look anything like one another. If you are striving for consistency among your documents, this can be a problem. Even though the document continues to be based on a certain template, the document matches the template as it was at the time the document was created, which may or may not be the way the template is now. If you change the template and create new documents, older documents won't match new documents.

How Templates Work

In Word, the document—not the template—is most important. To understand templates, you need to understand where they fall in the Word architecture. Unfortunately, if you don't understand how Word is set up, it can be all too easy to lose track of where your settings are stored.

Microsoft tells us that Word has a "layered" architecture. That sounds nice, but what does it mean? To understand the Word architecture, try thinking of Word as an onion (the frustration of losing document settings has been known to make people cry, after all).

The document is at the outside of the onion, and the Word application itself is at the inside. Any settings you add to the outer layers supersede the settings found in the inner layers. Here's a list of the layers from the inside out:

▶ *Word.* At the core of the onion is the Word application, which contains all the built-in commands and functions. The application controls basic function, such as left-justifying a paragraph or double-spacing text.

▶ *Global.* The next layer is the Global layer, which includes the global templates in the Startup directory, add-ins, and the Normal template (NORMAL.DOT). In addition to styles and templates, this layer includes macros, AutoText entries, and toolbars. For example, if you add macros to NORMAL.DOT with the same name as the built-in Word commands, your commands supersede the built-in functions (see Chapter 10, "Customizing the Workspace," for more information).

▶ *Custom Templates.* Your templates are located above the Global layer. The styles and other settings in your templates override the settings stored in the global templates and add-ins. For example, if you set up a Heading 1 style in your template, those settings override the settings stored in the Heading 1 style in NORMAL.DOT.

▶ *Document.* The outermost layer is the document. Settings in the document override the settings in templates. If you reformatted a Heading 1 paragraph with local formatting, those settings override the settings stored in the Heading 1 style in either NORMAL.DOT or your own templates.

Word goes through an elaborate set of steps to determine where to get the formatting for a given document. For example, on a small scale, if you type the word **Fred**, Word starts at the outermost layer (the document) and moves inward through the layers to find the settings it needs to lay out the word Fred on the page. First, Word checks to see if you applied any local formatting such as bold or italic to Fred. Next, it checks in your template, then in the global templates, for a character style or paragraph style you might have applied to Fred. Finally, it goes down to the Word application to figure out what it means to be left-justified.

If you don't use styles, Word finds all your document formatting information in the document (the outermost layer) and takes any other default settings from NORMAL.DOT or other global templates and add-ins it finds in the Global layer. Any settings it can't find in the Global layer, it takes from the built-in Word settings.

Conversely, if you set up your own styles in a template, Word first looks for local formatting settings in the document, then looks at the Custom Template layer for your style settings. It continues down to the Global layer and finally to the Word layer to get the other settings it needs.

9

Creating New Templates

Now that you know where your new templates will fall in the great scheme of Word, you can create templates secure in the knowledge that the settings in your new template will override the settings in NORMAL.DOT. Although many people live out their Word lives just adding more and more styles to NORMAL.DOT, this approach leads to more confusion the more documents you create. (See Chapter 10 for more on working with the NORMAL.DOT template.)

Creating your own templates gives you the freedom to store the styles for a particular type of document in the template. When you set up templates for specific purposes, you don't have to scroll through thousands of irrelevant styles to find the elusive style you need. Plus, you can leave your NORMAL.DOT alone and use it for storing global toolbar and macro information that you want to access when you work on *every* document.

You can create a template in two ways: directly (by creating a new file), or indirectly (by basing it on an existing document). If you want to create a template from scratch, choose File, New and click the Template radio button under Create New. You can base the new template on an existing template or on NORMAL.DOT (Blank Document). Add styles, formatting, macros, toolbars, and text just as you would to any other document and save the file as a template with a DOT extension.

If you already have a document that you think is just peachy, you can replicate it for future use by saving it as a template. Open the document and choose File, Save As. Choose Document Template (*.dot) from the Save As Type list box (see fig. 9.8). When you switch the file type to a template, Word automatically switches to the default template directory (usually WINWORD\TEMPLATE). Now, the next time you choose File, New, you'll be able to select your spiffy new template from the list.

Fig. 9.8

Creating a new template from an existing document saves all the styles you set up for the document into the new template, so you can use them again.

Remember that when you take an existing document and do a Save As to turn it into a template, Word leaves all the text in there, too. If you just want the styles, open the template again, delete the text that is specific to the originating document, and resave the template.

There really isn't much difference between a template and a document. The process works in reverse too. You can turn a template back into a document if you want to. For example, if you rename a template in the Explorer or File Manager so it has a DOC extension (instead of DOT), you can create a document that contains all the toolbars and AutoText entries that were stored in the template.

Attaching Templates

After you start working with templates, you might want to change the styles in your existing documents to the new ones you created in your new templates. In Word, this process is known as *attaching* a template to a document. However, when you start attaching templates to documents, it's important to note what the process does and does not do.

To attach a template, choose File, Templates and select the Automatically Update Document Styles check box (see fig. 9.9). When you click the OK button, Word overwrites the style formatting of styles in the document that have the same name as the styles in the new template you're attaching. All the matching styles magically change to the new settings and the styles in the new template are added to the style list. Text formatted with styles from the old template that don't match styles in the new template retain the old style. If you want to make sure that you remove all vestiges of the old template from the document, make sure all the text is formatted with style names that match across the two templates.

9

Fig. 9.9
Attaching templates updates the styles, but does not change page elements such as margins, headers, and footers.

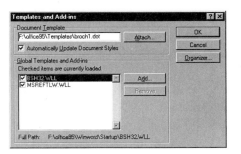

For example, if you have a document with the Normal style set to the font Arial and you apply a template with the Normal style set to Times New Roman, any paragraphs with a style set to Normal now appear in Times New Roman (unless you applied local formatting). You also now have access to all the styles in the newly attached template, but none of the styles from the old.

Sometimes, however, you might want to retain some of the styles from the old template. If so, before you attach the new template, you should check to see if the old style will get overwritten when you attach the template. Rename any matching styles you want to preserve by choosing Format, Style, clicking Modify, and typing a new name.

Applying templates has limitations, however. This procedure only changes the styles in a document to those of the new template. But there is more to the average document than just styles. Attaching a template does not change document elements such as margins, page size, headers, or footers. To ensure consistency among documents, transfer these settings to another document as well. Although this limitation is potentially confusing, it makes sense if you think about the Word hierarchy discussed earlier. Margins, headers, footers, and so on are document-level settings. Remember that document-level settings always supersede template-level settings. Therefore, when you attach a new template, because the page settings are stored at the document level, Word can't overwrite them with settings stored at the template level.

To change these document-level page elements, you have to approach the problem from a different direction. Because you cannot override document settings, you need to bring the document to be modified into the template. You end up using the document settings stored in the template. Create a new document based on your template and then choose Insert, File. From the Insert file dialog box, select your file from the list of files on the left and click OK (see fig. 9.10). Your new document contains all the document-level page elements stored in your new template.

Fig. 9.10

To reformat page elements, you need to insert the old file into your new template.

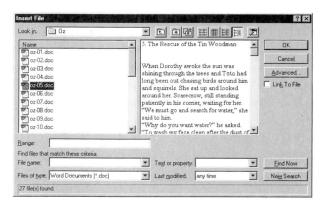

Adding Global Templates

When you work on a document, you can typically use only the AutoText entries, macros, custom toolbars, menu settings, and shortcut keys that are stored in the template attached to the document or in the global NORMAL.DOT template. To use items stored in another template, you can load the other template as a *global* template. This function is handy if you temporarily need a macro that you created for another template.

To load a global template, follow these steps:

1. Choose File, Templates.
2. Click the Add button.
3. Select a template from the list of files.
4. Click OK.

After you load a template as a global template, all of the macros, AutoText entries, toolbars, and so on that live in the template are available to any document you decide to open while you are working in Word. Word unloads all the global templates you add using the Templates command when you quit Word. Note also that if you only need a global add-in or template for a specific purpose, you should unload it when you're done to conserve system resources. The more global templates you have loaded in memory, the more likely Word is to have problems.

Alternatively, you can load an add-in or template every time you start Word by copying the add-in or template to the Startup folder in the Winword directory. You can change this startup location by choosing Tools, Options and changing the Startup location in the File Locations tab. Again, adding in a lot of global templates can drain system resources, so beware.

Copying Styles Between Templates

Rather than setting up the same styles repeatedly when you work on templates, you can just copy styles from existing documents or templates and modify them to suit the needs of the new template. This technique can be helpful for ensuring naming consistency across your templates. By copying styles, when you attach new templates, the styles will update correctly. You won't end up with any unexpected surprises because you spelled a style name slightly differently in one template than another.

To copy styles from one document or template to another, follow these steps:

1. Choose File, Templates.
2. Click Organizer and select the Styles tab (see fig. 9.11).

Fig. 9.11

Verify that the document or template names are correct on both sides of the Organizer dialog box before you start copying styles.

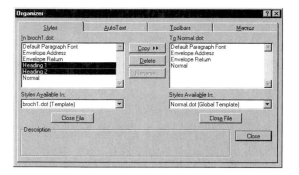

3. If necessary, close the document or template in Styles Available In on either side of the dialog box by clicking the Close button. The button changes to an Open button, so you can open the desired document or template. Verify that the names are correct before you start copying.

4. Select a style from the Styles In list box. You can select styles from either template (the Copy arrow changes direction). When you click a style name, a description appears in the description box below the list. To select more than one style, hold the Shift or Ctrl key while you select. Holding down the Shift key lets you select contiguous styles in the list. Holding down the Ctrl key lets you select non-contiguous styles.

5. After you select your styles, click the Copy button. The styles transfer to the document or template.

Copying styles can also be useful if you set up a style and forget to add it to the template. After you realize that your cool new style isn't stored in the template, you can just open the document with your perfectly crafted style and copy it to the template.

Using the Style Gallery

You can use the Style Gallery to test out styles without committing yourself to reformatting a document. The Style Gallery shows you a preview of what your document would look like if the styles in the template were applied to the document (see fig. 9.12).

To access the Style Gallery, choose Format, Style Gallery. You see a list of all the templates in your template directory on the left and a preview window on the right. When you select a template from the list, you see a preview of your document. Any styles applied in your document that have the same name as the styles in the template you're trying out appear with the formatting of the new styles. For example, if your document has its Normal style formatted in Arial, and you select the Manual style sheet, the Normal style appears in Garamond. If you click OK, the styles are imported into your document. Note that Word doesn't actually attach the template you select from the list; instead, it imports the styles into your document. Whatever template you had attached remains attached, but now it has a whole lot more styles in the list.

Fig. 9.12

You can use the Style Gallery to check out how a document would look formatted with the styles in a different template.

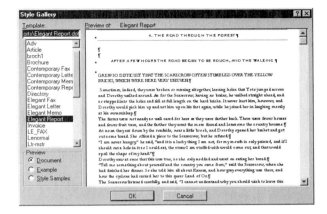

When you use the Style Gallery, if your documents have a lot of styles, many of the style names you use won't match the style names in other templates. It can be difficult to get a good feel for the styles in a template by looking at your document in the Preview Of window. So Microsoft set up its own templates so it can display sample text for the Style Gallery. If you click the Example button for a built-in template, you can see an example of text formatted with the selected template. Similarly, if you click the Style Samples button, you see the style names in the selected template with sample text formatted with the styles.

You will find, however, that if you click Example for one of your own templates, a message saying `There is no example for this template` appears in the Preview Of window. If you click the Style Samples button, you see an equally attractive message that says `There is no sample for this Template`. If you are industrious, you can add your sample text to your templates, so as you cruise the Style Gallery, your templates can look just as good as Microsoft's.

Adding Text Examples to Your Templates

The sample text that appears in the Preview Of window is actually set up with AutoText entries. To add examples to your template, you must open the template, add the AutoText entries, and resave the template. Just follow these steps:

1. Choose File, Open. Switch the Document Type to Template and select your template from the list.

2. Type some sample text that uses the styles in your template. Try to use as many of the styles in your template as possible (see fig. 9.13).

3. Select the text and create an AutoText entry by choosing <u>E</u>dit, AutoTe<u>x</u>t.

4. Type **Gallery Example** in the <u>N</u>ame text box in the AutoText dialog box. Make sure you change the <u>M</u>ake AutoText Entry Available To list box to Documents Based On your template (see fig. 9.14).

5. Now delete the text you typed to create the AutoText entry.

6. Save and close the template.

Fig. 9.13

When you create the AutoText entry for the Style Gallery preview, you can type in anything you want.

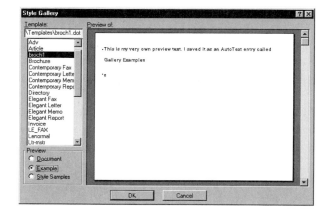

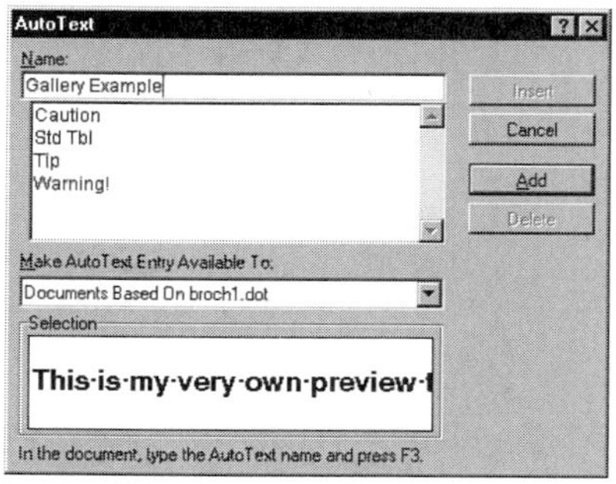

Fig. 9.14

If you want sample text to appear in the Style Gallery for your own templates, you need to add an AutoText entry in the template called Gallery Example.

Adding Style Samples to Your Templates

Adding style samples works almost the same way. Again, you create an AutoText entry. The only difference is the name of the AutoText entry and how you set up the text. To add style samples to your template, follow these steps:

1. Open your template and type the name of each style you want to include on a separate line. Now, apply the style to the style name text so that each line shows the formatting of the style.

2. Highlight the formatted sample text and create an AutoText entry called Gallery Style Samples.

3. Again, make sure the AutoText entry is available to your specific template rather than NORMAL.DOT.

4. Delete the text you typed for the AutoText entry and save the template.

Working with Wizards

A wizard is basically a template with an attitude. Wizards contain a complex macro that walks you through the construction of a document. The wizard asks you questions about the document and then creates the document based on your answers. Word comes with a number of built-in wizards you can install when you install Word.

Wizards are great for complicated documents you don't use very often. If you don't want to figure out how to create a perfectly formatted meeting agenda, for example, you can just run the Agenda Wizard and let Word do most of the formatting for you (see fig. 9.15).

9

Fig. 9.15
Using Word's meeting agenda wizard, you can set up a perfectly formatted agenda just by answering a few questions.

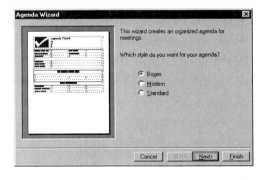

Of course, many people get grumpy about having Microsoft's font and layout choices foisted upon them in a wizard. For example, if you have a personal loathing for the Arial font, you'll be out of luck when you go rummaging through the wizards Microsoft provides. However, you can go off to see the wizard all by yourself. Like almost everything about Word, if you don't like it, you can change it. For those really adventurous souls who want total control, you can even create your own wizards.

Editing Wizards

Suppose for a moment that your company has standardized on a font other than Arial. (Imagine that!) You like the layout of the Contemporary Memo, and you love the flexibility that the choices in the wizard give you. The only problem is that you can't stand the font. What to do?

At heart, a wizard is really a template. Like any template, you can change it by opening it directly. Some wizards give you a choice between different layout styles, such as Contemporary, Modern, and Elegant. These wizards use a different template for each type of document. For example, if you create a "contemporary" memo, not surprisingly, it uses the CONTEMPORARY MEMO.DOT template. You'll notice these templates sitting in the Memos tab of the New dialog box when you go to run the wizard. You can change the styles in the template by opening the template directly.

1. Run the wizard and check the style name of the text you want to reformat. For example, if you want to change the font of the Message Head style, write it down somewhere.

2. Now open the template by choosing File, Open. Click Open and the template opens.

3. Choose Format, Style and make sure the drop-down List box displays All Styles.

4. Select the style you want to change and click Modify. Make sure you select the Add To Template check box.

5. Change the style formatting.

6. Change the formatting of all the styles you want to change and click OK.

7. Choose File, Close. When Word asks if you want to save the changes to the template, say Yes.

The next time you use the Memo Wizard, the Wizard uses your new styles. If you decide to go spelunking through these templates, however, be very sure not to touch any special formatting such as bookmarks. If you kill the wizard, you can always replace it by doing a custom installation. Of course, an easier approach is to just back up the Word templates to a safe directory before you start spelunking in the first place.

Creating a Simple Wizard

Wizards are easy to run, but they are *not* easy to create. If you have never worked with macros, you absolutely must learn how to create macros first and have quite a bit of familiarity with Word Basic. Refer to Chapter 8, "Word Macros," for more information on creating your own macros.

To create your own wizard, you should be familiar with the Macro Editor and the Dialog Editor, and have some experience creating custom dialog boxes and dynamic dialog boxes. If you have all that experience, you also already might have a copy of the *Word Developer's Kit* from Microsoft Press. This book is invaluable for anyone contemplating a foray into the world of wizards. Although this section gives you a glimmer at a possible approach to a short wizard, the wizard shown here is, by necessity, extremely stripped down.

In contrast, the *Word Developer's Kit* comes with a disk that includes two wizard templates: the Starter Wizard and the Wizard Maker Wizard. The Starter Wizard is a boilerplate wizard that contains routines common to all Microsoft Word wizards. These routines manage the user interface, including the functions that let you move back and forth through the wizard panels.

The Wizard Maker Wizard is a wizard Microsoft provides that you can use to get started. When you go through the wizard, it creates a StartWizard macro with the standard routines in the Starter Wizard, but it also lets you specify some of your own criteria. When you finish the wizard, you use the Macro Editor to add your own controls and routines, so your new wizard performs the task you set it out to do.

Anatomy of a Wizard

A wizard is merely a template that is saved with a WIZ extension. Every Word wizard contains an AutoNew macro that runs when the user creates a new document based on the wizard. The AutoNew macro is a three-line macro that does nothing more than call the StartWizard macro, like so:

```
Sub MAIN
    StartWizard
End Sub
```

The StartWizard macro is what does the work of the wizard. Although technically a wizard is a template, the StartWizard macro has a lot more to do with the wizard than the template itself. Although the template might contain the document formatting, its most important function is as a place to store the StartWizard macro, which does the work of the wizard.

So, now that you know what a wizard is, you can take a peek at an existing wizard. Instead of running a wizard, choose File, Open and open one of the wizards that comes with Word. In the template, choose Tools, Macro. Select StartWizard and click Edit. Now you can take a peek at the text of the wizard.

The StartWizard Macro

Now that you've been totally intimidated by a high-end wizard, you may want to look at a bare-bones version. The companion CD contains a listing called LE_WIZ.TXT. By looking at the code for this stripped-down wizard, it's easier to see the components that make a wizard work the way it does. The sample wizard creates a custom fax cover sheet. Although this wizard works just like the ones from Microsoft, it's not as complex. A few of the subroutines are included in the text that follows; however, because of space constraints, it wasn't possible to include the entire listing here. To get a feel for what the wizard does, please refer to the listing on the CD-ROM.

In the effort to make a generic template for the *Word Developer's Kit*, Microsoft added a level of complexity that isn't necessary for a simple wizard. For example, Microsoft identifies controls using numbers and uses an array to keep track of the controls on each panel. In contrast, the simplified wizard on the companion CD uses text IDs for the controls, which makes the code easier to follow. Microsoft wizards also often let you choose among different templates, which adds another layer of complexity as well.

In the effort to remove everything that isn't absolutely necessary, unlike a true Microsoft wizard, the sample wizard on the companion CD doesn't contain the cute flag on the final panel or the graphic lines above the buttons. (This is supposed to be a "simple" wizard after all.) To reduce complexity, the controls relating to the Hint button and showing and hiding the preview were eliminated as well.

The sample fax cover sheet wizard does show you several common wizard routines and gives you an idea of how wizards work (see fig. 9.16). Like every Microsoft wizard, it defines a dialog box with several panels. Each panel has its own set of controls where the user can make choices or enter information. Each panel also shares a common group of navigation controls that let the user move between the panels or leave the wizard.

Look at the code in LE_WIZ.TXT on the companion CD. As you can see, first the wizard defines global variables that will be used in the wizard, including variables to keep track of the current panel, the user dialog, and the wizard name. Next, the user dialog is defined. Because wizard dialog boxes include the controls for all the panels of the dialog, the dialog definition can get extremely long. First, the dialog box definition defines the standard controls (Next, Back, Finish, and the file preview) that are shared by every panel. Next come the controls for the first panel, then the controls for the second panel, and finally the controls for the third panel. Essentially, the different controls defined for each panel are overlaid over the shared dialog box that contains the navigation buttons and the preview window.

Fig. 9.16

This sample fax cover sheet wizard has many of the standard functions of a Microsoft wizard.

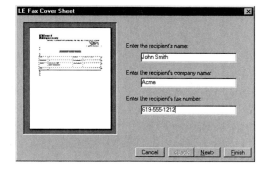

Several subroutines are used in the wizard to manage the panel controls. When a user presses a button to move to a different panel, the controls in the current panel are hidden and the controls in the new panel are displayed. If the user moves to the first panel, the Back button also must be disabled. Similarly, if the user moves to the last panel, the Next button must be disabled. The following subroutines are used to manage the controls.

▶ *DoClick.* Used to process dialog click events. Executes the appropriate button function or action depending on the button the user clicks.

```
Function DoClick(id$)
    ret = 0' (assume dialog will continue)
    Select Case id$
        Case "buttonNext"
            Next_Click
        Case "buttonFinish"
            Finish_Click
            ret = 1' Close dialog
        Case "buttonCancel"
            ret = 1' Close dialog
        Case "buttonBack"
            Back_Click
    End Select
    DoClick = ret
End Function' DoClick
```

▶ *Back_Click.* The click event for the Back button. This subroutine hides the current panel and shows the previous panel.

```
Sub Back_Click
    If CurPanel > 1 Then
        NewPanel = CurPanel - 1
        ChangePanel(CurPanel, NewPanel)
    EndIf
End Sub' Back_Click
```

▶ *Next_Click.* The click event for the Next button. This subroutine hides the current panel and shows the next panel.

```
Sub Next_Click
    If CurPanel < 3 Then
        NewPanel = CurPanel + 1
        ChangePanel(CurPanel, NewPanel)
    EndIf
End Sub' Next_Click
```

▶ *Finish_Click.* The click event for the Finish button. This subroutine inserts information input by the user into the document at specific bookmark locations.

```
Sub Finish_Click
    EditGoTo .Destination = "MarkRecipient"
    Insert DlgText$("textRecipient")
    EditGoTo .Destination = "MarkCompany"
    Insert DlgText$("textCompany")
    EditGoTo .Destination = "MarkFaxNo"
    Insert DlgText$("textFaxNo")
    EditGoTo .Destination = "MarkPageCount"
    Insert DlgText$("textPageCount")
    EditGoTo .Destination = "MarkRegarding"
    Insert DlgText$("textRegarding")
    EditGoTo .Destination = "MarkNewText"
End Sub' Finish_Click
```

▶ *ShowHideControls.* Shows or hides the controls for a specific panel.

```
Sub ShowHideControls(panel, show)
    Select Case panel
        Case 1' Panel 1 controls
            DlgVisible "labelRecipient", show
            DlgVisible "textRecipient", show
            DlgVisible "labelCompany", show
            DlgVisible "textCompany", show
            DlgVisible "labelFaxNo", show
            DlgVisible "textFaxNo", show
        Case 2   ' Panel 2 controls
            DlgVisible "labelPageCount", show
            DlgVisible "textPageCount", show
        Case 3   ' Panel 3 controls
            DlgVisible "labelRegarding1", show
            DlgVisible "labelRegarding2", show
            DlgVisible "textRegarding", show
    End Select
End Sub' ShowHideControls
```

▶ *ChangePanel.* Manages the transition of one panel to another. Calls ShowHideControls to hide the current panel; and calls it again to display the new panel. EnableControls is called to enable the buttons for the new panel.

```
Sub ChangePanel(old, new)
    ShowHideControls(old, 0)
    ShowHideControls(new, 1)
    CurPanel = new
    EnableControls
End Sub' ChangePanel
```

▶ *EnableControls.* Enables and disables common wizard controls depending on the current panel. This routine also determines which wizard control has initial focus. For example, when the first panel is displayed, the Next button is enabled and the Back button is disabled.

```
Sub EnableControls
    Select Case CurPanel
        Case 1    ' Panel 1
            DlgFocus "textRecipient"
            DlgEnable "buttonNext", 1     ' Enable Next
            DlgEnable "buttonBack", 0     ' Disable Back
        Case 2    ' Panel 2
            DlgFocus "textPageCount"
            DlgEnable "buttonBack", 1     ' Enable Back
            DlgEnable "buttonNext", 1     ' Enable Next
        Case 3    ' Panel 3
            DlgFocus "textRegarding"
            DlgEnable "buttonBack", 1     ' Enable Back
            DlgEnable "buttonNext", 0     ' Disable Next
    End Select
End Sub EnableControls
```

The fax form is stored in the template with bookmarks at each location that requires user input. In the Finish_Click subroutine, EditGoTo statements are used to position the cursor at the bookmarks in the fax form. The Insert statements in the subroutine insert the user's text from the dialog box into the appropriate places on the fax form.

The actual work of the wizard is done by the dialog control function (DlgControl). All of the user's actions are passed to this routine for processing. This function uses a Case statement to determine the appropriate response to the user's actions. The dialog control function can process many different types of dialog actions, but this wizard only processes the initialize (Case 1) and click (Case 2) events.

```
Function DlgControl(id$, iaction, wvalue)
    fRet = 1
    Select Case iaction
        Case 1 'Init
            CurPanel = 1
            ShowHideControls(2, 0)      ' hide panel 2
            ShowHideControls(3, 0)      ' hide panel 3
            EnableControls        ' enable/disable buttons
        Case 2 'Click
            result = DoClick(id$)
            If result = 1 Then
                ' User pressed "Finish" or "Cancel"
                fRet = 0
            EndIf
        Case Else
            'do nothing
    End Select
    DlgControl = fRet
End Function' DlgControl
```

9

For more information, refer to the Word Basic help topic called Dialog Function Syntax. This help topic lists all the possible actions you can process with the dialog function.

Summary

Styles and templates are fundamental to working efficiently in Word. Mastering these two tools is the first step in taking you from Word amateur to Word expert. In this chapter, you learned how Word constructs a document and how styles and templates fit into the great scheme of Word things.

Knowing how to create your own styles and how to use style controls, such as Based On and Style for Following, can help you automate some of the mundane aspects of document construction. Understanding what is and is not stored in your templates can help you keep formatting consistent across all the documents you create. Armed with this insight, you'll spend less time fiddling with formatting settings and more time getting your work done.

chapter 10

Customizing the Workspace

10

by Susan Daffron

In this chapter

◆ **Modifying toolbars**
Learn how to add, delete, and change buttons and toolbars to reflect the way you work.

◆ **Changing menus**
By changing menu commands and adding new menus, you can create your own Word interface.

◆ **Adding keyboard shortcuts**
Set up keyboard shortcuts for frequently accessed tasks to accelerate document production.

◆ **Changing Word commands**
By creating a macro with the same name as a built-in Word command, you can change the function of any Word command.

◆ **Using Word on a network**
Share global templates on a network to maintain a corporate identity with standardized fonts and layouts.

I f you're like most people, when you use Word, you stare at the same screen Microsoft gave you day after day. But, it doesn't have to be that way. You can change most elements of the Word screen to reflect the way you use Word. If you have ever wanted to design your own software interface, this is your big chance. Word's menus, toolbars, and commands are all subject to change. And, if you make a complete mess of the process, you can put everything back the way it was. So, very little risk is involved.

Changing View Options

Before you go wild changing interface functions, check out some of the options you can change in the Tools, Options, View tab (see fig. 10.1). For example, if you are short on screen space, you can tell Word not to show the status bar or the horizontal and vertical scroll bars. You will need to learn the keyboard navigation commands, but on a laptop screen or a 14-inch monitor, that extra few millimeters of screen real estate can be crucial.

Fig. 10.1

Changing the options in the View tab under Tools, Options can make Word easier to use.

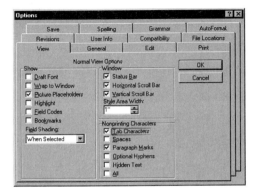

Conversely, if you have a big monitor and you work extensively with styles in Normal view, you may want to change the Style Area Width. The default setting is 0, but if you increase the width to about one inch, you can see your style names displayed in the left margin.

Exploring Other Options

Changing other options under the View tab can make your Word environment easier to use. For example, applying styles is much easier if you display the paragraph markers. Knowing where your styles begin and end is essential to working in Word. If you work with tables, you may want to display other nonprinting characters, such as spaces and tabs. You may soon discover, however, that when you display the space character, proofreading text on-screen is difficult and annoying. Generally, you want to leave the spaces turned off.

When you are working with fields, it helps to turn on hidden text and field codes to see what's going on. In addition, if you need to search and replace a term that appears in a book, for example, you can turn on hidden text so that the search can find the index entries.

If you are working with imported graphics, you probably want to turn on Picture Placeholders to reduce the amount of time Word spends redrawing the screen. When you select Picture Placeholders, Word hides the imported graphics and replaces them with an empty box. You can still see how large your graphic is, but if you have a sluggish computer, you no longer need to witness the painfully slow bitmap redraw process.

 Note

Turning field codes or hidden text on and off repaginates the document. If you have field codes or hidden text turned on, your document length does not reflect the actual length of the document when it's printed.

Using Word Command-Line Switches

Before you even begin running Word, you can tell it what to do. You can use *command-line startup switches* to control what happens as Word starts up.

Using switches in Windows 95 works a little differently than it did under Windows 3.1. In Windows 95, you add a switch to the target line in the shortcut to Microsoft Word. Using Explorer, you can modify the shortcut properties to include command-line switches.

To get to the target line, follow these steps:

1. Using Explorer, create a shortcut for Word, and drag the new shortcut icon to your desktop. Right-click the Word shortcut icon and choose Properties.

2. Click the shortcut tab. You see the path to Microsoft Word in the Target line. Depending on where you installed Office, this path is often C:\MSOFFICE\WINWORD\WINWORD.EXE.

3. Edit this line to add a space and any switches after WINWORD.EXE (see fig. 10.2). You can add more than one startup switch by separating the switches with a space.

If you need to set up Word to run different ways at different times, you can set up several different shortcuts on your desktop to take advantage of the different switches:

▶ */a*: Prevents Word from automatically loading add-ins and global templates. Global templates include any templates you have placed in the Startup folder and NORMAL.DOT. This switch also prevents the Registry from being read and modified.

▶ */n*: Prevents Word from starting with a new blank document (Document 1).

10

▶ */mMacroName*: Starts Word and runs the macro you specify. This switch also prevents the AutoExec macro from running. If you just want to prevent the AutoExec macro from running, use the */m* switch without passing it a macro name. You also can use the */m* switch to access Word's built-in commands. A handy target line is C:\ MSOFFICE\WINWORD\WINWORD.EXE /mFile1, which tells Word to open the first file on the recently used file list using the built-in File1 command.

▶ */lAddInPath*: Starts Word and loads the Word add-in you specify.

▶ */t TemplateName*: Starts Word and creates a new file based on the specified template.

Fig. 10.2

Adding switches to the Target line in the Word shortcut enables you to change the way Word starts up.

By passing a file name on the Target line, you can start Word and open a specific file. For example, to open a file called FRED.DOC that is located in the DOCS folder, you type C:\MSOFFICE\WINWORD\WINWORD.EXE C:\DOCS\FRED.DOC on the target line.

Working with Toolbars

Word comes with toolbars other than the Standard and Formatting toolbars you normally see. Depending on the type of work you are doing, you may want to display other toolbars, such as the Borders or Drawing toolbars. To see all your toolbar options, choose View, Toolbars, or point to a toolbar and click the right mouse button. Select the toolbars you want to try from the list (see fig. 10.3). You can display as many toolbars as you and your monitor can stand to fit on-screen.

Fig. 10.3

You can try Word's
toolbars by choosing
View, Toolbars.

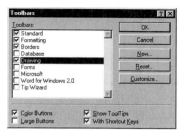

 Tip

Under View, Toolbars, choose Show ToolTips to see the commands associated with the toolbar buttons. You also can choose With Shortcut Keys to show shortcut keys for each button, which can help you learn Word's keyboard command shortcuts.

Toolbars are saved in the document template, so you can create toolbars geared to the activities you generally perform when you use a certain template. For example, if you use the INVOICE.DOT template to create your company invoices, you can include buttons for calculation, borders and shading, and table functions. You may not use these buttons very often on a day-to-day basis, but when you create invoices with this template, having these functions available on the toolbar can save time.

Creating New Toolbars

Changing the toolbars is the next step in tailoring your Word environment. You can create new toolbars and add and rearrange the buttons and toolbars to your heart's content. If you want to isolate the functions you use most frequently in a specific template, create a new toolbar and store it in that template. You also may want to make changes to the Standard or Formatting toolbars that appear every time you use Word. Be sure to store those toolbar changes globally by selecting NORMAL.DOT when you save the toolbar.

To create a new toolbar, follow these steps:

1. Open a document that uses the desired template. If the document is protected, you must unprotect the document (Tools, Unprotect Document) before you can add a toolbar.

2. Choose View, Toolbars.

3. Choose the <u>N</u>ew button. (If you have not unprotected the document, the New button is grayed-out.) The New Toolbar dialog box appears (see fig. 10.4).

4. Type a name for the new toolbar in the <u>T</u>oolbar Name box.

Fig. 10.4

Type the name of your new toolbar and select the template to which you want to attach it.

5. Select a template from the <u>M</u>ake Toolbar Available To drop-down box. If you select All documents (NORMAL.DOT), your new toolbar appears every time you create a new blank document. If you want to isolate the toolbar to a specific template, select the template name from the list.

6. Click OK. The Customize dialog box appears along with a tiny new toolbar (see fig. 10.5). The toolbar is a floating toolbar at this point. If you want to fix the toolbar in place amidst the other toolbars, drag it up to the top of the screen, and it snaps into place. Toolbars also snap to the sides or bottom of the screen.

⚛ **Tip**

If you want to permanently change any of Word's standard toolbars, save the changes into the NORMAL.DOT template.

Fig. 10.5

After your new tiny toolbar appears, you can move it into place anywhere on-screen.

New toolbar ——

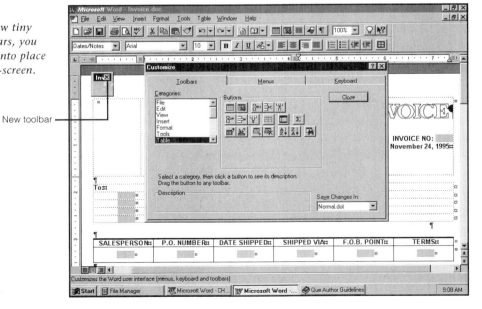

After you have created your new toolbar, you can move it around by clicking between the toolbar buttons and dragging the toolbar to the new location. You can return the toolbar to its original position by double-clicking its title bar.

Adding Buttons to Toolbars

You can add buttons to your new toolbars or to Word's standard toolbars. You use buttons to access commands, run macros, apply styles, insert AutoText entries, and change fonts. (See Chapter 7, "Critical Skills in Word," for more information about AutoText.) If you are tired of going through three levels of menus to get to your favorite Word functions, adding a button to the toolbar places that function just a mouse click away.

To add buttons to a toolbar, follow these steps:

1. Display the toolbar to which you want to add a button. If the toolbar is not displayed, choose View, Toolbars and place a check mark next to the name of toolbar.

2. Choose Tools, Customize, and then choose the Toolbars tab. Or place the mouse over a toolbar and click the right mouse button. Or click Customize on the shortcut menu.

3. In the Save Changes In box, select the template in which you want to store the toolbar changes. If you want to associate the toolbar with a certain template, make sure that you select the name of that template—do not select NORMAL.DOT.

4. In the Categories list, select a category. The buttons for the category appear in the box on the right. When you click a button, a description of its function appears in the Description box below. If you select the All Commands, Macros, Fonts, AutoText, or Styles categories, you see a list of commands rather than buttons because these categories do not have built-in buttons. (See the next section, "Creating New Buttons," for more information on creating buttons.)

5. Drag the button to the toolbar you want to modify. If you change your mind, you can drag the buttons back off the toolbar to remove them. You can rearrange the buttons by dragging them into a new position. Keep adding, removing, and rearranging the buttons until you are happy with your toolbar (see fig. 10.6). Be careful when dragging and dropping buttons—if you drag one button on top of an existing button, Word thinks you are replacing the button, which may or may not be what you intend to do.

6. When you finish, click the Close button in the Customize dialog box. Your changes are saved permanently when you save the template.

10

Fig. 10.6

This example shows dragging buttons to the new Invoice toolbar.

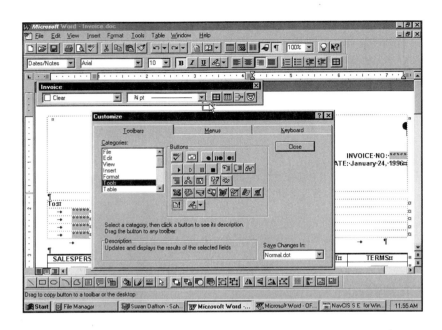

※ **Tip**

Certain toolbars, such as the Outline and Header and Footer toolbars, appear only when you change to a certain view. You can change these toolbars the same way you change any other toolbar. For example, to change the Header and Footer toolbar, choose View, Header and Footer. Right-click the toolbar and select Customize. Drag-and-drop buttons onto the toolbar just as you do for other toolbars. If you frequently change the fonts or styles in your headers or footers, having these buttons on the toolbar can be convenient.

Creating New Buttons

When you modify toolbars, you may discover that Word doesn't provide buttons for all its functions. If you select All Commands, Macros, Fonts, AutoText, or Styles from the Categories list, all you see is a list of command names. For those of you who find the pictures on buttons cryptic at best, take this chance to be creative and make your own buttons. Follow these steps:

1. Drag a font, style, or command name from the Customize dialog box to your toolbar. The Custom Button dialog box opens, and a blank button appears on the toolbar.

2. You have three choices. The Text Button is highlighted by default, and you see Word's proposed button name highlighted in the Text Button Name box, ready for you to edit (see fig. 10.7). Your first two choices are to type the text for the face of the button or select an image from the group.

3. If none of the images are appealing, or you want more than just text on your button, you can go to your third choice: choose the Edit button to access the Button Editor. (See the following section for information on using the Button Editor to create your own button images.)

4. After you have created or chosen a button, choose Assign. The button image is added to the blank button on the toolbar.

Fig. 10.7

To add a text button, change the highlighted text in the Text Button Name box.

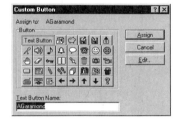

Editing Button Images

Word's Button Editor enables you to create or modify toolbar button images. Note that you have no way to save buttons except by placing them on a toolbar.

 Note

If you have an artistic bent and create many of your own button images, you should store them on a separate toolbar. That way you can copy your favorite buttons to new toolbars when you want them.

10

To use the Button Editor, follow these steps:

1. Choose Tools, Customize and drag a button or command to the toolbar.

2. If the button doesn't have an image and you want to start with a blank button, choose Edit. Or you can modify one of the standard images in the button box. Click the image first and then choose Edit. Any time the Customize dialog box is open, you can right-click any toolbar button you want to edit and select Edit Button Image from the shortcut menu. Any of these methods brings up the Button Editor (see fig. 10.8).

3. In the Button Editor, draw or edit the image in the image box. You may use these options:

   ▶ To add a color, select it in the Colors box and click or drag in the image to apply the color.

   ▶ To erase color, click the color labeled Erase.

   ▶ You can move the entire picture around in the square by clicking the move arrows.

   ▶ Click the Clear button to erase the image in the image box.

4. Click OK to exit the Button Editor and place your new image on the button.

5. Click Close to exit the Customize dialog box.

Fig. 10.8
You can create your own buttons in the Button Editor.

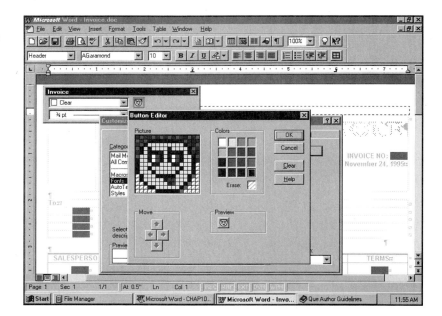

 Tip
You can paste bitmap images from the Clipboard onto a button and then edit the image in the Button Editor. With the Customize dialog box open, right-click a button and select Paste Button Image. Bear in mind that buttons are small, so you need to find tiny clip art for this process to work.

If you think that an image is not right for a particular button, you can copy the image to another button. The only limitation is that the other button must also be on a toolbar. With the Customize menu showing, follow these steps:

1. Place your mouse over the toolbar button that has the image you want to copy.

2. Click the right mouse button and select Copy Button Image from the shortcut menu.

3. Place your mouse over the button you want to receive the image.

4. Click the right mouse button and select Paste Button Image from the shortcut menu.

If you start moving these button images around, however, anyone else who uses your system may be completely confused. If this situation becomes universally unpopular, you can always restore the built-in buttons to their original images. With the Customize menu showing, place your mouse over the button you want to restore and click the right mouse button. Select Reset Button Image from the shortcut menu.

Modifying and Rearranging Toolbars

After you have added buttons to toolbars, you can modify the toolbars in a number of ways. For example, you can resize the drop-down boxes, such as the font or style names on the toolbars. With the Customize dialog box open, click a drop-down box on the toolbar to select it. When the cursor changes to a bar, you can drag the edges to size the box.

You also can modify toolbars without opening the Customize dialog box. While holding down the Alt key, you can drag toolbar buttons to a new position on a toolbar, to a different toolbar, or off the toolbar completely. If you want to copy rather than move the buttons, hold down the Alt and Ctrl keys and drag the button.

You can move toolbars between templates or rename toolbars using the Organizer:

1. Choose File, Templates.

2. Choose Organizer, and then choose the Toolbars tab (see fig. 10.9).

3. Select a toolbar from the Toolbars Available In drop-down box.

4. Choose Rename and type the new name. Or choose Copy to copy the toolbar to the template displayed on the right.

Fig. 10.9

You can use the Organizer to move toolbars between templates.

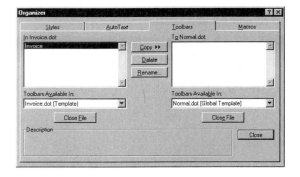

Removing Toolbars

You can remove toolbars in a number of ways. You can hide a toolbar by choosing View, Toolbars and deselecting the toolbar in the list.

If you have customized Word's toolbars to the point that everyone else is mystified by your system, you can reset the Word toolbars to the default settings. Choose View, Toolbars and select the toolbar from the list. Click the Reset button.

After you have created a custom toolbar, it appears in the list of toolbars when you choose View, Toolbars. You can always deselect your new toolbar from the list to hide it. If you are sure you never want to see this toolbar again and are positive you want to delete the toolbar, choose Delete.

> **Caution**
> Unlike Word's toolbars, you cannot reset your custom toolbars. If you delete a custom toolbar, it's really gone, and you need to start over.

Using Handy Toolbar Buttons

When you start modifying toolbars, it's wise to think about all the mundane tasks you perform when you create a document. Word's Standard toolbar has many functions you may never use taking up valuable toolbar space. If you cannot remember what the button does, you probably can remove it. As part of my own efficiency effort, I put the following tasks on my Standard toolbar:

▶ My favorite views: Normal, Page Layout, and Header and Footer

▶ The InsertPicture command

▶ The CreateEnvelope command, which was on the Word 2 toolbar (I missed it)

> ▶ The ToolsOptionsView command. I found that I was spending a lot of time in that dialog box turning hidden text, field codes, and nonprinting characters on and off.
>
> ▶ The FormatStyle command
>
> ▶ The Find and Replace commands, which I use constantly
>
> ▶ The Thesaurus, which I put next to the Spell Check button

To make room for my new buttons on the Standard toolbar, I removed the buttons that enable you to insert information from other applications. I am not much of a spreadsheet user, so I have to mentally prepare myself to go into Excel in the first place. Because I rarely add Excel spreadsheets to my Word documents, having that button on my toolbar was a waste of space. I also didn't want the ToolTip icon on my toolbar, so I dragged it off, too.

If you have trouble remembering what all those little button pictures mean, grouping your buttons together by function may help. For example, I put the Thesaurus button next to the Spell Check button. If you hold down the Alt key, you can drag and push your buttons around on the toolbar, so you can arrange them in a way that makes sense to you.

If the button images puzzle you, you can switch all your buttons to text buttons that show the command names. This approach is not very space-efficient, but anything that helps you work more easily is worth a try.

Changing the Menus

The menus in Word are just as flexible as the toolbars. You can add and delete commands from the menus and even create your own menus. Like the toolbars, you can add any command, AutoText entry, font, or style to any Word menu. You also can add separator lines so your menus are easier to read. Just as Word has a separator between the Close and Save options on the File menu, you can group your commands with a spiffy 3-D separator line.

10

Adding Commands

Adding commands to the menus is similar to customizing the toolbars. If you want the menus to be arranged a certain way for a specific template, make sure that you store the changes in the specific template and not NORMAL.DOT. You may want to add some extra commands to your menus or remove certain commands that you never use. For example, I added the ToolsRepaginate command to my Tools menu. As the name suggests, this command repaginates a document. It is useful if you work in Normal view and don't like to have background repagination turned on. This command was available on the Tools menu in version 2 of Word, but was removed in version 6 and remains gone in Word for Windows 95. I put it back.

To add a menu command, follow these steps:

1. Open a document that uses the desired template. If the document is protected, you must unprotect the document (Tools, Unprotect Document) before you can add any commands to the menus.

2. Choose Tools, Customize, and then choose the Menus tab. The commands are categorized the same way they are in the Toolbars tab (see fig. 10.10). Note that if you have not unprotected the document, the Customize button is grayed-out.

Fig. 10.10

You can add menu commands using the Menus tab in the Customize dialog box.

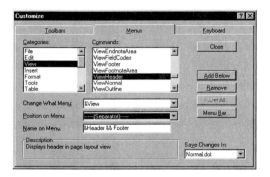

3. Use the Save Changes In drop-down box to select the template that will contain the new menu settings. Select NORMAL.DOT if you want the settings to be global.

4. Select a Category from the Categories list on the left. The list of available commands appears.

5. Select the item you want to add from the list of commands. You can select from AutoText entries, macros, fonts, styles, or commands.

6. Use the Change What Menu drop-down list to select the menu you want to contain the new command.

7. Use the Position on Menu drop-down list to select the position on the menu:

   ▶ *Auto.* Word decides where to place the command based on how the other commands are grouped in the menu.

   ▶ *At Top.* The new command is placed at the top of the menu.

   ▶ *At Bottom.* The new command is placed at the bottom of the menu.

   ▶ *Command Name.* The new command is placed below the command you select.

8. Type a command name or use Word's default command name. If you want your new command to have an Alt key shortcut, place an ampersand (&) in front of the character you want to use as the shortcut key. If you really want an ampersand in the command name, you must type two ampersands in a row (&&) to indicate to Word that you want an ampersand, not an underlined character. For example, if you want a menu name to appear Header & Footer, type &Header && Footer.

9. If you have specified that the menu be positioned automatically, the Add button is available. If you have specified a certain location in the menu, the Add Below button is available. The button name depends on the placement you specified for the new command in the Position On Menu box. In either case, when you click Add or Add Below, the new menu item is added to the menu.

10. Repeat these steps until you have added all the commands you want.

11. When you are done adding commands, click the Close button.

Adding New Menus

If you are used to the arrangement of Word's menus, you may find that adding a new menu is easier than changing the existing ones. If you have added many of your own commands to the menus, it may be easier to group them all in one menu. Similarly, you may want to create a menu for specific types of tasks. If you work with numerous AutoText entries, for example, you could create a new menu for them.

To add a new menu, follow these steps:

1. Open a document that uses the desired template. If the document is protected, you must unprotect the document (Tools, Unprotect Document) before you can add a new menu.

2. Choose Tools, Customize and choose the Menus tab.

3. Use the Save Changes In drop-down box to select the template that will contain the new menu. Select NORMAL.DOT if you want the settings to be global.

4. Choose Menu Bar.

5. Type a name for your new menu in the Name On Menu Bar box. Place an ampersand (&) in front of the letter you want to underline as a shortcut key.

6. Use the Position on Menu Bar drop-down list to select the new menu's position on the menu bar (see fig 10.11):

  ▶ *First.* The new menu is placed on the left side of the menu bar.

  ▶ *Last.* The new menu is placed on the right side of the menu bar.

  ▶ *Command Name.* The new menu is placed to the right of the selected menu.

10

7. Choose <u>A</u>dd or <u>A</u>dd After. The button name depends on the placement you specify for the new menu in the <u>P</u>osition On Menu Bar box. If you have specified that the menu be positioned First or Last, the <u>A</u>dd button is available. If you have specified a certain location, the <u>A</u>dd After button is available.

8. Click Close. The new menu appears on the menu bar. You can add commands to your new menu as described in the preceding section, "Adding Commands."

Fig. 10.11

Use the Menu Bar dialog box to add or remove menus.

You also can use the Menu Bar dialog box to remove or rename a menu. From this dialog box, select the menu from the list. Choose the <u>R</u>ename button and type your new name. Or choose the <u>R</u>emove button to delete a menu. Before you delete any of the standard Word menus, however, you may want to ponder the ramifications of that decision.

 Note

If you decide that changing the menus was a big mistake, you can always restore the Word menus to their original settings. Follow these steps:

1. Choose <u>T</u>ools, <u>C</u>ustomize and choose the <u>M</u>enus tab.

2. Use the Sa<u>v</u>e Changes In drop-down box to select the template you changed.

3. Click the Reset All button. The old familiar Word menus return. Note that this command deletes any custom menus you have created.

Assigning Keyboard Shortcuts

The standard NORMAL.DOT template contains shortcut keys for almost all Word commands. You also can assign shortcut keys for the macros and AutoText functions that you create. If you find that you work more quickly when you use keyboard shortcuts, you should assign them to your favorite tasks. If you can never remember that you use Alt+Shift+K to preview a mail merge, you also can simplify some of Word's more convoluted shortcuts to ones that are more meaningful to you.

Another reason to change Word's keyboard shortcuts is if you just started using Word after using an antique command-based word processor. You can ease the adjustment into Word by remapping Word's keyboard shortcuts to the keystrokes you're used to. To assign shortcuts, follow these steps:

1. Open a document that uses the desired template. If the document is protected, you must unprotect the document (Tools, Unprotect Document) before you can assign shortcuts.

2. Choose Tools, Customize and choose the Keyboard tab (see fig. 10.12).

3. Use the Save Changes In drop-down box to select the template that will contain the new shortcut. Select NORMAL.DOT if you want the settings to be global.

4. Select a Category from the Categories list on the left. The list of available commands appears on the right. You can select from AutoText entries, macros, fonts, styles, or commands.

5. Look in the Current Keys area to see if a keyboard shortcut is already defined for the command. Press your new keyboard combination. You need to use a letter in conjunction with one or more of the Alt, Shift, and Ctrl keys. If the shortcut combination you press is already assigned to another function, a message appears.

6. Click the Assign button. Repeat these steps until you have finished assigning shortcuts. When you are done, click Close.

Fig. 10.12

Use the Keyboard tab in the Customize dialog box to assign keyboard shortcuts to frequently used functions.

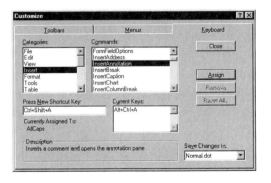

As with toolbars and menus, all this customization power comes at a price. You have the power to render your extremely personalized copy of Word unusable to anyone else. For example, remapping the Cut command to something other than Ctrl+X may be good for you, but others may be less pleased with your creativity.

In any case, a time may come when you question the wisdom of all this keyboard remapping. So, as with the other customization options, you can return to the Word default settings. To remove a single shortcut, in the Keyboard tab, highlight the command and click Remove. If you want to reset all the keyboard combinations, click the Reset All button.

Tip

If you cannot remember what a keyboard shortcut or toolbar button does, press Ctrl+Alt+plus (+) on the numeric keypad. The cursor changes to a four-leaf clover icon (which looks suspiciously like the "Apple" key on a Macintosh). Type your keyboard shortcut or click one of your toolbar buttons. The Customize dialog box appears and displays the command associated with the button or shortcut.

You can print a complete list of your keyboard assignments for reference. Choose File, Print and select Keyboard Assignments from the Print What drop-down list box.

Customizing Built-In Commands

To further customize your Word environment, you need to delve into the world of macros. This section discusses how you can create macros to change the workings of Word, but it does not describe how to create macros in detail. For that information, you should read Chapter 8, "Word Macros," which discusses the ins and outs of creating macros. If you are new to creating macros, refer to that chapter before you attempt any of the macro adventures described here.

Word's flexibility extends to the actual behavior of the program itself. For example, if you don't like how Word opens files, you can write a macro that changes the FileNew command. If you write a macro with the same name as a built-in Word command, Word uses your version of the command rather than its own built-in command.

You can see a list of the built-in Word commands by choosing Tools, Macro and changing the Macros Available In drop-down box to Word Commands (see fig. 10.13). This list displays the more than 500 Word commands. Many of the commands correspond to the commands you see on the menus (such as FileOpen). Other commands such as SaveAll cannot normally be accessed unless you add them to menus or toolbars, or unless you use them in macros.

Although the ability to change the inner workings of Word is incredibly powerful, it also has great potential for disaster. You can make a huge mess. So remember, if you do something dreadful, go to Tools, Macro, select the appropriate template from the drop-down list, and just delete your new macro. Word returns to using its built-in command.

Fig. 10.13

You can get a window on Word's command list by switching the Macros Available In drop-down box to Word Commands.

Changing the FileOpen Command

An extremely popular change to the Word interface is to modify the FileOpen command so that Word shows you all the files in a folder (*.* in DOS parlance) rather than just the files that end in .DOC (see fig. 10.14). While you're at it, if you don't want Word to search in the My Documents folder, you can have Word change to your favorite document folder.

Fig. 10.14

Using the macro editor, you can edit Word's built-in FileOpen command.

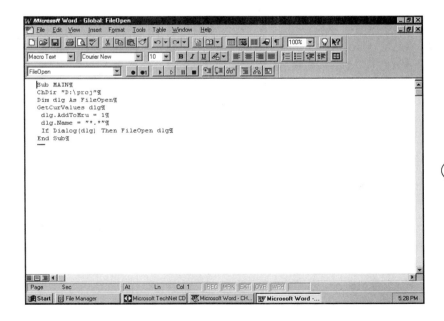

10

To create this macro, follow these steps:

1. Choose Tools, Macro.

2. Type **FileOpen** in the Macro Name box and choose the Create button.

3. The text of the current FileOpen macro displays in the window. Change the text so it looks like the following listing:

```
Sub MAIN
    ChDir "d:\proj" 'changes to your favorite document folder
    Dim dlg As FileOpen 'defines the dialog as the FileOpen dialog
    GetCurValues dlg
    dlg.AddToMru = 1
    dlg.Name = "*.*"
    If Dialog(dlg) Then FileOpen dlg
End Sub
```

4. Click Close and click Yes when you are prompted to save the macro.

If you decide to replace the built-in FileOpen command with this macro, notice that the recently used file list doesn't update unless you save a file after you open it. However, that price is small for the ability to see *all* your files.

 Tip

You may forget Word's cryptic command names by the time you get into the Macro dialog box. Instead of typing the command name directly into the Macro Name box, you can switch the Macros Available In drop-down box to Word Commands, choose a command, and then switch the Macros Available In box back to your desired template. The command name you selected appears in the Macro Name text box.

Using Automatic Commands

Certain Word commands can be run automatically. If you create a macro with a special name, you can run it automatically when you start Word or open a document. These five command names are reserved for Word's automatic macros:

▶ *AutoExec*: Runs when you start Word. You can prevent AutoExec from running by using the /m command-line switch when you start Word.

▶ *AutoNew*: Runs after you create a new document based on a current template.

▶ *AutoOpen*: Runs each time you open an existing document using the File, Open command, the find function, or the recently used file list.

▶ *AutoClose*: Runs each time you close a document.

▶ *AutoExit*: Runs when you quit Word.

Like other Word macros, you can save the AutoNew, AutoOpen, and AutoClose automatic macros with a specific template. Or you can define these macros globally by saving them into NORMAL.DOT or into a global template that you placed in the Startup folder. The AutoExec macro, however, doesn't run automatically unless you store it in NORMAL.DOT.

For example, if you often forget to spell check your documents, you can write an AutoClose macro to run spell check before you close them:

```
Sub MAIN
    ToolsSpelling
End Sub
```

Of course, a macro like this one can be potentially annoying if you don't want to spell check every document. If you want to get fancy, you can add dialog boxes that ask you whether you want to perform the tasks in the automatic macro. The following listing shows a slightly more complicated example of an AutoNew macro that presents a dialog box asking if you want to insert the date at the top of the page (see fig. 10.15). If you choose the Yes button, the macro inserts a date field.

```
Sub MAIN
    answer = MsgBox("Do you want to add the date?", 36)
    If answer = - 1 Then
        InsertDateField
    End If
End Sub
```

Fig. 10.15

*An automatic macro
can present a dialog
box that checks with
the user before
performing a task.*

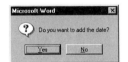

If you change zoom views and other options for different types of documents, you may want to reset those options to the original settings when you exit Word. The AutoExit macro shown here sets your display so when you return to Word, all your favorite settings are restored, no matter what you were doing when you left. The following example switches the display to Page Layout view, zooms to 100 percent, and shows the tab and paragraph markers. You can edit the macro to specify your own settings.

```
Sub MAIN
    If Not ViewPage() Then ViewPage
    ViewZoom .ZoomPercent = 100
    ToolsOptionsView .Tabs = 1, .Paras = 1
End Sub
```

If you occasionally don't want to use the auto macros, holding down the Shift key prevents the auto macros from running. For example, when you open a Word document that uses a template with an AutoOpen macro, hold down the Shift key until the

10

document appears on-screen. Make sure you are holding down the Shift key while you select the file from the file list.

Adding a Custom Interface

After you realize how easy it is to customize your own Word environment, you may want to spread the Word around (so to speak). Because you can attach toolbars, macros, and AutoText entries to a template, you can force anyone who uses your template to look at Word the same way you do.

Every company has necessary tasks that are unique to the company. If you often need to explain certain Word features to people, maybe you can make things a little easier for them by creating a custom interface. Combining AutoText entries and macros with Word's customization features can speed up repetitive tasks immensely.

Adding Features

Certain commands generally are not available in Word, or they are buried four levels deep in a menu somewhere. Of course, these features may be just the ones you need to use on a daily basis.

If your company has standard templates, you can add a menu or toolbar that lists your company's standard AutoText entries (see fig. 10.16). In a technical documentation department, for example, these AutoText entries may include text and graphics for Cautions, Warnings, and Tips.

Fig. 10.16
Adding AutoText entries to a menu or toolbar makes them easier to use.

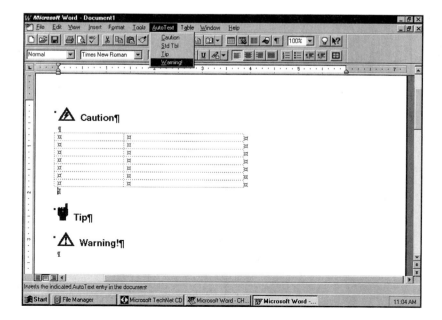

Automating Common Tasks

Learning all the functions of a large word processing program like Word can be time-consuming, and many companies don't allow much training time for people to get up to speed. The result is that new users often have to produce many documents before they really know how to use the program. If you work with people who are just getting started with Word, you can add a new menu to their NORMAL.DOT template with macros for creating simple letters, memos, fax cover sheets, expense reports, or other standard documents that users need to produce on a daily basis. After these people learn more about using Word and loading different templates, you can provide more sophisticated templates for these functions later on.

For example, the following letter macro adds a logo and date, and provides dialog boxes to add address and salutation information. Any novice user can run this macro and begin typing the body of the letter almost instantly (see fig. 10.17).

```
Sub MAIN
ChDefaultDir "D:\logexp\logos\", 1 'changes to the logo directory
REM This logo directory depends on the location of the graphic file on disk.
InsertPicture .Name = "RET-ADDR.TIF", .LinkToFile = "0" 'inserts the logo
REM The logo filename depends on the name of the graphic file on disk.
CharLeft 1, 1 'highlights the logo
FormatPicture .ScaleX = "86.5%", .ScaleY = "86.5%" 'scales the logo to the
➥correct size
CharRight
InsertPara
InsertPara
InsertPara
InsertField .Field = "DATE \@ " + Chr$(34) + "MMMM d, yyyy" + Chr$(34) 'inserts a
➥date field
CharLeft 1, 1 'highlights the field
UnlinkFields 'unlinks the field to keep it from updating later
CharRight
InsertPara
InsertPara
InsertPara
REM the following creates a dialog box where the user enters address information
Begin Dialog UserDialog 300, 224, "Address Information"'Address Info Dialog
    TextBox 90, 43, 160, 18, .Name
    Text 15, 70, 71, 13, "Address1", .Text2
    TextBox 90, 66, 160, 18, .Address1
    TextBox 90, 89, 160, 18, .Address2
    TextBox 90, 112, 160, 18, .City
    TextBox 90, 135, 160, 18, .State
    Text 13, 93, 71, 13, "Address2", .Text3
    Text 53, 116, 29, 13, "City", .Text4
    Text 42, 139, 41, 13, "State", .Text5
    Text 54, 162, 25, 13, "Zip", .Text6
    TextBox 90, 158, 160, 18, .Zip
    Text 40, 46, 44, 13, "Name", .Text1
    Text 9, 6, 204, 30, "Enter the Name and address of the recipient", .Text7
    OKButton 45, 191, 88, 21
    CancelButton 162, 191, 88, 21
End Dialog
```

10

```
Dim dlgAddress As UserDialog 'Defines the address dialog
On Error Goto UserClickedCancel 'Cancels the macro
Dialog dlgAddress 'displays the address dialog
On Error Goto 0
REM the following statements insert the dialog information into the document.
InsertPara
Insert dlgAddress.Name
InsertPara
Insert dlgAddress.Address1
If dlgAddress.Address2 <> "" Then
    InsertPara
    Insert dlgAddress.Address2
End If
InsertPara
Insert dlgAddress.City + ", " + dlgAddress.State + " " + dlgAddress.Zip
InsertPara
InsertPara
InsertPara
InsertPara
REM the following creates a dialog box where the user enters salutation
➥informationBegin Dialog UserDialog 404, 62, "Salutation"
    TextBox 106, 11, 263, 18, .Salutation
    Text 11, 15, 77, 13, "Salutation", .Text1
    OKButton 270, 36, 88, 21
End Dialog
Dim dlgSalut As UserDialog 'defines the salutation dialog
Dialog dlgSalut 'displays the salutation dialog
REM this statement insert the dialog information into the document.Insert
➥"Dear " + dlgSalut.Salutation + ":"
InsertPara
InsertPara
Insert "Sincerely,"
InsertPara
InsertPara
InsertPara
InsertPara
Insert "Susan C. Daffron"
UserClickedCancel:
End Sub
```

This example only scratches the surface of the things you can do to create (and share) a custom interface. After you realize that you can change or automate almost anything in Word, you'll find many ways to customize your environment so it works best for you.

Fig. 10.17

Adding menus can help new users get work done quickly while they are learning Word.

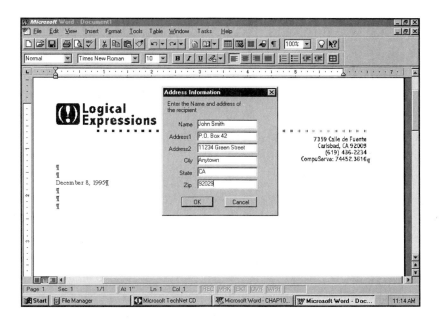

Sharing Templates on a Network

In a networked office, supporting multiple Word users is easier if they all are using the same templates. For organizational purposes, you may want to create corporate or workgroup templates and store them on a server. This approach helps maintain a corporate identity across departments with standardized fonts and layouts for common company documents.

When documents are based on shared templates, the styles and macros associated with the template remain available when the document is passed around to other users in the workgroup. You are less likely to have mysterious problems arise as documents are accidentally reformatted when two templates use the same style names but have different definitions associated with the styles.

10

Template Locations

To set up templates for network use, you need to place your company templates on a server or other universally accessible location. Then you must set up all the user workstations to point to the network drive and directory where the company templates are stored.

In the copy of Word loaded on each workstation, follow these steps to set the workgroup template location:

1. Choose Tools, Options and click the File Locations tab (see fig. 10.18).

2. Select Workgroup Templates from the list and choose the Modify button.

3. Select the drive and folder where your company templates are located. You select network locations the same way you do in Explorer. (This method may depend on the type of network you have installed.)

Fig. 10.18

You set the Workgroup Templates location in the File Locations tab.

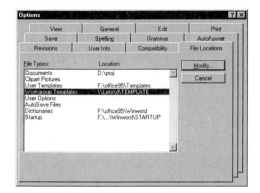

If you do not see your network drives listed, you may need to reconnect to the network drive. Click the Commands and Settings button in the Modify Locations dialog box and choose Map Network Drive. From the Drive drop-down box, select the network drive letter you want to use. The Workgroup templates appear along with the templates on the workstation every time the user creates a new file using File, New.

Network Tips

Set the templates on the server to read-only. Read-only templates cannot be changed, so you don't need to worry about anyone destroying your carefully crafted settings. Another thing to consider is that if the template has write access and a user opens a document based on that template, no one else can open a document based on that template until the first user closes the document. Users who try to access the template or documents based on the template get a `file in use` message. These error messages may cause users a great deal of frustration, which they may decide to take out on you.

If you store templates on a server and on workstations, you may want to give the templates on the server different names than the ones on the workstations. By establishing some kind of file naming convention, users can differentiate between templates loaded on their workstation and the company templates on the server. For example, the company templates in figure 10.19 all begin with LE_ to differentiate them from the templates stored on the workstation.

Fig. 10.19

Establishing a file naming convention makes it easier for users to distinguish company templates from their own.

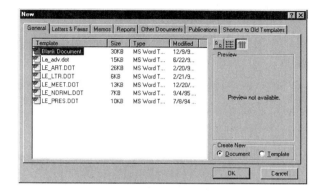

You also can set up a special template with company macros or AutoText entries and load it as a global template. Choose File, Templates and choose the Add button. You can select any template—including the templates you have set up on the server. These global templates close when you quit Word.

If you want a global template to be available always, you can put a copy of it in the user's Startup folder, which is located in the Winword folder. If you prefer, you can create a Startup folder on the server and change the location of the user's Startup folder in the File Locations tab to the network Startup folder location.

Changing Registry Options

You can change most Word options from within Word. However, some settings are buried deep within the Windows 95 Registry. Within the Registry, the Word settings reside under HKEY_CURRENT_USER\SOFTWARE\MICROSOFT\WORD\7.0. To access the Registry, select Run from the Start menu on the desktop. Type **REGEDIT** in the Open line and click OK. The Registry Editor appears.

Caution
Using the Registry Editor can be extremely dangerous. If you make a mistake, you may need to reinstall Windows 95. Always make a backup of the Registry before you do anything in REGEDIT.

Backing Up the Registry

You can back up the entire Registry by copying two hidden files, SYSTEM.DAT and USER.DAT, to a safe location. These files are located in the C:\WINDOWS folder. If you don't see these files in Explorer, you may need to change the setup in View, Options to Show All Files under the View tab. You also can use REGEDIT to export all or a portion of the Registry to a text file. If you change settings in other portions of the Registry frequently, you may want to back up just the Word portion of the Registry, so you don't overwrite changes in other parts of the Registry when you perform a restore operation.

To back up just the Word Data key in the Registry, for example, follow these steps:

1. Click the Start button and select Run. Type **REGEDIT** and click OK.

2. In the Registry Editor, select HKEY_CURRENT_USER\SOFTWARE\MICROSOFT\WORD\7.0\DATA.

3. Choose Registry, Export Registry File. Select the folder where you want to save the backup.

4. Make sure that Selected Branch is selected in the Export Range box.

5. Type a name for your backup file in the File Name box.

6. Choose the Save button. The file is saved with a REG extension.

After you have backed up the Registry, you can use REGEDIT to add, delete, and change values in the Registry. You right-click the value or key you want to change and select the action you want to perform from the list.

Using MACROS7.DOT

Word comes with a group of macros that are installed into the Macros folder located in the Winword folder. MACROS7.DOT, LAYOUT7.DOT, TABLES7.DOT, CONVERT7.DOT, and PRESENT7.DOT perform many useful functions. MACROS7.DOT includes a macro called RegOptions that enables you to edit the Word options in the Registry without resorting to REGEDIT.

To use RegOptions, you need to open the MACROS7.DOT template or copy the macro to one of your own templates. To copy the macro, open MACROS7.DOT and choose File, Templates, Organizer. In the Macros tab, copy the RegOptions macro by selecting it from the list on the left and choosing the Copy button to add it to the template on the right.

You can run the macro like any other macro:

1. Choose Tools, Macro and select RegOptions from the list.

2. Choose the Run button, and the Microsoft Word Registry Options dialog box appears (see fig. 10.20).

3. Select the option you want to change from the drop-down list.

4. Click the Change button and type the new entry in the Settings field. Note that some settings go into effect only after you restart Word.

Fig. 10.20

Changing Word's Registry options is easy using the RegOptions macro in MACROS7.DOT.

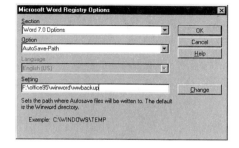

Checking for the Word Prank Macro

A new prank macro, unique to Word, has appeared on the scene lately. Although the prank macro does not harm your documents and is not really destructive, it is extremely annoying. The program replicates itself through Word. When a user opens a document that contains the prank macro, the macro copies itself into the Normal template and then replicates itself into new files, which it then saves as templates.

If you have noticed some very strange happenings, you may be the latest victim. Be sure to download the "fix" from Microsoft, if you are having any of the following problems:

▶ You suddenly find that Word is forcing you to save your files with a *.DOT extension (i.e., as a template). In other words, you can no longer save any of your files with a normal *.DOC extension.

▶ When you open a document, a dialog box with the number 1 appears.

▶ You have new macros called AAAZAO, AAAZFS, PayLoad, AutoOpen, and FileSaveAs in your list of macros. If you already had your own AutoOpen and FileSaveAs macros in the macro list, these new ones behave differently.

Because the prank macro is an automatic macro, you can ensure that the macro never gets a chance to replicate by holding down the Shift key every time you open a document. Holding down the Shift key prevents automatic macros from running.

If you think you have the prank macro, get Microsoft application note number WD1215, called "Prank Macro: Cleanup and Prevention." You can download the fix from the Word forum on CompuServe (GO! MSWORD) or from Microsoft's World Wide Web page on the Internet at **http://www.microsoft.com**.

Restoring the Default Settings

When you start changing a lot of settings within Word, it is possible to make a mess that confuses Word. If strange things start happening in your Word files, you may have corrupted a document. Corrupted documents may cause Word to repaginate a document indefinitely, incorrectly layout or format the document, spew forth unreadable characters, generate error messages, or crash your system when you try to open or view the file.

If things go bad—really bad—you can put all your settings back the way they were when you installed Word. When things get ugly, the first troubleshooting step you should take is starting Word using the /a switch. The /a switch forces Word to run without any templates or add-ins. Follow these steps to restore default settings:

1. On the Windows 95 desktop, right-click the shortcut icon for Word.

2. Choose Properties and select the Shortcut tab.

3. In the Target box, type the path to Microsoft Word. (This path is often C:\MSOFFICE\WINWORD\WINWORD.EXE.)

4. Add a space and the /a startup switch to the end of the path after WINWORD.EXE.

If this technique fixes the problem, rename the NORMAL.DOT template to NORMAL.OLD. If Word cannot find NORMAL.DOT, it rebuilds the template from the system defaults. In general, renaming NORMAL.DOT is a good first step in isolating problems in Word.

 Tip

Even if you have to go back to Word's default NORMAL.DOT, you can still copy macros, styles, and AutoText entries to the new NORMAL.DOT using the Organizer. (Choose Tools, Macros, Organizer.)

If you have big problems that won't go away, Word's Data key Registry settings may have become corrupted. You can try running the setup program again and removing, then reinstalling, Word. Another approach is to edit the Registry and delete the Data key. Deleting this key forces Word to regenerate the default settings.

Be sure to create a backup of the Registry before you delete anything, however. Backing up the Registry is described in "Backing Up the Registry" earlier in this chapter. After you have exported the file, go back to the Registry and delete the HKEY_CURRENT_USER\SOFTWARE\MICROSOFT\WORD\7.0\DATA KEY by right-clicking the key and selecting Delete.

After you delete this key, Word returns to its default settings.

Summary

If you take the time to customize Word, you can save hours of time in the long run. Think about how you use the program. Which commands do you use the most? Be sure that you set up your workspace so you have those functions close at hand. If you like to use the mouse, put these commands on a toolbar. If you prefer to use the keyboard, set up shortcuts.

After you set up your workspace, you'll wonder why you didn't do it sooner. If the changes you make save you just 10 minutes every day, that's almost an hour every week. That savings could add up to over a week's worth of work over the course of a year. What *will* you do with all that extra time?

10

chapter 11

Desktop Publishing with Word

by Susan Daffron

11

In this chapter

◆ **Setting up a Page Grid**
Learn how to visually organize your document with page grids.

◆ **Adding graphics**
Inserting graphics adds interest to your layout.

◆ **Working with Columns**
Setting up a document in a multicolumn format often aids readability.

◆ **Using Tables**
In Word, tables are used for everything from crop marks to business cards.

Although Word is not a desktop publishing program, you can use it for some forms of desktop publishing (DTP). You cannot create elaborate four-color ads with irregular text wraps and fancy graphics, but you can create many useful documents that fall into the realm of DTP. With Word, you can create one- and two-color documents that form the majority of the printed material you see everywhere.

If you don't consider yourself an artist, or you feel insecure about doing DTP work because the word *designer* isn't in your job title—*don't*! Much of graphic design is nothing more than a combination of common sense and an intuitive feel for what looks good. Effective design is often utilitarian: what looks good to the most people is the most effective graphic design. Unlike fine art where beauty is in the eye of the beholder, graphic design is about getting your documents read. The goal of graphic design is to create beauty for the eyes of many beholders.

Although graphic design has no hard and fast rules, most design decisions are based on the intuitive effect a document has on the reader. Designers take into account how the eyes and mind are going to assemble and arrange the elements in a design. A good designer can tell whether a design is pleasing or objectionable and whether the graphics message makes sense. The primary purpose of a document is to communicate an idea. If you find your document pleasing to view, others probably will too. If no one reads the document, the idea is lost and your design has failed.

As you forge ahead into the world of desktop publishing and graphic design, remember that the reader is the final judge. If you create a document that is legible and appealing to your readers, you have done far better than a lot of award-winning graphic designers.

Setting Up a Page Grid

Page layout is nothing more than the arrangement of type and graphics on a page. To start creating page layouts, you need to begin by dividing up the page. People derive a certain amount of security from the predictability of a balanced page layout. This quest for an organized, balanced layout is why graphic designers often use page grids.

A *page grid* is a set of imaginary lines, which form a pattern that divides the page vertically and horizontally. These lines help you organize and line up your text and graphics on the page, so they remain consistent throughout the document. At its most basic level, every page grid starts with margins and column settings. These imaginary lines define the placement of text on the page, keep your layout logical, and force you to look carefully at what you are doing.

Setting up your first page grid is easy in Word. You begin by setting the options in File, Page Setup. In the Paper Size tab, you select the paper size and orientation (portrait or landscape). You set your margins in the Margins tab (see fig. 11.1).

Fig. 11.1

When you start a new document, you set the page orientation, size, margins, and other layout options in the Page Setup dialog box.

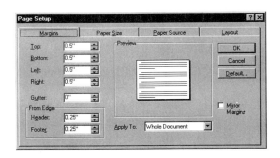

You can use *portrait* orientation for documents such as newsletters and proposals. Other documents, such as brochures, can be set up using a *landscape* orientation. If you want to create documents that are an unusual size, in the Paper Size tab, select Custom Size from the Paper Size drop-down box and type your own values for Height and Width. Usually, however, it's easier to leave the page size a standard size such as 8.5 by 11 and create your own crop marks as described in "Creating Crop Marks" later in this chapter.

Before you venture too deep into the Page Setup dialog box, ask yourself a few questions about your new document:

- Who is the intended audience for this document? Should the document be formal, informal, cutsey, happy, somber, flippant?

- Should the page be portrait or landscape orientation?

- Does the document need extra space in the margins to accommodate a certain type of binding?

- Do you want to add repeating elements such as headers and footers?

- How many columns appear on a page? How wide should they be? How much white space should I put between the columns?

- What typestyles am I going to use?

- How many photographs are there? How should they be placed? Do I need captions?

- What reproduction limitations are there?

 Tip

If you are having your document printed, make sure that the settings you choose in the Page Setup dialog boxes conform to the printer's needs. Many printers and service bureaus provide information on how to set this information correctly for their equipment.

Putting a little thought into the design of your document before you begin work can save you aggravation in the long run. In general, you need to tailor the design of the document to the type of message it conveys. A technical document has a different layout than an advertising piece. In generating either document, you need to consider the style or "look" as well as content. For example, in terms of layout, a legal document may use justified columns for a geometric, formal feel. An advertising piece, however, needs to be more visually accessible. An ad may use left-justified, ragged-right text to increase legibility and create a less formal feel.

11

Remember that white space is an important part of your design. White space is the blank space that surrounds your text and graphics. This negative visual space is as important as the positive. Using a consistent amount of white space at the edge of the page helps the reader focus on important text. You also can add white space around headings to help make them stand out. If you squint at a design, you can see the contrasting elements more easily. If the whole thing looks gray, you have not used white space to your advantage.

Many design decisions are derived from nothing more than common sense. For example, good design tends to be simple and uncluttered. Obviously, an uncluttered look helps convey the message of a document because you have fewer visual distractions. No one wants to wade through a document that is hard to read. Your page layout should lead the reader's eye to the most important elements first.

After you have created a workable page grid, you can break out! Too much symmetry in a layout tends to put people off. Without any visual interest or excitement, people get bored. After you have set up your balance and symmetry with a grid, breaking the grid with graphics or other special items can add interest to your layout.

Working with Columns

In Word, using columns is one way to vary your page layout. In conjunction with the margins, columns provide vertical structure in a page grid. If you create a document with a great deal of text, you may need to switch to a multicolumn format to help readability. Studies have shown that people can most easily read lines fewer than 55 characters long, so try and keep the lengths of text lines fairly short. If you don't switch to a multi-column format, the longer the line length, the more spacing (leading) you need to add between the lines of text. Otherwise, your document will have the visual character of a phone book.

You can use columns for more than just large, text-intensive tomes. A standard three-fold brochure is really just three equal columns on a landscape page (even though you normally may not think of it that way). This type of document is easy to set up in Word (see fig. 11.2).

To create columns, you choose Format, Columns and select the number of columns you want. Generally, the only tricky part is setting up your document's margins and columns so the document will print, fold, or bind correctly.

When you work with columns, you do not need to make them equal widths. You can change the look of your brochure substantially by creating multiple columns of unequal width. Technically, Word allows you to include up to 14 columns in portrait mode and 18 columns in landscape mode. The only restriction is that each column must be at least one-half inch (0.5") wide. If you try to make the columns smaller, Word displays an error message. Practically speaking, however, a document is unwieldy and unreadable if it has more than 3 or 4 columns of text on a portrait page or 5 or 6 columns on a landscape page. If you leave some of your columns blank, you can create interesting effects using the areas of white space.

Fig. 11.2

You set up a three-fold brochure by creating a three-column land-scape document.

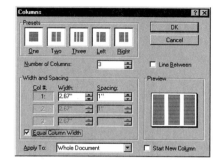

Choosing Type

Choosing the right typeface for the job is an important part of desktop publishing. If a corporate mandate has dictated that you use only one font, you don't have much to worry about. However, if you are like many people who have bought software that comes with hundreds of fonts, selecting the right type for the job can be an intimidating task.

Use a typeface that is right for the document you are creating. For example, wedding invitations use different fonts than billboards. If elegance is most important, you might choose script display font. If readability is most important, you might choose a bold sans serif font. A sans serif font is a font such as Arial that does not include the small "tails" at the ends of the letters. Most books use serif fonts (with little tails), such as Times New Roman or Garamond.

In general, think about where, why, and how the document will be used. For example, if older people are going to be reading your brochure, you should set the type at a point size large enough to accommodate those with poor vision.

In Word, you create typographic consistency throughout the document using styles. *Styles* enable you to save a group of formatting attributes that you can apply all at once to a particular line of text. With styles, you can make global changes to the layout all at once by just changing the style. Styles and templates are discussed in detail in Chapter 9, "Word Styles."

Tip

If you send your files to a service bureau, do not mix TrueType and PostScript fonts in a document. Many service bureaus have more experience with PostScript fonts, so if you have a choice, standardizing on PostScript fonts is a good idea.

Following are a few rules for selecting type:

▶ Use appropriate type for your piece (remember your audience).

▶ Use a single typeface family in a variety of weights (such as Arial Bold and Arial Regular) or two contrasting typefaces.

▶ Use 9- to 11-point type for body text (Normal) for the best readability.

▶ Use typographic symbols like em dashes and smart quotes.

▶ Create contrast by mixing serif type for headings with a sans serif typeface for body text.

▶ Watch out for widows and orphans. Although definitions vary, a *widow* generally is a single word or phrase left at the bottom of a page, and an *orphan* is a single word or line left at the top of a page. Some argue that the definitions are the reverse. Either way, you want to avoid widows and orphans.

▶ Don't mix typefaces or sizes of body text.

▶ Don't use too many special type effects like drop caps and decorative text.

▶ Don't mix very thick type with very thin type; doing so can make your document look out of balance.

▶ Don't use underlining; use italic instead.

▶ Don't set long blocks of all caps, italic, or bold text.

▶ Don't type two spaces after a period at the end of a sentence; use just one space.

Creating a Brochure

Now that you have had a quick introduction to some of the basics of DTP, you can get into the nitty gritty of creating a brochure. To create a three-fold brochure, for example, you set up a landscape page with three equal columns. As a guideline, start by setting the margins and columns so that the space between the columns is two times that of your outside margin. In other words, if you set the outside margin to one-half inch, make the Spacing setting in the Columns dialog box 1.00 inch. For equal columns, make sure that the Equal Column Width box is selected. If you find you need less space between the columns, you can adjust it later. Be sure to leave enough space for the brochure fold, however.

Before you start any DTP project, you may want to create a new template so you don't clutter up (and potentially destroy) your default NORMAL.DOT template with the new styles for this project.

To create a new template, follow these steps:

1. Choose File, Open. Switch the List Files of Type drop-down box to Document Templates and select a template name from your template folder. Click Open and the template opens.

2. Choose File, Save As and type a new name (see fig. 11.3). If you already know you want to make some changes to the styles, such as changing the font for the Normal style, close NORMAL.DOT. Open your new template and make those changes now.

3. Save and close the new template file.

4. Choose File, New and select your new template (do not select Blank Document). You are ready to create your brochure without worrying about having to later resurrect your old NORMAL.DOT from the abyss.

Fig. 11.3

Create a new template for your DTP projects so you don't end up unintentionally changing NORMAL.DOT.

Now you have a blank document. To transform it into a three-fold brochure, do the following:

1. Switch to Page Layout view. Choose File, Page Setup, then choose the Paper Size tab and change the orientation to landscape.

2. Click the Margins tab. Change the Top, Bottom, Right, and Left margins to 0.5 inch.

3. Create your columns by choosing Format, Columns. Click the three-column Preset icon and type **1"** in the Spacing amount. Place a check mark in the Equal Column Width box. To format the entire document as multiple columns, make sure that Apply to Whole Document is selected.

11

Note

You cannot insert columns in headers, footers, annotations, or frames. To arrange text in these places, you need to use a table.

You can see what's going on more easily if you switch to Page Layout view and choose Tools, Options, click the View tab, and then select Show Text Boundaries. You can see the outline of the columns, so you can see where to type your text. However, before you start merrily typing away, you need to consider the order of your text. Think about how you want to fold your brochure. As you add text, it snakes from the first column right on through to the sixth. The title of the brochure appears in the first inside column, which may not end up being the cover, depending on how you fold the brochure.

To help visualize your layout, take a scrap piece of paper and make a dummy of your brochure. Bend, fold, spindle, and mutilate the paper until you understand where your columns fall in relation to the folds. Think about whether you want a "barrel" fold (where the two sides fold in) or an accordion or "z" fold (where the paper is folded in alternate directions).

Usually the front of a brochure contains some form of special text or graphic, so if you decide on a barrel fold, make the cover page the last panel (the third column on page 2), as shown in figure 11.4.

Fig. 11.4

For a barrel-fold brochure, make the third column on page 2 the front cover.

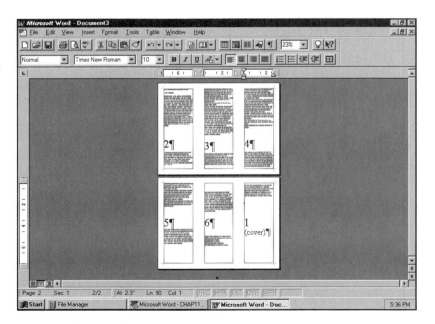

Word includes a number of prepared templates for common documents such as brochures, newsletters, forms, and reports. If you start running out of inspiration or ideas, you can always start with one of Word's templates and modify it to suit your own needs. Looking at the templates is also a good way to get a feel for how the experts decided to approach a complicated layout in Word.

Changing Column Width

After you have your brochure set up, you can still edit the column widths. In general, the narrower your columns are, the less space you need between the columns. Remember that if you create wide columns with long lines of text, be sure to add extra spacing (leading) between the lines. You don't want to make your columns too narrow, either. Narrow columns force the reader's eye to jump to the next line more frequently, which reduces readability. If you must reduce the column width substantially to fit more text on the page, you should reduce the size of the type as well.

To edit the column width, choose Format, Columns and edit the Width and Spacing amounts to specify the exact width of each column and the spacing between the columns. If you want to create text that crosses the columns, you can insert sections or framed text or graphics (see "Working with Sections" and "Working with Frames" later in this chapter). Always have your frames align with your column guides, however, so the page elements remain aligned with the grid. Also, keep in mind that reducing the space between columns makes the document appear darker because there is less white space to lighten up the page.

Balancing Columns

Unlike many desktop publishing programs, Word does not balance columns automatically. If you don't have enough text, the first two columns are filled and the last column is short. Word does not automatically distribute the text evenly among all three columns. You can force all columns on a page to balance, however, by inserting a continuous section break at the end of the last column.

If you have organized your brochure into topics, you can add column breaks to begin a new column or force a column to end in a certain place (breaks are discussed in more detail later in this chapter). Dividing the columns logically with column breaks helps make a document easier to follow. You can use the ragged bottom margin to provide contrast. The contrast between the text and white space acts as a visual cue to help guide the reader through the document.

11

Adding Intercolumn Rules

When you set up columns using Format, Columns, you can add lines between the columns (or intercolumn rules) by selecting the Line Between box. If you decide to add intercolumn rules, you probably shouldn't set your body type with justified alignment. The square blocks of type in conjunction with the vertical rules usually results in a rigid and boring layout. You can turn off the intercolumn rules at any time by choosing Format, Columns and deselecting the Line Between box.

Organizing Text

After you have a brochure set up, you need to organize your text. You can use headlines, subheads, captions, drop caps, headers, and footers to attract the reader's attention. These typographic tools make the document more visually interesting and add clarity for easier reading.

Headings break up the page into smaller sections and make it easier to read. Use a typeface that contrasts with the body text to give your document some variety. Leave more space above the heading than below it to help set it off from the surrounding text.

Change type sizes for a reason. Use different type sizes and weights to indicate captions, headings, and pull quotes, and to indicate the hierarchy of importance. Be consistent in your use of typefaces and sizes to keep readers from being confused.

Consider these tips for using typographic tools effectively:

▶ Don't use too many special effects on a page. You should place all the page elements for a *reason*.

▶ Format your headings and subheadings consistently. (Setting up styles helps ensure consistency throughout a document.)

▶ Keep headings short to improve readability. If your headings are long, do not let Word hyphenate them.

▶ Avoid setting headings in uppercase text. Uppercase text is more difficult to read than initial caps.

▶ Don't put more white space below a heading than above it. Keep the heading or subhead visually connected to its associated text.

▶ Use headers and footers to help your readers navigate long documents. (Readers expect to find page numbers in headers or footers.)

▶ Add contrast by setting headlines in a different typestyle, a larger type size, or a bold typeface.

In Word, you can set up your text formatting using styles. This approach saves time in the long run because you need to set up the formatting for your headings and subheads only once (see fig. 11.5). Another time-saver is to save a drop cap as an AutoText entry that you can insert into the text where you need it.

Fig. 11.5

Formatting text using styles ensures typographic consistency throughout a document. Select Format, Style to add or modify styles.

When you apply the built-in heading styles to your headings, you can easily generate tables of contents or cross-references later if you need to. Like any other style, you can change the formatting of the built-in styles to match your layout.

Working with Sections

Sections are another way to organize a document. Many documents need to switch back and forth between single and multiple columns. For example, a newsletter often has a single-column masthead and multiple columns in the body of the document. To make this task possible, you need to break your document into sections. To format a section of the document as multiple columns, you click in the section you want to format and choose Format, Columns.

To create a section in a document, you must insert a section break. The break stores the formatting for the section, including the settings for margins, page numbers, and headers and footers. So be careful about deleting empty paragraph markers, especially when you are in Page Layout view. If you are not careful, you can accidentally delete all your section formatting by deleting a seemingly unnecessary extra paragraph at the end of a document.

To insert a section break, follow these steps:

1. Place your cursor where you want to start a new section.

2. Choose Insert, Break.

3. Select the type of break. Clicking Next Page breaks the page at the section break. A Continuous section break starts a new section on the same page. Selecting Odd Page or Even Page starts the new section on the next odd- or even-numbered page.

Tip

Breaks are easier to see in Normal view, where a section break is displayed as a double dotted line that appears *above* the place you inserted it. This line marks the end of the preceding section.

Copying and deleting section breaks can be extremely confusing. For example, if you paste a section break, the text *above* the section break is affected by the formatting stored in the section break. Similarly, when you delete a section break, you delete the section formatting that was stored in it (see fig. 11.6). The formatting for the text above the old section break is now different. That text is part of the section that used to follow it, so the text acquires the formatting stored in that section. This confusion is compounded if your headers and footers are formatted with references to chapter names or numbers. Deleting sections can throw off these references, which can result in some embarrassing mistakes.

Fig. 11.6

To delete a section break, highlight the line by clicking in the left margin, then press the Backspace or Delete key.

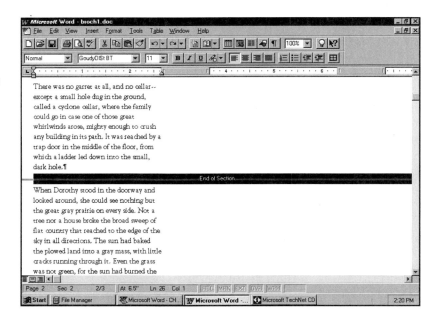

Adding Lines, Borders, and Shading

You can use lines, borders, and shading to add visual emphasis to a page. For example, in a newsletter, the table of contents is often enclosed in a box to separate it from the articles on the first page. You also can use lines, or rules, to join rather than separate blocks of text. Newspapers, for example, often extend a line across columns to indicate that the article continues across both columns. When used sparingly, graphic devices such as rules add to the readability of a document; when graphic devices are overused, they quickly overwhelm the document.

Make sure you keep your line widths consistent within a document. Randomly placing a two-point rule over one headline and a four-point rule over another for no apparent reason does nothing but confuse your readers. Also keep your boxes and rules aligned with your page grid. For example, in a multicolumn layout, boxes should span a full column width, not partial columns.

Borders and shading are easy to add to paragraphs and tables. You select your paragraph or table or position your cursor within the paragraph, and choose Format, Borders and Shading. The border and shading options you select are applied to the entire paragraph and span the width of the margin or column. For example, by adding black shading to a paragraph with a font color set to white, you can create reverse-out headings. To add a line across the page, select a blank paragraph and click the top or bottom of the sample box in the Border area of the Borders tab (see fig. 11.7).

Fig. 11.7

Adding a top or bottom border to a paragraph in a document set up with a single column places a line across the page.

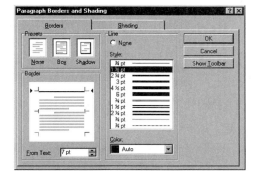

Adding a border around the entire page is another way to add interest to a document. Use these steps:

1. Display the Drawing toolbar by choosing View, Toolbars and selecting the Drawing toolbar box.

2. Click the Rectangle button and then drag the border to the size you want.

3. Change the fill and line attributes by choosing Format, Drawing Object.

Much to the dismay of former WordPerfect users, you cannot apply shading or a box to just one word using the Borders and Shading command, because this command is a paragraph format in Word. However, you can apply shading to a word using the highlight button on the Formatting toolbar. The default highlight color is yellow, which looks fine on-screen. If you are printing to a black-and-white printer, however, you may want to experiment with other colors by choosing <u>T</u>ools, Re<u>v</u>isions and clicking the <u>O</u>ption button. Try out a few colors until you find one that prints the way you want.

Another seemingly bizarre approach to borders is to use the Equation (Eq) field to place a border around a single word. Press Alt+F9 to view field codes, choose <u>I</u>nsert, Fi<u>e</u>ld, and choose Eq from the list. Add the \x switch and type your text between the parentheses, so you end up with code that looks like this:

```
{ Eq \x(word) }
```

 Tip

If you want to place a border around more than one word, make sure you do not include regular spaces in the text. Use nonbreaking spaces (Ctrl+Shift+spacebar) instead.

A text box is another more graphical way to create words with borders or shading, or both (see fig. 11.8).

Fig. 11.8

You can add shading and borders to text elements in a number of ways: using the Borders and Shading command, the Highlight button on the Formatting toolbar, an Equation field, or a text box. Each method has advantages and disadvantages, depending on what you want to do.

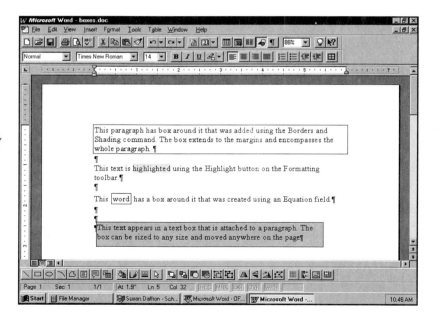

To create a text box, follow these steps:

1. Display the Drawing toolbar and click the Text Box button. The pointer changes to a crosshair.

2. Draw a rectangle and type some text into the box.

3. Modify the Line and Fill Colors of the text box by clicking these buttons on the toolbar or by choosing Format, Drawing Object.

4. Position the text box using the mouse. You also can nudge the text box using the arrow keys. (The nudge distance is affected by amounts you set in the Snap to Grid settings.)

5. If you want the text to flow with the paragraph, choose Edit, Cut. Place the cursor where you want the box to appear and choose, Edit, Paste Special. Select Picture and click OK.

Creating a Newsletter

Creating a newsletter involves putting together the elements discussed so far in this chapter. Most newsletters are set up with a page grid of one to three columns; they use sections to vary the layout; and they use typographic tools, lines, and borders to visually organize text (see fig. 11.9). Because most newsletters are largely text, you already have the information you need to get started.

Fig. 11.9

Continuous section breaks enable you to vary your newsletter layout with single and multiple-column formats.

11

When you set up a newsletter, try to make it accessible to the reader. Make your newsletter something people want to read (as opposed to something they *have* to read). Put the most interesting and preferably short articles on the front page. Try to avoid having articles jump from one page to another. In a newsletter, people don't like flipping through pages to find the end of an article. To make the articles more accessible to the reader, you can use graphic elements such as:

▸ *Kickers.* The text above a heading that helps lead the reader into an article.

▸ *Decks.* The text below a heading that contains additional information about an article.

▸ *Sidebars.* Short articles that contain specific information that relate to a topic in the main article they accompany.

▸ *Pull quotes.* A quotation or summary point from an article that is set in a larger type size than the rest of the body text for emphasis.

Set up your layout so it leads readers to the most important elements of the newsletter first. Always strive for visual and editorial consistency. Use the same terms throughout the document to provide continuity. Also be sure to use visuals to break up the page layout (see "Adding Graphics" later in this chapter). People reading newsletters love to look at pictures. Always add captions to describe the photos.

Editorially speaking, you should try to keep your paragraphs and sentences short. A long column of text is intimidating and hard to read in a newsletter format. Break up long articles into two or more shorter ones and use graphics to convey any complex data.

If the newsletter will be placed in a three-ring binder, be sure to add a wider margin in your layout. Set up your newsletter with facing pages and make sure you add an extra 5/8 to 3/4 inch for the rings. Plastic ring binding, spiral, or perfect binding (used for books) requires less space for a binding edge.

Fine-Tuning Text

When graphic designers lay out a document, they pay attention to small typographic details. Viewed individually, these minute elements may seem trivial. However, attention to these details is what separates professionally desktop-published documents from the thousands of odious 10-point-Courier documents generated daily.

Creating a Leading Grid

Leading grids improve a document's appearance by helping to create an orderly layout. Creating a leading grid involves keeping track of the vertical space between lines. If all the text is set based on a consistent point size, lines in adjacent columns align neatly across the page. As you set up your styles for a document, keep track of the settings for each style. In Word, the trick is to set the line spacing in the Paragraph dialog box to an exact setting.

By keeping track of the total vertical space occupied by each style, you can set all your styles in multiple amounts. In other words, for the Normal style, look in the Paragraph dialog box and add the point size of the exact Line Spacing to the space added above and below (see fig. 11.10). Then set the spacing settings for the rest of your styles so they are a multiple of the Normal style's total size. This technique seems like a giant pain, but for documents that will be reused constantly, this initial time investment is well worth the effort.

Fig. 11.10

When you create a leading grid, in all your styles, you must change the Line Spacing At drop-down box to Exactly, and make the amount a multiple of your body text (Normal) style.

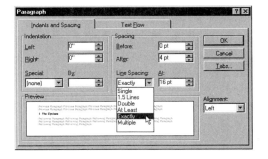

Adjusting Tracking and Kerning

TrueType aficionados take settings like tracking and kerning very seriously. Kerning involves adjusting the space between two letters so that part of one letter extends over the body of the letter next to it. Unkerned text is most noticeable between certain pairs of letters, such as an A and a V. Kerning these two letters slightly tucks the bottom of the A under the top of the V.

Perfectly kerned letter pairs are a hallmark of quality typography, and if you want people to think you are a real DTP pro, you can kern your letter pairs individually. Of course, this task is extremely painstaking (and arguably, boring) work. However, manually kerning headlines can improve the readability and appearance, especially if the headlines are set in a fairly large point size.

Word enables you to adjust kerning using the Spacing option in the Character Spacing tab of the Font dialog. In the Character Spacing tab, you can change the space between selected characters or turn on Automatic Kerning for the entire document (see fig. 11.11). Automatic Kerning adjusts the spacing between characters depending on the font

11

size you select. For example, if you select 10 points in the dialog box, Word automatically kerns all type larger than 10 points. Kerning works only with TrueType or Adobe Type Manager fonts that are larger than a certain size. This size depends on the individual font.

Fig. 11.11

Carefully adjusting the text spacing by adjusting the values in the Character Spacing tab adds the finishing touch to your layout.

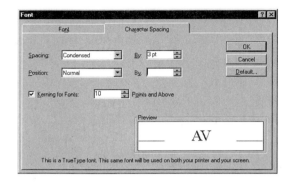

To adjust spacing between characters, follow these steps:

1. Highlight the characters you want to kern.

2. Choose Format, Font and click the Character Spacing tab.

3. You can choose Normal, Condensed, Expanded, or specify a number between 0.25 and 14 in the By box. To set automatic kerning, type a number in the Points and Above box.

4. If you want to save your new settings in the current template, click the Default button.

Using Typographic Characters

Another hallmark of good typography is using special characters such as em dashes rather than hyphens, and curly quotes rather than straight quotes. You can insert these special characters, international characters, and symbols using the Insert, Symbol command. (When you use this method, the character is protected so you cannot change the font manually.) You also can insert a character or symbol by typing the ASCII key combination on the numeric keypad.

If you use certain symbols often, you may want to create an AutoText entry or assign the symbol a shortcut key. You can set up Word to automatically replace some key combinations with symbols by adjusting the options in Tools, AutoCorrect and Tools, Options, AutoFormat. For example, you can tell Word to always replace two hyphens with an em dash. You also can turn on Smart Quotes, which automatically turns all your straight quotes to curly typographic quotes.

To insert symbols using the Symbol command, follow these steps:

1. Place your cursor where you want to insert the symbol.

2. Choose Insert, Symbol. Select the Symbol tab and choose a font from the drop-down list box.

3. Single-click or double-click a symbol character. Single-clicking the symbol shows you an enlarged view of the character. Word also shows you the ASCII key combination or shortcut key for the symbol, so if you need to use the symbol frequently, you can create a macro using that key combination.

    Double-clicking the symbol inserts it into your document.

Adding Graphics

A key element in page design, graphics add excitement to your layout. You can use photographs, callouts, and illustrations to give the reader's eyes a break from the text and add visual interest. To attract this elusive "visual interest," designers work with value and contrast. *Value* is the distribution of darkness and lightness across the page. You can achieve differences in value using various densities of type and photographs (both black and white and color). When you start adding graphics, it's especially important to use enough white space to convey a feeling of space.

Contrast also adds interest to a design by enhancing its feeling of dimension. You can contrast volume (big things versus small things) or form (horizontal versus vertical). Contrast in conjunction with the creative use of white space can guide the reader in the right direction (i.e., to the most important information).

When you add graphics to your documents, think about the organization of your page grid. The appearance and readability of your document is vastly improved if you go to the effort to fit your graphics into the grid. If you break the grid, make sure you do it intentionally for emphasis and variety. For example, bleeding a graphic off the edge of the page can create an interesting effect if you do it properly and for a reason. If you decide to add photos to your layout, be sure to crop them so they focus on the important element in the photo.

In Word, you add a graphic by choosing Insert, Picture. For example, the castle in the Emerald City News document shown earlier in figure 11.9 is a CorelDRAW symbol that was exported as a TIF file and inserted into Word.

When adding graphics, be sure to keep the design simple. Try to avoid cluttering your document with too many graphics. Too much of a good thing gets confusing. One well-placed graphic is far more effective than many little images strewn across the page at random. Also be sure to keep your layout unified. Keep the graphics near the text that describes them.

If you are running Word on an old, wimpy computer, graphics can drastically slow down the screen redraw process. If you find yourself clenching your fists as Word painfully repaints the screen, you may want to turn on picture placeholders instead of displaying the image (see fig. 11.12). Choose Tools, Options and click the View tab. Select the Picture Placeholders check box.

Fig. 11.12

Displaying picture placeholders can help you retain your sanity if you use many graphics.

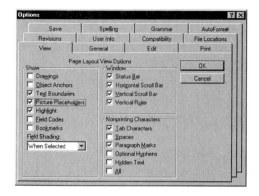

Cropping and Resizing

When you use photographs, it's important to focus the image on the most important elements. Sizing and cropping your pictures correctly aids in readability. Leaving extraneous detail in your images weakens the image and inhibits the reader's ability to understand what the graphic means.

Resizing imported graphics works much like it does in most graphics applications. To keep the original proportions of the graphic when you resize, drag a corner handle. Dragging one of the middle handles changes the proportions. While you are resizing, check the percentage of the graphic's original height and width in the status bar at the bottom of the screen.

If you make a mess resizing, you can always return a graphic to its original size by holding down the Ctrl key and double-clicking the graphic. Or you can choose Format, Picture and click the Reset button.

To crop graphics, you can use the Format, Picture command or hold down the Shift key as you drag a sizing handle. Cropping can dramatically change the appearance of a picture as the folks at the grocery store tabloids can attest.

In Word, for example, a few mouse clicks removes an entire feline in the photograph in figure 11.13. Cropping works from the outside in. In the bottom photograph, 3.1 inches was cut off the top of the original photo by specifying 3.1" in the Top box. You also can specify negative numbers to add white space around a photograph.

Fig. 11.13

Cropping pictures helps to isolate the subject of a photo. Be sure to select your photos carefully, however. Sometimes it isn't possible to crop out all incriminating evidence (the extra tail in the second photo- graph makes a reader wonder).

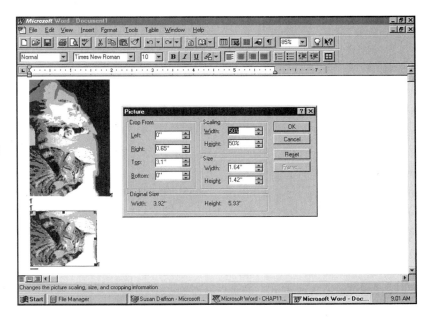

Linking Graphics

When you insert graphics into your document, the file sizes can get enormous. If you have many graphics, it may be better in the long run to link the graphics rather than embed them in the document. However, there is a trade-off. If you delete or move the original graphic files, Word will not be able to find them when you open the document, and you'll receive an error message. If you move your files around frequently, linking may not be a good option.

To link graphics, when you choose Insert, Picture, make sure that you select Link to File. This process inserts an IncludePicture field code with a \d switch. The \d means that the graphic is not stored with the document. If you view field codes by pressing Alt+F9, you can tell if your pictures are linked or embedded.

Linking graphics is also an advantage if your graphic files are updated frequently. If you embed graphics and the original graphic file changes, you need to reinsert the picture. If you link graphics, you can update them just by updating the field. Note that Word does not update the linked graphics in a document automatically. If your linked graphics change, you can update the graphics as you would update any other field. Highlight the field and press F9. To update all the links in a document, choose Edit, Select All and press F9. To selectively update links, choose Edit, Links and select the links you want to up- date. (Holding down the Ctrl key while clicking lets you select multiple links.) Choose the Update Now button and the graphics are updated from the latest version of the graphic files.

11

Even if you link your pictures, your files may still get unwieldy because Word maintains an internal screen representation of the picture within the document for display purposes. To keep your files small, you can specify that linked pictures not be saved in the document. When you choose Insert, Picture, make sure that the Save Pictures in Document check box is not selected.

 Note

If you move your linked graphics to a different folder, you can update the document by choosing Edit, Links. Select the file you want to update from the list and click the Change Source button. Select the file from the list in the Change Source dialog box.

Working with Frames

In Word, you use frames to position graphics in a specific location. If you just insert a picture, you can adjust what happens inside the picture box, but you cannot change what happens in the vicinity. With a frame, you can wrap text around a graphic in different ways and adjust the white space between the text and graphic. Putting a frame around an imported graphic and moving the frame gives you much more flexibility than just inserting a picture alone.

You need to be in Page Layout view to insert a frame. In fact, if you try to insert a frame while you are in Normal view, Word asks if you want to switch.

Frames are different from the text boxes you create using the Drawing toolbar, and you cannot use frames to position those drawing objects. When a frame is inserted into text on the page, the text flows around the frame. In contrast, a text box does not force text on a page to flow around it. Text boxes are good for placing text or a graphic behind other text (see "Creating a Repeating Graphic or Text" later in this chapter).

Frames help keep items separate from the text because as you add text or a graphic to a frame, it automatically resizes. With frames, you can add callouts, separate articles, or graphics into a layout and lock the frame in place if you want.

To insert a frame, choose Insert, Frame. Your cursor changes to a crosshair pointer. Now just draw a square in the margin. When you let go, you have an empty frame. As the text wraps around the frame, your layout often gets confused. You may be alarmed at first, but you can fix the problems by selecting the frame and choosing Format, Frame.

You can add a frame to text or a graphic that's already in the document. If you select an item and choose Insert, Frame, Word automatically sizes the frame to the item.

 Tip
You can place a frame around items to keep them together when you move them around. This feature is handy for keeping your figure captions with your figures.

Anchoring Frames

Frames have two primary uses: moving things around and keeping things in one place. As soon as you draw a frame, you probably notice that you can move it anywhere. Locking a frame, although not as obvious, is no less useful. Frames enable you to attach an item to a paragraph. If the paragraph moves during editing, the item automatically moves with it. Conversely, you can make the item remain exactly where you inserted it, even if the text around it moves during the editing process.

When you work with frames, you may want to show frame anchors. Choose Tools, Options, View and make sure Object Anchors is selected.

The key to anchoring frames is in the positioning controls of the Frame dialog box. To change the attributes of a frame, select the frame and choose Format, Frame. You can place frames vertically relative to the page, margin, or column. Or you can place frames horizontally relative to the paragraph, margin, or page.

When you draw a frame, it is anchored to the paragraph that it is closest to on the page. If you move the frame around on the page, the anchor moves to the paragraph that the frame is nearest to. To make sure a framed item always stays with the same paragraph, select the Lock Anchor check box. If you want the frame to flow with the paragraph, select Move with Text. If you want the frame to stay on a certain page and not move with the paragraph it is anchored to, deselect Move with Text and Lock Anchor.

Creating Side Heads

Another useful way to use frames is to set up *side heads*. A side head is text that appears in the left margin of your document. Side heads are a popular layout device because they are easy to read. When used correctly, side heads give a document an open, airy feel because of the large amount of white space in the margins (see fig. 11.14).

Fig. 11.14

You can use frames to create side heads in the margin of your document.

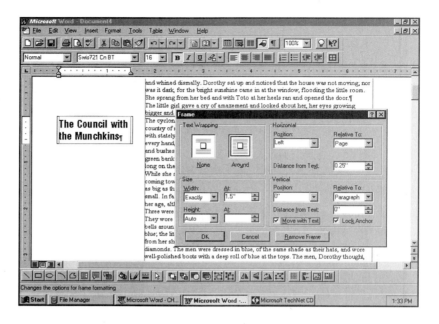

To set up a side head, you specify a large left margin that is big enough to handle your text or graphic. Next you create a frame that fits in the margin. Set the horizontal position to left, relative to the page, and the vertical position to 0", relative to paragraph. Be sure to select <u>M</u>ove with Text if you want the side head to move with the paragraph and Loc<u>k</u> Anchor if you want the side head text frame to be locked to a paragraph.

To extend other types of heading titles into the left margin, you need to set a negative indent for those styles. Similarly, you may need to adjust your header and footer styles with a negative indent while you are in the Header and Footer view (see "Using Headers and Footers" later in this chapter).

Adding Background Elements

Certain parts of a page can be integral to the structure of the document. Never underestimate the value of navigational tools such as headers and footers on readability. Think about it. When reading a book, just about everyone looks for the page number at the top or bottom of the page. Not finding a page number where you expect it can be downright annoying. You can add other informative graphics to the page using the drawing tools built into Word or the OLE-based WordArt add-in program.

Using Headers and Footers

Headers and footers are used to provide consistency and to help readers figure out where they are in a long document. In Word, you also can use headers and footers to include graphics or text that you want to repeat on every page.

To add headers and footers, follow these steps:

1. Choose View, Header and Footer. To switch between headers and footers, click the Switch Between Header and Footer button (the leftmost button on the toolbar). If you have set up your document in the Page Setup dialog box to contain different first page and odd and even pages, you can set up different headers and footers for those pages.

2. Enter text or graphics within the dashed line that surrounds the header or footer area. You also can insert page numbers, the date, or the time by clicking the toolbar buttons.

3. While you are working in Header and Footer view, you cannot edit text and graphics in the document, so click Close to go back to the main part of your document.

Using Drawing Tools

The tools on the Drawing toolbar enable you to create simple drawings in your document. You can draw many of the same things you can draw in a stand-alone application such as lines, circles, arcs, text boxes, and callouts. The Drawing toolbar also has grouping, aligning, and transformation functions so you can work with your objects after you draw them. When you use a button on the Drawing toolbar, that tool remains in effect until you select another button or start typing.

If you want to get fancy, you can access the stand-alone WordArt application. WordArt enables you to apply special effects to text, such as rotation, slanting, shaping, and arcing. To access WordArt, you choose Insert, Object and select WordArt from the list. WordArt is an add-in that comes with Word; however, you must have installed WordArt when you installed Word for this add-in to appear in the list.

As with all graphic treatments, you should exercise considerable restraint with tools like WordArt and the built-in drawing functions. Just because you can do something doesn't mean you should. A bizarre document filled with twisted, rotated type and distorted graphics is not going to be readable and will undoubtedly end up in the trash.

Creating a Repeating Graphic or Text

After you have mastered the joys of headers and footers for text and explored the Drawing toolbar, you can expand your horizons by combining these elements to create repeating text or graphics. Word calls a graphic that appears on every page of a document a *watermark* (which has little to do with the traditional meaning of the term, but that's another story).

To repeat the text or graphic on every page, you need to put it into the header or footer. The text or graphic is printed wherever you place it on the page. You don't need to limit yourself to keeping the element within the confines of the header or footer itself.

You can put your graphic in a text box so it appears behind the text. Or if you want the text to flow around the graphic, you can put the graphic in a frame instead.

To add a watermark, follow these steps:

1. Display the Drawing toolbar and choose <u>V</u>iew, <u>H</u>eader and Footer.

2. Create a text box and type the text. Or use the drawing tools to create your own graphic. To use an imported graphic, create a text box and then choose <u>I</u>nsert, <u>P</u>icture to put the graphic inside the text box. After the graphic is in a text box, you can position it like a normal drawing object.

3. Move and resize the watermark so it's the way you want it.

4. To place a graphic behind text, select the graphic and click the Send Behind Text button on the Drawing toolbar.

5. On the Header and Footer toolbar, click <u>C</u>lose.

 Tip

Text boxes don't resize automatically when you add text or graphics. If some of your text seems to have disappeared, you probably just typed more text than would fit in the box. Try resizing the box and see if that makes the text reappear.

If the watermark ends up being too dark, you can lighten it by changing the color. For text, choose F<u>o</u>rmat, <u>F</u>ont and change the text color. To change the color of objects, choose F<u>o</u>rmat, Drawing <u>O</u>bject. Be very careful about placing graphics or text behind the text of a document. As you can see in figure 11.15, text that is too dark can seriously impair the readability of the document.

Fig. 11.15
*You can use a
combination of
headers or footers and
text boxes to create
watermarks that
appear behind the
document text on
every page.*

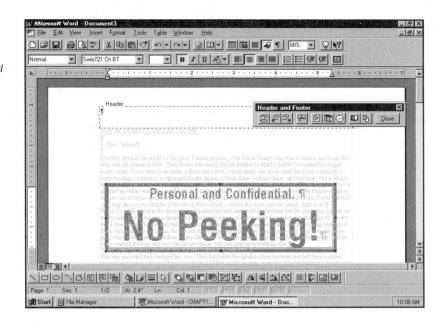

Using Tables in DTP

When you desktop publish in Word, you can use tables for more than just organizing boring, tabular data (although tables are certainly good for that, too). Tables are great for organizing your information using side-by-side columns of text and/or graphics. In many cases, tables may be easier to work with than frames or columns.

The Word table function works much like a spreadsheet. If the word *spreadsheet* makes you shudder, don't worry. Word's tables are nowhere near as intimidating as a mono-lithic application like Excel. However, the two applications are similar because in a Word table, you work with rows and columns. Like a spreadsheet, each square is called a *cell*.

Choose T<u>a</u>ble, <u>I</u>nsert Table to add a new blank table to your document (see fig. 11.16). Then you just fill in the empty cells with text or graphics.

Fig. 11.16
*You set the number of
rows and columns for
your new table in the
Insert Table dialog
box.*

If you have a great deal of text, converting existing paragraphs to a table may be faster than creating a new table. To convert text to a table, follow these steps:

1. If your text isn't formatted with separator characters between the columns, such as tabs or commas, make sure to add separator characters to divide columns and rows. Using tabs to divide columns and paragraphs to divide rows often is easiest.

2. Highlight the text to convert.

3. Choose Table, Convert Text to Table.

4. Under Separate Text At, select the separator characters you used. Click OK. The text appears formatted as a table.

If you have a large amount of data from other sources, such as databases or spreadsheets, you can use other methods to convert that data to a table. This subject is covered extensively in the Integration chapters in Part VII of the book.

Using Tables to Align Text and Graphics

Another use for tables is for aligning text and graphics. For example, if you look in a software manual, you often see this technique for lists of icons and their descriptions. You also can use tables to create side-by-side paragraphs as shown in figure 11.17.

Fig. 11.17

You can use tables to align graphics and descriptive text in your layout.

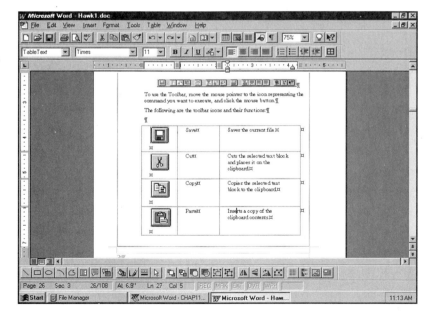

Setting Up Business Cards

Most Word users know that you use tables to set up repeating elements like labels or envelopes for a mail merge, but you can apply the same principle for documents such as business cards.

To set up a sheet of business cards, follow these steps:

1. Choose File, Page Setup and click the Layout tab. Set the top and bottom margins to 0.5 inch and the left and right margins to 0.75 inch.

2. Choose Table, Insert Table. Create a table with four columns and seven rows.

3. Select the first row and choose Table, Cell Height and Width and click Row. Make the row height .25 inch. Do the same thing for the last row in the table. Now select the five rows in between and make the cell height 2 inches.

4. Select the entire table by choosing Table, Select Table. With the entire table highlighted, choose Table, Cell Height and Width and click the Column tab. Make the first and fourth columns .5 inch wide, and the second and third columns 3.5 inches wide. Make sure that the Space Between Columns is set to 0 (see fig. 11.18).

5. Design one business card by adding text and graphics.

6. Copy your card and paste it into the other cells. If you are going to cut the cards yourself on a paper cutter, adding a light border to the table makes it easier to see where to cut.

7. Now add the crop marks by adding specific borders to the cells in the narrow outside columns. For example, click the upper-left cell and choose Format, Borders and Shading. Click the right and bottom borders in the Border box. The other three corners and the cut marks work the same way. Add borders to the appropriate cells to indicate where to cut the cards.

Now you have a set of business cards complete with crop marks. If you have a paper cutter, all you need to do is print the document on card stock and cut it. If you prefer, you can print the file and send it to a service bureau to be printed professionally.

Caution

Check your printer's user's guide before you attempt to feed card stock through your printer. Some printers are not designed to work with heavy paper such as card stock and attempting to print may damage the printer.

Fig. 11.18
Using a table, you can set up your own business cards complete with crop marks and cut lines.

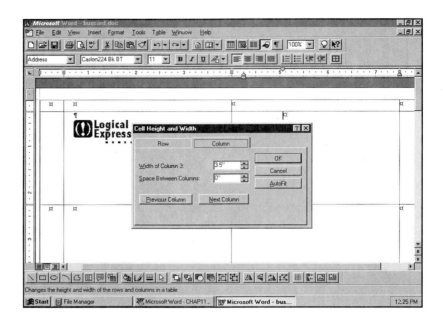

> ⚛ **Tip**
> Sometimes selecting a small cell in a table can be tricky. If you have trouble, try holding down the Shift key and pressing the right-arrow key.

Preparing Files for Service Bureaus

If you want to send your file to a service bureau for high-resolution output, you need to print your document to a file. Most service bureaus require PostScript output. If you are not using a PostScript printer, you need to set one up in Windows. Talk with the service bureau and find out what type of equipment they are using. Most service bureaus will take the time to tell you which Windows driver works best with their equipment. If someone does not take the time to explain this subject to you, find a new service bureau. It is not worth your time or money to deal with an outfit that refuses to run anything but perfectly formatted Macintosh QuarkXpress files. Worst of all, if any service bureau scolds, hints, or even suggests that you need to buy a Macintosh to send your files to an imagesetter, run, don't walk, to the nearest phone book and find a new service bureau.

People have been successfully running PC PostScript files to high-resolution imagesetters for years. However, you need to bear in mind that Word is very sensitive to the printer driver you have selected when you create your document. If you are going to send your document to a Linotronic or other high-resolution device, be sure to set up the driver early in the layout process so your pagination is correct before you go to film.

As you work on your document, make sure that the default printer is set to the device you eventually want to use for your output. You can switch to your default printer for printing, but unless you have a PostScript printer, you may experience some repagination as Word figures out what it needs to do to print to your printer.

To print your document to a file, make sure that you have selected the correct destination printer. Usually, you need to set up the printer in Windows so the Printer Port is set to File. In any case, when you print the document, make sure that the Print to File box is checked. Word places a file on the disk location you specify. You take this file to the service bureau.

Work closely with your service bureau the first time you try this procedure, because every system is different. You may find that you have some font-related issues to work out before the process becomes seamless. If you have a PostScript printer, testing your files (as described in "Testing Files" later in this section) can save you money and aggravation in the long run.

Creating Crop Marks

Unlike most DTP applications, Word does not have an automatic crop mark feature. If you set your page size to a larger size than your final document, you can add your own crop marks. This method is similar to the approach used to add crop marks in the earlier business card example. Basically, you just add a three-column, one-row table in the header and footer of your document.

The first trick is to set up your page with a standard paper size and use big margins to reduce the page to the finished size. The margins should provide the normal margin allowance, plus appear far enough in to account for the fact that the finished page to which you are printing is actually smaller than the paper size you have selected. For example, if you are going to print a 6 × 9 document with 0.5-inch margins, set up the document on a paper size of 8.5 × 11. You need to subtract 6 from 8.5, which leaves 2.5. Half of 2.5 is 1.25, plus you want a margin, so you need to add 0.5 to each side. So, your left and right margins are 1.75. You do the same thing for the top and bottom (11-9=2). Divide 2 by 2 (1) and add 0.5 for your margin, so your top and bottom margins are 1.5.

After all that math, choose File, Page Setup to go into the Page Setup dialog box. Select the Margins tab and change your margins for the whole document to 1.75 for the left and right and 1.5 for the top and bottom. Also make sure that you set the Footer to be 0 inch from the edge of the paper. To set crop marks, follow these steps:

11

1. Choose View, Header and Footer. In the header area, insert a table with one row and three columns.

2. Select the table. Choose Table, Cell Height and Width and click the Column tab. Make the second column the same width as the distance between the left and right margin of your page. In this example, that distance is 6 inches. Set the column width of columns 1 and 3 to 0.5 inch.

3. Click the Row tab. Type **-.75"** in the Indent From Left box. This number pushes the crop mark to the left by the margin amount plus the width of the crop mark (0.5 for the margin and 0.25 for the crop mark in this case).

4. In the Height of Row box, select Exactly. In the At box, type the margin size you set up in the Page Setup dialog box minus the amount of your true margin (in this case, 1.5"-.5"=1") and click OK.

5. Select column 1 and apply a right and bottom border. Select column 3 and apply a left and bottom border. Your header table should look like the one in figure 11.19.

6. Copy the header and paste it into the footer. In the footer table, change the border formatting in columns 1 and 3.

Fig. 11.19

Crop marks make printers happy. Unfortunately, setting them up in Word requires a bit of math to get the settings right.

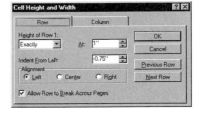

Creating Spot-Color Separations

Although you cannot print automatic color separations in Word, you can create spot color separations if you format your text in different colors. The method is quite a workaround, however. Word doesn't have any way to separate graphics, so you need to have a printer separate them traditionally. This technique also is cumbersome to use for more than two colors.

When you do spot color separations, you need to print a separate page for each color. This separate page contains only the elements you have designated to be a certain color on the page. When a printer runs a piece of paper through a press, each color is printed separately, so the printer needs a separate piece of art that contains just those elements. This separate piece of art is called a separation.

Basically, you use search and replace to format your entire multiple-color document to white except the text included in the separation (see fig. 11.20). You need to repeat the process for each color in the document. You change the text included in the separation to black. This method ensures that your text will line up exactly as you intended.

Fig. 11.20

Searching and replacing text color enables you to simulate a color separation.

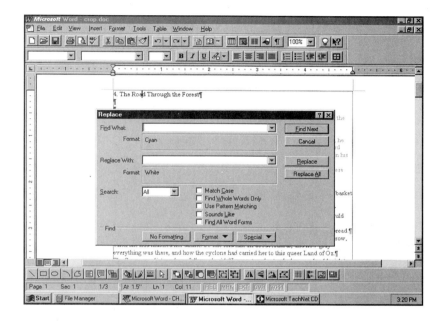

To create a spot-color separation, follow these steps:

1. Choose Edit, Replace.

2. Place your cursor in the Find What box and choose Format, Font. Under Color, select one of the text colors for which you are *not* creating the current color separation.

3. Place your cursor in the Replace With box and choose Format, Font. Select a text color of White.

4. Click Replace All. Repeat these steps for any colors you are not including in this separation.

5. Now do an Edit, Replace for the color you *do* want in the separation. Replace this color with black.

6. Print the document.

7. Close the document *without* saving the changes. (This is important!)

8. Reopen the document and repeat the steps to create a color separation for other text colors in your document.

11

Testing Files

If you have a PostScript printer, you can test your PostScript print files before you give them to a service bureau. Testing the files on your laser printer saves you time, aggravation, and money.

To test your files, follow these steps:

1. Print your document to a file as described in "Preparing Files for Service Bureaus" earlier in this section. You may want to give your file a PRN extension, so you can tell it apart from other files.

2. Open up an MS-DOS session under Windows.

3. Go to the directory that contains your file and type:

    COPY *FILENAME*.**PRN** *LPT1*:

    where *FILENAME*.PRN is the name of your file and LPT1 is the name of the port to which your laser printer is connected (see fig 11.21). This approach may seem archaic, but by bypassing the Windows printing system, this test simulates the environment at the printer or service bureau.

Fig. 11.21

Test your PostScript files on your laser printer before you send the files to a service bureau by copying them directly to your printer port from a DOS window.

When you change your printer driver to a high-resolution device such as a Linotronic, you may encounter unwelcome surprises. Some Word formatting is based on the printer driver you have selected, so you may be dismayed to find that Word has changed your document pagination or fonts when you switch printers. When you test your PostScript files, you can tell if your fonts were downloaded into the PostScript file and isolate other setup or pagination problems before you spend big money at the printer or service bureau.

Checking Proofs

The last part of the printing process is checking your proofs or bluelines against your own laser printed output. Strange things can happen at the printer, so always check your proofs carefully. On a document you've stared at a million times, looking at the proof upside down may help. Errors may pop out at you if you are not reading the text of the document. Check for sharpness, spots, marks, and flaws. Also check that nothing has been reversed or omitted.

When you give your corrections to the printer, be specific in your instructions. Circle the problem and describe what is wrong and how to fix it. If the problems are serious, request a second proof from the printer.

If, after approving the proof, something goes wrong with the job and the finished product is bad, *reject* the job. You are within your rights to reject a faulty print job. Many things are out of your control and are the printer's responsibility. For example, in humid weather, if a printer does not allow enough drying time between printing colors, the inks smear. That kind of thing is the printer's fault, not yours. A good printer graciously owns up to mistakes.

Summary

Many books have been written on desktop publishing; there is far more to the topic than the information presented in this chapter. However, when you start considering how your font and layout choices affect your readers, you have taken the first step toward thinking like a designer. Using Word, you have many of the tools you need to effectively convey a message to your reader.

By setting up your pages logically with your reader in mind, you can present a professional image that reflects well on you and the company you represent. Paying attention to whether or not your layout is pleasing to the eye makes the reader's job easier. Organizing your text and using repeating text elements such as headers and footers helps guide your readers through a document. If you plan your layout carefully, you also can incorporate graphics and special effects that complement the message in the text. Pulling these techniques together so that they work to create a cohesive message is what desktop publishing is all about.

PowerPoint

chapter 12

Critical Skills for Presentations

by Toni Messer

In this chapter

◆ **Presentation Skills**
Understand the impact of communications skills and visual communications on your presentations.

◆ **Planning Your Presentation**
Learn how to clarify your objectives and select the right points to emphasize.

◆ **Designing Visual Aids**
Learn when to use PowerPoint slides and other visuals, and what to include in them.

◆ **Delivering Your Presentation**
Understand the importance of your personal style to the success of your presentation.

PowerPoint enables you to easily create professional visual aids for your presentations—so easy, in fact, that it's natural to feel casual about throwing together a few overheads without putting much thought into them.

Visual images are very powerful. Visual aids can be an excellent addition to your presentation, but they can also detract from your message. Research has shown that good visuals increase the effectiveness of a presentation, but bad visuals *decrease* its effectiveness. To make your visuals work for and not against you, they should be designed with care.

Whether you're preparing visuals for your own use or designing them for someone else, you should think of them as a vital part of the presentation. This chapter discusses what you should think about *before* sitting down with PowerPoint to create your visuals.

The Importance of Presentation Skills

Of all the skills that are necessary in business—personal, technical, political, and so on—communications skills are the most important for success. You must be able to share your ideas with others in a way they can understand and accept. Your ability to influence others, to lead, to inspire, persuade, and educate, is governed by your communications expertise.

Many of us cringe at the thought of speaking in public. Stand-up presentations are intimidating. They are a complex form of communication that uses all of our verbal and non-verbal skills. Because they involve all our senses, presentations can be as engaging as live theater. As a presenter, you may not be an actor, but you are indeed on stage.

Developing your presentation skills is one of the most valuable things you can do for your career. A little training and practice will go a long way to help you conquer the fear of public speaking and help you shine in the corporate world.

The Power of Visual Communications

Communications experts say that people remember information differently, depending on how they acquire it. According to the Industrial Audio Visual Association, we remember:

▶ 10 percent of what we read

▶ 20 percent of what we hear

▶ 30 percent of what we see

▶ 50 percent of what we see and hear

We're a nation of watchers. Most of us learn by watching teachers in classrooms and newscasters on TV. We've become accustomed to the ease and rapid pace of professional delivery.

When you are standing in front of a group, whether two people or two hundred, your best visual aid is yourself—your appearance, your enthusiasm, your stage presence. Your visuals cannot replace you. Too many people try to hide behind their visuals, hoping the audience will not notice the speaker for the slides. That's what the huge stack of overheads is for!

Sorry, it doesn't work. You're the main attraction. Hundreds of books have been written about public speaking and the skills it requires. Visual aids are no substitute for these skills, or for planning, organizing, and practicing your speech. Visuals should not be used as a crutch, but as a tool. Used properly, they can improve your speech by making it more accessible to and memorable for your audience.

Visuals do the following:

- ▶ *Visuals get our attention.* They help break through the clutter of information overload and get us focused on the topic at hand.

- ▶ *Visuals take precedence.* Our eyes are quicker than our ears, and, for most people, more reliable. Faced with a conflict between our senses, when we see one thing and hear another, we will believe our eyes rather than our ears most of the time.

- ▶ *Visuals help us understand.* Abstract concepts are more easily grasped when visually illustrated (see fig. 12.1).

- ▶ *Visuals are remembered.* Our minds retain a visual image longer than they retain spoken words.

Fig. 12.1
A picture conveys a concrete example and makes it easier to understand the abstract words.

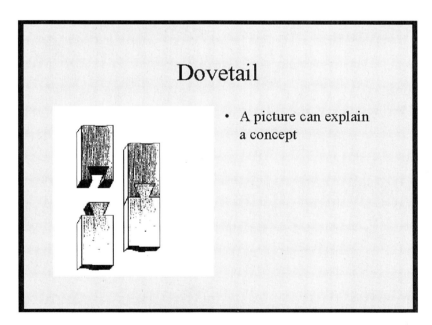

Understanding the Power of Speech

12

Enthusiasm, body language, and responsiveness can turn simple words into a moving speech. Nations have been inspired by great orators (as well as by scoundrels, but those scoundrels gave powerful speeches). Deals are won and lost on the quality of the presentation. Personal delivery skills are a critical element in any presentation.

The best way to develop your skills is by means of videotaped training sessions and regular practice with a group such as Toastmasters. There, you have an opportunity to practice your delivery—your posture and stance, your vocal tone and inflection, your pace, and so on—in a supportive setting. When it comes time to make a formal presentation, you will feel much more competent about it, and your audience will pick up on that.

Your audience is attuned to your emotions. They can hear anxiety in a voice that cracks. They can feel the uncertainty of a speaker who tries to buy time with "ers" and "ums." Similarly, they sense the confidence in a voice that uses the proper volume. A speaker who pauses for thought, instead of waffling with "um," is perceived as sure of the material.

The audience hears all these cues in your voice and in the flow of your speech. The audience labels you as confident and competent, or nervous and unsure, accordingly.

Planning Your Presentation

Planning your presentation involves knowing what you want to say and how you will say it to achieve your objectives. It involves allotting the proper amount of time to an introduction, body, close, and question and answer period. When planning your time, keep in mind that shorter is usually better. People have very short attention spans. Unless you're wildly entertaining, they'll appreciate a talk that won't keep them seated and captive for too long.

Clarifying Objectives

When you begin to prepare your presentation, the first issue to settle is the intent of your talk. Is it to persuade, educate, inspire? What message do you want to deliver? What main points do you want your audience to remember? How can you net out your message in a way people will understand, believe, and remember?

For example, you might be reporting on the results of a year of work by a task force. What highlights will you stress? What do you want your audience to walk away knowing, feeling, believing? Keep in mind that your audience will not remember your entire talk. They *will* remember the highlights. See figure 12.2 for an example.

If you haven't started by clarifying your objectives, your audience is likely to remember details that you didn't intend. Here are some techniques that can help you get to the heart of your topic:

▶ *Brainstorming*. Get all your ideas out on paper. Write down everything you think you want to talk about. Then review your notes with a critical eye. Group the topics that belong together, highlight the main points, and discard those that are marginal.

▶ *Outlining.* Design an introduction, a body, and a close. Focus on your main points and search for examples to illustrate them. Make sure the presentation has a logical progression.

▶ *Storyboarding.* Use thumbnail sketches and brief descriptions to work out the sequence of your presentation. Determine where visuals will help to emphasize or clarify a main point.

Fig. 12.2

Working from a wordy description to a concise outline often helps you plan the content and format of your visuals.

Presentation Objective: Educate management on task force results. Convince them that task force should be supported again next year.

What the task force did: Ten staff from Product Marketing, Finance and Sales met monthly during 1995 to discuss inventory levels, sales projections, sales actuals, and purchase plans. Arranged for monthly printouts on resale and service stock usage. Revised purchase plans based on sales projections in light of prior actuals. Spent about 240 staff hours, 10 programming hours.

Results: End-of-year inventory fell from $24M in 1994 to $16M in 1995. Reduction in carrying costs of nearly $1M. Increase of $9M in division's net income. We could cut another $4M from inventory next year.

Outline:

Inventory Task Force: 1995 Results

1. Inventory dropped from $24,000,000 to $16,000,000

2. Carrying costs dropped by $1,000,000

3. Bottom line: $9,000,000 savings

4. Cost: Roughly $10,000 in staff time and resources

5. Identified $4,000,000 in potential savings for 1996

Researching Your Subject and Audience

Part of being prepared is knowing your subject and your audience. To reach your audience, you need to project yourself into their world. What aspects of your subject are relevant to their concerns?

▶ *Knowing your subject.* When you stand in front of a group to talk, you're expected to be an expert on your subject. Assess your knowledge of the subject and understand your limitations. Restrict your talk to the aspects of the subject you know best. Be sure you're up on the latest developments in the area you're covering.

▶ *Knowing your audience.* Before, during, and after your talk, your audience should be foremost in your mind. Make sure you know their motivations and needs. Who are

12

they? Why are they there? What benefits will your talk have for them? Do you have a solution to one or more of their needs? Why should they pay attention to you?

▶ *Knowing what they know.* Anticipate your audience's level of knowledge of your subject. How much background information do they need? Try to bring them to a common level of understanding before you introduce new material.

Organizing Your Discussion

An agenda is an extremely useful device to help you lead your audience through your talk. Begin the presentation by showing them where you're going, and close it by reminding them where you've been. It's helpful to keep the agenda posted so that they can keep track of where you are. In a less formal setting, you might write the agenda on a flip chart, or tape it to a wall. In a more formal setting, you might display it from time to time on your slides. See the following for a sample agenda.

Today's Agenda

9:00 - 9:15	Introduction
9:15 - 9:30	Customer Requirements
9:30 - 10:00	Suggested Solution
10:00 - 10:15	Product Demonstration
10:15 - 10:30	Question and Answer Session

It's critical that your presentation have a clear, orderly flow. Oral presentations can be hard to follow. The audience will rely on your organization and emphasis to receive your message.

Again, it helps if you outline your presentation. It should have a clear introduction, body, and close:

▶ Use the *introduction* to establish rapport with the audience, and tell them what you're going to cover. One good way to establish rapport is to show them that you share a common background or experience. Doing so can set the stage for preparing them for your main message.

▶ Use the *body* of your presentation to deliver your message, selecting a few main points to emphasize with verbal examples and visuals. Make sure that these main points follow a logical sequence. If you're having difficulty making one or more points fit in the sequence, perhaps they don't belong at all.

▶ Use the *close* to review and summarize what you have already told them, and to suggest further action you'd like them to take. Don't be afraid to use terminology such as "Please remember and act on what we've discussed today, because if you do, you'll benefit."

Scheduling the Event

How large a crowd do you expect? Will it be a formal or informal presentation? Do you have a choice of rooms, seating arrangements, and presentation media? If you have choices, make them based on your objectives. The date, time, and place might have been arranged for you. Be sure that you know what else might have been arranged. What is the purpose of the meeting? Find out if you are the only speaker or if you're sandwiched between two others. The speaker who precedes you will have an effect on the audience, and you need to prepare yourself to deal with that effect. Will the audience have heard bad news? Good news? What of the speaker who follows you? Will the audience be anticipating what follows your presentation? Dreading it?

The best time for a presentation is usually in the morning—perhaps not so early that the audience feels rushed, but early enough that a prior appointment doesn't delay their arrival. Right after lunch is a notoriously difficult time to make a presentation: people tend to be drowsy. If you must present after a meal, it's even more important to keep things lively and brief.

Check out the room ahead of time. Will the seating arrangement allow everyone to see the screen? Will you need to bring an extension cord to place the equipment where you want it? The smallest details can make a big difference in the success of your delivery. The more you can anticipate, the more prepared you'll be.

It's a good idea to confirm your agenda with the audience during your introduction. For example, "I understand that we have 30 minutes for this part of the meeting. Is that right?" Then, pause to let them agree with your statement. Get a commitment from the audience that they will attend to you during your allotted time.

Using Visual Aids

A well-thought out visual provides interest and variety. Unnecessary visuals, however, just clutter your presentation. Use visuals to help your audience understand and remember what you want them to. Each visual should have a purpose. Use one to emphasize a point, to illustrate a concept, or to provide evidence for your assertions.

12

Prepared with care, visuals can:

▶ *Add interest.* Pictures, both black-and-white and color, can enliven almost any talk. They add variety and grab your attention.

▶ *Clarify.* Concepts, ideas, processes, and the organization of parts into a whole can be hard to convey with words alone. A simple, well-thought out diagram can depict a complex process that might be difficult to describe verbally.

▶ *Show proof.* Tables and charts with statistical evidence, such as the one shown in figure 12.3, reinforce your words and provide your talk with credibility.

▶ *Give examples.* Use your visuals to illustrate your message. It's easier for your audience to understand an abstract concept when you have provided a familiar example.

Fig. 12.3
Objective numbers and quantities particularly reinforce your audience's perception that you are reliable and credible.

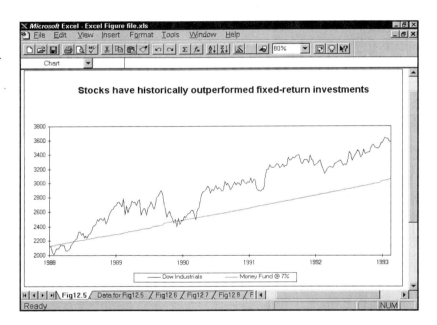

Designing Visual Aids

The basic design of your visuals will tend to flow from the type of presentation you prepare—that is, education, persuasion, or a call to action—and from the formats that your software provides. Beyond that basis, there are a few design rules that you should try to follow:

▶ *Be brief.* Net out your message with key words and phrases. Don't use complete sentences or full explanations; use your verbal explanation to expand on your visual. Don't try to display too much on one page. Put only one major point on a slide with a few supporting bullets, and never put more than seven bullets on a slide.

▶ *Be clear*. Use simple language. Avoid long words, acronyms, and jargon. The harder you make it for your audience to understand you, the less they will listen to you.

▶ *Be legible*. Make sure that your visuals can be seen from the back of the room. Use upper- and lowercase lettering. All uppercase is okay for headings, but it is not easy to read. Write labels horizontally, not vertically.

▶ *Be accurate*. Check for spelling errors with your software's Spelling feature and make sure proper names are spelled correctly. Then, ask someone else to proofread your slides for spelling and grammar errors.

▶ *Be selective*. Don't try to illustrate your entire talk with visuals. Select the points you want to emphasize and use visuals for impact. *You* must select what you want the audience to notice and remember.

▶ *Use pictures*. Drawings, graphs, maps, and diagrams can help your audience grasp your concepts and will make a stronger impression than words (see fig. 12.4).

▶ *Use restraint*. Don't make your slides garish and confusing with too many colors, fonts, symbols, logos, and so on.

Fig. 12.4

Which visual did you look at first?

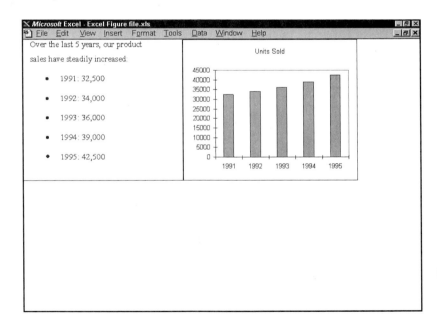

Deciding Which Type of Visual to Use

Your software provides you a variety of choices of the *type* of visual to present, for any given point. Here are some ground rules to help you with your options.

Using Text

Text is the most commonly used form of visual, as well as the most often misused. A copy of a memo, a page out of a book, or a laundry list of issues is *not* an effective visual aid.

But text is often appropriate on a visual. Consider using text to display an agenda, a simple table, or a short list of bulleted points.

Some guidelines for effective text are:

▶ Use no more than seven bullets.

▶ Use short, simple words.

▶ Make your phrasing parallel. That is, if your first point starts with a gerund, start your others with gerunds (Acting…, Managing…, Directing…, not Acting…, Managed…, Direct…)

▶ Avoid complex sentences or paragraphs

▶ PowerPoint's Wizards and templates supply you with default fonts and font styles for text. It's smart to use them to avoid a cluttered mix of fonts.

Using Column Charts and Bar Charts

You can use Column charts (oriented vertically) and Bar charts (oriented horizontally) to show relationships among variables. You can use them, for example, to illustrate the relationship between costs and revenues. You can also use charts to show relationships among different values of the same variable. For example, each bar could show revenue for a different year.

These charts can be dramatic and informative when you have quantitative information to convey. If you use them, however, keep the following points in mind:

▶ Be sure there are significant differences to show. What's the point of showing four virtually identical columns?

▶ Clearly label each bar. Few things chop up your presentation more than reading a litany of numbers or labels to your audience.

▶ Don't use vertical lettering—it is too hard to read. Use a chart title, or a chart legend, or a floating label instead of an axis title to explain the chart's vertical axis.

Using Pie Charts

Pie charts are excellent for showing how individual parts relate to the whole. For example, you might use a pie chart to show the relative headcount in different departments, or the relative contribution of different product lines to total revenue. Make sure you do the following:

▶ Focus your audience's attention on the main point. For example, Excel offers several different attractive pie chart subtypes. Ask yourself whether a 3D pie chart with value labels that separate one slice from the rest enhances or obscures the information.

▶ Group insignificant sections into one miscellaneous category.

Compare the charts in figure 12.5 to see how different chart formats can work to your advantage and disadvantage.

Fig. 12.5

Several unimportant categories distract from the important ones.

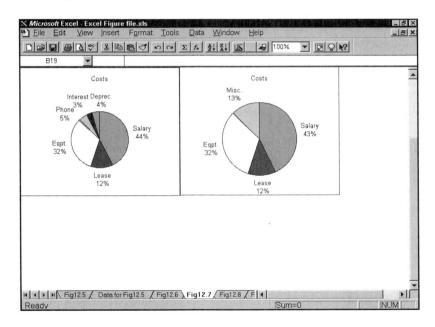

 Note

Notice the discrepancy in the percentages shown in the charts in figure 12.5. Excel's pie charts sometimes return slightly erroneous value labels, and you'll want to ensure that they display the intended percentages.

12

Using Line Charts

You usually use line charts to display changes in numeric data over time. They are an excellent way to show trends, cycles, changes, or patterns. For line charts, keep these two points in mind:

▶ It's easy to unintentionally mislead your audience with your vertical axis scale. Notice that the upper chart in figure 12.6 makes it appear that the monthly increase in unit sales is fairly strong. But this is an artifact of the scale's minimum value of 23,000. The lower chart uses a minimum value of 0 for the vertical axis and makes it clear that although sales are growing, the growth rate is fairly flat.

▶ Limit the number of data series to avoid confusion. Two or three data series is a useful maximum on any given chart. And you certainly should omit any data series that you don't intend to talk about.

Fig. 12.6

Be sure to set your chart scales so that they display their information accurately.

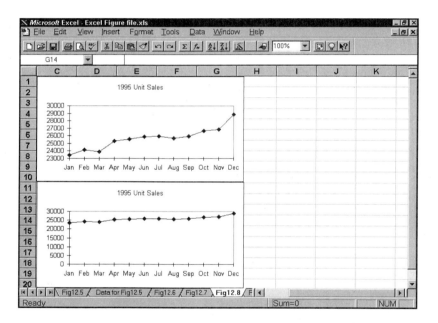

Using Other Chart Types

Don't neglect these other useful visuals if they advance your message or help to engage your audience:

▶ *Flow charts.* Use these to depict processes. With all charts, but particularly with flow charts, break up complex flows into separate charts.

▶ *Maps.* These are a great way to show how numeric variables—regional sales figures, for example—are distributed geographically. Consider using Excel's Map tool to create the visual, as shown in figure 12.7.

▶ *Organization charts.* These are occasionally necessary to depict how work flows among different groups and how a company allocates business responsibilities. However, use these types of charts sparingly and briefly. Watch for your audience's eyes glazing over.

▶ *Photographs.* Look for opportunities to put photographs into your presentation. Photos, especially of people, enliven your presentation.

Fig. 12.7
The density of the dots in the map can have a stronger impact than the raw numbers.

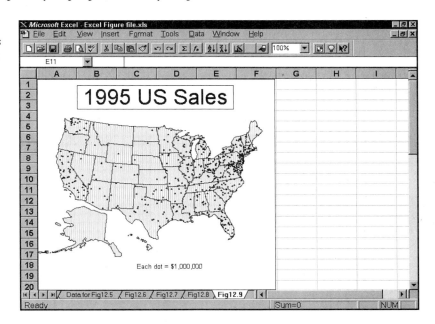

Delivering Your Presentation

Probably the most important guidance for your delivery is to practice, practice, practice. If you can, rustle up a sympathetic audience that will give you constructive feedback. Have yourself videotaped if at all possible. It's the best way to become aware of the distracting mannerisms we all seem to have that detract from our message.

At the very least, practice in front of a mirror. Time yourself. If you don't, it's difficult to judge how long your talk will really take.

12

Meeting Your Public

Anxiety about public speaking is normal. So normal, in fact, that it is the most frequently occurring phobia in the population. But you can blunt its effect, and even turn it to your advantage. Here are some ways you can do so.

Breaking the Tension

Many professional speakers take a brisk walk before their presentation to work off some nervous energy. Practice deep breathing before you go on to calm your nerves. Realize that your nervous energy can be transformed into enthusiasm!

Arriving Early

This is imperative. Give yourself time to check out the room, seating, and equipment. An extra 10 minutes can save your bacon if someone has commandeered the projector or if its bulb has burnt out. If possible, meet your guests as they arrive and introduce yourself to begin to establish rapport.

Being Aware of First Impressions

It takes seven seconds for people to form an impression of you. They take in your appearance, your demeanor, and your energy level in that period of time. Then, they form an opinion. Frightening, no? It needn't be. Just remember the following:

▶ *Your appearance counts.* Groom carefully and dress appropriately for the occasion.

▶ *Your attitude counts.* A friendly, likable speaker is hard to resist.

Establishing Rapport

Smile and greet your audience with enthusiasm. Welcome them and make them feel glad they came. Tell them something about yourself and why you're there. Tell a humorous story if you're comfortable doing so and if it leads into your talk. If not: *don't*. A lame joke is a bad way to start, and it's hard to recover.

Perfecting Personal Style

Your purpose is to direct your audience's attention to your message. You'll need to gain, and regain, their attention. Any distractions will dilute their attention and your impact. A strong personal style is one way to minimize distractions:

▶ *Display energy and enthusiasm.* Focused energy and enthusiasm capture an audience's attention and influence their emotions. Nothing you say is as important as how you say it in a personal presentation. Convert your nervous energy into enthusiasm for your topic.

▶ *Control nervous habits.* Do you jangle the change in your pockets as you talk? Empty your pockets ahead of time. The best way to learn to control nervous habits, like shuffling your feet or twirling your hair, is to become aware of them by watching and listening to yourself on videotape. This can be a humbling experience, but it usually humbles even experienced presenters.

▶ *Be aware of your posture and movement.* Stand comfortably erect with your arms relaxed at your sides. Avoid crossing your arms or putting your hands in your pockets. Use your arms for intentional emphasis and demonstration. Purposeful gestures and movement are very effective to guide your audience's attention. Unconscious fidgeting and pacing are distracting.

▶ *Project your voice.* Use a microphone if you need one. Make sure everyone can hear you. Checkpoint this with your audience shortly into your presentation.

 Tip

If you use a wireless microphone, be careful not to walk near the speakers. If the volume is high enough, the microphone can produce feedback.

▶ *Use vocal variety.* A monotone voice will lull your audience to sleep. Listen to your recorded voice with a critical ear.

▶ *Avoid "Ums" and "Ahs."* People who sprinkle their talks with "Ums" are afraid of the silence between words and phrases. There is nothing wrong with silence. It is far less distracting than nervous fillers. Practice by recording your talk ahead of time to become aware of fillers in your speech. Work to eliminate them.

▶ *Save your handouts for afterwards.* People will read ahead if you give them a handout, and that means they won't be listening to you. Tell them they'll have a copy of your slides after the talk. Then, they'll be free to pay attention to you and to your visuals.

12

Tip

You're likely to distract the audience by fiddling with anything you're holding, whether it's a pointing device or a sheaf of papers or a highlighter. Put it down when you're not using it.

▶ *Have a glass of water handy*. Nervousness causes dry throats. There's nothing wrong with stopping briefly to sip some water. Your audience will appreciate it.

 Tip

Be careful with water glasses or bottles, especially if you're making an electronic presentation. Spilled water shorts out computers.

Using Visual Aids Effectively

Even the best visuals don't completely speak for themselves. You must integrate them into your presentation by introducing and explaining them.

▶ *Introduce*. Explain what you're going to show before displaying it. For example, you might say, "I'd like to show you a graph of the stock I'm talking about."

▶ *Explain*. Describe what the visual depicts. "This is a graph showing the stock price fluctuation from January to December of last year."

▶ *Talk to your audience*. Always maintain eye contact with your audience. Don't turn your head to address the slide. Put a hard copy of your presentation on the table where you can glance down at it briefly, if you find it necessary.

▶ *Don't block their view*. This sounds obvious, but people do it all the time. Stand to one side of the screen (see fig. 12.8).

▶ *Don't let slides become a distraction*. Remove the visual when you finish talking about it. Turn off the projector or the computer when the last visual has been displayed.

Fig. 12.8
Using a pointer helps you to stay away from the screen but still direct the audience's attention to your visual's main topics.

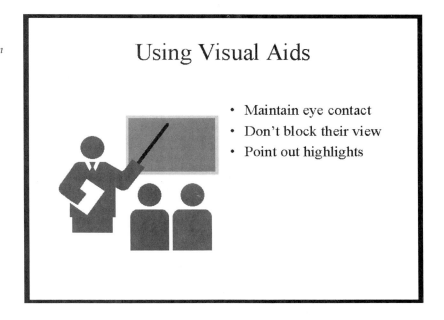

Closing the Presentation

Plan a strong ending for your presentation. Your closing is as important to your impact as is your opening. Remember that your closing is the final opportunity to have an effect. There are ways that you can arrange a strong closing:

▶ Earlier, this chapter advised you to use your introduction to tell the audience what you are about to tell them. Similarly, use your closing to summarize the main points that you made. This helps ensure that the audience remembers them after they leave.

▶ Allow time for a question-and-answer session. Even if you asked the audience to raise questions during the presentation, people may have hesitated to interrupt you. Give them a formal opportunity to request additional information or clarification.

▶ Thank the audience for attending. They almost certainly gave up an opportunity to do something else in order to listen to you, and they deserve your thanks.

▶ Distribute handouts or have the audience pick them up as they leave. Not before—you don't want them reading instead of listening and watching.

12

Summary

This chapter has advised you to begin a presentation by telling your audience what you're going to tell them, and to close by telling them what you told them. If you keep the following points in mind, you will be able to take maximum advantage of the visuals that you can make using PowerPoint:

▶ Use the visuals to emphasize the most important parts of your talk.

▶ Make sure that your visuals can be easily read and understood.

▶ Be selective so that the visuals don't become boring or overwhelming.

▶ Work—work *hard*—on polishing your personal mannerisms and vocal style.

PowerPoint takes the hard work out of producing good-looking visuals for your presentations. In order to work well, however, the visuals must be designed with care. The next chapter begins this book's discussion of PowerPoint itself.

chapter 13

Sharing PowerPoint Information

13

by Brian Reilly

In this chapter

◆ **Transfer presentations from one computer to another**
Moving presentations to other desktops, laptops, and across networks—even to Macs—can be done easily without unwanted surprises.

◆ **Manage color system idiosyncrasies**
Moving between 16 million and 256 colors or RGB and CMYK colors can be done, but the differences need to be understood.

◆ **Integrate presentations from other programs like Lotus Freelance into PowerPoint**
Translating presentations across programs is not as easy as translating text documents but can be done if you follow some guidelines.

◆ **Make your presentations truly portable**
When you need to distribute presentations on floppy disks, you can use the new Pack and Go Wizard to compress it and even include a PowerPoint viewer.

In this chapter, you learn about a number of pitfalls in sharing PowerPoint information and how to avoid them. The chapter covers how to deal with differences in sharing presentations on different types of equipment. You learn about differences in video and printer drivers, fonts, networks, service bureaus, ways of showing colors, sharing presentations between PowerPoint 7 and previous versions of PowerPoint, and using Macintoshes.

Transferring PowerPoint Files from One Computer to Another

If you've ever created most of a presentation in your office and then taken it home on your laptop to finish it, you may have found that on the laptop everything is suddenly out of position and the fonts are all wrong. You also may have found that the presentation won't print correctly, that the scans look awful, or even that you can't save the simple changes you made. Why presentations behave differently on different computers is a common cause of frustration, but it needn't be. You learn to understand and anticipate the problems that may arise and how to avoid those problems.

Printer and Video Drivers

A presentation you review on a different computer may not look at all like it did on your computer in the office. This may actually be a printer driver problem rather than a PowerPoint problem. The video driver relies on information from whatever printer driver is installed to determine how to display things. If the display doesn't look right, the laptop probably doesn't have the proper printer driver or even any printer driver installed. This is a common problem. Install a printer driver for a common mainstream printer, such as one of the HP laser printers, from the Windows 95 installation disk. Even though you don't plan to print from your laptop, PowerPoint relies on this driver to determine how to display the presentation.

Fonts

Designers often use special fonts to enhance the presentation. If your presenter doesn't have the same font installed on his or her computer that you used, PowerPoint will choose a font to substitute when he or she attempts to view the presentation. Although some of these substitutions work quite well, some can cause unpleasant surprises, such as words overlapping or running off the page.

PowerPoint enables you to easily identify what fonts are used in a presentation and choose others to replace those that are unavailable. To replace fonts, follow these steps:

1. Choose Tools, Replace Fonts.
2. Select the font you want to replace from the Replace pull-down list (see fig. 13.1).
3. Select the font you want to use from the With pull-down list.
4. Click the Replace button.

Fig. 13.1

Replace the unavailable fonts with those that you do have.

Understanding what fonts are installed with which program can help eliminate many font problems. Windows installs only Times New Roman, Symbol, and Wingdings as usable type fonts. Several Microsoft fonts are installed with Windows 95, but these fonts are available for use by the system only to display items like the menus. They are not fonts that applications can use. Office can install an additional 29 families of fonts; however, these fonts fill up nearly 3.5M on your hard drive. A laptop-user squeezed for space can get along just fine without Playbill, Braggadocio, Brush Script, Modern, and perhaps some other fonts. You are never sure what fonts are going to be installed on other machines. If you are creating a presentation for use on other computers, it is critical that you be aware of the fonts that will be available on those computers, or the presentation may not look like the presentation you created.

PowerPoint provides an option for embedding TrueType fonts within a presentation. But if you use a non-TrueType font, even if it came with Office 95, you cannot embed it. You will see the error message shown in figure 13.2.

Fig. 13.2

Only TrueType fonts can be embedded in presentations.

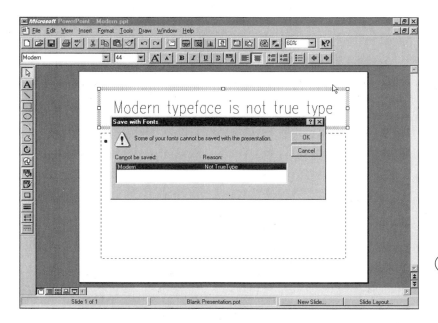

13

You can enclose the fonts that you used in the presentation with the file. This is useful when sending the file to a service bureau, but it may be a bit optimistic to send it to a salesman in the field or a client and expect him to be willing—or able—to install that font.

 Note

Managing fonts in Windows 95 is a great deal easier than it was in Windows 3.x. The fonts are now located in a Fonts folder inside the top-level Windows 95 folder. New fonts can be installed by merely dragging the font file into the Fonts folder. To distribute the fonts with your presentation, simply drag the appropriate fonts to a floppy disk and supply that disk with your presentation file. This copies the font file onto the floppy disk and leaves your original file intact.

Additionally, Windows 95 manages available fonts far better than Windows 3.x. Under Windows 3.x, a large number of fonts loaded in PowerPoint, whether they are used in a presentation or not, drastically slows down the operation of PowerPoint 4. Now you can have a great many more fonts installed and available without noticing a performance difference.

When a presentation is going to be shown on a variety of machines, it's a safe bet to use Times New Roman. It is a very readable typeface and is likely to be present on every Windows machine because it is the only text font automatically installed with Windows 95. Although the Microsoft TrueType font pack is available when a Mac user installs PowerPoint on a Mac, the Mac and PC will very likely substitute the correct font. It's difficult to imagine a Mac not having Times installed.

Although Arial generally is available on most PCs, it's actually not installed automatically by Windows 95. If you want to be really cautious, stick to Times New Roman.

Working on a Network

There are several critical issues to consider that can affect the success of moving your presentations across networks.

One of these issues is the speed of the network. If you are working on a fast network, you'll find it easy to share large files with others. But if you work on a network that was designed for moving small files, such as text files or small spreadsheets, don't try to open a large presentation from a network drive without expecting a long wait. Depending on the size of the presentation and the speed and traffic on a network, you may experience waits of 20 minutes or more. That is a function of the network and not of PowerPoint.

Using links to move a file across a network drive can also be a problem because PowerPoint looks for the links in the directories where they were established in the first place. The automatic links option will try to open every link when the file is opened—not finding the source, PowerPoint will complain about each link. Suppose that you create a page in PowerPoint with a link to an Excel spreadsheet and that you keep your spreadsheet data on your personal hard drive (drive C:). If you move that presentation to your boss to view on drive N, the PowerPoint presentation will look to your drive C:, which isn't necessarily available to the network to update the links. If it's not available, it can't update the links.

 Note

Moving linked files becomes a logistical issue that you need to solve based on your specific needs. A very good practice is to create a unique directory for the presentation and keep all data files in that same directory with the presentation. For most presenters, chances are very high that the presentation will move off the network to a laptop or to another computer off the network. In that situation, it makes sense to create the original presentation and data directory in drive C:, because virtually any computer is going to have a drive C:. When you then move the presentation, you only have to create a new directory in drive C: and copy the presentation and data files there. In this case, PowerPoint will look to that directory on drive C: for all links.

Transfer Speeds

Network transfer speeds can vary from very fast to very slow. While standing in front of an audience, one presenter had the unpleasant experience of opening a file from a network drive on a very slow network and waiting twenty minutes for it to open. The file was over 40M and contained a good number of high-resolution scans because it was prepared for slides. It would have been less embarrassing if the file had been moved to the local hard drive before the meeting. This would have been time-consuming, but it would have been the presenter's time rather than that of her audience. If it had been moved to the local C: drive, this file would have opened within two minutes.

Links to Other Files

If you plan to share your files across the network, be cautious about using links to Excel, Word, or other files. If the links were created originally on your own hard drive, remember to set the Edit Links option to manual updates rather than automatic. Otherwise, the program cannot locate the linked files, and you are bombarded with error messages. If you have to move linked files across various drives or machines, you can set the update links to manual to avoid the error messages. Simply choose Edit, Links and click Manual to do this (see fig. 13.3). If you want to reestablish the links for later updates, you can change the source of the link manually.

Fig. 13.3

Change the source of your linked files link by link.

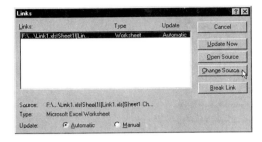

Sharing Files with a Service Bureau

Turning your presentations into 35mm slides or into color prints is often done by sending your files out to a service bureau. A service bureau is a company that specializes in this type of output. Because they prepare slides for many customers, they can afford high-speed color printers and expensive slide imaging cameras.

If you have already worked out the rough edges in dealing with service bureaus in the past several years, especially on operations performed frequently, you may still be in for a surprise or two when switching to PowerPoint 7.

Because there is currently no Mac version of PowerPoint 7 available, the first issue is whether the service bureau is really a full-service, PC-based operation, or if it is servicing PC files through a Mac system. If the service bureau is PC-based, a second issue is whether it is running PowerPoint 7. If the Service Bureau is Mac-based and not making the camera-ready files on a PC running PowerPoint 7, it will have to make these files as PowerPoint 4 files. You then will lose whatever features you may have used that are available only in PowerPoint 7, such as textured fills and transparent fills. Your files will revert to what is available in PowerPoint 4—in this case, a solid fill. The same would apply to a service bureau that is not using PowerPoint 7.

Another difference between PowerPoint 7 and PowerPoint 4 is the way PowerPoint determines colors and what color information is sent to the printer device. PowerPoint 4 uses a color system that combines red, green, and blue values in over 65,000 steps to determine a color. PowerPoint 7 uses a much more conventional 256 steps. Although there should be no problem with converting these colors between programs if you are using True color (16 million colors), there may be some significant differences if you are using only 256 colors.

If you will be creating either a large number of slides or prints for an extremely important meeting, or if you create this kind of output frequently, it is very important to establish a good relationship with at least one service bureau who understands what you want and what your limitations are. There are many ways to accomplish a task, and a service bureau can be a great source of knowledge because they deal with a wide variety of situations every day.

It's a good idea for the service bureau to print their file to a standard PostScript printer before making the Winslide file. If the application is spitting out bad PostScript information, you'll find out now rather than 12 hours before your deadline when the service bureau calls and says that there may be a problem with your file.

Service bureaus often can receive files by modem through a bulletin board or through their own custom bulletin board software. With a modem hookup, you can send the file over the modem with delivery and billing instructions automatically filled out on a simple form. An example of this kind of custom software is included on the CD-ROM that comes with this book.

 Note

Some service bureaus that do not run PowerPoint 7 have a perfectly valid solution to this dilemma. They provide printer drivers, free of charge, that will print your PowerPoint 7 files to a PostScript file. This PostScript file is not editable or viewable, but the file can be read by a PostScript printer device, whether it be a slide camera or a printer.

In a nutshell, there is nothing in PowerPoint 7 that should make output of files at a service bureau any more difficult than in the past, but this is a good time to output a few test slides or prints to be sure that your service bureau is staying as current as you are.

Dealing with Color

With more variety in the number of computers in use, presentations must be more versatile than ever. Along with more sophisticated ways to show color have also come special problems.

Less Capable Systems

When you plan to share your presentation with others, don't assume everyone has the same equipment, even in your own company. Keep in mind that others may view the

13

presentation on computers considerably less capable than the ones for which the presentation was designed. Another user's computer may be far less capable of displaying colors, be much slower, or may not even have enough memory to run a presentation.

Many nongraphics professionals have their computer set to show no more than 256 colors on-screen. You might even find that many can't show more than 16 colors. The scan that looks great in 16 million colors on the monitor in your office can look terrible when it's projected from a laptop that only shows 16 colors. A laptop's hard drive also may be so full that you have problems opening a file or resaving a file, even if you change only one letter of text.

This is not to say you have to prepare presentations for the lowest common denominator. Be aware, however, that what you want to present may not show up the same on another monitor or may not be able to be modified.

Color Printers

When you print to slides or to black and white, it is relatively easy to match color logos. But with new color printers, it may seem more difficult. This is because the color system for the slides and monitor is completely different from the color system for the printer.

Monitors and slides show all colors in combinations of red, green, and blue. A color printer prints all colors in combinations of cyan, magenta, yellow, and black. This is why slides and monitors are said to use an RGB system and the printer a CMYK system (K stands for black).

PowerPoint uses an RGB color system to describe every color it can show or print. When PowerPoint sends the color information to the color printer, it is the printer's job to translate the RGB value it is given from PowerPoint into a CMYK combination. This translation often is not a very close approximation of how it started out and will be unacceptable to color-critical users. Poor translation of RGB colors into CMYK is not a function that's specific to PowerPoint. All RGB-based programs have poor color translation on color printers.

Trial and error is the only way to get an RGB value in PowerPoint that is an acceptable CMYK value on your printer. At the same time, choosing this other value may change the RGB color on the monitor enough to make *that* unacceptable.

If you need both color renditions to be acceptable, a workaround is to create the art correctly for one version and then use a paint program to create a separate piece of art of exactly the same pixel size to place over the other piece of art for its other use. If you zoom the screen to a high magnification, you can nudge the artwork into place with the arrow keys. This way you can tell when the art is exactly located over the underlying art.

You will see edges to the overlying piece of art if it is not aligned exactly. By using the arrow keys, you can nudge the overlying piece of art, pixel by pixel, until you cannot see any edges between the overlying art and the background art. (Don't forget to take the overlying art out when it's not needed.) While this is a bit tedious, it is the easiest way to solve the problem without creating two separate presentations.

 Tip

Print a variety of test color swatches and start from there. It may take a little time, but you should be able to get a color that is very close to what you want. To shorten the time of creating color swatches to print as tests, you can also download a file called V7Palette.zip (193k) from the PowerPoint library on CompuServe. This file is a hand-created copy of the hexagon color picker in PowerPoint. Because you cannot copy the color picker to a file, this is the easiest way to print those color values.

To confuse printing issues even more, many color printers come with minimal memory installation. This can create problems in PowerPoint and other landscape-oriented programs. On one color printer with 2M of printer memory, a 4M file in Word would print fine. However, in PowerPoint and other landscape-oriented presentation programs, an `Out of Printer Memory` error might occur. The only solution is to add memory. 6M of printer memory seems to handle most files.

Sharing with Previous Versions of PowerPoint and with Macs

As noted previously, a PowerPoint 7 file can be saved as a version 4 copy, which then can be opened in either the PC or Mac version 4. But many of the special effects that are new in version 7 are converted to version 4 effects or dropped altogether.

In addition to the textured and transparent fills being converted to solid fills, all the new animation transitions in version 7 are dropped or converted to other transitions. If the file is reopened in version 7, those effects may be lost or changed to a completely different kind of effect. However, if you are familiar with the differences between version 7 and version 4, and you design entirely in version 4 techniques, you can move files seamlessly back and forth.

Some other effects new to PowerPoint 7 that get lost by saving as a PowerPoint 4 file are:

13

▶ Graphical builds—build effects such as fly from left, and sounds associated with those builds

▶ Interactive settings, including launching another program

▶ Sounds associated with slide transitions

There are also several special issues related specifically to moving files back and forth from PC to Mac. Recognizing these issues can make your life much easier:

▶ Files have to be named in the PC format of eight characters with a PPT extension. Version 7 does not recognize a Mac long file name—even with a PPT extension.

▶ Video clips (.avi files) will not work because they are incompatible file formats.

▶ Sound clips cannot play across multiple slides on the Mac, but they can on the PC.

▶ Adobe Illustrator EPS files with transparent whites from the Mac will not show on-screen on the PC, although they will print perfectly.

▶ Mac files that are sent to PCs via e-mail often cannot be opened on the PC. Zipping the file first on the Mac and unzipping it on the PC eliminates this problem.

▶ Fonts, as always, can be an issue. Use Tools, Replace Fonts if necessary.

▶ When pictures are reduced to 256 colors on the Mac, you can have some problems. The color palettes in the Mac and PC are different and can cause significant color shifts when moved across platforms. Also try to create the picture in 256 colors in a program such as Adobe Photoshop, which lets you save it with an adaptive palette rather than a system palette.

 Note

The essential difference between a system palette and an adaptive palette is the specific 256 colors that the computer displays for that image. In the system palette, the computer uses the Windows-defined 256 colors, which is based on a uniform sampling of the entire color spectrum available. The adaptive palette creates 256 colors to use based on a sampling of colors that are more frequently used in that specific image. Simplistically, if you show a red rose, a system palette will give you only approximately 30 or 40 colors of red to choose from to display the redness of that rose. An adaptive palette may give you well over 100 choices of red, which would give you a better representation of the red rose.

Sharing with Lotus Freelance, Harvard Graphics, and Other Programs

When you need to display other files that you don't have control over—say, files from another presentation package like Lotus Freelance or Harvard Graphics—don't despair. Translations of presentation files can be accomplished, but it is sometimes difficult. If you have to demonstrate another program—perhaps your own custom application—during a presentation, you are still in luck. Launching another program from within PowerPoint is quite easy.

Presentation Translators and Translations

Unfortunately, presentation files are complex animals and don't set themselves up for easy translations between programs. But, while there are some cautions to keep in mind about translating files, don't be timid about taking files into PowerPoint or moving them out to Lotus Freelance or Harvard Graphics. That is, as long as you don't expect it to be a perfectly smooth ride.

PowerPoint does have several file translators that ship with PowerPoint 7, the newest of which is for Lotus Freelance version 2.0, 2.1. If PowerPoint has a translator for the program you are trying to get into, by all means try that first. You may be able to use a large number of the slides from the file to be translated, depending on how complex they are. However, not every slide translates well. Some don't make it at all.

If you are trying to translate a Lotus Freelance file, for example, try the following:

1. Choose File, Open.
2. Select the location and proper file format from Files of Type (see fig. 13.4).

The file opens and goes through a translation process, which may take a couple of minutes depending on how complex the presentation.

Review the translation of your file and note the pages that are fine and those that aren't. Keep in mind that if the file imports but elements have been moved, it still may be faster to move the elements on that particular slide back into place than it would be to re-create the slide from scratch. These slides, including graphs, are now fully editable just as if they had been created originally in PowerPoint. You can even change the data in the charts, and they will redraw. This has now become a PowerPoint file, and all the PowerPoint tools are available for editing. Don't be shattered, however, if some elements shifted around.

13

Fig. 13.4

*Open files for transla-
tion with a translator.*

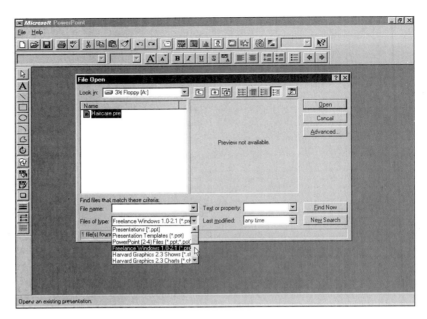

You may have two other situations facing you:

▶ The program you just tried to translate did not translate well or at all.

▶ There is no translator for the program you are trying to translate.

If either of these is the case, here are some general guidelines:

▶ Does the program Save As (Export) in another file format? PowerPoint saves pages, one by one, as Windows metafiles (WMF). Other programs may do the same or save in a file format that PowerPoint can insert as a picture. If this is possible, save/export the pages you need and import them into the new program as a picture, or whatever comparable command is appropriate for that program.

▶ If this fails, you can try the "slide viewer to slide viewer/slide" approach. All the major presentation programs have a way of viewing more than one slide at a time. Switch the file that you want to copy from to this view. You can either copy several slides at a time from this view to another program in the same view, or you can copy one slide at a time from this view to another program in "slide edit" view. This not only captures all the graphics and words, but will also capture the background.

Note

None of these methods works perfectly in every situation. You may want to copy some pages while you re-create some pages entirely from scratch.

You will also notice that the file is imported entirely on one level. The background is now part of the page in the new file. So you may want to delete the background master in the original file and create a new master in the new file. Files that are imported this way can often be ungrouped, but not always. Also, charts that are imported this way lose their attachment to the original data and will be uneditable.

 Tip

When you need to recreate a chart from another program because it will not import without losing its data, you may run into the problem that the x and y axes for the datasheets for the two programs are transposed. Such is the case in going from Lotus Freelance to PowerPoint. A simple workaround for handling this situation is to use the copy-and-paste functions a few times and transpose the data in Excel. You can copy from one program's datasheet and paste it into Excel with Edit, Paste Special, Transpose. Then copy that part of the Excel spreadsheet and paste it into the datasheet for the correct page in PowerPoint. This can be accomplished with no rekeying and no (or minimal) reproofing.

Running Other Programs from PowerPoint During Your Presentation

If you have a large number of presentations to translate from another program and run as a PowerPoint file, you're better off just running that part of your presentation from within its own program. Or, if you want to run a specific program during your presentation, you can do that as well without the hassles of translating the files to a PowerPoint format. Just launch the desired program from within PowerPoint and return to PowerPoint when you are done. All it takes is a touch of the mouse.

13

To launch another program from within PowerPoint, go to the slide from which you want to launch this other program and follow these steps:

1. Select an object you want to use as a launch button. It can be a graphical object like a rectangle or a picture. It can even be a selection of words such as the headline on the page.

2. Choose Tools, Interactive Settings from the menu (see fig. 13.5).

3. Click the Run Programs option button and enter the name and path of the program that you want to run, or choose Browse to select the file.

4. Click OK.

Fig. 13.5

Use Browse to set the path to the program to launch.

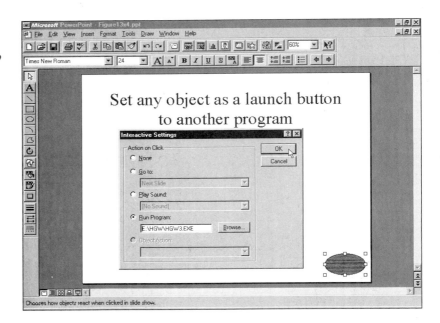

When you are in Slide Show view, the mouse pointer switches from an arrow to a hand with a pointing finger (see fig. 13.6) when the mouse is over the object set to launch your special application. Simply clicking the object activates the program you have selected. Closing or minimizing the program returns you immediately to PowerPoint.

Fig. 13.6
The cursor turns into a hand, indicating when you can launch the other program.

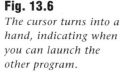

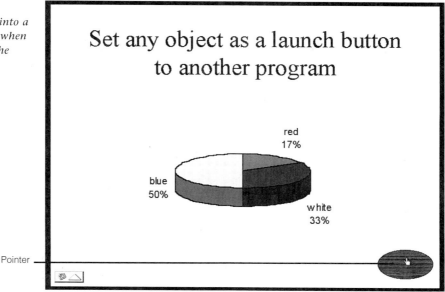

Pointer

Using the Pack and Go Wizard

Not too long ago, presentations had to be split up and put on disks to be moved to a laptop for travel purposes. File size was dramatically reduced when Harvard Graphics created a way to drop all the resolution down to 256 colors.

Now Microsoft PowerPoint has made a big step forward with its Pack and Go feature. Pack and Go lets you create a self-extracting file, which you can copy to multiple floppy disks (with prompting for a new floppy). To use Pack and Go, follow these steps:

1. Choose, File, Pack and Go, and Next to start. The Pack and Go Wizard dialog box appears.
2. Choose the presentation, and then choose Next.
3. Choose the drive to export to (see fig. 13.7) and again choose Next.
4. Click if you want to Include Linked Files or to Embed True Type Fonts, or leave blank if not (see fig. 13.8). Choose Next.
5. Click Include the PowerPoint Viewer if you want the PowerPoint viewer to be packed as well (see fig. 13.9).
6. Choose Next and then choose Finish.

13

Fig. 13.7
Pick the drive to pack to. You will be prompted for additional floppies for Drive A.

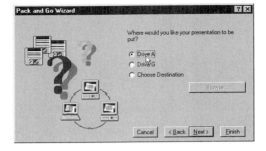

Fig. 13.8
Include linked files and Embed TrueType fonts if necessary.

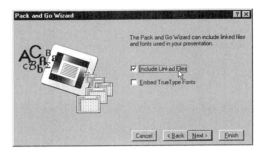

Fig. 13.9
You can pack the PowerPoint Viewer as well.

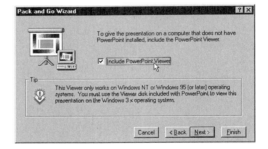

If you choose not to include the PowerPoint Viewer, you end up with an EXE file named PNGSETUP.EXE and a file named Pres0.png. The EXE file is what you double-click to install the entire presentation. The Pres0.png file is the data file in MS PowerPoint zipped format.

To unpack the presentation from Windows, you can double-click the PNGSETUP.EXE file even if the presentation is on floppy disks and the first floppy is in drive A. You will be prompted for a directory to place the presentation. Note the next warning because this process will overwrite any existing files of the same name. The presentation then will be unpacked automatically, and you can launch the presentation immediately in Slide

Show view. It is a very nice addition, but you should experiment with it before relying on it. For instance, the PowerPoint viewer that originally shipped with Office95 was a version 4 viewer and not a version 7 viewer. If you do not have the version 7 viewer, you can download it from Microsoft. The file name is P95VIEW.EXE.

Summary

The main purpose for presentations is to communicate. Clear communication is best accomplished when the format of the communication does not interfere with the content of the communication. As it becomes easier to create increasingly complex presentations quickly, you should never lose sight of the potential pitfalls of moving the presentation from inside your computer into the audience's mind.

No matter whether the presentation is going to circulate on networks, on laptops, via telephone lines, on floppy disks, or even on Macs, you should now have the tools to accomplish the true task at hand—getting the presentation presented.

Always be aware of how the presentation is going. It doesn't do any good if it only exists on your hard drive, no matter how impressive it might be. With the increasing proliferation of different computer capabilities, getting it there has become one of the latest areas for potential disaster. With the right planning, you won't be caught with a presentation that won't play in Peoria.

chapter 14

Creating Electronic Presentations

14

by Brian Reilly

In this chapter

◆ **Scan and prepare artwork**
The art and science of scanning images and choosing file formats is demystified.

◆ **Modify and create templates**
Follow easy guidelines to customizing templates or creating your own from scratch.

◆ **Create see-through logos**
Learn the right way and the wrong way to make logos transparent.

◆ **Add sound, video, and animation**
Add sophistication with easy-to-incorporate elements without filling your entire hard drive.

◆ **Link to Excel and Word data**
You can avoid re-keying of information if you use Copy, Paste Special and choose the Link option, permitting the presenter to control the content while you control the look.

◆ **Program interactive presentations**
Have backup slides ready to answer questions in more detail, without cluttering your presentation with detail that may not be needed; be prepared for every possibility with nonlinear programming.

◆ **Put your presentation in front of the audience successfully**
To get the presentation off your desktop and in front of the audience, you need to anticipate certain details when moving the actual presentation files from one computer to another.

PowerPoint provides a host of sophisticated tools for quickly creating and assembling effective electronic presentations. In this chapter, you learn how to create and assemble presentations for situations that require very large files. You also learn to prepare for those situations when the entire presentation has to fit on one floppy disk.

You probably receive information to create your presentations in a variety of ways. In many situations, when you receive the information in electronic files, you can dramatically increase your productivity by copying and pasting or paste linking the files directly into the PowerPoint page or the PowerPoint outline. A good understanding of the other programs in Office will be beneficial to accomplishing what you want quickly.

Additionally, understanding all the end uses of a presentation will help you create it correctly right from the start and avoid time-consuming revisions.

Keeping the End Result in Mind from the Start

How you prepare a presentation depends, to some extent, on how the presentation is ultimately going to be shown: In a big meeting? On machines you do or don't have control over? On Macs and PCs?

These different environments have different opportunities and limitations. Understanding the differences is critical to creating a successful electronic presentation.

So before you do anything else, consider the following points:

▶ How will the presentation be moved? On a slow network? Via telephone lines? By tape backup or other removable media such as a Syquest? Although most PC users are familiar with tape backup units, most Mac installations are more likely to have a Syquest drive than a tape backup unit. If you anticipate needing to go across platforms on a regular basis, it may be worth the investment to install a common media format that will permit this easily. Moving big files across slow networks or by telephone can be very time-consuming, so you may want to reconsider 24-bit scans (16 million colors) in favor of 8-bit scans (256 colors, also frequently referred to as indexed colors). Even compressing a file may or may not help much. If you are using removable media, you must make sure the recipient is exactly compatible.

▶ How many machines will you be using in your presentation? What control do you have over the hardware being used? Does your presentation also have to be cross-platform compatible? A wider variety of machines used for viewing probably means more variables to worry about. The issue of video resolution and whether all machines are multimedia-capable comes into play. If you must go cross-platform, you probably don't want to include AVI video files. These files probably won't show on the Mac because the AVI file format is a PC format. If you use Mac Quicktime Movies, you want to be sure the PC side has Quicktime for Movies drivers loaded. Chances are they won't be, unless they have been loaded specifically.

▶ Using movies in cross-platform situations is not for the faint of heart. It can be done, but should be attempted only after testing in every situation you anticipate your presentation being used. This is not a PowerPoint issue. It is actually an issue best addressed in a program that generates the final movie file. The safest alternative is to use a program that permits generating the movie file in both a Mac and a PC format and creating two versions of the presentation to accommodate the movie. The remainder of the presentation, however, does not have to be created twice. You just need to insert the correct movie version on the pages where you want them to play.

▶ Is your presentation going to be shown in more than one medium: Screenshows? Color prints? Or even overheads?

▶ Subtle shadings that are effective in screenshows are not readable on overheads—in fact, they look like mistakes. For example, if a new product screen show prepared for an electronic presentation to a sales force is then presented to the trade as overheads, the beautiful gradients you used and the subtle drop shadows on the type will not only be wasted, but will be detrimental and difficult to read.

Another key consideration before starting is to decide whether to create the entire presentation in PowerPoint or to create some elements by using other programs. Some programs perform certain tasks better than PowerPoint, and some elements PowerPoint may not be able to create at all.

Depending on your particular needs, I would recommend that you have several additional tools available to you that work in concert with PowerPoint. Use the tool that is best for the task at hand, given the quality needed and the time allowed. Keep in mind, however, that there are many ways to get to the end and sometimes the appropriate solution does not require the best quality. After all, you probably wouldn't construct a tree house with high-quality wood.

The tools in the following list are mainstream and work quite well. Other tools are also available that accomplish the same tasks. If you are already using some of these tools, you should probably continue to use what you know:

▶ A scanner and a scanning/retouching program such as Adobe Photoshop or CorelDRAW. Either program enables you to scan photos, logos, and more. You can also adjust the exposures and set the image sizes to the correct levels before importing the file into PowerPoint.

▶ A vector-based drawing program such as Adobe Illustrator, Adobe FreeHand, or CorelDRAW enables you to convert scans of logos into the vector-based artwork you need to properly produce transparent logos.

14

▸ A sound-editing program to record and mix sounds. There are many programs available, and one probably came bundled with your sound card.

▸ If you frequently need to capture your own videos, you need a video capture card and a video editing program, such as Adobe Premiere. Adobe Premiere enables you to edit the sound and the order of the frames in the video. (Another editing program may have come with your video capture card and may be sufficient for many situations.) If you plan to capture your own video only occasionally, you may be better off sending it out to a service bureau to do this for you.

You have decided how the presentation is going to be shown and you have the right tools available to accomplish what you need to do. The next step is to use the right process to get the best results for the presentation.

Scanning Pictures for Use in PowerPoint

Scanning pictures is an art frequently misunderstood, but a few simple guidelines can help take the mystery out of it. You want to quickly scan at the optimal file size without one wasted byte on the shrinking hard drive.

You need to understand three variables when determining a scan's "correct" size (in this case, "correct" size is the best quality image the eye can see at the smallest file size possible):

▸ The size of the page the image will cover (inches, millimeters, or pixels)

▸ The source of the art to be scanned; how big the art is to be scanned and whether it is a soft-focused picture or small type

▸ The number of colors necessary to accurately represent the image

First, let's look at page size. The first rule here is to measure in pixels and not in inches or millimeters. Although this can take a bit of getting used to for experienced paper-based designers who are used to measuring in inches, points, or picas, it is critical for managing file sizes in electronic publishing. It's not difficult to measure in pixels, it is only a different unit of measurement that directly relates to the video resolution of the monitor. Unfortunately, PowerPoint does not permit you to measure in pixels, so you should look to your scanning program for this feature.

Second, you need to scan different sized originals at different scales. Additionally, if the source of art is a photograph, you can use fewer dots per inch (dpi) than you can if the art is type. But with type, you need to place the dots closer together to make the eye think they are all connected. You control this with the dpi setting.

Third, not all computers display the same number of colors no matter how many colors are included in the file. If you are going to show your presentation on laptops that show only 256 colors, you'll want the file to contain only 256 colors, which will cut the file size roughly 66 percent.

Page Size and Resolution

The first thing to think about is what size page you are trying to cover with the finished scan. In spite of its tiny physical size, the biggest page you will work with is the 35mm slide. The 35mm slide is what many of us have been most familiar with. The need for high resolution on scans for slides is probably what is leading to larger-than-needed file sizes in many scans. Table 14.1 shows page sizes in pixels for the five most common outputs for PowerPoint presentations.

Table 14.1   Page Sizes in Pixels for Various Media

	35mm Slide	Color Print (8.5×11" paper)	Overhead Transparency (8.5×11" film)	Screen show	Screen show
Page size:	4096×2732	1375×1063	792×612	800×600	640×480

I've included two screen resolutions for screenshows because many people are now using bigger screens that display these higher screen resolutions.

 Note

If you're using more than one output, take the highest level dpi. For example, if you are using 35mm slides *and* overhead transparencies, use the dpi for 35mm slides.

Table 14.2 shows what dpi to use based on what the end use is going to be.

Table 14.2   DPI to Use for Various Media

	35mm Slide	Color Print	Screen Show 800×600	Screen Show 640×480	Overhead Transparency
Picture	125	125	96	72	72
Text	300	300	240	175	175

14

Note

These scanning guidelines come from testing conducted on the Kodak Q-60 Color Input Chrome, which includes color swatches, a soft focus photograph, and some fairly small type. Judgments were made at each resolution to determine where the quality was "respectable" versus where the quality started to diminish to the eye. If you have the time, you should conduct your own tests with the typical types of things you anticipate scanning. You might be surprised at how much lower you can go in resolution and still get good results.

Scaling

Remember, these scans are going to be bit-mapped images. *Bit-mapped* images are collections of dots that fool the eye into thinking they're actually a picture instead of many tiny dots. You have the correct page size and resolution for the scan, but not all the art to be scanned is the same size. You now have to determine how to scale the image at this resolution so that the dots still look like a picture.

Say that you have a 2-by-3-inch and a 1-by-1.5-inch picture, and you want to fill the page for a 800×600 screen show from top to bottom with each picture on two separate pages. If you scan the first picture at 100 scaling, it will measure 900 pixels high by 600 pixels wide, which is 100 pixels too high to fit exactly on-screen. So, you need to use the scaling adjustment in your scanner to scale it down to fit to 800 pixels high. Scaled at 88 percent (800/900) yields a scan very close to 800 pixels high. Because the smaller picture will measure half the size of the bigger picture—450 pixels high by 300 pixels wide—you will have to scale that up in order to make it measure 800 pixels high. In this case, you increase your scaling measure to 178 percent (800/450). Both scans will be the perfect resolution and basically the same file size. In fact, if you can, you should set your scanner to measure in pixels. Otherwise, just multiply the number of inches times the dpi for pixels.

What if you don't plan to fill the whole page with your image? Shouldn't the total number of pixels be smaller for less than a full page? That's exactly the point. The image size in pixels should only be the number of pixels the image is going to cover on the page. You can figure out precisely how much of the screen you are going to cover and measure those pixels as the target size for this scan.

Because PowerPoint measures the screen in inches and mm and not pixels, you have to do a little more calculating. If the image is going to cover about half the screen, multiply the full page size by the half. To continue with the previous example of two pictures 800 pixels high, if one of them is going to fill only half the screen vertically, you want the pixel measurement to be one half of 800. This works precisely, and you should follow these rules; however, you can usually round about +/- 10 percent and still be pretty safe. This is good to know when your boss or client says, "Make my picture a little bigger."

Number of Colors

The third variable to consider when scanning art is the number of colors in the art. You want to squeeze every wasted byte out of your scan without compromising quality. If you are shooting 35mm slides, you want all 16 million colors to get the best-looking image you can. If you are doing a screen show from a laptop, however, the laptop cannot display all 16 million colors. The best laptops display only 65,000 colors, and many laptops display only 256 colors. Therefore, you can cut your file size again according to the quality of the output. A correctly sized scan may vary in size from over 33M for a high-resolution scan of type to be used in a 35mm slide to as little as 1/3M for a 256 color picture in a 640×480 screen show. If you can't see it, why carry it? Look at the chart in figure 14.1 showing the different file sizes for correctly sized scans to get a better feel for the differences.

Fig. 14.1

File sizes can vary dramatically, depending on how you plan to use them.

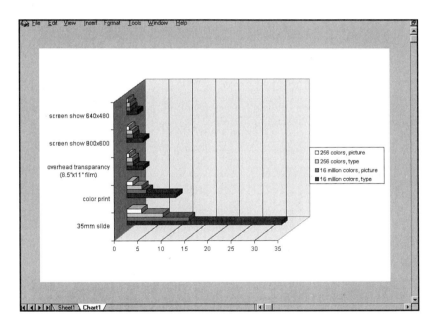

Another frequently asked question is what is the best file format to use when scanning for PowerPoint. Although it is a very important question with many desktop publishing programs, it is far less important in PowerPoint. The reason is that when PowerPoint imports a graphics file, it converts it to a PowerPoint file. So, an image that is 1M in TIF, BMP, or WMF format will still be a 1M file in PowerPoint. Even a JPG compressed file will expand back up to its non-compressed file size.

So, scan away. And put in a requisition for another bigger and faster hard drive.

Creating Your Own Templates

PowerPoint comes with many professionally designed templates, but it also enables you to easily create your own custom templates. You can do this by creating them entirely from scratch or by making modifications to the existing PowerPoint templates.

Modifying PowerPoint Templates

Any PowerPoint template can be easily modified and saved as a new template. To modify one of the existing PowerPoint templates, open the template by double-clicking the file in Explorer or by opening a new presentation in PowerPoint based on that template.

In the following example, you will open the template named BEDROCK.POT and make two modifications:

▶ Change the position of the existing artwork to the bottom of the page by rotating the art 90 degrees counterclockwise.

▶ Add the logo for the Rex Campsites, which, in this case, is a combination of clip art and type.

Figure 14.2 shows the original template, and figure 14.3 shows the revised template.

There are a few special enhancements added to the artwork. The existing bedrock art-work is made up of three elements to give it a shadow effect. You can add to this effect by ungrouping the art and placing the T-Rex figure between the layers to create the illusion of the dinosaur climbing out of the valley to come over the mountain. You need to convert a piece of clip art on a white background to make it appear that the artwork is on the existing blue background.

After rotating the art and ungrouping the layers, you can stretch the foreground art to fill the slide horizontally. In order for the logo of the T-Rex to appear transparent against the blue background, open the clip art in Photoshop and select only the background, which is white, fill it with exactly the same color as the PowerPoint blue background (RGB value 51, 102, 153), and save it as a TIF file.

Fig. 14.2
You will modify the original PowerPoint template BEDROCK.POT.

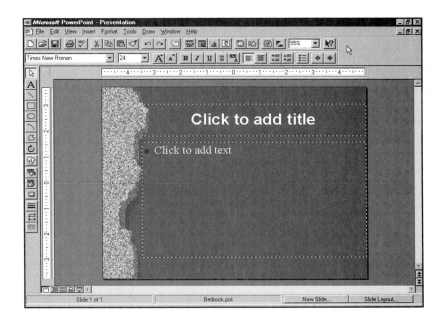

Fig. 14.3
The modified template has been saved as REXCAMPS.POT.

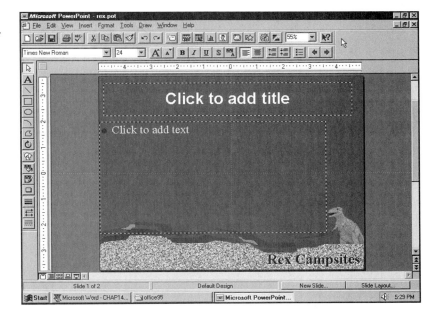

14

Because the shadow of the mountain and the mountain are separate elements, you can place the clip art, now on a matching blue background, behind the bedrock mountain. Then you can add the type for the logo and adjust the drop shadow to three points right and three points down to help it read against the mottled background of the mountain.

 Note

PowerPoint treats the Title slide completely different from the rest of the layouts. Changes made to templates do not apply to Title slides. To avoid this problem, just create a Title slide on a layout with the correct background and move the text where you would like it. (Forgive the programmers who make you do this because there's only one Title slide.)

To save the new file as a template, choose File, Save As. The File Save dialog box appears. Change the default of PowerPoint presentation to Presentation Templates, as shown in figure 14.4, and then place it in the Presentation Designs Folder.

Fig. 14.4

Save the new file as a presentation template.

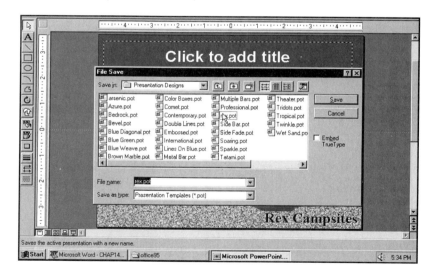

In the future, you can open this template just like any of the standard PowerPoint templates.

> **Note**
>
> Version 7 now saves the templates with the extension POT and locates them in the directory \Templates\Presentation Designs. The files located in the directory \Templates\Presentations are actually presentations that the Presentation Wizard uses; they are based on template designs.

Creating PowerPoint Templates from Scratch

As easy as it is to customize existing PowerPoint templates, it is also easy to create completely new templates. One way I like to think of the template is as a collection of graphical objects—pictures, logos, and so on—and a separate collection of copy areas for headlines, bullet points, charts, and tables.

You will create a completely new template for the Arsenic and... Company (see fig. 14.5). This template is comprised of the following elements:

▶ A scan of a lace handkerchief

▶ Type added on separate layers and one word rotated

▶ PowerPoint clip art of a mortar and pestle

▶ A rectangle filled with a semi-transparent gray

Fig. 14.5
The completed "Arsenic and..." custom template.

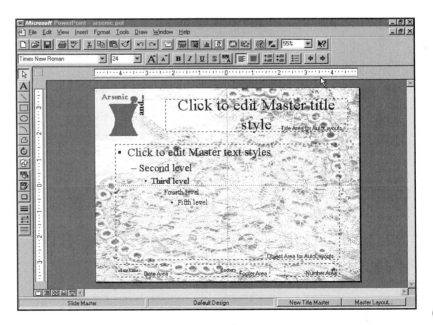

14

To create the new template, follow these steps:

1. Choose File, New and open a Blank Presentation.

2. Choose View, Master, and then choose Slide Master (see fig. 14.6).

Fig. 14.6

You use Slide Master to select files for the template.

3. On the Slide Master that appears, choose Insert, Picture and select the file you are going to place in the Slide Master. Choose Draw, Send To Back in order to place the picture behind the type.

4. Choose Insert, Clip Art and select the mortar and pestle in the Science and Medicine category. Resize the art and place it in the upper-left corner. The original clip art contains the letters RX in white. To change the RX from white to black, as done for this figure, choose Tools, Recolor and click the white check box under Original. Change the color to black under New.

5. Adding the type "Arsenic and..." has to be done in two separate steps because you are going to rotate part of the type and place the copy on separate layers. Use the Text tool and add **Arsenic**. Then use the Text tool again and add **and...**. Select the copy "and..." so that you can see the handles. Then choose Draw, Rotate/Flip, Rotate Left. You can now position both pieces of type on the picture of the mortar and pestle.

6. To soften the harshness of the word "Arsenic," use the Rectangle tool and draw a box over the pestle and the type in the left corner. Choose Format, Colors and

Lines and change the fill to a gray that is just darker than white, and then click the Semi-Transparent box (see fig. 14.7). If you choose Draw, Send Backward, you can send the soft rectangle behind the "and..." and keep it above "Arsenic" to emphasize the "and...".

Fig. 14.7
Semi-transparent fills are new in PowerPoint.

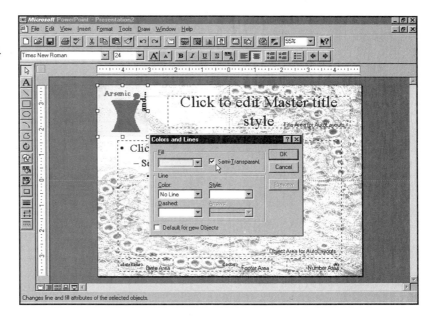

7. The last thing to do is to position the Headline text so that it does not cover the logo in the left corner.

Save the file as a Presentation Template just like you did when modifying an existing template, and you can use this as a new template any time.

Mixing Templates in One Presentation

One of the great strengths of PowerPoint—consistency of the master template—is also one of the great challenges to flexibility in good presentation design. Many people want to mix templates within one presentation for a variety of valid reasons:

▶ Custom looks for different divisions or departments

▶ A real need for different looks to present different types of information

▶ A need to mix landscape and portrait formats, and more

14

Unfortunately, PowerPoint will not let you change the template within a presentation, but there are several ways to work around this.

The first and easiest thing to do is to create separate presentations that meet your needs. You then can just insert the second presentation as an OLE object in the first presentation. This second presentation is then launched from within the first presentation at the appropriate time.

To do this, go to the slide in the first presentation where you want to start the second presentation, and follow these steps:

1. From the main menu, choose Insert, Object. The Insert Object dialog box appears.

2. Scroll down the dialog box and click Microsoft PowerPoint Presentation and then select the Create from File option button.

3. Choose Browse and click OK. Select the file you want to insert and click OK.

You now need to set the options on how to play this second presentation:

1. Choose Tools, Animation Settings. You see the Animation Settings dialog box.

2. Select Play Options, Show. A second level of options is behind the More button. You can select the box to Hide the object when not playing the presentation (see fig. 14.8).

Fig. 14.8

Look for buried levels of dialog boxes in PowerPoint 7.

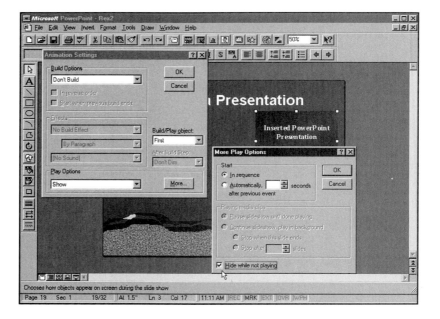

These steps will play the second presentation when you advance from this slide in the first presentation (you can think of this slide as a Jump From slide). At the end of the second presentation, you will be returned automatically to this slide (the Jump From slide). Remember to design a slide that is an appropriate transition slide.

If you are unhappy with the amount of time this method takes to launch the second presentation, especially if you have only a few slides that deviate from the template format, you can always save each individual slide in Presentation 2 as a Windows Metafile (WMF) and insert it as a picture over the template. However, if you only want to delete the graphics from the master template, you can do this by changing the option in Format, Custom Background, checking the box Omit Background Graphics from Master, and choosing Apply. This will omit the graphics on the master from just this one slide. Apply to All affects all the slides.

Using See-Through Logos

Nearly everyone has had to create logos of irregular shapes that need to appear as if they are part of the background instead of as an inset on a white background. The correct way to do this is to create the logo in a vector-based tracing program, such as Adobe Illustrator, Adobe FreeHand, or CorelDRAW. Unfortunately, working in any of those programs requires not only a substantial amount of time but a new level of drawing skills that the user may not have.

If you find yourself in one of these situations—especially if you need the logo only once or twice and it really isn't worth investing the time to do it the right way—there is a workaround method you can use to get the result you need very quickly. It involves using a paint program like Adobe Photoshop or Corel Photopaint and assembling the elements in PowerPoint.

The first key step is to create the entire background in this other program. Note that you can even use this method with gradiant backgrounds. Simply create a new file—for example, in Photoshop—at exactly the correct page size of your PowerPoint page. Insert that file into the Slide Master in PowerPoint and choose View, Master, Slide Master, and Insert, Picture. Next, choose Draw, Scale and use the arrows to scale up to the maximum size PowerPoint will let you to fill the frame exactly. Using the arrow keys is better than using the object handles to resize because you need to keep the proportions exactly the same as the original image. *Write down the exact amount you rescaled the image*. You will need that number again later, and it must be exactly the same.

14

Back in Photoshop, open your scan of the logo and using whatever technique you need, select just the artwork you want to copy to that background. Paste it into place on the Photoshop background file. Then crop very tightly around the image and save that file as a new file.

In PowerPoint, insert the picture and very carefully position it right over the portion of the background that it was cropped from. Viewing at a very high zoom level will make this easier. You can nudge it into place with the arrow keys. What you have to do is position this cropped version of the picture exactly on top of the original background.

Using Transitions and Animated Effects

The basic transitions that were previously available in PowerPoint are essentially unchanged. However, PowerPoint 7 has three new animated effects:

- Animated bullets
- Animated graphical builds
- Sound effects

Actually, PowerPoint has separated these effects into their own submenu under Tools, Animation Settings. So many options are available that a clear bit of restraint will be necessary to avoid using them just because you can. You can fly bullets and drawings from the top, bottom, and just about anywhere else you want. You can even add the sound of applause on each of these objects. Use these effects sparingly—your presentation can get cluttered very quickly!

To add an animated effect to either a bullet or an object, follow these simple steps:

1. Select the bullet text box or the object.
2. Choose Tools, Animation Settings from the menu, also available by right-clicking the mouse. The Animation Settings dialog box appears (see fig. 14.9).
3. Choose Build Options, Build.
4. Select Effects and choose a sound effect from the pull-down list.

Fig. 14.9
You can choose from several special animated effects.

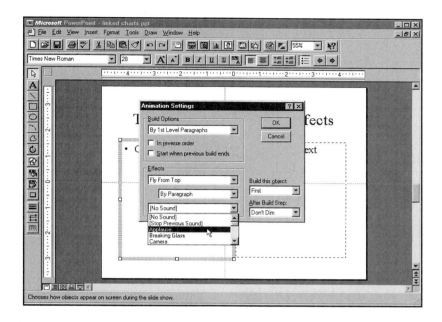

Using Sound

Sound is one of those things that really enhances a presentation. With PowerPoint 7, it is now easy to add sound files or even music directly from a CD without a great deal of time in a production studio. There are many options available for controlling how to play back the sound: as the slide starts, after a set amount of time, or even when you click a sound button.

The process is essentially very similar to adding pictures, with some minor differences. Basically, sound is just another kind of object. To add an existing sound that is a WAV file, follow these steps:

1. From the main menu, choose Insert, Sound and select the file you want to insert (see fig. 14.10).

2. With the sound object icon selected, right-click the mouse for Animation Settings, or choose Tools, Animation Settings from the menu.

3. In Play Options, choose Play.

4. Click the More button to set the Start and Play details. Click OK, and OK again, and you are set.

14

If you want to hide the sound icon when it is not playing, check the Hide While Not Playing box. Or, new in PowerPoint 7 is the capability to hide the unwanted object by holding the Alt key and dragging it outside the frame. It works for chart and picture objects as well.

Fig. 14.10

Adding sound is like adding a picture.

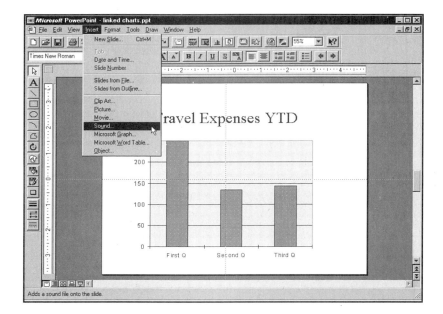

If you thought scanning pictures could occupy a lot of hard disk space, sound can be even worse. Depending on the quality level you record the sound at, much like dpi resolution for scans, a short 20-second sound recording may exceed 3M. If you are pressed for disk space and you have a CD-ROM in the machine you will present from, you can play the selected track right from the CD. Of course, you will have to have that CD loaded at the time of the presentation. While that might be cumbersome in some circumstances, such as when you want a lot of music from a wide host of CDs, it can work quite well for certain situations such as walk-in music or coffee break music.

To play a CD music track from a CD without recording it as a WAV file, follow these steps:

1. Choose Insert, Object and highlight Media Clip from the menu (see fig. 14.11).

2. When the menu switches to the Media Player menu, choose Insert Clip and choose CD Audio. Note that you must have the CD Audio option installed from Windows 95 in order to do this. If not available as an object, you will have to install that part of the multimedia options.

3. Move the slider bar to the track number that you want to start playing and click the Start Selection button.

4. Reposition the slider bar to where you want the track to stop playing and click the End Selection button. You will see the selected section highlighted on the slider bar.

5. Click back in the presentation frame to exit Media Player and return to PowerPoint.

6. Right-click the Media Clip Object, or choose Tools, Animation Settings from the menu and then choose Play in Play Settings.

7. Click the More button to set the Start and Play options. Click OK, and OK again, to return to your slide.

 Note

Although sound cards are frequently of good quality, multimedia speakers can often leave a lot to be desired in the area of quality reproduction. You can improve the playback quality by plugging the speaker out plug in your sound card directly into a decent-quality stereo system for much better results. This little extra effort is well worth the trouble for a permanently installed system in a conference room or at an important meeting in a big room.

Fig. 14.11

Insert the CD sound file as an Object and select Media Clip.

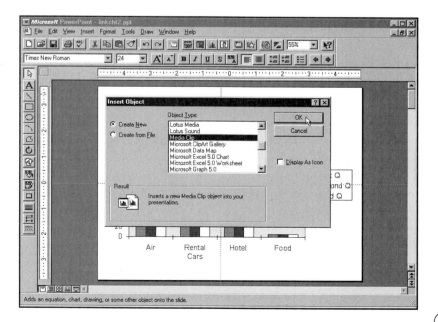

14

Using Video and Animation

Although sound can be easy to create and insert into your presentation, video is a bit more difficult to create—but just as easy to insert. If you need to add a video clip of your CEO speaking to your customers or if you need to show your TV commercials, the minor difficulties of digitizing the video can greatly enhance your presentation. And insertion and playback is really quite simple.

Describing how to capture your own video to digital files is beyond the scope of this book. Some of the things you will want to consider, though, are the percent of the screen you want to cover with your video image and how long the clip is because, again, file size is a significant issue. Video capture boards are no longer an extravagant expense for a busy presentation production department. But you will also want to consider whether the presenters have full-frame video playback capability on their machines.

Although PowerPoint enables you to create some animated effects in screen shows, it also makes it easy to add animations created in other applications. Like video, the safest kind of file to insert is an AVI file because that driver is available with the Windows 95 multimedia package.

A consideration when adding video or animation to PowerPoint 7 is the file format used and the drivers that will be installed on the machines showing the presentation. Windows 95 installs drivers that play AVI files, so the Autodesk (FLI and FLC) file formats may present some playback problems. When I encounter one of these situations, I use another program that imports the FLI or FLC files and exports them as AVI files. It's an extra step that eliminates a great deal of problems when my presentations will be shown on a variety of machines.

When you have an AVI video file, you can insert it into PowerPoint in much the same way you insert a picture. Just follow these steps:

1. Choose Insert, Movie and select the file you want to insert (see fig. 14.12).

2. Again, like you did with sounds, you have to set the Animation Settings. Right-click the object and choose Animation Settings, Play from Play Options; or choose Tools, Animation Settings, Play from the menu.

3. Click the More button to set Start and Stop options.

 Note

Many people often get all this correct and ask, "How can I get rid of the border and the control bar that show up around my video clip?" It's quite easy. Right-click the object and choose Edit Video Clip. Then choose Edit Options and set them the way you want them. See figure 14.12 for the choices available.

Fig. 14.12

Movie files in AVI format insert just like pictures.

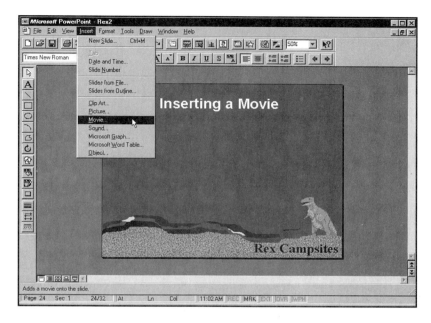

Investing in a Good Clip Art/Sound/Video/Animation Library

Creating first-class elements, such as clip art, sound clips, video, or animation clips, can be the ticket to success for a presentation. However, the amount of time and skill involved may preclude creating these elements in some situations. A good solution to this dilemma might be to purchase a good collection of professionally created clip libraries for the elements you expect will be useful. It will keep your presentations looking professional and fresh with a minimum of effort. There are many sources of clip libraries available now, and you should consider investing in one or several if you think they will help. An excellent source for these libraries are mail-order catalogs. Consider good clip libraries as just another tool for you to use.

Linking to Data in Excel and Word

One of the wonderful things about OLE is the ability to automatically update your presentation from an original document in Excel or Word with no re-keying of data in Excel. If your presentations are likely to be changed frequently, especially at the last minute, it is well worth the initial investment of time to copy the data from the original

14

document and paste-link it into PowerPoint. Then when you, or someone else, changes the original data, the presentation is automatically updated with the new data.

Consider the following example. A presentation of the division's quarterly financial results is given every quarter. Much of the data for charts comes from a variety of spreadsheets—such as sales by region, expenses by region, and so on—which are consolidated into other spreadsheets and then charted. If any of the expense numbers change at the last minute, you have to change a wide variety of the charts and tables because many numbers are affected. Or, when the next quarter's results are available, you have to re-do the entire presentation. With OLE linking, you can have those changes reflected as soon as they are made on the spreadsheets.

This example will illustrate linking an Excel spreadsheet and Excel chart to a PowerPoint slide. The same principle applies to Word documents and especially to Word tables. Having first created the Excel chart from the Excel spreadsheet, do the following:

1. Save the Excel file with a file name that will not change. When PowerPoint links to that file, it links knowing the file name and the path to the file. If either one changes, the link will be lost, although it can be re-established.

2. Select the entire chart from the Excel chart sheet (see fig. 14.13) and copy it.

3. Switch to PowerPoint and the appropriate page (it does not need to be a chart layout page), and choose Edit, Paste Special, Paste Link. Your choices of link options are shown automatically—in this case, Microsoft Chart Object.

4. Choose OK.

Fig. 14.13

Make sure that you select the entire chart.

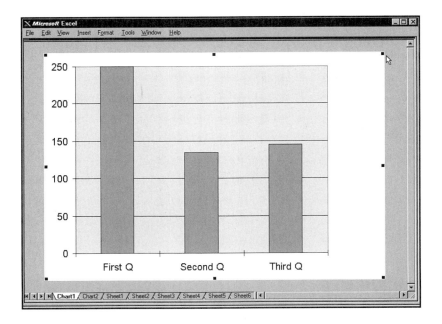

That's all there is to it. To test it, switch back to Excel and change some of the data in the spreadsheet. When you switch back to PowerPoint, the chart will be instantly updated.

Although linking is that simple to accomplish, there are a number of potential problems you should be aware of that frustrate many users. They generally have to do with lost links. An understanding of how the link is established and the rules of staying linked can eliminate those problems and make this an extremely productive tool.

When the link is made, PowerPoint knows and remembers the name and path of the file to link to. If that file is renamed or moved to another directory, the link is temporarily misplaced and cannot be established. This happens frequently in network situations when users are using files on a variety of drives or in private password-protected drives.

To re-establish a misplaced link, while in PowerPoint, do the following:

1. Choose Edit, Links from the menu.
2. Click the line containing the link for the file you want to re-establish as the source (see fig. 14.14).
3. Choose Change Source, which will let you find the file you want to link to.
4. Click that file when found and choose Update Now.

Fig. 14.14

Re-establishing links is possible but time-consuming.

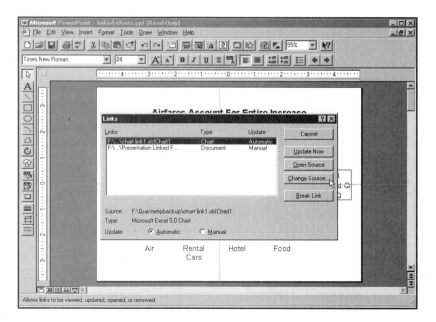

14

Note

One or two experiences of trying to find and re-establish lost links will reinforce the need for discipline in file management when using linking. With a little care, linking can be a tremendous productivity booster.

Planning Interactive Presentations

As the presentation moves from the linear medium of 35mm slides to the potentially non-linear electronic medium of the PC, you are afforded the opportunity to upgrade your presentations into interactive presentations. PowerPoint 7 has made this much easier. You have several simple opportunities for making presentations interactive:

▶ Branching to customize a core presentation to a specific audience

▶ Adding sound if you choose, depending on the audience's reaction

▶ Demonstrating another program without leaving PowerPoint

▶ Running what-ifs where data assumptions change

The first option, branching to other presentations, enables you to prepare more detail than you plan to show, but still be prepared for virtually any level of detail that may be required. Assume that you are showing the current travel expenses for a department in summary form. You probably wouldn't want to show detail such as airfares, rental cars, hotel bills, and restaurant bills. But if the need arises to show them, you're prepared.

If you are not sure what reaction your audience is going to have, you might prepare a sound track for a positive reaction and a different one for a negative reaction, and make it appear that you anticipated their objections. If the reaction is favorable, you can click the favorable object on-screen and play applause.

If you want to demonstrate a separate program from inside your presentation and return to the presentation seamlessly, you can set an object to launch that program. This option will launch your selected program and let you click back in the PowerPoint frame to return to the presentation. This can be especially useful if you want to access another or several other programs at various points in a presentation.

By launching an OLE object, you get to edit that data and examine what-ifs more easily than has been available in the past.

When programming a slide to be interactive, you have several options. To program an interactive object on a slide, select the object on the page and choose Tools, Interactive Settings (see fig. 14.15). You then have your choice of Go To, Play Sound, Run Program, or Object Action.

Fig. 14.15

Programming Interactive presentations can be "interactively challenging."

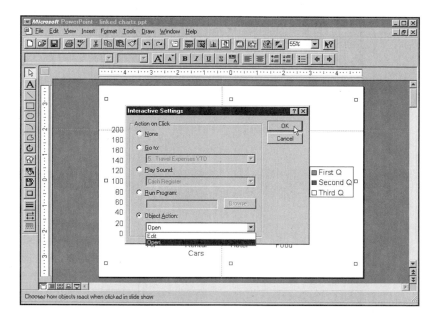

Your exact needs will dictate which method of interactive programming is the best for each situation. Just keep in mind exactly what you are trying to accomplish and stay disciplined. It is very easy for the undisciplined to get lost in all the options available. Your role in these interactive and linked presentations goes well beyond designer and begins to become programmer as well.

Summary

PowerPoint 7 is still one of the easiest presentation programs to use to assemble presentations. You can create a simple presentation or a very sophisticated one. PowerPoint provides many of the tools you need. At the same time, some tasks are accomplished with a bit more ease in other programs, whether they are Excel, Word, Photoshop, or whatever. You should use whichever tool accomplishes what you desire in the best manner that suits your own needs.

Most people use whichever tools they are most familiar with and ignore some other tools that might accomplish the task equally as well or maybe even better. The tools you are most comfortable with are usually more efficient to use rather than using new tools that you have to learn. But hopefully, some of the tricks in this chapter will help you learn new tools and create your own presentations more efficiently.

Some of those tools maximize the efficiency of the presentation file size, and some maximize the efficiency of the time needed to create the presentation. Use what you need to accomplish what you want.

chapter 15

Customizing PowerPoint

by Brian Reilly

In this chapter

◆ **Create custom toolbars**
Create your own custom toolbars with the tools you use most often and create new shortcut buttons for over 100 buried menu commands.

◆ **Customize paragraph spacing**
Following preset formats is great, but being able to deviate slightly may save you a lot of time.

◆ **Create custom color schemes**
When your company colors don't fit a PowerPoint template, create your own color scheme.

◆ **Monitor the workplace and work pace**
Find out how long it really takes to prepare a presentation and which of your coworkers really works the fastest at certain tasks.

◆ **Create master presentations that the presenter can customize to an audience in seconds.**
Don't let the need for customizable presentation limit the quality of the presentation.

There are many ways to accomplish the same task. The way you choose to accomplish a specific task may be very different from the way another user might accomplish the same task. Because the way you choose to do something depends on you, PowerPoint can vary the way it works to match your style. All you have to do is ask.

Customizing can mean different things to different people. To many it means more work, but it doesn't have to. In the case of PowerPoint and Microsoft Office 95, it can mean changing PowerPoint to fit your style—as unique as it may be. And it can also mean not having to sacrifice high production quality in order to create truly customized presentations, even ones that need to be customized in seconds.

Customizing Toolbars

Every user has different habits and therefore relies on certain features of a program more heavily than others. PowerPoint lets you customize the application to the user and even to the situation at hand. You can change which buttons are on which toolbars and create your own toolbars that let you work the way you like to work. You can even create your own toolbar button images if you find Power Point's buttons confusing or inadequate.

For example, if you are preparing a presentation with a lot of ®, ©, or Σ symbols, you will need the Character Map button available at all times. That button clutters up the screen if you are working on a presentation that doesn't use any of those symbols.

You can customize your toolbars in two ways:

▶ Mix the existing buttons to create a new toolbar that has just the mix of buttons you use most often.

▶ Create your own button, attach your own menu command to it, and then put it on a toolbar. This is especially helpful if you use a menu command frequently and it is buried under several levels of menu commands.

The first way lets you arrange any existing icons on the toolbar so that you can keep your screen free of clutter while keeping your frequently used icons at hand. Users who know many of the keyboard shortcuts or use the right-click shortcut menus might like to free up some screen real estate by deleting the icons for cut, copy, and paste, and so on.

The second way lets you make more accessible those menu commands that do not have keyboard shortcuts or are several keystrokes away. Figure 15.1 shows a new button being added to a custom toolbar—Screen Shows. It has some of the normal formatting buttons on this custom toolbar, along with Insert Picture, Insert Sound, Slide Transitions, and Text Anchor buttons. This toolbar also includes a custom-drawn button attached to the Format Colors and Lines command. You learn how to create such a custom drawing later in this chapter.

PowerPoint enables you to assign buttons to 260 different commands. Approximately 117 of these commands already have buttons assigned to them by PowerPoint. That leaves 143 commands to which you can assign your own custom buttons. You have four choices of how to assign an image to a button:

▶ Assign a predrawn button image to a command.

▶ Add special text to a text button.

▶ Draw your own button.

▶ Paste an image from another graphics package onto a blank button.

Fig. 15.1

Customize your own toolbars and add custom buttons.

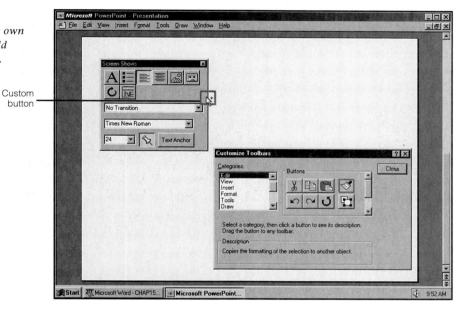

Clearly, not every command needs its own custom button. However, if you find yourself using a few commands frequently, such as Format, Colors and Lines, you can dramatically increase your productivity by assigning or creating your own custom buttons.

Assigning or creating a button is actually quite an easy task. Because you probably won't do this very frequently, however, it is easy to forget how to do this. To create a custom toolbar, follow these steps:

1. Choose View, Toolbars.
2. Choose New.
3. Type a name for the toolbar in the dialog box and click OK.
4. From the categories, select a choice, such as File or Edit, that contains the button you want to add to the new toolbar.
5. Drag the button to the new toolbar.
6. Repeat Steps 3 and 4 until you have added all the buttons you want to add to your custom Toolbar.
7. When you finish adding buttons to your custom Toolbar, click Close.

If there is no button image for a command, you can create your own button image by drawing a simple bitmap, as I have done with the Format Colors and Lines command. You can also paste a bitmap image from another program.

If you want to create your own icon for a command, follow these steps:

1. Choose View, Toolbars.

2. Click New or Customize, depending on whether you are creating a new toolbar or just customizing a button on an existing toolbar.

3. In the Categories box, choose All Commands. You see a scroll box containing many commands that you can assign to buttons (see fig. 15.2).

Fig. 15.2

You can assign commands to a toolbar.

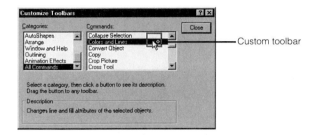

Custom toolbar

4. Select the command you want to make an icon and drag it to the new toolbar. If you choose Colors and Lines, or another command that does not have a button assigned to it, you see another dialog box showing a variety of unassigned custom buttons (see fig. 15.3).

5. Choose the button image you want to assign to that command and click Assign. The image you assigned immediately shows up on that blank button. Or click Edit and you get a third dialog box that lets you draw your own icon (see fig. 15.4).

To paste an image from a graphics program onto a button face, you first have to copy the image from the other graphics program to the Clipboard. Then, in PowerPoint, right-click the blank button on a toolbar and choose Customize. Right-clicking that blank button one more time gives you the option to Paste Button Image. Choosing Paste Button Image places the image from the Clipboard onto the button face.

Fig. 15.3
*Click Edit to draw
your own button
design.*

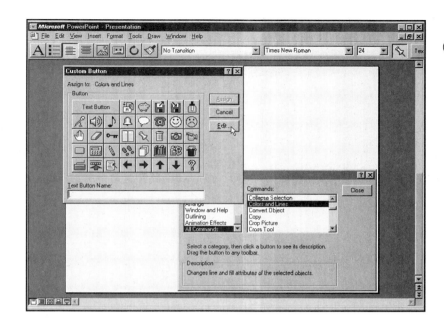

Fig. 15.4
*Design your own
button.*

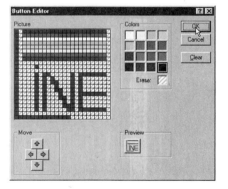

 Tip

When pasting a bitmap from another program, be sure to make the image size no bigger or smaller than the exact button size. The default button size is 16 pixels wide by 15 pixels high. The large button size is 24 pixels by 23 pixels.

If you expect to switch between large and small buttons, design the custom button at the small size. This permits accurate viewing of the button at both sizes with no distortion.

Here are some commands you might consider assigning to buttons:

▶ Black and White (includes ten different options for black-and-white settings)

▶ Links

▶ Break Link

▶ Update Link

▶ Change Link

▶ Open Link Source

▶ Find

▶ Find Next

▶ Search and Replace

▶ Paste Special

▶ Character Map Utility

▶ Recolor

▶ Colors and Lines

▶ Slide Color Scheme

▶ Disassemble Picture (converts picture or OLE object to PowerPoint Objects)

▶ Replace Fonts

▶ Save As

▶ Scale (for scaling inserted objects)

Customizing Paragraph Spacing

Make the line spacing between bullets slightly larger than the line spacing between the lines within a bullet. This makes it easier for the audience to read each bullet point as a separate thought. For example, you may choose to separate the lines within a bullet by normal spacing, such as one line, while separating each complete bullet with a line and a half.

Presentation preparers often want to say too many things on a single page. The dilemma is to include everything and not be able to read it, or figure out a way to break the content down or spread it over several pages. Sometimes the problem is marginal, and your text is just a bit too long or just one bullet too many.

When you have a situation like this, the quickest and easiest solution would seem to be reducing the type size to make it fit. But that can also make it more difficult to read. As an alternative, you can squeeze the line spacing a little and leave the font size alone. You can sometimes reduce the line spacing a bit either between the lines or between the paragraphs without affecting the readability. This helps the copy fit on the page. Changing the spacing on that page does not have to change the entire presentation. And because you have to select the lines you are going to change, you may need to change only a few lines in order to make your copy fit.

You have two choices of units for working with line spacing—either point sizes or line size in percent. The choice of which to work with is yours. If you have fairly consistent font sizes in a presentation, you will probably be able to use point-size spacing guides without many surprises. If your font sizes change frequently in a presentation, however, you may be better off using line sizing because it will be more proportional to the text on that page.

To customize your line spacing either on a single slide or on the slide master, select the lines you want to change and follow these steps:

1. Choose Format, Line Spacing.

2. Adjust the spacing either with Line Spacing, Before Paragraph, or After Paragraph (see fig. 15.5).

3. Click OK to accept your changes.

Fig. 15.5
Changing line spacing
can help you squeeze
a little extra copy
onto a page.

 Tip
When you are putting the finishing touches on a presentation, add a button for Format, Line Spacing to your toolbar, or for Increase Paragraph Spacing or Decrease Paragraph Spacing. The changes will go that much faster.

Creating Custom Color Schemes

PowerPoint's templates come with several different color schemes designed to provide good color mix and good contrast. However, you may want to create your own color scheme. You can even change any predetermined element along the way and then apply that new scheme to the entire presentation. You also can save your color scheme for reuse by saving the scheme as a new template.

Eight elements make up the PowerPoint color scheme. When you change any one to a new color, it is shown in a thumbnail preview. The eight elements are:

▶ Background

▶ Shadows

▶ Fills

▶ Title Text

▶ Text and Lines

▶ Accent 1

▶ Accent 2

▶ Accent 3

The default color of a fill is Accent 1. You have to manually apply Accent 2 or Accent 3 to an object to change its color.

Although this color scheme works for many situations, you may need to make some modifications when you are creating charts with a large number of data points. Oddly enough, some of the color schemes reuse the same color for two data points on a chart, which may confuse your audience. You may need to change the default colors that a chart uses. When charts are created, PowerPoint applies colors to each sequential data point in the following order:

data 1.   Fill

data 2.   Accent 1

data 3.   Accent 2

data 4.   Accent 3

data 5.   Shadow

data 6.   Title Text

data 7.   Other color from MS Graph

data 8.   Other color from MS Graph

data 9.   Other color from MS Graph

> ### Tip
>
> When PowerPoint plots more than six data points in a chart, the colors beyond the sixth point may look like some of the previously used colors. It is easy enough to change the colors manually, or you can change the default colors for charts in MS Graph. To change the default colors for all charts, double-click the chart to open MS Graph. Choose Tools, Options and click the Colors tab. By double-clicking a color in chart fills or chart lines, you can change the RGB value for the default color. If you enter more than eight values in your data series, PowerPoint uses the colors for Chart Lines for the color fills for the data series 9 through 16. Figure 15.6 shows the dialog box for changing color values for chart colors.

Fig. 15.6

Customize default chart colors in MS Graph.

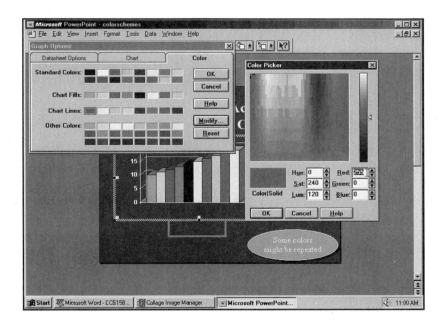

Customizing Screen Show Options

There are a few new additions to PowerPoint that help smooth out the rough edges of screen shows. In fact, there are so many additions that it may be a bit confusing.

Under Tools, Options, many of these options can be turned off ahead of time so that they are completely inactive. You will be presented with four tabs, as shown in figure 15.7. The third tab, View, is where you set the options for which commands are available during screen shows. It can get a little confusing because the options behave differently depending on what is set on or off in this dialog box. For instance, if P̲opup Menu On Right Mouse Click is checked, you must use the menu to select the Previous slide during a screen show, or use the keyboard keys P or Page Up. If P̲opup Menu On Right Mouse Click is not checked, a right mouse click during a slide show will back up to the previous slide as it did in version 4.

Fig. 15.7

Set the options for screen shows in this dialog box.

You can easily add a black screen at the end of a screen show if you want to end the screen show and not leave the final page showing. During a screen show, a right mouse click brings up a pop-up menu that gives you a variety of options, such as turning the on-screen pen on or off or changing the color of the pen (see fig. 15.8). So now you can emphasize different sections of a page during the presentation in different colors right during the presentation.

Fig. 15.8

Right-clicking the mouse during a screen show displays this menu with a wide variety of options.

Additionally, you can turn the screen black during the meeting without losing your place in the presentation. This can be especially handy in a presentation when the contents of a specific page gets the meeting participants launched into a lively discussion that is best encouraged by blanking the screen.

When advancing a slide show to the next slide, you have the option of using the left mouse button, the Page Down key, the Enter key, or the N key (the letter N). To back up to the previous slide, you can use either the Page Up key or the letter P. You can back up to the previous slide with the mouse, but it requires that the screen display the menu so that you can pick the *Previous P* option.

You can also hide the pointer with Ctrl+L—presumably the L stands for lose. Ctrl+A shows the arrow again.

There is also an option called Slide Navigator that allows you to jump to a slide out of order.

> ⚛ **Tip**
>
> Because PowerPoint 7 has added so many options you can use to control a screen show, you may want to coach your presenters on only a few of the options each is likely to use. Certainly every presenter should know how to go to a previous slide, because skipping to two pages ahead is probably the most frequent mistake nervous presenters make. At the same time, most presenters will not use the on-screen pen very often, so memorizing the keyboard command E to erase the on-screen pen marks may be a waste of time.

While you are looking at the options available under Tools, Options, you should also look at the other options you can set for yourself in PowerPoint, such as Maximum Number of Undos, rendering 24-bit pictures at highest quality (select this for the screen show and deselect it for faster repainting of the screen while editing), and setting a default file location.

> ⚛ **Tip**
>
> If you are creating a presentation on a memory-challenged computer, you should limit yourself to only one or two levels of Undo and definitely turn off the rendering of 24-bit pictures at highest quality. A large number of Undo levels and highest-quality rendering will both use up available memory and slow you down.

Using File Properties to Track Information

When a PowerPoint presentation is created, PowerPoint automatically updates and saves file properties. You might think of this as your automatic statistician taking notes for you. This can help you in a variety of ways. File Properties keeps track of a variety of valuable information, such as the fonts used, the time it took to edit the presentation, the time and date the file was last edited, and so on (see fig. 15.9). File Properties also describes your file with various classifications, such as a Client name, Editor, or one you name yourself. These classifications permit you to conduct very powerful keyword searches to find a file on your hard drive that might not be easy to locate by other means.

Fig. 15.9

The Custom tab of a File Properties dialog box keeps track of a variety of information about a file.

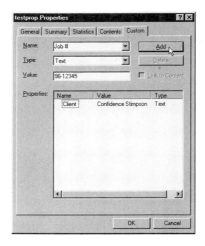

If you are sending files to a service bureau or another computer for viewing, you can check Properties on the Contents tab to see a list of all the fonts used in that presentation. This will help you determine whether you should send the fonts along with the file, because you should have a list of fonts supported by your service bureau. Editing the time and number of revisions are very useful pieces of information when dealing with clients or bosses who can't believe that it actually took all night to create a simple presentation. A custom tracking system for files allows you, in the future, to search for files nobody can remember the name of. You can save your file with searchable properties, such as the client's name, subject, or job number.

Figure 15.9 shows the Custom tab of the File Properties dialog box. To add a custom file property, follow these steps:

1. Choose File, Properties
2. Click the Custom tab.
3. In the Name box, enter the custom name you will want to search for, such as Job #.
4. Select the Type of data it will be: Text, Date, Number, or Yes/No.
5. Type in the Value of the data.
6. Click Add.
7. Click OK when finished.

Now you can search all or part of your hard drive for this file by its properties. To search for this file in the future, do the following:

1. Choose File, Open.

2. Click the Advanced button in the File Open dialog box.

3. In the Advanced Find dialog box, define the criteria for your search. In this case, it is a presentation file whose Job # is 96-12345 (see fig. 15.10).

4. Click Find Now and PowerPoint searches for this file and shows you the location. Now you can double-click the file to open it.

Fig. 15.10

File Properties can help find a file by various criteria, such as Job #.

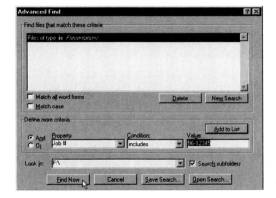

Standardizing Custom Reports

Although most of this chapter is focused on customizing PowerPoint to work around your preferences, you can also apply your design talents to standard reports. The result is a report/presentation that has good production values; it looks very well designed, but it only takes minutes to update.

For example, many people have to issue standard reports on a regular basis, such as monthly status reports with many charts and tables. This generally has been very time-consuming just to get the new information into PowerPoint. Additionally, the rush to publish has left little or no time for good design elements to be incorporated. However, the use of object linking and embedding (OLE) can help raise the level of the design of such reports, while shortening the time needed to get the report out the door.

One of the easiest ways to do this is to design a master presentation with actual, but outdated, data while you have the time. For example, suppose that you get a great deal of the information in an Excel spreadsheet every month, and it has already been charted in Excel. And, for this example, assume that each month you get a spreadsheet named

January Sales Results.xls, February Sales Results.xls, and so forth. It is very likely that these spreadsheet formats are going to be very similar from month to month. You can use that consistency of format to make your life easier.

First rename the file to something like Sales Results.xls and rename the sheet with the data Current Month. Then create the PowerPoint report by copying and pasting the Excel charts into PowerPoint using Edit, Paste Special and Paste Link. You can now design the entire report as appropriate. The design elements will always stay intact—all that will change is the chart data.

To update your PowerPoint Report, just copy the data from the new spreadsheet to your Sales Results.xls sheet onto the Current Month sheet (see fig. 15.11). When you open the PowerPoint report, it will automatically update your report/presentation with the new chart. No re-entering of data or replotting of charts.

Fig. 15.11

Copy the new data to the Current Month sheet for instant updating.

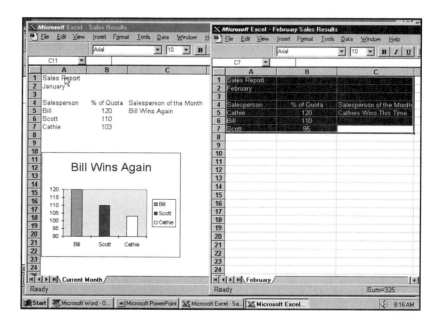

15

PowerPoint. Now she only has to rename the Excel file to SLIDES.XLS (the PowerPoint file is linked to SLIDES.XLS), and she instantly has every one of those charts in PowerPoint perfectly sized. She only needs to delete the pages she does not want as slides and change a headline if necessary, and the PowerPoint file is ready for the service bureau. In the past, this took several hours; now it is complete in minutes.

More Standardized Custom Presentations

Another good application for using the power of OLE with PowerPoint was developed for a client who had to present the same core presentation in a variety of languages, and sometimes even in different languages at the same time. This solution does present some design challenges because most of the design work is done in Excel, and PowerPoint is purely a client for that information. But this presenter could present the presentation in any language at any time. All one had to do is tell him what language to present in.

The solution, although actually quite simple, does take a bit of organizing. Essentially, column A in Excel was used to show a page number and was visible only when editing the presentation in Excel. Column AA was used to carry the copy for that page in English; Column AB was used for the translation of that page into French. This pattern continued for as many languages as he needed.

To create the original presentation, the English version was copied to Column B and formatted in Excel for font size and font color. Each cell in column B was copied into PowerPoint and paste-linked to the Excel sheet. In the case of bullet points, each bullet point was sourced from a new row in Column B. This pattern continued until the entire presentation was assembled in PowerPoint.

At that point, in Excel, a simple macro was written to copy an entire column—the appropriate column, depending on the desired language—and paste it using Edit, Paste Special, Value into Column B. This would paste only the content and not affect the underlying pre-formatted look in Column B. The PowerPoint presentation would be updated instantly into the new language. Figure 15.12 shows the Edit, Paste Special, Value dialog box just before pasting the French copy over the English copy. Figure 15.12 shows the result of that Paste Special, Value on the spreadsheet and in PowerPoint.

The presenter was even able to jump between languages mid-presentation. He just switched to Excel and ran the macro to change the language, which instantly updated the entire PowerPoint presentation. When he switched back to PowerPoint, in a mere matter of 5 or 10 seconds, he was still on the same slide but in a different language.

Fig. 15.12
In Excel, Paste Special, Values does not affect preset formatting.

Fig. 15.13
Excel instantly updates the presentation in PowerPoint.

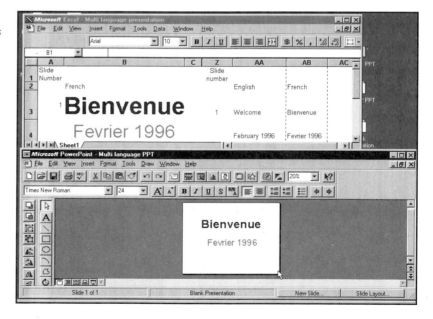

Tip

Although you may not need to be as flexible as this, you might be able to think of a wide variety of applications. A National Sales Manager could make quota review presentations in a series of markets on sequential days. Much of the presentation could be common from market to market. A great deal of information, however, could be linked to cells in an Excel spreadsheet so that the National Sales Manager could simply run a macro called NorthEast to change yesterday's data to the NorthEast data. Using this technique enables you to prepare and give extremely high-quality presentations that are truly customized to specific situations with a minimum of fuss.

Summary

Think of PowerPoint as an excellent tool to assemble presentations and as a tool that does everything for you for your presentation. You will be able to accomplish many objectives quickly and create presentations not only with good content, but also with a very high level of production value. The trick is to not try and use everything PowerPoint offers you. There are so many options, but there is also a high probability that some or many are inappropriate for your task at hand.

Identify the way you like to work and the kinds of needs you have for presentations, and then customize PowerPoint to suit your needs. Don't be afraid to use another tool like Excel to help organize your data. After all, even though some of us have done it, you wouldn't want to use a sledgehammer to drive in a tiny nail, would you?

Access

chapter 16

Critical Skills in Access

16

by Diane Tinney

In this chapter

◆ **Touring Access**
The fastest way to learn Access is to tour the application, learn the basic terminology, and identify when it is appropriate to use Access.

◆ **Creating a Database**
Access assists in creating a database by providing database templates that you can modify, by generating tables from datasheets, and by allowing you to define a table from scratch.

◆ **Adding Intelligence to a Database**
Access databases can be programmed to validate data, enforce relationships between tables, and automatically look up table data.

◆ **Extracting Information**
Queries and filters assist in the location and extraction of data that meets specific criteria.

◆ **Creating Forms & Reports**
Forms allow you to control and automate the data input process in a familiar graphical format. Designing and modifying custom reports requires planning and knowledge of how to use report controls.

The Professional edition of Microsoft Office contains Microsoft Access, a relational database management application. Whereas spreadsheet applications such as Excel perform complex computations quickly, database applications such as Access perform data management tasks such as storing, retrieving, and analyzing data. Over the past five years, Access has become the best-selling database application. Besides being closely integrated with the other Office applications, Access is easy to use and learn. Access also provides the tools necessary to create a sophisticated full-featured database program. If you've never used a database application before, or are new to Access, this chapter brings you quickly up to speed and builds a solid foundation in Access critical skills. If you have used Access before, you might want to glance through this chapter and only focus on areas where you may not have had much experience.

Touring Access

Experience is the best teacher, so turn on your computer and tour Access. As you venture through the application, you will cover key features, define basic terminology, and gain basic navigation skills. You can start Access from the Start menu or from the Office Shortcut Bar. To start Access, follow these steps:

1. Click Start.

2. Choose Programs, Microsoft Access.

Alternatively, display the Office toolbar in the Office Shortcut Bar and click the Microsoft Access button.

When Access opens, by default it displays a dialog box prompting you to either create a new database or open an existing database (see fig. 16.1).

Fig. 16.1

If you need to create a new database, consider using the Database Wizard as a quick way to learn Access.

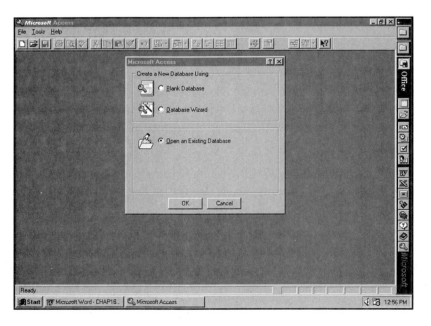

Working with an Existing Database

Access comes with a sample database named Northwind which is used in this tour. With the default option <u>O</u>pen an Existing Database selected, click OK in the Microsoft Access startup dialog box. A familiar Open dialog box appears (see fig. 16.2). Double-click the Shortcut to Northwind icon to open the existing sample database.

 Note

If you've previously opened the Northwind database, it will appear in a list box within the startup dialog box. You can select the Northwind database from here and bypass the Open dialog box. The same is true for any other databases with which you have recently worked.

Fig. 16.2

The Open dialog box works the same in Access as it does in the other Office applications.

 Note

If you don't see the Shortcut to Northwind icon in your My Documents folder, look in the Access\Samples folder for the Northwind.mdb file and open it. If the Samples directory does not exist, or if the Northwind.mdb file is missing, you can reinstall it from the setup disk(s). Open the Add/Remove Programs icon in the Control Panel and follow the prompts.

Unlike some other database applications, Access keeps an entire database in one file. The file extension is .MDB (Microsoft Database). As you can see in figure 16.3, the Database window for the open database lists all the objects in the database. Each tab is the name of a type of object in Access. *Tables* store data in column and row format. *Queries* extract data from a table based on criteria that you set. *Forms* provide graphical, user-friendly views of data and are usually used for data entry. *Reports* print data to the screen, a file, or to a printer based on the format you specify. *Macros* automate common repetitive tasks. *Modules* contain Visual Basic for Applications (VBA) code to automate more complex tasks and create full-featured, turn-key database applications.

Fig. 16.3

The Database window operates similarly to the Explorer in Windows 95.

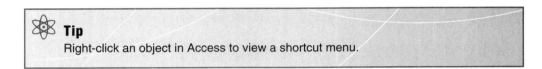

Tip

Right-click an object in Access to view a shortcut menu.

Click the desired tab to view a list of objects of that type in the database. Use the Open button to view the object (and enter or edit data as applicable). Choose the Design button to view or change design properties of an existing object. Use the New button to create a new object of that type.

Exploring Database Tables

Tables form the foundation of a database. The table structure is defined by the user in terms of fields and records. Conceptualize a table as a spreadsheet of columns and rows. Each column is called a *field* in database terminology. Each row is called a *record*. Before you can enter data into a table, you need to define the fields (columns). You will learn how to do this later in this chapter in the section "Designing a Table."

Select the Tables tab in the Northwind database and double-click the Customers table. A Datasheet view of the Customers table appears in a window entitled, "Customers: Table" (see fig. 16.4). Each column contains specific field information. The fields (columns) visible include Customer ID, Company Name, Contact Name, and Contact Title. Each row is a record of information about a customer. The first record has the Customer ID ALFKI, the second record has the Customer ID ANATR, and the third record has the Customer ID ANTON. All three records have a piece of data called Customer ID, but the value stored in Customer ID is different for each record. Notice the description of the current field location in the status bar of the Access application window ("Unique five-character code based on customer name."). You will learn later in this chapter how to provide these status messages and how to specify unique field values to identify records (called a *primary key*).

16

Fig. 16.4

The status bar of the table window lists the current record number, total number of records, and provides record navigation keys.

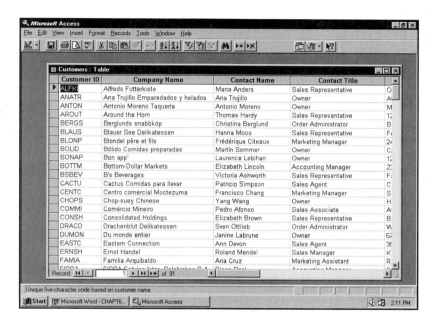

To view the definition of a table's fields, switch to Design view. Click the Design tool in the toolbar, or choose <u>V</u>iew, Table <u>D</u>esign. The Datasheet view of the table is replaced with a Design view (see fig. 16.5). The top grid lists the fields defined for a table. The bottom pane lists the properties for the selected field.

Fig. 16.5

In Design view, you can change the properties of a field, or add new fields to your table.

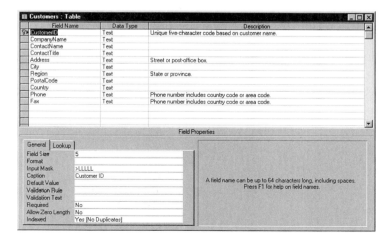

Each field name has a specific data type and description. When you create a database, you decide what to name each field. As you will learn later in this chapter, the name that you choose to use in the table design can be changed in Forms and Reports to be more descriptive, or abbreviated as needed. Access does enforce certain naming rules for objects, which is covered later in the section "Access Naming Conventions."

The *data type* predefines the kind of data that you want stored in that field. For example, names and addresses are usually alphanumeric and given the data type Text. For numerical data, you might use the Currency or Number data type. Access provides several special-purpose data types such as date/time, AutoNumber, and OLE. By specifying the data type, you let Access know what kind of data can be entered into a field. Access only allows valid data of that type to be entered into the database. For example, if a user tried to enter letters into a number field, Access would display an error message. Specifying the data type of fields also helps Access better manage memory and hard disk space for you. For instance, the memory and hard disk space needed by a date differ from that of a text field.

You can also (optionally) provide a description of a field. In Datasheet view, Access displays your description in the status bar of the Access window (refer to fig. 16.4). The description helps users understand what kind of data they should input in a field.

The lower pane of the Design window contains two tabbed property sheets. The General tab allows you to specify field size, captions, default values, and validity checks. The Lookup tab allows you to define properties for links to other tables (data appears in this table via a lookup feature). The Lookup feature is discussed later in this chapter in the section "Looking Up Data."

To return to Datasheet view, click the Datasheet tool in the toolbar, or choose View, Datasheet. If you have time, open the Products table in Datasheet view and then switch to Design view (you will use the Products table in the next section). When you are ready to move on to the next topic, Queries, close the table (click the x close button).

Exploring Queries

In Access, a query extracts information from a table (or multiple tables) and lists the data that meets your criteria in a datasheet format. You need to know three important facts about Access queries. First, the data is stored only once, in the applicable table. The list produced by the query exists in memory only. When you run a query, Access looks through the table(s) for data that meets your criteria. Matching records are then copied into memory and a list appears on-screen with the results of the query. Second, Access allows you to create Forms and Reports that are based on the results of a query. Third, Access can be instructed to produce live query results. In a live query, you can edit the query results and the underlying data stored in the applicable tables reflects your edits. The specifics of how queries work and the various types of queries are covered later in this chapter in the section "Getting Information Out."

Return to the Database window, and select the Queries tab. Double-click the Products Above Average Price query. After a brief delay, the query results display in Datasheet format (see fig. 16.6). The query lists the Product Name and Unit Price. This is an example of a simple query called a select query. Although the Products table, on which this query is based, contains many fields, this query creates a list that contains only two fields. Furthermore, only products that meet the criterion of having a price above average are included.

Fig. 16.6

A select query allows you to select which fields to include in the query results.

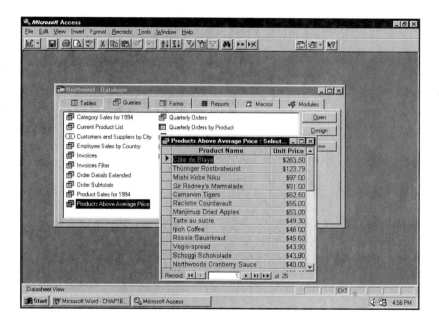

As with tables, queries are defined in Design view. To switch to Design view, click the Design tool in the toolbar. Figure 16.7 shows the Products Above Average Price: Select Query in Design view. The top pane contains boxes for each of the tables in the query. In this case, only the Products table is being used. The Products table box lists the fields defined in the Products table. The bottom pane lists the fields involved in the query. Each column is a field. For each field you can specify whether the field is shown in the query results, the sort order, and other criteria. Notice that this query sorts the results in descending order of the unit price. The formula in the Unit Price field's criteria row selects only those records that have a unit price that is higher than the average unit price.

Fig. 16.7

Design view for a query allows you to specify the tables and fields to be included in your query results.

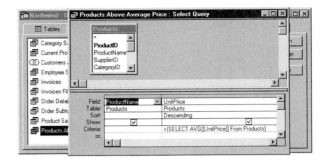

Exploring Forms

Just as paper forms allow you to capture and organize data, Access forms allow you to control data entry into tables and present data in a format other than the basic datasheet view. In Datasheet view, you can see multiple records at once, but not always a full record of information. Furthermore, Datasheet view only shows data from one table. Using forms, you can work with one record at a time, view information from multiple tables (or queries) at once, and select which fields to include on a form. Access forms can include graphics and other design elements to enhance appearance and usability.

Select the Forms tab in the Database window. Double-click the Customers form. Figure 16.8 shows the open Customers form window. Instead of the multiple record datasheet format, this form displays one record at a time. As users page up and down, other records display. In the background of this form, a picture of the world has been placed, which makes the screen more visually appealing. Each field name appears to the left of the data for that record. Pressing Tab moves you to the next field. In this case, all fields in the Customers table have been listed on the form.

Fig. 16.8

The status bar of the form window provides record navigation keys, and identifies the current record number and total number of records.

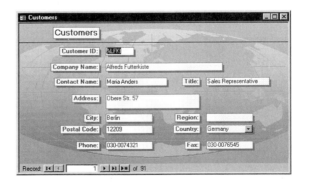

The View tool on the toolbar allows you to switch between Form view, Design view, and Datasheet view. Datasheet view lists the fields included in the form as a table (this is not the same as viewing a table in Datasheet view—remember, forms can be designed to only show a few of the fields in a table). Design view is where you create and modify forms. To switch to Design view, click the Design tool in the toolbar, or choose <u>V</u>iew, Form <u>D</u>esign. As you can see in figure 16.9, a form is divided into sections such as Form Header and Detail. The fields on a form are selectable objects with their own properties. A design Toolbox contains tools you can use to add controls (such as a label) to a form. The process of creating and customizing forms will be covered later in this chapter in the section "Creating Forms."

Fig. 16.9

Forms let you control how data is displayed on-screen.

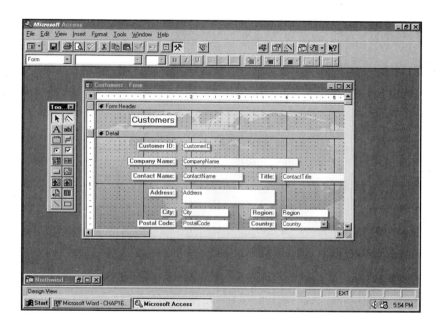

Exploring Reports

In Access, reports are used primarily for printing data from one or more tables (or queries) in a specified format. However, reports can be viewed on-screen or saved to a file. You cannot edit data displayed in a report. Instead of opening reports, you preview reports. A report preview shows you what the report looks like when printed. As with forms, you can add color and graphics to reports to enhance their visual appeal.

To preview a report, switch to the Reports tab in the Database window. Double-click the Customers report. Figure 16.10 shows a preview of the Customers report. Notice that only a few of the fields in the Customers table have been used in the Customers report.

Fig. 16.10
In Report Preview you can zoom in/out, and view one or two pages at once.

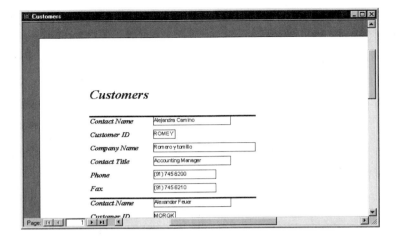

To switch to Design view, choose <u>V</u>iew, Report <u>D</u>esign. Access provides the same design tools as used in form design. As with forms, reports have sections such as Report Header/ Footer, Page Header/Footer, and Detail. In figure 16.11, the page footer lists the date and the page number. This information appears at the bottom of each page. The objects on a report have their own set of properties that you can modify. You can use the tools in the Toolbox to add controls (such as graphics and labels) to your report.

Fig. 16.11
Items in the Report Header section appear only once, on the first page of the report.

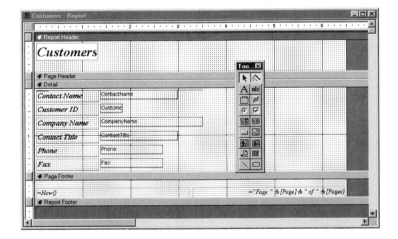

Exploring Macros and Modules

Macros and modules can be used to automate database tasks. A *macro* is a list of specific actions. Access executes the list of actions in order when you run the macro. Macros can be attached to events on forms and reports, such as a form opening, a button being clicked, or data being entered into a field. Unlike Excel, Access does not provide a macro recorder. Instead, you select an action from a drop-down list and then define arguments for the action. For example, to display a message you would select the MsgBox action and define arguments such as the title and message to be displayed. Macros stored in the currently open database are listed on the Macros tab of the Database window. For more information on macros, refer to Chapter 20, "Getting Started with Access Programming," the section entitled "Macro Programming."

Although macros provide many sophisticated application automation tools such as custom menus, auto execute macros, and event programming, for more complex turn-key applications you may need to use the programming language in Access, Visual Basic for Applications (VBA). VBA programs are stored in modules. The modules stored in the currently open database are listed on the Modules tab of the Database window. Access VBA is very similar to Excel VBA, the key difference being that Access VBA contains commands specific to the objects in Access. For more information on modules and Access VBA, refer to Chapter 20, "Getting Started with Access Programming."

Creating a Database

As discussed in the previous section, an Access database is a collection of all the related objects used to manage data: tables, queries, forms, reports, macros, and modules. An Access database is stored in a single file which has an MDB file extension. The initial Access dialog box that appears when you open Access (refer to fig. 16.1) gives you the option of opening an existing database or creating a new database. You can create a new database by using the Database Wizard or by using a Blank (empty) Database.

In either case, you have to name your database and identify a folder location in which to store the database file. The naming convention for Access database files follows the general Windows 95 file naming rules. Database file names can be as many as 255 characters and may include blank spaces (maximum of 260 characters including full folder path). Whereas in some other database applications you need to create separate folders in which to store each database, you don't need to do this in Access. Because all the objects for a database are stored in a single file, you can store different databases in the same folder without being confused as to which tables, forms, and other objects belong to which database.

Using the Database Wizard

The Database Wizard presents you with a selection of predesigned database templates from which you can choose as the basis for your new database. Just as Word templates help you get a jump start on creating a document, Access database templates help you quickly create polished databases. After you select a database template, the Access Database Wizard walks you through the process of customizing the database to better meet your needs. At the end, the Wizard modifies the template according to your specifications and saves the new database to the name and folder you specify.

The database templates that ship with Access include:

- Address Book
- Asset Tracking
- Book Collection
- Contact Management
- Donations
- Event Management
- Expenses
- Household Inventory
- Inventory Control
- Ledger
- Membership
- Music Collection
- Order Entry
- Picture Library
- Recipes
- Resource Scheduling
- Service Call Management
- Students and Classes
- Time and Billing
- Video Collection
- Wine List
- Workout

Each database template includes tables, forms, queries, and reports that are ready to use. You can modify some aspects of the database from within the Database Wizard, before the new database is created. Other aspects can only be altered after the new database is created from the Design view of the specific object (table, form, and so on).

To create a new database using the Database Wizard, follow these steps:

1. From the initial Access screen, choose <u>D</u>atabase Wizard, or from the Access menu, choose <u>F</u>ile, <u>N</u>ew Database.

>
> **Tip**
> From outside of Access, you can use the Start menu (choose New Office Document) or the Office Shortcut Bar (click the Start a New Document button).

16

2. Select the Databases tab (see fig. 16.12).

Fig. 16.12

The Database Wizard helps you customize a database template to meet your specific needs.

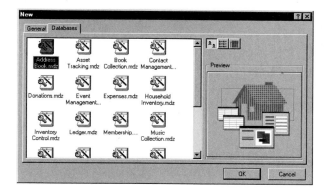

3. Double-click the database template that best matches the type of data you want to manage. Note that if you accessed the New dialog box from outside of Access, the first item listed is a Blank Database which is not a Database Wizard.

4. In the File New Database dialog box (see fig. 16.13), enter a File <u>N</u>ame and specify a folder to Save <u>I</u>n. The File New Database dialog box works the same as any Save As dialog box you have used in Office. Click Create to continue.

Fig. 16.13

Before the Wizard can start, you need to specify a name and folder location for the new database.

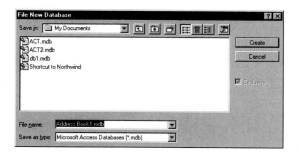

5. The Database Wizard opens. Follow the on-screen prompts to tailor the database template to better meet your needs.

The exact Wizard prompts differ depending on which template you selected. Some templates have multiple tables that are integrated, whereas others only have one table. All database templates prompt you to specify the following options:

▶ *Fields in the Table.* For each table in the database, you have the option of selecting which optional fields to include in your new database (see fig. 16.14).

▶ *Screen Display Styles.* The Database Wizard applies a screen display color and style scheme to the forms in the new database. You can preview choices such as Colorful, Clouds, and Evergreen before committing to one screen display style.

▶ *Printed Report Styles.* The Database Wizard applies a report print style scheme to the reports in the new database. You can preview report styles such as Corporate, Casual, and Formal before committing to one print display style.

▶ *Title of Database.* The Database Wizard places a database title that you enter on the forms and reports in the database.

▶ *Picture.* The Database Wizard allows you to select a picture to be placed on all reports.

Fig. 16.14

Besides adding optional fields to a table, you can also have the Wizard add sample data to the table.

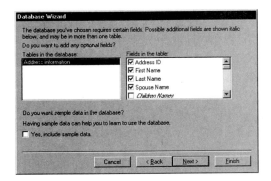

On the final Database Wizard screen, click Finish to have the Wizard create the new database based on your instructions. Two progress indicators appear on-screen. The top indicator shows the overall progress in creating the database. The bottom indicator shows the progress as each object (table, form, and so on) is created within the database. Figure 16.15 shows the Main Switchboard for a new database created using the Address Book template.

Fig. 16.15

The Database Wizard creates a Main Switchboard to guide users through the database features.

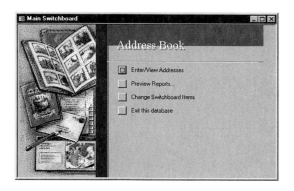

16

 Note

A *switchboard* is a form that displays a group of buttons used to perform common tasks. You can think of a switchboard in a database application as a main menu for that application. Often a main switchboard has choices that display another sub-switchboard, such as a switchboard that lists all the forms or reports in a database. Switchboards guide users who do not know Access through a database (users rely on the switchboard instead of the Database window to navigate through the database).

The switchboard created by the Database Wizard is customizable by end users. A table named Switchboard Items contains the settings for the switchboard. Users can change the text, command, or form/report displayed for each item on the switchboard. An autoexecute macro is used to open the Main Switchboard whenever the database opens.

Creating a Blank Database

If none of the database templates suit your database management needs, or if you have a specific database design in mind, you are better off creating a blank database. A blank database has no objects (tables, forms, reports, and so on). However, Access does provide wizards to help you create tables, forms, reports, and queries. Or, you can create these objects from scratch using blank tables, forms, reports, and queries.

To create a new database using a blank database, follow these steps:

1. From the initial Access screen, choose <u>D</u>atabase Wizard, or from the Access menu, choose <u>F</u>ile, <u>N</u>ew Database. From outside of Access you can use the Start menu (choose New Office Document) or the Office Shortcut Bar (click the Start a New Document button).

2. Select the General tab (see fig. 16.16).

Fig. 16.16

Use the Blank Data-base icon to create a new database from scratch.

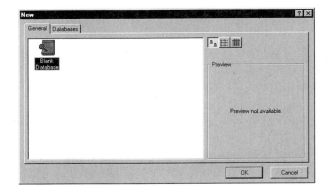

3. Double-click the Blank Database icon.

4. The File New Database dialog box appears (refer to fig. 16.13), prompting you to enter a File Name and specify the folder to Save In.

5. Click Create. An empty Database window appears for the new database.

Creating New Tables

In Access, you can create new tables by using the Table Wizard, by directly entering data into a datasheet, or by designing a table from scratch. Access also allows you to create a new table by importing data from external sources or linking to tables in an external file. To create a new table, open a database, select the Tables tab and click the New button. The New Table dialog box shown in figure 16.17 appears.

Fig. 16.17

If you are unsure of how to design a new table, consider using the Table Wizard.

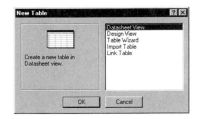

The following sections describe each method of creating a new table.

Datasheet View

Datasheet View creates a new table with twenty fields named Field1 through Field20 and displays it in Datasheet view (see fig. 16.18). You can immediately start entering data. When you save the table for the first time, Access looks at the data in each column and assigns an appropriate data type. You can at any time change the field names, data types, or other table design elements by using the skills discussed in the later section, "Designing a Table."

Fig. 16.18

Creating a table using Datasheet view allows you to start entering data immediately.

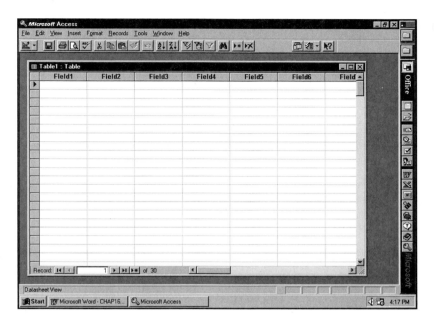

> χ **Caution**
>
> Although convenient, Datasheet view can lead to problems in the long run. If the initial data you enter is not representative of the information you need stored in a field, the data type will be wrong. Also, users unfamiliar with database design often put several items of information into one field, instead of breaking the parts down into several fields (such as First Name and Last Name). It is better to plan the database design and table design before entering data. Failure to properly design a table (the foundation of a database) could cause problems later.

Design View

Design View displays a blank table in Design view, ready for you to enter field names, data types, descriptions, and set field properties. For more information, see the later section, "Designing a Table."

Table Wizard

Table Wizard opens the Table Wizard, which contains templates of popular table designs for personal and business use. As you can see in figure 16.19, you can select the sample table, sample fields to include in your new table, and even rename fields. The Table Wizard can automatically set the primary key for you (the primary key is the unique field used to identify a record) or you can define the primary key yourself. When you select Finish from the last Table Wizard screen, you can modify the table design, enter data into the new table, or create a form for the new table.

Fig. 16.19

The Table Wizard allows you to select fields from more than one sample table, combining them in your new table.

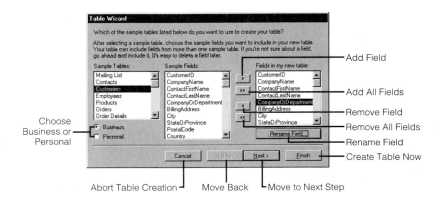

Import Table

Import Table displays the Import dialog box, which allows you to import data into a newly created table in your database. The supported file formats include:

- ▶ Access (.mdb)
- ▶ Excel (.xls)
- ▶ Text files (.txt, .csv, .tab, and .asc)
- ▶ dBASE III, IV, 5 (.dbf)
- ▶ FoxPro (.dbf and .dbc)
- ▶ Paradox (.db)
- ▶ Lotus 123 (.wk*)
- ▶ ODBC databases

To import data into a new table, follow these steps:

1. Open an Access database.
2. In the Database window, select the Tables tab.
3. Choose New.

4. Choose Import Table and click OK.

5. In the Import dialog box (see fig. 16.20), specify the folder to Look In.

Fig. 16.20

Rather than re-entering existing data, use the Import dialog box to import the data into a new table.

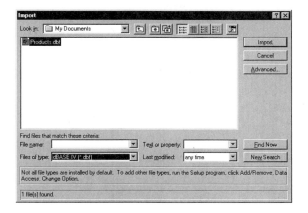

6. In the Files of Type drop-down list box, select the file type.

7. Choose Import. Access displays a message as to whether the import was successful.

8. Continue importing files as needed, or close the Import dialog box if finished. Imported tables appear on the Tables tab of the Database window.

Link Table

Link Table links external files to an Access database, so that the data can be used in Access, but remain saved in the external file. Use Link in situations where the data must reside in an external file; for example, when the data is primarily maintained in an external file. You can also use Link to work with tables in other Access databases. The file formats supported by Link are the same as those listed for Import. And the Link dialog box (see fig. 16.21) operates the same as for imported files.

Fig. 16.21

Use Link to create a new table that allows you to work with data stored in an external file.

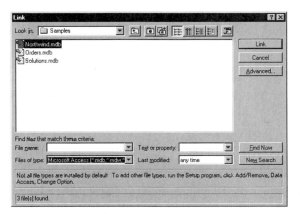

When you click the Link button in the Link dialog box, Access looks for the specified external file. If the external file is an Access database, a secondary Link Tables dialog box appears (see fig. 16.22). A similar dialog box appears if you are importing from an Access database. The dialog box lists the available tables. You can select specific table(s) or use the Select <u>A</u>ll, Deselect <u>A</u>ll buttons. Click OK when done and the Linked tables appear in the Database window on the Tables tab.

Fig. 16.22

The Link Tables dialog box lists the tables in the external Access database to which you can link.

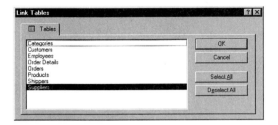

 Note

In the Database window's Tables tab, a black arrow appears to the left of the icon next to the table name to indicate that a table is linked rather than stored in the current Access database file.

Designing a Table

When you design a table, you specify the names of the fields, the data type of each field, optionally supply a description to be displayed in the status bar, and set field properties. In the quick tour you took of Access earlier in this chapter (refer to fig. 16.5), Design view for a table was discussed. This section reviews the Access naming rules, the available data types, specifying a primary key, and setting field properties.

Access Naming Conventions

Object names in Access (including table and field names):

▸ Can be as many as 64 characters long

▸ Can include any characters except square brackets ([ ]), period (.), exclamation point (!) or closing quote (').

▶ Cannot include control characters (ASCII values 0 through 31)

▶ Can include spaces, but cannot begin with a space

It also is not considered good programming practice to name objects with names that resemble (or are) reserved Access or VBA keywords. Also, most programmers choose to use brief but descriptive names without spaces as a matter of convenience when referring to objects in code. Furthermore, many Access programmers follow specific naming rules published by external sources, such as the Leszynski naming conventions, that make code easier to read and understand across applications and companies.

Data Types

A *data type* specifies the kind of information you can store in a field. If you define a field as a Date field, for example, Access does not permit you to enter text in that field. When you assign a data type, Access also knows how much storage space is needed. A date value requires eight bytes of storage space, whereas text requires one byte for each character (a 20-character name needs 20 bytes of storage). Based on the data type, Access also determines the types of calculations or other operations available for that field.

Access provides the following nine basic data types:

▶ *Text*. Alphanumeric characters, as many as 255 bytes (one byte per character).

▶ *Memo*. Alphanumeric characters, as many as 64,000 bytes.

▶ *Number*. Any numeric type; see table 16.1 for storage sizes and range of values permitted.

▶ *Date/Time*. Dates and times (eight bytes).

▶ *Currency*. Rounded numbers that are accurate to 15 digits to the left of the decimal point and to four decimal places.

▶ *AutoNumber*. Unique sequential (incrementing by one) or random numbering, automatically entered by Access for each record you add.

▶ *Yes/No*. Logical values (Yes/No, True/False, or On/Off).

▶ *OLE Object*. OLE objects, graphics, or other binary data.

▶ *Lookup Wizard*. Creates a field that displays a drop-down list of acceptable values from another table.

Table 16.1 gives the range of values that Access allows for numerical data, depending on the field and data type you select.

Table 16.1 **Numeric Values Permitted for the Number Data Type**

Field Size	Storage Size	Range
Byte	1 byte	0 to 255; no fractions
Integer	2 bytes	–32,768 to 32,767; no fractions
Long Integer	4 bytes	–2,147,483,648 to 2,147,483,647; no fractions
Single	4 bytes	Numbers with seven digits of precision. –3.402823E38 to 3.402823E38
Double	8 bytes	Numbers with 15 digits of precision. –1.79769313486232E308 to 1.79769313486232E308
Replication ID	16 bytes	Globally unique identifier (GUID) used for database replication

By default, Access assigns the data type Text to a new field. To assign a different data type, click the down-arrow button and select one from the Data Type drop-down list.

 Note

For numbers on which you don't need to perform calculations, use the Text data type to save processing time and space.

For numbers containing punctuation (such as hyphens in a Social Security or phone number), you must use the Text data type, because no punctuation is allowed in a Number data type.

 **Caution**

Be careful when choosing between the Number and the Currency data type. Entries in Currency fields are rounded, whereas Number fields use floating-point (the decimal point floats as needed) calculation. Currency uses a faster method of fixed-point (predetermined number of decimal places) calculation that prevents rounding errors.

Tip
To speed selection of data types, type the first letter of the data type and press Tab. Access fills in the rest.

16

Setting the Primary Key

Although the primary key is not required, every table should have a primary key so that it works efficiently in Access. The primary key identifies a record as being unique. In an Employee database, for example, each employee has a unique Social Security number. The Social Security number field would be the primary key.

The benefits of establishing a primary key include the following:

▶ *Speed*. Access creates an index based on the primary key, which enables Access to improve processing of queries and other functions.

▶ *Order*. Access automatically sorts and displays database records in primary-key order.

▶ *No duplicates*. Access does not permit users to enter data with the same primary key as an existing record.

▶ *Links*. Access maintains relationships between linked tables based on a common primary key.

Sometimes, the unique fact about a record is a combination of the information kept in several fields. In an Invoice table, for example, the primary key might consist of the invoice number and the customer number, because a customer might have more than one invoice number. Access enables you to key more than one field in a table to create a multifield primary key.

To set a primary key, follow these steps:

1. Click the field selector (first column) to select the field you want to use as the primary key. For a multifield primary key, hold down the Ctrl key and click the field selector for the remaining field(s).

2. Choose Edit, Set Primary Key. A key icon appears in the field selector column of each primary-key field. Figure 16.23 shows that the Order Details table in the Northwind database is keyed on OrderID (from the Orders table) and ProductID (from the Products table).

Later in this chapter, the section "Adding Intelligence to a Database" discusses how primary keys can be used to relate tables. Chapter 17, "Understanding Relational Databases," provides an in-depth discussion of relational database theory.

Fig. 16.23

Access displays a key icon in the field selector column to indicate the field(s) that define the primary key.

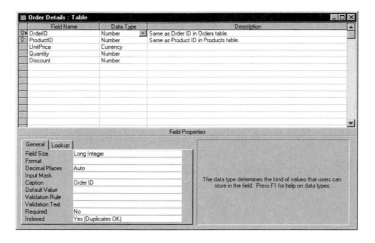

Setting Field Properties

Fields have properties that define the way data is stored and displayed. By setting field properties, you can provide the following:

▶ A default caption

▶ A default value

▶ A default format (display layout) for data entry

▶ Data-entry validation

▶ An index (for fields that can be indexed)

▶ Various display qualities, such as field size and formats

The field properties set at the table level are applied automatically to other database objects that use this table, such as forms, reports, and queries. Field properties are organized on two tabs, General and Lookup. The Lookup properties are discussed in the next section, "Adding Intelligence to a Database."

Following is an overview of the General field properties:

▶ *Field Size.* Limits Text fields to a specific number of characters (such as 2 for two characters in a State field); limits Number fields to a range of values.

▶ *New Values.* Specifies how new values for AutoNumber fields should be generated: incremental or random.

▶ *Format.* Specifies a specific display format for dates and numbers, such as 2/21/96 or Wednesday, February 21, 1996.

▶ *Decimal Places.* Sets the number of decimal places displayed in Number and Currency fields, such as 2.99.

▶ *Input Mask* (Text and Memo data only). Specifies formatting characters, such as dashes in a phone number field, to be filled in automatically during data entry.

▶ *Caption.* Supplies a label to be used in forms and reports instead of the field name, such as Movie Tag instead of MovieID.

▶ *Default Value.* Specifies a default value to be entered automatically in new records, such as the city and state in which a video-rental store is located.

▶ *Validation Rule.* Restricts data entry to values that meet specific criteria, such as the return date being greater than today's date.

▶ *Validation Text.* Specifies the error message that appears when data entry violates validation rule.

▶ *Required.* Specifies that data must be entered in the field, such as the member's ID number.

▶ *Allow Zero Length.* Permits Text and Memo fields to contain zero-length strings (""). By default, Access does not store string values that contain no characters or spaces.

▶ *Indexed.* Sets up an additional index based on this field.

 Tip

For help in entering a validation expression or an input mask, click the Build button in the toolbar while the insertion point is in the field property.

To set field properties in Table Design view, follow these steps:

1. Select the field for which you want to set properties. The bottom part of the window displays the General properties for that field.

2. Click the specific General property you want to set, or press F6 to move to the Field Property pane and tab to the desired property.

3. Enter the property value, or select it from a drop-down list of values (if available).

4. Continue setting other properties for the field.

5. Select the Lookup tab and set properties as needed.

6. Set properties for other fields as needed.

7. When you finish setting properties, save your table.

If the property box is too small for the value you need to enter, press Shift+F2, or click the right-mouse button and choose Zoom from the shortcut menu, to display the Zoom dialog box. The Zoom dialog box is available throughout most of Access.

Note

Right-clicking a field property displays a pop-up shortcut menu containing the Build, Zoom, Cut, Copy, Paste, and Help commands. (Some commands are disabled, depending on the property or data type.)

Adding Intelligence to a Database

As you may have noticed in the previous section which reviewed the field properties, Access provides many advanced methods of making your database smarter. This section focuses on the critical areas: validating data, relating tables, and looking up data. Before you start building queries and creating forms and reports, you should fully explore the tools available to you at the table level. Keep in mind that tables are the foundation of your Access database. In this section you learn how to strengthen the foundation of your Access database.

Validating Data

Access provides a variety of ways to control how data is entered into your database. For example, you can limit the data that can be entered into a field by defining a validation rule for that field. If the data that is entered into the field breaks the rule, Access displays an error message telling the user what kind of entries are allowed.

 Tip

Another method of controlling data entry is to create an input mask to restrict the kind of values that can be entered in positions across the field (input mask field property).

Data validation and restriction properties can be set at the table level in field properties, at the form level, or be controlled at runtime by macros and VBA code. By defining data validation and restriction at the table level in a field's property, you control data entry in Datasheet view, and whenever the field is used in a form. However, for controls on a form not bound to a table, you have to define data validation and restriction properties at the form level. For more complex validations, or to change the validation rules at runtime, you have to use a macro or VBA code.

Note

Your first line of defense is always the data type. Take the time to determine if you have chosen the correct data type for each field. For example, Date/Time fields only allow entry of valid date and time formats. If you are currently using a Text field for such information, it may be appropriate to change the field to a Date/Time field.

Furthermore, depending on the data type, you can specify other field properties to control the maximum field size, range of values, input masks, and allow/prevent duplicate values.

Validation rules allow you to define a rule to limit what data will be accepted into a field. Access allows you to define two kinds of validation rules: field validation rules and record validation rules.

▶ A *field validation rule* is used to check the value entered into a field as the user leaves the field. For example, you could define >=10 And <=100 as the validation rule for a Number field to allow only values from 10 to 100 to be entered.

▶ A *record validation rule* controls when an entire record can be saved. Unlike field validation rules, record validation rules can refer to other fields in the same table. This makes them useful when you want to compare values in different fields. For example, you could define [RequiredDate]<=[OrderDate]+30 as the validation rule for an Orders table. This rule makes sure that the date entered into the RequiredDate field is within 30 days of the date in the OrderDate field.

Both kinds of validation rules display a message that you define when the rule is broken to inform the user how to properly enter data. Field validation rules are enforced whenever you add or edit data, whether it is through Table Datasheet view, a control on a form that is bound to the field, an append query, an update query, Microsoft Access code, or by importing data from another table.

 Note

As you may know from working in Excel, an *expression* is a calculation composed of operators, constants, literals, functions, and identifiers that evaluate to a valid value. In Excel, the tool that helps you build expressions is called the Function Wizard. Access provides a similar tool called the Expression Builder that helps you build expressions by listing expression components and letting you select them from a list. For more information on expressions and using the Expression Builder, see Que's *Special Edition Using Microsoft Office for Windows 95*.

To define a validation rule for a field in Table Design view, follow these steps:

1. Open a table in Design view.

2. In the top pane of the window, select the field for which to set a validation property.

3. In the bottom pane of the window, click the Validation Rule property box (see fig. 16.24).

Fig. 16.24

The validation rule for the OrderDate field prevents users from entering future dates.

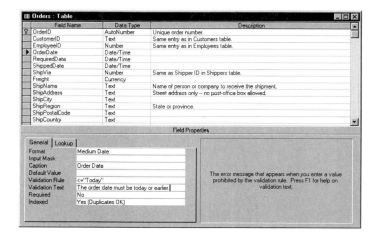

4. Type in the validation rule, or click the Build button to open the Expression Builder.

5. In the Validation Text property box, type in the error message that you want displayed if the rule is broken.

6. Save the table. Access asks you if you want to apply the new rule to existing data when you save the table.

 Tip

You can test to see if the data in a table meets validation rules by clicking the right mouse button on the title bar of Table Design view, and then clicking Test Validation Rules.

You can't refer to other fields or controls in a field's validation rule, or to user-defined functions, aggregate functions, Microsoft Access or SQL domain aggregate functions, or the CurrentUser or Eval functions. However, you can refer to other fields in the same

16

table using a record validation rule to control when an entire record can be saved. Record validation rules are enforced whenever you add or edit data, whether it is through Table Datasheet view, a form bound to the table, an append query, an update query, or Microsoft Access code, or by importing data from another table.

To define a record validation rule, follow these steps:

1. Open the table in Design view.

2. Choose <u>V</u>iew, <u>P</u>roperties. The Table Properties dialog box opens (see fig. 16.25).

Fig. 16.25

You can only enter one validation rule for a table.

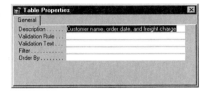

3. Click the Validation Rule property box.

4. Type in the validation rule, or click the Build button to open the Expression Builder.

5. In the Validation Text property box, type in the error message that you want displayed if the rule is broken.

6. Save the table. Access asks you if you want to apply the new rule to existing data when you save the table.

 Tip

To specify more than one validation rule for a table, combine expressions using the AND operator.

Relating Tables

A general rule of database design is "divide and conquer." Rather than creating one huge table that includes all the data, you divide your data into common groups and create a separate table to manage the data for each group. For example, most businesses have customers, employees, and products. Rather than creating one table that stores all the information for an entire business, it is more efficient (in terms of memory usage, hard disk space, and data management) to create a separate table for each group of information.

Some groups of information need to work together. For example, when a customer calls, you may want to view the customer's record at the same time that you view any orders that customer placed. Furthermore, you may want information on the salesperson who services that customer. Luckily, Access makes it very easy to pull these related pieces of data together from multiple separate tables.

As noted earlier, a primary key is a field or combination of fields that uniquely identifies each record. Access can retrieve data more quickly in keyed tables. Another benefit of keying tables is that you can relate the tables based on a piece of common data.

A relationship between tables works by matching data in key fields, usually a field with the same name in both tables. In most cases, this will be the "primary key" from one table, which provides a unique identifier for each record, being matched with an entry in the "foreign key" in the other table.

For example, the Orders table in the Northwind database (refer to fig. 16.24) is keyed on the OrderID. Each record can be quickly identified based on a unique value in the OrderID field. But you'll notice two other familiar fields listed right below the primary key field: CustomerID and EmployeeID. Including these fields in the definition of the Orders table allows you to relate the Orders table, the Customers table, and the Employee table.

You define a relationship by adding the tables you want to relate to the Relationships window, and then dragging the key field from one table and dropping it on the key field in the other table. The kind of relationship that Microsoft Access creates depends on how the related fields are defined. Here is an overview of the various relationship types:

▶ A one-to-many relationship is created if only one of the related fields is a primary key or has a unique index.

▶ A one-to-one relationship is created if both of the related fields are primary keys or have unique indexes.

▶ A many-to-many relationship is really two one-to-many relationships with a third table whose primary key consists of two fields, the foreign keys from the two other tables.

Chapter 17, "Understanding Relational Databases," explains how to use the Relation-ships window and the nuances of relational database theory.

Looking Up Data

Another way you can build intelligence into your tables is to automatically look up data for the user. Using the Lookup Wizard, you can create a field that displays either:

▶ A lookup list that displays values looked up from an existing table or query.

▶ A value list that displays a fixed set of values that you enter when you create the field.

The Lookup Wizard gives you the option to display the list as a combo box or a list box. If you use the list from a table's or query's datasheet, the list can be displayed only as a combo box, regardless of the choice you make. However, if you add the field to a form later, the list will be displayed in the format you select from the Wizard.

> **Note**
>
> After you've created a lookup or value list field, if you add the field to a form, Access copies its definition into the form. You won't have to create the combo or list box and its lookup or value list definition for the form. However, if you change the definition of a lookup or value list field in the table after adding it to a form, those changes will not be reflected in that form. To correct this, delete the field from the form and then add it again.

The most common lookup list displays values looked up from a related table. Figure 16.26 that shows that the Products table in the Northwind database has a lookup list defined for the SupplierID field. When the user arrives on the SupplierID field, a drop-down list appears listing all of the supplier names in the Suppliers table.

Fig. 16.26

The Lookup Wizard guides you through the process of setting lookup properties for a field.

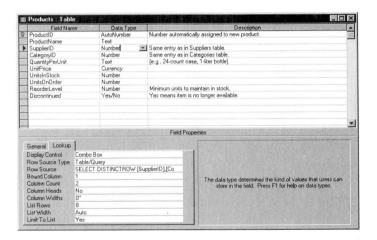

A value list resembles a lookup list, but consists of a fixed set of values you type in when you create it. A value list should only be used for values that do not change very often and don't need to be stored in a table. For example, a list for a Salutation field containing Mr., Mrs., or Ms. would be a good candidate for a value list. Choosing a value from a value list stores that value in the record—it doesn't create an association to a related table. For this reason, if you change any of the original values in the value list later, they will not be reflected in records added before this change was made.

You can add a new lookup or value list field in either Table Design view or Table Datasheet view. However, if the field you want to use as the foreign key for a Lookup field already exists, you must open that field's table in Design view to define the Lookup field. For example, if you have a Products table that has a SupplierID field already defined, and you want to change it to a Lookup field to display supplier names from your Suppliers table, you must open the Products table in Design view to change SupplierID to a Lookup field.

Getting Information Out

The true value of a computerized database management program such as Access really comes to light when you need to find stored information. Access provides two powerful data extraction features: filters and queries. Filters in Access work very similarly to the filters you may have used in Excel. However, a table or form can only have one filter associated with it at any given time. Queries, on the other hand, are separate objects, so you can have many queries for any given table. Queries are more powerful than filters.

Exploring Filters

Access provides three types of filters:

- *Filter By Selection*. Users highlight data to indicate the records to display.
- *Filter By Form*. Users fill out a form to indicate the records to display.
- *Advanced Filter/Sort*. Users fill out a query window to indicate the records to display.

To create a Filter By Selection, display the table or form window and highlight (select) the value you want to find. Then choose Records, Filter, Filter By Selection. Access only displays the records that have a matching value in the field you specified. For example, to display only customers in California, you could highlight the CA in the State field of a customer table. To remove the filter, click the Remove Filter tool on the toolbar.

The Filter By Form approach works in much the same way. The advantage of the Filter By Form method is that it allows you to specify criteria values in more than one field. To create a Filter By Form, display the table or form window and click the Filter By Form tool in the toolbar. Figure 16.27 shows a Filter Form for the Customers table in the Northwind database. Use the first tab, Look For, to specify logical AND criteria. Use the second tab, Or, to specify logical OR criteria.

Fig. 16.27
This Filter By Form instructs Access to show only records for Accounting Managers in Berlin.

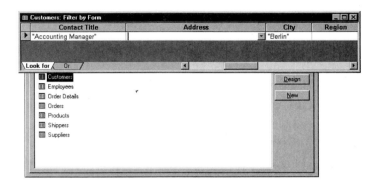

To use the Advanced Filter/Sort feature, choose Records, Filter, Advanced Filter/Sort. The Advanced Filter/Sort window which appears works the same as the Query window, discussed in the next section.

Exploring Queries

A *query* is a statement that tells Access what kind of information you need to extract from one or more tables. A query can also perform an action on the data in the table(s) and summarize data in spreadsheet format.

You can use queries, for example, to accomplish the following tasks:

- ▶ Compile a list of employees who live in a certain state
- ▶ Show customer names, demographics, and purchasing information in one report
- ▶ Determine the frequency of movie rentals
- ▶ Calculate the total cost of movies by category
- ▶ Purge the database of customers who have not rented in the past year
- ▶ Add old customer records to a history database

Queries can be used as a source of information for forms and reports. In such a case, the query enables you to include specific data from more than one table. Access executes the query each time you open the form or report, so you can be sure that the information you see is up to date.

Access enables you to create the following types of queries:

- ▶ *Select queries.* Used to extract data from tables based on criteria specified in the query object. This type of query is the most common. A select query could be used to list all customers in New York, for example.

▶ *Action queries*. Used to perform an action on records that meet criteria specified in the query object. This type of query enables you to change or move data, create new tables, or purge records from a table. You could use an action query to purge inactive customer records.

▶ *Crosstab queries*. Used to summarize data in a spreadsheet format based on criteria specified in the query object. Crosstab queries most often are used to show data in a graph.

▶ *Union queries*. Used to combine fields from two or more tables. For example, you could create a query that lists customer data from the customer table and invoice totals from the invoice table.

▶ *Pass-through queries*. Used to send commands to a Structured Query Language (SQL) database.

▶ *Data-definition queries*. Used to perform actions on Access databases with SQL statements.

For each query type, you can specify query parameters that prompt the user to specify query criteria before the query executes. Access places the results of a query or a filter operation in a dynaset. A *dynaset* looks and behaves like a table, but it actually provides a dynamic view of the data in one or more tables. You can enter and update data in a dynaset; after you do so, Access automatically updates the data in the associated table or tables.

 Note

In a multiuser environment, changes made by other users are reflected in the dynaset and its associated tables.

 Caution

Dynasets seem so much like tables that it is hard to remember that they really are not. Just keep in mind that the data is stored in the primary tables themselves, not in the dynaset.

To create a new query, click the New Object, New Query button in the toolbar, or switch to the Database window, select the Query tab, and then click the New button. The New Query dialog box appears.

Whichever method you decide to use, it helps to spend some time designing the query before actually creating it. Think about some of the following factors before getting started:

- ▶ Which table(s) contains the information you need?
- ▶ Table relationships (are the tables properly keyed?)
- ▶ The type of query you want to perform
- ▶ The field conditions and criteria that the records must meet
- ▶ Calculations, if desired
- ▶ Sort order
- ▶ The name under which you want to save the query

The New Query dialog box provides five types of generic queries:

- ▶ *Design View*. Enters Query Design displaying a blank query form for the table(s) you select.
- ▶ *Simple Query Wizard*. Creates a select query from fields you pick.
- ▶ *Crosstab Query Wizard*. Summarizes query data in spreadsheet format.
- ▶ *Find Duplicates Query Wizard*. Locates duplicate records in a table.
- ▶ *Find Unmatched Query Wizard*. Locates records in one table that do not have matching records in a related table.

Each wizard prompts you for specific information needed to create its particular type of query. In each case, you must identify the table(s) or queries on which the new query will be based.

To create a query from scratch, choose Design View in the New Query dialog box. Access displays the Select Query: Query1 window and opens the Show Table dialog box. As you select tables, Access places a field list for the table at the top of the Select Query window.

To select the table/query you want to add to your query definition, double-click the table/query name or highlight the table/query name and then choose the Add button. Access adds the table/query to the Select Query: Query1 window; the Show Table dialog box remains open so that you can add more tables, if necessary. Access automatically finds any relationships among multiple tables added to a query definition and shows those relationships by drawing lines between the related fields.

Access automatically finds table relationships and draws a line between the matching key fields (same field name and field type). These lines are called *join lines*. Join lines apply only to multitable queries. You can create join lines yourself by dragging and dropping a key field from one table to another.

The bottom half of the window contains the Query-by-Example grid, in which you define the criteria of the query. Query-by-Example (QBE) enables you to define query criteria by providing practical examples of the type of data you need. To find all employees in the state of New Jersey, for example, you would type the example element **NJ**.

After you finish adding tables, click C‌lose. To reopen the Show Tables dialog box, click the Show Table button in the toolbar, or choose the Query Show Table command.

 Note

By default, Access sets the query type to Select Query. You can change the query type by making a different selection from the Query menu, or by clicking the Query Type button on the toolbar.

For more information on queries and creating advanced queries, see Chapter 18, "Advanced Queries."

Creating Forms

You can create new forms via the toolbar or the New Form dialog box. The AutoForm button in the toolbar creates a simple columnar form based on the current table or query and displays the completed form with data in Form view. Columnar forms let you focus on one record at a time.

You create all other new forms in the New Form dialog box. To display the New Form dialog box, select New Form from the New Object drop-down button on the toolbar. Or, switch to the Database window, select the Forms tab and click the New button. Either way, the New Form dialog box appears.

The New Form dialog box allows you to select the table or query on which you want to base the form and provides the following new form options:

▶ *Design View*. Allows you to create a custom form design from scratch.

▶ *Form Wizard*. Assists you in creating a form by asking you questions and using predesigned form templates (see the following section, "Using the Form Wizard").

▶ *AutoForm: Columnar*. Displays one record at a time in a vertical format (each field label value on a separate line, in a single column). The resulting forms are the same as those generated by the AutoForm button on the toolbar.

▶ *AutoForm: Tabular*. Displays multiple records in a row and column format.

▶ *AutoForm: Datasheet*. Displays records and fields in the familiar row and column layout of the Datasheet view.

▶ *Chart Wizard.* Displays a form with a graph or chart of the data.

▶ *PivotTable Wizard.* Creates a form based on an Excel pivot table.

Using the Form Wizard

The Form Wizard generates a form design for you based on your specifications. The Form Wizard asks you a series of questions to determine what table(s) you want to use and what type of form you want to create.

To create a new form using the Form Wizard, follow these steps:

1. In the toolbar, click the New Object drop-down button and select the New Form button. The New Form dialog box appears.
2. Type or select the name of a table or query in the drop-down list box.
3. Choose Form Wizard and click OK.
4. Select the form type, and then choose OK. The Form Wizard appears.
5. In the Tables/Queries drop-down list, select the tables or queries you want to include on the form.
6. In the Available Fields list, select the fields to be included in the form. Choose Next to continue.

 Note

To select fields in the Available Fields list, use the arrow buttons to select individual fields (>) or all fields (>>). To remove fields from the Selected Fields list, use the < arrow button to remove one field, or the << arrow button to remove all fields.

When working with more than one table or query on the same form, select the table/query and select the fields, then select the next table/query and select the fields from that table/query, and so on.

7. In the next Form Wizard dialog box, select a layout (Columnar, Tabular, or Datasheet) and choose Next.
8. In the next Form Wizard dialog box, select a style for the form and choose Next.
9. In the next Form Wizard dialog box, enter a title for the form in the Form text box and select the Open the Form To View or Enter Information option or the Modify the Form's Design option.
10. If you want to display Help on working with the form, select that check box.
11. Choose Finish.

Designing a Form

You can use Design view to create a new custom form that displays data in specific locations, which cannot be achieved by using generic templates in Form Wizard. For example, you might need to create a form that matches a required government form, such as a W-4 form. Or, you might need to create a form that includes pictures in the employee application form. To create a new form using Design view, follow these steps:

1. In the toolbar, click the New Object drop-down and select New Form. The New Form dialog box appears.

2. In the drop-down list box, select the table or query for which you want to create a form.

3. Choose Design View and choose OK. Access displays a blank form in Form Design view.

Navigating Form Design View

Form Design view is where you can create and modify forms. Although new forms in Design view contain only a detail section, you can add other sections to your form design. To add a form header/footer or page header/footer to your form, choose Format, Form Header/Footer or Format, Page Header/Footer.

Following is an overview of each section that can appear in a form:

▶ *Form header.* Appears at the top of the screen. Prints at the top of the first page.

▶ *Page header.* Appears only when printed. Prints at the top of each page.

▶ *Detail section.* Displays data.

▶ *Page footer.* Appears only when printed. Prints at the bottom of each page.

▶ *Form footer.* Appears at the bottom of the screen. Prints at the bottom of the last page.

The design tools in the Toolbox and other design features in Form Design view are the same tools as used in the Report Design view.

Creating Reports

Report creation is very similar to form creation. To create a new report, display the Database window, select the Report tab, and click the New button. The New Report dialog box appears listing the following options:

▶ *Design View.* Enables you to create a custom report from scratch.

▶ *Report Wizard.* Assists you in creating a form by asking you questions and using predesigned report templates.

▶ *AutoReport: Columnar.* Displays one record at a time in a vertical format (same layout as AutoForm: Columnar).

▶ *AutoReport: Tabular.* Displays multiple records in a row and column format (same layout as AutoForm: Tabular).

▶ *Chart Wizard.* Displays a report with a graph or chart of the data.

▶ *Label Wizard.* Creates label reports in a variety of formats.

 Note

If you have an Access form that resembles your report design, you can save the form as a report. This feature is available as a toolbar button that you can add to any toolbar. First, open the form in Design view and select View, Toolbars. Click Customize and select the Form & Report Design category. Drag the Save As Report button to any toolbar and click Close.

Now you are ready to use the Save As Report Button. Click the Save As Report button and enter a name for the report. Click OK to save the form as a report.

To preview the new report, switch to the Report tab of the Database window and double-click the new report name.

Using the Report Wizard

When you select Report Wizard, Access presents a series of dialog boxes that ask you for the report specifications. The Report Wizard functions much the same as the Form Wizard, so many of the dialog boxes are familiar.

To create a new report using the Report Wizard, follow these steps:

1. Click the New Object button in the toolbar and select New Report.

2. Type or select the name of the table or query on which to base the report.

3. Choose Report Wizard and click OK.

4. Select the fields to be included in the report from the Available Fields pane (they appear in the Selected Fields pane). Then select Next.

5. Specify any desired grouping levels and select Next. If you specify grouping, you'll be asked to specify sort order and options.

6. Select the desired layout (Vertical, Tabular, or for grouped reports, various step, block, and outline layouts are available).

7. Select Portrait or Landscape orientation.

8. If desired, select to Adjust Field Width to fit on page.

9. Choose Next.

10. Select a style (Bold, Casual, Compact, Corporate, Formal, or Soft Gray) and choose Next.

11. Type in the report title and choose Preview the Report or Modify the Report's Design.

12. Select Report Help if desired.

13. Click Finish.

Previewing a Report

If you selected the Preview the Report option in the final Report Wizard dialog box, Access displays the print preview view of the report. Print preview shows on-screen how the printed report will look. The mouse pointer resembles a magnifying glass. Clicking the report zooms in the view. Click again to zoom out.

Designing a Report

At times, the generic Report Wizards may not provide the particular report format or layout that you need. In these cases, you can use a blank report to design a report that meets your needs. For example, you may need to create a report that matches a required document format in your business, such as a service contract, or you may need to create a report that includes special effects, such as pictures of products.

To create a new report using Design view, follow these steps:

1. Click the New Object button and select New Report. The New Report dialog box appears.

2. Choose Design View and click OK.

3. In the drop-down list box, select the table or query for which you want to create a report. Access displays a blank report in Design view.

4. Use the Toolbox to select and place controls on the form as needed.

The tools and features available in Report Design view are essentially the same tools and features as in Form Design view. The following list is an overview of the sections that can be used in a report design:

▶ *Report header.* Contains information, such as the report title, that appears at the top of the first page in a report.

▶ *Page header.* Contains information, such as column headings, that appears at the top of each page in a report.

▶ *Category header.* Contains information, such as a group title, that appears before each group of data.

▶ *Detail section.* Contains the body of the report. This area is where you display the data from tables and queries.

▶ *Category footer.* Contains information, such as group totals, that appears after each group of data.

▶ *Page footer.* Contains information, such as page numbers, that appears at the bottom of each page in a report.

▶ *Report footer.* Contains information, such as grand totals, that appears at the bottom of the last page in a report.

Although new blank forms contain only a detail section, new reports also have page header and footer sections defined. As with forms, you can add headers and footers to the report. To add a form or page header and footer to your report, choose Format Report Header/Footer or Format Page Header/Footer. In addition, reports can contain two new sections: category headers and footers for groups of data.

Summary

This chapter provided you with a good foundation in the critical skills necessary to use Access. You learned how to open and navigate an existing Access database. In touring Access, you learned the basic terminology and when to use Access in your work. You know how to create a database using predesigned database templates and using a datasheet format and how to design a database from scratch. This chapter examined the methods available to add intelligence to your database. You learned how to validate data, enforce relationships, and look up related data from other tables. In the section on queries, you learned how to extract information in the format you need. Lastly, this chapter showed you how to create forms and reports to present your data in a variety of ways.

Understanding Relational Databases

17

by Diane Tinney

In this chapter

◆ **What is a relational database?**
Before you can start joining tables together, you'll need a solid foundation in relational database theory, terminology, and how it applies to Access.

◆ **Designing a relational Access database**
Access provides a Relationship tool to help you create and maintain relationships between multiple tables in a database.

◆ **Working with related tables**
After the relationship between multiple tables has been defined, you can create queries, forms, and reports to join the data and maintain the database.

I n Chapter 16, you learned the critical skills necessary to create and use an Access database. This chapter builds on your understanding of the basic skills and expands your understanding of Access as a relational database management system. Access allows you to define relationships between tables to bring data together as needed in Forms, Queries, and Reports. This powerful feature allows you to build efficient databases without duplicating data entry and storage. Furthermore, the relational database features in Access can automatically keep records in multiple tables in sync. For example, if you delete a company's master record, Access can automatically delete any related records for that company stored in other related tables.

What Is a Relational Database?

Two types of database systems exist: flat-file database systems and relational database systems. In the flat-file database system, data is stored without indexing, which results in the data being processed sequentially. Users have very little flexibility in data manipulation. To compensate for this lack of data manipulation, users tend to store the same data in more than one place (data redundancy) to accomplish database tasks such as reporting.

Relational database management systems enable users to manipulate data in more sophisticated ways, without data redundancy, by defining relationships between sets of data. The relationship is a common element, such as a customer identification number or an employee's social security number. The data stored in each set can be retrieved and updated based on the data in the other set.

In Access, the common element is called the primary key. In Chapter 16, you learned how to define a primary key using one or more fields in a table (see the section "Relating Tables"). The process of breaking data down into sets which you then relate by using a common element is called *normalizing data*. Data normalization eliminates redundancy in your database (see section later in this chapter on "Normalizing Data").

Working with Multiple Tables

In most cases, your database application will have more than one table. Before you start creating the tables and defining relationships, you should take the time to plan the table relationships. Ask questions such as:

▶ What data needs to be stored?

▶ How should the fields be formatted?

▶ What reports need to be printed?

▶ Can the data be broken down into smaller sets?

 Tip
When designing a multitable database, divide and conquer is the rule!

Use basic pencil and paper (or Word or Excel) to plan the inputs and outputs. Make the plans available in printed form to everyone involved in the database design (involve end users if at all possible). Use a set of representative (not live) data to test your design and illustrate the output. Using the pencil and paper approach allows you to stay flexible and creative as your multitable database design takes shape.

> **Tip**
>
> Use a flow chart program to illustrate the common element used to relate tables together.

Dividing your data storage needs into manageable sets of data is the first step in normalizing your data. Next, you need to determine the common element which can be used to join the separate sets back together when needed. A fundamental rule of relational database design is that you shouldn't have duplicate records in the same table. It would be a waste of hard disk space (not to mention memory) to have a customer record for Jane Jones at 15 High Mt. Road in Walden, NY listed three times in the customer table. To prevent duplicate records from being entered into a database, you define a *primary key* for each table in the database. A table's primary key can be one or more fields. The primary key contains a unique, non-duplicated value. For example, in a customer table, you might assign each customer a unique customer number. In an orders table, each order may have a unique order number.

In addition to preventing the storage of duplicate records, a table's primary key serves as a default sort order for the table. Just like page numbers in a book uniquely identify each page and provide order, a primary key does the same. You will never find two pages in a book with exactly the same page number, and you can quickly find a page number within a book.

Reviewing Relationship Types

In order to join tables together correctly, you need to determine the nature of the relationship between the tables. Relationships between tables fall into one of the three relationship types:

- ▶ One-to-one (1:1)
- ▶ One-to-many (1:M)
- ▶ Many-to-many (M:M)

We will use the NorthWind sample database to illustrate the differences between the three relationship types (\Samples\NorthWind.mdb).

One-to-One Relationships

In a one-to-one (1:1) relationship, each record in one table has exactly one matching record in another table. One-to-one relationships are rare because in most situations the one-to-one data relationships are kept in a single table. However, there may be business reasons for separating the data into two tables. For example, rather than keeping all of the confidential employee information such as salary and performance ratings in a public employee table, you could split the data into two tables. Access to the table containing private information would be restricted to authorized users only.

The NorthWind database does not contain any tables with a one-to-one relationship, so we created a new table called Confidential Employee Data and related it to the Employee table by adding the Employee ID field to the new table. As you can see in figure 17.1, for each employee record in the Employee table, one, and only one, related record exists in the Confidential Employee Data table. Furthermore, for each confidential employee record in the Confidential Employee Data table, one, and only one, related record exists in the Employee table.

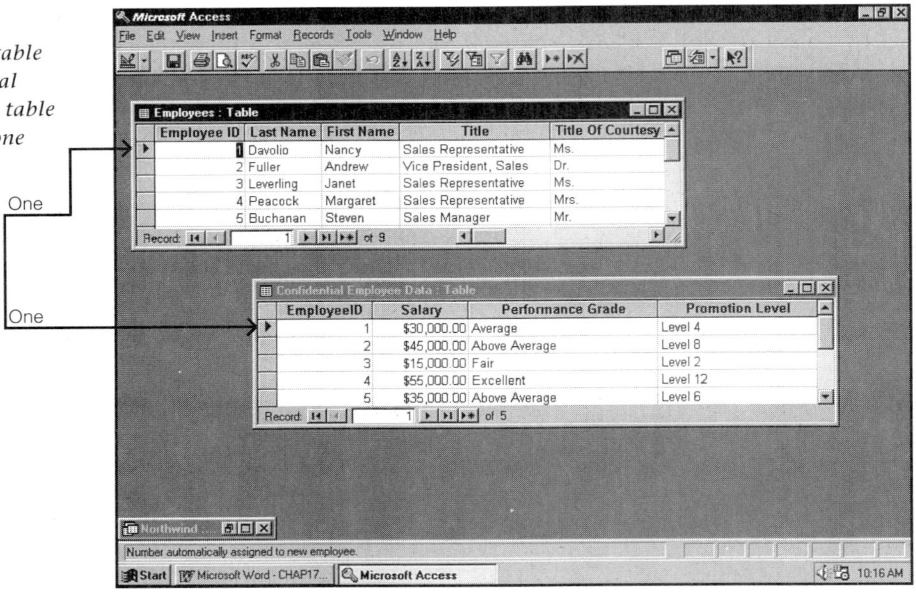

Fig. 17.1

The Employee table and Confidential Employee Data table have a one-to-one relationship.

If your database design contains a one-to-one relationship between two tables, consider why you need to keep the data separated. Keeping the data in one table usually is easier to maintain and more efficient. If you need to keep the data separate for a business or design purpose, use the same primary key for both tables, or if the two tables have different primary keys, choose one (either one) primary key and use in both tables.

One-to-Many Relationships

The most frequently occuring relationship in databases is the one-to-many (1:M) relationship. In a one-to-many relationship, each record in one table can have many related records in another table. Consider a business which has customers. Each customer (1) could order many (M) products from the business. Figure 17.2 shows the Customers and Orders tables from the NorthWind database. For the company ALFKI in the Customers table, the Orders table has many Order records. But for each Order in the Orders table, only one matching record exists in the Customers table.

Fig. 17.2

The Customers and Orders tables have a one-to-many relationship.

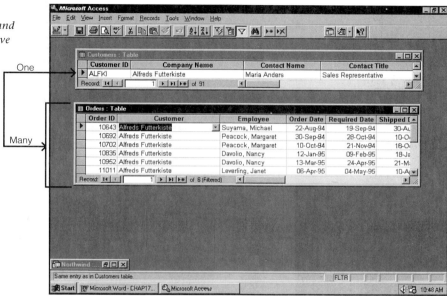

If your database design has tables that contain one-to-many relationships within a table, you should break the table down into two tables. Set up one table as the single record (the "one" side of the relationship). Set the other table up to store the set of related records (the "many" side of the relationship).

You may find that a one-to-many relationship blooms into another one-to-many relationship. Figure 17.3 illustrates how the Customers, Orders, and Order Details tables are related. For each Customer record (1), the Orders table can store many (M) orders. For each Order record (1), the Order Details table can store many (M) items ordered.

To set up a one-to-many relationship, add the field or fields that form the primary key on the "one" side of the relationship to the table on the "many" side of the relationship. For example, the primary key for the Customer table is the Customer ID. To relate the Customer table to the Orders table, the Customer ID field is added to the Orders table. To relate the Orders table to the Order Details table, the Order ID field is added to the Order Details table.

Fig. 17.3
Customer ID ALFKI has placed many orders, one of which (Order ID 10643) orders many products.

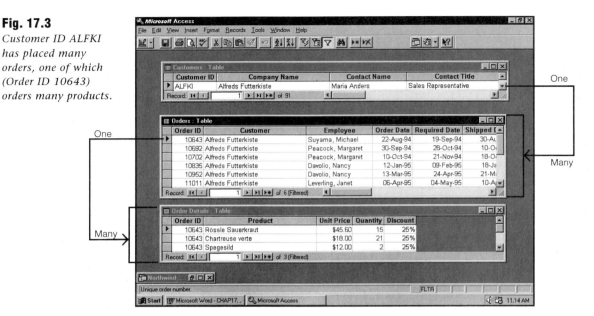

Many-to-Many Relationships

In a many-to-many relationship, each record in a table can have many matching records in another table, and vice versa. The many-to-many relationship is a two-way street. Although not as common as the one-to-many relationship, your database design may very well include a many-to-many relationship between two tables. To illustrate this relationship further, consider the Orders and Products tables in the NorthWind database. Each order can list many products, and each product can be listed on many different orders (see fig. 17.4).

If the Orders table is keyed on Order ID and the Products table is keyed on the Product ID, which key field do you add to which table to create the many-to-many relationship? The answer is neither. If you add one of the keys to the other table, you will duplicate data entry resulting in an inefficient database design. Instead, when two tables have a many-to-many relationship, you break the relationship down into two one-to-many relationships. This is done by creating an intermediary table which has a one-to-many relationship with both of the original tables. Figure 17.5 shows the intermediary Order Details table, which has a one-to-many relationship with the Products and Orders tables.

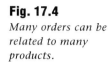

Fig. 17.4

Many orders can be related to many products.

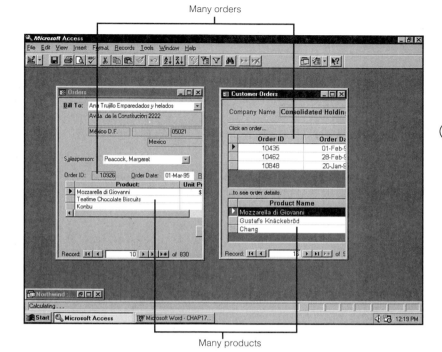

Fig. 17.5

Splitting the many-to-many relationship into two one-to-many relationships eliminates data duplication.

Instead of the Orders table and the Products table being directly related, they are related through the Order Details table.

Normalizing Data

The process of data normalization applies common sense to the design of your database in order to obtain the best performance using the least amount of resources (physical storage and memory). The five rules of database normalization that you can apply to your database design are:

▶ Eliminate repeating groups of data.

▶ Eliminate redundant data.

▶ Eliminate fields not dependent on the primary key.

▶ Isolate independent multiple relationships.

▶ Isolate semantically related multiple relationships.

To help us explore these data normalization rules further, we'll use the following scenario. The Marketing department decided to create a database to manage contacts at various companies and the activities with those companies. Table 17.1 shows the initial database design. The data is organized into two sets (Company and Contacts), and the fields within each set are defined by name and data type.

Table 17.1 Initial Marketing Database Design

Company Data Set

Field Name	Data Type
Company Name	Text
Address	Text
City	Text
State	Text
Zip	Text
Phone	Text
Fax	Text
Annual Sales	Currency
Employees	Number
Industry	Text
Locations	Number

Contact Data Set

Field Name	Data Type
First Name1	Text
Last Name1	Text
Title1	Text
Phone1	Text
Fax1	Text
Action Date1	Date/Time
Action Time1	Date/Time
Action Description1	Text
First Name2	Text
Last Name2	Text
Title2	Text
Phone2	Text
Fax2	Text
Action Date2	Date/Time
Action Time2	Date/Time
Action Description2	Text
First Name3	Text
Last Name3	Text
Title3	Text
Phone3	Text
Fax3	Text
Action Date3	Date/Time
Action Time3	Date/Time
Action Description3	Text

Eliminating Repeating Groups

This is our divide and conquer rule. Applying this rule to your database design provides you with a much more flexible database that is easier to modify and maintain. As you review your initial database design, look for repeating groups of data. For example, the

Contact data set in table 17.1 contains two sets of data. The contact information of name, title, phone, and fax forms one distinct set. The action information of date, time, and description forms another separate data set. According to the rules of data normalization, the two groups of data should reside in separate tables.

"Separate, yet united" and so shall our tables be thanks to the primary key. This is the other benefit of defining primary keys in each table. Using the primary key you can retrieve all data related to a specific company, such as contacts and actions. In the Company table, none of the existing fields would provide a unique element to serve as the primary key. So a unique Company ID field could be added and defined as the primary key.

 Note

Access allows you to define text as the primary key. However, it is usually not a good idea to define a name as the primary key in a table. Doing so presents many potential problems. First, it is possible to have more than one company or person with the same name. For example, John Jones lives at 22 Elm Street with his son John Jones and father John Jones. The name and address do not result in a unique key. A second familiar problem occurs when you need to change the name. If a company table is keyed on the company name, and you need to change the name, you will lose the related records. Third, using a name requires that you spell the name correctly, otherwise a misspelled name won't find the related data.

Access helps you create unique primary keys by providing the AutoNumber field type, which automatically generates a unique value whenever you add a record to the table. AutoNumbers are integers that by default have a field size of Long Integer. The New Values field property of AutoNumber defaults to Increment, but you can set this property to Random if you prefer to have random numbers generated.

In reviewing the Contacts table, none of the existing fields seems unique. You could have more than one contact with the same name or title. The phone number and fax number fields, although unique, would not make good primary keys since a contact could change his or her phone number or fax number at any time. So here again, we need to add a new field called Contact ID and assign each contact a unique number. In addition, we need to relate the Contact table to the Company table. This is done by listing the Company ID field in the Contact table and creating a composite primary key (more than one field makes up the unique primary key). Each record in the Contact table will have a Company ID and a Contact ID value.

Since none of the fields in the Actions table is unique, a new field called Action ID needs to be defined using AutoNumber. Since the Marketing department wants to track actions for each contact at each company, we need to relate the Actions table to the Company and Contacts table. This is done by listing the primary keys Company ID and Contact ID with Action ID. Table 17.2 illustrates the revised database design after eliminating repeating groups, defining primary keys, and relating the tables. Notice that when you use a key field from another table to relate the tables together, the key field from the other table is called a *foreign key*. Also, notice that the data type is Number, not AutoNumber.

Table 17.2　Revised Marketing Database Design

Company Table

Primary Key	Field Name	Data Type
Key	Company ID	AutoNumber
	Company Name	Text
	Address	Text
	City	Text
	State	Text
	Zip	Text
	Phone	Text
	Fax	Text
	Annual Sales	Currency
	Employees	Number
	Industry	Text
	Locations	Number

Contacts Table

Primary Key	Field Name	Data Type
Foreign Key	Company ID	Number
Key	Contact ID	AutoNumber
	First Name	Text
	Last Name	Text
	Title	Text
	Phone	Text
	Fax	Text

Table 17.2   Continued

Actions Table

Primary Key	Field Name	Data Type
Foreign Key	Company ID	Number
Foreign Key	Contact ID	Number
Key	Action ID	AutoNumber
	Action Date	Date/Time
	Action Time	Date/Time
	Action Description	Text

 Note

Note that by defining a primary key for the Contacts table, the redundancy in field names (First Name1, First Name2, First Name3) was eliminated. Furthermore, if the Marketing department needs to manage more than three contacts in the future, the capability has been built into the database.

Eliminating Redundant Data

In the revised Marketing Database design (refer to table 17.2), most of the redundant data has been removed. Only the Company table contains potentially redundant data. The Phone and Fax number fields appear in both the Company table and in the Contacts table. Unless the Marketing Department needs to keep track of a general company phone and fax number that is different than the phone and fax numbers maintained in the Contacts table, the redundant fields should be eliminated.

Redundant data could also be found in a table. Suppose the Marketing department creates an Invoice table to track company invoices and divides the invoice data into the two tables shown in table 17.3.

Table 17.3   Initial Design for Invoice Tables

Invoice Table

Primary Key	Field Name	Data Type
Foreign Key	Company ID	Number
Key	Invoice Number	AutoNumber
	Invoice Date	Date/Time

Invoice Table

Primary Key	Field Name	Data Type
	Action Time	Date/Time
	Action Description	Text

Items Table

Primary Key	Field Name	Data Type
Foreign Key	Company ID	Number
Foreign Key	Invoice Number	Number
Key	Item Number	AutoNumber
	Product ID	Number
	Product Name	Text
	Quantity	Number
	Price	Currency

The redundant data is hard to see by just looking at the table design definition. This is where working with representative data helps you during the design process. Table 17.4 shows some sample data in the Items table.

Table 17.4   Items Table Sample Data

Items Table Sample Data

Company ID	Invoice ID	Item ID	Product ID	Product Name	Quantity	Price
200	8076	1	8855	Widget	10	$59.99
200	8076	2	6437	Nuts	48	$ 1.95
367	8102	1	8855	Widget	8	$59.99
367	8102	2	6437	Nuts	5	$ 1.95

Notice the duplicate product information (Product ID, Product Name and Price) Company numbers 200 and 367 both ordered the same products (8855 and 6437). The Items table contains not only the product ID numbers, but also the Product Name and Price. Every time a product is sold, the product name and price is also listed, duplicating data already in the Items table from the last time the product was sold. Duplicate data means duplicate storage needs, which result in slower, less efficient database systems. The solution is to carve out the duplicate data and create a new related table which stores the data once. Table 17.5 shows the revised design for the Items table and the new Products table design. A side benefit of creating the new Products table is that if a product name or price changes, it is easy to update in one location, knowing that all related tables will automatically use the new data.

Table 17.5   Revised Design for Invoice Tables

Items Table

Primary Key	Field Name	Data Type
Foreign Key	Company ID	Number
Foreign Key	Invoice Number	Number
Key	Item Number	AutoNumber
	Product ID	Number
	Quantity	Number

Products Table

Primary Key	Field Name	Data Type
Foreign Key	Company ID	Number
Foreign Key	Invoice Number	Number
Foreign Key	Item Number	Number
Key	Product ID	Number
	Product Name	Text
	Price	Currency

Table 17.6 shows the sample data after normalizing the Items table to eliminate the duplicate data. Keep in mind that the product name and price are stored only once in the Products table. Only the Product ID data is "duplicated" to provide the relationship between the two tables. Notice also, that the Product ID field included in the Items table is not used to define a primary key.

Table 17.6   Normalized Item and Products Table Sample Data

Normalized Item Table Sample Data

Company ID	Invoice ID	Item ID	Product ID	Quantity
200	8076	1	8855	10
200	8076	2	6437	48

Normalized Item Table Sample Data

Company ID	Invoice ID	Item ID	Product ID	Quantity
367	8102	1	8855	8
367	8102	2	6437	5

Normalized Products Table Sample Data

Product ID	Product Name	Price
8855	Widget	$59.99
6437	Nuts	$ 1.95
8855	Widget	$59.99
6437	Nuts	$ 1.95

Eliminating Fields Not Dependent on the Key

The third rule of data normalization is to eliminate fields in a table that are not dependent on the primary key for that table. In other words, store only information that relates to the primary key in that table. For example, only product information is stored in the table keyed on Product number. You wouldn't store invoice information in the Products table (invoices to customers are not dependent on product information). The same concept applies to the Company table. Only company information is stored in the table keyed on Company number. Although related to the Company table, the demographic information now contained in the Company table (see revised design in table 17.2), Annual Sales, Employees, Industries, and Locations, do not belong in the Company table. Thus, a new table, Demographics, is created and keyed on the Company ID.

Table 17.7   Revised Company and Demographics Tables

Company Table

Primary Key	Field Name	Data Type
Key	Company ID	AutoNumber
	Company Name	Text
	Address	Text
	City	Text
	State	Text
	Zip	Text

continues

Table 17.7   Continued

Demographics Table

Primary Key	Field Name	Data Type
Key	Company ID	AutoNumber
	Annual Sales	Currency
	Employees	Number
	Industry	Text
	Locations	Number

Now the Company table contains only data that depends on the key. The first three rules of normalization have been met.

Isolating Independent Multiple Relationships

No table may contain two or more one-to-many (1:M) or many-to-many (M:M) relationships that are not directly related. When this happens, it creates a situation known as *multi-valued dependency*. In these cases, usually the fields in the table actually represent separate tables with the data becoming the fields in that table. Let's use a new scenario to illustrate the application of this rule. In this scenario, the Marketing department wants to create a table to track and manage product demonstrations. Table 17.8 shows the initial design of the Demo table which records the name of the Demonstration, the Representative who will do the demo, and the PowerPoint demo file name. Notice that a composite key consisting of all three fields forms the primary key.

Table 17.8   Initial Design of the Demo Table

Demo Table

Primary Key	Field Name	Data Type
Key	Demo Name	Text
Key	Rep	Text
Key	PPT File	Text

Let's look at this table design with some data entered (see table 17.9). Notice the duplication of data (always a bad sign), and how complicated and unorganized the table appears. This is because the table contains two one-to-many (1:M) relationships. For every demo, there are many reps who could give the demo. For every demo, there are many PowerPoint files that could be used by the sales rep.

Table 17.9   Sample Data for Demo Table

Sample Data for Demo Table

Demo Name	Rep	PPT File
Widgets	Jones	How To Install Widgets.ppt
Widgets	Anderson	Using Widgets.ppt
Widgets	Keene	Expert Widgets.ppt
Surfing	Anderson	Easy Surfing.ppt
Surfing	Dillahunty	Expert Surfing.ppt
Surfing	O'Donnell	Easy Surfing.ppt

In order to normalize this table, we need to apply the fourth rule of data normalization. Find the multiple relationships within a table and isolate them into separate tables. Divide and conquer once again! In this example, the Demo table actually contains data for two additional tables, Reps and Files. Table 17.10 illustrates the revised database design to manage demos. In addition to splitting up the three fields into three tables, two new tables had to be created:

▶ *DemoFile*. Indicates which PowerPoint files are used in which demo, independent of the Sales Rep.

▶ *DemoRep*. Indicates which Sales Rep is assigned to which demo, independent of the files used in the demo.

Table 17.10   Revised Tables for Demos

Demo Table

Primary Key	Field Name	Data Type
Key	Demo ID	AutoNumber
	Demo Name	Text

Rep Table

Primary Key	Field Name	Data Type
Key	Rep ID	AutoNumber
	Rep Name	Text

continues

Table 17.10 Continued

Files Table

Primary Key	Field Name	Data Type
Key	File ID	AutoNumber
	PPT File Name	Text

DemoFile Table

Primary Key	Field Name	Data Type
Key	Demo ID	Number
Key	File ID	Number

DemoRep Table

Primary Key	Field Name	Data Type
Key	Demo ID	Number
Key	Rep ID	Number

Isolating Semantically Related Multiple Relationships

Once your table meets the fourth normalization rule, you most probably have also met the fifth normalization rule. The fifth normalization rule basically says that you need to identify the multiple relationships and separate them into three or more tables of data items with similar meaning.

 Note

If you correctly applied the data normalization rules to your database design, the only fields in your database which are duplicated from one table to another are the fields which provide relational links between tables.

Defining Relationships in Access

Once you complete defining the tables in your database design (including relating primary keys and normalizing data), you can join the related table data together as needed in queries, forms, and reports. Access provides a Relationships dialog box that helps you define and manage relationships in a graphical flowchart format. Once the relationships are defined, Access will automatically relate data whenever it can in queries, forms, and reports.

Caution

If you are still unsure of the relationships between the tables, diagram the proposed relationships on paper or in a flowchart diagram application. Don't start defining or changing the relationships in Access until you are sure of the consequences. Changing some relationship settings could result in lost data (Access alerts you before deleting the data and gives you the option of canceling). Other relationship settings will not be allowed until the table definition or records are modified to fit the new relationship.

Exploring the Relationships Window

The Relationships Window allows you to create a relationship between two tables that have matching fields. Only one relationship can be defined between any two given tables. If you add a second relationship, it replaces the existing relationship (only one relationship can exist between two tables). To open the Relationships window, choose Tools, Relationship. Figure 17.6 shows the Relationships window for the NorthWind sample database.

The toolbar provides new buttons to help you navigate the Relationships Window. Table 17.11 lists the new toolbar buttons and describes each one.

Table 17.11 Relationship Toolbar Buttons

Relationship Toolbar Buttons

Name	Description
Show Table	Allows you to add tables to the relationship layout window.
Show Direct Relationships	Shows only tables with direct relationships.
Show All Relationships	Shows all relationships in the Database.
Clear Layout	Removes all tables from the layout (doesn't delete the relationships).

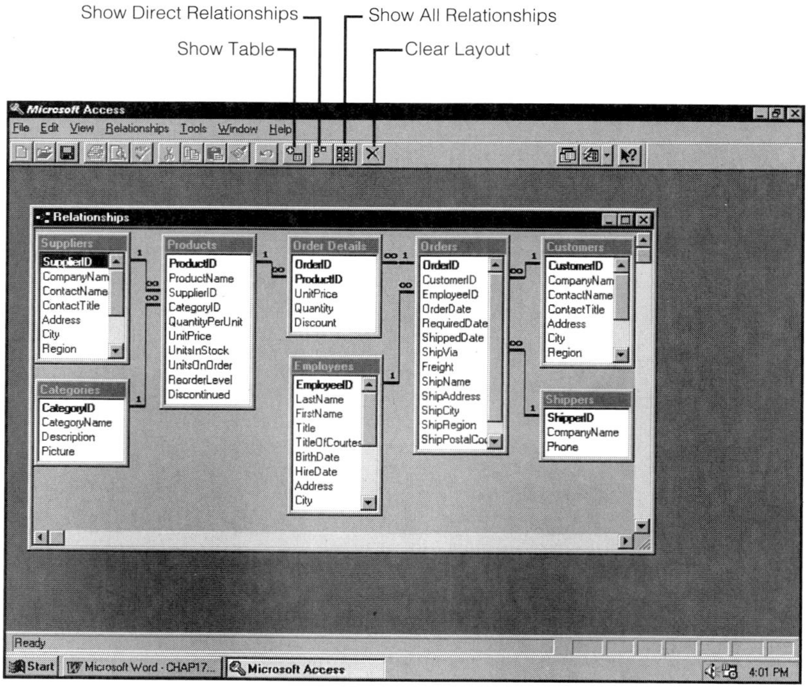

Fig. 17.6

Access displays the relationships between tables using lines and symbols.

In order to understand the relationship layout diagram, you need to know the symbols used. Table 17.12 lists the symbols and describes each one.

Table 17.12   Relationship Symbols

Relationship Symbols

Symbol	Description
1 _____ ∞	A one-to-many relationship.
1 _____ 1	A one-to-one relationship.
∞ _____ 1	A many-to-one relationship.

α Note

Many-to-many relationships are achieved in Access by creating a one-to-many relationship between an intermediary table (the "one" side) and the two original tables (the "many" side). For more information, see the topic "Many-to-Many Relationships" earlier in this chapter.

Creating Relationships

You can think of the Relationships window as a canvas on which you can diagram the relationships between tables. This makes the process of creating relationships easier to do and easier to understand. Before you can start defining relationships, you need to display the related table and/or query boxes on the Relationship layout. Once the tables/queries appear on the Relationship layout, you can draw a line between the two tables by dragging the field(s) that you want to relate from one table to the related field in the other table.

In most cases, you drag the primary key field (which is displayed in bold text) from one table to a similar field in the other table (the foreign key). When determining which field(s) to use in the relationship, consider the following:

▶ You can drag more than one field.

▶ The related fields can have different names.

▶ The related fields must be the same data type.

▶ Related fields of the Number data type must have the same Field Size (with the exception of an Increment AutoNumber field which can be related to a Long Integer Number field, and a Replication ID AutoNumber field which can be related to a Replication ID Number field).

After you drag the field to the related table, Access displays a dialog box prompting you to further define the relationship. Once the relationship is defined, Access stores the relationship in the Database for use in all areas of Access (forms, queries, and reports).

 Note

Keep in mind that the layout window is just a diagram. Clicking the Save button on the toolbar or choosing File, Save merely saves the layout as is and defines the relationships.

To create relationships, follow these steps:

1. Close any tables you have open. You can't create or modify relationships between open tables.

2. Switch to the Database window and choose Tools, Relationships, or click the Relationship button on the toolbar.

3. If your database doesn't have any relationships defined, the Show Table dialog box appears (see fig. 17.7).

Fig. 17.7
The new Marketing database has four tables that can be related.

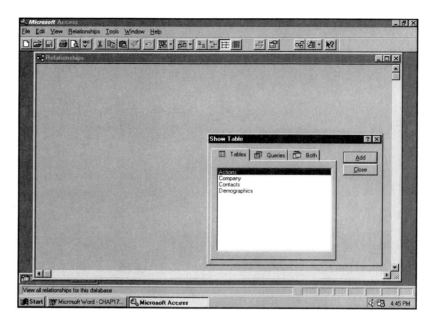

4. Double-click the tables you want to relate, then click Close to close the Show Table dialog box. Figure 17.8 shows the Company and Contacts table boxes added to the Relationships window for the Marketing database.

Fig. 17.8
Each table or query added to the Relation-ships window appears as a field list box.

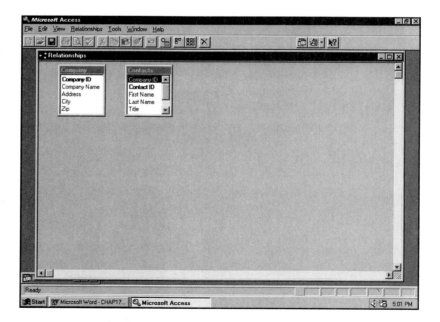

5. To add tables/queries to the Relationships window at any time, click the Show Table button to redisplay the Show Table dialog box.

6. Drag the field that you want to relate from one table to the related field in the other table. To drag multiple fields, press the Ctrl key and click each field before dragging them. Access displays the Relationships dialog box (see fig. 17.9).

Fig. 17.9

The Relationships dialog box displays any existing relationships found and describes the relationship type.

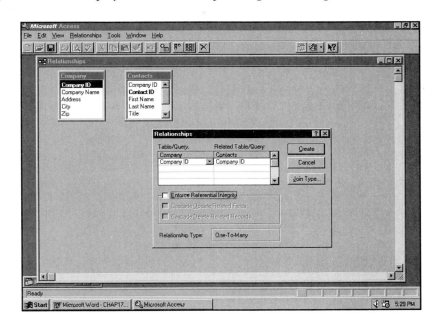

7. Set any desired relationship options. Table 17.13 briefly describes the relationship settings available. See the next two sections, "Enforcing Referential Integrity" and "Selecting a Join Type," for more information.

Table 17.13   Relationship Settings

Setting	Description
Table/Query	Lists the table/query field(s) selected for the relationship. You can edit as needed.
Related Table/Query	Lists the matching fields found in the related table/query. You can edit as needed.
Join Type	Displays the Join Type dialog box.
Enforce Referential Integrity	Instructs Access whether to enforce referential integrity (checked) or not.

continues

Table 17.13   Continued

Setting	Description
Cascade Update Related Fields	When Enforce Referential Integrity is selected, instructs Access whether to update related fields (checked) or not.
Cascade Delete Related Fields	When Enforce Referential Integrity is selected, instructs Access whether to delete related fields (checked) or not.
Relationship Type	Describes the current type of relationship defined between the two tables.

  8. Click the Create button to create the relationship. Access draws a line between the
      related tables and adds symbols to indicate the relationship type (see fig. 17.10).

Fig. 17.10
*The Company and
Contacts table have
a one-to-many
relationship.*

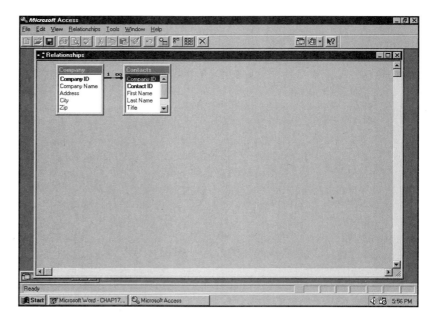

> ⚛ **Tip**
> To edit an existing relationship, double-click the join line; Access displays the Rela-
> tionships dialog box.

Caution

Access allows you to create relationships using queries as well as tables. However, Access cannot enforce referential integrity with queries. See the next section, "Enforcing Referential Integrity," for more information.

Note

You may need at some point to create a relationship within a table. This is usually done when you need to perform a lookup within the same table. For example, in the NorthWind database, the Employee table has a relationship defined between the Employee ID field and the Reports To field. This allows the Reports To field to display employee data from a matching Employee ID.

To create a relationship between two fields in a table, add that table to the Relationships window twice. Then drag the related field to the target field.

Enforcing Referential Integrity

The integrity of your database, the integrity of table relationships, and the validity of data contained in each table are important issues to consider when designing your database. The term *referential integrity* means that the integrity of the related tables within the database is protected through a set of predefined update and delete function rules. According to relational database theory, these rules are called restricted, cascade, and nullify.

The *restricted* rule states that a parent key cannot be changed if foreign keys depend on it. For example, if records in the Orders table depend on a specific Customer record, you would not be able to delete that Customer record. If you were allowed to delete the Customer record, the integrity of your database would be compromised. The Order records left in the Orders table would be called *orphans* because they no longer have a parent (Customer) record to relate to.

The *cascade* rule says that when a parent key value is changed, all dependent foreign keys will also be changed. For example, suppose you want to change the method used to assign customers a Customer ID. The cascade rule makes sure that whenever you change the Customer ID in the Customer record, any related records in other tables, such as Orders, will have the Customer ID value updated too. If the cascade rule was not applied, you would lose all dependent records, and the dependent records would become orphans.

The *nullify* rule states that when a parent record is deleted, null values are placed in all foreign key fields of dependent tables. Executing the nullify rule creates orphan records in dependent tables, which is probably why Access does not support the nullify rule.

Access supports the restricted and cascade rules via the Relationships dialog box (refer to figure 17.9). If you check the option Enforce Referential Integrity, Access automatically makes sure that there are no orphan records. Access will not let you:

▶ Add a record to the related table unless there is a matching record in the parent table.

▶ Change a value in the primary key field of the parent table if there are records in the related table that use that value as their foreign key.

▶ Delete a record from the parent table if there is a record in the related table that refers to it.

Tip

Unless you have some special reason not to, you should check Enforce Referential Integrity to make sure you do not enter invalid foreign keys by mistake.

Note

The Enforce Referential Integrity check box only protects the integrity of the foreign key in the related table. It does not protect the primary key of the parent table.

Furthermore, the parent table must be the "one" side of a one-to-many relationship in order to use the Enforce Referential Integrity check box. The "many" side of the relationship contains the foreign key which this feature protects.

When you check Enforce Referential Integrity, the other two options below that become enabled. If you check the option Cascade Update Related Fields, you can edit the primary key field in the parent table, and Access will automatically make the same change to the foreign key in the related table. This keeps the records related.

If you select the Cascade Delete Related Records option for a relationship, you can delete records in the parent table, and Access will automatically delete any related records in the related table.

Caution

Cascade update and delete are powerful tools for database application developers. However, cascade update and delete overrides many protections built into Access. Novice users should exercise care, since they may delete or modify records in the related "many" table without realizing that they have changed the other table.

Alternatively, novice users could use an Action query to accomplish the same task. This method focuses the user on the task at hand and the effect of updating or deleting related records, rather than doing it automatically behind the scenes.

Selecting a Join Type

The last relationship option in the Relationships window that you can set is the join type. When you click the Join Type button, Access displays the Join Properties dialog box (see fig. 17.11). The Join Properties dialog box describes three types of joins possible in Access.

Fig. 17.11

Selecting the correct join type affects table relationships and query results.

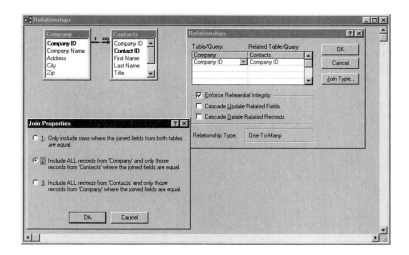

Access defaults to a one-to-one, equi-join (also called inner-join in database terminology). As described in the first choice, only records in which the joined fields are the same are included. For example, the NorthWind Customers table is related to the Orders table. If the join type property 1 is selected, only records which have the same Customer ID would be included.

The second and third properties are not as straightforward and are more difficult to understand from the description given. The second property (called a left outer-join in database terminology) includes all records from the parent table and only the records from the related table that have the same key. However, when a record exists in the parent table that has no matching records in the related table, the parent record is still listed. For example, an outer-join between the Customers table and the Orders table would list all the Customer records and only the matching records in the Orders table. This technique is helpful in identifying Customers who had not placed orders.

The third property (called a right outer-join in database terminology) is the reverse of the second property. All records from the related table are listed and only those records with the same key in the parent table are listed. In this case, you would find any orders that did not have a corresponding Customer record.

 Note

Choose the join property that you will use most often. Your selection here will be the default for your database. You can always change this default selection in the individual forms, queries, and reports as needed.

Working with Related Tables

Once the table definitions have been set, and the relationships between tables created, you are ready to create multitable queries, forms, and reports. Each object automatically reads your database relationship information and automatically applies that information to the task at hand. You can, however, override or change relationship data within each object when necessary.

 Note

If you need to change a global relationship or relationship setting that applies to all objects in the database, you should make the change in the Relationships window, not in each object. For example, if you are working on a multitable form and realize you forgot to relate two subtables, stop working on the form, create the relationships, and then return to the form (recreate the objects if necessary). This will save you work in the long run.

Creating Multitable Queries

As you can see in figure 17.12, Access automatically finds any defined table relationship when you create a new query. The relationship line and symbols appear just as they did in the Relationships window. Unless you need to change the relationship for purposes of this specific query, you are ready to design your query. For basic information on how to create a basic select query, see the section "Exploring Queries" in Chapter 16's "Critical Skills in Access."

Fig. 17.12

The new select query shows the one-to-many relationship between the Company and Contacts tables.

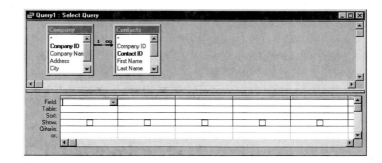

If needed, Access allows you to modify the relationship used as the basis for a query. Changes made here only apply to the query being worked on, and do not affect other queries or the relationship settings made in the Relationships dialog box. You can add tables by using the Show Tables dialog box (click Show Tables). You can relate those tables by clicking and dragging a key field from one table to another as you do when you create a default relationship in the Relationships window. If you need to remove a table from the query design, select the table box and press Delete.

The most common modification to a relationship is to change the Join Properties. To change the Join Properties, you can double-click the join line, or choose <u>V</u>iew, <u>J</u>oin Properties. Access displays the familiar Join Properties dialog box (refer to fig. 17.11).

Creating Multitable Forms and Reports

As you learned in Chapter 16, "Critical Skills in Access," you can create a form or report based on either a table or a query. Now you can see why it would be beneficial in a multitable relational database to create a form or a report based on a query.

You can use the Form Wizard and Report Wizard with a multitable query to create the form or report. Or you can select fields from multiple tables. The Wizards also help you create a form with subforms and reports with grouping.

In Form and Report Design, you can use the Subform/Subreport tool to imbed a related table in a master form or report design. Access will automatically display only those records which apply to the key of the master table. For example, you could create a Customer form which has embedded in it an Orders form. As you page through the Customer form, only the Orders related to the current Customer would appear.

Caution

When working with a Form based on a query, remember that changes made in the "one" table in one record can cause changes in the same field in other records, and changes you make in the foreign key of the "many" table can cause changes in the fields of the same record that are taken from the "one" table.

Working with Subforms and Subreports

Subforms and subreports are usually used to display data from tables or queries that have a one-to-many relationship. The main form/report contains the data for the "one" side of a one-to-many relationship. The subform/report contains the "many" side of the "one-to-many" relationship.

Note

The Form and Report Wizards relate the tables based on the default relationship defined in the Relationships window. To change the default relationship, you should return to the Relationships window and make the adjustment before using the Wizard.

The main form/report is synchronized with the subform/report so that the subform/report shows only records related to the record in the main form/report. If you use a wizard to create a subform or subreport, or if you drag a form or datasheet from the Database window to another form or report to create a subform/report, Access automatically synchronizes the main form/report with the subform/report if *both* of the following are true:

▶ The tables you select have relationships that you've set in the Relationships window. This is usually a one-to-many relationship.

▶ The main form/report is based on a table with a primary key and the subform/report is based on a table that contains a field with the same name as that primary key and with the same or a compatible data type.

If you select a query or queries, the underlying tables for the query or queries must meet the two conditions outlined above.

Microsoft Access uses the LinkMasterFields and LinkChildFields properties of the sub-form or subreport control to link the main form/report and subform/report. If, for some reason, Microsoft Access doesn't link the form/report and subform/report, you can set these properties directly.

To manually link a form/report and subform/report, follow these steps:

1. Switch to Design view.
2. Right-click the subform/report control to display its property sheet.
3. In the LinkChildFields property box, enter the name of the linking field in the subform.
4. In the LinkMasterFields property box, enter the name of the linking field in the main form.
5. Save your form or report design.

Tip

If you're unsure what the linking field is, click the Build button to open the Subform/Subreport Field Linker. To enter more than one linking field, separate field names with semicolons. If you enter more than one linking field, you must enter the fields in the same order in the LinkChildFields and LinkMasterFields properties.

Note

Remember that the linking fields must contain the same kind of data and have the same or a compatible data type or field size. For example, an AutoNumber field is compatible with a Number field whose FieldSize property is set to Long Integer. Refer back to the section "Normalizing Data" for the specific rules on compatible primary keys and foreign keys.

Optimizing Form/Report and Subform/Report Performance

There are several things you can do to make your forms and reports run faster. In addition to the tips listed below, you can use the Performance Analyzer to analyze specific forms in your database. For information on using the Performance Analyzer, search the Help system for that topic.

▶ If you want to use a form or subform primarily for entering new records, set the DataEntry property of the form to Yes. This causes the form to open to a blank record saving the time Access usually spends reading each record into memory before displaying. You can also choose Records, Data Entry to switch to the blank record display as needed, instead of changing the property permanently.

▶ Base subforms/reports on queries rather than on tables, and include only fields from the record source that are absolutely necessary. Extra fields can decrease subform/report performance.

▶ Index all the fields in the subform/report that are linked to the main form/report.

▶ Index any subform/report fields that are used for criteria.

▶ Set a subform's AllowEdits, AllowAdditions, and AllowDeletions properties to No if the records in the subform aren't going to be edited. Or set the RecordsetType property to Snapshot.

▶ Close forms, tables, queries, or other objects not being used.

▶ Use black and white rather than color bitmaps in form and report designs.

▶ Convert unbound object frames that display graphics to image controls.

▶ Avoid overlapping controls.

Summary

This chapter provided you with a good foundation in relational database theory and how it applies to Access. You learned how to plan table relationships, determine the unique primary key for each table, and relate the tables. This chapter examined the data normalization rules and reviewed the basic types of relationships between tables. You know how to use the Relationship tool in Access to create and maintain relationships between multiple tables in a database. In the section on working with related tables, you learned how to create multitable queries, forms, and reports. Lastly, this chapter provided some tips for optimizing the performance of multi-tabled forms and reports.

chapter 18

Advanced Queries

18

by Susann Novalis

In this chapter

◆ **Expressions in query criteria and calculated fields**
You learn how to create complex expressions to select records and perform calculations.

◆ **Nesting queries**
Nesting one query inside another allows you to create complex queries and improve performance.

◆ **Queries with self-joins and parameters**
Joining a table to itself allows you to solve several common but tricky problems. Parameter queries allow the user to change search values.

◆ **Advanced query wizards**
Access wizards help you create queries to find records with duplicate values and records without matching records in related tables.

◆ **Query performance**
You learn how Access determines an optimal query plan and tips for faster queries.

When you design an Access database, you normally spend considerable time making sure the data is properly separated into a set of tables. A well-designed relational database typically has many tables and minimizes duplication of data storage. Ideally, only the values needed to relate tables are duplicated. Ironically, the next problem is putting the atoms of data stored in different tables back together again in order to answer questions and turn your data into useful information. This is the role of the query.

This chapter introduces some of the more advanced features of Access queries and focuses on showing you how to use queries as problem-solving tools. After a brief review of the basic terms and query building blocks, the chapter builds on your knowledge of queries by examining several query-building tools that include creating complex expressions, nesting queries, and joining a table to itself. You learn how to create interactive queries that obtain selection criteria from the user and queries that answer advanced data management problems. The chapter concludes by discussing how Access processes queries and what you can do to make your queries run faster.

 Note

The queries discussed in this chapter are based on the sample Northwind Traders application that ships with Microsoft Access for Windows 95. Queries with names that begin with the letter *q* are new queries created as an example for the chapter and are based on the tables and queries in the Northwind database. The three or four letters that begin the names used for the new database objects and form controls are part of the Leszynski naming standard and are called *tags*. Most developers in Access adopt a naming standard to make applications easier to work with by packing as much information as possible into each object name using an arrangement of naming pieces that other developers will easily recognize. In the Leszynski naming standard, some of the tags for queries include `qry`, `qapp` (append query), `qdel` (delete query), `qupd` (update query), and `qxtb` (crosstab query). Examples of basic tags for other objects include `tbl` (table), `frm` (form), and `rpt` (report). You can obtain the document "The Leszynski Naming Conventions for Microsoft Access for Windows 95" from Kwery Corporation via CompuServe at 71573,3261 or by fax to 206-644-8409.

Reviewing Basic Terms

You create most queries using the graphical features in the Query Design window. Figure 18.1 shows the Query Design window for a select query that retrieves the names of recently hired salespeople in the Northwind database.

The upper pane displays field lists for the tables and other queries that supply the data for the query you are designing; the qryNewSalesPeople query is based on the Employees and Orders tables. The join line shows that the tables are related on their EmployeeID fields; the bold line-ends indicate that the tables were related using the Relationships window and that the option to enforce the referential integrity rules was elected.

Fig. 18.1

The Query Design window displays an upper pane for field lists and a lower pane with a design grid with special cells for designing the query.

Field lists

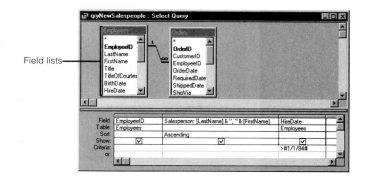

18

The lower pane displays the design grid with its special cells for designing the query. You place in the Field cells any fields that you want to use in the query for any reason: for displaying in the query result, for selecting or sorting records, or for performing calculations. You also use Field cells to create custom calculated fields such as Salesperson in the qryNewSalesPeople query. If a Field cell contains a field from one of the lists in the upper pane, the Table cell below the Field cell displays the name of the field list; the Table cell below a calculated field is blank.

 Tip

To show the Table row, choose Tools, Options, select the Tables/Queries tab in the Options dialog box, and then check the Show Table Names check box.

You use the Sort cell below a Field cell to sort the result by the values in the field; you can sort by any field including a calculated field. The check box in the Show cell indicates whether the column is shown or hidden in the query result. You use the Criteria and Or cells below a Field cell to enter one or more search conditions that limit the records returned by the query. When you use a select query to perform calculations on groups of records, an additional Totals row is added below the Table row. When you create an action query for batch operations, the design grid changes to include the rows appropriate for the batch operation. In an update query, an Update To row replaces the Sort and Show rows; in an append query, an Append To row replaces the Show row; and in a delete query, a Delete row replaces the Sort and Show rows. (A make table query displays the same design grid rows as a select query.)

Elements of Expressions

When you create a query, you can enter expressions in Field and Criteria cells (and in Update To cells of an update query). An *expression* is a combination of operators and values that Access evaluates and then returns a value. A *condition* is an expression that returns the value **True** or **False**. *Operators* are symbols or special reserved words that act on the values that precede and follow them and produce a result. An expression must have at least one operator. Access uses four kinds of operators for creating expressions:

▶ *Arithmetic operators* perform mathematical calculations: addition (+), subtraction (-), multiplication (*), division (/), exponent (^), integer division (\) (divides two numbers and returns an integer), modulus (Mod) (divides two numbers and returns the remainder).

▶ *Comparison operators* perform comparisons: less than (<), less than or equal to (<=), greater than (>), greater than or equal to (>=), equals (=), not equals (<>).

▶ *Logical operators* perform logical operations: And, Or, Not, Is, Between...And, and Like.

▶ *Concatenation operators* combine character strings: &, +.

The values in an expression can be constants, the names of objects that have values such as field and control names, and functions. A *function* is any procedure or rule that returns a value. Access includes a large set of built-in functions including the following categories:

▶ *Date functions* perform date procedures: for example, Date(), DatePart(), DateAdd(), DateDiff(), and Now().

▶ *Math functions* perform mathematical procedures: for example, Sqr(), Abs(), Sgn(), and exponential and trig functions.

▶ *String functions* manipulate character strings: for example, Len(), Left(), and Mid().

▶ *Conversion functions* perform various conversions: for example, Format() converts an expression to a specified format, and data type conversion functions, such as CCur(), convert an expression to a specified data type.

▶ *SQL aggregate functions* calculate summary values based on a group of values in a query column or in the record source of a form or report: for example, Avg(), Sum(), Min(), Max(), and Count().

▶ *Domain aggregate functions* calculate summary values based on a group of values in specified set of records called the *domain*: for example DAvg(), DSum(), DMin(), DMax(), Dcount(), and Dlookup().

Note

To create expressions in queries, type directly into the cell or use the Expression Builder. To start the Expression Builder, right-click in the Field or Criteria cell where you want to enter an expression and choose the Build command. The lower pane of the Expression Builder contains lists of all of the expression elements (both the built-in operators, constants and functions, and the names of all of the objects in the current database). To create an expression, you select expression elements and paste them into the upper pane. When the expression is complete, the Builder pastes it into the cell (replacing whatever expression was in the cell). The Expression Builder is context-sensitive: the lower pane displays only the objects and functions that are appropriate to the context from where you started the Builder.

Missing, Unknown, and Inapplicable Data

In any real database, certain pieces of data in a table record may be missing, unknown, or not be applicable to a specific record. For example, in the Customers table in Northwind, the records for some customers have no data in the FAX field for one of the three reasons:

▶ If you know a customer has a FAX number, but you don't know what it is, the data value is *missing*; the record will be complete when you enter the FAX number.

▶ If you don't know whether the customer has a FAX number, the data value is *unknown*.

▶ If you know a customer does not have a FAX number, then no data value is appropriate; in this case the FAX field in *inapplicable*.

Relational databases use the Null *value* to indicate missing, unknown, or inapplicable data. The special Null value is not a real value, like "Exotic Foods" or 12/23/95, but is only an indicator that the data value is missing, unknown, or inapplicable. You can differentiate between the case of information that exists (but is missing or unknown) and the case where information does not exist. If data doesn't exist, store a *zero-length string* (double quotation marks without a space, "") in the field. If the data is missing or unknown, leave the field blank instead. When you leave a field blank, you are actually storing a Null value. Keep in mind that you can only make this distinction for text or memo fields.

Note

By default, both Null values and zero-length strings are displayed as blanks. You can distinguish between the two and display the word "Unknown" for a Null value by typing the expression **@;"Unknown"** for the field's Format property. With this setting, a zero-length string is displayed as a blank, a Null value is displayed as "Unknown", and text that you enter is displayed as you entered it.

Null values require special handling for the following reasons:

▸ If you use an arithmetic operator in an expression and one of the fields has a Null value, the result of the expression also has the Null value. This is called *propagation of nulls*. For example, if a record in the Products table has a Null value in the [UnitsInStock] field, then calculating the Inventory as the product [UnitPrice]*[UnitsInStock] gives a Null value for Inventory for this record.

▸ If you use an SQL or domain aggregate function to calculate a summary value for a field, records with Null values in the field won't be included in the calculation.

▸ When you sort on a field in ascending order, the sort order is: records with Null values in the field first, followed by records with zero-length strings in the field, followed by records with neither Null values nor zero-length strings in the field.

▸ When you create a relationship and enforce referential integrity, you can create unrelated records in the child table by leaving the matching fields blank. For example, the relationship between the Customers and Orders tables has referential integrity enforced, but you can add new unrelated orders to the Orders table that have Null values in the CustomerID field.

▸ When you join tables in a query, records that have Null values in the join field won't be included in the query result. For example, if you create a query based on the Customers and Orders tables, the query's result will contain only records for customers who have placed orders and for orders that are related to specific customers; the query won't include records for customers without orders or for unrelated orders.

Here are some guidelines for working with Null values:

▸ Use a field's DefaultValue property to set a numerical field to zero or a text or memo field to the zero-length string when a new record is created.

▸ Use the Nz() function to convert a Null value to zero or a zero-length string. If the argument is not Null, the Nz() function returns the value itself, otherwise, the Nz() function returns zero or the zero-length string depending on whether the context requires a number or a text string. For example, if the argument is `Null`, `Nz(FAX)` returns a zero-length string because FAX is a text field. In addition, you can use the function's second argument to specify another value to be returned if the original value is `Null`. For example, `Nz(FAX, "No Fax")` returns `No Fax` when the value is `Null`.

▶ Use the `IIF()` and `IsNull()` functions to convert a value to a zero or a zero-length string. For example, the function `IIF(IsNull[Amount],0,[Amount])` returns zero if the value of the Amount field is `Null` and otherwise returns the value.

▶ You can prevent unrelated records in a child table that can occur if the matching field is allowed to be null by setting the Required property of the matching fields in the child table to Yes.

▶ When you are combining fields with text values, use the & operator instead of the + operator if you want the result to display one of the values when the other value is null.

▶ You can search for null values for a field in a query by setting the Criteria cell to `Is Null`. You can search for zero-length strings by setting the Criteria cell to the zero-length string, "".

▶ You can search for records that do not have a `Null` value in a field by setting the Criteria cell to `Is Not Null` or `Not Null`. The result will include records with a zero-length string in the field because the zero-length string is not null. You can also use Like"*" to search for records with non-null values.

18

Creating Expressions for Criteria

The search conditions for limiting the records returned by a query can be very complex. This section gives examples of complex query criteria for select and action queries.

When you want to limit the records returned by a query, you enter expressions in the Criteria and Or cells in the query design grid. When the query runs, Access tests the selection criterion for each record; if the value of the criterion is `True`, the record is included in the query result, otherwise the record is excluded. As an example, you can create a new query called qryCustomers based on the Customers table that displays all of the fields. In the simplest case, you enter a specific value, called a *literal value*, as a search criterion. For example, to display customers from Argentina, enter **Argentina** in the Criteria cell below the Country field. Because the Country field has the Text data type, Access encloses the value in quotation marks. To search for records with values in a field that match any one of a set of literal values, use the `In` operator; for example, to display customers from Argentina or Brazil, enter **In(Argentina, Brazil)** in the Criteria cell. When you press Enter, Access changes the expression to `In("Argentina","Brazil")`.

You create query criteria using literal values in only the simplest cases. More generally, criteria expressions are the results of calculations that include operators, references to fields, references to controls on forms, and functions.

Using Wild Cards and the *Like* Operator

If you want to search for records with a specific pattern, such as customers from countries beginning with the letter C, you can use *wild-card characters* as placeholders for other characters and specify a *wild-card search* criterion using the Like operator followed by the pattern. In the example, you would enter Like"C*" in the Criteria cell below Country. You can do wild-card searches only on fields with Text, Memo, and Date data types. Access uses the set of wild-card characters shown in table 18.1 as placeholders.

Table 18.1   Wild-Card Characters

Characters in pattern	Matches in the expression
?	Any single character
*	Zero or more characters
#	Any single digit
[*list*]	Any single character in *list*
[!*list*]	Any single character not in *list*

When you enter a value with one or more wild-card characters in a Criteria cell, for example **a***, Access assumes you are doing a wild-card search and replaces your entry with the Like operator followed by the entry enclosed in quotation marks—for example, Like "a*". When you want to search for any specific character in a list, you enclose the list in square brackets; for example, to search for either *b* or *f*, use **[bf]**. To search for a range of characters, use a hyphen to separate the beginning and the end of the range; for example, to search for any letter in the range *b* through *f*, use **[b-f]**.

As examples, you can perform the wild-card searches on the CustomerID field in the qryCustomers query shown in table 18.2. Note that wild-card searches are not case-sensitive, so you can use Like"m*" to search for values beginning with m or M.

Table 18.2   Examples of Wild-Card Searches

Expression	Selects records
Like "m*"	Customers with ID beginning with M
Like "*m"	Customers with ID ending with M

Expression	Selects records
Like "[as]*"	Customers with ID beginning with A or S
Like "[!as]*"	Customers with ID beginning with any letter except A or S
Like "?o*"	Customers with ID whose second letter is O
Like "[a-fr-t]*"	Customers with ID beginning with any letter in the range A-F or the range R-T

Using the *Is Null* and *Not* Operators

To search for records that do not satisfy a criteria for a field, enter the Not operator followed by the expression in the Criteria cell. For example, enter the expression **Not "Brazil"** in the Criteria cell under the [Country] field to display customers from every country except Brazil.

To search for records with Null values in a field, enter the expression **Is Null** in the Criteria cell below the Field cell; for example, enter **Is Null** in the Criteria cell under FAX to display customers with Null values for FAX. To search for all records that do not have a Null value in a field, type the expression **Is Not Null** or **Not Null** in the Criteria cell. To search for zero-length strings in a field, enter the expression **""** (without a space between the quotation marks) in the Criteria cell. If you use Like "*" in a search expression, the query returns records with zero-length strings but does not return records with Null values; for example, if you enter **Like "*"** in the Criteria cell for Region in the qryCustomers query, the 31 records with non-Null values for Region are returned.

Multiple Criteria and Query Operators

Often you want to use more than one field value to limit the records returned by a query. For example, if you want to find all products in the beverage category with a price greater than $10, you need criteria for both the Category and UnitPrice fields. If you enter expressions into more than one cell in the same Criteria row, Access combines the expressions with the And operator and returns records that satisfy both criteria. If you enter expressions into cells in different Criteria rows, Access uses the Or operator and returns records that satisfy either criterion.

In terms of the Venn diagrams of set theory, if each circle in figure 18.2 represents the set of records that satisfy a criterion, the intersection of the two circles represents the result of the And operator, and the union of the two circles represents the result of the Or operator. Figure 18.2 also shows Venn diagrams for the *minus* and *difference* operations. The minus operation is the result of the And Not operators and returns records that satisfy the first criterion, but do not satisfy the second criterion. The difference operation is the result of taking the minus operation on each criterion to find the records that satisfy the first criterion but not the second and the records that satisfy the second criterion but not the first, and then taking the union of the two results.

Fig. 18.2

Venn diagrams illustrate the query criteria.

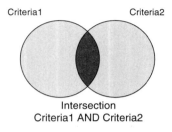

Intersection
Criteria1 AND Criteria2

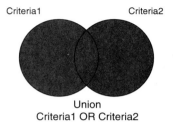

Union
Criteria1 OR Criteria2

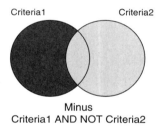

Minus
Criteria1 AND NOT Criteria2

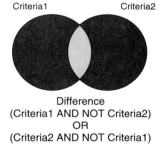

Difference
(Criteria1 AND NOT Criteria2)
OR
(Criteria2 AND NOT Criteria1)

As examples, use the qryCustomers query to display the customers records that satisfy the criteria shown in table 18.3.

Table 18.3　Multiple Criteria for a Query

	Criteria for Customer ID	Criteria for Country	Operation Query	CustomerID of Records in Query Result
Criteria:	Like "a*"			ALFKI, ANATR, ANTON, AROUT
Criteria:		"Mexico"		ANATR, ANTON, CENTC, PERIC, TORTU

	Criteria for Customer ID	Criteria for Country	Operation Query	CustomerID of Records in Query Result
Criteria:	Like "a*"	"Mexico"	Intersection	ANATR, ANTON
Criteria: **Or:**	Like "a*"	"Mexico"	Union	ALFKI, ANATR, ANTON, AROUT, CENTC, PERIC, TORTU
Criteria:	Like "a*"	**Not** "Mexico"	Minus	ALFKI, AROUT
Criteria:	**Not** Like "a*"	"Mexico"	Minus	CENTC, PERIC, TORTU
Criteria: **Or:**	Like "a*" **Not** Like "a*"	**Not** "Mexico" "Mexico"		ALFKI, AROUT, CENTC, PERIC, TORTU

Note

When you create a query in query Design view, Access automatically converts the query definition into a *string expression* and passes the string expression to the Jet database engine for processing. In the conversion, Access uses a data language called Structured Query Language (SQL) and creates an equivalent SQL statement for the query. You can view the SQL statement by clicking the Query View button on the toolbar and choosing SQL view. Access translates the criteria in the Criteria and Or cells below the Field cells in query Design view into string expressions that follow the word WHERE in the SQL statement. For example, the equivalent string expressions for the criteria in table 18.3 are:

```
[CustomerID] = Like "a*"
[Country] = "Mexico"
([CustomerID] = Like "a*") And ([Country] = "Mexico")
([CustomerID] = Like "a*") Or ([Country] = "Mexico")
([CustomerID] = Like "a*") And (Not [Country] = "Mexico")
([CustomerID] = Not Like "a*") And ([Country] = "Mexico")
((([CustomerID] = Like "a*") And (Not [Country] = "Mexico")) Or
((([CustomerID] = Not Like "a*") And ([Country] = "Mexico"))
```

> Converting to an SQL statement, Access always includes the name of the data source when referring to a field. Access uses the syntax *datasource.fieldname*—for example, Customers.CustomerID. However, when there is only one data source, you can omit its name in the reference to the field when you write your own SQL statements. You can learn more about SQL in Chapter 19, "Understanding the Data Languages in Access."

Using Domain Aggregate Functions as Criteria

Suppose that you want to find each product in the Products table whose price is greater than the average price of all products in the table. In this case, the search expression for [UnitPrice] depends on the prices for all of the products in the table. Or, suppose you want the products whose price is greater than the average price of current products, only without including discontinued products. In this case, the search depends on only some of the products. One way to solve these problems is using domain aggregate functions.

You use a domain aggregate function to do a summary calculation on a column of values from a group of records selected from a larger set of records. The domain aggregate functions require that you specify three pieces of information as arguments:

▶ the set of records (*domain*)

▶ the criterion (*search condition*) that restricts the set to a smaller group (restricted domain)

▶ the field or field expression (*column*) you want to use for the summary calculation.

All three arguments must be expressed as strings. The domain can be a table or the result of a query (in the examples, the domain is the Products table, or "Products"). The search condition is a string expression that specifies the rows to be included in the smaller group (in the first example, there is no search condition because you are using the entire set of records). If you don't specify a search condition, the function uses the larger set of records. The column can be either a field name for one of the fields in the domain or an expression based on at least one of the fields (in the examples, the column is the UnitPrice field, or "[UnitPrice]"). The domain aggregate functions have the syntax

```
DFunction(column, domain, search condition)
```

or

```
DFunction(column, domain)
```

when a search condition isn't specified.

We'll use the DAvg() function to solve the two examples. Create a new qryProducts query based on the Products table and display all the fields. To find the products with a price greater than the average price for all products, enter the expression >DAvg("[UnitPrice]","Products") in the Criteria cell below the [UnitPrice] field. When you run the query, 25 products are returned. To base the average only on products not discontinued, use the third argument of the domain aggregate function to restrict the domain with the search condition "[Discontinued] = No". Change the expression in the Criteria cell below the [UnitPrice] field to **>
DAvg("[UnitPrice]","Products","[Discontinued] = No")**. When you run the query, 26 products are returned.

The domain aggregate functions are listed in table 18.4.

18

Table 18.4   The Domain Aggregate Functions

DFunction	Returns
DAvg	The average of the column values in the restricted domain.
DCount	The number of records with non-null column values in the restricted domain. If you want the total number of records in the restricted domain, use the asterisk (*) wild-card character instead of the name of a field: DCount("*",domain,search condition).
DSum	The sum of the column values in the restricted domain.
DLookup	A column value in the restricted domain. If the search condition limits the restricted domain to a single record, the column value of this record is returned. If the restricted domain has more than one record, the column value of the first record in the restricted domain is returned. If a search condition isn't specified, a random column value in the domain is returned. If the restricted domain has no records, a Null value is returned.
DMin, DMax	The minimum or the maximum of the column values in the restricted domain.
DFirst, DLast	The first or the last of the column values in the restricted domain.
DStDev, DStDevP	The standard deviation for the column values in the restricted domain.
Dvar, DVarP	The variance for the column values in the restricted domain.

The real power of the domain aggregate functions lies in their capability to do calculations based on a different table or query. For example, suppose that you want to find each product in which the current price exceeds by 10 percent the average price at which the product was sold. To understand what is being requested, you need to know that the UnitPrice field in the Products table stores a product's current price, and the UnitPrice field in the Orders Details table stores the actual sales prices for the product as it is sold in different orders. This means the DAvg() function is based on the Orders Details table as the domain. The search condition must select only those records in the Order Details table with the same ProductID as the record you are examining in the Products table. The search condition is "ProductID = "&[ProductID]. In this expression, Access first determines the value in the [ProductID] field of the current record, treats the value as a string, and then concatenates the two strings to obtain the search condition. In qryProducts, change the expression in the Criteria cell below the [UnitPrice] field to **>** **1.10 * DAvg("[UnitPrice]","[Order Details]", "ProductID = "&[ProductID]).** When you run the query, three products are returned.

 Note

Using a domain aggregate function in a search criterion is equivalent to using a *subquery*. See Chapter 19 for a discussion of subqueries.

You can also use domain aggregate functions in the criteria for action queries. Action queries allow you to perform batch operations on groups of records: to append records to an existing table (append query) or a new table (make table query), to delete records from an existing table (delete query), or to modify specific field values in a group of records based on one or more tables (update query). Creating an action query is similar to creating a select query. You drag the fields involved to the design grid and enter expressions in Criteria and Or cells below Field cells to specify the records that the action query operates on. In an update query, you also enter expressions in the Update To cells for the fields you want to update. You can use the built-in functions including domain aggregate functions but not the SQL aggregate functions in the Update To cells of an update query. For example, to update the price for each product in the Products table to the minimum price at which the product was ordered, the search condition must select from the Order Details table only the records with the same ProductID as the record you want to update in the Products table. Enter the expression **DMin("[UnitPrice]","[Order Details]", "ProductID = "&[ProductID])** in the Update To cell under the [UnitPrice] field.

Creating Expressions for Calculated Fields

When you use the Query Design view to create a query, you can use fields from the field lists in the upper pane, or you can create your own calculated fields.

A *calculated field* is a field that displays the result of a calculation instead of a data value stored in an underlying table. There are two categories of calculations: calculations for a single record based on the other fields in the same record (*row calculations*) and summary calculations based on the values in a column of a group of records (*column calculations*). For example:

▶ When you create a calculated field to concatenate an employee's first name and last name into a single name column, you are doing a row calculation.

▶ When you create a custom field to sum the sales revenue for each product in an order and use the result as the order subtotal, you are doing a column calculation based on a group of records.

18

> **Tip**
>
> By default, a calculated field is unformatted. You can define the format in the query by setting the calculated field's Format property to one of the predefined settings or to a custom format expression. You can also define the format in a form or report by setting the Format property of the control that displays the calculated field.

Calculations for a Single Record (Row Calculations)

You create a calculated field in a query by typing an expression in an empty Field cell in the query design grid. An expression for a row calculation can include operators, references to other fields in the query and to other objects that have values such as controls on forms, and functions. Note that according to their definition, the SQL aggregate functions can be used only for column calculations. However, you can use the domain aggregate functions in row calculations. The expression for a calculated field can also include subqueries (see Chapter 19).

You can name the calculated field by typing in a name followed by a colon to the left of the expression. If you don't name the calculated field, Access uses the default field name ExprN, where N is an integer that Access increments for each new calculated field in the query. Some examples of calculated fields for row calculations are shown in table 18.5:

Table 18.5   Examples of Calculated Fields for Row Calculations

Calculated field	Description
AllowedTime: DateDiff("d",[OrderDate],[RequiredDate])	Returns the number of days between the order date and the required date.
FreightCharge: IIF(IsNull(Freight),0,Freight)	Changes a null value to zero in the Freight field.
EmployeeName: "[LastName]&", "&[FirstName]"	Returns the value of the LastName and FirstName fields separated by a comma and a space.
NameCode: Left([CompanyName],5)	Displays the first five characters of the value in the CompanyName field.

Using Domain Aggregate Functions in Row Calculations

You can use domain aggregate functions in calculated fields when you want to display a summary value for each record in the query results. Here are a few examples for the qryProducts query:

▶ To display the average product price based on the prices in the Products table, create a calculated field AveragePrice: DAvg("[UnitPrice]","Products")

▶ To display the average product price based on the order prices for all the records in the Order Details table, create a calculated field AverageOrderPrice: DAvg("[UnitPrice]","[Order Details]")

▶ To display the lowest and highest order prices for each product, create calculated fields based on summary values from the Order Details table: MinimumPrice: DMin("[UnitPrice]","[Order Details]", "ProductID = "&[ProductID]) and MaximumPrice: DMax("[UnitPrice]","[Order Details]", "ProductID = "&[ProductID])

Calculations for a Group of Records (Column Calculations)

The second type of calculation uses the SQL aggregate functions to calculate summary or total values based on a group of records. We'll call this kind of calculation a *totals calculation*, and we'll call the resulting query a *totals query*. To perform a totals calculation, you display the Total row in the query design grid by clicking the Totals button on the toolbar, and then you use the cells in the Total row to design the calculation. Click the down arrow in a Total cell to select a purpose for the cell. Each cell in the Total row below a Field cell is used for one of four purposes:

▶ To specify that the field is a grouping field by selecting Group By in the field's Total cell. When there is at least one grouping field, Access arranges the records into groups *before* doing the totals calculations. If no field is specified as a grouping field, the totals calculations are based on all of the records.

▶ To specify one of the SQL aggregate functions for calculating the summary value for the field. There are nine SQL aggregate functions in the Total cell list that you can choose from. Access calculates the selected summary values for each of the groups defined with the Group By fields.

▶ To specify that you are using a calculated field for a totals calculation involving SQL aggregate functions. In this case, you select Expression in the field's Total cell and define the calculated field using one or more SQL aggregate functions.

▶ To specify criteria that limits which records are included *before* performing the totals calculations. In this case, you select Where in the field's Total cell.

Caution
When you add the Total row to the design grid, you must specify each field as serving one of the four purposes by selecting a value for each Total cell from the list. If you leave a Total cell blank or enter a value not on the list, Access displays an error message and does not run the query.

As an example of a column calculation, suppose you want to calculate the average freight charge for all orders. Create a new query called qryOrders based on the Orders table. There are two ways you can calculate the average. One way is to enter the SQL aggregate function directly in a new calculated field as **AveFreight: Avg([Freight])** and enter **Expression** in the field's Totals cell. The second way is to drag Freight to a Field cell and select Avg from the combo list in the Total cell. Figure 18.3 shows the two ways to use SQL aggregate functions in a query.

As another example, you can count the number of records using the Count() function. To count the number of records with non-null values in a particular field, use Count([ColumnName]); the Count() function counts the records with non-Null values in the field and ignores those with Null values. To count all of the records, use the asterisk (*) wild-card character as the argument instead of the name of a particular field; for example, enter **Number: Count(*)** in an empty Field cell and select Expression in the field's Total cell.

Fig. 18.3

*Two ways to use an SQL
aggregate function: (a)
use the function in the
Field cell and select
Expression in the Total
cell or (b) select the
function in the Total cell.*

(a)   (b)

 Tip

The `Count(*)` function is especially optimized in Access and is much faster than
`Count([ColumnName])`.

The summary calculation in figure 18.3 is based on the freight values for all of the orders
because there are no grouping fields. To calculate average freight values for each of the
three shippers, you group the records first by dragging the Ship Via field to the grid.
When you drag a field to the design grid of a Totals query, by default it is a grouping
field with Group By in its Totals cell.

You can limit the records used in a totals calculation by adding criteria in the Criteria
and Or cells below Field cells. There are three ways you can specify criteria, and each way
results in a different totals calculation as shown in figure 18.4:

▶ *Limit the Group By fields.* Limit the groups of records for which you calculate summary values by entering expressions in the Criteria cells of the Group By fields. For
example, if you want the average freight values for each of the three shippers for
orders shipped to Argentina or Brazil, drag the Ship Country to the design grid to
the right of the Ship Via field and enter the condition `In(Argentina,Brazil)` in the
Criteria cell. The order of the Group By fields determines how the summary records
are displayed but doesn't effect the totals calculations themselves. When you run
the query, the records are grouped first by their values in the Ship Via field, and
then by their values in the Ship Country field. Next, the criteria expressions for the
grouping fields are used to select only the groups for Argentina or Brazil. Finally,
the summary calculation is performed on the selected groups of records to give the
values shown in figure 18.4a.

- *Limit the totals fields.* Specify which records to display after the totals calculations are performed by entering expressions in the Criteria cells of totals fields. (A *totals field* has either Expression or one of the SQL aggregate functions in its Total cell.) Continuing the same example, if you want to display only the average freight values that *exceed $40* for each of the three shippers for orders shipped to Argentina or Brazil, enter the expression **>$40** in the Criteria cell of the calculated field. When you run the query, Access performs the groupings, restricts the groups, does the totals calculations, and then limits the records displayed to give the values shown in figure 18.4b.
- *Limit the Where fields.* Specify which records will be included in the groups before grouping and performing calculations by entering expressions in the Criteria cells of fields that have Where in the Totals cell. Continuing with the same example, if you want to display only the average freight values that exceed $40 for each of the three shippers for orders shipped to Argentina or Brazil *during 1995*, drag the ShippedDate field to the design grid, select Where from the combo box list in the Totals cell, and enter the expression **Between 1/1/95 And 12/31/95** in the field's Criteria cell. When you run the query, Access first limits the records to only those shipped during 1995, then performs the groupings, restricts the groups, does the totals calculations, and finally limits the records displayed to give the values shown in figure 18.4c. Notice that the field with Where in the Totals cell is not displayed in the query result because Access automatically clears the Show check box of a Where field.

Fig. 18.4
Specifying a search condition gives a different result depending on whether the field is a Group By field (a), a summary field (b), or a Where field (c).

qryOrders : Select Query

Ship Via	Ship Country	AverageFreight	Number
Speedy Express	Argentina	$26.39	5
Speedy Express	Brazil	$49.77	31
United Package	Argentina	$58.72	7
United Package	Brazil	$71.81	35
Federal Shipping	Argentina	$13.89	4
Federal Shipping	Brazil	$48.46	17

Record: 6 of 6

(a)

qryOrders : Select Query

Ship Via	Ship Country	AverageFreight	Number
Speedy Express	Brazil	$49.77	31
United Package	Argentina	$58.72	7
United Package	Brazil	$71.81	35
Federal Shipping	Brazil	$48.46	17

Record: 4 of 4

(b)

qryOrders : Select Query

Ship Via	Ship Country	AverageFreight	Number
Speedy Express	Argentina	$46.85	2
Speedy Express	Brazil	$43.74	14
United Package	Argentina	$83.12	4
United Package	Brazil	$55.15	9
Federal Shipping	Brazil	$42.45	5

Record: 5 of 5

(c)

Note

You can use a field as both a totals field and a Where field by including the field twice in the query design grid, once as a totals field and the second copy as a Where field. An expression entered in the Criteria cell of the Where field copy limits records before groupings and *before* the totals calculations. An expression entered in the Criteria cell of the totals field copy limits the records that are displayed *after* the totals calculations.

Distinguishing Between SQL and Domain Aggregate Functions

The SQL and domain aggregate functions are similar in that each takes a group of records and performs a summary calculation on the group; they differ in how the group is defined. For SQL aggregate functions, the group is based on the recordset of the object you are working with: the records in the active query (as in this chapter) or the records in the underlying recordset of the active form or report. The domain aggregate functions are a generalization in that you can define the group of records based on *any* table or query and not just the recordset of the active object. For example, you use an SQL aggregate function in a calculated control on a form based on the Customers table in order to calculate a value based on all of the records in the Customers table. By contrast, you use a domain aggregate function in order to base the value on a restricted set of Customer records or on the records from another table or query.

Table 18.6 shows when you can use the SQL and domain aggregate functions:

Table 18.6   Using the SQL and Domain Aggregate Functions

	SQL Aggregate Functions	Domain Aggregate Functions
Queries: Field cells	Yes	Yes
Queries: Criteria and Update cells	No	Yes
Forms: Calculated controls	Yes	Yes

	SQL Aggregate Functions	Domain Aggregate Functions
Reports: Calculated controls	Yes	Yes
Macros: Conditions and Action Arguments	No	Yes
VBA Modules	Only as part of an SQL statement	Either as part of an SQL statement or called directly

Nesting Queries

A powerful feature of Access queries is that you can base a query on other queries. When you use a query as a data source for a second query, the first query is a *nested query*. You can build complex queries by nesting simpler queries within each other; Access allows up to 50 levels of nesting. As an example, the Category Sales for 1994 query in Northwind is based on the nested query Product Sales for 1994. Building a complex query as a sequence of simpler nested queries is helpful in understanding how the query works. However, there are other reasons for nesting queries. This section explores two of those reasons.

Nesting a Totals Query to Improve Performance

When a totals query includes joined tables, you can often improve the query's performance by breaking the query into two. You create a query that selects the records for the groups and then nest this query within a second query that performs the joins and the totals calculations. By splitting the tasks this way, you can often reduce the total number of joins that have to be formed.

As an example, we'll create a totals query and compare it with a pair of nested queries that give the same final result.

1. Create a totals query called qryCustomersOrders based on the Customers and Orders tables. In the design grid, place the Country field from Customers as a Group By field and enter the expression **In(Argentina, Brazil)** in the Criteria cell below the Country field. Place ShipVia as a Group By field, place Freight as a totals field with Avg selected in the Totals cell, and place ShippedDate as a Where field, and enter the expression **Between 1/1/95 And 12/31/95** in the Criteria cell below the ShippedDate field. When you run this query, the query must create the joins between the 91 customers and their related orders before applying the search conditions and performing the totals calculations.

2. Create a query called qrySelectCustomers based on the Customers table. The purpose of this query is to select the records for the groups. Drag CustomerID and Country to the design grid and enter the expression **In(Argentina, Brazil)** in the Criteria cell of the Country field. Run the query. This query selects the twelve customers from the specified countries. You'll nest this query.

3. Switch to Design view for the qryCustomersOrders query. Delete the Customers table in the upper pane and add the qrySelectCustomers query to the upper pane to nest the query. Join the two field lists on their respective CustomerID fields. Drag the Country field from qrySelectCustomers to the first field column as a Group By field. Run the query and note that it runs faster. This query creates joins only between the 12 customers selected by the nested query and their related orders.

The nested totals query runs faster because it has fewer joins to form. Each join that is formed takes time; creating a separate query to select the records that are in the groups reduces the number of joining operations in the totals query from 91 to 12. See the later section "Optimizing Query Performance" for more information on query performance.

Resolving Ambiguous Outer Joins

When a query contains three or more tables with at least one outer join, you may get the error message `Query contains ambiguous outer joins`. Access displays this message whenever the results of the query differ depending on the order in which the joins are formed. Unfortunately, there is no way to specify the order of the join operations using query Design view, so Access is unable to process the query.

We'll create an example using the Customers, Orders, and Employees tables in Northwind.

1. Create a query with the Customers, Orders, and Employees tables in Northwind and drag CustomerID, OrderID, and EmployeeID from the respective tables to the design grid. By default, both joins are inner joins: Customers—Orders—Employees. When you run this query, each of the 830 records in the result corresponds to a specific order with a specific employee for a specific customer.

2. Right-click the join line between Customers and Orders, click Join Properties, and change the join to an outer join that selects all records from Customers and only the records from Orders that match the records in Customers (the join arrow points to Orders): Customers→Orders—Employees. When you try to run this query, the error message is displayed.

By changing the join between Customers and Orders to an outer join, you might expect that the query will include records for Customers whether or not they have matching records in Orders. However, Access can't tell from the Design view specifications whether it should start with the Customer records, the Order records, or the Employee records. If it starts with the Order or Employee records, only a subset of the Customer records is returned because not all Customers have placed orders. If it starts with the Customer records, then all of the Customer records are returned due to the way you defined the outer join. These two outcomes are in conflict, so Access calls the outer join ambiguous and cannot run the query. You must make the starting point explicit by nesting two queries. The first one evaluated constitutes the starting point.

We can observe the two results, depending on the order in which Access performs the joins by creating and nesting queries.

1. Create a new query called qryCustomersOuterOrders based on Customers and Orders. Drag CustomerID from Customers and OrderID and EmployeeID from Orders to the design grid. Change the join to an outer join that selects all records from Customers. When you run the query, 832 records are returned. (You can find the customers who haven't placed orders by entering Is Null in the Criteria cell below OrderID: there are two such customers with CustomerID FISSA and PARIS, respectively.)

2. Create a new query based on qryCustomersOuterOrders and add the Employees table. Drag CustomerID, OrderID, and EmployeeID to the design grid and run the query. The query performs the join in the nested query first to produce records for all customers (including the two records with null values for OrderID), and then performs the inner join with Employees to return records with matching values in OrderID (disregarding the two records with null values for OrderID):(Customers→Orders)—Employees. When you run this query, 830 records are returned.

18

3. Create a new query called qryOrdersEmployees based on Orders and Employees. Drag OrderID and CustomerID from Orders and Employee ID from Employees to the design grid. Each record that this query returns corresponds to a specific order and a specific employee. (As an inner join, this query would not return orders that don't have matching employees or employees who don't have any orders.)

4. Create a new query based on qryOrdersEmployees, add the Customers table, and change the join to an outer join that selects all records from Customers. Drag CustomerID, OrderID, and EmployeeID to the design grid and run the query. The query performs the join in the nested query first to produce records with specific values for OrderID and EmployeeID, and then performs the outer join with Customers to return all records from Customers:

> Customers→(Orders—Employees)

When you run this query, 832 records are returned (including records for the two customers who don't have orders).

The general rule is this: The results of a query involving outer joins between three tables depend on the order of the joins whenever the join arrows point toward the middle table. Queries with joins as follows:

> Customers→Orders—Employees
>
> Customers—Orders←Employees
>
> Customers→Orders→Employees

are all ambiguous and require that you specify the order of the joins by using nested queries.

Using Self-Joins in Queries

Occasionally, you need to join two copies of the same table. You create a *self-join* that combines records from the two copies when there are matching values in the joined fields. This section explains three situations where self-joins are required.

Joining Rows to Other Rows in the Same Table

When the rows of a table are related to other rows in the same table, you can use a self-join in a query to display the relationship. For example, the Employees table in Northwind has a Reports To field for each employee's record that stores the ID of the employee's supervisor (and displays the supervisor's name because the field is a Lookup field). Another way to display the supervisor's name instead of the ID, is to create a query with a self-join that joins the Reports To field in the table to the EmployeeID field in the copy of the table.

1. Create a query called qrySupervisors based on Employees and drag EmployeeID, LastName, and FirstName to the design grid.

2. Add a copy of Employees to the query. By default, Access displays the name of the copy as Employee_1 in order to distinguish between the two copies; we'll rename the copy. Right-click the field list, choose Properties, and then set the Alias property to Supervisors.

3. Join the Reports To field from Employees to the EmployeeID field in Supervisors (a self-join between the two copies of the table). Drag the LastName field from Supervisors. The design grid has LastName fields from each copy see fig. 18.5a. To distinguish between the two fields in Datasheet view or in any form or report based on the query, right-click the LastName field from Supervisors and set the Caption property to Supervisor.

4. Run the query. Figure 18.5b shows the query results.

Fig. 18.5

Using a self-join to join rows to other rows in the same table.

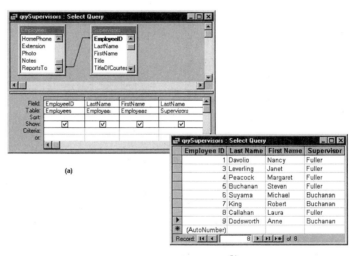

(a)

(b)

Using Self-Joins in a Many-to-Many Relationship Table

When two tables are in a many-to-many relationship and you want to find all records in one table corresponding to two or more records in the other table, you can use a self-join between two copies of the relationship table.

As an example, the Order Details table in Northwind is the relationship table for the many-to-many relationship between the Orders and Products tables. Each record in Order Details corresponds to a specific order placed by a customer and to a specific product in the order. Suppose you want to find all orders that contain two specified products, for example, all orders that have both Alice Mutton (ProductID=17) and Chai (ProductID=1). To solve this problem, we use a self-join to find the records in the *intersection of two sets*: the set of orders with Alice Mutton and the set of orders with Chai. Follow these steps:

1. Create a new query called qrySelfJoinTwoProducts based on Order Details. Set the Alias property of the field list to Orders with Alice Mutton and drag OrderID and ProductID to the design grid. Set the Criteria cell for ProductID to 17 to select all orders with Alice Mutton. Running the query at this point returns records for the 37 orders with Alice Mutton.

2. Drag a second copy of Order Details to the query and set the Alias property to Orders with Chai. Drag ProductID to the grid and set the Criteria cell to 1 to select all orders with Chai. Note that Access doesn't join the copies of the table. If you run the query without joining the tables you get the *Cartesian product* of the two sets of records containing 1406 records (the Cartesian product contains a record for each pair selected from the 37 orders with Alice Mutton and the 38 orders with Chai). Create a self-join by joining the two copies of the relationship table on the OrderID (see fig. 18.6a).

3. Run the query to produce the result: there are two orders with both Alice Mutton and Chai as shown in figure 18.6b.

Fig. 18.6

Using self-joins in a relationship table for tables in a many-to-many relationship to find all records in one table corresponding to two records in the other table.

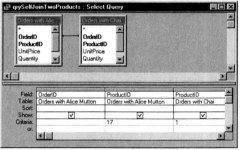

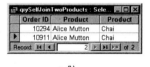

(a)

(b)

Using Self-Joins with Transactions Tables

When a table records events over time, it is called a *transaction table*. In a transaction table each event occurs only once, but the transactions are repetitive in some sense. When you want to find all occurrences in a specific time interval, you can use a self-join as part of the solution. As an example, the Orders table in Northwind is a transaction table with each record recording a unique event—a particular order. Because customers generally place more than one order, the Orders table contains many records for a customer. Suppose you want to find customers who ordered in both 1993 and 1994. Using the self-join technique of the example in the last section, you can find the records of customers who ordered in both 1993 and 1994 as the intersection of the set of customers who ordered in 1993 and the set of customers who ordered in 1994.

1. Create a new query called qryOrdersin93and94 based on the Orders table. Set the Alias property to Ordersin93. Drag CustomerID and OrderDate to the design grid. Enter **Between 1/1/93 And 12/31/93** in the Criteria cell and clear the Show check box for the OrderDate. Running the query at this point displays the 67 customers who ordered in 1993. (If you check the Show check box, running the query displays the 157 orders placed by the 67 customers.)

2. Add a second copy of the Orders table to the query. Set the Alias property to Ordersin94 and drag OrderDate to the design grid. Enter **Between 1/1/94 And 12/31/94** in the Criteria cell and clear the Show check box for the OrderDate. Create a self-join by joining the copies on the CustomerID field (see fig. 18.7a).

3. Run the query. Figure 18.7b shows several of the 65 customers who ordered both in 1993 and 1994.

Fig. 18.7

You can use self-joins in a timeline problem to find customers who ordered both in 1993 and in 1994.

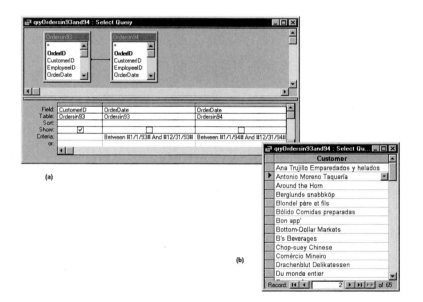

(a)

(b)

Creating Parameter Queries

When you want to run a query repetitively using different values for the query criterion, instead of changing the criterion in the query Design view for each value, you can convert the query to a parameter query that gets the different values from a dialog box (a Default dialog box is often called an input box in the other Microsoft Office applications). In the simplest case, you convert the query by replacing the specific value in the expression in the Criteria cell with a *prompt* (a prompt is the text you display in a dialog box to prompt the user to enter a value). You designate the prompt by enclosing its text in square brackets in the Criteria cell. The value that the user enters is called a *parameter*. As an example, we'll create new query based on the Products table that selects records based on the value of UnitsInStock.

1. Create a new query called qparProducts based on the Products table and drag all of the fields to the design grid. Enter the expression **>20** in the Criteria cell below the UnitsInStock field. Running the query returns the products that satisfy this expression.

2. In the Criteria cell, replace the number 20 with the prompt **[Enter a lower stock limit]**.

   When you run the query, Access displays a dialog box with the title Enter Parameter Value. After you enter the value in the text box and click OK, the query runs using the value you entered and retrieves the records that satisfy the criterion. When there is more than one parameter, Access displays separate dialog boxes in an order that depends on the arrangement of the prompts in the Criteria and Or cells. By default, the data type assigned to the prompt value is Text.

   You can also include a prompt in a calculated field expression. As an example, we'll add a second prompt to test product price adjustments for different inflation rates.

3. Insert a new column to the right of the UnitPrice field and enter the expression **NewPrice: UnitPrice*(1+[Enter an inflation rate])**. When you run the query, the first dialog box prompts for the inflation rate, a second dialog box prompts for the lower stock limit, and then the query displays the result.

Setting the Parameter Query Parameters

You can override the default prompt order and data type. Right-click in the upper pane in query Design view and choose Parameters to display the Query Parameters dialog box (see fig. 18.8). Enter each prompt in the desired order. Each prompt entry must match the prompt text exactly. The square brackets are optional in the Query Parameters list, but not in the design grid. Select a data type from the drop-down list in the second column of the Query Parameters dialog box. In most cases, setting a prompt's data type is optional. An exception is a field with the Yes/No data type; if you don't set the data type of the prompt to Yes/No, Access responds with the error message Can't evaluate expression if you enter Yes or No as the prompt.

Fig. 18.8

Specify the data type and an order for the parameter prompts in the Query Parameters dialog box.

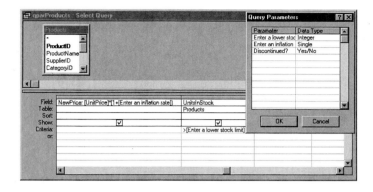

Continuing with the example:

1. Enter the prompt **[Discontinued?]** in the Criteria cell of the Discontinued field. Try to run the query by entering **No** when the third prompt is displayed.

2. Display the Query Parameters dialog box, enter the prompts and the data types shown in figure 18.8. Run the query by entering a lower stock of **20** in the text box of the first Enter Parameter Value dialog box and **Yes** in the text box of the second dialog box to display the three products.

Obtaining the Prompt from a Form

When you enter prompts in the query design grid, Access displays a separate default Enter Parameter Value dialog box for each prompt. You enter a value manually in the Default dialog box to satisfy the prompt. There are limitations of the default procedure:

▶ There is a separate dialog box for each parameter so working with more than a few prompts is cumbersome.

▶ You have to type a value in the text box of the Enter Parameter Value dialog box. You have to type the value correctly, and you often have to know which values are appropriate. Both of these problems could be avoided with a combo or list box displaying the choices. In other cases, an option group or check box might be more appropriate.

You can overcome these limitations by creating a custom form that prompts for all parameters at once and that uses the particular type of form control appropriate to each parameter. The technique of using a form to supply parameter values to a query is called *Query By Form (QBF)*. You modify each prompt in a Criteria cell of the query to refer to the corresponding control on the form. The form must be open in Form view when you run the query. As an example, we'll create a form called frmQBF to collect the parameter values for selecting products.

1. Create an unbound form called frmQBF and set the form's Caption property to Products Parameter Query.

2. Place a text box named txtLowerLimit, a text box named txtInflation, a check box named chkDiscontinued (set the TripleState and the DefaultValue properties to No), and a combo box named cboCategory. Enter appropriate captions in the labels for each control.

3. For the combo box, click the Build button in the RowSource property, select the Categories table for the query, drag the CategoryName and CategoryID to the design grid, and close the window. Set the ColumnCount and the BoundColumn properties to 2 and set the ColumnWidths property to 1.0;0.2 and the ListWidth property to 1.4. Switch to Form view (see fig. 18.9).

4. Click in the query and modify the query as follows (type the form control references or use the Expression Builder to create the references):

Query cell	Expression That Refers to Form Control
Criteria cell	>Forms!frmQBF!txtLowerLimit for UnitsInStock
Criteria cell	Forms!frmQBF!chkDiscontinued for Discontinued
Criteria cell	Forms!frmQBF!cboCategory for Suppliers
Calculated field cell	NewPrice:UnitPrice* (1+Forms!frmQBF!txtInflation)

5. Display the Query Parameters dialog box and delete all entries. Switch to Datasheet view; no records are displayed.

6. Enter choices in the controls of the form. Click in the query and press Shift+F9 to run the query with the choices on the form. The query runs and displays the records satisfying the choices made in the form (see fig. 18.9).

Fig. 18.9

Use a custom dialog form to collect parameters for the query (Query By Form).

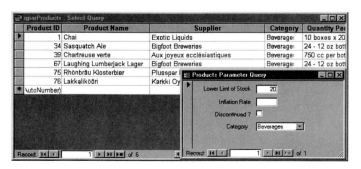

Using the Advanced Query Wizards

There are three query wizards that you can use to create more complex queries. These wizards are discussed in the following sections.

Using the Crosstab Query Wizard

A crosstab query is a special kind of totals query that you can use to display totals calculations in a compact row and column format. In a crosstab query, you specify a field as Group By field for the Column headings, at least one field as a Group By field for the Row headings and a field for the totals calculation. When you run the query, the cell at the intersection of a column and a row contains the summary value. The Quarterly Orders by Product query in Northwind is a crosstab query that displays the total orders of a product by a customer in each quarter of the 1994 order year. The query uses product name and customer name as grouping fields for the row headings.

You can create a crosstab query from scratch in query Design view, or you can use the Crosstab Query Wizard. We'll use the wizard to create a simple crosstab query that displays the total number of orders by employee and by ship country.

1. Click the New Object button on the toolbar, choose New Query, choose Crosstab Query Wizard, and then click OK.

2. Choose Orders as the table that contains the fields you want to display and click Next. The lower half of the wizard screens display a model of the crosstab query results.

3. Choose EmployeeID as the row heading and click Next.

4. Choose ShipCountry as the column heading and click Next.

5. Choose OrderID in the first list box and Count in the second to count the number of orders. Leave the Yes, Include Row Sums check box checked.

6. Name the query qxtbOrders and click Finish. Figure 18.10a shows the Design view, and figure 18.10b shows the Datasheet view for the query.

18

Fig. 18.10
*The Crosstab Query
Wizard creates a totals
query to display the total
number of orders by
employee and by ship
country.*

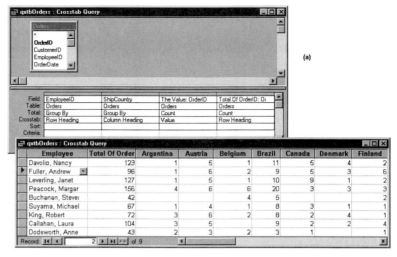

Creating a Find Unmatched Query

Sometimes you need to find records in one table or query that don't have related records in another—for example, customers who have never ordered or products that have never sold. You can create these queries to find *orphan records* (a record in a child table that has no corresponding record in the parent table; for example, an order without a matching customer record) and *widow records* (a record in the parent table of a one-to-many or one-to-one relationship that doesn't have a corresponding record in the other table; for example, a customer without matching orders). You can create a Find Unmatched Query whenever you want to find records that have no corresponding records in another table. First, we'll use the Find Unmatched Query Wizard to find customers without matching orders, and then we'll create a query from scratch.

To find customers without matching orders, do the following:

1. Click the New Object button on the toolbar, choose New Query, choose Find Unmatched Query Wizard, and then click OK.

2. Choose Customers as the table that contains the records you are looking for and click Next.

3. Choose Orders as the table that contains the related records and click Next.

4. In this dialog box, you specify the matching field. Accept the default match on CustomerID and click Next.

5. Choose to display the CustomerID and CustomerName and click Next.

6. Accept the default name Customers Without Matching Orders and click Finish. The query displays the two customers without orders with CustomerID FISSA and PARIS, respectively.

To see how the query works, switch to Design view (see fig. 18.11). The wizard creates an outer join to select all records from the Customers table. To observe the effect of the Is Null criterion, temporarily delete the expression and check the Show check box under the CustomersID field from the Orders table. Running the query (now just a simple outer join without a limiting criterion) displays a list of all customers; for customers with no orders (FISSA and PARIS), the third column displays a Null value. To find the records for customers with no orders, the Wizard enters the Is Null expression in the Criteria cell. Switch back to Design view, enter the expression Is Null in the Criteria cell, and clear the Show check box under the CustomerID from Orders field.

Fig. 18.11

Design view of a Find Unmatched query finds records in a table without matching records in a second table.

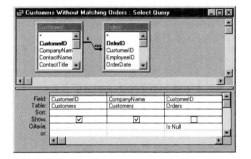

In terms of sets, the shaded region in figure 18.12a depicts the outer join of two related sets of records, here Customers and Orders. The Find Unmatched Query works when you have two overlapping sets of records from two related tables or queries and you want to find the records in one set that are not in the intersection (the shaded region in figure 18.12b). The records you want are those with Null values in the matching field; in the current example, you want the records in the outer join that have Null values in the matching field from Orders.

As another example, suppose that you want to find customers who placed orders in 1993 but did not order in 1994. In a previous section, "Using Self-Joins in Transaction Tables," we used a self-join to find customers who ordered in both 1993 and 1994. If the circle on the right in figure 18.12 represents the customers who ordered in 1993 and the circle on the left represents the customers who ordered in 1994, then the customers who ordered in both 1993 and 1994 are represented by the intersection depicted in figure 18.12. We'll find the customers who ordered in 1993 but are not in the intersection (the shaded region in figure 18.12b) as follows:

1. Create a new query called qryOrdersIn93Not94 based on Orders. Drag the CustomerID and OrderDate to the design grid. Enter the expression **Between 1/1/93 And 12/31/93** in the Criteria cell and clear the Show check box below OrderDate.

2. Right-click in the upper pane, choose Properties, and set the UniqueValues property to Yes. With this property set to No, the query displays a record for each order placed in 1993; set this property to Yes to display a single record for each customer who placed one or more orders in 1993. Running the query at this point displays the records for the 67 customers who ordered in 1993.

3. Add the qryOrdersIn93And94 query (you nest the query you created in the earlier section "Using Self-Joins with Transaction Tables"), create an outer join on CustomerID, and drag CustomerID to the grid. Running the query at this point displays 67 records for the customers who ordered in 1993. These records have null values in the second column for those customers who did not order in both 1993 and 1994.

4. Enter the expression Is Null in the Criteria cell and clear the Show check box under the CustomerID field from qryOrdersIn93And94. Running the query displays records for the two customers who ordered in 1993 but not in 1994.

Fig. 18.12
The Find Unmatched Query finds records in the outer join (a) that are not in the intersection of the two sets (b).

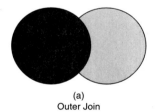

(a)
Outer Join

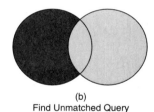

(b)
Find Unmatched Query

Using the Find Duplicates Query Wizard

When you want to find records that have duplicate values in a specific field, you use a Find Duplicates Query Wizard. As an example, you can use a Find Duplicates Query Wizard when you are working with a table that contains data but does not have a primary key. When you try to define a primary key, Access may display the following error message: Duplicate values in index, primary key, or relationship. Changes were unsuccessful. This means that there are records with duplicate values in the field or the group of fields that you are trying to use as the primary key.

As an example, we'll use the Find Duplicates Query Wizard to find records in Employees for employees from the same city.

1. Click the New Object button on the toolbar, choose New Query, choose Find Duplicates Query Wizard, and click OK.

2. Select Employees as the table with the duplicate records and click Next.

3. Choose City as the field that contains the duplicate values and click Next.

4. Click Next without selecting additional fields to display.

5. Accept the default name Find duplicates for Employees and click Finish. The wizard builds the query and displays the results shown in figure 18.13a. The query displays the value that is duplicated and the number of records with the duplicated value.

6. Switch to Design view (see fig. 18.13b).

Fig. 18.13

When you include only the field with the duplicated value, the Find Duplicates Query Wizard uses a totals query to find the duplicates.

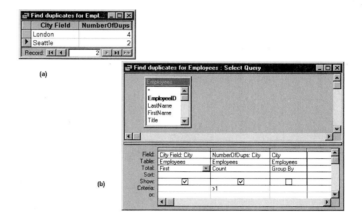

(a)

(b)

If you include only the field with the duplicated value in the result, the wizard automatically adds a field to count the duplicates. Figure 18.13b shows that the wizard creates a totals query that groups records by city, counts the number of records in each group and includes only groups with more than one record, and displays the City value of the first record in the group.

If you step through the Find Duplicates Query Wizard a second time, but choose to display additional fields such as the LastName, the wizard produces the result shown in figure 18.14a. Because the additional fields have different values (in this example, different last names), the wizard uses a different strategy. Figure 18.14b shows the Design view of the query. Design view shows that the wizard has created a select query without a Total row and has entered an expression in the Criteria cell for City. Notice that the criteria expression contains a statement that you may recognize as an SQL statement for a subquery. A *subquery* is a query that is expressed as an SQL statement and included within another query. Chapter 19, "Understanding the Data Access Languages in Access," explains both SQL and subqueries.

In this example, the subquery groups records by their City value, counts the number of records in each group, and then selects only groups with more than one record. The subquery returns its selected records to the main query. The main query returns each record whose City value matches one of the values returned by the subquery.

Fig. 18.14

When you include fields in addition to the field with the duplicated value, the Find Duplicates Query Wizard uses a subquery to find the duplicates.

(a)

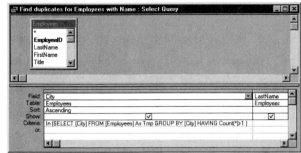

(b)

Running Queries

There are many ways to run a query interactively.

▶ You run a query whenever you open a query in Datasheet view by selecting the query in the Database window and clicking Open.

▶ If the query is a select query that is already open in Design or SQL view, it runs when you switch to Datasheet view.

▶ An action query open in Design or SQL view runs when you click the Run button on the toolbar or choose Query, Run.

▶ If the query is a select or crosstab query, the query runs when you open a form or report that has the query as its record source, or a form that has a combo box, list box, or lookup field that has the query as its row source.

When two database objects (tables, queries, or forms) are open and you change the data in one of them, the other object refreshes automatically to display the changes when it receives the focus. (The automatic update that occurs when you modify an existing record is called *refresh*.) However, if you add a new record to the first object, the other open object does not display the new record automatically. If you delete a record from the first object, the other open object displays the word #Deleted in each field or control that previously displayed data from the deleted record. (Refresh occurs only when you modify an existing record.) Interactively, you can force the updating of the second object by pressing Shift+F9 to read the underlying table again or run the underlying query again.

You can also run a query programmatically. In macro programming, you run the OpenQuery macro action, and in VBA programming, you can use the OpenQuery method. By default, the OpenQuery action or method opens a select or crosstab query in Datasheet view and simply runs an action query. See Chapter 19, "Understanding the Data Languages in Access," and Chapter 20, "Getting Started with Access Programming," for more information on creating and running queries programmatically.

Optimizing Query Performance

In order to make your queries run faster, you need to know how they are processed in Access.

18

How Access Processes Queries

When you install Microsoft Access, you are actually installing three groups of files:

▶ The first group of files deals with the user interface and handles all of your direct interactions for creating and modifying tables, queries, forms, reports, macros, and modules. This group of files is referred to as the Microsoft Access application.

▶ The second group is Visual Basic for Applications (VBA), the programming language you can use to automate database operations and create custom applications.

▶ The third group is the Joint Engine Technology (JET) database engine that handles all of the interactions with the data, including running the queries. The database engine is referred to simply as Jet.

There are several ways you can define a query. Interactively, you can define a query in query Design view, in query SQL view, or by using Filter By Form or Filter By Selection to create a filter to select records and then save the filter as a query. You can also define a query programmatically.

However you create the query, it is stored in the form of an SQL statement (see Chapter 19). When you run the query, Access sends the SQL statement to the query engine part of Jet which is responsible for compiling, optimizing, and executing the SQL statement. To execute a query, two operations must occur: tables must be read and joins between tables performed. During optimization, the query engine determines the most efficient way to perform these two operations. The optimizer selects one of three different ways to read each table and one of five different join strategies for each join. The query engine bases its decisions on statistics, such as the size of the table, the existence of search conditions and indexes, and the presence of nested queries. After assigning a cost to each task based on the statistics, the engine chooses the least expensive strategy and creates a *query plan*. After optimizing, Jet executes the SQL statement according to the query plan.

Using Indexes for Speed

In Access, a database is organized and stored as a set of pages with each page holding up to 2K of data. The records in the tables are stored in pages. When you want to find records with a particular value, for example, all products in the beverage category, Access must search through all the pages for the Products table to find the records. You can speed the search process by creating an index for the Category field. An *index* is a lookup table (stored in its own set of pages) that relates the value of a field in the lookup table to its page number and the location of the page. In the index, the field values are arranged in ascending order so Access can look up an indexed value quickly. By reading the index pages, Access can quickly determine which data page contains the requested value.

An index in a database plays exactly the same role as an index for a book (a book's table of contents is also an index). Without a book index of any kind, if you want to find a topic in a book, you must scan through every page of the book until you find all instances of the topic. With a good book index, you only need to look up the value in the index because the index points to all of the book pages that refer to the topic. Some books have several indexes to help you find information quickly. So, with an Access database, you can create an index for each field or combination of fields that you expect to use for finding and sorting records. Without an index, if you are trying to find records with a particular value in a field, Access must read all the pages of a table to find all the records. When an index is defined on the field, Access first reads the pages of the index. Because the values are in order and the index is physically small, Access finds the value very quickly and looks up the data pages that contain the desired records. As a result of using the index, Access then reads only the specific data pages to find the records.

You can create an index for each field that participates in joining operations to speed up the process. Without an index on a join field, Access must read all of the pages of the table in order to create the join. Using indexes can dramatically decrease the amount of the table that has to be read for joining and finding records and dramatically improve the query performance.

While indexes are necessary for better performance in retrieving records, there are costs: the index lookup tables take up space on the disk, and it takes time to update the index tables every time a record is added, edited, or deleted. You can experiment to determine the best trade-off between increasing the use of indexes to improve retrieval and decreasing the use to improve update performance.

Taking Advantage of Rushmore Query Optimization

In the first versions of Access, the query optimizer could work only with a single index. In particular, earlier versions could optimize queries that had simple search criteria set on fields which were indexed and used only one of the following comparison operators: <,>,=,<=,>=, Between...And, Like, and In. Examples of these simple optimizable expressions are:

> [LastName] = Like "m*"
>
> [Quantity] Between 10 And 50
>
> [HireDate]> #1/1/95#
>
> Suppliers.[CompanyName] = Shippers.[CompanyName]

This assumes that the fields are indexed. More generally, a simple optimizable expression has the form

> Indexed field   Comparison operator
> Expression

where Expression can be any valid expression including constants, functions, and fields from other tables.

Access 2.0 introduced the use of Rushmore query optimization as a set of techniques that involve using multiple indexes. With Rushmore, Access can optimize complex expressions that consist of two simple optimizable expressions combined with the And or Or operator. Examples of complex optimizable expressions (assuming the fields are indexed) include:

> [LastName] = Like "m*" And [HireDate]> #1/1/95#
>
> [LastName] = Like "m*" Or [Quantity] Between 10 And 50

To take advantage of Rushmore query optimization, include only simple and complex optimizable expressions and avoid using other kinds of expressions in queries.

Optimization Tips and Strategies

The Performance Analyzer is a new feature in Access for Windows 95 which can analyze a set of database objects and provide recommendations, suggestions, and ideas for improving performance. You start the Performance Analyzer by choosing Tools, Analyze, Performance. You specify the database objects you want the Performance Analyzer to look at (only closed objects can be analyzed). Some examples of the Analyzer's recommendations for queries are:

> Add an index to field(s) 'fieldname'
>
> Use a saved query as the record source
>
> Use a saved query as the row source for the control 'fieldname'

18

Here are some tips for improving query performance based on the previous sections:

▶ Index fields on both sides of a join. With both fields indexed, the query optimizer can use more sophisticated joining strategies (two of the five join strategies require indexed join fields).

▶ In defining table fields, choose the smallest data type appropriate for the data.

▶ In creating a query, display only the necessary fields. If you use fields for sorting or setting search criteria only, clear the Show box.

▶ Avoid calculated fields in queries that are nested within other queries.

▶ In creating a totals query, minimize the number of GROUP BY fields. Each GROUP BY requires a sort of the data so the more GROUP BY columns you include the longer the query takes.

▶ If a totals query includes a join, consider splitting the query: group the records in one query and nest this query within a second query that performs the join.

▶ Index fields with criteria.

▶ Avoid setting criteria on calculated fields if possible.

▶ If you set a criterion on a field used in a join, consider adding the criterion to the field on the "one" side of the join rather than the field on the "many" side of the join.

▶ Avoid using the domain aggregate functions in a query to access data in another table or query. Instead, add the table or query to your query if appropriate, or use a subquery (see Chapter 20).

▶ Index the fields that use the Between...And, In, and the equals (=) operators (to take advantage of Rushmore technology.)

▶ Use Count(*) instead of Count([ColumnName]) whenever possible. There is a special optimization strategy for Count(*).

Summary

Queries are the heart of Access. In this chapter, you learned how to create complex queries that combine the data stored in table records and perform calculations that turn the data into useful information.

The next chapter introduces the two data languages in Access: Structured Query Language (SQL) and the Data Access Objects (DAO) language. All of the queries you have learned to create in the query Design view in this chapter can be expressed in SQL. In the next chapter, you learn about queries that can be created using only SQL and that have no query Design view counterpart. Most of the time you create tables and queries interactively in their respective Design windows. In the next chapter, you also learn that tables and queries can be created programmatically.

18

chapter 19

Understanding the Data Languages in Access

19

by Susann Novalis

In this chapter

◆ **Structured Query Language**
Learn the role of SQL as the standard language of relational databases and how to write SQL statements.

◆ **SQL Queries**
Expand your query skills by learning about queries that can't be created graphically.

◆ **Data Access Objects (DAO)**
Read about the data access objects that enable you to "talk" to the Jet database engine using VBA.

◆ **Performance Considerations**
Learn the performance differences between stored queries and SQL statements, and between SQL and DAO techniques.

Microsoft Access includes two different methods for organizing, retrieving, and managing data: Structured Query Language (SQL) and data access objects (DAO). Both are languages with elements that you use to interact with data. SQL is the fundamental language for interacting with any relational database. DAO is the language that Visual Basic uses to interact with the Jet database engine, the component of Access that is responsible for managing the data.

When you work interactively with Access, you don't need to know much about SQL and DAO. Instead, you use the powerful Access interface to work with data. You create queries to retrieve data graphically. The query Design view shields you from SQL. However, when you need the power that programming gives you, you must at least learn the basics of these two data languages.

The two data languages are not independent: although you can use SQL independently, DAO requires SQL for creating queries. Neither language is a programming language because each lacks the basic components of a programming language, such as the capability to test conditions and to create loops for carrying out repetitive operations.

The fundamental difference between the two methods is that SQL is a *relational model* based on retrieving and manipulating a *set* of records as a batch; DAO is a *navigational model* based on moving around within a set of records and working with one record at a time. For example, in SQL you retrieve a group of records by defining criteria that the records must satisfy to be in the result; with SQL you specify what you want done, but not how to do it. In contrast, you write a program in DAO to move from record to record in a set testing individual records to determine whether they satisfy the selection criteria.

Understanding SQL and Why You Should Learn It

SQL (pronounced *ess-cue-ell* or *sequel*) is a tool for interacting with the database in any relational database management system. Although SQL has several different functions, the primary role is as a query tool: when you want to retrieve data from any relational database, you use SQL to make the request. Your request contains the names of the tables and the fields holding the data you want returned; your request might also contain information that defines the search so only specific data are retrieved.

You can create the request interactively or programmatically using macros or Visual Basic. Interactively, you can create the request graphically in query Design view or by writing a statement in query SQL view. Access for Windows 95 has two new *ad hoc query* features for creating requests interactively. One new method uses a special Filter By Form view of a form or datasheet for entering search values in blank fields. The other new method uses a special Filter By Selection view of a form or datasheet for selecting search values. Programmatically, you create the request as a data access object using VBA.

However you create it, the request is formulated ultimately as a statement in SQL and sent to the Jet database engine. Jet accepts SQL statements from many sources, including the interactive query window, the ad hoc query views of forms and datasheets, Visual Basic code, macros, and properties of controls, forms, and reports.

 Note

SQL was developed in the late 1970s as the data language for IBM's DB2 database management system. Two standards organizations, ANSI (American National

Standards Organization) and ISO (International Standards Organization), promote SQL as the standard cross-platform tool for managing data. The current version of the standard is known as ANSI-92, which this chapter refers to as ANSI SQL. In practice, the vendors of the major database management systems use different SQL dialects with differing capabilities. This chapter describes Access SQL, the dialect used by Microsoft.

When you create a query interactively, you usually create it using the query Design view. Access automatically translates your query definition into an SQL statement that you can view by switching from Design view to SQL view.

Why learn how to write SQL statements yourself? The principal reason is to expand your ability to create queries; you cannot graphically create queries called *SQL queries* or *SQL-specific queries* in the Design view. A second reason is convenience, if you intend to do much programming in Visual Basic. Although you can switch to query Design view to define a query, switch to SQL view to copy the SQL statement, and then switch to the Module window to paste the SQL statement into the VBA code, an easier method is to learn enough SQL to write simple SQL statements directly. Finally, most business applications are developed in a client-server environment requiring that you have a working knowledge of the server's SQL dialect.

The Structure of SQL

As a language, SQL has a vocabulary of English words and abbreviations called *keywords* or *reserved words*. Access SQL has about 100 keywords (search "reserved words, Microsoft Jet SQL" in online help for a complete list). Keywords are usually shown in uppercase, although they aren't case-sensitive in Access. SQL consists of statements built from sets of commands, clauses, operators, and group aggregate functions.

Access SQL is based on seven commands shown in table 19.1. Each command requests a specific action from Jet.

Table 19.1   The Access SQL Commands

Command	Description
SELECT	Retrieves stored data as a set of records from tables
INSERT	Adds new records to a table
DELETE	Removes records from a table

continues

Table 19.1 Continued

Command	Description
UPDATE	Modifies specific fields in existing records
CREATE	Adds a new table to the database or creates an index for a field or a group of fields
ALTER	Adds new fields or deletes existing fields
DROP	Deletes an existing table or an existing index for a field or a group of fields

Each SQL statement begins with one of the commands as a *verb*, such as SELECT or INSERT, describing the requested action. The command is followed by one or more *clauses* that specify which data the command applies to and provide additional information for carrying out the command. Each clause begins with a keyword, such as FROM, INTO, HAVING, or WHERE, and may include field, table, or query names, expressions, constants, references to controls on forms and reports, other SQL keywords, and built-in functions (see Chapter 18, "Advanced Queries," for the operators, functions, and basic query terms). Each SQL statement ends with a semicolon.

Access SQL uses the following punctuation:

▶ Semicolons end each SQL statement.

▶ Commas separate names in lists, such as LastName, FirstName.

▶ Square brackets enclose a name when the name includes spaces or special characters, such as [Full Name].

▶ Periods separate a table or query name from a field name, such as Employee.LastName.

▶ Wild-card characters used with the Like operator include ?, *, #, [...], and [!...].

▶ Double quotes (") and single quotes (') enclose literal values such as "Canada," and the number symbol (#) encloses date/time values such as #1/1/95#.

Observing SQL Statements

Even if you have never written an SQL statement, your Access database has many examples. This chapter works with the queries in the sample Northwind Traders application that ships with Microsoft Access for Windows 95.

Observing the SQL View of a Query

When you create a query in query Design view, Access automatically converts the definition to an SQL statement. You can view the equivalent SQL statement by clicking the Query View button on the toolbar and choosing SQL view. You can view the SQL statements for all but one of the queries in Northwind by selecting a query in the Database window, clicking the Design button to open the query in Design view, and then switching to SQL view. Figure 19.1a shows Design view for the Current Product List query and figure 19.1b shows the corresponding SQL view. The English language request for this query is as follows:

List the ID number and the product name of all products that aren't discontinued, sorted in alphabetical order.

Fig. 19.1

You can view the Current Product List query in the Northwind database in Design view and in the equivalent SQL statement in SQL view.

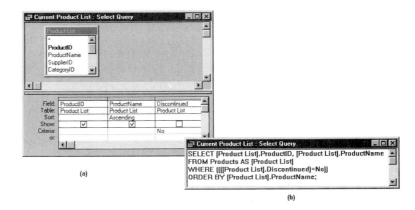

(a)

(b)

For most of these queries, Design view displays the kinds of expressions you learned to create in Chapter 18, "Advanced Queries." The Design view of the Products Above Average Price displays a new feature: the expression in the Criteria cell for UnitPrice includes an SQL statement (see fig. 19.2). An SQL statement contained in another query is called a *subquery*. The English language request for this query is as follows:

List the products and the price where the price for the product exceeds the average price of all products.

Fig. 19.2

In the Products Above Average Price query, a Criteria cell contains an SQL statement.

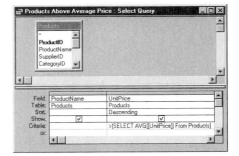

When you try to open the Customers and Suppliers by City query, it opens directly in SQL view (see fig. 19.3a). This query has no representation in Design view and is an example of an SQL-specific query called a *union query*. In the Database window, union queries are indicated with the interlocking-circles icon (see fig. 19.3b). The English language request for this query is as follows:

> List the city, company name, contact name, and relationship for all customers and suppliers, sorted alphabetically by city and company name.

Fig. 19.3

The Customers and Suppliers union query has only the SQL view in (a). The Database window in (b) shows the special union query icon.

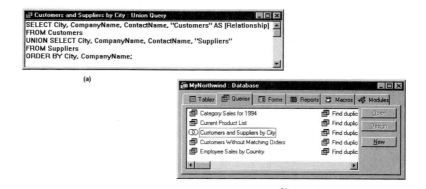

Observing the SQL Statements of Properties

You can observe SQL statements in Northwind or in your own databases as settings for certain properties. By default, the Form and Report Wizards create SQL statements for RecordSource properties, and the Lookup, Combo Box, and List Box Wizards create SQL statements for RowSource properties. The Find Duplicates Query Wizard often creates an SQL statement as part of an expression in a Criteria cell (see Chapter 18, "Advanced Queries").

When you click the Build button at the right of the property box in the property sheet, Access displays the query Design view for the SQL statement. If the SQL statement doesn't have a Design view, Access displays the SQL view for the statement. For example, figure 19.4a shows the SQL statement that the Lookup Wizard creates for the RowSource property of the SupplierID lookup field in the Products table. Clicking the Build button displays the statement's query Design view shown in figure 19.4b. You can switch to SQL view to see the SQL statement shown in figure 19.4c. If the statement is for an SQL-specific query, clicking the Build button opens query SQL view directly.

Fig. 19.4
The Lookup Wizard creates the RowSource property in (a) as an SQL statement shown in Design view in (b) and SQL view in (c).

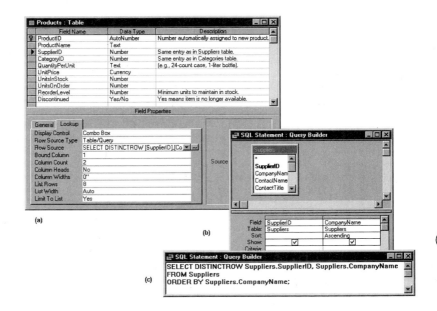

(a)

(b)

(c)

19

Learning SQL

As with any language, the best way to learn SQL is to start with simple statements and add additional features to create more complex queries. This section begins with simple select queries that retrieve data from a database and return it as a set of rows. The SQL statements for these queries contain the SELECT command. You start by writing simple select SQL statements based on a single table, learn how to join tables into multitable queries, and then learn how to perform summary calculations and create crosstab queries. (For a hands-on approach to learning SQL, create each of the example SQL statements in SQL view and then switch to Datasheet view to observe the query results.)

After discussing select queries, this section looks at the following action queries:

▶ *Update queries* change values in specified fields using the UPDATE command.

▶ *Append queries* add records to a table using the INSERT INTO command.

▶ *Delete queries* delete records from one or more tables using the DELETE command.

▶ *Make-table queries* add records to a new table using the SELECT...INTO command.

You can use query Design view to create the queries discussed in this section. You'll probably find that much of this chapter parallels and extends the discussions in Chapter 18, "Advanced Queries"; however, this chapter does not include discussions of parameter and crosstab queries (search the PARAMETERS and TRANSFORM reserved words in online help for information on SQL statements for these queries).

Note

This chapter uses the word *record* when referring to tables and queries used as data sources for the SQL statements you create. The word *row* refers to the results created by clauses of the SQL statements.

Selecting Records in Simple Queries

When you write the SQL statement for a select query, you must specify what tables and fields you want to see. You can also specify that you want to see only some, but not all, of the records, and you can specify an order for the records. The basic SELECT statement for a simple query contains four clauses to define the data you want returned:

```
SELECT select items
FROM table names
WHERE search condition
ORDER BY sort specification;
```

The SELECT clause lists the data items to be selected and displayed in the query results. The *select items* can be fields from tables in the database, constants, or items that are calculated by Jet when it performs the query. The *select items* are separated by commas and displayed as columns in the order listed in the query result. To select all the fields in a table, use the asterisk (*). The *select items* can also be fields from another query used as a nested query. You can replace a field name with an alternate name as an *alias* in the query results using the AS reserved word followed by the alternate name.

The FROM clause lists the tables (and queries) that contain the data. The names of the tables and queries are separated by commas.

The WHERE clause is an optional clause that you use to specify which of the rows satisfying the SELECT clause is to be included in the query result. The *search condition* is a condition that tests each selected row using any of a set of tests described later in this section. If you don't specify a search condition, all of the rows that satisfy the SELECT clause are returned.

The ORDER BY clause is an optional clause that sorts the rows based on one or more fields. You cannot sort by fields with Memo or OLE object data type.

Only the SELECT and FROM clauses are required. In most cases you display these two clauses on a single line and display additional clauses on separate lines for readability. As an example, this query lists the last name and country for each employee:

```
SELECT LastName, Country FROM Employees;
```

In processing this statement, Jet goes through each record in the Employees table. For each record in the table, Jet takes the values from LastName and Country and creates a single row in the query result.

 Note

If you create the example query in query Design view and then switch to SQL view, Access includes references to the table name such as Employees.LastName and Employees.Country. Even when only one table exists, Access includes the table name for each field in the SQL statement.

This query lists all fields from the table for each employee:

```
SELECT * FROM Employee;
```

To display a different column name in the query result, use an alias. The following query lists the last name and the date of birth using DOB as an alias for each employee:

```
SELECT LastName, BirthDate AS DOB FROM Employees;
```

In addition to selecting fields that come directly from a table, you can create your own calculated columns. You define a calculated column using expressions based on field values in the table or nested query. When you create a calculated column, you must include an AS clause to provide an alternate name; if you omit the AS clause, Access provides ExprN, where N is an integer, as a default alias. As an example, this query lists the full name and hire year for each employee:

```
SELECT LastName&", "&FirstName AS [Full Name], Year(HireDate) AS Hired
FROM Employees;
```

In processing this query, Jet goes through each record of the Employees table and calculates the Full Name and Hired values based on the data values in the current record. Jet returns the calculated values in a query row.

Use the ORDER BY clause to display the query rows in a particular order. The sort specification can include a list of the items, separated by commas, that you want to use in the sort. The query rows are sorted first by the values in the first item listed. Then rows with the same values in the first item are sorted by the values in the second item listed, and so on. The default sort order is ascending (A to Z or 0 to 9); to sort an item in descending order, follow the item name with the reserved word DESC. The following query lists the employees in the order of country and then by descending hire date:

```
SELECT * FROM Employees
ORDER BY Country, HireDate DESC;
```

19

By default, Jet returns a query row for each table record that satisfies the criteria in the SELECT statement. If the query contains duplicate rows, you can use the DISTINCT reserved word to omit duplicate rows and return only one row for each set of duplicate rows. For example, this query lists the country for each employee using the SQL statement:

```
SELECT Country FROM Employees;
```

Jet returns nine query rows, with a row for each employee. USA appears in five rows and UK in four rows. By contrast, the following SQL statement returns two rows, one for USA and one for UK:

```
SELECT DISTINCT Country FROM Employees;
```

A query that uses the DISTINCT reserved word is not updatable, because each row in the query result may correspond to more than one table row. If you don't include the DISTINCT reserved word in a query based on a single table, Jet assumes you want all rows returned.

 Note

When you create a query in query Design view and switch to SQL view, Access includes the DISTINCTROW reserved word by default. When the query is based on a single table, DISTINCTROW is ignored and all rows including duplicates are returned. The DISTINCT and DISTINCTROW reserved words are called *predicates*.

Specifying Search Conditions

Usually you want to include only some of the rows satisfying the SELECT clause in the query result. To limit the rows, specify a search condition in the WHERE clause. The search condition is an expression that evaluates to True, False, or Null. The search condition can contain up to 40 expressions linked by logical operators. For example, the following query lists employees hired before 1/1/94, sorted by last name:

```
SELECT LastName FROM Employees
WHERE HireDate <#1/1/94#
ORDER BY LastName;
```

If the HireDate for an employee has not been entered, the search condition HireDate <#1/1/94#" returns a Null for that employee.

Conceptually, in processing a simple query based on a single table, Jet selects data values and calculates values as specified in the SELECT clause to create a candidate query row corresponding to each record in the table. Then Jet applies the search condition in the WHERE clause to each row. If the search condition is True, the row continues as a candidate for the query result; if the search condition is False or Null, the row is excluded. If DISTINCT is included, Jet tests the query rows and eliminates duplicate rows. If an ORDER BY clause appears, Jet sorts the remaining query rows.

These examples show SQL statements with WHERE clauses:

▶ List customers with company names beginning with the letter *r* from Argentina or Brazil:

```
SELECT CompanyName FROM Customers
WHERE CompanyName LIKE ("r*") AND Country IN("Argentina", "Brazil");
```

▶ List ship countries for orders placed in the last quarter of 1993:

```
SELECT DISTINCT ShipCountry FROM Orders
WHERE OrderDate BETWEEN #1/10/93# AND #12/31/93#;
```

If you omit the DISTINCT reserved word, the query returns a row for each order placed in the last quarter of 1993.

19

>
> **Note**
> When you enter dates in Criteria cells in query Design view, you can enter a variety of date formats, and Access automatically converts the value to the U.S. short date format. For example, Dec 1, 1993, is converted to #12/1/93# in the design grid. However, when you write an SQL statement, you must use the U.S. short date format and enclose the date in number (#) symbols.

Joining Tables

Many queries are based on data from more than one table. The real power of SQL as the language of relational databases is that SQL enables you to combine and retrieve data from two or more related tables (or queries) and return rows in a query result as if you had a single table. For example, the Northwind database contains separate tables for employees and orders. The tables are related because each record in the Orders table contains the EmployeeID of the employee who handled the order. You have several ways to combine two tables with Access SQL.

You can combine the two tables in a product (called the *Cartesian product*) by including all possible pairs of records from the two tables. Each pair of records is combined into a row in the product. For example, the following query lists all possible combinations of employees and orders:

```
SELECT Employees.EmployeeID, Orders. OrderID FROM Employees, Orders;
```

This query produces a total of 7,470 rows (9 employees×830 orders), but this result has no real significance. Normally, Cartesian products have no meaning in database applications. When you create a query based on two tables in the query Design grid and omit the join lines between the tables, the result is the Cartesian product.

When you create *joins*, you are removing rows from the Cartesian product. When you select from the Cartesian product only the rows where an *exact match* occurs between two columns, the result is an *inner join* (also called an *equi-join*). When you join two tables in query Design view by dragging between matching fields, you are creating an inner join.

Access SQL has two ways to express an inner join operation. One way is to create a search condition for the match. For example, this query lists all orders with the last name of the employee who handled the order:

```
SELECT Employees.LastName, Orders. OrderID FROM Employees, Orders
WHERE Employees.EmployeeID= Orders.EmployeeID;
```

The second way to express the join operation uses a modified FROM clause:

```
SELECT Employees.LastName, Orders. OrderID
FROM Employees INNER JOIN Orders ON Employees.EmployeeID= Orders.EmployeeID;
```

In this version, the two tables to be joined are explicitly connected with the INNER JOIN operation, and the join search condition is specified in an ON clause in the modified FROM clause. More generally, the join search condition can be any condition that specifies criteria used to match rows in the two tables. The syntax for a modified FROM clause is shown here:

```
FROM table1 INNER JOIN table2 ON join search condition
```

Conceptually, in processing a simple query with two tables, Jet considers each row of the Cartesian product formed as a pair of records from the two tables specified in the FROM clause. For each row, Jet determines or calculates the values in the select items list and creates a candidate row for the query results.

The search condition in the WHERE clause or the join search condition in the modified FROM clause compares the value of a field in a record in one table with the value of a field in a record in the second table. If the search condition is True, the row is kept; if the search condition is False or Null, the row is discarded. If DISTINCT is included, Jet tests for duplicate candidate rows and eliminates duplicates. If the DISTINCTROW reserved word is included and the select items list includes values from only one of the tables, Jet tests for duplicate records in that table and eliminates the corresponding candidate query rows. If an ORDER BY clause appears, Jet sorts the remaining candidate query rows and produces the query result.

If you omit OrderID as a display field in the earlier example, the query result contains duplicate rows. To see the difference between DISTINCT and DISTINCTROW, first add a new employee (EmployeeID = 10) with last name King and first name Mary to the Employees table. Then add a new order (OrderID = 11078) handled by the new employee to the Orders table. You now have 831 orders and 10 employees, including two employees with King for the last name. This query displays 831 rows with a separate row for each order:

```
SELECT Employees.LastName
FROM Employees INNER JOIN Orders ON Employees.EmployeeID= Orders.EmployeeID;
```

This query displays nine rows with a separate row for each different last name:

```
SELECT DISTINCT Employees.LastName
FROM Employees INNER JOIN Orders ON Employees.EmployeeID= Orders.EmployeeID;
```

Using DISTINCT omits rows that contain duplicate data in the displayed fields. By contrast, the following query displays ten rows with a separate row for each employee:

```
SELECT DISTINCTROW Employees.LastName
FROM Employees INNER JOIN Orders ON Employees.EmployeeID= Orders.EmployeeID;
```

Using DISTINCTROW omits rows from the query that are based on duplicate records in the table containing the displayed fields, not just on duplicate displayed fields. In this example, the displayed field is from the Employees table, which contains no duplicate records, so the query produces a row corresponding to each row in the Employees table. In a two-table query, DISTINCTROW has an effect when you display records from only one of the tables; DISTINCTROW is ignored if you display records from both tables.

When Jet performs the inner join operation, it creates a candidate query row for each pair of table records that satisfy the join search condition. In contrast, in an *outer join* operation, Jet creates a candidate query row corresponding to each record in one table, whether or not the record matches a record in the second table. For each record in the first table that has a matching record in the second table, Jet creates a query row based on the two matching records.

 Note

When you create a query with joined tables in query Design view, you can change the join to an outer join by clicking the join line, selecting Join Properties, and selecting an outer join option in the Join dialog box.

In the *left outer join* operation, for each record in the first table that doesn't match a record in the second table, Jet creates a query row using null values for the fields from the second table. In the *right outer join* operation, for each record in the second table that doesn't match a record in the first table, Jet creates a query row using null values for the fields from the first table. As an example, the following query to list customers and matching orders with unmatched customers is a left outer join:

```
SELECT Customers.CustomerID, Orders.OrderID
FROM Customers LEFT JOIN Orders ON Customers.CustomerID = Orders.CustomerID;
```

The query result includes 832 rows, one row for each of the 830 orders with a matching customer and two rows for the two customers without matching orders. (These two query rows have null values in the OrderID column.) The query to list customers and matching orders with unmatched orders is a right outer join:

```
SELECT Customers.CustomerID, Orders.OrderID
FROM Customers RIGHT JOIN Orders ON Customers.CustomerID = Orders.CustomerID;
```

The query includes 831 rows, one row for each of the 830 orders with a matching customer and one row for the one order without a matching customer (you added this order with OrderID = 11078 earlier in this section).

Figure 19.5 shows the relationship between the clauses in a SQL statement and the cells in query Design view for the Quarterly Orders query, with the original query modified to sort the rows by country.

Fig. 19.5

Each clause in an SQL statement corresponds to specific cells in the query Design window.

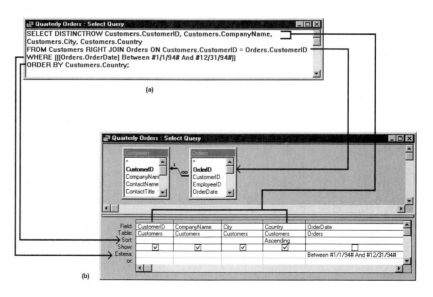

When you want to create a query that involves a relationship between a table and itself, include a second copy of the table and use an AS clause in the modified FROM clause to specify an alias that distinguishes between the two tables (see Chapter 18 for information on self-joins). For example, the following query lists the names of the employees and their supervisors:

```
SELECT Employees.LastName, Employees.FirstName, Supervisors.LastName
FROM Employees INNER JOIN Employees AS Supervisors
➥ON Employees.ReportsTo = Supervisors.EmployeeID;
```

Performing Summary Calculations

You can perform summary calculations on a column of values using the SQL aggregate functions. Use these functions to calculate summaries for the values in a column for all rows that satisfy the selection criteria. (See Chapter 18 for a parallel discussion.)

In the simplest case, you perform summary calculations on a column's values for all the rows. For example, this query finds the average value of the product price:

```
SELECT AVG(UnitPrice) AS [Average Price] FROM Products;
```

This query returns a single row with the Average Price.

When you use an SQL aggregate function (or any expression) in an item in the select list, you must include a name for the calculated column using an AS clause in the SELECT clause. You can use SQL aggregate functions in expressions in the select list, but Access does not allow you to use an SQL aggregate function as an argument of another SQL aggregate function. Also, if any item in the select list includes an SQL aggregate function, then all items in the select list must include SQL aggregate functions. For example, suppose that you want to display a list of products and the average product price, and you try to execute this SQL statement:

```
SELECT AVG(UnitPrice) AS [Average Price], ProductID FROM Products;
```

Access displays the error message `'ProductID' not part of aggregate function or grouping.` Instead, you can achieve the desired result by using the DAvg() domain aggregate function as follows:

```
SELECT DAvg("UnitPrice", "Products") AS [Average Price], ProductID FROM Products;
```

See Chapter 18 for a discussion of the domain aggregate functions.

You can perform summary calculations on several columns. For example, the following query finds the highest and lowest product prices and counts the number of products ordered:

```
SELECT MIN(Products.UnitPrice) AS Minimum, MAX(Products.UnitPrice) AS Maximum,
➥COUNT(*) AS [Number of Products]
FROM Products INNER JOIN [Order Details]
➥ON Products.ProductID = [Order Details].ProductID;
```

This query produces a single row containing the summary values. Using the asterisk instead of UnitPrice as the argument of the COUNT() function ensures that all products are counted even if the UnitPrice fields for some products have null values.

When you want to calculate summaries for some, but not all of the rows, you use a WHERE clause to limit the rows. For example, to calculate the same summaries for current products only (not discontinued products), use this query:

```
SELECT MIN(Products.UnitPrice) AS Minimum, MAX(Products.UnitPrice) AS Maximum,
➥COUNT(*) AS [Number of Products]
FROM Products INNER JOIN [Order Details]
➥ON Products.ProductID = [Order Details].ProductID
WHERE Products.Discontinued = No;
```

Conceptually, in processing a query with SQL aggregate functions to calculate summary values based on all the rows, Jet considers each row of the Cartesian product based on the tables in the FROM clause. Jet applies the join search condition in the modified FROM clause and excludes the rows for which the join search condition is False or Null. Jet applies the search condition in the WHERE clause to each remaining row and excludes the rows for which the search condition is False or Null.

If DISTINCT is included, Jet tests the remaining rows for duplicates and omits duplicate rows. If DISTINCTROW is included and the select list includes fields from some (but not all) of the tables, Jet tests for duplicate records in the tables that contribute fields to the select list and omits corresponding candidate query rows. Finally, Jet calculates the summary value for each SQL aggregate function using all the column values for the remaining rows and displays the summary values in a single summary row as the query result.

In the preceding SQL statement example, Jet creates the candidate rows satisfying the modified FROM clause, applies the WHERE search condition to retain only the rows corresponding to the current products, and then performs the summary calculations. The query Design view for this SQL statement is shown in figure 19.6a. If you create the query in query Design view, you can include a Total row to select the SQL aggregate functions and to display the WHERE condition for the Discontinued field (see fig. 19.6b).

In these examples, the SQL aggregate functions are used to produce a single Total row containing the summary calculations based on the values in columns for all the selected query rows. You can also create sets of subtotal rows by grouping the selected query rows according to values in one or more columns, as described in the next section.

Fig. 19.6
Two versions of query
Design view corre-
spond to the SQL
statement: (a) without
a Total row and (b)
with a Total row.

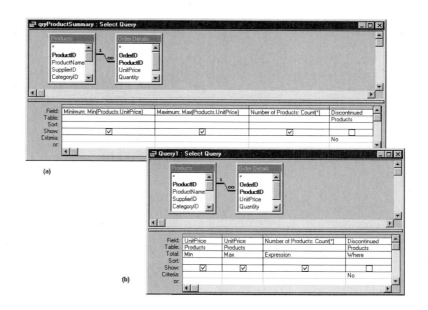

(a)

(b)

19

Grouping Records

You can use SQL to group records that have identical values in one or more fields using the GROUP BY clause. After you create groups, you can use a HAVING clause to specify a group search condition for including or excluding groups. The basic SELECT statement for a grouped query based on two tables contains six clauses:

```
SELECT select items
FROM table1 [LEFT¦RIGHT¦INNER] JOIN table2 ON join search condition
WHERE search condition
GROUP BY grouping select list
HAVING group search condition
ORDER BY sort specification;
```

The SELECT clause for a grouped query lists the data items to be displayed in the query result. The select items can be fields from tables, constants, or calculated items that may include SQL aggregate functions. Calculated items must include an AS clause with an item name for an alias. Each select item in the list either must include an SQL aggregate function or must be included in the GROUP BY list.

The GROUP BY clause lists the data items to be used for grouping. The grouping select items can refer to any fields from the tables listed in the FROM clause, but they cannot refer to fields with the Memo or OLE Object data type and cannot contain SQL aggregate functions. You can include up to ten grouping select items.

The HAVING clause is an optional clause that you use to specify which groups created with the GROUP BY clause you want to include in the query results. The group search condition tests each group; if you don't specify a group search condition, all groups are included. The group search condition can contain up to 40 expressions combined with logical operators.

As an example, suppose you want to display the OrderID and the total value of the Order for all Orders that totaled more than $500. The Order Detail table contains information about the prices charged to customers, so that's the table you need to query.

But the records in Order Details do not provide information about the Order total—just about the individual products included in the Order. The level of detail you want is each Order, and you want to display the sum of the price charged for each product in that Order.

The solution is to group the records in Order Details by OrderID, and display the sum of the price charged in each of those records. The result will be the sum of the price of the products sold in that Order. Here is the SQL statement to get that result:

```
SELECT OrderID, Sum(UnitPrice*Quantity) AS Subtotal FROM [Order Details]
GROUP BY OrderID;
```

You want to display the OrderID and the sum of the order, so those are included in the SELECT clause. To get the sum, use the SQL aggregate Sum function. To display the sum, you must provide an AS clause to give the sum an alias. Here, choose the alias Subtotal.

As usual, the FROM clause tells Access which table to use. The GROUP BY clause tells Access to base each subtotal—the total Order amount—on the OrderID. Access will return the total of the UnitPrice times the Quantity for each Product in the Order.

This isn't quite what you want, though. There's a discount applied to each product in each record of Order Details. Also, you want to display the results in currency format. So, complicate the first line of the statement to account for the discount and to obtain the currency format as follows:

```
SELECT OrderID, Sum(CCur(UnitPrice*Quantity*(1-Discount/100)*100)) AS Subtotal
FROM [Order Details]
GROUP BY OrderID;
```

Now suppose you want to display only those Order totals that came to more than 500 dollars. That's where the HAVING clause comes into play:

```
SELECT OrderID, Sum(CCur(UnitPrice*Quantity*(1-Discount/100)*100)) AS Subtotal
FROM [Order Details]
GROUP BY OrderID
HAVING Sum(CCur(UnitPrice*Quantity*(1-Discount/100)*100) > 500;
```

Conceptually, in processing a grouped query with SQL aggregate functions, Jet considers each row of the Cartesian product based on the tables in the FROM clause. Jet applies the join search condition in the modified FROM clause and excludes the rows for which the join search condition is False or Null. Jet applies the search condition in the WHERE clause to each remaining row and excludes the rows for which the search condition is False or Null.

If the query has a GROUP BY clause, Jet arranges the remaining rows into groups according to the grouping select list; the rows in each group have identical values for every grouping select item. If the query has a HAVING clause, Jet applies the group search condition to each group and excludes groups for which the group search condition is False or Null. If DISTINCT is included, Jet tests the remaining rows for duplicates and omits duplicate rows. If DISTINCTROW is included and the select list includes fields from some (but not all) of the tables, Jet tests for duplicate records in the tables that contribute fields to the select list and omits corresponding candidate query rows.

For each remaining group, Jet calculates the summary value for each SQL aggregate function using all the column values for the rows in the group. Jet creates a query row with the summary values. If the query has an ORDER BY clause, Jet sorts the summary query rows and displays the summary rows as the query result.

Continuing with the example, suppose you want to include only order items with a discount greater than 20 percent in the order subtotals, and display only the orders with restricted subtotals exceeding 500 dollars. To solve this problem, you need a WHERE clause to restrict the order items before grouping them into orders and a HAVING clause to select the orders for the final result, as follows:

```
SELECT OrderID, Sum(CCur(UnitPrice*Quantity*(1-Discount/100)*100) AS Subtotal
FROM [Order Details]
WHERE Discount > .20
GROUP BY OrderID
HAVING Sum(CCur(UnitPrice*Quantity*(1-Discount/100)*100) > 500;
```

This query returns records for the 44 orders with subtotals that are based on items with discounts exceeding 20 percent; each subtotal must also exceed 500 dollars.

Modifying Tables

You can use SQL to create the four action queries: append, update, delete, and make-table queries. In each type of action query, you use an optional WHERE clause to restrict the records that the action query operates on.

The following SQL statement creates an append query that copies existing records from another table or query and adds them to a table or query in the same database:

```
INSERT INTO target [(fieldlist)]
SELECT select list FROM sourceexpression
WHERE append condition;
```

In this statement, *target* is the name of the table or query to which you want to append records, and *fieldlist* is the optional list of fields to which you are appending data. The *sourceexpression* is the name of the table or query from which you are copying existing records, and *select list* is the list of fields with the data you are copying in the *sourceexpression*. The *sourceexpression* can also be the result of join operations on tables.

If individual fields being copied are not specified in the select list, then the names of the fields being copied must match the field names in the table to which you are appending the records. As an example, if Import List is a table of imported customer data with the same structure as the Customers table, then the SQL statement to append the imported records looks like this:

```
INSERT INTO Customers
SELECT [Import List].* FROM [Import List];
```

The SQL statement to create a delete query that removes records from a table looks like this:

```
DELETE [tablename.* ] FROM sourceexpression
WHERE delete condition;
```

In this statement, *sourceexpression* is the name of the table or the result of join operations on tables from which you are deleting records. When *sourceexpression* includes only one table, the *tablename* in the DELETE clause is optional; otherwise you must specify the *tablename* as the name of the table from which records are deleted. As an example, this SQL statement deletes the records for the customers from Germany:

```
DELETE * FROM Customers
WHERE [Country] = "Germany";
```

This SQL statement creates an update query to change the values of specified fields in a table:

```
UPDATE tableexpression
SET valueexpressionlist
WHERE update condition;
```

In this statement, *tableexpression* is the name of the table or the result of join operations on tables that contain the fields you want to update. The *valueexpressionlist* is a list of expressions that determine the value to be inserted in a particular field; the expressions in the list are separated with commas. As an example, this SQL statement increases the unit price for all beverages by five percent:

```
UPDATE Categories INNER JOIN Products ON Categories.CategoryID = Products.CategoryID
SET Products.UnitPrice = UnitPrice*1.05
WHERE Categories.CategoryName = "beverages";
```

The following SQL statement produces a make-table query that creates a new table and copies existing records from another table in the same database:

```
SELECT fieldlist INTO newtable FROM sourceexpression
WHERE append condition;
```

In this statement, *fieldlist* is the list of field names to be copied, and *newtable* is the name of the new table you are creating. The *sourceexpression* is the name of the table or the result of join operations on tables from which you are copying records. As an example, this SQL statement creates a new table called tblBeverages that contains product information for beverages:

```
SELECT Products.* INTO tblBeverages FROM Categories INNER JOIN Products
➡ON Categories.CategoryID = Products.CategoryID
WHERE Categories.CategoryName = "beverages";
```

You can use an IN clause to modify these statements so they create or modify tables in another database (search INSERT INTO, DELETE, UPDATE, and SELECT...INTO in online help for more information).

19

Understanding SQL-Specific Queries

You can create all the queries discussed in the preceding section in query Design view or SQL view. However, you cannot create the queries called SQL-specific queries (or SQL queries) in query Design view (at least in the current version of Access). This section discusses five kinds of SQL-specific queries.

Using Non-Equi Joins

All the join search conditions used in the join operations in the preceding section are based on equality. In some cases, you may need to create joins that are not based on equality; such *non-equi joins* cannot be created or displayed in query Design view. As an example, the following query lists orders where the quantity of an item ordered exceeds the stock quantity for that item:

```
SELECT [Order Details].OrderID, [Order Details].ProductID
FROM Products INNER JOIN [Order Details]
➡ON Products.ProductID = [Order Details].ProductID
➡AND [Order Details].Quantity > Products.UnitsInStock;
```

Using Single-Record Append Queries

A SQL-specific version of an append query enables you to specify the value of each field in a single new record and then append the record to an existing table or query. The SQL statement for a single-record append query is as follows:

```
INSERT INTO target [(fieldlist)]
VALUES valuelist;
```

In this statement, *target* is the name of the table or query to which you are appending the new record, and *fieldlist* is the list of the field names, separated by commas, to which you are appending the values. The *valuelist* is the list of the values you are inserting into the specific fields of the new record; separate the values with commas and enclose text values in double quotes. Values are inserted into fields by their corresponding position in the lists. As an example, this query adds a new category to the Categories table:

```
INSERT INTO Categories (CategoryName, Description)
VALUES ("Packaging Products", "Plastic jars, paper wrappings");
```

Using Union Queries

Sometimes you want to merge the results of two or more independent queries or tables into a single query result. Here are two examples:

▶ Merge the lists of customers and suppliers into a single list.

▶ List the products where the unit price exceeds $100 or a single order includes an order for more than $5,000 of the product.

Access SQL includes the UNION operation to create a merged list as a *union query*. You can use the UNION operation to merge the results of two or more tables, queries, or SELECT statements. This SQL statement merges two tables, queries, or SELECT statements:

```
[TABLE] query1 UNION [TABLE] query2
[ORDER BY sort specification];
```

In this statement, *query1* and *query2* can each be the name of a query, a table (in which case the table name is preceded by the TABLE reserved word), or a SELECT statement. The items being merged must contain the same numbers of fields, but the fields need not have the same name or data type. The column names of the first item are used in the result. The *sort specification* in the optional ORDER BY clause must be based on the column names of the first item. No duplicate records are returned when you use the UNION operator; to return duplicate records use the UNION ALL operator instead. For example:

▶ Merge the lists of customers and suppliers into a single list and sort by company name:

```
TABLE Customers UNION TABLE Suppliers
ORDER BY CompanyName;
```

▶ List the products where the unit price exceeds $100 or a single order includes an order for more than $5,000 of the product:

```
SELECT ProductID FROM Products
WHERE UnitPrice>100
```

```
UNION
SELECT ProductID FROM [Order Details]
WHERE UnitPrice*Quantity>5000;
```

Using a Subquery: a Query within a Query

A *subquery* is a query whose results are passed on to another query. Often requests are expressed in terms of the results of another query. As an example, in Chapter 18, the query created by the Find Duplicates Query Wizard to list employees from the same city contained a subquery in a Criteria cell. Here are some other examples of requests that use subqueries:

▶ List the products whose unit price exceeds the average price of all products.

▶ List the products whose unit price is greater than the price of any product sold at a discount exceeding 20%.

▶ List the products that sold at a discount exceeding 20%.

▶ List the products whose unit price exceeds the average of all products in the same category.

In this section, you can create queries for these examples.

You can use a subquery in the select list of a SELECT statement, the search condition of a WHERE clause, or the group search condition of a HAVING clause. A subquery must be a SELECT statement following the rules of any SELECT statement, except that the ending semicolon is omitted and the subquery is enclosed in parentheses. Not all queries can be subqueries: a subquery must produce a single column of data and cannot contain the UNION operator or an ORDER BY clause. Some subqueries can be run as stand-alone queries independent of the main query; other queries refer to column names in the main query and cannot be run independently. Not all queries can contain a subquery: the main query can be a select or an action query but not a crosstab or a union query. You can create the main query in the query Design grid and type in the SQL statement for the subquery.

When the subquery is part of a search condition of a WHERE clause or is part of the group search condition of a HAVING clause, you can use any of the *subquery search conditions*:

Comparison. Compares the value of an expression to a single value produced by a subquery using any of the comparison operators: <, >, =, <=, >=, <>.

Membership. Tests the value of an expression to determine if the value matches any of a set of values produced by a subquery using the IN operator.

Existence. Tests to determine if the subquery produces any values using the EXISTS reserved word.

Quantified Comparison. Compares the value of an expression to each value produced by a subquery. When you use the ANY reserved word, if any one of the comparisons is True, the search condition is True. When you use the ALL reserved word, if all of the comparisons are True, the search condition is True.

This section creates the queries with subqueries for the following examples:

▶ List the products whose unit price exceeds the average price of all products:

```
SELECT * FROM Products
WHERE UnitPrice > (SELECT AVG(UnitPrice) FROM Products);
```

The subquery is a summary query that produces a single value: the average price of all products. The main query compares the unit price to the calculated average.

▶ List the products whose unit price is greater than the price of any product sold at a discount exceeding 20 percent.

This time, you want to compare the current price of each product with the actual sale prices of products that sold at a large discount. You only want to consider products that sold at a discount of at least 20 percent. The current prices are stored in the Products table, but the actual sales prices and the discount rates are in the Order Details table. The subquery searches the Order Details table to find actual sales prices for any item that sold with a discount greater than 20 percent. The result of the subquery is a list of the sales prices for these items. The main query compares the current price of a product to this list keeping the product if its price exceeds all values in the list and discarding the product otherwise. Here is the query:

```
SELECT * FROM Products
WHERE UnitPrice > ANY (SELECT UnitPrice FROM [Order Details]
➥WHERE Discount > .20);
```

You use the ANY keyword to retain a product if its current price is greater than at least one of the sales prices returned by the subquery (76 such products exist). Use the All keyword instead if you want to keep a product only if its current price is greater than the largest of the prices returned by the subquery (only one such product exists).

▶ List the products that sold at a discount exceeding 20 percent.

As in the last example, the subquery searches the Order Details table, but this time the subquery returns a list of IDs for products that sold at a discount greater than 20 percent. The main query returns product information for each of the product IDs in the list. Here is the query:

```
SELECT * FROM Products
WHERE ProductID IN (SELECT ProductID FROM [Order Details]➡
WHERE Discount > .20)
```

In each of the preceding examples, the subquery is independent—you can copy the subquery to a new SQL view window and run the query as a stand-alone query. Next, look at an example where the subquery depends on a field in the main query and cannot be run as a stand-alone query. Because this query is more complex, you build it piece by piece.

▶ List the products whose unit price exceeds the average of all products in the same category.

For each product in the Products table, the subquery must calculate the average price of all the products in the same category. The main query includes the product only if its current price is greater than the category average. For example, when the main query considers Aniseed Syrup, a condiment, the subquery computes the average price for all condiments as $23.06. Then, the main query tests and rejects Aniseed Syrup because its current price of 10 dollars is less than the average condiment price. The subquery depends on the main query because the subquery must refer back to the main query to get the product's CategoryID. The subquery looks through a copy of the Products table to find all the products with the same CategoryID; you use an alias to refer to the subquery's copy to distinguish it from the main query's copy. The subquery calculates the average price using the following SELECT statement:

```
SELECT AVG(UnitPrice) FROM Products AS Copy
WHERE Copy.CategoryID = Products.CategoryID;
```

The main query includes a product only if its price is greater than the category average as follows:

```
SELECT * FROM Products
WHERE UnitPrice > (SELECT AVG(UnitPrice) FROM Products AS Copy
➡WHERE Copy.CategoryID = Products.CategoryID);
```

This query produces a listing of 27 products.

Creating Tables and Indexes

Using SQL, you can create new tables, define new indexes for fields in an existing table, alter an existing table, create relationships, and delete existing tables or existing indexes. You can use Access SQL's data definition language to create data definition queries for these tasks as shown in Table 19.2.

Table 19.2   SQL Statements for Data Definition Queries

SQL Statement	Description
CREATE TABLE	Use to create a new table and specify the name, data type, and field size of each field. Use the CONSTRAINT clause to define indexes, a primary key, and foreign key fields.
ALTER TABLE	Use to modify the design of an existing table including adding new fields and deleting existing fields. Use the CONSTRAINT clause to add new indexes or keys and delete existing indexes or keys.
CREATE INDEX	Use to create a new index for an existing field in a table.
DROP	Use to delete an existing index from a table or to delete an existing table from the database.

As a simple example, the following SQL query creates a new table called tblFriends with LastName, FirstName, and SSN as three Text fields.

```
CREATE TABLE tblFriends (LastName TEXT, FirstName TEXT, SSN TEXT)
```

Considering Performance: Stored Queries versus SQL Statements

After you create a query in query Design view or in SQL view, you can save it as a *stored query* under a name listed in the Database window. You run a stored select query in one of several ways: by opening it in Datasheet view from the Database window, by opening a form or report that has the stored query as its record source or as the row source of a control, or by opening a query or table that has the query as the row source of a lookup field. You can run a stored select query or an action query programmatically using the OpenQuery macro action or method. You can also run a stored action query as a QueryDef object using the Execute method (see the following section).

As an alternative to storing a query as a separate database object, you can enter the equivalent SQL statement directly as the RecordSource or RowSource property setting for an object, as a macro argument, or as part of VBA code. In these cases, the SQL statement runs when it is called by the object it is part of. For example, if you enter an SQL statement as the RecordSource for a form, the statement runs when you open or requery the form. You can run an SQL statement that modifies data using the RunSQL macro action or method. Additionally, you can use the Execute method to run an SQL statement in a query you created in code using the CreateQueryDef method (see the following section).

As a general rule, running a stored query is faster than running an SQL statement. A stored query runs faster because it is optimized. The first time you run a new or modified query, Jet creates a query plan to optimize the execution; when you save the query, you also save the query plan. When you run the query subsequently, you run the optimized version. On the other hand, when you execute an SQL statement, the SQL statement must be optimized each time. See Chapter 18 for more information.

 Note

Similar performance considerations apply to the domain aggregate functions: a domain aggregate function is a special form of an SQL statement that returns a single value. When you use a domain aggregate function, you are actually running an unoptimized SQL statement. As a result, avoid using the domain aggregate functions if another method is available.

Creating and Modifying Database Objects Programmatically

You can create all the Database window objects (tables, queries, forms, reports, macros, and modules) interactively using the Design views in Access. When you want to create objects programmatically, you can use the programming language of Access, Visual Basic for Applications.

Beginning with Access 2.0, Microsoft added the data access objects (DAO) language that enables you to create and modify not only tables and queries, but also databases and security objects. You can use DAO to add, edit, and delete records by navigating through the records of the database. DAO is a special-purpose language component that Access VBA uses to work with the data access objects.

In Visual Basic you work with objects such as forms, reports, and controls. Each object has its own set of *properties* that define its characteristics such as size, color, and caption, plus its own set of *methods* that define the actions the object can do such as Close, Requery, and PrintOut. Some objects also have a set of events (an *event* is a change in the object's state that the object recognizes and that you can respond to with code or a macro). VBA is not a stand-alone programming language; VBA is embedded within a host application, and you must run the host application to run a VBA program. VBA is currently embedded in two of the Microsoft Office for Windows 95 applications: Excel and Access. VBA is also embedded in Microsoft Project. When you are running Access as the host application, you can use Access VBA to manipulate four kinds of objects:

▶ Objects that Access itself provides as the Access application objects: Application (refers to the Access application itself), Screen, DoCmd, Control, Form, and Report, and their collections Controls, Forms, and Reports.

▶ Objects provided by other applications (for example, the 131 objects of Microsoft Excel and the one object of Microsoft Word). Any application that conforms to the OLE Automation standards can provide objects that you can manipulate with VBA.

▶ Objects that you create using the NEW capability in VBA, which was added in Microsoft Access for Windows 95.

▶ Objects provided by the Jet database engine. Jet provides objects for defining and manipulating a database: tables, queries, indexes, relationships, security objects. These objects are the data access objects, or DAO. The Jet database engine conforms to the OLE Automation standards.

Talking to the Jet Database Engine with DAO

You can think of the data access objects as the language that the Jet database engine uses for communication. You use VBA to "talk" to Jet when you want to manipulate programmatically the objects that Jet manages. The kinds of operations you can control programmatically include running queries to select or modify records; finding individual records; creating databases, tables, indexes, relationships, and queries; moving among individual records in a set to update, add, or delete individual records; and connecting to remote sources of data.

There are 31 data access objects, including the DBEngine object that represents the Jet engine itself, 15 objects in collections, and the corresponding 15 collections. (The collections are named using the plural of the object name. For example, Errors is the name of the collection object for the Error object.) The following table describes the three objects that Jet uses to manage security and multiuser use:

Object	Description
User	Refers to information about an individual user. This object is stored in the workgroup information file and used to establish access permissions for individual objects by assigning a user to a group. This object also is used to establish passwords for the user.
Group	Refers to a group of users. This object is stored in the workgroup information file and used to establish access permissions for users assigned to the group.
Workspace	Refers to a Jet *session* (a session begins when a user logs in and ends when the user logs off). All Jet operations during the session are governed by the user's permissions. This object is created as needed, not stored.

The following table describes the eight objects Jet uses to manage the database:

Object	Description
Database	Refers to an Access database (an .MDB file) or an external data source (an ODBC data source). Saved in the database.
TableDef	Refers to tables stored in a database as local tables or linked tables in external databases. Saved in the database.
QueryDef	Refers to a query stored in a Jet database (.MDB file). Saved in the database.
Field	Represents a column of data contained as a field in a TableDef, QueryDef, Index, Relation, or Recordset object. Saved in the database only for the first four objects.
Index	Refers to the object used to specify the order of records retrieved from a TableDef object. Saved in the database.
Relation	Refers to the object used to establish relationships between fields in tables or queries. Saved in the database.
Parameter	Refers to the parameter you supply to a parameter query before it can run. Saved in the database.
Recordset	Refers to a set of records in a table in a Jet database or records that result from running a query. You use two kinds of Recordset objects (Table and Dynaset) to retrieve, update, add, or delete records, and a third kind of Recordset object (Snapshot) to retrieve only. This object is created as needed, not saved.

19

There are two DAO objects for keeping track of all of the objects you create and save in an Access database: the Document object and the Container object. There is a Document object for each saved object. An object's Document object holds administrative details for the object. For example, there is a Document object for each saved query that holds the query's name, the date and time it was created, and who has permission to use the query. There are Document objects for the database itself and for each of the tables, queries, and the relationships you create in the Relationships window. Additionally, there are Document objects for each of the forms, reports, macros, and modules.

There is a Container object for each category of saved object. Jet puts tables and queries in the same category, so the categories are databases, tables and queries, saved relationships, forms, reports, macros, and modules. A category's Container object holds the administrative details for the category. For example, the Tables Container object holds administrative details for the collection of Document objects for the tables and saved queries. The details held in a Container object include who owns the object and who has permission to use it. Although the Document and Container objects contain information about saved objects, it is interesting to note that Document and Container objects are not saved—they are recreated each time you open the database.

The Error object refers to the information describing an error that occurs during an operation with a data access object; the Error object is not saved to the file.

Finally, the Property object refers to a property of a data access object; the property may be built-in or one that you create. If an object is saved to a file, so are its Property objects. Each data access object except the Error object has a built-in Properties collection. Figure 19.7 shows the data access objects hierarchy as displayed in online help. Note that the figure doesn't display the individual object's Properties collection containing the Property objects.

Fig. 19.7

The data access objects hierarchy shows the relationships between the objects. Note that the Properties and Property objects are not shown in this figure.

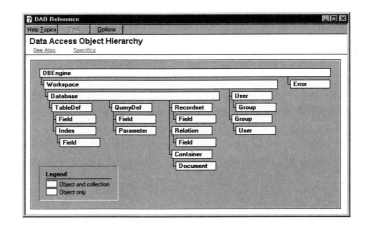

The 31 data access objects represent, or model, the physical objects that make up the database. When you manipulate a data access object programmatically by setting its properties or asking it to complete one of its methods using VBA, the result is that the physical object is actually manipulated when you run the VBA program. The property of the physical object changes or the physical object executes the behavior you requested.

To manipulate an object, you must first refer to it. To refer to a specific data access object, you start at the top of the hierarchy and traverse to the object, using the dot operator to move along the path. To refer to a specific object in a collection, you can use any of the references shown in Table 19.3.

Table 19.3   Ways to Refer to an Object in a Collection

Syntax	Purpose
collectionname!objectname	To refer to the object in the collection by its name using the exclamation point operator.
collectionname("objectname") or collectionname (objectvariable)	To refer to the object in the collection by its name or by using a String variable to refer to the object.
collectionname(index)	To refer to the object in the collection by the index number assigned to the object. The index number for an individual object is assigned according to the order in which it is created or loaded into memory. The index number may change when other objects in the collection are unloaded. The index is zero-based.

The syntax you use depends on your purpose. When you open an Access database, a Workspace object is opened automatically as the first object in the Workspaces collection. You can use this index reference: `Workspaces(0)`. You can refer to the current database explicitly by its name using either of the first two references, or because Workspace is the first object in the Databases collection, you can use the index reference: `Databases(0)`. Therefore, when you want to talk to Jet from Visual Basic, you can traverse the hierarchy to the current database using this syntax:

```
DbEngine.Workspaces(0).Databases(0)
```

When you write a VBA program, you usually create variables to assign temporary storage locations in memory for the values you want to modify in the program. You use an *object variable* to refer, or *point to*, an object. You declare, or *dimension*, the object variable and specify the type of object the variable refers to using a `Dim` statement as follows:

```
Dim object variable As object type
```

Object type is either the generic Object data type or any of the data access object types such Database, QueryDef, Recordset, or Field. You use the `Set` keyword to point the object variable to a specific object. For example, if you use `MyDb` as an object variable that points to the current database, you declare the variable and assign the variable to the current database as follows:

```
Dim MyDb As Database
Set MyDb = DbEngine.Workspaces(0).Databases(0)
```

Access 95 provides another way to refer to the current database. The CurrentDb function returns an object variable that represents the current database. Using the CurrentDb function, the Set statement is as such:

```
Set MyDb = CurrentDb
```

Defining New Data Access Objects

You can programmatically create and modify databases; create and modify tables, fields, and indexes; and create and modify relationships between the tables. You can also programmatically link tables from external databases and maintain the database by compacting and repairing it. When creating or modifying objects, you can define new custom properties. You can create objects to manage multiuser environments and to provide security.

Objects that know how to create other objects have Create methods. As examples, the Database object has CreateTableDef, CreateRelation, and CreateQueryDef methods, and the TableDef object has CreateField and CreateIndex methods. You create a new object by following these steps:

1. Use one of the Create methods to create the object.

2. Define the object's characteristics by setting its properties.

3. Use the object's Append method to append it to its collection.

For example, you can create a new table using these steps:

1. Use the CreateTableDef method of the Database object. Enter a unique name of the new TableDef object as a string.

2. Use the CreateField method of the Database object. A table must have at least one field.

3. Use the Append method of the Fields collection to append the Field object to the Fields collection of the TableDef object.

4. Use the Append method of the TableDefs collection to append the TableDef object to the TableDefs collection of the Database object. The TableDef's Append method saves the table to the database file.

To try the method, follow these steps:

1. Choose the Modules tab in the Database window and click the New button to open a new module window in NORTHWIND.MDB.

2. Choose Insert, Procedure. Enter **NewTable** as the name and choose the Sub
   option to create a new subroutine. Enter the following subroutine:

```
Public Sub NewTable()
Dim MyDb As Database, MyTable As TableDef, MyField As Field
Set MyDb = CurrentDb
Set MyTable = MyDb.CreateTableDef("Carriers")
Set MyField = MyTable.CreateField("CarrierName", dbText, 30)
MyTable.Fields.Append MyField
MyDb.TableDefs.Append.MyTable
MyDb.TableDefs.Refresh
End Sub
```

A new table isn't displayed immediately in the Database window unless you use the
Refresh method to update the TableDefs collection.

3. To run the subroutine, click the Debug window button on the toolbar, enter the
   name of the subroutine (without the parentheses), and press Enter.

4. Open the new table.

To define a new query, use the CreateQueryDef method of the Database object. Set the
method's first argument to a unique name expressed as a string. To define the query, set
the method's second argument to an SQL statement expressed as a string. As an example,
click the Insert Procedure button on the toolbar, type **NewQuery** as the name, choose
the Sub option, and then enter the following subroutine:

```
Public Sub NewQuery()
Dim MyDb As Database, MyQuery As QueryDef, MySQL As String
Set MyDb = CurrentDb
Set MySQL = "SELECT * FROM Customers WHERE [Country] = 'Brazil'"
Set MyQuery = MyDb.CreateQueryDef("BrazilianCustomers", MySQL)
End Sub
```

> **α Note**
>
> When an SQL statement includes text enclosed in double quotation marks, you
> must replace the double quotes with single quotation marks when you embed the
> SQL statement in a string.

As soon as you create a QueryDef object, it is automatically saved and stored in the database file. You don't have to append a new QueryDef object to the QueryDefs collection.

Tip

You can create a temporary query by setting the name argument of the `CreateQueryDef` to the zero-length string (""). Because a zero-length string isn't a valid name for a stored query, a temporary QueryDef isn't stored in the database file and ceases to exist when the procedure ends.

Manipulating Data

When you work with data programmaticallly, you don't work directly with the TableDef or QueryDef objects. Instead, you create a Recordset object that represents the records of the table or query you want to work with. You create a Recordset object by using the `OpenRecordset` method of the Database object. When you create a Recordset object, you are placing rows of data in a buffer and pointing to one row at a time. The rows are held in memory and are not displayed on-screen. The row you are pointing to is called the *current record.*

When you create a new Recordset object, it is added automatically to the Recordsets collection (the set of open Recordset objects), and you don't need to take any action to append it. A Recordset object is not saved; instead, you create a new Recordset object each time you want to interact with data and destroy it when you are finished using the Close method. A Recordset object created in a VBA procedure exists only while the procedure is executing; when the procedure ends, so does the Recordset object.

There are three kinds of Recordset objects:

▶ *Table Recordset objects* are used to interact with records in a single table in the .MDB file of the open database (but not on a linked external table). Table Recordset objects can retrieve, add, update, and delete records. Indexing and the `Seek` method are allowed only on table Recordset objects.

▶ *Dynaset Recordset objects* are used to interact either with records in a single table or with records returned from a query. Dynaset Recordset objects can retrieve, add, update, and delete records in a single table or tables defined by the query. If you want to manipulate data in a linked table, you have to use a dynaset Recordset object.

▶ *Snapshot Recordset objects* are used to retrieve records from a single table or records returned from a query. Snapshot Recordset objects contain a static, read-only copy of the records stored in the table or tables. This type of recordset is faster than dynaset Recordset objects but is not updatable.

The following examples show how to use the different Recordset objects.

This example opens a dynaset Recordset object for the Customers table and closes the object at the end of the procedure:

```
Sub NewRecordsets()
Dim MyDb As Database, rstCustomers As Recordset
Set MyDb = CurrentDb
Set rstCustomers = MyDb.OpenRecordset("Customers", dbOpenDynaset)
...[statements]
rstCustomers.Close
End Sub
```

To open a dynaset Recordset object based on a query defined as an SQL string, replace the table name with the SQL statement. For example:

```
Set rstCustomers = MyDb.OpenRecordset("SELECT * FROM Customers
➥WHERE [Country] = 'Brazil'" , dbOpenDynaset)
```

To open a dynaset Recordset object based on a stored select query, replace the table name with the name of the stored query:

```
Set rstCustomers = MyDb.OpenRecordset("qryCustomers", dbOpenDynaset)
```

Opening a Recordset object on a select query runs the query and returns the query's result to the buffer. When you want to run an action query, you use the Execute method instead of the OpenRecordset method because there are no records to return when an action query runs.

Note

It is usually faster to open a recordset on a stored query than on an SQL string because the stored query is stored in a compiled state.

When you manipulate data programmatically, remember that the Recordset object points to one record at a time so you must know how to navigate from record to record. You navigate among records using special properties and methods of the Recordset object as follows:

- Use the Sort property to sort a dynaset or snapshot Recordset object. For example, to sort a dynaset Recordset object based on the Customers table by country, use this code:

  ```
  rstCustomers.Sort = "Country"
  ```

- Use the Filter property to apply a filter to a dynaset or snapshot Recordset object. When you set the Filter property, the records of the Recordset object aren't affected and you must open a second Recordset object based on the first one to see the effects of the filter. For example, to apply a filter to a dynaset Recordset object opened on the Customers table that selects only the customers from Brazil, use this code:

```
rstCustomers.Filter = "Country = 'Brazil'"
Set rstCustomers = rstCustomers.OpenRecordset()
```

▶ Use the Index property to sort a table Recordset object. For example, to order a table Recordset object based on the Customers table by an existing index for CompanyName, use this code:

```
Set rstCustomers = MyDb.OpenRecordset("Customers", dbOpenTable)
rstCustomers.Index = "CompanyName"
```

▶ Use the Find methods to move the current record pointer to the first, next, previous, and last occurrences of a record in a dynaset or snapshot Recordset object that meets your criteria. If no such records exist, Jet sets the NoMatch property to True. For example, to find the first record in a dynaset Recordset object for a customer from Brazil, use this code:

```
Set rstCustomers = MyDb.OpenRecordset("Customers", dbOpenDynaset)
rstCustomers.FindFirst "Country = 'Brazil'"
```

▶ Use the Bookmark property to identify a record to which you want to return. Set a string variable to the current record's bookmark (when you create or open a Recordset object, each record has a unique identifying string called a *bookmark*). To return to that record, set the Recordset object's Bookmark property to the value of the variable. For example, after finding the first customer from Brazil, you can store the bookmark for the record in the bmk variable using this code:

```
Dim bmk As String
bmk = rstCustomers.Bookmark
```

Later, to return to the record, you just set the Bookmark property to the stored value as follows:

```
rstCustomers.Bookmark = bmk
```

▶ Use the Seek method to find the first occurrence of a record in a table Recordset object that meets your search condition. The Seek method uses an index to find records. Before you can use the Seek method, you must set the Index property to the name of the index you want to use. The search condition is expressed as a comparison operator (expressed as a string) followed by a comma and the search values in the index field. For example:

```
Set rstCustomers = MyDb.OpenRecordset("Customers", dbOpenTable)
rstCustomers.Index = "CompanyName"
rstCustomers.Seek "=", "The Big Cheese"
```

▶ Use the Move methods to move the current record pointer to the first, next, previous, or last record in a Recordset object. You use the BOF and EOF properties to detect the beginning and end of a recordset. If BOF (or EOF) is True, the current record pointer is before the first record (or after the last record) of the recordset.

You can use the following Recordset methods to modify an individual record:

- ▶ Use the Edit method to modify the current record. After you modify the record, use the Update method to save the changes.

- ▶ Use the AddNew method to add a new record. After you modify the new record, use the Update method to save the changes and add the record to the recordset.

- ▶ Use the Delete method to delete the current record.

The data access object methods are navigational methods because they enable you to move the current record pointer to a record, take action on the record, and then move to another record. Typically, you use a loop to move one by one through the records in a recordset.

As an example of the DAO navigational method, the following code deletes records in the Customers table for all customers from Canada:

```
Sub DeleteCanada()
Dim MyDb As Database, rstCustomers As Recordset
Set MyDb = CurrentDb
Set rstCustomers = MyDb.OpenRecordset("Customers")
Do Until rstCustomers.EOF
    If rstCustomers![Country] = "Canada" Then
        rstCustomers.Delete
    End If
    rstCustomers.MoveNext
Loop
End Sub
```

You start with the first customer record and test the Country field. If Country field is Canada, use the Delete method to delete the record, use the MoveNext method to move to the next record, and repeat the process. You repeat the loop until all the records have been tested; that is, until the EOF property returns the True value indicating the current record is after the last record in the recordset.

Considering Performance: SQL versus DAO

The navigational approach using DAO described in the preceding section usually is slower than the equivalent set approach using SQL. As a general rule, use the SQL approach whenever possible. For example:

- ▶ To sort or filter a recordset or to find a specific record, open the recordset using an SQL string to define the sort or filter or the search condition for the specific record. For example, to open a dynaset Recordset object based on Customers from Brazil and sorted by CompanyName, use this code:

```
Set rstCustomers = MyDb.OpenRecordset("SELECT * FROM Customers
➡WHERE {Country] = 'Brazil' ORDER BY [CompanyName]")
```

▶ To update or delete records that satisfy a criteria, create a new action query or a temporary query using an SQL string to modify the records. Then run the query using the Execute method. For example, to delete the customers from Canada, the following code creates a temporary delete query:

```
Sub DeleteCanadaSQL()
Dim MyDb As Database, MyQuery As QueryDef
Set MyDb = CurrentDb
Set MyQuery = MyDb.CreateQueryDef("",DELETE Country FROM Customers
➥WHERE Country = "Canada")
MyQuery.Execute
End Sub
```

These examples use SQL strings, but using a stored query is even faster because a stored query has been compiled and optimized. To run an existing select query, you open a Recordset object based on the query. To run an existing action query, you first refer to the query in the QueryDefs collection and then use the Execute method. For example, if qdelCustomers is a delete query that deletes customers from Canada, you can use this procedure:

```
Sub DeleteCanadaSQL()
Dim MyDb As Database, MyQuery As QueryDef
Set MyDb = CurrentDb
Set MyQuery = MyDb.QueryDefs("qdelCustomers")
MyQuery.Execute
End Sub
```

The navigational methods of DAO are particularly inefficient when you are working with large recordsets and with external tables. If you do need the navigational model of DAO, you can take advantage of the efficiency of SQL by using an SQL SELECT statement to create as small a recordset as needed for the problem. Then use the DAO navigational methods to step through the records.

Summary

This chapter has introduced the two data languages in Access. SQL is the language you use in interactive and programmatic mode to retrieve and manipulate data. DAO is the language component you use in Visual Basic to interact with the Jet database engine. The two data languages are not independent: DAO uses SQL to retrieve data. After the data has been retrieved, VBA can use SQL techniques to manipulate the retrieved set of records or DAO navigational techniques to manipulate one record at a time.

The chapter considers the performance of the various approaches to data retrieval and manipulation. You have learned that stored queries are typically faster than the equivalent SQL statements because stored queries are compiled and optimized. SQL techniques are typically faster than equivalent DAO navigational techniques.

chapter 20

Getting Started with Access Programming

20

by Susann Novalis

In this chapter

♦ **The Access Event Model**
Events are changes that controls, forms, and reports recognize that you can use as signals to run programs.

♦ **The Two Automation Tools**
Access has two programming languages: macros and VBA. You learn how they are related, why you should start your study of Access programming with macros, and when you need to learn Access VBA.

♦ **Referring to Objects**
Using the correct references to objects is necessary for successful programming.

♦ **Macro Programming**
Macro programming is the easiest way to start automating an Access database.

♦ **Access VBA**
You learn the basics of Access VBA and explore the programs that the Access wizards create.

When you work interactively, you give Access commands one at a time. Access responds to each command by carrying out the action you requested, such as opening or closing a form, running a query, or running a report. In contrast, when you work with Access programmatically, you create *programs* as lists of detailed instructions you want Access to carry out. You store the programs as separate objects in the database file. You can run a program using customized versions of the interactive methods by choosing a custom menu command, clicking a custom command button, pressing a custom keystroke combination, or clicking a mouse button.

Additionally, you can run a program when the application starts up, or when a specified object recognizes an event. (An *event* is a change in the state of an object that is made available for programming.)

Although you can create complex Access databases without programming, it is more efficient to learn basic Access programming techniques, so you can create your own custom functions and transfer much of the manual labor of repetitive operations to the computer. You can also use Access programming techniques to replace the default error messages with your own custom messages. Finally, you can create database applications that can be used by people who don't know how to use Access.

The Access Event Model

The Access programming environment is a collection of visual objects and a provision for creating programs that run when the objects recognize events. The visual objects are graphical controls, forms, and reports.

What Is an Event?

At every instant, an object has a state. A *state* is a set of characteristics recorded in memory that define the object (such as its color or size, or whether it's open or closed). When you interact with an object, you can change its state. For example, when you open a form, you change its state from closed to open; when you click a command button, you change its state from unclicked to clicked. Access makes some of these changes in state available as opportunities for you to run programs; these special changes in state are called *events*.

In Access for Windows 95, events are defined for controls on forms, forms and form sections, and reports and report sections. Each of these objects recognizes its own set of events. For each event there is a corresponding *event property*. The event properties of an object are listed in the Event category of the object's property sheet. For example, figure 20.1 shows the 29 event properties for a form and the 12 event properties for a command button (the Products command button on the Main Switchboard form in the Northwind database).

For most events, the corresponding event property is named On followed by the event's name; for example, OnClose is the property corresponding to the Close event. You link a program to an event by assigning the program to the event property; this is also called *trapping* the event. When a user action changes an object's state and triggers an event, the object recognizes the event and Access runs the linked program. In figure 20.1b, a program called OpenForms is linked to the OnClick property of the command button and runs when you click the button.

Fig. 20.1

Event properties for the events an object recognizes are listed in the object's property sheet.

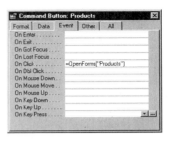

(a)

(b)

Categories of Events

20

In all, there are 39 events defined in Access 95 (by comparison, Excel 95 has 15 events). Table 20.1 shows how the events can be arranged in nine categories.

Table 20.1   Access Events Arranged by Category

Event Category	Recognized by
Mouse	Form controls, form sections, and forms when you click (Click), double-click (DblClick), press (MouseDown) or release (MouseUp) a mouse button, or move the mouse pointer (MouseMove).
Keyboard	Form objects, form sections, and forms when you press (KeyDown) or release (KeyUp) a key on the keyboard, or when you press and release a key or key combination that produces a standard ANSI character (KeyPress). Also recognized when you programmatically send keystrokes.
Window	Forms and reports when you open (Open) or close (Close) a form or report, load (Load) or unload (Unload) the records for the form or report, or resize (Resize) the window for the form or report.

continues

Table 20.1   Continued

Event Category	Recognized by
Focus	Form controls and forms when the object gains or loses the focus (Enter, GotFocus, Exit, LostFocus). Also recognized by forms and reports when the object becomes active (Activate) or inactive (Inactivate).
Data	Form controls and forms when you change data in controls (BeforeUpdate, AfterUpdate, Change, Updated, NotInList), change data in a record (BeforeUpdate, AfterUpdate), add or delete a record (BeforeInsert, AfterInsert, Delete, BeforeDelConfirm, AfterDelConfirm), or move the focus to another record (Current).
Filter	Forms when you apply or remove a filter (Filter, ApplyFilter).
Print	Report sections and reports when Access determines what data goes in a section (Format) and lays out a report for printing (Retreat, NoData, Page, Print).
Error	Forms and reports when an error occurs (Error) in the Access interface or in the Jet engine.
Timing	Forms when a specified time interval has passed (Timer).

Understanding the order in which events are recognized is crucial to successful event-driven programming in Access. If you create an error-free program to carry out a task, and then trigger the program with the wrong event, you usually get the wrong result. To complicate the matter, a single user action often triggers a sequence of several events; for example, when you double-click a form in the Database window, the form recognizes the following sequence of events:

Open→Load→Resize→Activate→[GotFocus]→Current

The GotFocus event is shown in brackets, because the form recognizes this event only if the form has no controls that can receive the focus. If the form has a control that can receive the focus, then the control—but not the form—recognizes the GotFocus event when the form opens. As another example, when you enter new data or change existing data in a control then move the focus to another control, the changed control recognizes the following sequence of events:

BeforeUpdate→AfterUpdate→Exit→LostFocus

Note

Search "Events, Order of Events" in the online Help for information on other event sequences.

Two Automation Tools

Access 95 provides two tools for writing programs: Visual Basic for Applications (VBA) and Access macros.

Visual Basic for Applications

VBA is a comprehensive programming language with the following features:

20

▶ *Variables.* The capability to create a *variable* as a temporary storage location in memory for a value or a reference to an object. You use variables to hold and modify values while a program is running. Variables can have any of the following types of values (called *data types*): numeric types, strings, objects, variants, and custom data types you define yourself.

In VBA, you use *object variables* to refer (or point) to objects such as forms, reports, and controls. Use custom (or user-defined) data types to store multiple values of different data types in the same variable. You use *variant variables* to refer to any data type except custom data types. (The variant variable is a chameleon that can hold different data types—Access handles the data type conversion automatically.)

Each data type is stored differently in memory. Normally you *declare* (or *dimension*) a variable and specify its data type at the beginning of the program to set aside memory. If you don't specify a data type, the variable is assigned the variant data type. When you use variables, you can write a program more quickly, and the result is easier to read. An additional benefit of using variables is that the program runs faster, because Access processes the reference only once when you assign the variable in the program, instead processing the reference repeatedly each time you need the value in a program.

▶ *Decisions.* The capability to test a condition and change the program execution depending on the results of the test. VBA uses If...Then...End If to test a condition and to provide two program branches (you can add a test for a second condition using an ElseIf statement), and uses Select Case...End Select to provide several program branches.

▶ *Looping*. The capability to repeat a section of the program. VBA uses three basic looping control structures: `For...Next` to repeat a set of instructions a specific number of times, `Do While...Loop` to repeat the set while a specific condition is true, and `Do Until...Loop` to repeat the set as long as a specific condition is satisfied.

▶ *Run-time errors*. The capability to determine what error occurred, and to intercept the default behavior and replace it with your own instructions to be carried out if the error occurs.

When you write a VBA program (called *code*), you work with objects. In programming, the word *object* refers to an element with two components: data that describes the element (*properties*) such as its size, color, name and data source, and a set of small programs for all of the operations the element can perform (*methods*). In a VBA program, you read and change properties, and you execute methods. Access includes a large set of built-in objects with built-in properties and methods. You work with objects created both by the Access application and by the Jet Database Engine. You can also create your own objects with custom properties and methods.

The individual VBA programs are called *procedures*. There are three kinds of procedures you can create: a *function procedure* returns a value, a *subroutine procedure* performs actions without returning a value, and a *property procedure* reads or sets a property value or sets a reference to an object. Another way to classify procedures is by the way they are run: an *event procedure* is a subroutine procedure you link to an event, and a *general procedure* is any procedure that is not linked to an event.

Procedures are stored in *modules*. A module has two sections: a *declarations section* where you enter statements that affect all of the procedures in the module, and a *procedures section* where you enter and store the procedures. There are two kinds of modules:

▶ *Standard modules* are module objects that are listed in the Modules pane of the Database window. Typically, you use standard modules to store the common procedures that are used by several forms or reports. You can store both *event procedures* and *general procedures*. You can open a standard module by selecting the module in the Database window and clicking the Design button. For example, Utility Functions is a standard module in NORTHWIND.MDB.

▶ *Form* and *report modules* are not displayed as separate objects in the Database window. When you create a form or report, Access automatically creates a form or report module as is an integral part of the form or report. By default, Access names the module after the form or report. For example, if `frmName` is the name of the form, the corresponding form module is `Form_frmName`. The primary purpose of a form or report module is to contain the event procedures linked to events recognized by the form or report (or the form's controls or sections or the report's sections), but you can also store general procedures in a form or report module. You can open a form or report module by selecting the form or report in the Database window and clicking the Code toolbar button. For example, the form module for the Orders form contains three event procedures. Figure 20.2 shows part of the Form_Orders form module.

> **Tip**
>
> By default, Access displays the declarations section and the code for each procedure separately in the Module window. You can quickly view the contents of the module by changing how Access displays the module. Choose Tools, Options, choose the Modules tab, select the Full Module View check box, and deselect the Procedure Separator check box.

Fig. 20.2

The form module for the Orders form in Northwind.mdb *shows the declarations section and the first few procedures because Full Module view was selected.*

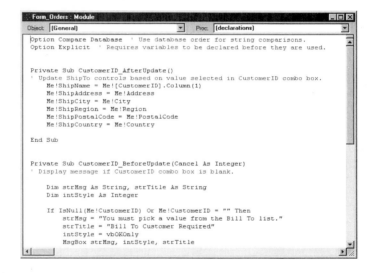

> **Note**
>
> Standard modules are opened and prepared for execution when you first open the database. In contrast, a form or report module isn't opened and processed until you open the form or report. You can improve the "perceived" performance of an application by placing all VBA procedures in standard modules—the initial opening of the application is slower, but the forms and reports open faster. To make the initial opening appear faster, you can display an informative splash screen to give the user something to read while the application opens.

Procedures and variables can be public or private. A *public procedure* or variable is available to all other procedures in the database; public procedures stored in standard modules are also available to other databases. A *private procedure* or variable is available only to procedures stored in the same module. By default, event procedures you create in a form or report module are private, and all other procedures are public.

Access Macros

The Access macro language is a simplified automation tool. While it lacks some of the powerful features of VBA, the macro programming language is easier to learn and provides enough power to create sophisticated database applications. The following list describes the simplified macro programming features:

▶ *Separation of objects and actions.* Conceptually, in macro programming, macro actions are separate entities that operate directly on the physical objects in the database. Macro actions are not stored inside the objects they affect. This separation of objects and actions contrasts the way methods are stored inside the VBA programming objects.

▶ *Simulated variables.* In macro programming, you can't create variables as temporary storage locations for values in memory. Instead, you can simulate a limited version of variables by creating temporary storage locations for values using controls on forms. You can work only with numeric and string values; object, variant, and user-defined variables are not part of macro programming.

▶ *Decisions.* Macro programming uses a special version of the If condition: if a condition is True, Access runs a set of instructions as the "true branch." There is no provision for a "false branch." If a condition is False, Access skips the true branch and jumps to the next instruction following the true branch. If you want to run a set of instructions when a condition is False, you must create another condition that is True when the original condition is False (called the *opposite condition*).

▶ *Looping.* Macro programming provides versions of the three basic looping control structures as part of the RunMacro action.

▶ *Run-time errors.* Macro programming lacks VBA's capability to trap specific errors and replace default behavior with custom behavior.

 Tip

Because macro programming lacks the capability to trap specific errors, the best approach is to design macros that avoid potential errors. You avoid the error by testing conditions before running a macro instruction that could cause an error and stopping the macro before it runs the instruction. For example, the macro instruction to save a record fails if the primary key has a null value. You can avoid the error by testing the value of the primary key before running the save instruction and aborting the instruction if the value is null.

Access 95 provides 49 macro actions you can use in writing programs called *macros* (analogous to VBA subroutine procedures; there are no macro programming analogs to function and property procedures). In the simplest sense, the 49 macro actions can be viewed as a reduced set of the 121 Access VBA methods.

When you write macro programs, you work directly with the Database window objects: you display forms and reports, and modify their properties by running macro actions. In macro programming, you work with a reduced set of an object's properties. Many of the built-in properties are available only in VBA programming; for example, a form's CurrentRecord property that you use to identify the current record is available only in VBA.

Macros are stored in *macrosheets* (analogous to VBA modules). Each macrosheet is saved as a macro object in the Database window. Although you can store each macro as a separate macro object, a more effective way to organize individual macros is to create two kinds of macrosheets (analogous to the two kinds of modules): *standard macrosheets* store some or all of the individual macros, and *form and report macrosheets* store the event macros. An *event macro* is a macro that is linked to an event (analogous to an event procedure). All individual macros are available to all other macros and to all VBA procedures in the database. All simulated variables you create using form controls are available to all macros and VBA procedures as long as the form is open. You can display a macrosheet by selecting the Macros tab in the Database window and clicking the Design button. Figure 20.3 shows the Customer Labels Dialog macrosheet containing the event macros for the form with the same name.

α Note

Although you can create an automated database application using only macro programming, you can't create one using only VBA. In Access 95, you must use macros to create custom menus and key assignments. In addition, many Access VBA operations are really macro actions that you execute in VBA as methods of the DoCmd object. The DoCmd object of VBA provides the link between the two programming tools by allowing you to execute 41 of the 49 macro actions from VBA. Of the remaining eight macro actions, all but one (the AddMenu action) have VBA equivalents.

Fig. 20.3

The Customer Labels Dialog macrosheet contains the event macros for that form.

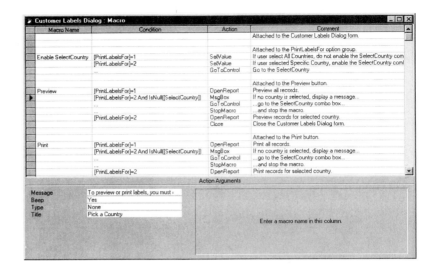

Where Do You Start?

Unfortunately, and in contrast to Excel and Word, Access does not have a recorder for either VBA or macro programs. Microsoft takes a different approach to helping you get started with Access VBA. Access provides a set of wizards that create custom VBA programs. You can study and modify these simple programs in the same way you would pick apart and alter a recorded program. To help you learn Access macro programming, Microsoft provides the macro design window (called the *macrosheet* in this book). This window has a special structure that hides the details of macro programming syntax and specialized cells that minimize typing. You write macro programs in the macro design window by pointing to the special cells and clicking to select from lists. Because macro programming is both very easy to learn and extremely powerful, you'll begin programming with macros in the section "Learning Macro Programming," then move to using the wizards to explore Access VBA. However, before learning any kind of programming, you need to know how Access wants you to refer to objects.

Referring to Objects

Whether you are using macro or VBA programming, the programs you create involve objects. A program runs as a response to an event property of some object. The instructions in the program change the properties of other objects. Access requires that you refer to objects in a specific way.

The Access 95 Object Model includes only 40 objects (compared to the Excel 95 Object Model with 160 objects and the Word 95 Object Model with a single object). There are nine Access application objects to represent the Access application, interface, open forms and reports, and 31 data access objects to represent the tables and queries. (See Chapter 19, "Understanding the Data Languages in Access," for an introduction to the data access objects.) Access organizes the application objects into a hierarchy. In the hierarchical arrangement, objects contain other objects, and objects of the same type are grouped into collections. Figure 20.4 shows the hierarchy for the Access application objects.

Fig. 20.4

The Access application objects hierarchy shows the relationships between the objects.

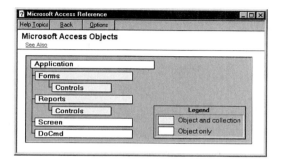

You use the Application object to refer to the Access application. As the top object in the hierarchy, the Application object also encompasses all of the other Access objects below it in the hierarchy. The DoCmd object refers to the special object that VBA uses to run 41 of the macro actions as VBA methods. The remaining objects refer to open forms and reports as follows:

Object	Collection Object	Description
Control	Controls	Refers to a control on an open form or report. The Controls collection refers to the set of controls on an open form or report.
Form	Forms	Refers to an open form. The Forms collection refers to the set of all open forms.
Report	Reports	Refers to an open report. The Reports collection refers to the set of all open reports.
Screen		Refers to the form, report, or control that currently has the focus or the control that last had the focus. There is no corresponding collection.

Caution

Unfortunately, Microsoft often uses the same word for two concepts. For example, the word *Forms* is used both for the `Forms` collection (which is an application object that refers to the set of all open forms) and for the `Forms` container object (which holds administrative information for all of the forms in the database).

An object that contains other objects also contains a set of references to these objects. For example, a form contains a list of references to all of its controls. To refer to a specific object, start at the top of the hierarchy and traverse to the object using the dot operator to move along the path. When you get to a collection on the path, you use the exclamation point operator to refer to a specific object in the collection as follows:

```
collectionname!objectname
```

The exclamation point operator indicates that the object is an element of the collection. (The section, "Referring to Objects in VBA," later in this chapter describes two other ways to refer to an object in a collection when you write VBA programs.) For example, using the full hierarchical path, `Application.Forms!Customers.Controls!CustomerName`, refers to the `CustomerName` control on the open Customers form. If the object name includes spaces or special characters, you must enclose the name in square brackets. You can refer to a form or report only if it is open; if the form or report you are referring to isn't open, Access displays an error message. Normally, you don't have to include all the components of the reference, because Access assumes certain defaults. The `Application` object is assumed when you are creating macros or VBA code that execute inside Access so you can remove the `Application` reference. In addition, objects may have a *default collection* of objects that Access assumes when you don't name the collection explicitly. For example, forms and reports have the `Controls` collection as the default collection. Taking defaults into account, the reference simplifies to `Forms!Customers!CustomerName`. The simplified version is called the *full identifier*.

If you are familiar with Excel's Object Model, you know that Excel does not use the exclamation point operator. Excel uses the dot operator both for moving along the object hierarchy and for referring to an object in a collection.

 Note

You refer to a field in the table or query that is the record source for an open form using the full identifier:

```
Forms!formname!fieldname
```

You can use this syntax to refer to a field whether the form contains a control bound to the field or not.

To refer to the property of an object, use the following dot operator syntax:

```
objectname.propertyname
```

For example, `Forms!Customers.RecordSource` refers to the *RecordSource* property of the Customers form and, `Forms!Customers!CustomerName.Text` refers to the current value (as a formatted string) of the *CustomerName* control on the Customers form. Objects may have a *default property* that is assumed when you don't name the property explicitly. For example, `Text` is the default property for a text box control, so the full identifier `Forms!Customers!CustomerName`, refers to the *CustomerName* control and, by default, the current value displayed in the control.

Depending on the context, you can often use a shorter reference instead of the full identifier for an object. For example, to refer to a control on the active form, you can use the following *short identifier*:

```
controlname
```

So, if Customers is the active form, you can use the short identifier, `CustomerID`, to refer to the text box control (or its current value).

Ⲁ **Note**

Normally, you can use the full identifier any time you refer to an object, but there are a few exceptions where you must use the short identifier instead. For example, you must use the short identifier in the `GoToControl` macro action to specify the name of the control on the active object you want to move the focus to; using the full identifier in this situation causes the macro action to fail.

Interestingly, some objects have properties you can use to refer to either the object itself or to another object. Table 20.2 shows these objects and properties.

Table 20.2   Properties of Objects that Refer to an Object

Object	Property	Refers to
Screen	ActiveForm or ActiveReport	The form or report that contains the control that has the focus, or the form or report that has the focus.
Screen	ActiveControl	The control that has the focus.
Screen	PreviousControl	The control that had the focus immediately before the control that currently has the focus.

continues

Table 20.2 Continued

Object	Property	Refers to
Form or Report	Form or Report	Refers to the form itself or the report itself.
Form or Report	Me	Refers to the form or report itself (in VBA only).
Form or Report	Module	Refers to the form's module or the report's module.
Form or Report	RecordsetClone	Refers to a clone of the recordset underlying the form or report (in VBA only).
Control or Section	Parent	Refers to the object that contains the control or section.
Control	Section	Refers to the section of a form or report where the control is located.
Subform/ Subreport Control	Form or Report	Refers to the form or the report displayed by a subform/ subreport control on a form or a report.

The following examples use properties that refer to an object:

▶ If Customers is the active form and the CustomerID control has the focus, you can refer to the control as Screen.ActiveControl.

▶ To refer to a control on a subform, use the Form property of the subform control to refer to the form displayed in the subform control, and then refer to the control as follows:

    Forms!*formname*!*subformcontrolname*.Form!*controlname*

For example, Forms![Quarterly Orders]![Quarterly Orders Subform].Form!Year is the full identifier for the Year control on the subform of the Quarterly Orders form.

▶ To refer to a control on the main form if you are working in a subform, use the following syntax:

    Parent!*controlname*

For example, to display the company name in a calculated control on the Quarterly Orders subform, enter the expression =**Parent!CompanyName** as the ControlSource of the control.

▶ In a VBA procedure, use the Me property to refer to the current form or report; for example, in an event procedure in the form module for the Customers form, Me.Caption refers to the form's Caption property, and Me!CustomerID refers to the CustomerID control.

▶ In a VBA procedure, use the RecordSetClone property to refer to a copy of the form's underlying table or query. You can use this property to navigate through or operate on the clone's records independent of the form's records. For example, you can use the FindFirst method to find the first customer from Brazil in the Customers form as follows:

```
Forms!Customers.RecordSetClone.FindFirst "Country = 'Brazil'"
```

Or, if Customers is the current form, use

```
Me. RecordSetClone.FindFirst "Country = 'Brazil'"
```

> ### α Note
>
> You can use the Expression Builder for help in creating object references in macro and VBA programming. The Expression Builder always creates the full identifier for an object, so you must modify the reference for those cases where the short identifier is required. Also, you have to modify the reference if you want to use the Screen object in a macro or VBA program to refer to an active object, or use the Me property to refer to the form or report in which a VBA program is running.

Learning Macro Programming

The best way to learn programming in Access is to start with macro programming. Most applications can be created using only macros. By starting with macros, you can become comfortable with the complex Access Event Model and develop simple program logic without having to deal with the complexities of VBA. You can learn how to use the macro actions, nearly all of which are also used in VBA (as analogous methods). Additionally, you learn the tasks that can be performed only using macros, not VBA. The macros-only tasks include creating custom menus, creating custom key assignments, and running VBA procedures from toolbar buttons.

When you use the Access macro environment, you work in a special macro design window and create programs by selecting actions from lists. You enter additional information required to carry out actions in special cells. You can automate the standard database operations such as data entry, importing data, and archiving records. You can use macros to automate basic application techniques such as navigating among controls on a form and between open forms, finding individual records, selecting groups of records, and synchronizing two forms to display related records.

Creating a Macro

To open a new macrosheet, click the Macro tab in the Database window, and then click the New button (see fig. 20.5).

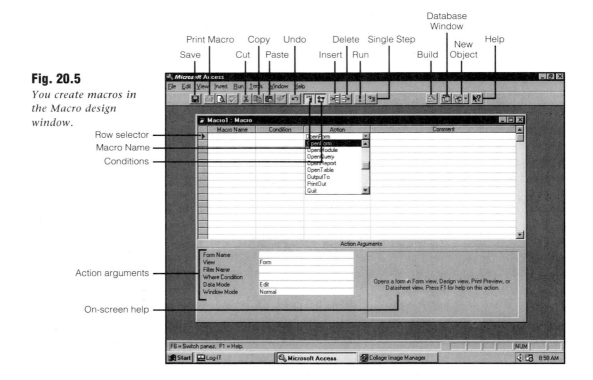

Fig. 20.5

You create macros in the Macro design window.

The upper pane of the macrosheet contains four columns. By default, Access displays only two columns, so you may need to toggle the Macro Names and Conditions buttons in the Macro toolbar to display all four columns. You enter the name of an individual macro in a Macro Name cell. You test a condition by entering it in a Condition cell. You enter macro actions in the Action column in the sequence you want them executed. Finally, you enter descriptive comments in the Comments column to explain the program's logic. Access ignores your entries in the Comments column and any blank rows. When you enter an action by typing or selecting from a drop-down list in the Action cell, the lower pane changes to display a list of the additional information, called the *action arguments*, needed to carry out the action. The right side of the lower pane displays on-screen help for each argument. For example, the action arguments for the OpenForm action shown in figure 20.5 require that you specify what form is to be opened and the desired view and modes. You also can use the optional Filter Name or Where Condition arguments to filter or select the records to display. You don't need to enter a macro action to end the macro; the macro ends when there are no more rows with actions to execute or when there is a row with an entry in the Macro Name cell signaling the start of another macro.

The Macro toolbar includes toolbar buttons for editing, running, and troubleshooting macros. You can edit the entry in a cell or text box of the macrosheet by selecting the cell and using the normal Windows editing operations including Cut, Copy, and Paste. You can select one or more rows by clicking the Row Selector box at the left of the first row and dragging to select additional rows. You can copy, paste, delete, and insert rows in the same or in another macrosheet in the same way you manipulate rows in a spreadsheet. When you paste an entire row, the action arguments are pasted also; but when you paste the contents of a single action cell, the action arguments are not pasted.

After entering one or more individual macros, you save the macrosheet as a macro object displayed in the Database window. A macrosheet that stores more than one individual macro is called a *macro group*. You refer to an individual macro in a macro group using the syntax

```
macrogroupname.macroname
```

If you use the macro organization recommended in the last section, each form and report has its own macro group containing the individual macros for automating the form or report. A typical automated application can have dozens of forms, reports, and macro groups with dozens of individual macros. To use macros effectively, you need to adopt a consistent naming convention that packs documenting information into the name. This chapter uses the conventions shown in table 20.3.

Table 20.3   Naming Conventions for Macros

Name	Description
objectname_eventname	An individual macro triggered by an event recognized by a control.
mformname	A macro group for a form named *formname*.
mreportname	A macro group for a report named *reportname*.
mcrStandard	A macro group for macros not associated with a form or report.
mmnumenugroup	A macro group for a menu on a custom menu bar.

For example, a macro triggered by the `Click` event of a command button named `cmdReview` on the Customer Orders form is named `cmdReview_Click` and is stored in a macro group named `mCustomerOrders` (I deleted the space for convenience). You refer to this macro by using the syntax `mCustomerOrders.cmdReview_Click`.

You can copy part or all of an individual macro to another macro group and reuse at least part of the macro program. You can import or export a macro group to another database just as you import or export any Database window object.

Macro Actions and Arguments

Access 95 provides 49 macro actions you can use to create macros. The actions can be arranged in categories of specific tasks as shown in table 20.4 (all macro actions except the eight actions marked with an asterisk [*] have corresponding VBA methods for the `DoCmd` object).

Table 20.4   Macro Actions Grouped by Task Categories

Category	Tasks	Macro Actions
Manipulating Database window objects	Select, copy, rename, or delete the object.	`SelectObject, CopyObject, Rename, DeleteObject`
	Open a table, query, form, report, or module.	`OpenTable, OpenQuery, OpenForm, OpenReport, OpenModule`
	Save, close, or print.	`Save, Close, PrintOut`

Category	Tasks	Macro Actions
Working with data	Update data or the screen.	`RepaintObject, Requery, ShowAllRecords`
	Set the value of a field, control, or property.	`SetValue*`
	Find a specific record, or select or sort a group of records.	`FindRecord, FindNext, ApplyFilter`
Execution	Run a query, macro, VBA procedure, or another application.	`OpenQuery, RunSQL, RunMacro, RunCode*, RunApp*`
	Stop execution of the current macro, all currently running macros, or Access.	`StopMacro*, StopAllMacros*, Quit`
	Carry out a menu command.	`DoMenuItem`
	Stop execution of default behavior following an event.	`CancelEvent`
Navigation	Move to a particular location.	`GoToControl, GoToPage, GoToRecord`
Importing and exporting data	Output data from a table, query, form, report, or module in XLS, RFT, or TXT formats or include in an e-mail message.	`OutputTo, SendObject`
	Transfer data between Access and other data formats.	`TransferDatabase, TransferSpreadsheet, TransferText`

20

continues

Table 20.4   Continued

Category	Tasks	Macro Actions
Miscellaneous	Create a custom menu bar or change how a menu command is displayed.	AddMenu*, SetMenuItem
	Sound a beep or display an hourglass.	Beep, Hourglass
	Show or hide a custom toolbar.	ShowToolbar
	Send keystrokes to Access or another application.	SendKeys*
	Display or hide screen updates or system information while a macro is running.	Echo, SetWarnings
	Display a custom message.	MsgBox*

Most of the macro actions are equivalent to the menu commands, such as FindRecord, Save, and Close. Some actions mimic manual user interaction, such as SendKeys and GoToControl. Other actions provide capabilities not available interactively, such as Beep and MsgBox. For more information about the syntax, arguments, and use of an individual macro action, search the index of online help for the name of the action.

Triggering a Macro with an Event

After you create and save an individual macro, there are 10 ways you can run it:

- ▶ From the macro design window
- ▶ From any active window
- ▶ From the Database window
- ▶ From another macro
- ▶ From a custom toolbar button
- ▶ From a custom menu command
- ▶ From a shortcut key
- ▶ At startup

▶ From VBA code

▶ By trapping an event on a form or report

The most important way to run a macro is by trapping an event. When you use an event to trigger a macro, you minimize the need for users to learn how to use your application. You can make the trap for the event obvious by linking the macro to the Click event of a command button. Or, you can hide the trap by running a macro in response to a user action that would not be expected to trigger a macro, for example, by trapping the Current event that a form recognizes when the user clicks into a different record.

To run a macro by trapping an event on a form or report, follow these steps:

1. Decide what event of a control, form or form section, or report or report section you want to trigger the macro.

2. Open the form or report in Design view, select the control, section, or the form or report.

3. Click in the corresponding event property and select the macro from the drop-down list.

4. Switch to Form view or Print Preview, and perform the user action that is required to trigger the event.

As an example of the process of creating a macro and linking it to an event, you add a *drill-down* capability to the Product List form in Northwind. You place a command button named cmdViewProduct in the detail section of the Product List form and create a macro that opens the Products form that displays the product you selected when you clicked the command button. Just follow these steps:

1. Open the Product List form in Design view and set the PopUp property to No. (With the PopUp property set to Yes, the form stays on top.)

2. With the Control Wizards tool deselected, select the Command Button tool in the toolbox, and place a command button in the detail section. Set the Name property to cmdViewProduct and the Caption property to &View Product.

   When you type the ampersand (&) character before a letter in the Caption property, you define a standard Windows keystroke combination Alt+[*letter*], called an *access key*. Pressing the access key combination is equivalent to clicking the command button.

3. Open a new macrosheet, type **cmdViewProduct_Click** in the first Macro Name cell, and select the OpenForm macro action. Set the Form Name argument to Products. If you don't enter additional arguments, Access uses the defaults and opens the Products form displaying the first record in the recordset. Instead, you synchronize the two forms by having the macro action find the record for the Products form with the same ProductID as the selected record in the Product List form.

20

4. To synchronize the records displayed in the two forms, set the `Where Condition` argument to the following expression: `ProductID = Forms![Product List]!ProductID`.

   In this synchronizing expression, the left side refers to the value of the ProductID in the recordset for the form being opened (Products). The right side refers to the value of the ProductID in the recordset for the Product List form. Note that the Product List form doesn't have a control bound to the ProductID field in the underlying table, so the object reference points directly to the table field. Save the macrosheet as `mProductList`.

5. Click in the Product List form, select the `cmdViewProduct` command button, click in the `OnClick` property, and select the `mProductList.cmdViewProduct_Click` macro from the drop-down list. Save the form and switch to Form view.

6. Select a product and click the View Products button. The Products form opens, displaying the synchronized record. If you click in a different record in the Product List form and do not click the command button, the Products form continues to display the previous product. The Products form does not remain synchronized to the Product List form.

Conditional Macros

You test a condition and run a set of macro actions if the condition is `True` by doing the following:

1. Enter the condition in a Condition cell and the first action of the set in the Action cell in the same row as the condition.

2. Enter an ellipsis (**...**) in the Condition cell and an action in the Action cell of the subsequent row for each remaining macro action in the set.

Conceptually, when you run the macro, the macro tests the condition. If the condition is `True`, the macro executes each of the macro actions in the set and moves to the next row after the final row in the set. If the condition is `False`, the macro ignores all of the actions in the set and moves directly to the next row after the final row of the set.

As an example, modify the drill-down process to keep the Products form synchronized. If the Products form is open when you select a different record, you can run the `OpenForm` action with the same arguments to resynchronize the Products form. However, if the Products form isn't open when you select a different record in the Product List form, you don't run the action, because the Products form should open only when you click a drill-down button. The macro must test to determine if the Products form is open. You can use the custom `IsLoaded()` function that is stored in the Utility Functions standard module in Northwind. To use the `IsLoaded()` function, enter the name of the form enclosed in quotation marks as the function's argument. If the form is open in Form view (and its records are loaded), the IsLoaded() function returns the True value; if the form isn't open in Form view, the function returns False. The event that occurs when you move the focus to a different record is the form's Current event, so use this event to trigger the synchronizing macro.

1. Click in the mProductList macrosheet, click in the Macro Name cell of a new row, and enter the macro name **Form_Current**.

2. Click in the Condition cell and enter the condition **IsLoaded("Products")**.

3. Click in the Action cell of the same row and select the Open Form action. Set the Form Name argument to Products and the Where Condition argument to the synchronizing expression

```
ProductID = Forms![Product List]!ProductID
```

In this case, there is only one macro action to execute if the condition is True. The macro runs the action and moves to the next row. If the condition is False, the macro jumps to the next row. In either case, the next row and all subsequent rows are blank, so the macro terminates.

4. Save the macrosheet.

5. Click in the Products List form and switch to Design view. Select the form, click in the OnCurrent property and select the mProductList.Form_Current macro from the list. Save the form and switch to Form view.

6. Select a product, and click the View Products button. The Products form opens, displaying the synchronized record. Click in a different record in the Product List form, but do not click the command button. The Products form resynchronizes to display the correct record.

7. Close the Products form. Click in a different record in the Product List form, but do not click the command button. (As planned, the Products form doesn't open.)

Limitations of Macro Programming

Macro programming is surprisingly powerful; you can use the 49 macro actions to create extremely complex applications. Nevertheless, there are limitations to macro programming that you need to be familiar with so you'll know when you have to include VBA in an application. The important limitations of macro programming are:

▶ *Lack of error handling in macro programming.* In macro programming, when a fatal run-time error occurs, you can't intercept the Access default behavior, so you can't prevent the macro action from failing. The only recourse is to try to redesign the macro to prevent the error from occurring at all. If a non-fatal macro error occurs, you can trap the form's `Error` event with a macro. For example, you can trap the `NotInList` event of a combo box and supplement the default error message with a custom message.

 Note

A *run-time error* in macro programming is any error that occurs when a macro is executing; a *fatal run-time error* is one that causes the macro action to fail and the macro to terminate. Some errors are non-fatal because the macro action doesn't fail after Access displays an error message.

▶ *Lack of variables*. Although macro programming lets you use form controls as simulated variables, the use of variables is extremely limited. Complex programs usually depend on liberal use of variables to make the programs easier to create and read, and faster to execute. Also, by using variables you can make sections of a program or an entire program reusable in different situations.

▶ *Editing and documenting programs*. VBA provides superior editing and documenting. For example, you can easily view and edit the entire contents of a module; in contrast, you can't view the entire contents of a macrosheet in a single glance because the action arguments are hidden (you must click in a row to view the arguments of one action at a time). In VBA, you can print the module in the same layout that you view it (WYSIWYG). In contrast, the Documenter prints a macro using a special macro layout that is complete, if not compact.

▶ *Debugging*. VBA provides superior debugging tools that are convenient and absolutely necessary for complicated programs.

▶ *Tunnel vision*. Although you can start up another application using macros, you can't use macros to control the application after it opens. Additionally, you can't communicate directly with Windows. With VBA, you can actually control another application, if it conforms to the OLE Automation standards. Also, you can communicate with Windows using the Windows Application Programming Interface (API) functions.

▶ *Creating and modifying objects programmatically*. In macro programming, you are limited to using the data definition queries to create and modify tables (see Chapter 19, "Understanding the Data Languages in Access," for more information). In VBA, you can use the methods of the data access objects to create and modify most of the data access objects.

▶ *Limited operations*. VBA provides operations that don't exist in macro programming. For example, in VBA you can group a set of statements together as a transaction and run the set in memory. A *transaction* is a set of operations you handle as a single unit: if one operation in the set fails, then none of the operations carry out. By default, Access runs an individual action query as a transaction, but if you want to run a set of action queries to archive records to a historical table and delete them from the current table as a single transaction, you have to use VBA. Additionally, VBA provides alternates to the macro actions that run much faster. For example, the Seek method is much faster than the FindRecord macro action (or method), and using the Bookmark property is the fastest way to return to a record.

▶ *Optimize performance*. If you want to get optimal performance, you have to use VBA. Individual macro actions are optimized; however, the equivalent VBA method may run faster. Each time you run a macro, Access interprets the macro line by line; in contrast, you can compile VBA modules (*compiling* a VBA module means translating the code you write into faster *pseudo-code* and does not mean true compiling with code translated into machine-readable form). Each time you run a VBA procedure, Access interprets the faster pseudo-code instead of the original code.

When you decide to include VBA programs in your application, you can use the new capability of Access 95 to convert some of your macros to VBA code. (Search for "Converting Macros" in online help for more information).

Exploring Access VBA

This section assumes that you are familiar with the basic features of the Visual Basic for Applications language, as described, for example, in *Special Edition Using Microsoft Office for Windows 95* by Que. The current chapter focuses on those features that are either especially important or are unique in Access VBA. You will begin by looking at additional ways to refer to objects in Access VBA.

Referring to Objects in Access VBA

The section "Referring to Objects" earlier in this chapter introduced the exclamation point operator syntax for referring to an object in a collection in Access VBA. That syntax is useful when you refer to the object explicitly by its name as you do in query expressions, macro conditions, and macro arguments. Table 20.5 shows that Access VBA provides two more ways to refer to objects.

Table 20.5   Referring to an Object in a Collection

Syntax	Description and Purpose
`collectionname!objectname`	Refers to the object in the collection explicitly by its name.
`collectionname("objectname")` or `collectionname (objectvariable)`	Refers to the object in the collection explicitly by its name, or by using a String variable to refer to the object.
`collectionname(index)`	Refers to the object in the collection by the index number assigned to the object. For the Forms and Reports collections, the index numbers for individual open forms and reports change because the numbers are assigned according to the order in which they are loaded and change when other forms and reports are unloaded. The index is zero-based; if Customers is the first open form, its index number is 0 and Forms(0) refers to it.

The syntax you use depends on your purpose: for example, when you want to process each element in a collection one by one, it is most efficient to refer to the elements by index number and loop through the objects of the collection.

 Note

There is an inconsistency between Excel VBA and Access VBA in the way items in a collection are indexed. In Excel VBA, the list is one-based: the first item in a collection list is assigned the number 1. In Access VBA, a collection's list is zero-based instead.

When you write VBA code, you can avoid explicit object names by using the parenthesis syntax with a variable representing the name of the object. For example, in an event procedure for the Customers form, you can use any of the following references for the CustomerID control:

```
Forms!Customers!CustomerID
Me!CustomerID
Me("CustomerID")
```

and any of the following references for the form's `Filter` property:

```
Forms!Customers.Filter
Me.Filter
Screen.ActiveForm.Filter
```

 Note

You use the `Me` property to refer to the form or report in which the VBA procedure is executing. `Screen.ActiveForm` refers to the active form, which is not necessarily the same as the form in which the procedure is running. For example, the procedure can open a second form and make it the active form.

Working with Variables and Objects

By default, you can create variables just by using them in your code; however, this method (called *implicit declaration*) would create a new variable if you should misspell a variable and could cause hours of tedious troubleshooting to find out why your "perfect" code isn't working. Instead, create variables by declaring them explicitly. To change the default to require explicit declaration of all variables, choose Tools, Options, select the Modules tab, and select the Require Variable Declaration check box. All new modules you create will have an `Option Explicit` statement in the declarations section just below the `Option Compare Database` statement that controls the sort order in the database. The remainder of this chapter assumes you have changed the default to require explicit declaration.

You can declare (create) variables in the declarations section of a module or in an individual procedure; where and how you declare a variable determines what other procedures can use it. The range of availability of a variable is its *scope*. You can declare a variable in either the declarations section or within a procedure as follows:

▶ *Declaring a variable in the declarations section.* When you declare a variable in the declarations section of a module, you can restrict the availability of the variable to the procedures stored in the module by using the `Private` (or `Dim`) keyword, or you can make the variable available to all procedures in all modules in the application by using the `Public` keyword. When you declare a variable in the declarations section, the variable exists only while the module is loaded into memory. Standard modules are loaded the entire time the database is open, so variables declared in the declarations section of a standard module exist as long as the database is open. In contrast, a form or report module is loaded only when the form or report is loaded, so variables declared in the declarations section of a form or report module

20

exist only when the form or report is loaded. The interval during which a variable exists (and can hold a value or point to an object) is its *lifetime*.

▶ *Declaring a variable in a procedure.* When you declare a variable in a procedure, you can refer to the variable only in that procedure—other procedures, even procedures in the same module, are unaware of the variable. You can restrict the lifetime of the variable to be the same as the lifetime of the procedure by using the Dim keyword or to the lifetime of the module by using the Static keyword. When you use the Dim keyword, the variable exists only while the procedure is running and ceases to exist when the procedure is finished. When you use the Static keyword, the variable keeps its value after the procedure is finished as long as the module is loaded.

Normally, when you declare a variable, you use the As keyword to specify the data type for the values that the variable can hold. If you don't specify a data type, Access assumes the Variant data type. The following table gives some examples of declaration statements to create variables.

Declaration	Location of Declaration	Scope and Lifetime of Variable
Dim MyDb As Database	Procedure	Available only to the procedure and exists only while the procedure is running.
Dim MyForm As Form	Declarations section of form module	Available to all procedures in the form module and exists while the form module is loaded.
Private DocName As String	Declarations section of standard module	Available to all procedures in the module and exists while the database is open.
Public UserID	Declarations section of standard module	Available to all procedures in all modules and exists while the database is open.
Static Counter As Integer	Procedure in a standard module	Available only to the procedure and exists while the database is open.

You assign a regular variable to a value using either of the following assignment statements:

```
variable = value
Let variable = value
```

and you point an object variable to an object using the Set keyword:

```
Set objectvariable = value
```

Here are examples that use the variables declared above:

```
Counter = 2
Let DocName = "Customers"
Set MyForm = Forms!Categories
```

When you are finished with an object variable, you can disassociate the object variable from the physical object by using the syntax

```
Set objectvariable = Nothing
```

to point the object variable to nothing.

When you change the value of a property of an object variable, you actually change the property of the physical object. The syntax for changing a property is

```
object.property = value
```

For example,

```
MyForm.RecordSource = "qryCustomers"
```

changes the record source of the Customers form to qryCustomers.

When you execute a method of an object variable, you actually perform the operation on the physical object. The syntax for executing a method of an object is

```
object.method [arguments]
```

Here are a few examples:

Execution Statement	Description
Forms!Customers!CustomerName.SetFocus	Moves the focus to the CustomerName control on the Customers form.
DoCmd.Close	Closes the active object.
Screen.ActiveForm.Requery	Requeries the active form.
DoCmd.OpenForm "Products"	Opens the Products form.

Exploring the Module Window

You write declaration statements and procedures in the Module window. Here are the ways to open Module windows:

▶ To open an existing standard module, click the Modules tab in the Database window, select the module, and click the Code toolbar button.

▶ To open an existing form or report module, select the form or report in the database window and click the Code toolbar button.

▶ To open a new module window, click the Modules tab in the Database window and click the New button.

Figure 20.6 shows the module window in Full Module view for the form module of the Products form in Northwind.

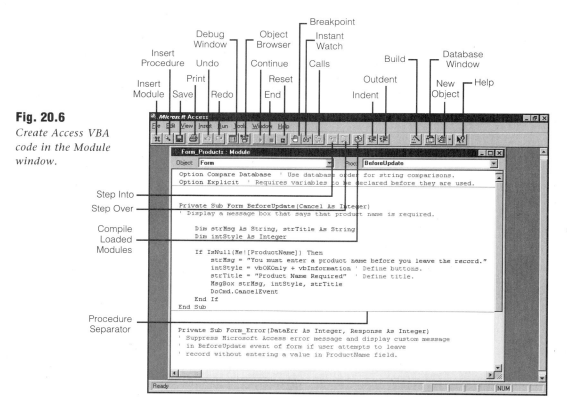

Fig. 20.6
Create Access VBA code in the Module window.

In figure 20.6, Form is selected in the Object drop-down list. The Object list also includes (General) as the first item. This item corresponds to both the declarations section and the section containing general procedures. The (General) item is followed by the names of all of the objects on the Products form that can recognize events (including the form itself).

When you select the (General) item, the Procedures list displays a list with (declarations) as the first item followed by the names of the general procedures stored in the module. The (declarations) item corresponds to the declarations section.

When you select an object in the Object drop-down list, the Procedures drop-down list changes to display the list of events that the selected object can recognize. Only events shown in bold have event procedures stored in the module. In this example, only the BeforeUpdate and Error events of the Form object have associated event procedures in the module. Selecting an item in the Procedures list moves the insertion point to the beginning of the corresponding procedure.

In a standard module, the Object drop-down list displays (General) as a single item. The Procedures drop-down list displays (declarations) as the first item followed by the names of the procedures stored in the module.

When you write code, you should indent statements to make your code more readable. Also, you should include comments to document and explain your logic (see fig. 20.6). Precede each comment by an apostrophe ('). You can place comments in a separate line or embed them in lines of code.

The Module window toolbar includes buttons for creating new modules or procedures, printing, editing, compiling, running, and debugging your code.

You create a new general procedure by choosing Insert, Procedure or clicking the Insert Procedure toolbar button. Figure 20.7a shows the Insert Procedure dialog box where you enter the name of the procedure; specify its type as Sub, Function, or Property; specify its scope as Public or Private; and specify the lifetime of its variables.

You create a new event procedure by selecting an object in Design view, clicking in the event property in the property sheet, and clicking the Build button to display the Choose Builder dialog box (see fig. 20.7b). When you choose Code Builder and click OK, the form module opens displaying two lines of a *code template* containing the first and last lines for the event procedure. For example, when you create a new event procedure for the AfterUpdate event of the ProductName text box on the Products form, the code template is

```
Private Sub ProductName_AfterUpdate()
End Sub
```

Fig. 20.7

Use these dialog boxes to create new procedures: the Insert Procedure dialog box for a general procedure (a) and the Choose Builder dialog box for an event procedure (b).

(a)

(b)

The `Private` keyword indicates that the procedure is available only to other procedures in the same module. `Sub` and `End Sub` are keywords that indicate the beginning and the end of a subroutine. The name of the event procedure follows the naming convention

    objectname_eventname

The name of the subroutine is followed by a parenthesis that holds the parameters you want to pass to the subroutine. (Subroutines and function procedures can receive parameters, but only a function procedure can return a value.)

If the form module is already open, you create a new event procedure by selecting an object and an event using the two drop-down lists in the Module window; after making your selections, the insertion point moves to the first line of the code template for the new procedure.

Running Procedures

You can run a function procedure in these ways:

▶ *In an expression.* Use function procedures the same way you use built-in functions in property settings of queries and filters, in macro conditions and arguments, and in other VBA statements.

▶ *Trigger by an event.* Enter the expression `=functionname()` in the event property; include any arguments in the parentheses. The function's return value, if there is one, is discarded. For example, see the form module for the Main Switchboard form in NORTHWIND.MDB.

▶ *Run from a macro.* Use the `RunCode` macro action entering the expression `functionname()` including any arguments in the parentheses (do not enter an equal sign). The function's return value, if there is one, is discarded. If you want to run a subroutine from a macro, you must create a function procedure that calls the subroutine and run the function from the `RunCode` macro action.

▶ *Call from another procedure.* To call a function procedure from a subroutine or another function procedure, use either syntax as follows:

```
functionname argumentlist
Call functionname(argumentlist)
```

In either case, the function's return value is discarded.

▶ *In the Debug window.* Enter the name of a function procedure in a standard module using any of the following:

```
Call functionname (argumentlist)
? functionname (argumentlist)
functionname argumentlist
```

and press Enter. To run a function procedure stored in a form or report module, you must enter the full identifier of the function; for example:

```
Form_formname.functionname argumentlist.
```

You can run a subroutine procedure in these ways:

▶ *Trigger by an event.* When you create the event procedure by clicking the Build button of an event property and entering the subroutine in the code template provided, the subroutine is automatically associated with the event and runs with the event is triggered.

▶ *Call from another procedure.* To call a subroutine procedure from a subroutine or another function procedure, use either syntax as follows:

```
subroutinename argumentlist
Call subroutinename(argumentlist)
```

▶ *In the Debug window.* Enter the name of a subroutine in a standard module using either syntax

```
subroutinename argumentlist
Call subroutinename(argumentlist)
```

and press Enter. To run a subroutine stored in a form or report module, you must enter the full identifier of the subroutine; for example (shown for a form module): `Form_formname.subroutinename argumentlist`. If the subroutine is an event procedure, the form must be open in Form view.

Using the Wizards to Create Access VBA Code

A good way to learn how to create VBA programs is to analyze programs written by other people. In this section, you look at the event procedures that two of the wizards create. You observe how and why the "experts" define regular and object variables, use the Screen object and the Me property, run macro actions as methods, and create SQL expressions as part of the VBA code. First, however, you examine the components of a simple event procedure produced by the Command Button Wizard.

Anatomy of an Event Procedure

When you use the Command Button Wizard to create a command button (called cmdFirst) to go to the first record in a form, the wizard produces the event procedure shown in figure 20.8. We'll use this procedure as a model and examine its parts.

Fig. 20.8

The Command Button Wizard creates simple event procedures with error handling.

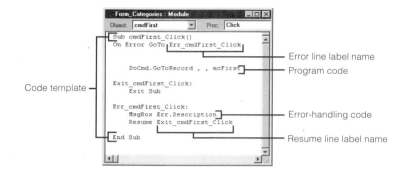

The first statement, the On Error GoTo *line* statement, turns on error handling. If a subsequent statement attempts an invalid operation while the procedure is executing, the following sequence occurs:

▶ A VBA run-time error occurs

▶ Access assigns a unique integer error code to the Number property of the VBA Err object

▶ The program branches to the line with the error-handling label followed by a colon

The statements between the error-handling label line and the Resume statement are the *error handling routine*. In this simple example, the error handling routine is a single line: a MsgBox function that displays a description of the error as the Description property of the Err object. More generally, you can test to determine what error occurred and write one or more sets of instructions you want carried out depending on the specific error. After the error handling routine is finished, the Resume *line* statement resumes execution of the procedure at the line with the resume label followed by a colon. In this example, there is a single program statement Exit Sub that causes immediate exit from the procedure. You can include a set of statements that you want to execute. If an error does not occur, the following sequence occurs:

▶ The program statements between the On Error GoTo *line* statement and the first label line are executed

▶ The Exit Sub statement is executed

▶ The procedure ends

If you don't include an On Error statement and error-handling code, any VBA run-time error is fatal to the procedure: an error message appears and the procedure terminates.

In this event procedure, the program statements section contains a single line of code that uses the DoCmd object to run a method equivalent to a macro action. Most of the methods of the DoCmd object have arguments—some required, and others optional. When you specify an argument in the argument list, all arguments before it in the list must be accounted for and separated by commas as placeholders, whether or not you enter values. If you don't enter a value for an optional argument, the default value is assumed. Omit the comma after the last specified argument, and omit the placeholder commas for optional arguments after it in the list.

In this example, the GoToRecord method has the same four arguments as the GoToRecord macro action: Object Type, Object Name, Record, and Offset. Only the third argument is required to specify the record you want to go to. Although the macro action argument provides a drop-down list of choices, the method argument requires you to enter either the number corresponding to the position of your choice in the list (the list is zero-based), or an intrinsic constant representing the choice. An *intrinsic constant* is a constant supplied by Access, VBA, or DAO and has a two-letter prefix indicating the source: ac for Access, vb for VBA, and db for DAO. To specify the First record, you could enter **2** (because First is the third choice in the macro action argument list for Record) or the intrinsic constant **acFirst**. In this example, the wizard omits the first two arguments (but includes the required placeholders), uses the intrinsic constant in the third argument to specify the record, and omits the fourth argument.

Using the Object Browser

An excellent way to learn about the objects, properties, methods, a method's arguments and syntax, and intrinsic constants is to use the Object Browser. The Object Browser is a new feature in Access 95. You start the Browser by clicking the Object Browser toolbar button when the Module window is active. Figure 20.9 shows how the Object Browser arranges its information. The Libraries/Databases drop-down list includes your database as the first item followed by the three built-in libraries:

▶ VBA contains references to all of the commands and constants of VBA.

▶ Access contains references to all Access constants and application objects including their properties and methods.

▶ DAO contains references to all DAO constants and objects including their properties and methods.

You can add references for other library databases to the list. After selecting your database or a library, the Modules/Classes list box displays the kinds of objects or categories of information available. When you select an object, the Methods/Properties list box displays the properties and methods for the selected object or a list of items for the selected category.

Fig. 20.9

The Object Browser displays the syntax for the GoToRecord method of the DoCmd object.

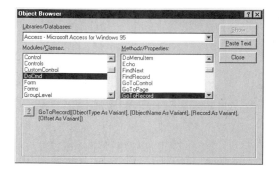

In figure 20.9, the Object Browser is looking up information in the Access library. The DoCmd object is selected in the Modules/Classes list box, and the GoToRecord method is selected in the Methods/Properties list box. After you make a selection, the lower pane displays information about the selection. In this example, the lower pane displays the syntax for the GoToRecord method. Clicking the question mark button summons online help for the selection. Clicking the Paste Text button pastes the expression into the module at the current location of the insertion point.

Using the Command Button Wizard

You can use the Command Button Wizard to automatically create a command button and attach a VBA event procedure for the Click event. With the form in Design view, you start the wizard by clicking the Control Wizards tool, clicking the Command Button tool in the Toolbox, and then clicking in the form where you want the button. The first screen displays a list of six categories of tasks, and a list of tasks for each category (see fig. 20.10).

In all, there are 32 tasks for which the wizard can create command buttons. If the task requires you to specify additional information, the wizard displays one or more screens to collect the information. For example, figure 20.11 shows the screens for the Open Form task. Figure 20.11a shows the screen where you specify what form to open, figure 20.11b shows the screen where you specify whether you want to synchronize the records in the form being opened, and figure 20.11c shows the screen where you specify the matching fields when you choose to synchronize the records.

Fig. 20.10

Use the first screen of the Command Button Wizard to select the task you want to carry out.

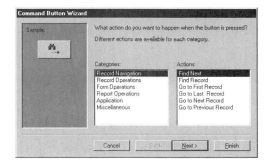

Fig. 20.11

The screens for the Open Form task gather information for synchronizing the records in the form the command button opens.

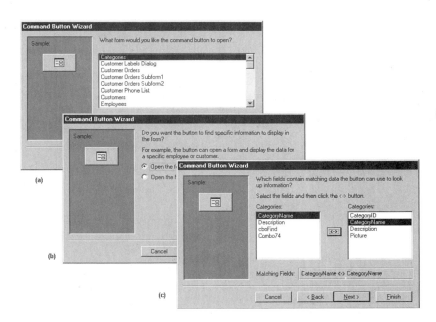

After supplying the additional information, you use the next screen to specify whether you want to display text or a picture on the command button (see fig. 20.12a). You use the final screen to name the command button (see fig. 20.12b). When you click the Finish button, the wizard creates the event procedure and the command button to your specifications. The wizard automatically links the event procedure to the command button. To observe the event procedure, click the Code toolbar button and locate the procedure in the form module. To test the wizard's work, switch to Form view, click the button, and follow these steps:

1. Using the Command Button Wizard, create command buttons in the footer of the Categories form for each of the 32 tasks. Supply additional information as needed. Figure 20.13 shows the completed form (it also shows a Lookup combo box created in a later section of the chapter).

2. Click the Code toolbar button. Select File, Print to print the entire module.

3. Study the event procedures observing the use of the DoCmd, Screen, and Application objects and the Me property, the declaration of regular and object variables, the use of intrinsic constants, and the Call statements.

Fig. 20.12

You can choose to display text or a picture on the button's face, and you can name the command button.

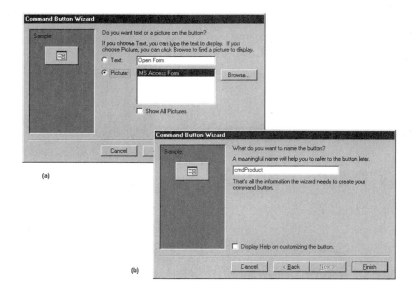

Fig. 20.13

The Categories form displays examples of all of the buttons you can create with the Command Button and the Combo Box Wizard.

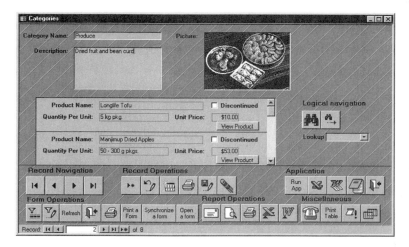

Table 20.6 lists the 32 tasks you can automate with the Command Button Wizard and describes the VBA event procedure the wizard creates.

Table 20.6   Tasks Automated with the Command Button Wizard

Category	Task	Description of VBA Event Procedure
Record Navigation	Go to First, Last, Next, or Previous Record Find Record, Find Next	Uses DoCmd to run the GoToRecord method for physical navigation. Uses DoCmd to run the DoMenuItem method to open the Find dialog box for logical navigation.
Record Operations	Add New Record	Uses DoCmd to run the GoToRecord method.
	Delete Record	Uses DoCmd to run the DoMenuItem method twice; first to select the record, then to delete it.
	Duplicate Record	Uses DoCmd to run the DoMenuItem method three times to select the record, copy it, and paste the record.
	Print Record	Uses DoCmd to run the DoMenuItem method to select the record and then use the PrintOut method to print the record.
	Save, Undo Record	Uses DoCmd to run the DoMenuItem method to save the record or to undo the record.
Form Operations	Apply Form Filter	Uses DoCmd to run the DoMenuItem method to apply the current filter for selecting or sorting groups of records.
	Edit Form Filter	Uses DoCmd to run the DoMenuItem method to open the Advanced Filter/Sort window for editing the current filter.
	Close Form	Uses DoCmd to run the Close method to close the active form.

20

continues

Table 20.6   Continued

Category	Task	Description of VBA Event Procedure
Form Operations (continued)	Open Form	Creates a string variable for the selected form name and a second string variable for the Where Condition synchronizing expression; creates the synchronizing expression if you chose to find specific data, and then uses DoCmd to run the OpenForm method.
	Print a Form	Creates a string variable for the selected form name, creates an object variable to refer to the active form, and then uses DoCmd to run the SelectObject method to select the form in the Database window, the PrintOut method to print the selected form, and the SelectObject method to select the active form.
	Print Current Form	Uses DoCmd to run the PrintOut method to print the active form (all records).
	Refresh Form Data	Uses DoCmd to run the DoMenuItem method to refresh the form.
Report Operations	Print Report	Creates a string variable for the selected report name and uses DoCmd to run the OpenReport method for printing the report (without opening the Print Selection dialog box).
	Preview Report	Creates a string variable for the selected report name and uses DoCmd to run the OpenReport method for displaying the report in Print Preview.

Category	Task	Description of VBA Event Procedure
	Mail Report	Creates a string variable for the selected report name and uses DoCmd to run the SendObject method for displaying the Send dialog box (for selecting a format).
	Send Report to File	Creates a string variable for the selected report name and uses DoCmd to run the OutputTo method for displaying the Output To dialog box (for selecting a format).
Application	Run Notepad	Uses the Call statement to run the Shell function to run the Notepad application.
	Run MS Word, MS Excel	Uses the Run method of the Application object to run a procedure in the UTILITY.MDA library database that starts Word or Excel as a toolbar application. Clicking the command button mimics clicking the Word or Excel toolbar button.
	Quit Application	Uses DoCmd to run the Quit method and quit Access.
	Run Application	Creates a string variable for the specified path to the application (you can include command line options) and uses the Call statement to run the Shell function to run the application.
Miscellaneous	Print Table	Creates a string variable for the selected table name, creates an object variable to refer to the active form, and uses DoCmd to run the SelectObject method to select the table in the Database window, the PrintOut method to print the selected table, and the SelectObject method to select the active form.

continues

Table 20.6 **Continued**

Category	Task	Description of VBA Event Procedure
Miscellaneous (continued)	Run Macro	Assigns the selected macro to the OnClick property of the command button (and doesn't create a VBA event procedure).
	Run Query	Creates a string variable for the selected query name and uses DoCmd to run the OpenQuery method to run the query.
	AutoDialer	Creates a string variable for the specified phone number, creates an object variable for the previous control (which is supposed to contain the phone number), tests the validity of the value in the previous control and sets the string variable to the value in the control or to the zero-length string depending on the test, then uses the Run method of the Application object to run a procedure in the UTILITY.MDA library database that starts the AutoDialer. Clicking the command button mimics clicking the AutoDialer toolbar button.

Note that all but six of the event procedures created by the wizard use the DoCmd object to run methods equivalent to macro actions. As exceptions:

▶ The event procedures for the Run Application and Run Notepad tasks use the Call statement to run the Shell() function. Shell() is a built-in function you can use to run any executable program.

▶ The event procedures for the Run MS Excel, Run MS Word, and AutoDialer tasks use the Run method of the Application object to run existing procedures in UTILITY.MDA, an Access library database. (A *library database* is a collection of custom functions, database objects, macros, and procedures you can call from any other Access database.)

▷ The sixth exception is the Run Macro task: in this case, the wizard attaches the macro directly to the event property and doesn't create an event procedure.

When you enter information, such as the name of a form or report, in one of the wizard screens, the wizard uses a Dim statement to create a string variable to hold the value. For example,

```
Dim stDocName As String
```

appears at the beginning of the eight event procedures for which you selected the name of a table, query, form, or report.

In automating three of the tasks, the wizard creates object variables. In the Print a Form and the Print Table tasks, the wizard automates the interactive sequence of selecting a form or table in the Database window and choosing the Print menu command. The wizard creates the object variable, called *MyForm*, to refer to the active form so that when the print task is finished, the previously active form can be made active again. The event procedures for these tasks include statements to declare and assign the object variable as follows:

```
Dim MyForm As Form
Set MyForm = Screen. ActiveForm
```

In addition, these event procedures include statements to execute the SelectObject method that selects the specified object in the Database window, the PrintOut method that prints the specified object, and the SelectObject method that selects the original form using the object variable to refer to it.

In the AutoDialer task, the task's design requires that you click the control that has the phone number you want to dial before clicking the command button. The wizard needs to refer to the value in the phone number control, so it creates an object variable to refer to that control as follows:

```
Dim PrevCtl As Control
Set PrevCtl = Screen.PreviousControl
```

The next step in learning Access VBA is to create simple event procedures of your own. For example, you might create an event procedure for the Current event of the Product List form that keeps the Products form synchronized (see the section "Conditional Macros" for the analogous event macro). Or, you can modify the procedures that the wizard creates. For example, create an event procedure that closes another open object instead of the active object, or modify the error-handling routine to display the error code number as well as the description.

20

Using the Combo Box Wizard

A new feature of the Combo Box Wizard is that it can create a Lookup combo box you can use to select a value from a list and display the corresponding record. Finding a record based on specific information is called *logical navigation*. You start the wizard by clicking the Control Wizards tool, clicking the Combo Box tool in the Toolbox, and then clicking in the form where you want the combo box. Select the third option button in the first screen to create a combo box for logical navigation (see fig. 20.14a). In the second screen, select the fields to display in the combo box from the Available Fields list (see fig 20.14b). The last screen gives you the opportunity to specify the combo box label but, unfortunately, not the combo box name.

As a specific example, create a Lookup combo box for the Categories form that includes both fields in the combo box list and displays the caption Lookup in the label (refer to fig. 20.13). When you select a value from the list, the form displays the synchronized record. The wizard creates the following event procedure for the AfterUpdate event of the combo box with the default name Combo74 (the number part of the default name will depend on the number of controls on the form):

```
Sub Combo74_AfterUpdate()
    'Find the record that matches the control.
    Me.RecordsetClone.FindFirst "[CategoryID] = " & Me![Combo74]
    Me.Bookmark = Me.RecordsetClone.Bookmark
End Sub
```

Fig. 20.14

You can use the Combo Box Wizard to create a lookup combo box for logical navigation.

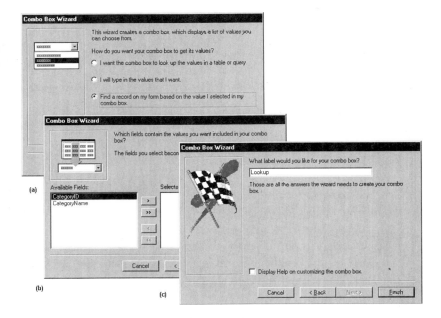

This elegant piece of code uses the form's RecordsetClone property to refer to the form's Recordset object as a clone for the form's underlying record source. Using the RecordsetClone property allows you to manipulate the records in the Recordset object independently of the records displayed in the form. The first statement uses the FindFirst method to find the first record in the Recordset object with a CategoryID that matches the value in the combo box and makes it the current record in the Recordset object. The second statement synchronizes the form's current record with the current record in the Recordset object: the right side of the statement returns the bookmark of the current record in the Recordset object, and the statement sets the bookmark of the current record in the form (Me.Bookmark) to the returned bookmark of the Recordset object.

If you change the name of an object, for instance to cboLookup, the object becomes disassociated from its event procedures. The event procedures previously associated with the object automatically move to the module's general procedures section. To make the event procedures work again, you have to rename the procedures and reestablish the links manually. You can rename an event procedure for the object by replacing all references to the object with the new name (including the procedure name). After renaming an event procedure, you can relink it to the object by clicking in the event property in the object's property sheet and selecting [Event Procedure].

Summary

This chapter has introduced you to the two programming languages in Access. Access macro programming is a simple programming language that includes only a few of the features of its more powerful parent; nevertheless, you can use macros alone to create complicated applications, and you should use macros as an effective way to learn the basic concepts of the Access programming environment. Visual Basic for Applications is a comprehensive programming language that uses objects arranged in hierarchies and manipulates objects by setting properties and executing methods.

Chapters 16 through 20 have given you a brief introduction to the advanced features of Access. For a more complete treatment of the features covered here, as well as comprehensive coverage of the many additional capabilities in Access 95, see *Special Edition Using Access 95* by Roger Jennings and *Microsoft Access Expert Solutions* by Stan Leszynski, both from Que Corporation.

Schedule+

chapter 21

Critical Skills in Schedule+

21

by Heidi Sullivan-Liscomb

In this chapter

◆ **Introduction to Schedule+**
You get a brief overview of the features and capabilities of Schedule+.

◆ **Starting Schedule+**
Schedule+ has several different log-on options. This section discuss group mode versus stand-alone mode and includes a discussion on profiles and passwords.

◆ **Using the Schedule+ Interface**
Schedule+ has many elements to its interface. Learn to use the different tabs found in Schedule+.

◆ **Printing**
Print reports for those times when you can't bring your computer with you.

Most people today use some type of calendar system. It may be a spiral-backed notebook, a preprinted wall calendar, a pocket organizer, or an electronic personal information manager. Schedule+ can replace your current paper or calculator-style calendar system, or it can augment your current system. Like more traditional time-management systems, Schedule+ enables you to schedule and track meetings, tasks, contacts, events, phone calls, and reminders.

Although there are a lot of similarities between Schedule+ and more traditional time-management systems, Schedule+ does not have the limitation that traditional time-management systems have: accessibility by others.

Introduction to Schedule+

Schedule+ 7.0 is an upgrade to the popular Schedule+ 1.0. Schedule+ has the appearance of a paper-base time-management system. Like your paper pocket or notebook organizer, Schedule+ has several tabs to organize itself into different sections:

▶ *Daily*. A one-day-at-a-time view of your appointments.

▶ *Weekly*. A weekly view of your appointments.

▶ *Monthly*. A monthly view of your appointments.

▶ *Planner*. The meeting planner enables you to see when other users are available for meetings, if you have access to their schedules.

▶ *To Do*. The To Do list enables you to track tasks that need to be completed but that do not have a specific scheduled time associated with them.

▶ *Contacts*. Think of this as an online address book. This feature is new to Schedule+ version 7.0.

The majority of scheduling challenge is eliminated when using Schedule+ due to its integration with both networks and Microsoft Mail, giving it group-enabled features. By being a *group-enabled application*, Schedule+ allows you to interact with other users. Most of us are familiar with the typical computer-based way of interacting with other users through an electronic mail system such as Microsoft Mail. Schedule+ takes this interaction to another level, allowing you access to other schedules and giving others the ability to access your schedule. You control the level of access to your schedule. Access permissions are set through Set Access Permissions found in the Tools menu. If you want to set it up as such, you can make sure that some people can have no access to your schedule. Others can see your appointments but cannot make changes to them, and still others have full access. Even those who have full access can be excluded from viewing more confidential appointments. You have full control over access.

This access can be controlled further with a group of special user roles. One assignable user role is Delegate. By assigning a user the role of Delegate, you allow that user to read existing items and modify them in the area chosen, including items marked Private. Another role is owner. An Owner can modify all your schedule. In addition, Owners can view and modify private items in your schedule, and they can change user access permissions for your schedule. To give someone complete control over your schedule, assign him the user role of Delegate Owner. This allows the selected user to modify all of your schedule—including private items and access permissions—as well as send and receive meeting messages on your behalf. This functionality is discussed in detail in Chapter 24, "Maintaining Security with Schedule+."

Starting Schedule+

Just as your traditional calendar is personal to the way you work, so is your Schedule+ schedule. Because Schedule+ is a group-enabled application, it interacts with Microsoft

Exchange. Because it interacts with Exchange, you need to have a profile set up before you can use all the features of Schedule+. A *profile* is a set of configuration options used by Microsoft Exchange and other messaging applications, such as Microsoft Fax and Microsoft Mail. A profile contains information such as the location of your Inbox, Outbox, and address lists. After selecting the profile to work with, you are required to log on with your user name and password. This is also necessary because Schedule+ integrates with your electronic mail system, which requires a user name and password. Some of these steps are skipped if you install Microsoft Office on a stand-alone machine.

 Note

At the time this book goes to press, Schedule+ 7.0 runs only in stand-alone mode on Windows NT. Schedule+ 7.0 requires the Exchange Client to run in group-enabled mode, which is not available at this time for Windows NT.

The first time that you run Schedule+ in stand-alone mode, Schedule+ asks whether you want to create a new schedule file or use an existing one. If you have been working group-enabled, you should use your existing SCD file, which is stored by default in the \Msoffice\Schedule folder. If you choose to create a new schedule file, which is recommended only for first-time users of Schedule+, Schedule+ presents a dialog box for you to enter a name and location for the file. The default location is the \Msoffice\Schedule folder, and the default name for the schedule files is your logon name. If you are running in group-enabled mode, the default name of the schedule file is the name of your mail profile, as configured through Microsoft Exchange.

 Note

If you are migrating from Schedule+ 1.0, your schedule file has the extension CAL instead of SCD.

The Group-Enabling Dialog Box

The group-enabling dialog box prompts you before starting Schedule+ as to whether you want to work in group mode or stand-alone mode. This dialog box is not available to all users of Schedule+. It is available to users running Schedule+ on a network and who have set up Microsoft Exchange. If you do not see the Group Enabling dialog box when you start Schedule+ and you know you should, see your mail administrator.

Working in a Group

If you connect to a network and install Microsoft Exchange, Schedule+ automatically starts in group-enabled mode. This allows you, if you have the correct access permissions, to view other users' schedule information. Unless you are in group-enabled mode, you cannot schedule meetings with other users using the meeting planning features of Schedule+. Also, when you are working in group-enabled mode, your local schedule automatically synchronizes with the copy of your schedule stored on the network server. This is how you receive updates to your schedule that other authorized users may have made.

If you want to log on in group-enabled mode, follow these steps:

1. Choose the Start button from the taskbar.

2. If the Group Enabled dialog box displays, select Yes, work in group-enabled mode, and click OK.

>
>
> **Tip**
>
> If you do not want to be prompted by the Group Enabled dialog box each time you start Schedule+, select the Don't Ask Me This Question Again check box.

3. Choose Programs, Microsoft Schedule+. This displays the Choose Profile dialog box (see fig. 21.1).

Fig. 21.1

The Choose Profile dialog box allows you to select the profile for this session of Schedule+.

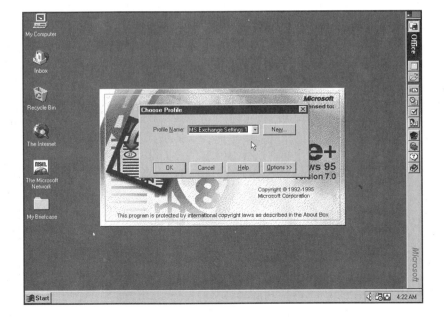

4. In the Profile Name box, type or choose your profile name, if it is not already displayed.

 Note
If you are running on a stand-alone machine without a MAPI electronic mail system, this dialog box does not appear.

 Tip
If you do not want to do this step in the future, choose the Option button and select the Set as Default Profile check box.

5. The Microsoft Mail dialog box appears. In the Password box, type your password.

 Note
If you select the Remember Password check box, the Microsoft Mail dialog box will not display in the future.

6. Click the OK button to complete the log-on process.

This procedure works if you have installed and implemented Exchange and have selected to work in group-enabled mode. If you accidentally selected not to work in group-enabled mode and selected not to be asked again, you can reset the option using REGEDIT and modifying the registry. Please use extreme caution whenever modifying the registry.

To modify the registry to prompt you for the Group-enabled option, follow these steps:

1. From the Start menu, select Run.

2. Type **regedit** and press Enter.

3. Select \HKEY_LOCAL_MACHINE.

4. Select \Software.

5. Select \Schedule+.

6. Select \Application.

7. From the right pane, double-click MAPIPresent.

8. Modify the value from 1 to 0.

9. Exit REGEDIT.

Working Alone

If you connect to a network and you have not installed Microsoft Exchange, then Schedule+ starts in stand-alone mode. You will not be able to view other users' schedules or schedule meetings with other users via Schedule+. This configuration is typical of a stand-alone home PC—there are probably no other user schedules.

If you connect to a network, but have installed Microsoft Exchange, you are prompted whether or not you want to work in group-enabled mode or stand-alone mode. Select the option that meets your needs.

To work in stand-alone mode, follow these steps:

1. Choose the Start button from the Taskbar.

2. Choose Programs, Microsoft Schedule+.

3. In the Logon Schedule+ dialog box, type your user name if it is not already displayed.

4. Choose the OK button to complete the logon process.

Recovering the Dialog Box

If the Choose Profile dialog box does not display and you would like to have the option of selecting your profile, you need to reset the Prompt for a Profile To Be Used option through Microsoft Exchange by following these steps:

1. Log on to Exchange.

2. Choose Tools, Options, and then the General tab (see fig. 21.2).

3. Choose Prompt for a Profile To Be Used.

4. Choose OK to close the Options dialog box.

Fig. 21.2

If you want to be prompted for a Profile when using Schedule+, use Exchange's Option dialog box.

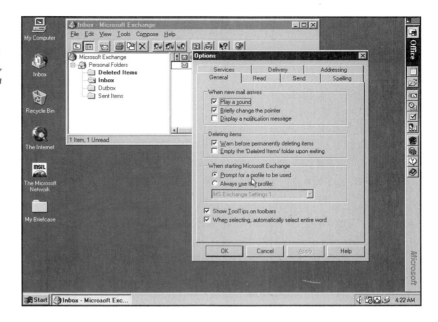

Logging on to Schedule+

As you have seen, a few things are needed to log on: a profile if you want to run in group-enabled mode, a logon name, and a password. The logon name identifies you as the user to Schedule+. The password secures your schedule from unauthorized use.

 Tip

You can bypass the prompt for logon name by creating a shortcut to Schedule+ and adding the switch: */u Name*, where *Name* is your logon name. If there is a space in your user name, you must enclose the name in quotation marks.

User Profile

Because Schedule+ is a group-enabled product, it relies on Microsoft Exchange for its transport mechanism. This means that you first must create a profile for Microsoft Exchange before you can use Schedule+. Remember that a profile contains your configuration information, such as your personal address book and whether your incoming mail is located locally or on the network. Information on creating a profile is found in Chapter 25, "Installing and Configuring Exchange."

Passwords

If you use Microsoft Exchange, your Schedule+ password is the same password you use to log on to Microsoft Exchange. You can change your password at any time. If you change your password through Schedule+, you are changing your local password. The local password is used when you need to work offline—for example, when you disconnect your laptop from the network.

If you want to change your password, follow these steps:

1. Choose Tools, Change Password to display the Change Password dialog box.

2. In the Old Password box, type your current password. Your old password will not display in the box as you type for security reasons.

 Tip

The first time you log onto Schedule+, you will not be prompted for a new password.

3. In the New Password box, type your new password.

4. In the Verify New Password box, type your new password again to verify it.

5. Choose OK to save the change to your password.

If the password you type in the Verify New Password box doesn't match the one you type in the New Password box, Schedule+ asks you to type your password again until they match.

Understanding the Schedule+ Interface

When you have successfully logged on, the Schedule+ window displays with the Daily tab for the current day selected (see fig. 21.3). The Schedule+ window has the graphic interface elements you would expect: a menu bar, a toolbar, and a status bar. It displays one of several views of your schedule. The currently displayed tab is the daily view. Each view is associated with a tab located to the left of the window. By default, there are six views and, therefore, six tabs:

▶ Daily

▶ Weekly

▶ Monthly

▶ Planner

▶ To Do

▶ Contacts

You can add or remove tabs to reflect the way you work. This ability is discussed in later sections.

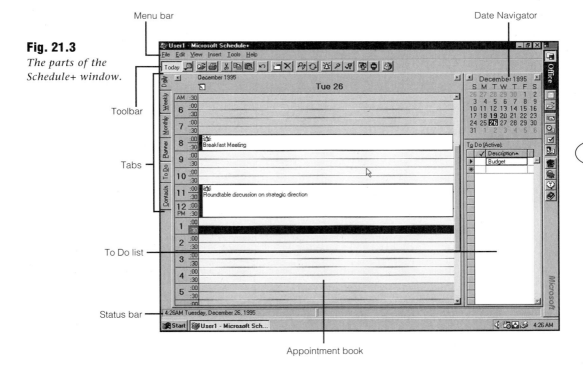

Fig. 21.3

The parts of the Schedule+ window.

The Menu Bar

Because Schedule+ is a Windows 95 application, it has a menu bar at the top of the window (refer to fig. 21.3). The menu structure has been changed in Schedule+ 7.0 from Schedule+ 1.0 to make it easier to use. See table 21.1 for a comparison of Schedule+ 1.0 and Schedule+ 7.0 menu structures.

Table 21.1   A Comparison of Menu Structures for Schedule+ 1.0 and 7.0

Schedule+ 1.0 Menu Structure	Schedule+ 7.0 Menu Structure
File	File and Options
Edit	Edit
Appointments	Edit, View, and Insert
Tasks	Edit, View, and Insert
Options	Tools and View
Window	[none]
Help	Help

The first menu item is File. The File menu enables you to do basic file operations, such as opening a schedule, exporting and importing schedules, printing, and exiting Schedule+.

The Edit menu has the standard menu items such as Cut, Copy, and Paste, as well as some appointment management options such as Move Appointment.

View controls the look of Schedule+, allowing you to customize the interface. For example, you can elect not to display the status bar or toolbar.

Insert enables you to create the elements used by Schedule+. You can use the Insert menu to create tasks, appointments, contacts, and more.

The Tools menu is where your utility functions reside such as Change password, Set access permissions, and Make Meeting. This menu is also used to access the Seven Habits Tool, which will be discussed in detail later in this book.

Finally, the Help menu is the menu you use to access online help for Schedule+ and the Seven Habits Tool.

The Toolbar

Like most Windows 95 applications, Schedule+ has a toolbar that displays just below the menu bar (refer to fig. 21.3). You click the buttons on the toolbar to perform commonly used commands quickly as shortcuts to the menu system. If you forget what a button does, position the pointer over the button. In a moment the button's ToolTip (name) displays in a yellow box. Table 21.2 shows the buttons on the Schedule+ toolbar.

Table 21.2   The Schedule+ Toolbar Buttons

Button	Description
Today	The Today button displays information for the current day in that view. This is a quick way to return to today's date if you have been working on scheduling or reviewing other dates. (Holding down shift as you click Today gives you the current time.)
	The Go To Date button indicates the date you want to display. It is a quick way to go to a specific date without having to scroll through the calendar. It is identical to the Go To command on the Edit menu.
	The Open button opens another user's Appointment Book if you have appropriate access permissions. It is identical to the Other's Appointment Book command on the Open menu of the File menu.
	The Print button prints the parts of your schedule that you specify. It is identical to the Print command on the File menu.
	The Cut button cuts the selected text to the Clipboard. It is identical to the Cut command on the Edit menu.
	The Copy button copies the selected text to the Clipboard. It is identical to the Copy command on the Edit menu.
	The Paste button pastes from the Clipboard text to the location of the pointer. It is identical to the Paste command on the Edit menu.
	The Undo button reverses or undoes the last action you took. There are times when this is a lifesaver. When in doubt, Undo! It is identical to the Undo command on the Edit menu.
	The Insert New Appointment/Task/Contact button opens a dialog box for you to insert a new appointment, task, or contact, depending on which view and what part of the view you are using. For example, if the active focus is on the Appointment Book portion of the Daily view, the button is called Insert New Appointment, and it displays an Appointment dialog box. It is identical to the Appointment, Task, or Contact commands on the Insert menu.

continues

Table 21.2 Continued

Button	Description
	The Delete button deletes the selected item or text. It is identical to the Delete Item command on the Edit menu when an item is selected or when the Delete key is pressed.
	The Edit button opens the dialog box for the selected item, such as appointment, task, or contact, so that you can edit the item. It is identical to the Edit Item command on the Edit menu.
	The Recurring button makes the selected item recurring. It is identical to the Make Recurring command on the Insert menu.
	The Reminder button switches the current reminder setting for the selected item. For example, if the selected item has a reminder, you can turn off the reminder by choosing the Reminder button. It is identical to the Set Reminder command on the Edit menu.
	The Private button switches the current privacy setting for the selected item. For example, if the selected task is private, you can make it visible by choosing the Private button. When the Private button looks as if it is pressed down, the item is marked private. It is identical to the Private command on the Edit menu.
	The Tentative button switches the current tentative setting for the appointment. It is identical to the Tentative command on the Edit menu.
	The Meeting Wizard button starts the Schedule+ Meeting Wizard to help you schedule a meeting, step by step. It is identical to the Make Meeting command on the Tools menu.
	The Timex Watch Wizard button starts the Timex Watch Wizard to help you copy (export) your schedule information to your Timex Data Link watch. It is identical to the Timex Watch command on the Export menu of the File menu.
	The View Mail button displays your Inbox, so you can read your meeting messages.

The Status Bar

At the bottom of the Schedule+ window is the status bar (refer to fig. 21.3). Typically, the current date and time displays on the left side of the status bar. If you are using the Daily tab, the time period you selected displays on the right side of the status bar. When you select a menu item, the status bar gives you a brief description of what the menu item does.

Adjusting the Screen Real Estate

Each area within the view can be resized and adjusted to your preferences. To the right of the Appointment book and between the Date Navigator and To Do List window regions is a dark line representing the window region's border. When you position the pointer over one of these lines, the pointer arrow changes to a resizing pointer that has a double-headed arrow with two lines.

To resize the different Window Regions, follow these steps:

1. Maximize the Schedule+ Window.
2. Position your pointer over the window region separator bar to the right of the Appointment Book.
3. Drag the separator bar to the right about two inches. The Appointment book area is now larger.
4. Drag the separator bar back to its original location.
5. Drag the separator bar located between the Date Navigation region and the To Do List down about three inches. The Date Navigation region now displays two months.

The Daily Tab

The tab that displays automatically when you open Schedule+ is the Daily tab. This means that you are ready to work with the Daily view. The Daily view is simply a one-day view of your appointments, meetings, and events. By default, you are looking at the items for today. There are three window regions in the Display view: the Appointment Book, the Date Navigator, and the To Do List (refer to fig. 21.3).

The Date Navigator

The Date Navigator enables you to quickly change the date that you are viewing in the Appointment Book by clicking the date you want to view. The current date is in a shaded box, and the date displayed in the Appointment Book is in a highlighted box. At the top of the Date Navigator are the month and year associated with the selected date. To the left and right of the month and year are arrow buttons that enable you to move to the previous or next calendar month (refer to fig. 21.3). To select a date from the Date Navigator, choose the desired date by clicking it.

 Tip

Right-click the Date Navigator to quickly go to Today or to some other date.

To Do List

In the lower right corner of the Daily view is the To Do List (refer to fig. 21.3). The To Do List displays the To Do list items that are not completed.

The Appointment Book

The primary region of the Daily view you work with is the Appointment Book (see fig. 21.4). The Appointment Book displays your appointments, meetings, and events. The Appointment Book is divided into 30-minute increments known as time slots. Nonwork hours appear shaded. The default working hours are 8:00 through 5:00.

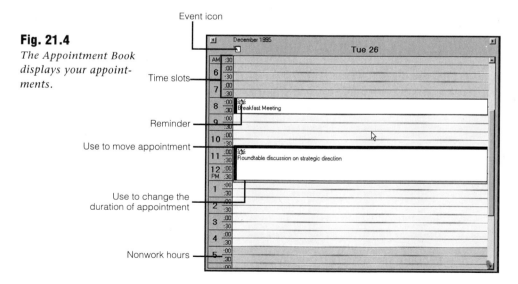

Fig. 21.4

The Appointment Book displays your appointments.

Tip

If you want to set your time slots to be a length other than 30 minutes, choose Tools, Options. Select the General tab and set the Appointment Book Time Scale to your preference.

 Tip

If you want to set your default work day to something other that 8:00 to 5:00, choose Tools, Options. Select the General tab and change the Day Starts At and Day Ends At options.

Scheduling an Appointment

The main function of Schedule+ is to maintain your own personal schedule. This is done primarily by scheduling appointments. After you schedule an appointment, you can modify it by changing its description or time. You can also give others permission to add or change appointments if you want to do so.

21

With appointments, you can do the following:

▶ Set a reminder for that appointment so that the appointment reminder displays a message box and a sound (alarm) is made.

▶ Invite other people to an appointment. This is a meeting.

▶ Set up an appointment as a recurring appointment so that you don't have to enter it repeatedly. For example, if you have a staff meeting every Friday at 2:00 p.m., or you go to aerobics every Monday, Wednesday, and Thursday, set these up as recurring appointments.

▶ Mark an appointment as private. When an appointment is marked as private, even those who have permission to view and change your appointments cannot view it.

▶ Mark the appointment as tentative. This feature is useful when you have an appointment that is tentative or easily rescheduled and you want others to be able to include you in a meeting for that time period if necessary.

You can schedule an appointment by either typing directly in the Appointment Book, or by using the Appointment dialog box.

You can schedule an appointment by doing one of the following:

▶ Double-click the desired starting time slot to access the Appointment dialog box (see fig. 21.5).

▶ Right-click the starting time slot and select New Appointment.

▶ Select the starting time slot and choose Insert, Appointment.

Fig. 21.5

The Appointment dialog box is used to add and edit appointments.

Editing an Appointment

After you create an appointment, you can easily edit it. To edit the description of an appointment, click the appointment and start typing. If you want to edit more than the basic information, you need to access the Appointment dialog box. To access the Appointment dialog box for an existing appointment, do one of the following:

▶ Double-click the appointment

▶ Select the appointment and choose Edit, Edit Item

▶ Select the appointment and press Ctrl+E

▶ Right-click the appointment and select Edit Item

▶ Use drag and drop

Schedule+ has a drag-and-drop feature that enables you to change the starting time or the length of the appointment. To use drag and drop to change the starting time and length of an appointment, choose the appointment you just created. Take a close look at it. At the top of the appointment is a dark shaded bar, and at the bottom of it is a lighter shaded bar. The top bar is used to move the appointment to a new time. The bottom bar is used to change the duration of the appointment.

Working with Events

There are times when you want to note an occurrence and associate it with a day but not a specific time. Examples of this are birthdays, anniversaries, and holidays. To include these types of dates, you add an event to your appointment book. Events are not listed with a time in your appointment book. Instead they are listed at the top of the appointment page.

There are actually two kinds of events. The first kind is the type of event that occurs the same time every year. An example of this is your birthday. It occurs the same calendar day every year. The other kind of event is one that doesn't occur the same time every year. An example of that may be a special sale that is going on at the store you work at, or if you want to make a note of the charity bake sale, or perhaps you want to note when your kids are off school. These are examples of events that do not happen the same calendar day of the year.

Adding Annual Events

There are two ways to add an annual event. One way to add an event is through the Insert menu; the other way is by using the Event icon. To add an annual event using the Insert menu, follow these steps:

1. Choose Insert, Annual Event. This displays the Annual Event dialog box (see fig. 21.6).

Fig. 21.6

*The Annual Event
dialog box allows you
to add and edit events.*

2. If the annual event is not occurring on the date that displays in the Annual Event dialog, choose the correct date.

3. Select the Description field type the name of the event.

4. If you want to set a reminder for the annual event, choose Set Reminder.

5. If you want to hide the annual event description from other users, choose Private.

6. Choose the OK button to save the information for the annual event.

The steps for creating an one-time event are very similar to creating a annual event. The difference is that instead of selecting Annual event, select Event.

Tip

If you do not want your events to display, from the Tools menu choose Options. Choose the Display tab and deselect Show Events.

At this point, you have covered the basic skills associated with working with the Daily view. You can create an appointment, move the appointment to a new time and/or day, make an appointment private, make an appointment recurring, and create an event, whether it is annual or not.

The Weekly Tab

Now that you are comfortable with the Daily view, let's work with the weekly view. The Weekly view has the same feature as the Appointment Book region of the Daily view. The main difference between the two is that you display more than one day's worth of appointments and events at a time. And just like the Daily view, you can add appointments, move them, add events, and perform other basic appointment management tasks. Figure 21.7 illustrates the Weekly view.

Fig. 21.7

The Weekly view enables you to view multiple days of your calendar.

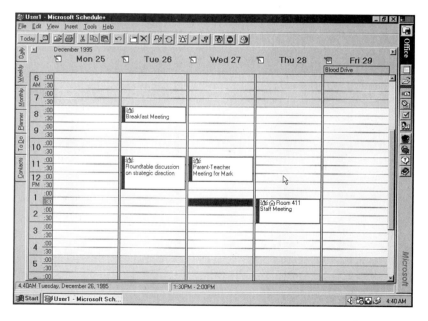

Notice that your appointment is listed in its time slot and the event is listed before the time slots.

Changing the Default Number of Days and Navigating the Weekly View

When you select the Weekly tab, you see the default number of days displayed, which is five days. You can easily change this if you want to see seven days, for example. Your choice for number of days displayed range from one to seven.

Most of us expect to see seven days at a time when we are in a week view. To change the number of days displayed from five to seven, follow these steps:

1. Choose <u>V</u>iew, Number of <u>D</u>ays.

2. Choose 7. Now all seven days are displayed.

You can easily select as many or as few days as you want to see in the Weekly view. This feature is available in the Daily view.

The Monthly Tab

As you can imagine, because you know how to work with the Daily view and the Weekly view, you know how to work with the Monthly view. The Monthly view is just another way to look at your appointments and events.

There are a couple of things to notice on this view. Events are not at the top of the window. They are listed on each day and prefaced with an asterisk. Appointments are listed in chronological order of occurrence within the day. If you have more appointments occurring than can be displayed within the day's box, a scrollbar displays. Figure 21.8 illustrates the monthly view.

Fig. 21.8

The Monthly view enables you to view a month's worth of appointments and events.

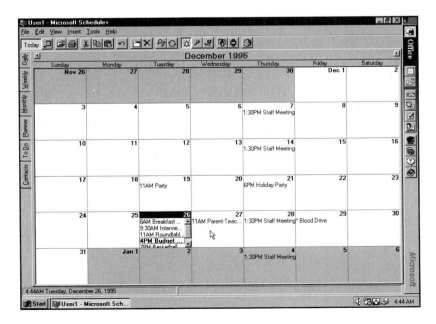

Changing the Day the Week Starts on and Navigating the Weekly View

By default, the first day of the week displayed in the Monthly view is Sunday. If you prefer a different day for the first day of the week you can change this through the Options menu item found in the Tools menu.

To change the first day of the week to Monday, follow these steps:

1. Choose Tools, Options, and then the General Tab (see fig. 21.9).

Fig. 21.9

The General tab is used to change the day the week starts on in the Monthly view.

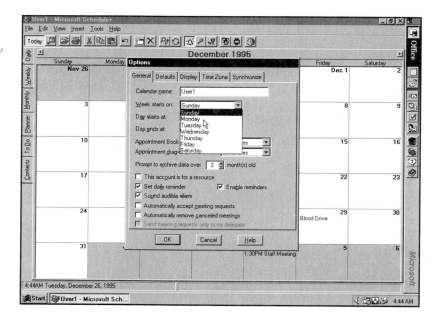

2. Change the Week Starts On to Monday.

3. Choose the OK button to exit the Options dialog box.

Navigating the Monthly view is very much like navigating any other view. If you want to move to the previous month or the next month, you can use the Previous and Next navigation buttons, which are found to the left and right of the month and year displayed.

Adding and Modifying Appointments in the Monthly View

Adding and modifying appointments in the Monthly view is similar to the way you do it in the Daily and Weekly views. There is one difference, however. You can't double-click to add an appointment. You have to use the Insert menu or the shortcut menu to add them. Another feature found in the Daily and Weekly views that is missing from the

Monthly view is drag and drop. You can't drag and drop appointments to move them to a new location. You need to select Move Appointment from either the appointment's shortcut menu or the Edit menu.

The Planner Tab

The last way to view your schedule is through the Planner view. The Planner gives you a graphical representation of your busy periods over several days. Your busy times are represented by bars (see fig. 21.11). This view does have an advantage over the other views. If you are running Schedule+ in group-enabled mode, you can also see other users' free and busy times. This is because the Planner is used to schedule meetings. The Planner adds other users' busy times to the view so that you pick the best time to have a meeting with those users. This feature is discussed in Chapter 24, "Maintaining Security with Schedule+." At this point, you are just going to take a brief look at the Planner view, as shown in figure 21.10.

Fig. 21.10

The Planner view is used with the meeting planning features of Schedule+.

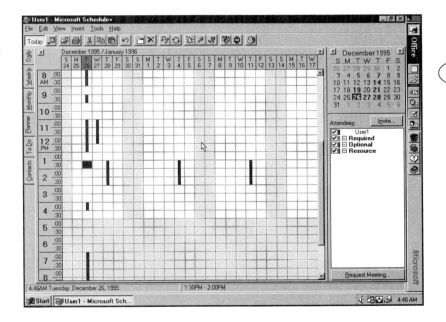

Navigating the Planner View

The free/busy display on the Planner view shows several days by default. The number of days shown depends on your screen resolution and the size of the Schedule+ window. If the window is maximized, more days show. If the window isn't maximized, less days are shown. When you switch to the Planner from another view, the Planner shows the same time frame as was displayed in the previous view. You can use the left and right arrows at the top of the display to move to different days, or you can click a date in the Date Navigator. The vertical bars indicate busy times.

The Attendees box displays the attendees you have selected by choosing the Invite button. This is part of the meeting planning feature that is discussed in Chapter 24, "Maintaining Security with Schedule+." In stand-alone mode, the Invite button isn't part of the Planning view. The Request Meeting button becomes the New Appointment button when running in stand-alone mode.

Adding Appointments and Events through the Planner View

Just as you can with the other views, you can add appointments and events to your calendar through this view. To add an appointment, simply highlight the time span for the appointment and from the Insert menu or the shortcut menu, select New Appointment. To add an event, select Event from the menu instead. You can't double-click to add an appointment. You have to use the Insert menu or the shortcut menu to add them. And is as the case with the Monthly view, you can't drag and drop appointments to move them to a new location. You need to select Move Appointment from either the appointment's shortcut menu or the Edit menu.

The Contacts Tab

A feature new to Schedule+ 7.0 is the contact list. The Contact view gives you a place to enter, manage, and track both your personal and business contacts. Think of it as an online address book or business card file. As a matter of fact, each contact is assigned a business card. Contact information is group-enabled just as your appointments are. You can give other users permission to view or modify your contact information. And, just as with an appointment or task, you can mark a contact as private to keep other users from viewing the information. This is on the right side of the Contact view and is called the business card. The left side is called the contact grid (see fig. 21.11).

The Business Card

Each contact has a business card associated with it. Each business card has several tabs:

- ▶ Business
- ▶ Phone
- ▶ Address
- ▶ Personal
- ▶ Notes

Business card

Fig. 21.11
Parts of the Contact view.

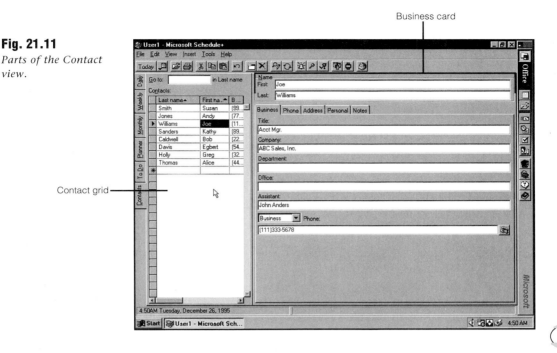

Contact grid

The Contact Grid

Each tab has several fields that correspond to a column on the contact grid on the left side of the Contact view. You can enter contacts into either side of the Contact view. Contact information can be updated easily.

Using the contact grid, you can group or sort your contacts. By grouping your contacts, you get a visual outline that you can expand and collapse based on how much detail you want. Sorting allows you to quickly organize your contacts in the way that you want. For example, you could sort by Last Name, Company, or Birthday.

Adding a Contact

Schedule+ allows you to add contacts in a variety of ways. You can type directly into the contact grid or the business card region. You can also add a contact using the Contact dialog box. Adding a contact through any of these ways updates the other portions of the Contact view.

To add a contact the three different ways, follow these steps:

1. Choose the first cell under the Last Name column in the contact view.

21

2. Type the name of your first contact. A contact could be a friend, a coworker, a vendor, or a family member.

3. Press Tab. This positions you in the First Name column. Notice that the business card area updates as you move to a new field.

4. Type in the first name of your contact.

5. Press Tab. This positions you in the Business Phone column.

6. Type a phone number for your contact.

At this point you have added a contact with minimum information. To add a contact with detailed information, follow these steps:

1. Select the blank line below the last contact.

2. In the business card region, choose First Name.

3. Enter the contact's first name.

4. Press Tab to move to the Last Name field and type the contact's last name.

5. Press Tab. This selects the Business tab. Press Tab again to select the Company field.

6. Enter the company for this contact.

7. If you want to, under Department enter their department name or code.

8. Another optional field is the Office field. This field enables you to assign an office such as "Northwest region" or "Detroit," for example.

9. If the contact has an assistant, enter their name in the Assistant field.

10. The next field is Phone. Select from the following types of phone numbers: business, home, fax, mobile, pager, assistant, business2, and home2.

11. Enter a phone number to correspond to the phone number type selected in the previous step.

12. Choose the Phone tab. The phone numbers you entered on the previous two steps are listed on this tab.

13. Choose the Address tab. You can enter two addresses per contact: a business address and a home address. Enter the address information you want for this contact.

14. Choose the Personal tab. This tab enables you to track more personal information, such as spouse, birthday, and anniversary. It also allows you to mark this contact as private. When you enter a birth date, a cake appears by that contact's name in the contact grid. When you enter an anniversary, wedding rings appear by that contact's name in the contact grid.

15. Choose the Notes tab.

16. The notes tab gives you a free-form area to enter additional notes on this user.

The last method you are going to use to enter a contact is through the Insert menu. You can enter the same basic information that you entered through the business card. The advantage of this approach is that you do not have to be on the Contact tab to add a contact. This could be done from the Daily view, for example:

1. Choose the Daily tab.
2. Choose Insert, Contact.
3. Enter a first name, last name, and business phone for the contact.
4. Choose the OK button to save the information.
5. Choose the Contact tab.

The contact grid reflects the recently added contact.

After you enter your list of contacts, you can easily manage them. Managing contacts can be the process of using the contact grid to facilitate making appointments. Managing contacts is also sorting and grouping your contacts. Perhaps you need to view them to make them easier to read and use.

Adding an Appointment from the Contact View

Let's say you are on the Contact tab and have just looked up a contact to get her phone number. After locating her record and number, you call her. She wants to schedule a meeting. Rather than going to another view, create the appointment in the Contact view.

You can create an appointment or a task from a contact by completing the following steps:

1. Choose the contact you need set an appoint with at this time.
2. Choose Insert, Related Item, Appt. From Contact. The contact's name you selected is automatically included in the description.
3. Enter the time and date for the meeting.
4. Choose the OK button.

Sorting and Grouping Contacts

The contact grid has three columns displayed: Last Name, First Name, and Business Phone. You can change the columns displayed or add to them. Sorting contacts is extremely easy. Each column has a column heading above it. To sort on that column, simply click it. If you want to sort by first name, click the First Name column heading. If you want to sort on last name, click the Last Name column heading. After a column is sorted, a sort button appears in the column heading, pointing upward if the sort is in ascending order or downward if the sort is in descending order. Ascending order is the default sort order. To sort in descending order, hold the Ctrl key while clicking the column heading. To sort on that column, simply click the column heading.

 Tip

You can choose the columns you want displayed in the Contacts, Projects or To Do lists. Double-click in any column to view the Columns dialog box. Use this box to customize your columns.

You can sort up to levels. This sorting is done through the Sort menu item found on the View menu. If you want, you can sort by company, and within company by last name, and then by first name. Just follow these steps:

1. Choose <u>V</u>iew, <u>S</u>ort. The Sort dialog box appears (see fig. 21.12). You can also access this dialog box by right-clicking the column heading.

Fig. 21.12

The Sort dialog box is used to organize your contacts.

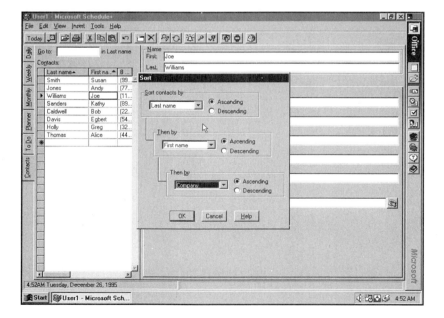

2. Choose up to three categories by which you want to sort your Contact List and indicate whether you want to sort in ascending or descending order. If you want to sort primarily by Company, and then by last name and first name, you select Company for the first key, Last Name for the second key, and First Name for the last key. Notice that you sort on columns that are not displayed in the contact grid.

3. Choose the OK button to complete the sort.

If you want Schedule+ to automatically resort your contacts whenever you insert a new one, use Autosort, which is in the Insert menu. From that point forward, the contact grid automatically sorts your contacts in alphabetical order by last name.

 Note

When you turn Autosort on, your contacts will not automatically resort. You still need to sort on the Last Name column one time. After that, Schedule+ resorts every time you insert a new contact.

Another option you have for organizing your contacts is by grouping them. This allows you to organize your contacts in an outline format.

You can group by up to three categories. You may want to group mainly by company and within each company by department. Group names are bold and display in outline form. This means that you can collapse or expand group lists to hide or show detail.

To group contacts, follow these steps:

1. Choose <u>V</u>iew, <u>G</u>roup By. The Group By dialog box appears (see fig. 21.13).

Fig. 21.13

The Group By dialog box gives you additional flexibility in organizing your contacts by allowing you to put them in groups.

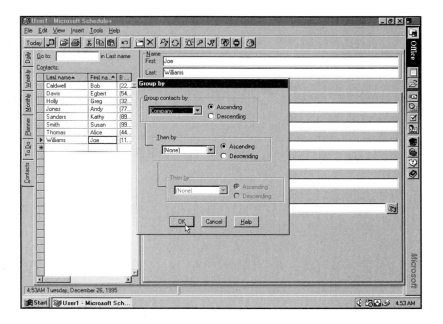

2. Choose up to three categories for grouping by selecting from the drop-down lists.

3. Choose the OK button to complete the grouping. Figure 21.14 shows an example of grouped contacts.

Fig. 21.14

These Contacts have been grouped by Company.

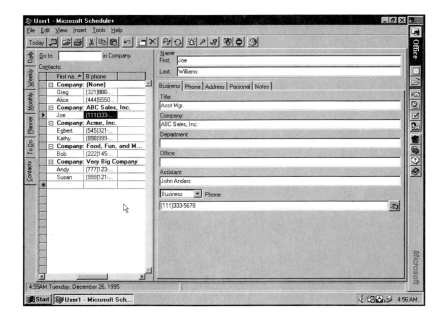

 When you have grouped your contact list and you delete a group, you delete the contents of that group. For example, say that you grouped by company and had the contacts Sue Smith, Joe Brown, and Alex Anders in the ABC Company. If you deleted that company, you would delete the contacts Sue, Joe, and Alex. If you do this in error, immediately choose Edit, Undo.

The To Do Tab

The To Do list view shows your tasks and projects on a spreadsheet-like grid. A task is something you want but isn't tied to a specific time like an appointment. Typically, a task needs to be done by a certain date, not at a specific time. An example of a task is buying gifts for the holidays. The To Do List allows you to enter, manage, and track tasks. The To Do List is found on the To Do and Daily tabs (see fig. 21.15).

You can assign tasks, end date, and duration. This is optional. If a task isn't completed by its end date, it appears in the To Do List as red. When you mark a task as completed,

Schedule+ draws a line through it. Schedule+ allows you to assign a priority to the task. Acceptable priority levels range from 1-9, A-Z. 1 is the highest priority and Z is the lowest. The default priority is 3.

Fig. 21.15

The To Do List helps you track tasks you need to complete.

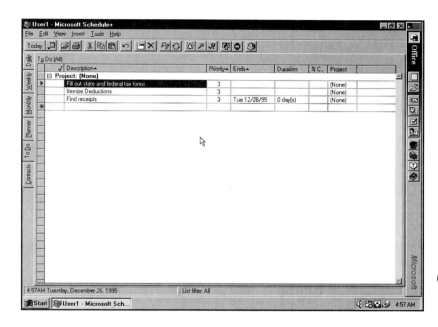

α **Note**
You can also use letter-number combinations, such as A1, A2, K3, and so on.

Inserting a Task

You can create a new task by either typing directly in the To Do List grid or by choosing Insert, Task. The ability to type directly in the To Do List is available from the Daily and To Do tabs. The ability to add a task via the Insert menu is available from all of the tabs. If you add a task through the Insert menu, the Task dialog box appears (see fig. 21.16).

Creating a Project

Just like contacts, tasks can be sorted and grouped. They can be sorted by completion date or grouped by priority. There is a special type of group for tasks, called a project. An example of a project is filing your income taxes. They are due on April 15, but you may (or may not) finish them before that date. When you do your income taxes, there are several steps involved: finding all of your receipts, itemizing your deductions, filling out the form, and so forth. You can create a task for each of these steps, and then you can organize them into a project called Income Tax. When you finish, you then have an idea of how long it took to do your taxes.

Fig. 21.16

The Task dialog box allows you to add detailed information about a task.

By default, you have a project named None. If you group your To Do List by project, which is the default, the project names are bold and preceded by an expand or collapse button. You can show or hide the tasks associated with a project using these buttons. A project is added through the Insert, Project menu (see fig. 21.17).

Fig. 21.17

The Project dialog box is used to add a project.

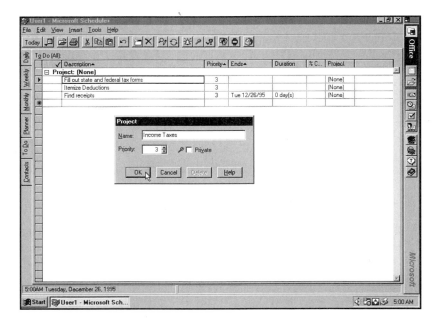

Printing

As you would with most Windows applications, you use the Print command from the File menu to print appointments, to-do lists, and contacts. You have a variety of layout choices and paper formats so that you can print the way that best suits how you work (see fig. 21.18).

Fig. 21.18
The Print dialog box allows you to choose the layout and paper format for printing.

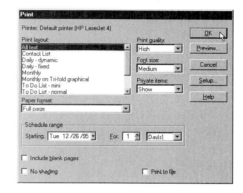

Print Layouts

Schedule+ has a variety of print layouts for you to choose so that you can print just the information you need. There are print layouts for contacts, appointments, and events as well as to-do lists. All print layouts include your name at the top. These available layouts are as follows:

▶ *Contact List.* This layout prints your contacts in the order they are sorted and grouped by.

▶ *Daily - Dynamic.* This layout is similar to the Daily - Fixed print layout but does not have an area to write other appointments.

▶ *Daily - Fixed.* Along with your name at the top of the Daily layout is this month's calendar. Along the left side of the report are the appointments and events for the selected day. On the right side is a section for you to write in other appointments and a listing of your active tasks.

▶ *Monthly.* The upper corners of this print layout are the previous and next months' calendars. The main body of this layout has the entire month's listing of appointments and events.

▶ *Monthly on Trifold Graphical.* The first trifold area displays the selected day's appointments and events. The middle trifold area shows your name and the next twelve months' calendars. The final trifold area lists your outstanding to-do list items.

▶ *To Do List - Mini, To Do List - Normal, To Do List - Text.* The to-do list layouts list your active to-do list items with various levels of detail.

▶ *Weekly - 5, Weekly - 7.* These layouts show you a five-day or seven-day week-at-a-glance view of your appointments and events.

 Note

If you have a description for a task, event, and so on, and it does not fit in the column, it will not wrap to the next line. Schedule+ does not wrap lines in printouts. It truncates the item at the end of the line.

Other Print Options and Selecting a Range

There are several other options you have when printing from Schedule+:

▶ Print Quality is dependent on your print driver and typically allows you to select high, medium, low, or draft quality.

▶ Font Size lets you pick a font size such as 10 or 12 points.

▶ The Private option lets you select from Show, which prints private items; Hide, which does not print private items; or Hide Text, which replaces the text of private items with the word *Private*.

▶ Paper Format allows you to select the paper size you want.

▶ Schedule Range is used to enter the starting date and the duration of the schedule you want to print. The larger the range, the more pages printed.

▶ Include Blank Pages, when selected, enables you to print pages with no appointments or tasks scheduled.

▶ No Shading, when selected, suppresses shading in graphical printouts. This can help to increase printing speed and increases legibility on certain printers.

▶ Print To File, when selected, prints the schedule to a file name you specify.

 Tip

The No Shading option is particularly useful when you're using a dot-matrix printer or when you're printing to a fax driver.

Previewing the Print

As with most Windows applications, you can Print Preview before actually sending the output to your printer. Set the options you want to print, select the Print Preview button, and review the output on your screen. If you need to have a closer look at the output, select the Zoom In button. When you finish previewing, choose the Close button.

Summary

Schedule+ is many things: an appointment book, a contact management system, a meeting planning tool, and a task manager. It is strongly integrated with Microsoft Exchange, giving you the ability to work as a group member and share your appointments, tasks, contacts, and events. You have the flexibility to set up appointments, events, and tasks as one time or recurring items. You can view this information through the Daily, Weekly, Monthly, and Planner tabs. Contacts are just as easy to work with and are easily sorted and grouped to meet your information needs.

21

chapter 22

Exchanging Information Using Schedule+

by Sue Mosher

In this chapter

◆ **Converting from an earlier version of Schedule+**
You can convert your old CAL schedule file to the new version of Schedule+.

◆ **Working in a mixed version environment**
Expect some limitations until everyone is converted to Schedule+ 7.0.

◆ **Interfacing with PIMs and palmtops**
You can exchange data directly with other systems and export to the Timex Data Link watch.

◆ **Importing and exporting text files**
If your PIM can write a delimited text file, you can probably import it into Schedule+.

◆ **Managing Schedule+ files**
Store group data, archives, and backups in their own files.

A ppointments, addresses, phone numbers, tasks, and projects are some of the most frequently used elements of your workday. Schedule+ offers many tools to help you redeploy those facts in other ways. You can exchange data with personal information managers (PIMs), download information to a Timex Data Link watch, or extract data into auxiliary Schedule+ files for backup, archiving, and interchange. Figure 22.1 shows the many possible types of direct information exchange.

Previous users of Schedule+ 1.0 have special interchange concerns. Although they will be able to convert their schedule files to Schedule+ 7.0, this chapter also advises them of the limitations involved in workgroups with a mixture of Schedule+ 1.0 and 7.0 users.

Basic file management is as important to Schedule+ as to most other applications. This chapter describes the built-in functions that help you archive, exchange data with other Schedule+ users, and make backups of your schedule for safekeeping.

Converting Schedule+ 1.0 CAL Files

Schedule+ 1.0 used a different file layout with a CAL extension for its primary schedule file. This difference presents some limitations when using Schedule+ 1.0 and 7.0 together in a workgroup, as the next section explains.

However, you should have no problem converting your existing CAL file to the new Schedule+ 7.0 format, which uses the SCD extension. Therefore, you can maintain all your previous appointments and tasks. Follow these steps the first time you run Schedule+ 7.0:

1. If Schedule+ can detect a previous CAL file, you see the dialog box in figure 22.1, which asks you to confirm the update process. Choose Yes.

2. If Schedule+ cannot find a CAL file for you, you see the Welcome to Schedule+ 7.0 dialog box (see fig. 22.2). Click the middle choice, I want to use an existing sched- ule file. Then choose OK.

3. Use the Select Local Schedule dialog box to browse your system and select your old schedule file (see fig. 22.3). The file should have a CAL extension. Choose Open.

4. If you are asked for a password, enter the password you used with your old Schedule+ 1.0 schedule file.

5. The next dialog box (similar to fig. 22.1) asks you to confirm the update process. Choose Yes.

Fig. 22.1

Choose Yes to move appointments and tasks from your old CAL file into your new Schedule+ 7.0 schedule file.

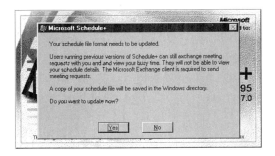

Fig. 22.2

If you have used an earlier version of Schedule+, choose to use your existing file so you can convert all your appointments and tasks.

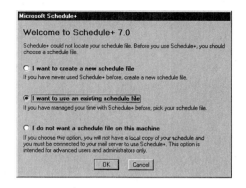

Fig. 22.3

Browse your system to locate the CAL file you used with Schedule+ 1.0.

Schedule+ 7.0 creates a new schedule file with the same name as your CAL file, only with an SCD extension.

Schedule+ 7.0 doesn't support backwards conversion. That is, you cannot open the new SCD file with the old version of Schedule+. However, the old CAL file is saved in its original location. If you choose to revert to the older version, the old file is available. Of course, the file doesn't contain any new appointments made since you converted to Schedule+ 7.0.

 Note

The Calendar program included with Windows 3.x (but not with Windows for Workgroups, which incorporated Schedule+ instead) also used a CAL extension for its files. You cannot convert these files directly to Schedule+ 7.0 schedule files. A Windows Calendar filter is included in the IntelliLink Plus add-in. Look at how to get it and use it in the later section "Exchanging Data with PIMs and Palmtops."

22

Working with Mixed Versions of Schedule+

If you are in a large group environment, with many users sharing schedules or booking meetings, you will confront some limitations until you get all users converted to Schedule+ 7.0. The file structures of the two versions are quite different, leading to differences in the way the two programs operate, as outlined in table 22.1.

Table 22.1   Differences Between Schedule+ 1.0 and 7.0 in a Mixed Environment

Task	Schedule+ 7.0	Schedule+ 1.0
View free or busy times	Yes	Yes
Open Schedule+ 1.0 users' appointment books	Only for read-only access	For read/write, depending on access rights
Open Schedule+ 7.0 users' appointment books	For read/write, depending on access rights	No

One strong point of Schedule+ as a group scheduling application is the ability to schedule conference rooms and other resources and to delegate control of your schedule to someone else. (Schedule+ 1.0 used the term assistant rather than delegate.)

Using resources and delegates in a mixed environment, however, is tricky. If a Schedule+ 7.0 user invites a 1.0 resource to a meeting, the invitation goes only to the resource, not to the resource's delegate. In the same fashion, an invitation sent by a Schedule+ 1.0 user to a 7.0 user does not go to the resource's delegate, but only to the resource.

You probably shouldn't use delegates with resources. Instead, set up resource accounts so that meeting requests for them are booked automatically—at least when the person setting up the meeting is working with the same version of Schedule+ as the resource. For Schedule+ 1.0, you set the default access privilege to Create Appts and Tasks. For Schedule+ 7.0, use the Tools, Options, General dialog box and check Automatically Accept Meeting Requests.

For the person scheduling the meeting to receive confirmation that the resource has been booked, you need to log in as that resource, accept the meeting request, and send a response.

Whether you set a resource up as a 1.0 user or a 7.0 user depends on two factors:

▶ Do you want all users to be able to view details of the resource's schedule? If so, then make the resource a Schedule+ 1.0 user.

▶ What version of Schedule+ is used by the person responsible for logging in as the resource and confirming meeting invitations? Set up the resource with an account using the same version.

Exporting to the Timex Data Link Watch

The Timex Data Link watch is not just a timepiece, but also a personal information manager storing up to 70 entries (such as appointments, anniversaries, phone numbers, tasks, and alarms). This section shows you how to upload these entries to the watch directly from Schedule+ without any cable or infrared connection. You also learn how to synchronize the watch with your PC's time.

The data is transferred by turning your computer display into a blur of special flashing bars. (The Data Link watch is not compatible with portable computers because their LCD monitors can't transfer data in this manner.)

Downloading Data Options

To transfer data from Schedule+ to your Timex Data Link watch, follow these steps:

1. Choose File, Export, Timex Data Link Watch to display the Timex Data Link Watch Wizard, shown in figure 22.4.

Fig. 22.4

Choose what data to export from Schedule+ to the Timex Data Link watch.

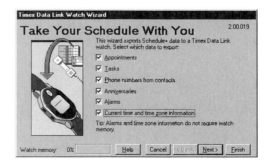

2. Select the type(s) of data you want to export, then choose Next.

3. On subsequent screens, you can choose options for each type of data (such as how many days of appointments and tasks to export, which phone numbers and anniversaries to transfer, what alarms to set, and how to handle time zones). Continue choosing Next to go through the screens.

 Note

Be sure you choose all the data you want the watch to hold. The watch cannot append to the information it already contains, so you must do a complete export each time.

4. After you complete your selections, the Data Summary screen tells you how much of the watch memory you will use with this export operation (see fig. 22.5). You can choose Back to revise your choices or Finish to prepare for the export.

5. After you choose Finish, press the Mode button on the watch until it says COMM mode. In a couple of seconds, it will switch to COMM READY mode. When it does, hold the watch up so that the little "eye" on the watch is directed toward the screen.

6. Choose OK in the Export to Watch dialog box. Schedule+ sends the selected data to the watch with the flashing bars.

Fig. 22.5

The Data Summary screen shows how much watch memory your transfer selections will use.

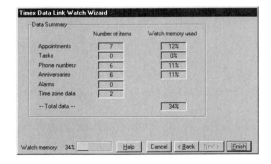

Calibrating the Screen

If the data does not transfer to the watch, you may need to first calibrate the watch to the screen. Follow these steps:

1. Choose File, Export, Timex Data Link Watch.

2. Choose Finish.

3. In the Export to Watch dialog box, hold down Ctrl key and choose Cancel, then click OK to continue.

4. Put the watch in COMM READY mode, as described in step 5 under "Downloading Data Options," and hold it up to the screen.

5. Adjust the lines with the arrow keys until the watch starts beeping at regular intervals. Then press any key to end the calibration procedure.

Synchronizing the Time

One of the choices on the Watch Wizard is to export current time and time zone information. This feature is especially useful if you are traveling to another time zone.

For example, if you normally work in the Eastern time zone in the U.S. but are traveling to the Central time zone, you can use the custom time zone settings to force all the appointments you're exporting to adjust by an hour (see fig. 22.6). Your watch also sets to Central time.

Fig. 22.6

Use the time export function to synchronize your watch with your PC and to adjust the times of appointments at your destination.

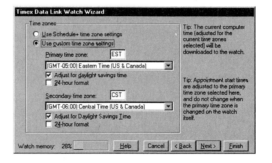

To synchronize your watch to the second, open the DATALINK.INI file found in your Windows folder and add the line **SyncTime=1** to the [Settings] section. Without this line, the times on your PC and watch will be several seconds apart.

 Note

All appointments stored in the Timex Data Link watch are rounded to the nearest quarter-hour. This means that, if you're going on a trip and list your departure time in Schedule+ as 11:10, the data downloaded to the watch will show 11:15. Because you certainly don't want to be five minutes late for your flight, you should probably set the time in Schedule+ for 11:00, instead. You can include the real departure time (11:10) in the description of the appointment.

Exchanging Data with PIMs and Palmtops

You can directly exchange data from several personal information managers (PIMs) and palmtop computers with Schedule+. This capability enables you to easily convert from your previous PIM or to take your appointments and tasks on the road in your pocket.

Obtaining Conversion Tools

The only converters included with Schedule+ are those for the Sharp palmtops. Microsoft is planning the release of additional import-only converters free of charge.

Table 22.2 shows where you can get converters for various applications and palmtops.

Table 22.2   Sources for Application and Palmtop Converters

Applications	Sources
ACT! for Windows 1.1 & 2.0	IntelliLink Microsoft add-in (import only)
Advantage	IntelliLink
CaLANdar	IntelliLink
Commence 2.0	IntelliLink
dBASE III/IV	IntelliLink
ECCO	IntelliLink Microsoft add-in (import only)
Excel 5.0 & 7.0	IntelliLink
Lotus Organizer 1.x & 2.x	IntelliLink Microsoft add-in (import only)
PackRat 4.1+ & 5.0	IntelliLink Microsoft add-in (4.1, import only)
Paradox	IntelliLink
Sidekick 2.0 for DOS	IntelliLink
Windows Calendar	IntelliLink
Windows Cardfile	IntelliLink Microsoft add-in (import only)
Word 6.0 & 7.0	IntelliLink
WordPerfect for Windows	IntelliLink

Palmtops		Sources
Casio	SF-4/5000 SF-5300B SF-7/9000 SF-7900 SF-R10/R20	IntelliLink
HP	100/200LX 95LX OmniBook	IntelliLink
Newton		LandWare (Sync+)
Psion	3 & 3A	IntelliLink
Sharp	5000/7400 Series 6500/9000 Series 7600 Series 8000/8200 Series 8600/YO-600 Series	Included with Schedule+
Sharp	Zaurus	IntelliLink
Tandy	Z-PDA/Casio Z-7000	IntelliLink

IntelliLink plans to expand the list of PIMs and palmtops it supports with Schedule+ data interchange. For an updated list, contact IntelliLink:

Voice:	(603) 888-0666
Fax:	(603) 888-9817

The Sync+ program for use with the Newton is available from LandWare:

Voice:	(201) 347-0031
Fax:	(201) 347-0340
Email:	sales@landware.com

Importing and Exporting with a PIM or Palmtop

To use the Sharp import/export filter included with Schedule+ or any of the IntelliLink add-in filters, follow these steps:

1. Choose File, Import or Export, then Other Systems.
2. From the Select Target System list shown in figure 22.7, highlight the application or palmtop you want to exchange data with, then choose OK.

Fig. 22.7
The IntelliLink Plus add-in enhances your import/export options with links to other palmtops plus a variety of PIMs and other applications.

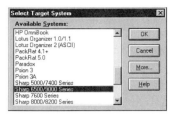

3. The Schedule+ 7.0 Import or Export dialog box has three tabs with selections you need to review. On the Main tab, shown in figure 22.8, choose what you want to import or export and where you want to direct that data. The choices vary depending on the palmtop or application to which you're linking.

Fig. 22.8
You must select what you want to export and to which area of your palmtop or application. The Import dialog box works the same way, only in reverse.

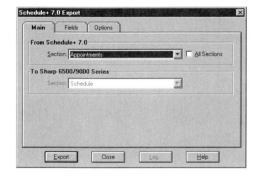

4. The Fields tab shown in figure 22.9 is extremely important. You must map the fields in Schedule+ to those available in your application or palmtop. Select a field from the left column and one from the right, then choose Map. (This button changes to Unmap when you map a pair of fields.)

Fig. 22.9
Use the Fields tab to match up Schedule+ fields with those in your palmtop or application.

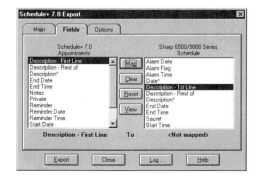

5. Click each of the choices in the Options tab (<u>G</u>eneral, <u>D</u>ate Range, your linked application or palmtop, and Schedule+ 7.0 if importing) and make any necessary changes. The available options are shown in table 22.3.

6. Choose <u>I</u>mport or <u>E</u>xport to complete the operation. If you are interfacing with a palmtop, you get instructions on how to connect to it.

Table 22.3   Import and Export Options for Applications and Palmtops

General	Description
Fan-out unknown recurring items	If the target system doesn't support recurring items, this setting transfers an individual entry for each instance of a recurring appointment. If you uncheck it, only the first instance transfers.
Auto-disconnect handheld after transfer	(Palmtops only) Disconnects after the import/export operation
Include completed To Do items	Transfers tasks that have been marked completed
Transfer To Do items with Appointments	Transfers tasks at the same time as appointments

Date Range	Description
Type	Date Range choices, including: 　　All 　　Today 　　This Week 　　This Month 　　This Year 　　Relative Date Range before and 　　after today 　　Absolute Date Range
Week Starts On	Used with the This Week range
From/To	Used with all (except All and Relative Date Range)
Days Before/After Today	Used with Relative Date Range

continues

22

Table 22.3 Continued

Target Application or Palmtop	Description
Com Port	For palmtops, set the communications port used for palmtop interface
Other settings	Various, depending on the target application, including conflict resolution, executable application, and so on

Schedule+ (Import Only)	Description
Conflict Resolution	Determines how Schedule+ deals with conflicting tasks or contacts and with overlapping appointments:
	Add: Retains the original record and adds the new one
	Ignore: Keeps the original record and ignores the new one
	Notify: Enables you to resolve each conflict individually. This setting is the normal default.
	None: Duplicate records are added where conflicts occur.
	Replace: Removes the original conflicting record and replaces it with the new record.
	Update: Changes any fields in the original record to reflect information in the new record.

 Note

If you are using the Sharp import/export filter or the IntelliLink Plus add-in, be aware of a couple of limitations:

When exporting appointments or tasks from Schedule+, all recurring items are exported, including any dates you may have excluded. For example, if you have a weekly staff meeting every Wednesday except December 27, Schedule+ exports the meeting for every Wednesday including December 27.

To import to Schedule+, make sure you have not selected Disallow Recurring Items or Disallow Overlapping Appointments in the Tools, Set Access Permission, Global dialog box. If you have either of these items checked, some appointments may not transfer.

Even if you do not find your PIM or other application on the list in table 22.2, you probably can exchange data with it using Schedule+'s capability for importing and exporting text files using a delimited format. The following section describes this technique.

Exchanging Data with Text Files

What if no direct converter exists for your PIM or other application? All is not lost. If your PIM or application can read and write a delimited text file, also known as a comma-separated value (CSV) file, you can exchange at least part of its information with Schedule+.

If you have never worked with delimited text files before, you can think of them as representing columns and rows in a table or spreadsheet. (In fact, Excel is a great tool for generating a delimited text file.) Each pair of commas marks the beginning and end of a column of data, and each line in the file is a new record—an appointment, event, task, or contact.

To work with a delimited text file, you need to perform several tasks with Schedule+:

▶ Tell Schedule+ what file to use for importing or exporting.

▶ Indicate what kind of Schedule+ data you want to exchange (only one type at a time).

▶ Select the separators used to delimit the data.

▶ Either choose the fields to be exported or match the fields being imported with those available in Schedule+.

These steps take place in a different order, depending on whether you're importing or exporting. This section looks at importing first.

Importing Text Files

Time spent carefully preparing your import file is time well-invested. Check your application's documentation for instructions on how to generate a delimited text file or CSV file. You get the best results if you limit the exported fields to those that you actually plan to bring into Schedule+ and export only one type of data—appointments, events, tasks, contacts—at a time.

If the application gives you the option of including field names with your data, use them. Then you can more easily match the fields with the Schedule+ equivalents.

 Tip

When you save the delimited file, use the extension TXT rather than CSV (Comma Separated Values). If you subsequently open the file using Excel, as discussed in the next section, the TXT extension automatically invokes Excel's Text Wizard. This Wizard lets you define the format of each column: General, Text, and Date. You can also choose to ignore a column. If you save the file with a CSV extension, the Text Wizard is not invoked.

Manipulating the Import File

If you cannot control the output from the source application, open the data in Excel or import it into Access and clean it up there. Use text functions, sorting, filtering, and formatting to build one or more clean import files with these characteristics:

▶ Single data type (appointments, events, tasks, or contacts)

▶ Consistent format for dates and times

▶ Data broken into fields that Schedule+ can use. For example, some PIMs put street address, city, and state into a single address field. Schedule+ needs to see those items as separate fields.

▶ Fields limited to only those you plan to use in Schedule+

 Tip

An easy way to see what your import file should look like is to do an export from Schedule+ first. Then open the file in WordPad or NotePad and examine the layout and the format of the individual fields.

Note

If you are planning to export from Microsoft Access 7.0 to Schedule+, take a look at the design of the table from which you're exporting, not just at the data in the table. Access 7.0 enables you to define table fields as lookups with links to other tables. The information in those linked fields displays in the data view of the original table. However, the actual data stored in that table may be completely different. In many cases, the data is an ID or other value that has no meaning for Schedule+. If you have an Access table with a linked field whose data you want to export, use a make table query to create a new table with the exact data you want to use in Schedule+.

Performing the Import

To import data from a delimited text file into Schedule+, follow these steps:

1. Choose File, Import, Text to open the Text Import Wizard, shown in figure 22.10.

Fig. 22.10

The Text Import Wizard first asks for the location of the import file.

2. Specify the location of the import file. (For this example, we created a CSV file by exporting the Employees table from the Northwind Traders sample Access database.) Choose Next to continue.

3. Indicate whether the first line of the data consists of field names (see fig. 22.11). Choose Next to continue.

4. The wizard continues to display the text sample to help you determine the delimiters for the file (see fig. 22.12). Make your selection, and then choose Next to continue.

Fig. 22.11
The Text Import Wizard displays the first few lines of your text file so that you can indicate whether the first line contains field names or data.

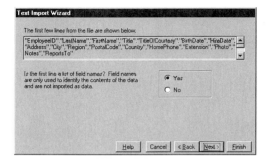

α **Note**
Comma separators and quotation marks around text fields are the most common delimiters, but don't blindly assume they apply to your file. Take a close look to confirm.

Fig. 22.12
With the initial text still displayed for reference, the Text Import Wizard asks you to choose the delimiters for the import file.

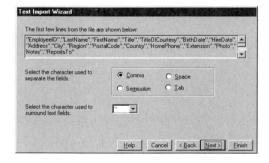

5. From the dialog box shown in figure 22.13, choose the type of data to import—only one type at a time. Choose <u>N</u>ext to continue.

Fig. 22.13
Choose the single type of data the import file represents.

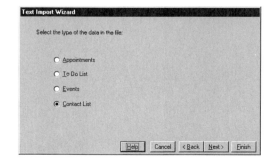

6. Match the source file's fields, shown on the left in figure 22.14, with the corresponding fields in Schedule+ on the right. The left column shows the field names if you chose Yes in step 3. If you picked No, then you see the first line of actual data from the import file. Click in the right column to activate the drop-down list for each field. If a field from the source file has no match in Schedule+, leave the right column set for IGNORE THIS FIELD. When you complete your selections, choose Finish to import the data.

Fig. 22.14

Each field in the source file (on the left) must be matched with a Schedule+ field (on the right) or marked IGNORE THIS FIELD.

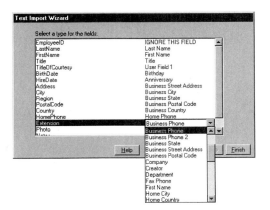

22

Figure 22.15 shows the data from our sample file imported into the Contacts section of Schedule+. Notice that the courtesy title, from the TitleOfCourtesy field matched with User 1 in figure 22.14, now appears in the User 1 field in Schedule+.

Also, see how the Notes field contains more than a full line of information and includes commas. Because the entire field was enclosed in quotation marks in the source file, the field could use commas without risk of it being interpreted as additional import fields.

Fig. 22.15

The data from the import file is appended to your Schedule+ schedule file.

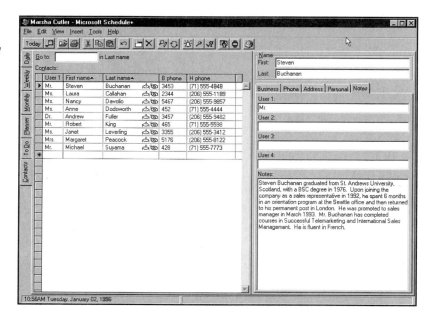

Exporting Text Files

Exporting from Schedule+ works much the same as importing, only in the opposite direction. Most word processors, spreadsheets, database programs, and PIMs can read delimited text files, giving you a way to extend the reach of your Schedule+ data.

For example, you may get so many contacts in Schedule+ that you want to move some or all of them to a departmental or company-wide database. A delimited text export transfers all that information with ease.

To export data from Schedule+, follow these steps:

1. Choose File, Export, Text to launch the Text Export Wizard.

2. Select the type of data you want to export—Appointments, To Do List, Events, or Contact List. Choose Next to continue.

3. If you chose Appointments, To Do List, or Events, you need to choose the range of dates defining the information you want to export. Choose Next to continue.

4. Select the delimiters, usually a comma between fields and quotation marks to surround text fields. Choose Next to continue.

5. Decide how to handle entries that contain carriage returns. (This doesn't mean items that span multiple lines because they're so long, but rather only those fields where you pressed Enter to start a new line while entering data.) If the application

where you're planning to use the Schedule+ data can handle fields with carriage returns, click No in the top box shown in figure 22.16. But if the application cannot handle carriage returns, choose Yes to export only the first line of each field.

Fig. 22.16

Two important export choices are how to handle fields containing carriage returns and whether to include field names on the first line.

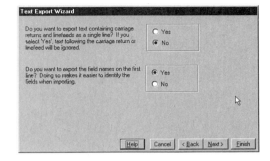

6. Decide whether to export field names as the first line of your delimited text file. As you saw in the import process, having the field names available can be very handy. After you make your choice, choose Next to continue.

7. In the dialog box in figure 22.17, you see the available fields for the data type you have chosen to export. Select the fields you want in the export file from the left column and use the Add button to place them in the right column. Use the Remove button to move any unwanted fields from the right column back to the left column. Then, reorder the fields if you like with Move Up and Move Down. After you have the right column's fields arranged in the order you want, choose Next to continue.

8. Provide a file name for the export file, then choose Finish to complete the export operation.

Fig. 22.17

Choose the fields to export, then adjust their order with Move Up and Move Down.

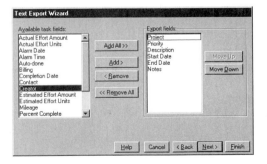

22

After you have exported the delimited file, you can use it as an import file for other programs, even for import by other Schedule+ 7.0 users. However, if you're exchanging information with other Schedule+ users, you can use an easier way. The next section takes a look at managing some of Schedule+'s special files, including interchange files.

Managing Files

This chapter has covered a lot of ground involving exchange of data with other applications and devices. This section explains how Schedule+ manages its own data with several special file types, detailed in table 22.4.

Table 22.4   Special Schedule+ Files

File Type	Extension	Uses
Interchange	.SC2	Exchange with other users.
	.SCH (Schedule+ 1.0 interchange)	Re-create your schedule file.
Archive	.SCD	Clean up schedule file.
	.ARC (Schedule+ 1.0 archive)	Review old schedule data.
Backup	.SCD	Back up schedule. Transfer schedule to another computer.

Note that Schedule+ 7.0 also can handle interchange and archive files generated by Schedule+ 1.0 users.

Using Schedule+ Interchange Files

Schedule+ interchange files are useful for exchanging data with other Schedule+ users. For example, Schedule+ does not have a facility for maintaining a global contact list or a list of company holidays. However, you can create a new Schedule+ file with File, New. Enter your holidays as events, and add the contacts you want everyone to have. Then export the data as an interchange file, following these steps:

1. Choose File, Export, Schedule+ Interchange.

2. In the Export Schedule+ Interchange dialog box, give a path and file name for the interchange file (see fig. 22.18). If you plan to make the file available to other users, be sure it's on a network drive that everyone can access.

3. Select the date range, choosing All Dates or specifying a range.

4. Choose what to export. Pick All Calendar Data if you want to exchange everything in the schedule file. Or select just one of the four types of schedule information.

5. Choose OK to complete the export, storing the data in the file you specified.

Fig. 22.18

Choose the location, date range, and type of data for your interchange file.

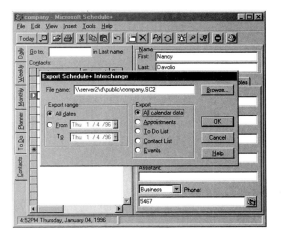

To import a Schedule+ interchange file, follow these steps:

1. Choose File, Import, Schedule+ Interchange.

2. Select the interchange file, then choose Open.

Caution

If you export to an interchange file, make changes in your schedule, then import the same interchange file; those appointments and other data that were changed revert to the way they were before you exported. This condition is due to the way Schedule+ stores pointers to the different appointments, events, tasks, and contacts.

Archiving Files

Last month's schedule may be of historical value, but it's probably not something you need to view every day. Schedule+ recognizes this situation by building in an automatic archive function. You also can archive manually at any time.

Archived items are automatically deleted from your schedule file at the same time they're appended to the archive file, thus shrinking your schedule file so it loads faster.

You can open any archive file directly in Schedule+ without any conversions, so you can quickly review last month's meetings when you need them.

Using Automatic Clean-Up

You get your first clean-up reminder about a month after you install Schedule+ 7.0. Figure 22.19 shows you what to expect.

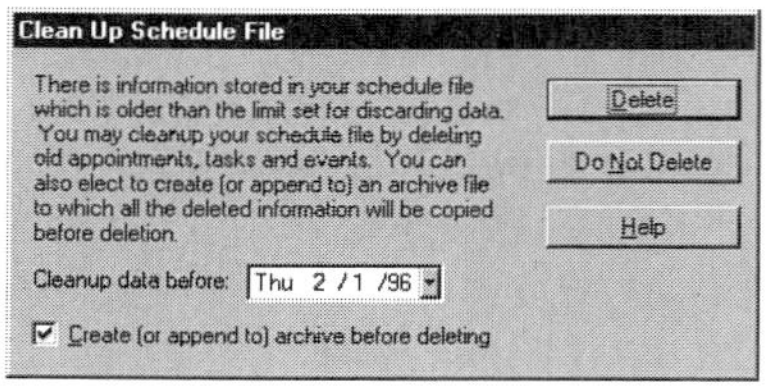

Fig. 22.19

Schedule+ automatically reminds you to clean out old information from your schedule file.

To cancel the automatic deletion, choose Do Not Delete.

To delete without archiving, clear the check box labeled Create (or Append to) Archive Before Deleting. Then choose Delete.

If you leave the archive box checked, then choose Delete, Schedule+ prompts you for a file name. You can keep one big archive or make one for each month, each quarter, and so on.

By default, Schedule+ prompts you to clean up the schedule file on the first day of the current month. To change this interval, choose Tools, Options, General and change the number of months under Prompt to Archive Data over # Month(s) Old, as seen in figure 22.20. Choose OK to save the change.

Archiving Manually

In addition to automatic archiving, Schedule+ gives you the ability to archive anytime you like:

1. Choose File, Archive to bring up the Create Archive dialog box.
2. Give a file name and date you want to use for archiving.
3. Choose OK to complete the archive process.

Fig. 22.20

Change the interval between automatic clean-up sessions on the General tab.

Opening Archives

Schedule+ 7.0 can open archives with an SCD extension (Schedule+ 7.0) or an ARC extension (Schedule+ 1.0).

To open an archive in its own Schedule+ window, choose File, Open, Archive or Project Schedule.

 Tip

As you've probably figured out, File, Open, Archive is used not just for opening archives, but for looking at any Schedule+ 7.0 file with an SCD extension (assuming you have permission from the owner). Another way to open a schedule is to double-click the SCD file either when you find it in a folder or if you receive one via e-mail.

Backing Up and Restoring Files

In addition to using interchange and archive files, you can make a complete backup of your schedule file.

If you create a backup, you can have your backup software copy the file when it backs up your system, even while you continue to work in Schedule+. Backup software cannot copy your schedule file when it's open, but it can copy a backup file.

A backup is also a good way to transfer the complete contents of your schedule file to your laptop or home computer and then back to your office computer. Be sure you do regular archives so the schedule file doesn't get so large that this transfer process takes too long.

To make a backup, choose File, Backup and type in a file name.

To restore from a Schedule+ backup, choose File, Restore and specify the file from which you want to restore.

Caution

Restoring completely replaces the data in your existing Schedule+ schedule file. If you want to append data (like new contacts) and not replace it, use interchange rather than backup and restore.

Summary

You now should have a good picture of the tools available to convert data into different formats as you expand your use of Schedule+ into exchanging information with other applications, with palmtops, and with other Schedule+ users.

Keep in mind the limitations of mixed Schedule+ 1.0 and 7.0 environments as you learn more about Schedule+ in a group situation in the next two chapters and in Chapter 34.

When you exchange data with PIMs, palmtops, and the Timex Data Link watch, you'll want to pay attention to the special settings that apply to each different target system.

Text import and export is one area where Schedule+ enjoys a good fit with other Office applications. Try Excel or Access as a preprocessor for delimited text files that you want to import into Schedule+. Or, if you find that the contact list in Schedule+ doesn't quite meet your needs, export your contacts as a delimited text file and use them to build a new database—perhaps one the whole office can share—in Access.

Schedule+ is a good housekeeper, prompting you to delete old data and archive regularly and making that process all but automatic. It also has an easy backup facility so that you can copy your schedule data and contacts to your traveling notebook computer.

chapter 23

Managing Workgroups Using Schedule+

23

by Sharon Podlin

In this chapter

◆ **Setting up a workgroup**
If you want to use the group-enabled features of Schedule+, you need to set up a workgroup and a postoffice, as well as profiles in Exchange.

◆ **Setting up resources**
Resources give you the ability to schedule resources, such as conference rooms and equipment.

◆ **Using passwords**
Whether you are working in Stand-Alone mode or Group-Enabled mode, you need a password to maintain the security of your schedule.

◆ **Adding more tabs**
You can customize your Schedule+ window by adding and deleting tabs.

◆ **Remote scheduling**
Windows 95 has tools to help you keep your schedule synchronized on multiple computers.

Whether or not you're in an office, you may want to use the group-enabled features of Schedule+. In this chapter, you learn to set up a workgroup and a post-office and create user profiles in Exhange. You also learn to create schedule files and set up access permissions to your schedule. In addition, this chapter shows you how to maintain your schedule on remote computers.

Setting Up a Workgroup

A *workgroup* is made up of the computers you communicate with to exchange files, schedules, or electronic mail, as well as to share resources, such as files and printers. Even in the home environment, you may want to set up a workgroup. If you have two or more computers, you can easily set up a peer-to-peer network with cheap network cards and some cable. You don't have to have a network operating system other than Windows 95. After you have set up a workgroup, you can use Exchange functionality to send messages to other machines and use the group-enabled functions of Schedule+.

Even if you have a stand-alone computer in your home or business, you may want to set up a workgroup and a postoffice if you have multiple users using the same machine. This allows you to exchange messages easily as well as manage schedules. A great example of this is managing the schedules of a typical busy family. Mom has work, exercise class, and parent association meetings to juggle. Dad has work and softball league. Their daughter has school, dance class, basketball, and Girl Scouts. Setting up a postoffice with each person having a mailbox would let them exchange messages with each other, such as, "Mom, don't forget I have practice on Thursday."

You can set up a profile for each person who uses the computer. By setting up a profile, you can customize which services each user can access. For example, maybe Mom and Dad want to be able to use the Fax service, but the kids don't need access to it.

The last thing to do is to set up Schedule+ so that each person has his/her own schedule. This allows everyone to know what's going on as far as schedules are concerned. Mom and Dad can decide who needs to pick the kids up after practice, as well as decide when to schedule the monthly family meeting!

Setting Up a Postoffice

To use Exchange, which is needed to use the group-enabled functionality of Schedule+, you need a postoffice. The Control Panel has an icon for MS Mail Postoffice, which enables you to create and administer postoffices.

The basic steps for creating a postoffice are as follows:

1. From the Start menu, choose <u>S</u>ettings, <u>C</u>ontrol Panel.

2. When the Control Panel group appears, open Microsoft Mail Postoffice. The Microsoft Workgroup Postoffice Admin dialog box appears (see fig. 23.1).

 Note

The Microsoft Mail Postoffice option is available only if you chose to install Mail when you installed Windows 95. If you did not do this during the original installation of Windows 95, you can access Microsoft Mail Services by double-clicking the Add/Remove Programs icon from the Control Panel. Click the Setup tab and from the

Components list box, choose Microsoft Exchange. Click Details to display the Microsoft Exchange dialog box. Select the Microsoft Mail Service check box and click OK. Click Apply to implement the changes. You will be prompted to restart your computer.

Fig. 23.1

The Microsoft Workgroup Postoffice Admin dialog box is used to create a new postoffice.

3. Choose Create a New Workgroup Postoffice and click Next.

4. The next window prompts you for a Postoffice location. Accept the default or enter a different location. Click Next. If a default location is not listed, click Browse and select the directory location for your postoffice.

5. After you click Next, the location of the Postoffice appears. Make a note of the location and click Next.

6. Enter your Administrator Account details, such as the name, mailbox, and password. Click OK. When the account information has been saved, you receive a message to share the postoffice with other users.

7. After creating the postoffice, you need to add users to the postoffice.

These are the basic steps for creating a postoffice. For more detail and information on this topic, see Chapter 25, "Installing and Configuring Exchange."

Network-Based and Single-Computer-Based Postoffices

There are two areas to set up a postoffice: on the local computer or on a network. If you are using a computer that is attached to a network, you should join the postoffice on the network that your administrator has set up. Otherwise, you get to be the administrator of your own private postoffice rather than belonging to the network postoffice. For more details and information on this topic, see Chapter 25, "Installing and Configuring Exchange."

If you do have a stand-alone computer, you may opt for setting up a postoffice for the reasons discussed earlier. A stand-alone computer is not always a single-user computer. Creating a postoffice gives you additional functionality to exchange messages and schedules.

Adding Users

After the postoffice has been created, you need to add users. Each user gets a user name and a mailbox. The basic steps for creating a user are as follows:

1. From the Start menu, choose Settings, Control Panel.

2. When the Control Panel group appears, open Microsoft Mail Postoffice. The Microsoft Workgroup Postoffice Admin dialog window appears.

3. Choose Administer an Existing Workgroup Postoffice.

4. You are prompted to enter the user name and password for the administrator. Enter this information and click Next.

5. At this point, the Postoffice Manager window appears (see fig. 23.2). From this window you can add, delete, or change user information.

Fig. 23.2

The Postoffice Manager window is used to update user information.

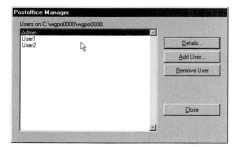

Setting Up Exchange Profiles

You may want to set up different kinds of Exchange profiles for different types of users. One profile may allow for full access to all services, including Mail, Personal Address Book, Fax, and Microsoft Network Online Service. You may want to set up other profiles that limit the user of that profile from using some services, such as Fax or Microsoft Network Online Service. For group-enabled usage of Schedule+, create a profile with the minimum services of Mail, Personal Address Book, and Personal Folders. You may want to set up a profile for each user so that you can assign individual personal address books and folders. To get detailed information on setting up profiles, see Chapter 25, "Installing and Configuring Exchange." For more information on profiles and how they relate to Schedule+, see Chapter 34, "Integrating Schedule+ and Exchange."

Note

If you have installed the Exchange Window 95 client, you can still use Schedule+ 1.0. However, the functionality will be diminished. You will not be able to use the group-enabled features of Schedule+, and you must run in Stand-Alone mode. To use group-enabled features after you have installed the Exchange Windows 95 client, you need to upgrade to Schedule+ 7.0.

Creating Schedule Files

Now that you have created yourself as a user of Exchange, you are ready to work with Schedule+. When you start Schedule+, it checks to see if you already have a schedule file. The schedule file contains your appointments, events, tasks, and contacts. If Schedule+ does not find a schedule file for you, it displays the Welcome to Schedule+ 7.0 window (see fig. 23.3).

To create your own schedule file, follow these steps:

   1. From the Start menu, choose Programs, Microsoft Schedule+. The Welcome to Schedule+ 7.0 window appears (see fig. 23.3).

Fig. 23.3

The Welcome to Schedule+ 7.0 window appears the first time you use Schedule+.

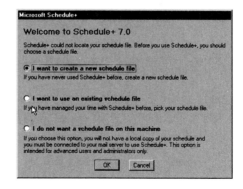

   2. Choose I Want To Create My Own Schedule File.

   3. Click OK to display the Select Local Schedule window (see fig. 23.4).

   4. Select the location for the schedule file. The default location is \MSOFFICE\ SCHEDULE.

   5. Enter a file name for the schedule file. You may want to use your name, for example.

   6. Click Save to create the schedule file.

Fig. 23.4

The Select Local Schedule window is used to create your schedule file.

Setting Access Permissions

After you have created your schedule file, you should set up your global access permissions. With Schedule+ in Group-Enabled mode, you can grant users different levels of access permissions to your schedule. Schedule+ has two kinds of access permissions: user and global. Through user access permissions, you set default access permissions and give specific users additional or restricted access. This type of access is discussed in detail in Chapter 24, "Maintaining Security with Schedule+." The second type of access permission—global—enables you to set access options for all users in spite of any user permissions you may assign.

You have three options when assigning global access permissions. Two options have to do with whether you want overlapping or recurring appointments in your schedule. If you do not want overlapping or recurring appointments, Schedule+ will not allow you and other users to create appointments that overlap with your other appointments. You can also decide how many months of your free/busy information you want to publish at a time. The default for this setting is three months.

To use global access permissions to disallow overlapping appointments, follow these steps:

1. Choose Tools, Set Access Permissions.
2. Select the Global tab (see fig. 23.5).
3. Select the Disallow Overlapping Appointments check box.
4. Choose the OK button to save the changes.

 Note

If you choose to publish your free/busy times on the Global tab, users assigned the role of None can still see when you are free and busy in their Planner. They simply do not have access to any details about your schedule.

Fig. 23.5

The Global tab of the Set Access Permissions window is used to set the Disallow Overlapping Appointments option.

Setting Up Resources

People aren't the only things that need scheduling when you have a meeting. You typically need a location for the meeting, such as a conference room. If your organization is like most, you have to schedule the conference room for your meeting, or someone else may plan their meeting at the same time in the same room. After you get the room, you may need other items for your meeting. Maybe you need a television and an VCR, or an overhead projector. These have to be scheduled, too. It seems somewhat inefficient to have to call someone to schedule a room or piece of equipment so that they can write it down in an appointment book or enter it into another system. Rather than using this scenario, you can use Schedule+ to set up rooms and equipment as resources.

Resources are rooms, equipment, or any other items that needs to be scheduled. Resources are treated like any other user in that they need to be scheduled for meetings.

Create a resource as you would any other user. The only extra step you need to do is to let Schedule+ know that this is a resource. This is done by following these steps:

1. Choose Tools, Options. The Options dialog box appears.
2. Choose the General tab (see fig. 23.6).
3. Select the This Account Is for a Resource check box.
4. Click OK to save the change.

Beyond creating the resource, you need to decide how you want to manage the resource. You have two options. If someone needs to know when a resource has been scheduled, then you want to set a delegate owner for the resource. Making someone a delegate owner allows the selected user to modify all of the resource's schedule, including private items and access permissions. In addition, delegate owners can send and receive meeting

23

messages on behalf of the resource. An example of using this feature is if you set a resource for an overhead projector. The projector itself may be available during a certain
time, but someone needs notification about scheduling it so that it can be delivered.

Fig. 23.6
The General tab in the
Options dialog box
enables you to mark an
account as a resource.

To set up a delegate owner for a resource, follow these steps:

1. Choose <u>T</u>ools, Set A<u>c</u>cess Permissions. This displays the Set Access Permissions
window (see fig. 23.7).

Fig. 23.7
The Set Access
Permission window
can be used to assign
a user as a delegate
owner.

2. Choose the user who is to be the delegate owner.

3. From the User R<u>o</u>le drop-down list box, choose Delegate Owner.

4. Make sure that User Receives <u>M</u>eeting Requests Sent To Me is checked.

5. Click OK to save changes.

Another option when creating a resource is to have Schedule+ do the resource management. This option would be useful, for example, for a conference room. No one may need to be notified when it is scheduled. Its schedule is being maintained to avoid conflicts. You want to set this account to automatically accept meetings and automatically delete canceled meetings. This is done by choosing Tools, Options.

To set up a resource account to automatically accept meetings and delete canceled meetings, follow these steps:

1. Choose Tools, Options.
2. Choose the General tab (refer to fig. 23.6).
3. Choose Automatically Accept Meeting Requests.
4. Choose Automatically Remove Canceled Meetings.
5. Click OK to save the changes.

After setting these two options, you should set the account so that it cannot schedule overlapping appointments:

1. Choose Tools, Set Access Permissions.
2. Choose the Global tab.
3. Select Disallow Overlapping Appointments.
4. Click OK to save the changes.

Passwords

When you log on to Schedule+, you are required to enter your user name and password. This is done to make sure that your schedule is private. If you use Exchange, your Schedule+ password is the same as the password you use to log on to Exchange. Your administrator assigns your initial password. You can change your password at any time. There are two types of passwords: local and server.

Local Passwords

The *local password* is actually the password used by users working Schedule+ in Stand-Alone mode without Exchange. If you are using Exchange, Exchange actually maintains the password for Schedule+ when you are using Schedule+ in Group-Enabled mode.

If you are using Schedule+ in Stand-Alone mode and want to change your password, complete the following steps:

1. Choose Tools, Change Password.
2. In the Old Password box, type your current password.

 Note

For security, your password does not appear in the box as you type it. If you do not currently have a password, you won't be prompted to type your old password.

3. In the New Password box, type your new password.
4. In the Verify New Password box, type your new password again to verify it.
5. Click OK to save changes to your password.

If the characters you type the second time do not match those you enter the first time, Schedule+ asks you to type your password again.

 Caution

If you change your password while in Group-Enabled mode, you are not changing your Mail password. If you exit and log off and log on again, you are prompted for your Mail password. The password you entered in the previous step is not the password it will accept. When working in Group-Enabled mode, it will accept only your Mail password. The above steps are for users working in Stand-Alone mode.

Server Passwords

If you are using Schedule+ in Group-Enabled mode, you should change your password through Exchange. You actually want to change your Mail password. Just follow these steps:

1. Start Exchange and log on.
2. Choose Tools, Microsoft Mail Tools.
3. Select Change Mailbox Password.
4. In the Old Password box, type your current password.
5. In the New Password box, type your new password.
6. In the Verify New Password box, type your new password again to verify it.
7. Click OK to save changes to your password.

Adding More Tabs

Up to this point, you have worked only with the standard views and their tabs: Daily, Weekly, Monthly, Planner, To Do, and Contacts. These tabs are useful for the majority of things you want to do with Schedule+. But what if you never use the Weekly view and do not want to have the Weekly tab in the Schedule+ window? Have you been wanting to see a yearly view? These tasks are handled easily with the Tab Gallery.

Using the Tab Gallery

The Tab Gallery is where you can add, rename, reorder, or remove tabs for views in the Schedule+ window. The Tab Gallery is available through the tab shortcut menu or the View menu. The Tab Gallery allows you to select from 14 tabs. When you select a tab from the Tab Gallery window, a preview and description of that view appears.

 Tip

To see the Tab shortcut menu, right-click the Tab bar. You can also jump directly to the Tab Gallery by double-clicking the tab bar.

The following selections are available through the Tab Gallery:

▶ *Contact List.* Displays the contact list only on the view. This differs from the default tab named Contacts. Contacts displays the contact list and the business card for each contact.

▶ *Contacts and To Do Lists.* Displays the contacts list and the related tasks for the selected contact. When you create a To Do List item, you have the option of assigning a contact to that item. The top portion of this view is a listing of contacts. The bottom portion of this view is a list of the To Do items assigned to the selected contact. Using this view, you can quickly find what tasks have been assigned to a contact.

▶ *Contacts.* One of the tabs installed as a default with Schedule+.

▶ *Cover Page.* Displays a view with a bitmap on it. Any BMP file can be used for this tab view. Use this view if you want to have a tab display a picture—for example, to quickly "cover" what you are entering in your schedule if someone comes into your office. You could also create a graphic to let people know that you are out of your office and place it on a cover tab.

▶ *Daily Schedule.* Displays the daily calendar, Date Navigator, and To Do list. This is a default tab.

▶ *Monthly Calendar.* Displays a month of appointments. This is a default tab.

23

▸ *Monthly Schedule*. Displays a month of appointments and the To Do list. This is a default tab.

▸ *Planner*. Displays the Planner showing free and busy times, the Date Navigator, and the meeting attendees list. This is a default tab.

▸ *Projects and To Do List*. Displays the Project list and related tasks. In this view, the top pane lists all projects. The lower pane lists the To Do items associated with the selected project. This differs from the To Do list tab, which shows To Do list items in outline form with projects being the outermost hierarchy.

▸ *Seven Habits Planner*. Displays appointments for as many as seven days and a To Do list organized by the Seven Habits roles.

▸ *To Do List*. Displays the To Do list. This is a default tab.

▸ *Weekly Appointments*. Displays appointments for as many as seven days. This is a default tab.

▸ *Weekly Schedule*. Displays appointments for as many as seven days in the upper pane, and the To Do list in the lower pane.

▸ *Yearly Calendar*. Displays up to 12 calendar months. Dates with appointments are in bold.

Adding a Tab Using the Tab Gallery

Any of the tabs discussed in the preceding section can be added easily by using the Tab Gallery. There are two ways to access the Tab Gallery. One way is to choose <u>V</u>iew, T<u>a</u>b Gallery. The other way is to select Tab Gallery from the tab shortcut menu.

One tab you may want to add is the Yearly Calendar. To add this tab, follow these steps:

  1. Choose <u>V</u>iew, T<u>a</u>b Gallery. The Tab Gallery window appears (see fig. 23.8).
  2. Scroll to the last item in the A<u>v</u>ailable Tabs list box, which is Yearly Calendar.
  3. Select Yearly Calendar.
  4. Click <u>A</u>dd.
  5. Click OK to add the new tab. The Yearly Calendar tab appears (see fig. 23.9).

Caution
In the Daily, Monthly, and Planner views, you can press Alt and one of the arrow keys to move between dates. This functionality currently does not work with the Yearly view. Alt+arrow does work after you add the Yearly tab, but, if you then change to another view and return to the Yearly view, Alt+arrow no longer works. This is a reported bug.

Fig. 23.8

The Tab Gallery dialog box is used to add and delete tabs in the Schedule+ window.

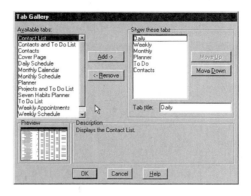

Fig. 23.9

The newly added Yearly Calendar tab gives you an additional way to view your schedule.

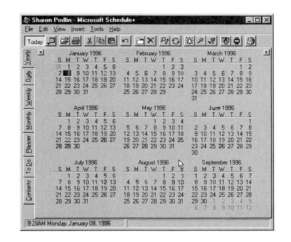

Another tab you may want to add is the Cover Page tab. Just follow these steps:

1. Choose <u>V</u>iew, T<u>a</u>b Gallery.

2. Select Cover Page.

3. Click <u>A</u>dd.

4. Click OK to add the new tab. The Cover Page tab appears (see fig. 23.10).

The default image on the Cover Page tab is the Schedule+ start-up screen graphic. This may not be your first choice for a cover page. The Cover Page tab has the added feature of letting you select the image on the view so that you can personalize it to your tastes. You can select any bitmap (BMP) file to use as a cover page image.

23

Fig. 23.10
One of the available tabs from the Tab Gallery is the Cover Page tab.

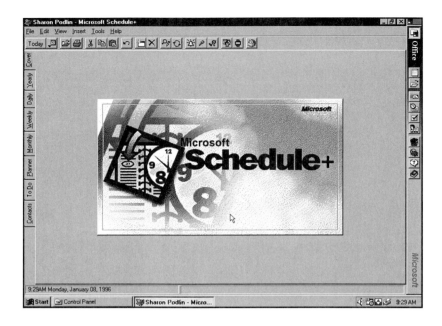

To choose your own cover page, follow these steps:

1. Right-click the image on the cover page to access the shortcut menu.

2. Choose Select Cover Page. The Select Cover Page dialog box appears (see fig. 23.11).

3. Select the file you want to display. From the Windows directory, for example, you could choose Forest.

4. Choose Open to change the image on the Cover Page. The updated cover page appears (see fig. 23.12).

Fig. 23.11
The Select Cover Page dialog box allows you to customize the image on the Cover Page tab.

Fig. 23.12

You can customize the graphic displayed on the Cover Page tab.

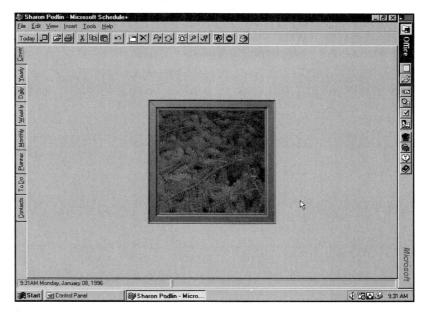

Removing a Tab

You may have a tab that you never use and do not want in the Schedule+ window. You can remove a tab by selecting the tab from the Tab Gallery window and choosing Remove, or you can choose Remove Tab from the tab shortcut window, or from the View menu.

To remove the Yearly Calendar tab, follow these steps:

1. Select the Yearly Calendar tab.

2. Choose View, Remove Tab.

3. When prompted, "Do you want to remove the current tab?", choose Yes.

Remote Scheduling

Many users today do not use just one computer. They have a desktop computer and a laptop computer. If you are one of these users, you don't want to maintain two separate versions of Schedule+. Imagine if you were using Schedule+ on both of your computers and you wanted to schedule an appointment on Tuesday. On your desktop, you enter the appointment. On your laptop, you enter the appointment. You hope that you enter the appointment correctly and identically on both machines. If you are a particularly busy person, this situation of doing double-entry keeps you even busier!

Setting Up Your Laptop or Home Computer

If you have two computers—a desktop computer and a laptop computer, for example—you probably want to keep your schedule synchronized between the two computers. A Windows 95 tool that you can use to do this is Briefcase. Briefcase helps you keep various copies of your files updated.

To use Briefcase, the two computers must be connected, either through a network or by a cable. To use Briefcase, drag files from shared folders on your main computer to the Briefcase icon on your portable computer. When you finish working on the files on the portable computer, reconnect to your main computer, and then click Update All in Briefcase to automatically replace the unmodified files on your main computer with the modified files in your Briefcase. The file you want to use with Briefcase for Schedule+ is your schedule file. Remember that your schedule file has the extension SCD.

A second way to support your schedule on two machines is to use export and import capabilities of Schedule+. You can export your Schedule+ information to a floppy disk so that you can work on your schedule at another computer such as your home computer. When you export, you can select to export all dates or a range of dates. You can also choose what to export. You may, for example, want to export all of your calendar data or just your appointments.

To return the changes you made to your schedule, you import the information from your other Schedule+ schedules. When you import information to your schedule, any conflicting appointments are added to your Appointment Book. These conflicting appointments are displayed side-by-side with existing appointments.

If you want to export schedule information, follow these steps:

1. Choose File, Export, Schedule+ Interchange to display the Export Schedule+ Interchange dialog box.
2. Enter a file name for the export file.
3. Select the Export range. All Dates is the default for this option.
4. Select one of the export options. All Calendar Data is the default.
5. Click OK to complete the creation of the export file.

To import schedule information using Schedule+ Interchange, follow these steps:

1. Choose File, Import, Schedule+ Interchange to display the Import Schedule+ Interchange dialog box.
2. Select the file to import.
3. Click Open to complete the import.

Working Remotely

Many network operating systems have tools to allow remote users to access the local network. Examples of these tools include Novell's Netware Connect and Microsoft's Remote Access Server (RAS). These tools allow the user to log on to the file server via a modem and act as if they are locally attached. Through the connection, users can access files, print, check their electronic mail, use Schedule+, and so on. See your network administrator for additional information on remote access options on your network.

Another option is to use an option available when you purchase Microsoft Plus!. Microsoft Plus! gives you additional functionality to Windows 95 Dial-Up Networking. This additional functionality lets you dial in to your computer from a remote location, and then use the network resources available on it. Dial-Up Networking has password protection so that other people who know the password can also dial into your computer.

Summary

Schedule+ is an application heavily integrated with Exchange. Because of this integration, you need to configure both Schedule+ and Exchange to take advantage of the group-enabled capabilities of Schedule+. Once configured, however, you can view other users' schedules and plan meetings with them, a feature that is discussed in detail in the next chapter. For additional information on Schedule+'s integration with Exchange, see Chapter 34, "Integrating Schedule+ and Exchange."

In today's environment, you may have the need for remote computing to help you maintain your Schedule+ schedule. There are Windows 95 tools for doing this, including Briefcase and Dial-Up Networking.

chapter 24

Maintaining Security with Schedule+

24

by Sharon Podlin

In this chapter

◆ **Access Permissions**
The security for Schedule+ relies on you to set up how you want users to access your Schedule.

◆ **Working in Group-Enabled Mode**
Group-enabled mode allows you to access other users' schedules indirectly by using the meeting planning features of Schedule+ or accessing the schedule directly through the File menu.

chedules seem to be independent objects with no connections to anything else. In reality, this could not be further from the truth. When you schedule a meeting, you need to consider the schedules of other people who will be attending the meeting. If you want to have a meeting concerning the budget, you invite those who need to have input on that topic. If you need to invite several people who have full schedules, trying to schedule a time convenient for them all is a challenge.

Access Permissions

With Schedule+, other users can read, create, modify, and delete information from your schedule. And the best news is that you have control over what a user can do to your schedule. Should Shirley be able to make changes to your schedule directly? You can set it so that Sam can modify existing appointments, and David can delete appointments for you. Maybe you want to set it up so Mark can only read your appointments but not see your contacts. It's up to you to determine to what extent you want other users to access your appointments, events, and contacts. Do this with *access permissions*.

You modify these permissions in the Set Access Permissions dialog box (see fig. 24.1). This dialog box has two tabs: Global and User. To open the Set Access Permissions dialog box, choose Tools, Set Access Permissions.

Fig. 24.1

The Set Access Permissions dialog box allows you to give users different access permissions to your appointments, events, and contacts.

Global Settings

Use the Global tab to set global defaults. These global defaults include the following:

▶ Whether to allow overlapping appointments. This applies to you and to other users.

▶ Whether to allow recurring appointments. A recurring appointment is one that happens regularly—every Friday at 2 p.m., for example. The ability to create recurring appointments applies to you and to other users.

▶ How many months of your schedule to publish and allow other users to view. The default is three months.

To set the global access permissions for your schedule, follow these steps:

1. Choose Tools, Set Access Permissions.
2. Click the Global tab (see fig. 24.2).
3. Select or deselect the Disallow Overlapping Appointments check box.
4. Select or deselect the Disallow Recurring Appointments check box.
5. Type or select a number in the Publish text box to specify the number of months of your free/busy information you want to make available to other users.
6. Click OK to save the changes you made.

Fig. 24.2

The Global tab of the Set Access Permissions dialog box is used to set options for the group-enabled features of Schedule+.

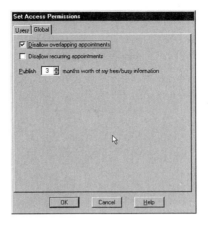

> **Note**
>
> Publishing your free/busy information shows other users only a colored bar in their Planners when you are busy. If you have not given users specific access permissions, they will not have access to any details about your schedule.

Default Setting

The majority of security for Schedule+ lies in the area of user permissions. You decide what permissions to give to all users or to a specific user. Schedule+ gives you a set of individual access permissions you can combine and assign.

▶ *None.* Gives users no permissions to view or modify your schedule. They cannot view details about items and cannot add, change, or delete appointments, to-do list items, contacts, or events.

> **Note**
>
> If you selected to publish your free/busy times on the Global tab, users assigned access permissions of None still see when you are free and busy in their Planners. They cannot view any details about your schedule.

▶ *Read.* Allows users read-only access, except for items marked Private. They cannot add, delete, or modify items in your schedule. They can view details about appointments, to-do list items, contacts, or events.

24

▶ *Create*. Allows users to read existing items and add new appointments, to-do list items, contacts, or events. However, they cannot read items marked Private.

▶ *Modify*. Allows users to read and modify existing appointments, to-do list items, contacts, or events, except for items marked Private.

▶ *Delegate*. Allows users to read existing items and add, delete, or change them, including items marked Private.

▶ *Owner*. Allows selected users to modify all of your schedule. In addition, Owners can view and modify Private items in your schedule, and they can change other users' access permissions for your schedule. Owners can do everything you can do, but cannot send or receive mail on your behalf.

▶ *Delegate Owner*. Allows selected users to modify all of your schedule, including Private items and access permissions. In addition, Delegate Owners can send and receive meeting messages on your behalf.

▶ *Custom*. Use this option if you want to give users a specific kind of access for a specific kind of item.

The easiest approach for setting up security for Schedule+ is to assign the permissions you want most users to have as the default. Default is used by all users who do not have specific permissions.

To assign default user permissions, complete the following steps:

1. Choose Tools, Set Access Permissions.
2. Click the Users tab (refer to fig. 24.1).
3. From the Users list, select Default.
4. From the User Role list box, select the permission you want to assign as the default permission.
5. Click OK to assign the default permission.

Individual Settings

After setting the default permission for user access, you want to assign permission to specific users who you want to have additional or restricted permissions. For example, you might want your assistant to accept meetings for you. In that case, depending on whether you want him to see your private items, you make him a Delegate, an Owner, or a Delegate Owner. These roles allow him not only to view private items, but to change them as well. Remember that unless a user has the role of Owner or Delegate Owner, he cannot view items you marked as Private.

The Delegate, Owner, or Delegate Owner doesn't need to know your password to access your schedule. You can have more than one Delegate. And, as with any other role, you can select a new Delegate or delete an existing Delegate.

Appointments your Delegate adds as well as meeting requests and responses sent by your Delegate are identified to message recipients as having been handled by a Delegate on your behalf. If a Delegate sets up a meeting in your Appointment Book and then sends meeting requests for that meeting, the responses are automatically sent to the Delegate, and your schedule is automatically updated to reflect the responses. If other users invite you to meetings, your Delegate receives copies of the requests and can view your schedule for conflicts and respond on your behalf. This type of functionality is useful if your administrative assistant is responsible for maintaining your schedule. You can specify that your meeting messages be sent only to your Delegate or to both of you in the Global tab in the Set Access Permissions dialog box.

Setting an individual user's access permissions is very much like assigning access permissions to Default. The only thing you need to do differently is add the user:

1. Choose Tools, Set Access Permissions.

2. Click the Users tab.

3. If the user's name isn't in the Users box, click the Add button. The Add Users dialog box appears (see fig. 24.3). Select the user from the list, and click the Users button. Click OK to add the user.

Fig. 24.3

The Add Users dialog box lets you add specific users to assign permission to in the Set Access Permissions dialog box.

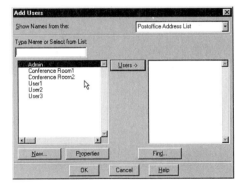

4. In the Set Access Permissions dialog box, select the user's name from the Users list.

5. From the User Role list box, select a role for the user. For example, if you selected Modify, Modify appears for Appointments, Contacts, Events, and Tasks. These selections are grayed. You can only make changes to individual items if you select Custom as the role.

6. If you want the user to receive meeting requests sent to you, select the User Receives Meeting Requests Sent to Me check box.

7. Click OK to save the access permission changes.

In the previous steps, I pointed out that the individual access items are grayed out if you select any role other than Custom. Use the Custom permission if none of the predefined roles meets your needs. Custom lets you grant a custom set of access permissions for a user. Users can be assigned a different access permission for appointments, contacts, events, and tasks. You can grant users different Custom access permissions by assigning them the Custom role and then selecting the specific permissions you want them to have.

To assign a Custom user permission, follow these steps:

1. Choose Tools, Set Access Permissions.

2. In the Users list, select the name of the user whose permissions you want to set. If the user's name is not listed in the Users list, add it by using the Add button.

3. In the User Role list box, select Custom.

4. In the Appointments list box, choose the permission you want the user to have for your appointments.

5. In the Contacts list box, choose the permission you want the user to have for your contacts.

6. In the Events list box, choose the permission you want the user to have for your events.

7. In the Tasks list box, choose the permission you want the user to have for your To Do List.

8. Click OK to save the access permissions.

After you set a user's access permissions, you can change them at any time using the following steps:

1. Choose Tools, Set Access Permissions.

2. From the Users list, select the name of the user whose permissions you want to change.

3. From the User Role list box, select a new role for the user.

4. Click OK to save the changes to access permissions.

Working in Group-Enabled Mode

When you work in Group-Enabled mode, the local copy of your schedule automatically synchronizes with the server copy of your schedule. This allows you to take advantage of the group-enabled features of Schedule+, including meeting planning. This functionality is available because Schedule+ uses the mail capabilities of Exchange. Because of this, Exchange has to be installed and running for you to use group-enabled features.

Scheduling Meetings

Schedule+ gives you the capability to interact with other users for joint appointments. These joint appointments are called *meetings*. With a meeting, attendees are invited with a Schedule+ Meeting Request form. To use this functionality, the attendees must also use Exchange and be connected to a mail server as well as being Schedule+ users working in Group-Enabled mode. Attendees also need to enable free/busy time publishing.

You can schedule a meeting in one of three ways:

▶ Through the Appointment dialog box by selecting the Attendees tab

▶ Using the Meeting Wizard, a tool that prompts you through the steps of creating a meeting

▶ From the Planner view

After you set up the meeting, you receive the attendee's responses to the request in your Exchange Inbox. If you need to, you can add or delete invitees from the meeting.

Using the Meeting Wizard

The easiest way to set up a meeting is to use the Meeting Wizard. The Meeting Wizard first requires that you know who you want to invite to the meeting. The Meeting Wizard then prompts you for additional information. Just answer the questions that Meeting Wizard displays.

To schedule a meeting using Meeting Wizard, follow these steps:

1. Choose Tools, Make Meeting to open the Meeting Wizard (see fig. 24.4).

Fig. 24.4

The Meeting Wizard gives you an easy way to organize meetings. Notice the tip at the bottom of the window to select at least required attendees and a location.

24

2. This window prompts you to organize your meeting. By default, it has selected the options Required Attendees Who Must Attend and A Location Such As a Conference Room. You can also select the Optional, 'FYI' Attendees Who Are Not Required to Attend check box and the Resources Like Computers or Audiovisual Equipment check box. Note the tip concerning selecting at least required attendees and a conference room. Make your selections and click Next.

3. The wizard prompts you to select the required attendees (see fig. 24.5). Click Pick Attendees.

Fig. 24.5

You can select required attendees by clicking Pick Attendees or typing directly into the Attendees box.

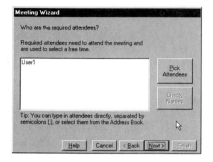

4. Select an attendee you want to invite and click Required. Do this for each required attendee (see fig. 24.6).

Fig. 24.6

On the left side of the Meeting Wizard window is the list of possible attendees.

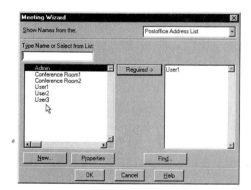

5. When you are finished selecting the attendees, click OK.

6. You return to the page prompting for required attendees. Review the list and click Next.

7. If you selected the Optional 'FYI' Attendees Who Are Not Required to Attend check box in the first Meeting Wizard screen, the next page asks you to select optional attendees. Select the optional attendees and click Next.

8. The wizard prompts you for the location of the meeting (see fig. 24.7). Click Pick Locations.

Fig. 24.7
*The Meeting Wizard
allows you to select the
location for the meeting
in much the same way
you selected attendees.*

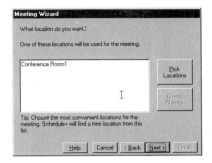

9. Select the location from the list and click Locations. Click OK to return to the Meeting Wizard. If there are no locations defined, you can add a new location by selecting New.

10. Click Next to move to the next page.

11. If you selected the Resources Like Computers Or Audiovisual Equipment check box from the first screen of the Meeting Wizard, the next screen prompts you to select resources. Select the resources and click Next.

12. The Wizard asks you for information concerning the duration of the meeting (see fig. 24.8).

Fig. 24.8
*Tell the Meeting Wizard
how long the meeting
needs to last.*

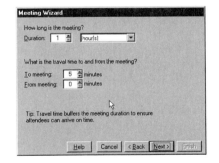

13. Select a number and time frame for the Duration list boxes, such as one hour.

14. If needed, enter travel time to and from the meeting.

15. Click Next to move to the next screen, which prompts you for acceptable meeting times (see fig. 24.9).

16. Select the acceptable Meeting Starts After time and the And Ends Before time.

Fig. 24.9
This page asks you for starting and ending time limitations.

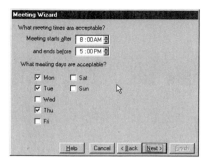

17. Select the acceptable meeting days.

18. Click <u>N</u>ext to move to the Planner view. This page shows you the first possible time that the meeting can be scheduled in the Next Available Time area (see fig. 24.10).

 Tip

Right-click a blocked-out area in the Planner view to find out whose appointment it represents. If you have permission, you can click the arrow on the pop-up to obtain additional details.

Fig. 24.10
You can accept the meeting time Schedule+ displays or choose another.

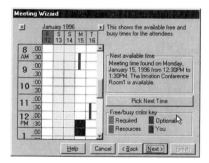

19. If you do not want to schedule the meeting at the displayed time, click Pick Next Time.

20. When you have selected the time for the meeting, click <u>N</u>ext.

21. The final screen lets you know that the Meeting Wizard is finished (see fig. 24.11). Click <u>F</u>inish to exit the Meeting Wizard. Notice that the Send button appears as a small envelope. Meeting Wizard is pointing this out to you because the next thing you do is create a meeting request. After you have completed the meeting request form, click the Send button to send it to the meeting's attendees.

22. The Meeting Request form automatically appears (see fig. 24.12). The T<u>o</u> text box includes all of the invitees. You can add additional names to the message if you want.

Fig. 24.11

At this point, the meeting is scheduled, and the Meeting Wizard is finished.

Fig. 24.12

When you set up a meeting, you send a meeting request to attendees letting them know the subject of and the proposed time and date for the meeting.

Send button

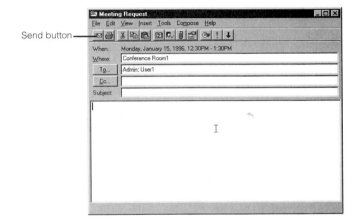

23. Optionally, you can select users to receive a copy of this message by clicking the Cc button. Schedule+ automatically places the optional attendees in the Cc text box.

24. Type a brief description of the meeting in the Subject text box.

25. Type any additional comments in the body of the message.

26. When you finish, click the Send button from the toolbar.

The invited attendees receive mail messages concerning the meeting. Invited attendees receive meeting requests in their Inboxes. These messages are differentiated from other messages by a Schedule+ symbol. The invited attendees can reply with an automatic meeting response by clicking either the Accept, Decline, or Tentatively Accept button. After they respond to the message, Schedule+ automatically books the meeting.

Using the Planner

The Planner view gives you an easy way to see when you are busy or free over several days. If you are running Schedule+ in Group-Enabled mode, you can see other users' free and busy times as well. You can also use the Planner as a tool to plan meetings. A smaller version of the Planner appears when using the Meeting Wizard.

The main part of the Planner view is the free/busy display on the left side of the Schedule+ window. You can move to different days in this display by using the left and right arrows at the top or by selecting a date in the Date Navigator. Vertical bars represent busy times. Time slots without vertical bars are referred to as free times. To see detailed information about a busy time, right-click the vertical bar and click the arrowhead displayed. The detail information appears.

When working in Group-Enabled mode, you can use the Planner to check another user's or resource's busy times to see when you can schedule a meeting. If a user or resource has given you Read permission, you can see details about their appointments; otherwise, you can only see their free/busy times.

To see other users' and resources' schedules in the Planner view, follow these steps:

1. From the Schedule+ main window, open the Planner tab, and click Invite to display the Select Attendees dialog box (see fig. 24.13).

Fig. 24.13

Use the Select Attendees dialog box to select the users who need to attend the meeting you are scheduling.

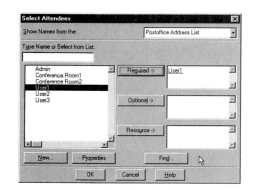

2. Select a name from the list of users on the left side of the window.

3. Click either the Required, Optional, or Resource button.

4. Continue selecting users and resources and choosing either Required, Optional, or Resource.

5. When you finish adding attendees, click OK to return to the Planner view. The Planner view appears and shows the busy times of the attendees (see fig. 24.14).

    Each category (Required, Optional, and Resource) of attendee is represented by a different color displayed in the lower-right corner. The attendees are listed under their individual categories. If you select a time period from the calendar and an attendee is not available during that time period, an x appears by that attendee's name.

Fig. 24.14

*The Planner view
shows the busy times
of the attendees.*

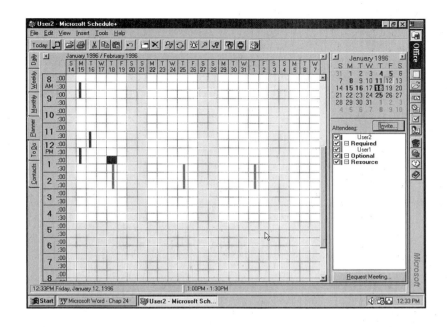

 Note

If you are running in Stand-Alone mode, the Invite button does not appear. The Request Meeting button is replaced with the New Appointment button.

After you select the attendees for the meeting you are trying to set up, their names appear in the Attendees list in the lower-right corner of the Planner view. Their busy times are shown in the busy/free times area. Depending on their status (Required, Optional, or Resource), they have different colored bars in the Planner. The following describes the bar colors:

▶ Blue bars represent your busy times.

▶ Gray bars represent the busy times of the required attendees.

▶ Purple bars represent the busy times for the optional attendees.

▶ Green bars represent the busy times for resources.

 Tip

If you want to override the default color settings for the busy bars, choose Tools, Options. Click the Display tab and make the desired changes.

24

A check mark appears in the check box to the left of a user's name if his or her schedule is displayed. A question mark in the check box appears if the schedule is not available. An X appears if the attendee is not available during the selected time slot.

 Note

If the attendees selected are located in another time zone, their busy times are automatically adjusted to your time zone.

After displaying the attendees' schedules, you are ready to schedule the meeting. You can do this one of two ways: by scheduling the meeting manually or by using the Schedule+ Auto Pick feature.

If you want to select a meeting time manually, follow these steps:

1. Click the Planner tab and select the time slot you want for the meeting.
2. Click Request Meeting to display the Request Meeting form.
3. Complete the form and click the Send button in the toolbar.

To select a meeting time using Auto Pick, follow these steps:

1. Click the Planner tab and select one or more time slots to represent the length of the meeting. Don't worry about the starting time you select—Auto Pick ignores this. It's simply looking for a duration.
2. Choose Tools, Auto Pick.
3. Auto Pick finds the earliest time available for all of the attendees. If you want to accept this as the meeting time, click Request Meeting. If you don't want this as the meeting time, choose Tools, Auto Pick again to get a new time.
4. After you select the time for the meeting and click Request Meeting, the Meeting Request form appears.
5. In the Subject text box, type a brief description of the meeting.
6. Optionally, you can add recipients.
7. Type any necessary message text.
8. When you are through with the message, click the Send button on the toolbar to send the message.

At this point, Schedule+ marks the meeting time in your Planner and adds it to your Appointment Book. If needed, you can reschedule the meeting, cancel it, or pick a new time. Schedule+ automatically guides you through the steps for notifying the attendees

of the change. Schedule+ updates your Appointment Book and asks if you want to notify attendees of the change or cancellation. If you do, Schedule+ displays the Meeting Request form and addresses it to the attendees. It also creates
a note that the original meeting time has been changed or that the meeting has been canceled.

Reviewing the responses to your meeting is easy. Use the Attendees tab in the Appointment dialog box for the meeting. Also, you can review the responses in your Exchange Inbox.

To view responses to your meeting request from Schedule+, follow these steps:

1. In the Appointment Book (accessed through the Daily, Weekly, or Monthly tabs), double-click the meeting description in your Appointment Book. The Appointment dialog box appears.

2. Select the Attendees tab (see fig. 24.15). A check by an attendee's name means he has accepted; an x means he has declined; a check with a question mark means that the attendee has tentatively accepted the meeting. Those attendees' names with no marks beside them have not replied to the meeting request form.

3. Click OK to close the dialog box.

Fig. 24.15

Use the Attendees tab to track the responses to meeting requests.

Directly Accessing Another Schedule

Up to this point, you have been indirectly modifying other users' schedules by scheduling meetings. Schedule+ also allows you to directly modify another user's schedule. This feature is available only if another user has given you access permission to her schedule. There are several reasons to use this functionality. For example, if you are on vacation, you might need someone else to manage your schedule. Or you might be responsible for maintaining another user's schedule, such as that of your boss. Resources also need someone to maintain their schedules. A conference room can't do that by itself! Depending on the access permission the user has given you, you can view, create, and modify appointments, tasks, events, and contacts.

To open another user's schedule, follow these steps:

1. Choose File, Open.

2. Choose Other's Appointment Book to display the Open Other's Appt. Book dialog box (see fig. 24.16).

Fig. 24.16

The Open Other's Appt. Book dialog box lets you directly access another schedule.

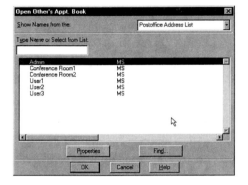

3. From the list of users, select the name of the user whose schedule you want to open.

4. Click OK to open the schedule.

If you do not have the correct access permission, Schedule+ notifies you that the user's schedule is unavailable. Don't forget—unless a user gives you Owner or Delegate Owner permission, you can't see items the user has marked as Private. You can now view, create, delete, or modify items depending on your permission.

When you finish with the other user's schedule, close it by choosing File, Close from the user's schedule window.

Summary

The security features of Schedule+ give you a great deal of flexibility. You can decide anything from allowing no access to your schedule to allowing someone else to create, delete, or modify items in your schedule, including private items. This functionality is available not only on a user-by-user basis, but allows you to assign different permissions to different items.

Because of this functionality, planning a meeting is easy with Schedule+. You can either plan a meeting manually or let the Meeting Wizard walk you through the process.

24

Exchange

VI

chapter 25

Installing and Configuring Exchange

by Kathy Ivens

In this chapter

◆ **Exchange components**
There are several elements in Exchange; you can install some of them or all of them.

◆ **Hardware installation**
Depending on the options you choose, you might need to install hardware such as a modem or a network controller.

◆ **Software installation**
Use the installation programs available in Windows 95 to add the Exchange components to your system.

◆ **Understanding profiles**
Create a specific set of configuration options to use when you want to access Exchange programs.

◆ **Configuring the services**
Customize the way you use e-mail messages, faxing services, and other Exchange services.

M icrosoft Exchange is a robust message service, capable of handling messaging by e-mail and fax. The e-mail services include *local* (the mail exchanged between users connected to the same network) and *external* (messages from outside services, such as the Internet).

The messages can be notes while you're working in the Microsoft Exchange software or files you've created in Microsoft Office software.

To use the features in Microsoft Exchange, you need certain hardware and peripherals, and you also need to make sure your operating system can find them. All of that is discussed in this chapter.

Deciding on Components

You can choose the individual parts of Microsoft Exchange that you want to install and use. The following sections give you a brief look at what those elements are and what they do.

E-Mail

If your computer is attached to a network, you can exchange messages with other users on the network. Those messages can contain more than a note that was composed in the Microsoft Exchange software window. You can also attach files created in application software, such as the programs you're using in MS Office. You can even include OLE objects in your e-mail messages.

Composing a message in Microsoft Exchange is a straightforward, simple process. There are many formatting options available, and you can use MS Office tools, such as the Speller, to make sure that your messages are perfect.

An *address book* enables you to keep a database of the people with whom you correspond by e-mail. Your network administrator can create an address book containing the entire user list for your network. When you log on, you have access to that address book in addition to any personal address books you want to keep on your local drive.

You can create folders, locally or on the network server, in which to store messages and files. This gives you the option of keeping e-mail in a scheme you prefer—by subject matter, by month, or by any criteria you want to apply.

 Note

For the technically curious, or for network mail administrators, take a look at some of the requirements for running the e-mail services in Microsoft Exchange:

▶ The first requirement is to accept Microsoft's spelling. In the Exchange language, post office (two words, the way Webster's spells it) is one word, *postoffice*.

▶ You need at least 8M RAM to run the software, and the swap file may need as much as 20M of free disk space during a session.

▶ Users running Exchange can access mailboxes if the postoffice containing the mailbox was created by Microsoft Mail version 3.0 or later, Microsoft Windows for Workgroups 3.1 or later, or Microsoft Windows NT version 3.1 or later.

Fax Services

You can use Microsoft Fax from the Exchange program window or as a stand-alone program (choose Fax from the Accessories group). Either way, you must install Microsoft Exchange to access fax services.

Caution
You must specifically choose Fax Services while you're installing Microsoft Exchange. If you use the default settings that are presented in the Add/Remove Software program, Fax Services is not selected.

You can create faxes and cover sheets in the Fax program or you can use a document created in a Windows application. If the recipient of your fax has the same application software, you can send an editable fax, which is pretty amazing.

Note
To send an editable fax, you and the recipient must use fax services on a computer. This obviously won't work if you're faxing to a fax machine. The computers must use Class 1 fax/modems.

The Microsoft Fax software fools the fax transport into sending a document instead of a bunch of dots by using a process called binary file transfer (BFT), which was developed by Microsoft for this purpose.

You can create cover pages or edit sample cover pages by using the Cover Page Editor. This is a stand-alone program included when you install Fax services. The program allows you to create fields that will be filled in as you create a fax. Because the program is an OLE 2 application, you can even create graphical items (I like to play with Microsoft Paint).

The Fax Viewer is a robust program that lets you save faxes anywhere you want, not just in your message folders.

25

If you use a fax service, there's a Request A Fax program that dials into your service and fetches your stuff for you.

Receiving faxes is as easy as telling the software when to answer the phone. While it's annoying that you can't tell Microsoft Fax to answer automatically on the first ring (the minimum is two rings), you can click the Answer Now icon on the Fax Status window as soon as the phone rings, if you're sure the call coming in is a fax.

System administrators will be happy to learn that setting up shared fax services on the network is fairly simple.

The Microsoft Network

The Microsoft Network (MSN) is an online service you can use to communicate with people outside your organization. Through MSN you can access Internet e-mail, chat sessions, information, and files. You can send e-mail to anyone with an Internet address, whether or not they are using MSN. There's additional (free) software available and you'll have to obtain it if you want to visit World Wide Web sites.

At the time of this writing, Microsoft was still developing and enlarging the capabilities of MSN, but it's probably safe to assume that eventually you'll be able to access news-groups, Web pages, and other Internet features.

There's a period of free time on MSN, followed by reasonable charges if you continue to use MSN after your free time expires.

Installing Hardware

If you're on a network and want to use the Microsoft Exchange e-mail service to commu-nicate with other users on the network, there's a network adapter (sometimes called a Network Interface Card or NIC) in your computer. However, the physical installation of that card (which was probably done by a network administrator) isn't all there is to the installation process. You also have to install the card in your Windows 95 system, config-uring it so that the system can access it.

Likewise, if you are planning to use fax services or access The Microsoft Network, you need to install your modem in Windows 95.

Installing a Network Adapter

Before you can install your network adapter in Windows 95, you should know its settings—specifically the Interrupt Request level (usually referred to as IRQ) and Port Address. If you did the physical installation yourself, you already have this information; otherwise, you can get it from your network administrator. To begin the Windows 95 installation, follow these steps:

   1. Click the Start menu and choose Settings, Control Panel.

2. Double-click the Add New Hardware icon to display the introductory page of the Add New Hardware Wizard. Click Next to begin the installation.

3. The Wizard offers to detect your hardware, or you can tell the system manually which hardware device you're installing. Choose <u>Y</u>es to have the Wizard find the hardware, or choose <u>N</u>o to install it yourself. Click Next.

 Tip

Although the Windows 95 hardware detection process is clever and handy (it will frequently find the hardware and determine the configuration), it can be time consuming. (A message displays to warn you that it takes awhile and also explains what to do if the system hangs up during the process). If you're comfortable with installation routines and configuration options, it's perfectly okay to say you'd rather do it yourself.

4. If you told the Wizard to detect the hardware, you'll see a progress indicator (a bar that moves from left to right) and, when the computer has been thoroughly searched, the Wizard announces that it is ready to install support for the devices it found (see fig. 25.1).

Fig. 25.1

The Add New Hard-ware Wizard has found some devices and is ready to configure them—you might want to ask the Wizard what it found.

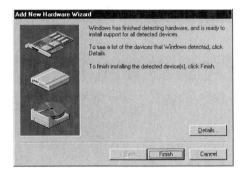

5. If you have blind faith in computers and operating systems, click the Finish button to complete the installation process for all the devices the Wizard found. If you want to see what the Wizard found, however, choose <u>D</u>etails.

25

 Tip

Not all hardware can be automatically detected. The detection program uses a list that it matches against the hardware it finds. If your device isn't on the list (which means it isn't supported), it won't appear on the list of hardware found.

6. When the list appears, highlight the device and click Finish. Confirm the configuration; if it's incorrect, you can change it later.

7. If you told the Wizard you want to pick the new hardware manually, a list of hardware types appears. Highlight the hardware type you want to install, and then click Next (see fig. 25.2).

Fig. 25.2

If you opted to skip the automatic detection, you have to choose the type of hardware you want to install.

8. A list of manufacturers appears. Highlight the appropriate one, then pick the specific model for your device. Click OK after you select the correct network adapter. The Wizard displays the configuration settings (they may be incorrect, but keep going). Choose Next to continue the installation.

9. Insert your Windows 95 CD-ROM or disk (the Wizard tells you which disk to insert) and the appropriate drivers will be transferred to your hard disk.

10. When the Wizard finishes installing the files, choose Finish to complete the installation process. You will be informed that to have the new settings take effect, you have to restart your computer. Choose No because you're not finished installing software for network services. The next section discusses the rest of the installation process.

 Note

If your network adapter isn't listed, you'll need drivers from the manufacturer of the adapter. These drivers frequently are included in the package, so look for a disk. If not, you can call the manufacturer or dial into a BBS run by the manufacturer and download the drivers you need. Some manufacturers maintain forums on CompuServe for this purpose.

Tell the Add New Hardware Wizard you want to choose your device rather than have the Wizard search for it. Then choose Network Adapters as the Hardware

Type and move to the Select Device page. Choose Have Disk and follow the instructions for inserting the disk into a floppy drive. The Wizard will transfer the files and complete the installation of the adapter.

Configuration Settings

You may find that the Install New Hardware Wizard is sometimes wrong about configuration options for a device. It occasionally presents the options that are the default for the device, even if you've changed the settings.

During the installation process, it isn't always possible to correct the Wizard, especially if you elect to skip automatic detection. The solution is to finish the installation process with the incorrect settings. You can correct the settings by using other Windows 95 features. You can also use these features to change configuration options if you change a device. You might, for instance, move a device to a different serial port, or purchase a later model of a device. This happens frequently with modems. When you have a large number of devices in your computer, you sometimes run into roadblocks with IRQ assignments. Some devices have limited IRQ choices, so you end up changing other devices to fit a new device into your system. IRQ and Port Address configuration can be a major problem when you buy a great deal of bells and whistles.

Changing Configuration Options for Hardware

Anytime you install a hardware device in your system, you can amend the configuration information. Suppose that the Wizard incorrectly configured your network adapter. To change the hardware configuration, follow these steps:

1. Click the Start menu and choose Settings, Control Panel.

2. Double-click the System icon to display the System Properties dialog box, and then click the Device Manager tab to see the devices in your system. Highlight the device you want to change (see fig. 25.3).

25

 Tip

Another way to get to the System Properties dialog box is to right-click on My Computer, and then choose Properties.

Fig. 25.3

A graphical representation of the devices in your system lets you manipulate your hardware configuration—you can even remove a device.

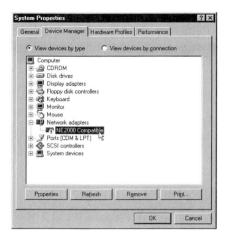

3. Choose Properties to see the configuration for the network adapter, and then click the Resources tab to view the current settings (see fig. 25.4).

Fig. 25.4

You also use this dialog box if you want to manually change the adapter to use a different IRQ or Port Addresses.

4. Highlight the incorrect setting in the Resource Settings area, and then choose Change Setting. Enter the correct information and choose OK (see fig. 25.5).

5. Repeat the process for any other setting that needs to be changed, and then choose OK. For some devices, such as a network adapter, you must shut down and restart the computer for the settings to take effect. Choose Yes to restart the system.

Fig. 25.5

The network adapter setting is changed to IRQ 15 and doesn't conflict with another device's setting.

Installing Network Services

The network adapter is one device that needs more installation processes than most other devices. It isn't enough to install the adapter and the drivers—you have to set up your system for the network services you'll be using.

The first step is to install the correct software and drivers to use network services. This involves installing client software, which is software specific to the type of networking you'll use. You have to install software and drivers for the protocol(s) you'll use to access other computers.

You also have to tell the system which client service you want to use for your primary network logon and create an ID for logging on.

 Note

A *protocol* is a form of language that computers use to talk to each other. All computers have to talk the same language or they can't communicate.

Windows 95 supports the following protocols:

▶ NetBEUI (NetBIOS Extended User Interface), which is Microsoft's workgroup protocol. It's used for communication between computers running Microsoft operating systems.

▶ IPX/SPX (Internetwork Packet Exchange), which is Novell Netware's protocol. You can access any Netware server or a Windows NT 3.5 server with this protocol.

▶ Protocols specific to other manufacturers, such as Banyan VINES (EtherNet and Token Ring); DEC PATHWORKS (EtherNet and Token Ring); IBM DLC; Novell IPX ODI; and SunSoft PC-NFS.

25

> ▶ TCP/IP (Transmission Control Protocol/Internet Protocol), which is used as the standard protocol for UNIX and also for the Internet.

To install network services, follow these steps:

1. Click the Start menu and choose Settings, Control Panel.

2. Double-click the Network icon. If no network services have been installed, only the network adapter is listed. Choose Add to install network services.

3. From the Select Network Component Type dialog box, begin adding the network services you need (see fig. 25.6).

Fig. 25.6

There are multiple components to install to make sure you have complete access to network features.

4. Highlight Client and choose Add to install client (workstation) software (see fig. 25.7). Highlight the client manufacturer you need, and then choose the appropriate network client. Choose OK. Repeat this if you want to install more than one client component.

Fig. 25.7

Install multiple client services if you use different servers for different services. Perhaps you have an NT server for e-mail and applications stored on a Novell server.

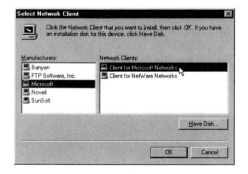

5. Most of the time, the system will automatically install the appropriate protocols for the service you just added. If not, choose Add, highlight Protocol in the Select Network Component Type dialog box, and choose Add. Check with your network administrator to determine the protocols you need. Select the protocols you need and add them to your system. When you finish, choose OK.

6. When you return to the Network dialog box, the network components in your system are listed. You now can begin the last steps of the network configuration process (see fig. 25.8).

Fig. 25.8

The hardware and software network components installed are displayed in the Network dialog box.

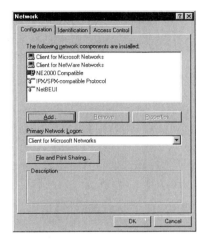

7. You now have to select a client service from the Primary Network Logon list box. This establishes the network service and logon procedure your system will use when it starts. Even if you only installed one client service (either Microsoft Networks or Novell Netware), you will also be given the option to have your primary logon as a Windows logon, which means you're logging on to your own computer. Choose the logon you want to use for system startup.

8. Click the Identification tab of the Network dialog box to display the computer name, the workgroup the computer belongs to, and a descriptive phrase for your computer. By default, the system uses the information you entered about your computer when you installed Windows 95. Make sure that your computer name is the same as it's configured on the server, or change it to match the computer's login that your network administrator established.

9. The system will inform you that you need to restart your computer for the new settings to take effect and will offer to restart it for you. Choose Yes to restart your computer.

When your system starts again, you'll see a Logon dialog box before the Windows 95 desktop appears. That logon depends on the primary logon you chose. The dialog box is waiting for a password. Enter one (or press Enter if you don't want to use a password) and this will become your permanent password.

You have completed the installation of network services. Thank goodness you only have to do this once.

25

Installing a Modem

If you want to use the Fax and/or MSN features in Microsoft Exchange, you need a modem. Luckily, the installation of a modem is not as complicated as the installation of a network adapter and network services.

First, physically install the modem. If it is an external modem, attach a modem cable to the modem and one of your serial ports. Then plug in the power cord and attach a telephone cable between the modem and the wall jack. If it is internal, insert the modem card in a slot in your computer and attach a telephone cable between the modem and the wall jack.

To install the modem in your Windows 95 system, do the following:

1. Click the Start menu and choose Settings, Control Panel. Make sure your modem is physically installed and, if it's external, is turned on.

2. Double-click the Modems icon to see the Install New Modem Wizard introductory page. You can let the Wizard find and detect your modem, or choose Don't Detect My Modem to install it yourself. Then choose Next. For this example, you install the modem manually.

3. The next page of the Wizard displays two panels. Choose a manufacturer from the Manufacturer list, and then select the specific modem from the Models list. Choose Next when you have made your selections.

4. Specify the port the modem is attached to. Internal modems usually are assigned to COM3. Choose Next.

5. The Location Information page appears, which lets you configure the way you'll use the modem:

   ▶ In the What Country field, specify the country you're dialing from.

   ▶ In the What Area Code field, specify the local area code.

   ▶ If you dial a number to access an outside line (commonly a 9), enter it in the Outside line box.

   ▶ Specify whether the phone system uses Tone or Pulse dialing.

6. Choose Next after you fill in the Location Information, and then choose Finish to complete the process.

Modem Configuration

As soon as you finish with the Install Modem Wizard, the Properties dialog box for the new modem automatically appears (see fig. 25.9).

Fig. 25.9

Use the Modems Properties dialog box to check or change the configuration for your modem and the port it's attached to.

Click the Properties button to see the configuration options for this specific modem. The General page of the modem's dialog box appears:

▶ Make sure that the Port setting is correct.

▶ Adjust the Speaker volume by moving the slider bar.

▶ Choose a Maximum speed for the modem.

 Tip

You don't have to stick with the modem's rated speed as a maximum speed—choose a higher speed. In fact, for all modems that are rated at 9,600 or higher, choose a speed of at least 38,400. This is advantageous because when modems transfer data, they use compression and as a result can frequently achieve speeds faster than their speed ratings.

Note that 14,400 is not available. If you have a 14,400 modem, choose 38,400. Never choose 14,400 for any modem configuration in any communications software. The reason for this is that modems really have two speed ratings: the rate at which they communicate with another modem, and the rate at which they communicate with the computer. There are industry standards that set existing, available rates for each of those two speed ratings. There is no 14,400 rate available in the speed ratings deemed acceptable for communicating with the computer. As a result, your software will frequently respond with error messages if you tell a configuration program that your modem is configured to work at 14,400.

25

Click the Diagnostics tab of the Modem Properties dialog box to see configuration settings for the serial ports in your computer. Make sure your modem is turned on, highlight the port that has the modem attached, and choose More Info. The system queries the modem and returns information about the configuration of the port and the modem in the More Info dialog box (see fig. 25.10).

Fig. 25.10

The port configuration and the modem's command strings are displayed, which can be useful if you're trying to get help from a technical support desk.

Fine-Tune the Modem's Configuration

You make configuration changes to the modem and the port through the System icon. If any of the configuration information displayed in the More Info dialog box is inaccurate or you want to change other properties such as your connection preferences, follow these steps:

1. Click the Start menu and choose Settings, Control Panel (or right-click on My Computer, then choose Properties to move right to the System Properties dialog box).

2. Double-click the System icon, and then click the Device Manager tab.

3. To configure the modem, click the plus symbol (+) to the left of the modem device to list the specific modem installed in this computer.

4. Highlight the modem, and then choose Properties. Click the Connection tab to see the connection settings (see fig. 25.11).

5. Enter the connection information that matches the software you'll use or the host computer you'll dial into.

6. Enter your preferences for calling out. You can select the following:

   ▶ Wait for a dial tone before dialing (usually necessary).

   ▶ Cancel the call if you don't reach a connection in an allotted amount of time—specify that time in seconds.

   ▶ Disconnect a call if the connection is idle for more than a specific number of minutes—enter the number of minutes you want to elapse before this automatic disconnection occurs.

Fig. 25.11

You have to set connection preferences and dialing preferences for your modem.

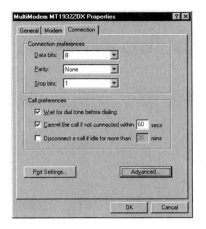

7. Choose A**d**vanced to configure additional settings (see fig. 25.12). Choose OK when you finish changing any of these options:

   ▶ Select Use **E**rror Control to enable error control features. This makes your connection more reliable.

   ▶ Select **R**equired to Connect to force error control features for connection. This is not always necessary and, depending on the connection at the other end, can be a problem. Enable this option only when you have been informed that your connection requires it.

   ▶ Select **C**ompress Data to speed up communications. If your modem doesn't support compression (which would only be the case if your modem is quite old), deselect this option.

   ▶ Select Use **F**low Control, then specify whether XON/XOFF (software controls) or RTS/CTS (hardware controls) should be used to control the flow of data between the modem and the computer. If either your modem or your cable doesn't support hardware controls (RTS/CTS), then you can choose XON/XOFF. Some software documentation will advise that XON/XOFF is not desirable. If you cannot use either flow control methods, deselect Use **F**low Control.

   ▶ Use the E**x**tra Settings text box to enter additional modem initialization settings (additional means more then the initialization strings that are normally sent to this modem). If you enter extra settings, these strings will be sent to the modem after the standard strings, and they will override the standard strings.

25

Tip

The use of extra settings is rarely necessary. The only time I used this feature was when a modem I was trying to install wasn't listed and I didn't have driver disks. I installed a modem driver that was similar to the modem I was installing, then used the E_xtra Settings text box to send the correct initialization string to the modem (which I copied from the documentation). Apart from this use, I don't know of any other reason to select this feature.

> ▶ Select Reco_rd a Log File if you want to keep a log of modem activity. The file, named MODEMLOG.TXT, is created in the folder where Windows is installed.

Fig. 25.12

Configuring the settings that control the way data moves through a modem connection.

8. You can choose P_ort Settings on the Connection tab of the modem's Properties dialog box to configure the way the modem's port works, using these guidelines:

> ▶ Select Use _FIFO buffers to use memory buffers for data. Your port must have a 16550 UART to take advantage of this feature.

> ▶ If you can use FIFO buffers, use the slider bars to change the settings of the _Receive Buffer and the _Transmit buffer to optimize your connections. The higher the setting, the faster the performance. However, high settings also bring the possibility of errors in transmission. Experiment with the permutations and combinations until you're happy with your modem sessions.

Installing the Exchange Software

Now that your hardware is installed and configured, you can install Microsoft Exchange. Microsoft Exchange is included in your Windows 95 software media, but depending on your installation decisions, it may not have been installed when you put the operating system on your computer. For the purposes of this discussion, assume that you have installed Windows 95 and have not yet installed Microsoft Exchange.

Before you begin, have your original Windows 95 CD-ROM or disks at hand.

Using the Add/Remove Programs Feature

One of the cool features of Windows 95 is that you can add programs, remove programs, and install specific parts of the operating system through the easy-to-use Add/Remove Programs component. To begin, follow these steps:

1. Click the Start menu and choose §ettings, §ontrol Panel.

2. Double-click the Add/Remove Programs icon, and then click the Windows Setup tab to see the list of components available for Windows 95 (see fig. 25.13).

Fig. 25.13

The Add/Remove Programs Properties dialog box provides an easy way to add or remove specific components of the Windows 95 operating system.

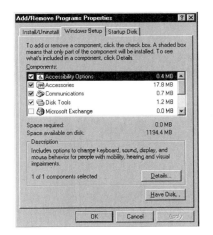

3. Begin adding components as described in the following section, "Installing Specific Components."

Before you add any components, you need to understand the Add/Remove Programs Properties dialog box:

▶ A listed component with a check mark in a white check box is completely installed.

▶ A listed component with a check mark in a gray check box is partially installed. That means there are multiple components or features available in that component and only some of them are currently installed.

▶ A listed component without a check mark in its check box is not installed; you can install it from your Windows 95 media.

As you highlight each choice in the list, the following specific information about that component appears in the dialog box:

▶ A description of the software component

▶ The number of available components in this software and the number of those components currently installed

In addition, you can choose <u>D</u>etails to see more information about the highlighted software selection. The Details dialog box describes each component and provides a check box so you can add it.

Installing Specific Components

For the purpose of demonstration, I'll walk through the installation of the possible components that Microsoft Exchange supports. You can choose the features you want to use.

 Note

To use the Windows 95 fax services, you have to install Microsoft Exchange. However, you only have to install the specific components that support fax services. You could skip this by installing third-party software, but you'll probably find that the fax application in Microsoft Exchange is as good as or better than anything else you'll find. Personally, I think the fax viewer is one of the coolest around.

Incidentally, the same response applies if you say you just want to use MSN for Internet access. You have to install Microsoft Exchange to install the Microsoft Network.

Because Microsoft Exchange is required for other software components, such as fax services, install that first. Follow these steps:

1. Highlight the Microsoft Exchange entry and choose <u>D</u>etails. The two components are listed and you can select one or both for installation by clicking the check box:

▶ Choose Microsoft Exchange to install the basic software. This permits access to other components of Windows 95, such as fax services, mail services, and the Microsoft Network.

▶ Choose Microsoft Mail Services to access Microsoft Mail postoffices. This is a workgroup version of Microsoft Mail and you can exchange messages with other users in your workgroup. To use a mail server outside your workgroup, you need to upgrade the server's operating system to include those facilities. The new Microsoft Exchange Server will fulfill this purpose and, at the time of this writing, was being tested for release.

2. After you choose the components you want, choose OK to return to the Windows Setup tab.

3. Highlight the Microsoft Fax entry and click the check box to install it. You don't have to choose Details because the two components are interrelated: if you choose one, you have to choose the other. Microsoft Fax Services send and receive faxes. Microsoft Fax Viewer permits you to view fax images.

4. Select The Microsoft Network and then click the check box. There are no subcomponents for this software.

5. Choose OK when you finish selecting new software components.

The necessary files are copied from the Windows 95 media. When the file transfers are complete, the Inbox Setup Wizard appears. The Inbox is the desktop icon that launches Microsoft Exchange. In effect, you will be configuring your Microsoft Exchange software with the Wizard.

1. The first question the Wizard asks is whether you've used Microsoft Exchange before. This isn't a question of your experience, and the Wizard doesn't care if you've used it on a different computer. The Wizard is really asking whether there's an existing version of Microsoft Exchange on this system. Because you already installed Microsoft Exchange and are just modifying the components, answer Yes, and then choose Next.

2. The Wizard lists the Microsoft Exchange services you chose to install. You can deselect any of them if you want. The listing indicates the services that will be included in your configuration profile, which will be set up automatically (you can make changes anytime). If this isn't your first installation of Microsoft Exchange and you're comfortable with the configuration options, select Manually Configure Information Services. Choose Next when you are ready to move to the next step.

3. If you selected fax services, the next three Wizard pages concern the setup of Microsoft Fax. Here, a list of the modems you've installed in your system is displayed so that you can choose the one you want to use for Microsoft Fax. Usually, there's only one modem. If you want, you can choose Add to add another modem. Choose Next when you have highlighted the appropriate modem.

4. If you selected fax services, the next page of the Wizard asks if you want Microsoft Fax to answer incoming calls. Choose Yes or No, then choose Next:

25

▶ Answer N<u>o</u> if you don't want this phone line answered by Microsoft Fax. If the same phone line is used for voice calls, you can click the icon for fax machine answering when someone calls to say the next call will be a fax.

▶ Answer <u>Y</u>es if this line is dedicated to Microsoft Fax services. Then specify the number of rings before answering.

5. On the next Wizard page, enter your name and fax number. This will be used on your fax cover page, along with other information you can design. Then choose Next.

6. The next Wizard page concerns Microsoft Mail. The Wizard needs to know the path of the location of the postoffice for your mail services.

If you don't know, ask a system administrator. If you cannot find a system administrator, enter any path you want or choose B<u>r</u>owse and pick a folder (the Wizard won't accept a blank field). Choose Next. You'll get an error message on the next Wizard page, but you can choose Next to keep moving. Don't forget to reconfigure your Microsoft Mail settings when you get the information.

Caution

If you try to use Microsoft Exchange before you have a valid postoffice in the configuration files, you'll get an error message. Choose Work Offline to permit the program to launch. You won't be connected to a postoffice, but you can create mail (you can't send it until you make a valid connection to a postoffice) and use the other components of Microsoft Exchange.

7. The Wizard then wants to know the name of your <u>M</u>ailbox and also wants a <u>P</u>assword. Get instructions for entering that information from your system administrator (or make something up and go back and correct it later). The Wizard will not accept an Enter key instead of a password, so invent one and enter it, and then choose Next.

8. Choose Next after you've read the explanation of The Microsoft Network on the next Wizard page. There's no setup for MSN in this Wizard. You'll configure MSN when you use it the first time.

9. The Wizard wants to know if you want Microsoft Exchange to start automatically when you start your computer. Choose <u>A</u>dd Inbox to the StartUp group or Do N<u>o</u>t Add Inbox. Then choose Next.

10. The last page of the Wizard lists the Microsoft Exchange Components that have been included in this configuration process. You can't change anything on this page, so choose Finish.

Windows 95 spends a few seconds (or longer, depending on the speed of your computer) setting up the appropriate files and desktop shortcuts. You can close the Control Panel when the hourglass goes away and the mouse pointer returns. When you next open the Control Panel, a Mail and Fax icon will be included in the group of icons displayed.

Understanding Profiles

When you worked with the Wizard to configure your Microsoft Exchange Services, you created a Microsoft Exchange profile.

A *profile* is a file that contains configuration information about your use of Microsoft Exchange. It has the location of your incoming mail, your address book, the Microsoft Exchange components you can access, and other information necessary for using the software.

You can edit a profile to change the configuration for a Microsoft Exchange session. And, you can have multiple profiles, configuring each one for a specific method of using Microsoft Exchange. Rather than mess around with the only existing profile, you may want to add a profile and then edit it to suit your tastes.

Adding Profiles

To work with profiles, you use the MS Exchange Settings Properties dialog box (see fig. 25.14). There are two ways to open this dialog box:

▶ Right-click the Inbox icon on your desktop, and then choose Properties.

▶ Click the Start menu and choose Settings, Control Panel. Double-click the Mail and Fax icon.

Fig. 25.14

Use the MS Exchange Settings Properties dialog box to manipulate the configuration of your Microsoft Exchange profiles.

25

When the dialog box appears, you can create a new profile by following these steps:

1. Choose <u>S</u>how Profiles to display a list of the existing profiles (unless you already created more profiles, there's only one).

2. Choose A<u>d</u>d to create a new profile. This launches the Inbox Setup Wizard you used to create your original profile. Let the Wizard guide you through the creation of the profile. Choose one of the following:

   ▶ Using only those information services you want accessible when you use this profile (for example, you may want a profile for fax services only).

   ▶ Using all the available services, but you will configure them differently for this profile (see the discussion "Configuring Profiles" that follows this section).

3. Choose a name for this profile that reminds you of its contents and configuration.

When you complete the steps, you can choose one of the profiles as the default profile used when you launch Microsoft Exchange.

Configuring Profiles

You can manipulate the elements and options in a profile to customize it for yourself by following these steps:

1. Click the Start menu and choose <u>S</u>ettings, <u>C</u>ontrol Panel.

2. Double-click the Mail and Fax icon to display the MS Exchange Settings Properties dialog box. The Services tab lists the information services established for the current profile, as seen earlier in figure 25.14.

3. If you want to configure a different profile, choose <u>S</u>how Profiles, then double-click the profile you want to configure.

4. If the selected profile is missing a Microsoft Exchange service you installed in your system, choose A<u>d</u>d. A list of installed services appears, and you can select the one you want to add to this profile.

5. If the selected profile has a service you don't want available when you're using this profile, choose R<u>e</u>move.

6. To configure a service for this profile, highlight the service you want to change, and then choose P<u>r</u>operties. For example, you may want to configure the basic options for The Microsoft Network (see fig. 25.15).

7. Move through each field, for each tab in the dialog box, selecting or deselecting the options you desire.

Fig. 25.15

*Before you launch
MSN, you can
establish some
configuration options
by manipulating your
profile.*

> **α Note**
>
> If you have problems with any of the services and a technical support person needs
> information about the service, you can get facts about the drivers, version number,
> file dates, size, and so on by highlighting the service and choosing About from the
> Services tab in the MS Exchange Settings Properties dialog box.

Configuring E-Mail

There are a number of configuration options available after you launch Microsoft
Exchange. You can start the program in one of two ways:

▶ Double-click the Inbox icon on your desktop.

▶ Click the Start menu and choose Programs, Microsoft Exchange.

Either way, the Inbox window appears (see fig. 25.16).

Fig. 25.16

*In the Inbox, you can
compose, send, and
read e-mail and faxes.*

25

To configure the way the Inbox behaves, choose Tools, Options. The Options dialog box
appears, which has six tabs. The following sections cover the options on all six tabs.

Configuring the General Tab

Specify the actions that occur when new mail arrives in your mailbox. Select one or more of the following options:

▶ Select Play a Sound to hear an alert sound (you specify the sound itself by selecting New Mail Notification and choosing a sound from the Sounds icon in the Control Panel).

▶ Select Briefly Change the Pointer to have your mouse pointer change into an envelope.

▶ Select Display a Notification Message if you want a message to appear when new mail is received in your mailbox.

You also have to decide how you want to deal with the deletion of items while you're using the software. Items can be anything from a message, an entry in the address book, or a folder. When you delete an item, it is placed in the Deleted Items folder. The choices are:

▶ Select Warn Before Permanently Deleting Items if you want Microsoft Exchange to display a dialog box so you can confirm or cancel the deletion.

▶ Select Empty the Deleted Items Folder Upon Exiting if you want everything in your Deleted Items folder to be permanently removed when you exit the program. It's probably not a good idea to select this item unless you also selected the previous item, just as a safeguard against accidental, disastrous deletions.

Caution

Don't confuse your Deleted Items folder with the Recycle Bin. The Deleted Items folder is only accessible while you're using Microsoft Exchange. If you delete a message, placing it into the Deleted Items folder, you won't find it in the Recycle Bin of your Windows 95 system. Microsoft Exchange is a separate, independent program that sometimes (as with deleted items) acts as if it doesn't know about Windows 95 features.

You can set the conditions for the profile selection at startup of the Microsoft Exchange program:

▶ Select Prompt for a Profile to have Exchange ask which profile you want to use before opening the program window.

Tip

Prompting for a profile is useful, for example, if you created separate profiles for a portable computer. When you're in the office and can hook directly into your work-group or network, your profile can let you work with the mailboxes on your system. You can send mail, receive mail, and so on.

When you're on the road, you can use a profile specifying that you want to work offline (unconnected to a mailbox). Then, any messages you create will wait in your Outbox folder until you connect to the office.

> Select Always Use This Profile (and select a profile from the list box) to skip the step of choosing a profile so the program launches automatically.

There are two options you can select that affect the way the program window behaves:

> Select Show ToolTips on Toolbars to see an explanation for any toolbar button you place your pointer on.

> Select When Selecting, Automatically Select Entire Word to select entire words when you drag the mouse across text.

Configuring the Read Tab

This is where you configure the way you read and reply to messages. When you open a message in the viewer so you can read it, you can move it to a folder. You can use your personal folder or a folder you create to hold specific types of messages. You can also delete the message. What happens after you move or delete a message depends on your configuration options:

> Select Open the Item Above It to have the message immediately above the current message move into the viewer. This works if you start viewing messages from the bottom of the message list and want to see the next message immediately.

> Select Open the Item Below It to accomplish the same thing if you start reading messages from the top of the list.

> Select Return to Microsoft Exchange if you want to return to the program window and pick a message from the list by yourself.

If you want to reply to a message you received, you can design the way the message looks when the recipient gets it:

> Select Include the Original Text to have the original message displayed after the text you enter as a reply. This is different from some of the mailing services you might be used to, where the original message appears before your reply.

25

▶ Select Indent the Original Text to offset that text and make it easy to distinguish from your reply.

▶ Select Close the Original Item if you want your reply to stand by itself in the message back to the sender.

▶ Click the Font button and select a font if you want the font of your reply to differ from the font of the original message.

Configuring the Send Tab

Use this tab to customize the messages you send and what happens when they're sent.

▶ Click the Font button to select a font for the text of your messages.

▶ Request a receipt either when the item has been read by the recipient (opened in the recipient's software) or delivered to the recipient's mailbox.

Caution
Even though the return receipt option is available, you may not be able to get return receipts for messages sent through an SMTP (Internet) gateway.

You can also specify a default sensitivity level for the mail you send. You can change this for any individual message as you compose and send messages. Choose one of the following levels from the Set Sensitivity list box:

▶ *Normal* has no particular sensitivity.

▶ *Personal* indicates that this message is not about a business matter.

▶ *Private* means that the recipient cannot modify the message during a reply or if it is forwarded to another user.

▶ *Confidential* can mean whatever your workgroup administrator (guided by company policy) wants it to mean. The issues that surround the handling of confidential e-mail are guided by company rules and protocols.

In the Set importance section of the dialog box, you can indicate the default level of importance of a message. This helps recipients decide which messages have to be attended to immediately and which can wait.

The setting you choose here is merely a default. It's just a convenience so that you don't have to set a level for each message. You can change this setting for any message you compose or send.

▶ Selecting High places an exclamation point on the message.

▶ Selecting Normal means no special marking appears on the message.

▶ Selecting Low places a down arrow on the message.

The Send tab also lets you opt to save a copy of every message you send. Select Save a Copy to place all your messages in the Sent Items folder. This is an excellent idea, but you have to remember to go into the folder and do some housekeeping once in a while.

Configuring the Services Tab

This tab is a duplicate of the dialog box for configuring a profile. See the section on configuring profiles earlier in this chapter.

Configuring the Delivery Tab

This is where you determine the place of delivery (the folder) for your incoming mail, and the way in which your outgoing messages are sent to their recipients.

▶ In the Deliver New Mail list box, choose a location. Unless you created additional folders, the only available choice is Personal Folders.

▶ You can choose an optional Secondary Location as an alternative delivery site in case something occurs that makes the primary delivery site unavailable.

▶ For Recipient Addresses, specify the order in which you want your outgoing mail processed. This page of the dialog box (the Delivery tab) lists the information services available for this profile; you can choose which service should have its outgoing mail processed first, which next, and so on. Select the service and then click the up or down symbol to move around the pecking order.

Configuring the Addressing Tab

This is where you establish options for using your address book. Specify your configuration preferences for the choices available:

▶ In the Show this Address List First list box, specify the address list you want to use as your default. Generally, the choice is between your personal (local) address book and the network address book. The latter has the names of all the users who log on. If you create additional address books, you may want to return to this tab of the Options dialog box and change the default.

▶ In the Keep Personal Addresses In list box, specify the address book you want to use when you're adding new names. Unless you created additional local address books, select your personal address book.

25

> In the <u>W</u>hen Sending Mail box, specify the order in which address books should be checked when you want to send a message. This is part of the verification procedure used before a message is sent. If most of your messages are sent to network users, you probably want the network address book checked first to speed things up.

 Tip

If not all the existing address books are listed, choose A<u>d</u>d to see a complete list and add one to the <u>W</u>hen Sending Mail list box. If there's an address book you don't want to use for verification, choose R<u>e</u>move. This does not remove the address book from your system, just from the <u>W</u>hen Sending Mail list box.

In addition, you can highlight an address book and choose P<u>r</u>operties to view and manipulate the selected address book (see fig. 25.17).

Fig. 25.17

Use the Properties dialog box for an address book to change its name and the way it displays the listings.

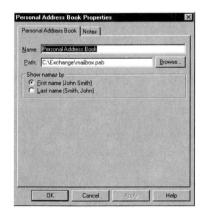

You can also choose whether you want the names in the address book displayed with first name first or last name first.

Creating a Postoffice

Before you do anything else, you have to make sure you have a postoffice. In most cases, this was accomplished well before you began the installation and configuration of your Microsoft Exchange software. However, if these setup steps haven't been taken or if you are acting as an e-mail services administrator, it is presented here.

Administrators for a workgroup can create and maintain postoffices. A postoffice is the place where mail is held for all the users in a workgroup. If there isn't a postoffice, you can create it by following these steps:

1. Click the Start menu and choose Settings, Control Panel.

2. Double-click the Microsoft Mail Postoffice icon. This launches the Postoffice Administration Wizard. The Wizard inquires whether you want to do one of the following:

   ▶ Administer an existing Workgroup Postoffice

   ▶ Create a new Workgroup Postoffice

3. Choose Create, and then choose Next. Enter the Postoffice Location. Use a directory on your own computer or on another computer in your workgroup. Choose Browse to look around.

Caution

You must be currently connected and able to see the postoffice location if you are placing it on another computer.

The postoffice directory must be marked as being shared, and you'll see a system message telling you that you must enable sharing for this folder (you get the message even if the folder is marked shared).

4. The Wizard creates the postoffice, displaying the directory and the postoffice name (WGPO0000 for the first postoffice). Choose Next to have the Wizard create the postoffice and present the Enter Your Administrator Account Details dialog box (see fig. 25.18).

Fig. 25.18

Each postoffice has information about the administrator, which makes it possible to find her or him when necessary.

25

5. Fill in the text boxes of the dialog box (only <u>N</u>ame and <u>M</u>ailbox are required, the rest are optional), and then press OK.

Creating New Folders

You can create as many folders to hold messages as you want. Some people create a separate folder for reports, and another one for questionnaires that have been sent to all users. Your own work habits, as well as the type and volume of messages you receive, determine your need for additional folders.

After you create additional folders, you can move or copy messages into the new folders.

To create a new folder, follow these steps:

1. Make sure the folders appear in the Inbox window. If not, choose <u>V</u>iew, Fo<u>l</u>ders (a check mark appears when the active view is Folders). You can also use the Show/Hide Folder List icon on the toolbar.

2. Select the folder that will be the parent of the new folder. Usually, that is the Personal Folders folder, which is the parent folder for the standard folders in Exchange. You may, however, decide that your new folder should be a subfolder under the Inbox.

3. Choose <u>F</u>ile, New <u>F</u>older to open the New Folder dialog box.

4. Enter a <u>F</u>older Name, and then choose OK. The new folder appears in the Exchange window.

Configuring Fax Services

Faxing with Microsoft Exchange is extremely flexible, so the first decision you have to make is how you want to get there. There are three ways to get to the software that lets you compose and send a fax:

▶ Double-click the Inbox icon, where composing and sending faxes are menu items.

▶ Click the Start menu and choose <u>P</u>rograms, Accessories, Fax, Compose New Fax.

▶ Choose a command for sending faxes from the File menu of a Windows program that is configured to link to your fax services (such as your Microsoft Office software). That command is usually Send.

Note

You can also fax a document from any MS Office software application with the Print command. When you installed Microsoft Exchange, a printer named Microsoft Fax was established for faxing. The printer driver installed is the Microsoft Fax Driver. Check the properties of the Microsoft Fax printer in your printer folder to make sure everything is set up properly.

Choose Printer Setup or Select Printer from your software and select the Microsoft Fax printer. Then, when you choose Print, the Fax Wizard will appear and walk you through sending the fax.

Configuring Default Options

The way to configure your fax services is to open Microsoft Exchange. The Inbox-Microsoft Exchange window appears and you can begin configuring your fax software. Remember that your preferences are defaults, and you can change any individual fax to match the options needed for it.

To configure your fax services, follow these steps:

1. Choose Tools, Microsoft Fax Tools, Options. The Microsoft Fax Properties dialog box displays with the Message tab in the foreground (see fig. 25.19).

Fig. 25.19

You can set default specifications for the fax messages you compose—the defaults are operative regardless of how you launch fax services.

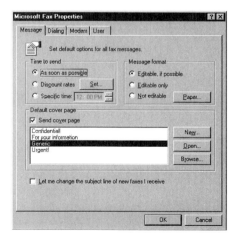

25

2. In the Time To Send section of the Message tab, specify your preferences for sending faxes:

   ▶ Select As Soon As Possible to send a fax immediately after you compose it.

   ▶ Select Discount Rates to send long-distance faxes when lower rates are in effect. Don't forget to specify your carrier's discount hours in the Set box.

   ▶ Select Specific Time to send the fax at a certain time.

3. In the Message Format section, choose your formatting preferences. These specifications are only important when the recipients have computer-based faxing. If the fax is going to a stand-alone fax machine, none of these options matter.

   ▶ Select Editable, If Possible to format your fax so that recipients who use the same software you do (Microsoft Fax) can edit the message. All other recipients receive a bitmap image that cannot be edited.

   ▶ Select Editable Only to insist that the message be editable, meaning the recipient must use Microsoft Fax. Any recipient who does not have Microsoft Fax will get an error message when he or she tries to receive your fax.

   ▶ Select Not Editable to send only bitmap images.

   ▶ Select Paper to specify a default Paper size, a default Image quality, and either Portrait or Landscape orientation.

4. Select Send Cover Page if you want one, then choose one of the cover pages provided. Look in the section "Configuring Fax Cover Pages" later in this chapter to learn how to edit the existing cover pages and design your own from scratch.

5. Select Let Me Change the Subject Line of New Faxes I Receive if you want to be able to edit incoming fax subject lines. If you select this option, any faxes you receive will be attachments to a mail message, because it is only in mail messages that you can change the subject lines.

6. Click the User tab to configure the information for your cover page. The data you enter is used to fill in fields when you design or edit cover pages. For example, if you opt to enter your home telephone number, and you choose to have that field display in your cover page, the data you enter here will be filled in.

7. The Dialing tab and Modem tab display information set up in your modem and port configurations, so you don't need to discuss them here. You might want to view the information to check its accuracy. If you make changes, the changes are also made to all other configuration pages connected to the modem.

Configuring Fax Cover Pages

You can customize a cover page for your faxes or customize multiple cover pages to send one that's appropriate to the type of fax you're sending. Just follow these steps:

1. Click the Start menu and choose <u>P</u>rograms, Accessories, Fax, Cover Page Editor.

2. The Cover Page Editor launches, and the program window resembles that of a word processor.

3. Choose <u>F</u>ile, <u>O</u>pen to open an existing cover page you can alter. When the Open dialog box appears, look in your windows directory for cover page files, which have an extension of CPE. By default, the Cover Page Editor shows only CPE documents in the Open dialog box.

   Or, choose <u>F</u>ile, <u>N</u>ew to create your own cover page from scratch.

Whether you opt to edit and customize an existing fax cover or build your own, it's important to understand that the fax cover is similar to a database entry window. It has fields, and the data connected to each field fills in automatically. In addition, you can insert on your cover page text and graphics that are not connected to the default information.

The fields cover two different types of information:

▶ Data fields about the sender are filled in using information from the User tab in your fax setup (see the previous section).

▶ Data fields about the recipient are filled in using information from your address book.

The easiest way to learn how to use the editor is to edit an existing cover page. The steps used to change the fields and the layout are the same ones you'll use to create your own cover page. It's easier to discuss it here if you have an existing cover page to view as you go over the steps. If you want to follow along, open a cover page and make changes as they are discussed here. To begin, open the Generic cover page (see fig. 25.20).

Fig. 25.20

The top of the Generic cover page has basic information about the sender and the recipient—you can add or change fields or insert some cool graphics.

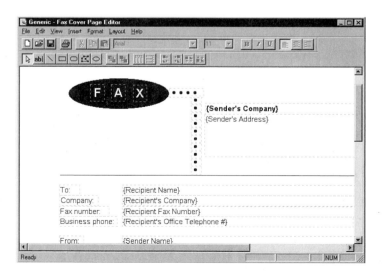

25

Adding, Deleting, and Moving Fields

To add a field to your fax cover, follow these simple steps:

1. Choose Insert, Recipient, Sender or Message, and then choose the field you want to add for that category.

2. The field and the field's caption are inserted in the fax cover. They are selected—editing handles surround the entry—and ready for editing (see fig. 25.21).

Fig. 25.21

The sender's title is inserted and needs to be moved to an appropriate place on the fax cover

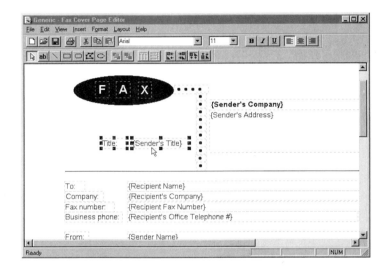

3. Drag the new field to the proper position. As you drag, both parts of the field (the field and the caption) move. When it is in position, click on any blank spot to deselect it.

4. You can eliminate the caption by clicking it to select it, and then pressing Delete.

Tip
To delete a field, select it and press Delete. To move a field, select it and drag it to the new position.

Adding Objects and Graphics

You can insert objects from documents, graphics from documents, or graphics you create in a drawing program. Follow these steps:

1. Choose Insert, Object to open the Insert Object dialog box.

2. Select Create New to create an object or select Create from File to insert an existing file from a software program.

3. If you are creating an object, double-click the object type you want to create. The appropriate software launches, along with the necessary toolbars.

   If you are bringing in an object from an existing file, choose the file by entering its path or use the Browse button to search your drive and find it.

 Tip

You can insert a variety of objects in a fax cover, including sounds and moving video. If you design a fax cover with these objects, however, only use it when the recipient is receiving faxes on a computer. It doesn't make a lot of sense to send a sound file to a stand-alone fax machine.

---

4. Select Link if you want to link the file object rather than insert its contents into the fax cover. Linking the file means that any changes you make to the object in either place (the fax cover or the original document) will change both.

5. Select Display as Icon to have the embedded object appear as an icon, as opposed to the real contents of the object. If you select this option, double-click the icon to see the actual object.

Configuring The Microsoft Network

The Microsoft Network (MSN) is the built-in software for Internet access. Besides information about Microsoft products, MSN provides e-mail capabilities—including exchanging messages through the Internet—software, other files you can download to your own system, and chat sessions with other members.

The software configuration for MSN involves setting up an account and creating a name and password. You accomplish all of that automatically when you launch the software for the first time:

1. Double-click the MSN icon on your desktop to see the opening screen. Choose OK to begin the configuration.

2. In The Microsoft Network dialog box that appears, enter the first three digits of your telephone number (your area code should already be displayed, but if it's not, you must enter it). This is how MSN finds the nearest access number for you. Choose OK after you enter the information.

25

3. The Calling dialog box appears, which explains that MSN will dial a central number to fetch a local access number for you and download information about the free trial period you'll have.

 Tip

If this is the first time you've used your modem, you might want to select <u>S</u>ettings to take a peek at your modem settings before telling MSN to connect. Make sure the modem brand and the port are correct and check to see whether you should select special dialing sequences to reach an outside line or to disable call waiting.

4. Choose <u>C</u>onnect to begin. After connection, you will see a note that MSN is beginning a transfer of files. After a minute or so (depending on the speed of your modem), the opening MSN registration dialog box appears.

 Tip

When the registration dialog box appears, the software disconnects you from MSN, so don't panic if you don't see lights flashing on your modem. After you fill in the information that MSN needs and elect to join, the software reconnects you to MSN.

5. Click each of the three items and fill out the associated dialog box. As you complete the following items, a check mark appears next to the icon.

▶ Enter your name, address, and voice line number.

▶ Enter the information about the credit card you want to use to pay for your MSN usage.

▶ Read the member agreement, then choose I <u>A</u>gree to indicate you've read and agreed to the MSN rules and regulations.

6. Choose <u>P</u>rice to read information about the free trial period and the cost to use MSN after the free period expires.

7. Choose <u>J</u>oin Now when you are ready to connect to MSN to begin your membership configuration, and then choose OK from the local access number dialog box that displays.

Tip

You can cancel the process at any time without losing the information you enter. To begin the process again, if any Microsoft Network dialog box is displayed, you can choose <u>B</u>ack to Signup. If you closed The Microsoft Network dialog box and left the software to do something else, use Windows 95 Explorer to find the Signup icon in the \Program Files\The Microsoft Network folder. Double-click on it to start the process.

 Note

Before the connection process begins, a dialog box displays the local number for MSN. In some areas, you will also have a backup number. The numbers are selected by choosing the nearest number to your area code and telephone exchange. The numbers are also selected for the baud rate of your modem, with a set of numbers for modems operating at 2,400 baud and other numbers for 9,600 and higher. If your modem is older and operates at less than 2,400 baud, don't join any Internet service—you'll lose your mind.

8. Follow the instructions to connect to MSN. When the connection is made, enter a member ID and a password (see fig. 25.22).

   ▶ Your member ID cannot include spaces, but you can use an underscore (_) to indicate a space. I don't know the maximum number of characters permitted, but I've never known anyone who got an error message that his ID was too long.

   ▶ Your password can contain up to 16 characters and must have at least eight characters.

   If your ID is already in use (which happens to people with common names), you are asked to choose another ID. You may have to do this more than once, or resort to an ID that isn't based on your name.

That's all there is to it. After your credit card information is verified, you'll be entered in the rolls of Internet travelers. Stick your ID on your business cards, stationery, and any place that seems relevant.

25

Fig. 25.22

Create an ID for yourself, which will become your Internet e-mail name throughout the world.

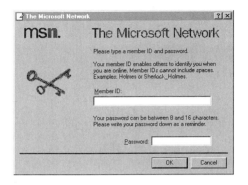

Summary

E-mail, fax services, and the Internet are important productivity tools for any user. The capability to combine these utilities with your Microsoft Office applications enhances that power. While it takes some time to install and set up your communications features, it's a one-time task from which you accrue a great deal of power and quite a bit of fun.

chapter 26

Managing Faxes

26

by Sue Mosher

In this chapter

◆ **Advanced configuration**
Learn how to set up and use a network fax server and recreate the fax printer driver.

◆ **Sending faxes**
This chapter covers generating faxes from Office applications, transmitting data (not just documents), dealing with special dialing problems, and managing the fax queue.

◆ **Receiving faxes**
This section describes how to use the fax viewer and retrieve documents from fax-on-demand services.

◆ **Security**
Use encryption, signatures, and public keys to secure your faxed documents.

The fax machine has grown in the past few years from a hard-to-use tool to an essential of doing business. The advent of desktop fax solutions makes it easy to exchange ideas and data without standing in line at the fax machine.

But it also introduces the need to master new skills for troubleshooting modem problems, designing cover pages, and attaching security to sensitive information. This chapter builds on the configuration and installation expertise you gained in the last chapter on Exchange.

Checking Your Setup

Microsoft Fax is set up as a service in Exchange (Inbox) (see Chapter 25, "Installing and Configuring Exchange"). You can use Microsoft Fax with a modem on the local machine or a modem on another PC on the network that also runs Exchange.

In addition to the modem functions, Microsoft Fax includes a printer driver, because many faxes are sent as images rather than as the documents themselves. If you have a problem printing to the fax printer driver, it's easy to recreate the driver.

Using a Network Fax Server

Where two or more PCs are linked in a network, but only one phone line for faxing is available, one machine can be set up as a network fax server. The other systems will be able to send faxes through the server just as if they had a locally installed modem.

To act as a fax server, your PC must have file sharing enabled in Control Panel, Network.

To set up your PC as a network fax server, follow these steps:

1. In Exchange, choose Tools, Microsoft Fax Tools, Options, then click the Modem tab. You see the dialog box shown in figure 26.1.

2. Be sure you have a modem installed and designated as the active fax modem.

3. Click the box labeled Let Other People on The Network Use My Modem to Send Faxes.

4. In the Select Drive dialog box that appears next, select the drive on your local system where you want outgoing faxes to be queued. Click OK to complete the process of sharing your fax modem, then click OK again to close the Microsoft Fax Properties dialog box.

Caution

Do not choose Cancel in the Select Drive dialog box, or you may not be able to share your fax modem without first removing, then reinstalling the Microsoft Fax service in your Exchange profile. If you are not sure where you want to put the fax folder, pick a drive anyway. You can later move the folder to a new location and share it again.

Tip

If your PC is a busy network fax server, you may want to install a second modem and phone line for non-fax calls. Your other communications programs can use this second line, even while the fax line is handling incoming and outgoing transmissions.

Fig. 26.1
*Make your PC a fax
server by installing a
modem, then allowing
others on the network
to use it.*

When you share the modem, Exchange creates a \Netfax folder on the drive you designated and shares it under the share name Fax with full access rights. You can confirm
these settings by choosing Properties on the Modem dialog box. In the dialog box shown
in figure 26.2, you can change the sharing characteristics by adding a password if you
want to restrict access or entering a comment to provide a better description of the
shared folder. Also note the name of the share. Other users will use this share name (not
the name of the folder itself) when they connect to your shared fax.

Fig. 26.2
*The \Netfax folder is
shared for full access
so others can use it to
queue their outgoing
faxes.*

Once you have shared the fax modem, you should leave Exchange running at all times.
Other users will not have access to the shared fax modem if Exchange is not active.

Setting Up a Client to the Network Fax Server

With a fax server installed, other users can now add Microsoft Fax to their Exchange
services and start sending faxes through the server. To set up a PC to access the network
fax server, follow these steps:

1. In Exchange, choose <u>T</u>ools, Microsoft Fa<u>x</u> Tools, <u>O</u>ptions, then click the Modem tab. Again, you see the dialog box shown in figure 26.1.

2. Choose <u>A</u>dd to bring up the Add a Fax Modem dialog box (see fig. 26.3).

3. Select Network Fax Server, then click OK.

Fig. 26.3

If you don't have a modem on your machine, you can fax through any installed network fax server.

 Tip

Check Network Neighborhood on your Windows 95 Desktop before setting up the shared fax clients to be sure you have the exact computer name and share name needed to construct the path to the shared network fax folder.

4. In the dialog box shown in figure 26.4, enter the path to the shared fax directory. For example, if the name of the computer (as shown in Network Neighborhood) is SERVER2, and the name of the share is FAX, then the path will be \\SERVER2\FAX. Click OK to complete the connection process.

Fig. 26.4

Before you connect to a network fax server, you need to know the server name and the share name for the fax folder.

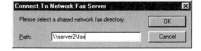

 Tip

When selecting a machine to act as the network fax server, be sure that someone will be available to print out incoming faxes or route them from that system to other Exchange users on the network.

With Microsoft Fax set up to use the network fax server, outgoing fax transmissions will be queued to and sent by the server. However, incoming faxes to the server are not automatically routed to recipients. Whoever uses Exchange on the network fax server will need to be responsible for forwarding incoming faxes to the right people. Alternatively, you may choose to use your network fax server only for outgoing faxes.

 Note

When you're trying to connect to a network fax modem, you may get a message, `The specified network server is not running. Please contact the administrator of the server.`

This message may occur if you're trying to connect to a shared fax directory that was created on a Windows for Workgroups machine. While Windows for Workgroups also has the capacity to share its fax services, it cannot share them with Exchange users, only with other Windows for Workgroups systems. Similarly, Windows for Workgroups systems cannot use a shared fax modem set up on a Windows 95 machine. Microsoft has indicated that a patch will be made available to allow these two operating systems to use each other's shared fax modems.

If, on the other hand, the shared network fax directory you gave was on a Windows 95 machine, then make sure that fax server is actually running Exchange before you try to connect to it.

Re-creating the Fax Printer Driver

The Microsoft Fax service in Exchange includes a printer driver so that you can fax any document that can be printed from a Windows application. If you accidentally delete the printer, you may need to recreate it. This may also be necessary if you can send a fax by composing an Exchange message but not by printing to the Microsoft Fax printer driver, or if you see any of the following messages when you try to fax from an application:

`WPSUNI.DRV could not be found or is not a valid printer driver.`

`Could not start print job.`

`Windows cannot print due to a problem with the current printer setup.`

`Not enough memory to print.`

WPSUNI.DRV is the name of the Microsoft Fax printer driver. Removing, then reinstalling, the Microsoft Fax service using Add/Remove Programs will not reinstall this printer driver. To replace or reinstall this driver, you must follow these steps:

26

1. Choose Start, Settings, Printers to bring up the Printers folder.
2. If the Microsoft Fax printer is present, delete it. Then, close the Printers folder.

3. Choose Start, <u>R</u>un. Type in `AWADPR32.EXE`, then click OK to reinstall the Microsoft Fax driver.

 Note

If you get a different message that seems related to the printer driver (such as `WordPad caused a General Protection Fault in WPSUNI.DRV`) and reinstalling the driver doesn't help, then you may have an old file on your system that you don't need.

Use Start, <u>F</u>ind to see if you have more than one version of FAXCODEC.DLL on your system. This file was also used in the Microsoft Fax component of Windows for Workgroups, so if you upgraded, you may have an extra copy. There should be only one version in your \Windows\System folder. If you find an older copy, possibly in your \Windows folder, delete it.

Coexisting with Other Exchange Services

If you have Microsoft Mail in your profile as well as Microsoft Fax, you may get a message when you try to fax that the e-mail address cannot be found.

All you need to do is change the order in which Exchange tries to deliver messages. In <u>T</u>ools, <u>O</u>ptions, choose the Delivery tab. Make sure that Microsoft Fax Transport is at the top of the list of information services.

If you have both Microsoft Fax and Internet Mail (another Exchange service available from Microsoft) installed in your Exchange profile, you can get the message `Internet Mail: Port already in use` when Exchange starts.

What's happening is that the fax modem is trying to initialize at the same time the Internet Mail service is trying to check for new mail. The message can be ignored if you have no messages waiting to be sent. If you do have Internet Mail messages pending in your Outbox folder, however, delivery of these messages will fail and you'll get a message from the System Administrator in your Inbox. You'll then have to resend each message.

To solve this problem, you will need to change the settings for the Internet Mail service so that it does not automatically check for new messages. Choose <u>T</u>ools, <u>S</u>ervices, then select Internet Mail and choose <u>P</u>roperties. On the Properties sheet, choose Work <u>O</u>ffline and Use Remote Mail.

Sending Faxes

There are two ways to send a fax—compose an e-mail message or print to the Microsoft Fax printer driver. Table 26.1 shows the best method to use, depending on who you're faxing to and what you're sending.

Table 26.1   Best Fax Methods for Sending Office Documents

To Do This	Use This Method
Send one document to a mixture of recipients on e-mail and fax.	From within the application, use File, Send. *or* From Exchange, choose Compose, New Message.
Send one document to one or more fax recipients with a note starting on the cover page.	From within the application, use File, Print to print to the Microsoft Fax printer driver. *or* From Exchange, choose Compose, New Fax
Send multiple documents to a mixture of e-mail and fax recipients.	From Exchange, choose Compose, New Message.
Fax multiple documents to one or more recipients with a note on the cover page.	From Exchange, choose Compose, New Fax.
Send only a few pages or a particular selection from a document, not the whole thing.	From within the application, use File, Print to print to the Microsoft Fax printer driver.
Fax a document as an editable file, including documents with security added.	From within the application, use File, Send. *or* From Exchange, choose Compose, New Message.

The last item in table 26.1 refers to the concept of an editable file. Yes, you can send documents not just as rendered fax images, but also as files that can be opened and run. This important feature, called binary file transfer (BFT), makes Microsoft Fax work just like person-to-person e-mail. BFT is covered in detail later in "Using Binary File Transfer."

We look first at your options for sending from within your Office applications, then examine the methods from within Exchange itself.

Sending from Office Applications

You do not need to start Exchange to send a fax. Just choose either File, Send (to send an e-mail message) or File, Print to send the document as a fax image with an optional cover page. If the fax service is not running, it will start automatically.

 Note
Remember that if your PC is acting as a network fax server, it must have Exchange running at all times.

Sending as an E-Mail Message

Using File, Send from within an Office application transmits a copy of the current document as part of a normal e-mail message. (For more information on sending normal e-mail messages, see Chapter 27, "Managing Electronic Mail.") Fax machines will get an image—the equivalent of a printed copy of the document.

To address a fax created using File, Send, use one of these methods:

▶ Enter a name from your address book in the To text box. Exchange will check for the fax address for this name when you send the fax.

▶ Use Tools, Address Book or Ctrl+Shift+B to open the Address Book. Select the recipient you want, then choose To, Cc or Bcc.

▶ Choose Tools, Fax Addressing Wizard and enter the name, country, and number in the fields provided in the dialog box shown in figure 26.5. Then choose Add to List. Repeat as many times as needed to enter all the recipients. Note that you can access your Address Book from the wizard, too, by choosing Address Book. Choose Finish when your recipient list is complete.

▶ Enter the fax names and numbers directly in the To field using the format [FAX:name@number], as seen in figure 26.6.

Fig. 26.5

The Fax Addressing Wizard makes it easy to send faxes to people who aren't already in your Address Book.

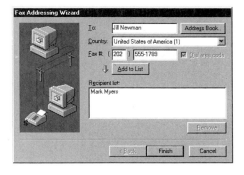

Fig. 26.6

You can enter fax numbers directly using the [FAX:] address format.

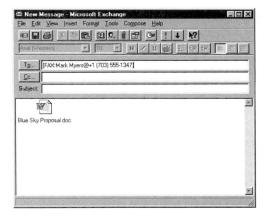

One important thing to remember about using File, Send is that it does not give you the opportunity to include a note on the fax cover page. Anything you write in the message body will appear on a separate page. Remember that on a fax machine using thermal paper, the fax paper is sized to exactly the length of the message. If you're sending a short message, the recipient will get a short piece of paper, which may not be desirable. (Those little slips of paper are hard to file.)

Another crucial point is that, to fax to a name from your Address Book, that person must be set up with a fax address. Even though Exchange lets you store fax numbers for each person in your Address Book, it sends faxes only to those whose entry type is set as Fax. To enter a new fax address in the Address Book, follow these steps:

1. Choose Tools, Address Book or Ctrl+Shift+B to open the Address Book. You can also click the Address Book button.

2. Choose File, New Entry or click the Index Card icon.

3. Select Microsoft Fax–Fax as the entry type, and then click OK.

26

4. In the New Fax Properties dialog box shown in figure 26.7, enter at least the name and number.

5. Click OK to save the new fax recipient to the Address Book.

Fig. 26.7

If you want to be able to send faxes to a person in the Address Book, you must enter that person with a fax address.

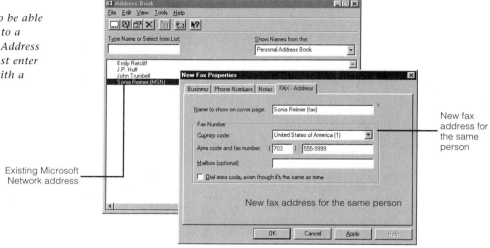

Existing Microsoft Network address

New fax address for the same person

New fax address for the same person

> ⚛ **Tip**
>
> If you send both faxes and e-mail to a person, you will need two addresses, one for each type. Put (fax) and (e-mail) in one of the name fields so you can tell them apart (see fig. 26.7).

Printing to the Microsoft Fax Printer Driver

If you are not sending to a mixture of e-mail and fax recipients and you do not need to send your document as an editable file, then you can print to the Microsoft Fax printer driver and be able to include a note on your cover page. Sending a fax this way also lets you control whether you send the entire document, just one page, or only the currently selected portion of your document.

To send a fax by using the printer driver and the Compose New Fax Wizard, follow these steps:

1. Choose File, Print.

2. From the Printer list, select the Microsoft Fax printer, as shown in figure 26.8.

Fig. 26.8

Use the Microsoft Fax printer driver to send a fax from virtually any Windows application.

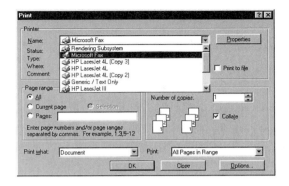

3. Make any other desired changes in your print settings, then click OK.

4. On the Compose New Fax Wizard, either enter a name from your Address Book in the To field or enter a name in the To field, a country code in the Country field, and the phone number in the Fax # field (see fig. 26.9). Then choose Add to List.

5. Repeat Step 4 until all recipients are shown in the Recipient List. Then choose Next to continue.

Fig. 26.9

The Compose New Fax Wizard appears when you print to the Microsoft Fax printer driver.

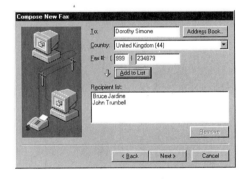

6. On the next dialog box of the wizard, choose whether to use a cover page (see fig. 26.10). Also, if you need to change any of the default options for the fax, choose Options to see the dialog box shown in figure 26.11. When you've selected your cover page and options, choose Next to continue.

7. Enter a subject line on the next dialog box and a note to appear on the cover page of your fax (see fig. 26.12). If you uncheck the Start Note on Cover Page box, the note will appear on a separate page.

8. Choose Next to continue, then Finish to begin preparing the fax for transmission.

Because this is a wizard, you can choose Back at any time to return to a previous dialog box and change your entries.

Fig. 26.10

The wizard continues by prompting you for a cover page choice and allowing you to change various options.

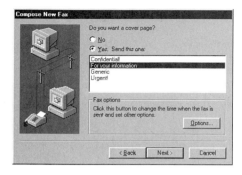

Fig. 26.11

Specify the send time, add security, or change other options on the Send Options For This Message dialog box. You can also choose Editable Only or Editable If Possible to send your document as a binary file.

Set transmission time

Enable/disable cover page

Select cover page   Add encryption or electronic signature

Enable binary file format

Set paper size and orientation

Disable binary file format

Set dialing properties

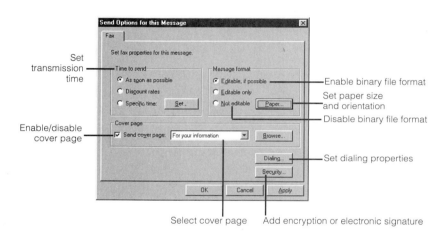

Fig. 26.12

The subject line and note will appear on the cover page of your fax.

Faxing the Contents of an Office Binder

And now a word about faxing a complete Office Binder: Don't. Trying to fax the contents of a Binder produces inconsistent and often frustrating results. If you use File, Send, usually only one or two sections are transmitted, not the entire binder. If you use File,

Print, each section is printed to the Microsoft Fax printer driver as a separate document. So, if you have six sections, you'd have six separate faxes to each recipient.

A much more satisfactory solution for faxing the contents of a Binder is to save the sections as individual files and attach them to a single fax, as described in the next section.

Sending from Exchange

The same Compose New Fax Wizard that appears when you print to the Microsoft Fax printer driver also can be run from within Exchange by choosing Compose, New Fax. You get one extra option when you run the wizard from Exchange—the ability to include more than one file in the fax. Figure 26.13 shows an example of a fax where two documents are being sent together.

Fig. 26.13

If you run Compose, New Fax from Exchange, you get the option of including more than one document.

From Exchange, you can also use Compose, New Message to send to both fax and e-mail recipients and to include multiple documents in the fax, as you saw in table 26.1.

 Tip

If you want to use a fax cover page that you created in Word, attach it as a separate document, along with the other document(s) you're faxing.

Using Binary File Transfer

We've hinted several times that binary file transfer is one of the great features of Microsoft Fax. It really solves the problem of trying to deliver editable documents to colleagues and clients in a timely fashion. You don't have to wrestle with making different communications programs link up, and you aren't at the mercy of third-party e-mail providers to deliver your documents.

26

Binary file transfer, or BFT, is a protocol that allows you to send the actual document, not just an image, to a compatible system. What does compatible mean in this case? You can exchange documents with any recipient using Exchange or the version of Microsoft Mail that comes with Windows for Workgroups or Delrina's WinFax Pro. It's likely that makers of other fax software will also add BFT capability.

What can you send with a BFT fax? Not just documents, but even executable files! You can compose complex messages with embedded objects and attached files and have them appear to the recipient in exactly the same form as you composed them.

After you have learned to send a fax, you can use those same skills to send a document modem-to-modem to another Microsoft Fax user. If you have ever wrestled with getting two modems to connect or tried to walk the person on the other end of the line through a file transfer, you'll understand what a time-saver this can be.

If you have the default message format set to Editable, If Possible, then Fax will always create both e-mail and rendered image versions of your faxes and deliver the binary document (e-mail version) whenever it encounters a compatible receiver. Recipients using Exchange or Windows for Workgroups Mail will see it as an e-mail message. Instead of a cover page, they'll get whatever note you included in your message.

You may also have situations where you want to force BFT-compatible systems to receive an uneditable fax image. In that case, just change the message format to Not Editable. If you're using the Compose New Fax Wizard, select Options to get the dialog box shown earlier in figure 26.11. If you're composing a regular e-mail message with one or more fax recipients, choose File, Send Options.

One caveat for BFT: you must have a Class 1 modem. BFT does not work with Class 2 modems. Both your modem and the recipient's modem must be Class 1.

Special Dialing Issues

Exchange normally uses the dialing properties set up for your modem. But these don't fit every situation. If you travel a lot, then you probably wrestle with hotel phones, send faxes using credit cards, and have trouble remembering what area code you're in today.

We'll look at several instances where you may need to work around the normal dialing properties or set up new dialing identities for yourself as you travel about.

Multiple Local Area Codes

In a growing number of North American cities, more than one area code is used for local calls. Windows 95 does not automatically handle cases where you need to dial a different area code without the usual 1 prefix for long distance.

The easiest way to handle this situation is to trick your modem into thinking you're in the same area code as the 10-digit number you need to dial. Either in the Address Book or in the Compose New Fax Wizard, enter your normal area code. Then in the number section, enter the area code plus the number; i.e. the full 10 digits.

For example, if you're in Toronto area code 416 but need to make a local call to 555-1379 in area code 905, enter 416 as the area code and 905-555-1379 as the number. Fax will dial your normal outside line access and call waiting codes, but will not dial a 1 before it dials 905-555-1379.

Adding Dialing Locations

When you land in a new city, the first thing you should do before sending your first fax is to give Exchange your new location. To create a new location, follow these steps:

1. Choose Tools, Microsoft Fax Tools, Options, Dialing, then choose Dialing Properties to bring up the dialog box shown in figure 26.14.

Fig. 26.14

The dialing properties include your location and the calling card and codes you use.

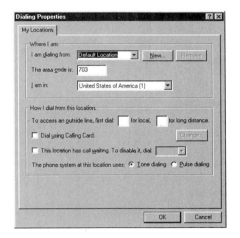

2. On the Dialing Properties dialog box, choose New.
3. Enter the name of your new location, and then click OK.
4. Enter the area code and country code of the new location.
5. Enter the information needed under How I Dial From This Location: outside line access, calling card settings, call waiting, and type of dialing.
6. Click OK to save the settings for the new location and make it the current location used by Windows 95 for all its dialing functions.

26

In figure 26.14, Default Location is the location created when you installed the Microsoft Fax service. Switch to other locations by picking from the I Am Dialing From list.

Using Calling Cards

Each location can have its own calling card setting. For example, when your laptop is docked in your office, your location settings may include the number you need to access an outside line. When you travel, you'll switch to a new location set up for calling card dialing.

Windows 95 includes calling card templates for many popular cards, including 10+ and 1-800 access options. You can use any of these templates to build your own personal card settings.

Set up a new personal calling card from the Dialing Properties dialog box by following these steps:

1. Choose Tools, Microsoft Fax Tools, Options, Dialing, and then choose Dialing Properties (refer to fig. 26.14).

2. Click Dial Using Calling Card.

3. In the Change Calling Card dialog box, choose New and enter the name of your new card entry (see fig. 26.15). Then, click OK to return to the Change Calling Card dialog box.

Fig. 26.15

You will need to use both the New and Advanced buttons to create a new calling card entry.

4. Now choose Advanced and then Copy From to get the list of dialing rules templates shown in figure 26.16. Click OK to continue.

5. In the Dialing Rules dialog box, you can make any changes you need (see fig. 26.17). Table 26.2 is a key to the different letter and symbol codes. Click Close when you're satisfied with the rules.

6. You can now enter the Calling Card Number in the Change Calling Card dialog box, then click OK to make this card the active calling card (refer to fig. 26.15).

Fig. 26.16
Pick the dialing rules template closest to your needs from the list of ready-made rules.

Fig 26.17
Starting from the dialing rules you copied, you can make any necessary changes to your calling card definition.

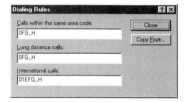

Table 26.2   Codes Used in the Calling Card Dialing Rules

Code	Description
E	Country code
F	Area code
G	Local number
H	Calling card number
W	Wait for a second dial tone
@	Wait for a ringing tone, followed by five seconds of silence
$	Wait for a calling card prompt tone (assuming your modem supports it)
?	Display an on-screen prompt to the user to continue dialing
,	Include a two-second pause

Tip
You can also use calling cards to set up custom dialing rules, like omitting the initial 1 if you're dialing long distance through a PBX. Instead of copying one of the rules templates, just enter your own rules for local (within the same area code), long distance, and international calls.

The example shown in figure 26.17 depicts a simple personal calling card used for dialing 0, then the number, followed by a four-second pause (two commas), then the calling card number.

Specifying an Exact Fax Number

There may be cases where you either want to specify the exact sequence of digits that will be dialed or simply want to override your normal dialing properties. You can do this by using Compose, New Message (or File, Send from within an application) and entering the fax number in the To text box.

Two different formats are available. To completely override the normal dialing properties (outside line access, call waiting, and so on), enter the recipient as **[FAX:name@XXX-XXX-XXXX]** where XXX-XXX-XXXX is the number. You can use as many digits as you need. Be sure to include the brackets.

 Tip

Using the [FAX:name@XXX-XXX-XXXX] format is another solution to the problem of dialing multiple local area codes, since it lets you enter the exact number to dial, without the leading 1.

To use your normal dialing properties but specify the number without using the Address Book or Fax Address Wizard, use the format [FAX:name@+1 (XXX) XXX-XXX] where +1 is the appropriate country code and (XXX) represents the area code. Your calling card, call waiting, and other settings will be used to make the call.

Working with Cover Pages

One of the more elegant features of the Microsoft Fax service is the ability to dress up your faxes with cover pages that include the recipient's name and number, your name and contact information, and details about the fax itself.

Exchange includes four cover pages for you to use, shown in figure 26.18. You can create your own either from scratch or by modifying any of those four with the Cover Page Editor application included with Windows 95.

Fig. 26.18

Exchange includes four cover pages you can use either as-is or as the basis for your own custom pages.

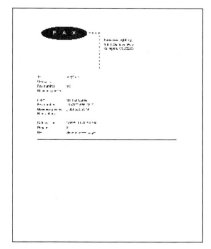

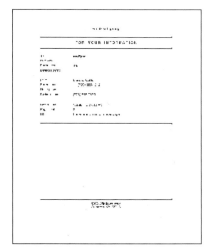

Creating and Modifying Cover Pages

To start working with cover pages, choose Tools, Microsoft Fax Tools, Options. In the Message tab shown in figure 26.19, you'll find the list of cover pages installed by Exchange.

To launch the Cover Page Editor, select a cover page, then choose Open. You can also choose New to begin with a new, blank cover page or Browse to locate other cover pages, perhaps one placed on the network server for company-wide use.

26

Fig. 26.19
Select a cover page to edit or start a new one.

 Tip
You can also launch the Cover Page Editor when Exchange isn't running. Click the Start button, then choose <u>P</u>rograms, Accessories, Fax, Cover Page Editor.

 Tip
It's easier to create a new cover page by using one of the existing ones as a model than by starting with a blank page.

If you have opened an existing cover page that you want to use as a template for one of your own, you should immediately choose <u>F</u>ile, Save <u>A</u>s to give it a new file name. That will preserve the original cover page untouched. Cover pages are normally stored in your Windows directory with a CPE extension.

Adding Fields to the Cover Page

Figure 26.20 shows the Cover Page Editor working with the Generic cover page. Notice the text surrounded by braces, such as {Sender's Company} and {Recipient Name}. These are fields that Microsoft Fax will fill in with values from Exchange. The sender information comes from the user properties entered when you first set up the Microsoft Fax service. Recipient information is extracted from the data in your Personal Address Book.

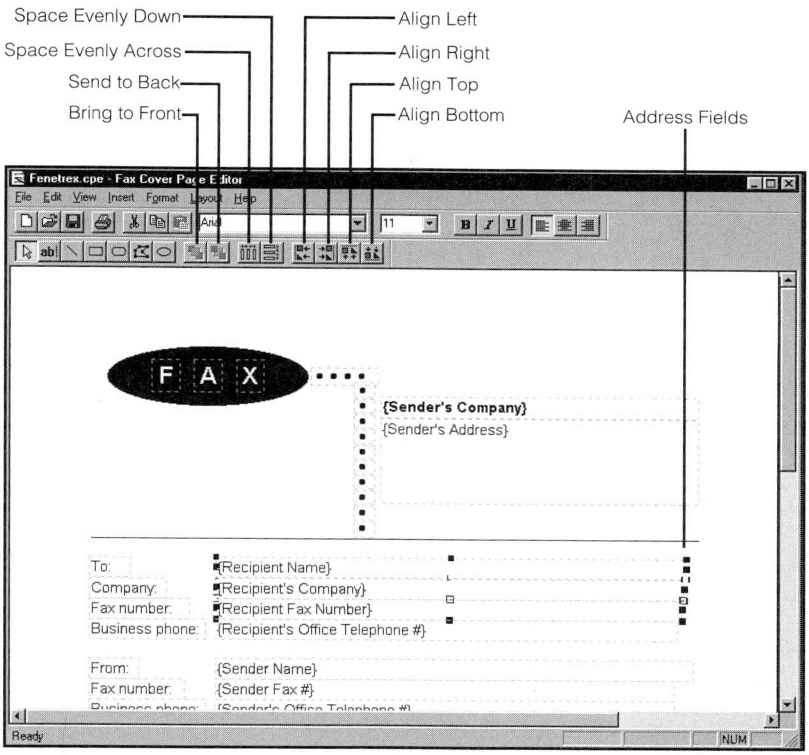

Space Evenly Down ——— ┐ ┌——— Align Left
Space Evenly Across ——— ┤ ├——— Align Right
Send to Back ——— ┤ ├——— Align Top
Bring to Front ——— ┘ └——— Align Bottom   Address Fields

Fig. 26.20

The Cover Page Editor includes drawing tools and controls for changing text formats. Use the Insert menu to add objects and address fields.

You can also include fields that give information about the fax itself, such as the number of pages, and the subject that you enter either in the Compose New Fax Wizard or in the Subject field on a normal Exchange message. Table 26.3 lists the fields available to you. Those that you should use on every fax cover page are marked with an asterisk.

α **Note**

Microsoft Fax does not put a one-line header on each page of a fax as some fax programs and most fax machines do. This makes it doubly important for the cover page to include recipient information and the number of pages to be expected.

26

Table 26.3   Fields Available for Use in the Cover Page Editor

Recipient Fields

* * Name
* * Company
* * Fax Number
* Street Address
* City
* State
* Zip Code
* Country
* Title
* Department
* Office Location
* Home Telephone Number
* Office Telephone Number
* List of To: Recipients for the Fax
* List of CC: Recipients for the Fax

Sender Fields

* * Name
* Fax Number
* * Company
* Address
* Title
* Department
* Office Location
* Home Telephone Number
* * Office Telephone Number

Fax Message Fields

* Note
* * Subject
* * Time Sent
* * Number of Pages
* Number of Attachments

* = recommended as essential for all outgoing faxes

To insert a field, choose Insert, then Recipient, Sender or Message, depending on the type of field. Pick from the list of fields on the menu. The field and an appropriate text label will be added to the fax as text frames. Click and drag if you need to move them to a different location.

Insert plain text and graphics using the icons on the Drawing toolbar. To insert objects created with other applications, such as a company logo, choose Insert, Object.

Arranging Cover Page Objects

The menu and toolbars offer a number of techniques to help you arrange the cover page objects. Table 26.4 lists the most important ones.

Table 26.4   Techniques for Arranging Cover Page Objects

Effect	Technique
Select multiple objects (#1)	Use the Select tool to draw a line completely enclosing the Objects.
Select multiple objects(#2)	Hold the Ctrl key down as you click each element.
Align objects	Select multiple objects, then choose Layout, Align Objects or click the appropriate icon on the Drawing toolbar.
Space objects evenly	Select at least three objects, then choose Layout, Space Evenly or click the appropriate icon on the Drawing toolbar.
Show layout grid lines	Choose View, Grid Lines.
Center selected object(s)	Select one or more objects, then choose Layout, Center on Page. You can center vertically or horizontally.

Changing the User Properties

As you saw in table 26.3, various fields with data about you, the sender, can be included on your cover page. You can change this information on the User tab in the Microsoft Fax Properties dialog box shown in figure 26.21.

To open the User properties, choose Tools, Microsoft Fax Tools, then click the User tab.

26

Fig. 26.21

Change the sender information on your fax cover sheets using the User properties.

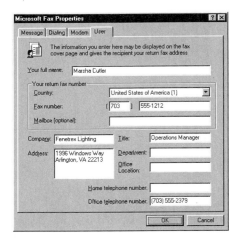

Using the Note Field

The cover pages shown in figure 26.18 all have a {Note} field. If you enter text for a note in the Compose New Fax Wizard (refer to fig. 26.12), this {Note} field is the location where that text will appear.

Only faxes created with the Compose New Fax Wizard—either by launching it from Exchange or by printing to the Microsoft Fax printer driver—will contain a note on the cover page. Message text created in a normal Exchange message form will appear on a separate second page, after the cover page.

If you want a note on all your cover sheets, make sure the cover page you are using includes a {Note} field. Additionally, always use the Compose New Fax Wizard or print to the Microsoft Fax printer driver.

 Tip

To force your cover pages to always fill a full sheet of paper, rather than cut off after the note on non-plain paper machines, put one or more fields at the bottom of the page after the {Note} field.

Solving Common Cover Page Problems

There is a bug involving cover pages that can be very frustrating. If the archive attribute is not set for the cover page files, then you cannot select a cover page. Instead, you get a message that the cover page is already in use (which, of course, it isn't).

The easiest way to fix this problem is to use Start, Run and enter the command **attrib +a C:\Windows*.CPE** where C:\Windows is your Windows 95 folder. To prevent a recurrence, either exclude *.CPE cover page files from your backups, add this command to AUTOEXEC.BAT, or create a batch file containing this command and run it after every backup to reset the archive attribute for the files.

Another vexing cover page issue is how to get the recipient's company name on the cover page when the Compose New Fax Wizard asks only for the name of the recipient and the fax number.

If you want information other than the name and number to appear on the fax, you must enter the recipient in the Address Book, adding the appropriate details on the Business tab, and select the address from there. To do this while using the wizard, choose Address Book in the dialog box shown earlier in figure 26.9.

The final problem in this collection occurs when you try to send a fax but get an error message, `Failed to create cover page`.

The way to fix this problem is to run the Cover Page Editor. Click the Start button, then choose Programs, Accessories, Fax, Cover Page Editor. Sometimes you need to actually open each cover page in the Cover Page Editor.

Previewing Faxes

Once you've created a cover page or two and started sending faxes regularly, you'll probably want to know how they look on the receiving end.

Unlike many fax programs, Microsoft Fax does not include any mechanism for viewing faxes before you send them. However, it is possible to send a fax to yourself without using the modem. This won't let you see how each recipient's fax will look with their name and number on the cover page, but it will show you how the cover page looks in general, and—most important—how your attachments or documents printed to the Microsoft Fax printer driver will be rendered.

The trick to this expert solution is in the address and the editable setting. If you're composing a fax with the normal Exchange message form, address it to [FAX:me]. If you're using the Compose New Fax Wizard or the Fax Addressing Wizard, address it as you see in figure 26.22.

You must also set the Send Options of this fax so that the fax is sent as Not Editable (refer to fig. 26.11).

26

Fig. 26.22
*Use this special
address to send a fax
image to your own
Inbox.*

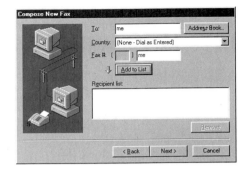

Include any cover page note and/or attachments that you want to see in the finished
product. After you send the fax, it will be rendered and placed in your Inbox, where you
can view it with the Fax Viewer, as we'll discuss in the next section on receiving faxes.

Receiving Faxes

You can set up your modem for outgoing fax transmissions only or for incoming transmissions as well. If you are working at a system set up as a network fax server, be sure to
forward incoming faxes to other people on your network.

If you're going to be receiving faxes, be aware that other communications applications
may have trouble accessing your modem. For example, you cannot have a modem set up
to auto-answer fax calls and also answer calls as a Dial-Up Network server.

Using the Fax Viewer

After you receive a fax, you can view, print, and copy it with the Fax Viewer included
with Exchange.

 Note

Microsoft has released an enhanced fax viewer, Imaging for Windows 95, developed by Wang. The viewer is available for download from the usual locations,
including **www.microsoft.com** and GO MSL on CompuServe.

Imaging adds several of the features that fax users really want: scanner support,
annotations, and the ability to save received faxes as TIF images. Most optical
character recognition (OCR) programs can read TIF files, so this means you can
finally use OCR on the faxes you get with Microsoft Fax.

Depending on how you have the Microsoft Fax service set up, you may see incoming faxes in the Inbox with either a fax machine icon or a paper clip, showing that a file is attached. See figure 26.23 for an example of each possibility. To view a fax marked with a fax icon, double-click it.

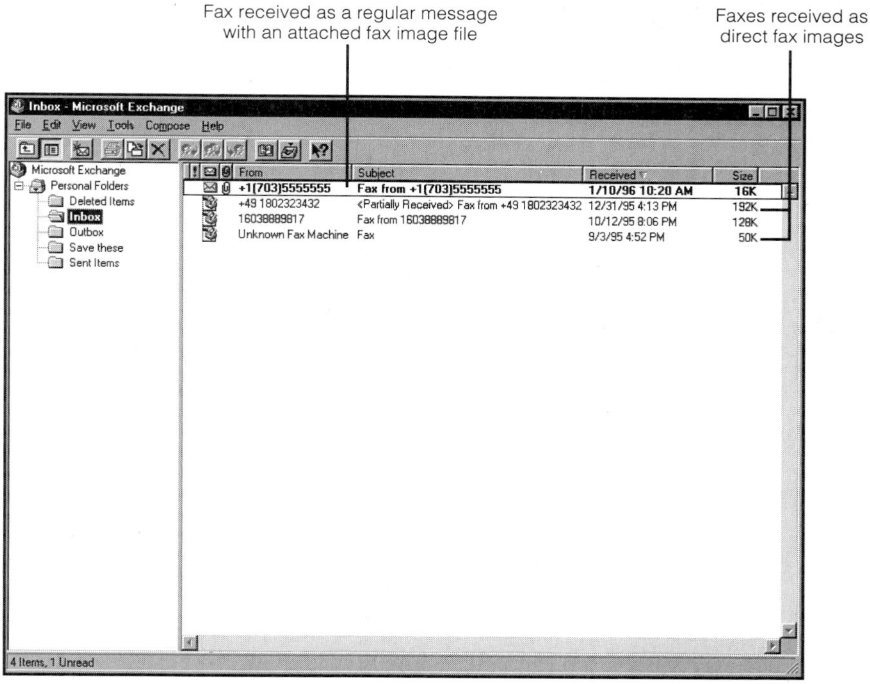

Fax received as a regular message with an attached fax image file

Faxes received as direct fax images

Fig. 26.23

Faxes may appear in your Inbox either with fax icons or with paper clip icons, depending on your setup.

To view a fax marked as a message with a paper clip, double-click the message to open it. You'll see a fax icon for the attached file. Double-click that icon to view the fax.

To change the way the Inbox displays incoming faxes, choose Tools, Microsoft Fax Tools to open the Message properties sheet (refer to fig. 26.19). If you want to view incoming faxes directly, uncheck the box labeled Let Me Change the Subject Line of New Faxes I Receive. If you prefer to see incoming faxes as messages with attachments and later be able to archive them with new subject lines, make sure that box is checked.

Figure 26.24 shows the Fax Viewer in action, with thumbnails on the left that you can use to quickly go to the page you want to view.

26

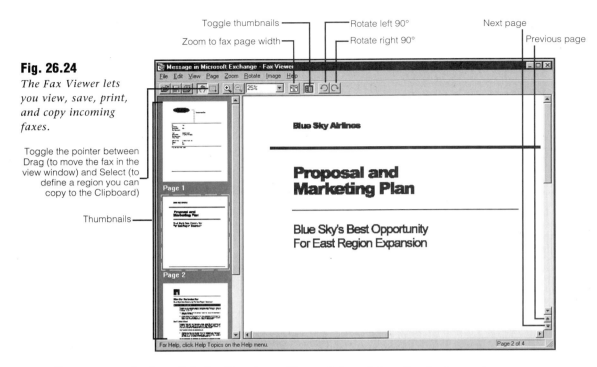

Fig. 26.24

The Fax Viewer lets you view, save, print, and copy incoming faxes.

To see more of a fax, click the Drag icon. Then, click and drag the fax image to a new position in the Fax Viewer window.

Another way to see more of a fax is to zoom in. Use the toolbar icons, or choose Zoom, Fit Height or Fit Both.

To keep a copy of the fax separate from your Inbox, choose File, Save Copy As.

You can't annotate faxes in the Fax Viewer, but you can copy a region or a full page as a bitmap to another Windows application and apply annotations there. Follow these steps:

1. Choose Edit, Select or click the Select icon in the toolbar.

2. If you want to copy the entire current page, choose Edit, Copy Page.

3. To copy just part of a page, drag the pointer across the area, then choose Edit, Copy.

4. Switch to Word or another Windows application and use Edit, Paste to paste the fax image into the current document.

Retrieving Faxes from Fax-on-Demand Services

It's possible to grab faxes from fax-on-demand services with Exchange. These services typically make one or more faxes available to anyone who dials in on a special number.

To retrieve a fax, follow these steps:

1. Choose Tools, Microsoft Fax Tools, Request a Fax to launch the Request a Fax Wizard, shown in figure 26.25.

Fig. 26.25

The Request a Fax Wizard walks you through the process of getting a fax from a fax-on-demand service.

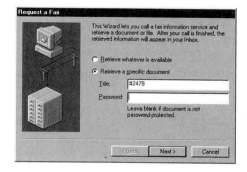

2. Select what you want to receive, either any available fax or a specific document. Choose Next to continue.

3. Enter the name and number of the fax-on-demand service, just as you'd address an outgoing fax. Choose Next to continue.

4. From the dialog box shown in figure 26.26, select when you want to place the call to retrieve the fax. Choose Next to continue, then Finish to complete the retrieval process.

Fig. 26.26

When you request a fax, you can choose when to make the call.

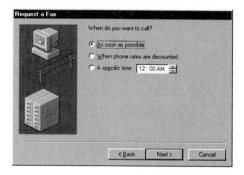

Managing Fax Transmissions

Microsoft Fax offers only rudimentary tools for managing your faxes. Your ability to alter the queue of outgoing items is limited to canceling a fax. No log is kept of fax transmissions, though you can obtain a delivery receipt in some cases.

On the other hand, Microsoft Fax provides detailed messages about failed fax deliveries that can help you address any problems. It also gives you an easy way to retransmit those faxes. Figure 26.27 shows two System Administrator messages, one a delivery receipt, the other a notification of an undelivered fax.

Fig. 26.27

Instead of keeping a log, Microsoft Fax places messages in your Inbox to advise you of successful and failed faxes.

Delivery record for successful transmission
Notice of undeliverable message

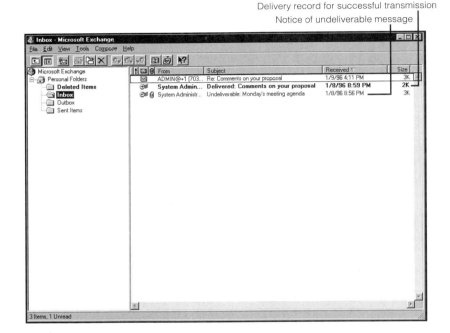

Managing the Fax Queue

When faxes are pending, the Outgoing Faxes icon will appear in the system tray on the taskbar. Double-click this icon to see the Outgoing Faxes queue. You can also view the queue by choosing Tools, Microsoft Fax Tools, Show Outgoing Faxes.

The fax queue, shown in figure 26.28, looks much like a printer queue and displays the following information:

Item	Description
Sender	Name of the computer from which the fax was sent.
Subject	Subject line for the fax
Size	Size of the fax
Recipients	Number of recipients
Time to send	Scheduled transmission time for the fax

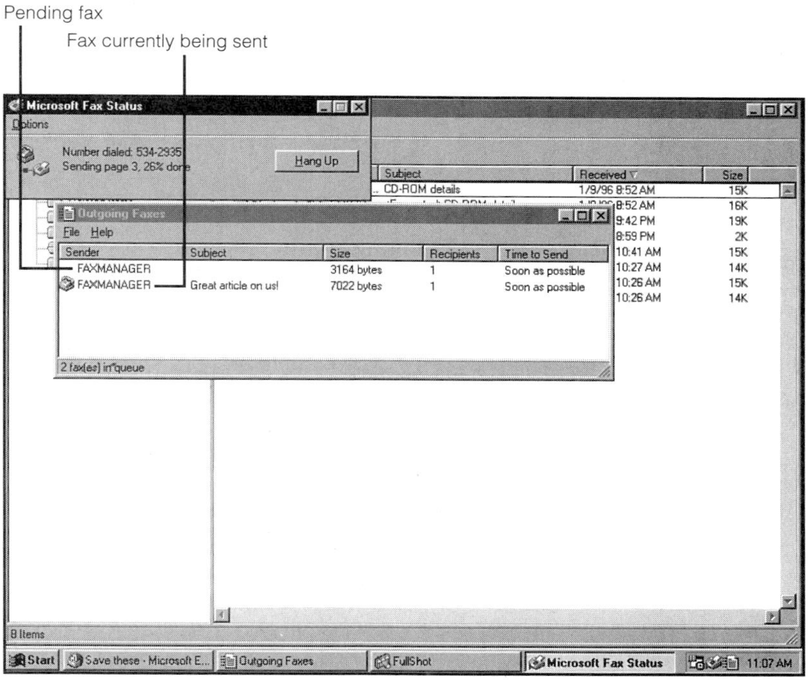

Pending fax

Fax currently being sent

Fig. 26.28

Pending fax transmis-
sions can be monitored
and canceled from the
Outgoing Faxes queue.

To cancel a fax, choose File, Cancel Fax. You can also right-click a fax and then choose Cancel Fax.

Getting a Delivery Receipt

For faxes sent with File, Send from an application or with Compose, New Message from Exchange, you can choose to be notified when the fax is successfully transmitted. Follow these steps:

1. Choose File, Properties to bring up the Properties dialog box shown in figure 26.29.

2. Click Delivery Receipt.

3. Click OK to add the delivery receipt request to the message.

You can request delivery receipts for all messages by choosing Tools, Options. On the Send tab, you find Delivery and Read Receipt options. Read receipts do not apply to faxes.

26

Fig. 26.29

On the Properties dialog box for a fax created as a normal Exchange message, you can choose to get a delivery receipt.

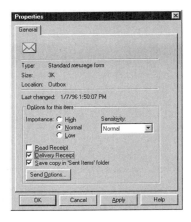

 Note

Delivery receipts are not provided for faxes created with <u>C</u>ompose, New Fa<u>x</u> or by printing to the Microsoft Fax printer driver. Even if you have made delivery receipts a default for all messages, Exchange ignores that setting for these faxes.

When a fax with a delivery receipt request is successfully transmitted, you'll get a Delivered message in your Inbox, as seen earlier in figure 26.27. An example of a delivery receipt appears in figure 26.30.

Fig. 26.30

Delivery receipts are available for faxes created as regular Exchange messages.

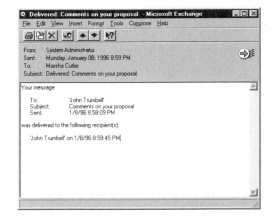

When a Fax Transmission Fails

To find out what happened to a fax that couldn't be delivered, open the Undeliverable message found in the Inbox (refer to fig. 26.27). Figure 26.31 is an example, showing you the kind of detailed information you'll get for each failed recipient.

Fig. 26.31

A fax that failed to be delivered to multiple recipients will get a follow-up message telling you exactly what went wrong at each site.

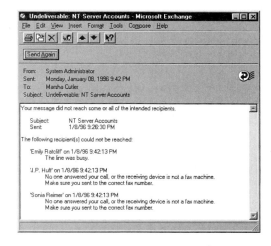

Once you have resolved the problems noted in the Undeliverable message, choose Send Again to resend the fax just to those recipients who didn't get it the first time. You'll have the opportunity to add new recipients (see fig. 26.32), but you will not be able to change the message.

Fig. 26.32

When you retransmit a previously failed fax, you can add new recipients, but you cannot change the message.

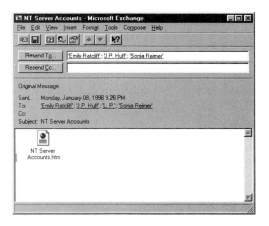

26

Adding Security to Your Faxes

With the ability to exchange editable files with binary file transfer comes the need to keep those files confidential until they reach the right recipient. Microsoft Fax supports three security methods, outlined in table 26.5.

Table 26.5   Security Methods Available with Microsoft Fax

Method	Description	Implementation
Password encryption	Simplest method, can be used on any fax without prior exchange of keys.	Sender encrypts the fax with a password. Recipient must know the password to decode the fax.
Key encryption	More secure, requires an exchange of private keys with intended public recipients.	Sender encrypts the fax with his key and the key of each recipient. Recipient unlocks the fax with his private key and the public key of the sender.
Digital signature	Not an encryption method, but a way to verify that the fax was actually sent by the supposed sender and prevent the document from being modified while it is being sent.	Sender "signs" the fax with his key. Recipient must have the sender's key in order to verify the fax.

Security is available only for faxes sent as editable files, that is with binary file transfer. It must be invoked on a message-by-message basis. It can't be set as an option for all faxes.

While Microsoft Fax security may appear complicated, it is actually rather easy to implement. Password encryption can be done on any message. To decode the message, all the recipient needs is the password. Key encryption and digital signature involve some preparation, but Microsoft Fax simplifies that task, as you see in the next section.

Implementing Key-Based Security

A key set is a unique collection of digital "words" that can be used to encrypt and decode messages. For each person that you want to send a key-encrypted fax, you will need to send her your keys and add her keys to your Address Book.

To enable key encryption and digital signatures for your Exchange profile, follow these steps:

1. Choose Tools, Microsoft Fax Tools, Advanced Security to bring up the dialog box shown in figure 26.33. If you are using fax security for the first time, only the New Key Set button will be enabled.

Fig. 26.33

With Advanced Fax Security, you can create encryption keys for yourself and add those from other people to your Address Book.

2. Choose New Key Set to bring up the New Key Set dialog box (see fig. 26.34).

3. Select and confirm a password to be used for security on your Exchange profile. You have the option of saving that password in your Windows 95 password list, so you won't be prompted for it again.

4. When you've entered and confirmed your password, click OK to create your key set.

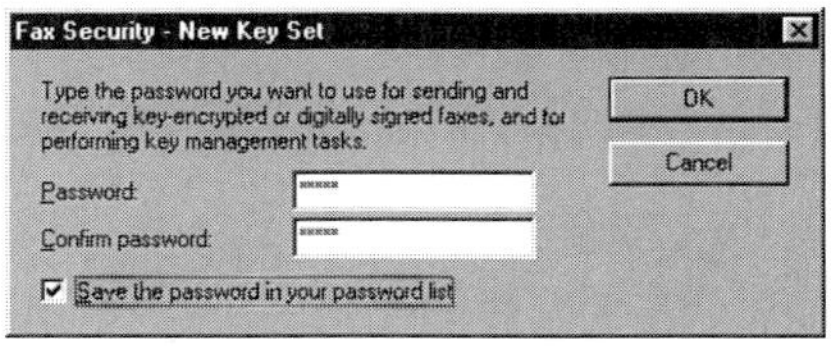

Fig. 26.34

Your set of encryption keys is password-protected.

5. Back at the Advanced Fax Security dialog box (refer to fig. 26.33), choose Public Keys to display the Managing Public Keys dialog box seen in figure 26.35.

6. Choose Save. You'll see the Save Public Keys dialog box, shown in figure 26.36. Highlight your own name, then choose To in order to place your name in the Save These Keys column. (You can also export public keys that you've received from other people.) Click OK, then give a file name for the public keys file, and click OK again.

Fig. 26.35

Before you can use key encryption, you must send your public keys to other users and add their keys into your Address Book.

Fig. 26.36

Use the To button to put your name in the Save These Keys column.

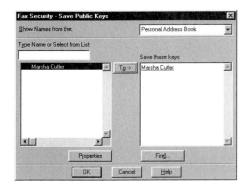

7. Back at the Managing Public Keys dialog box (see fig. 26.35), choose Add if you have already received key files from your fax recipients. If you haven't received their keys yet, proceed to step 9. You will need to return to this step (step 7) and complete it and step 8 before you can send key-encrypted or digitally signed faxes.

8. After you choose Add, you'll see the Add Public Keys dialog box (see fig. 26.37). Highlight the key(s) you want to add, then click OK to add them to your Address Book and return to the Managing Public Keys dialog box.

Fig. 26.37

Add public keys to your Address from lists provided by your recipients.

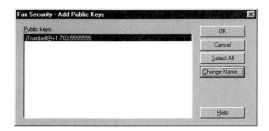

9. Click Close twice to exit the Managing Public Keys and Advanced Fax Security dialog boxes.

10. Send your public key file, the one you created in step 5, to people whom you want to be able to decode your encrypted faxes and verify your digital signature. You can mail it to them on a disk or fax it with binary file transfer.

Sending Secure Messages

Even if you have not enabled advanced fax security, you can use a simple password to scramble a fax message. The basic procedure for sending a confidential fax is the same whether you're using password encryption or the more advanced key encryption. Follow these steps:

1. Create a fax message with the New Message icon or Compose, New Message or Ctrl+N.

2. Choose File, Send Options to display the Send Options dialog box shown earlier in figure 26.11.

3. Make sure the message type is set for Editable Only or Editable, If Possible.

4. Choose Security to bring up the Message Security Options dialog box (see fig. 26.38).

5. Click the security method you want to use for this message.

6. Click the Digitally Sign All Attachments box if you want recipients (those with a copy of your public key) to be able to verify that you actually sent the attachments.

Fig. 26.38

Choose the type of encryption you want for this message, and add a digital signature if you prefer.

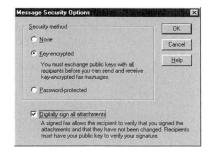

 Tip

If you use a digital signature on your attachments, it's a good idea to say so in the body of your fax message, so recipients will know that they can verify your signature.

7. Click OK twice to close the Message Security Options and Send Options dialog boxes.

8. Complete the addresses, text, and attachments for your message and send it as usual.

26

Receiving Secure Messages

When you receive a confidential fax, it will appear in your Inbox with a subject line marked <Encrypted>, as shown in figure 26.39. When you double-click the item to open it, Exchange will prompt you for a password or ask you to select a key from your Address Book that can be used to unscramble the message.

Encrypted, undecoded message

Fig. 26.39

To access an encrypted fax, you will need to supply a password or choose a key to decode it.

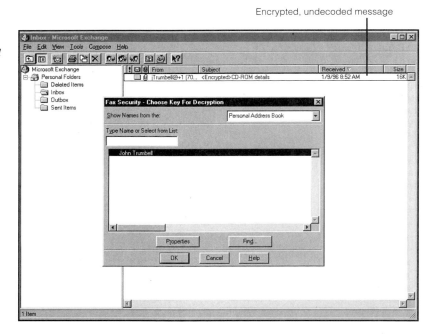

To verify that an attachment has been digitally signed, open the message, then choose Tools, Microsoft Fax Tools, Verify Digital Signature. Each attachment will be listed along with its digital signature. An example is shown in figure 26.40.

 Note

If you are operating a Microsoft Fax server to receive secure faxes, the person using Exchange at that workstation will need access to any passwords required. He or she will also need to add public keys for everyone in your organization to his or her Address Book. Encrypted faxes cannot be forwarded. Each one must be decoded before it can be sent to its intended recipient via e-mail.

Fig. 26.40

A valid digital signature verifies that the attachment was actually transmitted by the sender and that it has not been altered in any way during transmission.

Summary

Desktop faxing may change the way we do business just as much as machine faxing has. The Microsoft Fax service in Exchange helps you work more efficiently by sending reports, spreadsheets, presentations, and even databases right from your PC.

This chapter has covered how to transmit those documents both as images to regular fax machines and as editable files using binary file transfer (BFT). BFT also opens the door to secure faxing and the use of an electronic signature to assure your recipients that the documents indeed came from you.

In addition, you have learned about two applets included with Microsoft Fax, the Fax Viewer and the Cover Page Editor, which are essential tools in desktop faxing.

26

chapter 27

Managing Electronic Mail

27

by Sue Mosher

In this chapter

◆ **Sending and receiving mail**
Learn about composing, addressing, and reading messages, remote access to mail, and sending mail from Office applications.

◆ **Using the Personal Address Book**
In the Personal Address Book, you can keep a list of the addresses to which you send mail the most and organize the addresses into distribution lists.

◆ **Using personal folders**
Customize Exchange by changing the folder views, and discover how to archive messages and perform other file maintenance.

There's more to managing electronic mail than just sending and receiving simple messages. With Exchange, you can dress messages up with complex formatting and attach files or objects.

There's also more to Exchange than just e-mail, as you'll see when you learn about the features of the Personal Address Book and Personal Folders.

Sending and Receiving Mail

Sending e-mail is a very straightforward process. After starting a message (there are a couple of ways to do this), you address it, give it a subject, and compose the message. Then you send it. Depending on the kind of mail message, it will be sent either immediately or when you connect to your mail service.

The way you receive mail can vary, depending on what services you have in your profile and whether you're directly connected to your mailbox or you are dialing in remotely. After a message arrives in your Inbox, you can reply to it, forward it, and save it for later reuse.

Figure 27.1 shows the Microsoft Exchange window. Everything you need to send and receive messages is right here. Check out the basics of sending mail from Exchange.

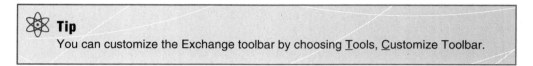

Tip
You can customize the Exchange toolbar by choosing Tools, Customize Toolbar.

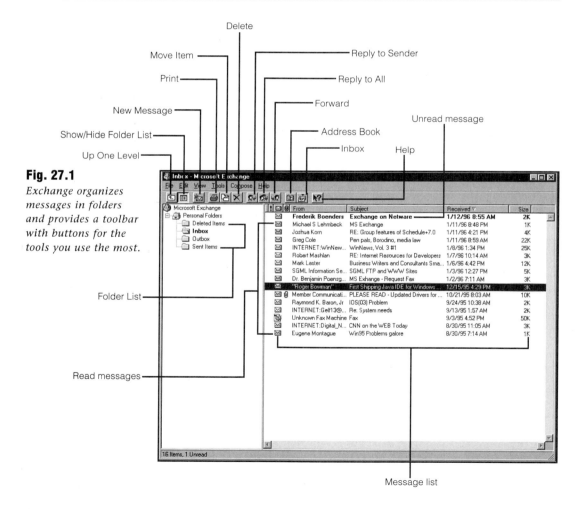

Fig. 27.1
Exchange organizes messages in folders and provides a toolbar with buttons for the tools you use the most.

Tip

If you don't see the list of folders on the left side, choose Tools, Folders.

Composing, Addressing, and Sending Messages

Start a new message by clicking the New Message button, choosing Compose, New Message, or pressing Ctrl+N. You see a message window similar to the one shown in figure 27.2.

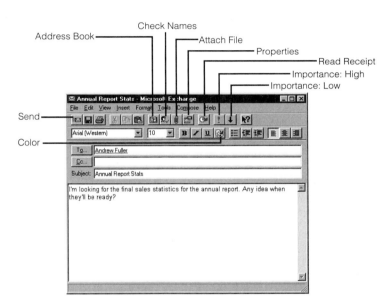

Fig. 27.2

The message window is Exchange's standard form for addressing and composing messages. It's also used to display messages you receive.

On the message window, you can use the second toolbar, the Formatting toolbar, to give your messages a snazzy format, using color, different fonts for emphasis, and even bullets. Recipients using Exchange will see the full formatting of your messages. Those reading your messages with other mail programs will get the same text, only without the formatting.

Addressing Messages

In the To and Cc text boxes, enter the names of the people you want to receive your message. If you need to look up addresses in the Address Book, choose To or Cc or click the Address Book button.

27

Tip

When you send the message, Exchange will match the To and Cc names with names in your Address Book. This means that if there's only one Randy listed in your Address Book, you can enter "Randy" on the To line and have Exchange look up the full name automatically. The Check Names button does the same thing.

Exchange also lets you send blind carbon copies (Bcc). This way, you can send a copy to someone without anyone in the To or Cc list knowing. In the message window, choose View, Bcc Box if you want to enter blind carbon recipients.

There might be times when you don't want to use the names in your Address Book. Table 27.1 lists the formats you can use to enter addresses directly. Make sure you include the brackets where they're indicated; they're an essential part of the address format.

Table 27.1   Address Formats

Type	Format
Microsoft Mail	Name of addressee, as shown in the Postoffice Address List
Microsoft Network	[MSN:<msn alias>]
CompuServe	[COMPUSERVE:<user id>]
Microsoft Fax	[FAX:<name>@+1 (xxx)xxx-xxxx] to use TAPI settings or [FAX:<name>@xxxxxxxxxx] to dial exactly the number indicated
Internet	address@domain
Internet via Microsoft Network	[MSNINET:<address@domain>]
Internet via Internet Mail	[SMTP:<address@domain>]

 Note

Other services besides those included with Windows 95 will have their own address formats (such as the Internet via Internet Mail format listed in table 27.1). Internet Mail is included only in the Microsoft Plus! pack and with Internet Explorer, but you can also send mail to the Internet through the Microsoft Network or CompuServe. See "Reaching the Internet If You Don't Have Internet Mail" later in this chapter.

Including Files and Objects in Mail

Not only can your messages be richly formatted, they can also include more than just text. To attach a file to your message, follow these steps:

1. Click the Insert File button or choose Insert, File.

2. In the Insert File dialog box, choose the file you want to insert (see fig. 27.3).

3. If you want the text of a text or Word document to be pasted into your message, select Insert as Text Only.

4. To attach the document or file (even an executable file), select Insert As an Attachment.

5. Choose OK to insert the file into your messages.

Fig. 27.3

You can insert a file as an attachment or, in the case of text documents, as text.

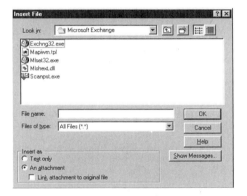

> ### ⚛ Tip
>
> If the file you're attaching already exists on a network server where everyone can see it, you can insert just a pointer to that file, rather than the whole file. To do this, select Link Attachment to Original File. This will make your mail message much smaller.

Notice that figure 27.3 also has a Show Messages button. Yes, you can also insert Exchange messages into your message. Either choose Show Messages from the Insert File dialog box or choose Insert, Messages from the main menu. In the Insert Message dialog box, you can select messages to add to the one you're composing (see fig. 27.4).

27

> **Tip**
> If you want to select more than one message to insert, hold down the Ctrl key as you click each one.

Fig. 27.4

Browse your message folders to find messages to insert in the message you're currently editing.

A third element you can insert into your message is an object created with another Windows application. Choose Insert, Object to open the Insert Object dialog box (see fig. 27.5). For more on objects, see Chapter 28, "Critical Skills for Integrating Applications."

Fig. 27.5

When you insert an object in your message, you must choose whether to create a new one (by selecting a particular object type) or use an existing file.

You can create an embedded object from scratch or use an existing file as your source material. Edit the object in its application, then close it to update the mail message.

Sending Messages

When you finish composing and addressing your message, click the Send button, choose File, Send, or press Ctrl+Enter. Exchange checks the addresses to make sure they are valid, then places the message in your Outbox.

It's very important to realize that sending a message is not the same as delivering it. Even though the message is in the Outbox, delivery is delayed until you actually connect to your mail service.

One exception to the delayed delivery phenomenon is Microsoft Mail. (Another is Microsoft Fax, which sends a fax immediately.) If you are working on the network and are connected to your Microsoft Mail postoffice, any messages intended for other Microsoft Mail users are sent from your Outbox automatically.

 Tip

Messages that are ready to be delivered are shown in italic in your Outbox. If you open a message, make sure you send it again, rather than close it. If you just close it, it will be listed in the Outbox in normal font, indicating that it is not ready for transmission. It won't be sent until you open it and send it.

For other mail services, or if you are not connected to the network, you will need to make a remote connection to send your mail and retrieve incoming messages. The simplest method is to choose Tools, Deliver Now Using and choose either All Services or the specific service you want to send mail to. You can also press Ctrl+M to deliver to all services. If you're working offline, Exchange will make a separate phone call to connect to each service in turn.

 Tip

When you choose Tools, Deliver Now Using, Exchange sends the items in your Outbox and retrieves any new mail being held for you.

You learn another method for sending messages in the section "Downloading and Marking Headers," later in this chapter.

Saving Drafts

Sometimes you might be half finished with a message and want to save it for completion at a later time. To save a message, click the Save button, choose File, Save, or press Ctrl+S. The message will be saved in your Inbox, but the From field will be blank (which makes sense, because you didn't receive this message from anyone—you created it).

You can also choose File, Save As when you want to save the message as a separate file—not in Exchange.

Reading and Responding to Messages

New messages are placed in your Inbox. They're shown in bold until you open them. Table 27.2 shows some of the different icons you can expect to see for different types of messages, and figure 27.6 shows an example of an opened message.

Table 27.2   Icons for Inbox Message Types

Icon	Description
	Normal message
	Routing slip
	Incoming fax
	Message returned to sender as undeliverable
	Successful delivery receipt
	Fax retrieval failure notice
	Schedule+ meeting request
	Schedule+ meeting acceptance
	Schedule+ meeting declined
	Schedule+ meeting tentative acceptance
	Microsoft Project assignment notice
	High-priority message
	Low-priority message
	Attached file

Fig. 27.6

While viewing a message from your Inbox, you can print it, move it to another folder, reply to it, or forward it to someone else.

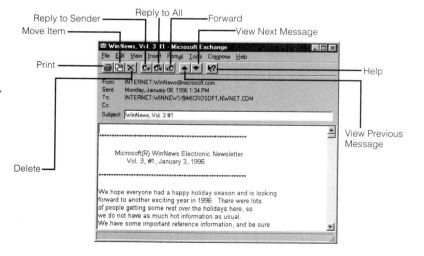

Notice that you have two reply choices. To send a reply just to the person who sent you the message, choose Co_m_pose, _R_eply to Sender or press Ctrl+R. Or, you can choose Compose, Reply to _A_ll or press Ctrl+Shift+R to include all the To and Cc addresses in your reply.

 Tip

If you want to reply to just some people, use Reply to All, then delete the addresses you don't want to use.

To forward a message to someone else, choose Co_m_pose, _F_orward or press Ctrl+F.

Replying to or forwarding a message brings up a message window like the one you saw earlier in figure 27.2. For a reply, you might see the text of the incoming message, depending on what options you chose on the Read tab in the Options dialog box, which you open by choosing _T_ools, _O_ptions. (You'll always see the text of the incoming message when you forward, of course.)

Complete the reply or forwarding note and send it just like you would any other message.

Sending to and Receiving from The Microsoft Network

Assuming you've set up The Microsoft Network (MSN) as one of your Exchange services, you can use MSN to send and receive mail not just with other MSN members, but with anyone who can be reached with an Internet address. I'll cover the details of setting up Internet addresses in the section "Reaching the Internet If You Don't Have Internet Mail" later in this chapter.

One special feature of exchanging mail with other MSN users is that you can format your message with fonts, bullets, and colors and the people receiving it will see exactly what you sent.

To get all of your MSN mail and send any outgoing items, choose _T_ools, _D_eliver Now Using, Microsoft Network.

Alternatively, you can download the "headers" for your mail (such as a list of the pending items), then pick and choose what to receive and what to delete. That is covered in the upcoming section "Downloading and Marking Headers."

Another point about MSN: Although you can schedule times to get your Microsoft Mail messages and even your CompuServe Mail messages if you're working remotely, you

27

cannot schedule connections to MSN. I don't know why Microsoft left out that function—that's just the way it is.

Another mystery is that there's no way to bypass the Microsoft Network login screen. When you want to access your mail, you must click the Connect button, even if you have MSN set up to remember your password.

Sending to and Receiving from CompuServe

Exchange is designed to accommodate many kinds of mail systems, not just those from Microsoft (like Microsoft Mail and Microsoft Network). The first addition to the family of Exchange clients is one that lets you download your mail from CompuServe.

Setting Up the CompuServe Client

To add CompuServe Mail access to Exchange, you must install additional software. You need to know your user ID, password, and access number.

The CompuServe client software is buried on the Windows 95 CD-ROM in the \Drivers\Other\Exchange\Compusrv folder. You can also download it from CompuServe at GO CSMAIL. If you download it, copy the file you download to an empty directory and run it to extract all the necessary files.

Then, whether you have the CD-ROM or downloaded version, run the SETUP.EXE program. It copies the necessary files to your system, then asks if you want to add CompuServe Mail to your default Exchange profile. You can choose Yes and go through the configuration now, or choose No and add it later.

If you choose Yes, the Inbox Setup Wizard will walk you through the settings you need, starting with the screen shown in figure 27.7. If you have WinCIM or another CompuServe software product, choose Browse to indicate where it is installed; Exchange will be able to read your WinCIM address book.

Fig. 27.7

If you already have CompuServe-provided software, such as WinCIM, choose Browse to tell the Wizard where that software is located.

Choose Next to proceed to the next step of the Wizard. Even though Exchange can read your CompuServe address book, it doesn't automatically pick up your user ID, password, and preferred dial-up number. You need to enter those in the screen shown in figure 27.8.

Fig. 27.8

Because the Inbox Setup Wizard always asks for the details of your CompuServe account, it's a good idea to have them handy before you start the CompuServe Mail installation.

Choose Next to proceed to the next step of the Wizard, shown in figure 27.9. Here you can set the following options:

Option	Description
Create Session Activity	Places an event log in your Inbox detailing the activity of every CompuServe Mail login session.
Delete Retrieved Messages	Automatically deletes messages from your online mailbox after you retrieve them.
Accept Postage Due Messages	Tells Exchange to accept messages sent to you with a postage due surcharge.

Fig. 27.9

The final step of installing the CompuServe Mail client is to set various options.

You can change these and other CompuServe Mail options later. Choose Tools, Services, CompuServe Mail, and choose Properties.

After you set the options in the Wizard, choose Next, then choose Finish to complete the setup of the CompuServe Mail client. You need to exit and restart Exchange before you can access your CompuServe mail.

Scheduling Automatic Mail Delivery

Unlike with The Microsoft Network, with CompuServe you can schedule automatic delivery of all incoming messages and transmission of outgoing messages. Follow these steps:

1. Choose Tools, Services, CompuServe Mail, Properties.

2. Click the Advanced tab, then choose Schedule Connect Times.

3. Choose any or all of the three connection modes shown in figure 27.10:

> ▶ When Exchange starts up

> ▶ At regular time intervals

> ▶ At a specific time of the day

4. Choose OK three times to close the dialog boxes and save your new connection time settings.

Fig. 27.10

The CompuServe Mail client gives you three ways to schedule connections.

 Tip
You can also access all of your CompuServe mail at any time by choosing Tools, Deliver Now Using, CompuServe Mail.

Using CompuServe Mail

Just as with mail sent via the Microsoft Network, you can get all your CompuServe mail at one time (choose Tools, Deliver Now Using, CompuServe Mail) or download just headers, then pick what ones you want to read.

There are a couple of important things to remember when sending mail via CompuServe:

▶ Mail sent from CompuServe to the Internet cannot include binary attachments, such as document files or embedded objects.

▶ Most of the people you'll be sending mail to via CompuServe won't be able to see some of the rich formatting you can put in an Exchange message. Keep the formatting to a minimum.

 Note

If some people to whom you send via CompuServe Mail complain about the formatting of your messages, you can tell Exchange to always use plain text. Open the Address Book and double-click a name to open the properties for that address. Click the check box labeled Always Send to This Recipient in Microsoft Exchange Rich-Text Format to uncheck it.

Remote Access to Your Mail

When you set up the Microsoft Network and CompuServe Mail clients, you're automatically setting up everything you need for remote access to those mail services.

However, if you need to access your Microsoft Mail server remotely—say, if you're traveling or working from home—you must set up a Dial-Up Networking connection to reach your postoffice.

 Note

The Microsoft Mail Remote program does not work with Exchange, and Exchange cannot access the same kind of dial-up as Mail Remote. Instead, Exchange must connect just like another node on the network. This means that, before you can dial into your Microsoft Mail postoffice with Exchange, a dial-up must be established on the network to handle incoming Dial-Up Networking calls.

Setting Up Remote Access to Microsoft Mail

To establish the Dial-Up Networking settings for a remote connection to Microsoft Mail, follow these steps:

1. Choose Tools, Services, and then select Microsoft Mail and choose Properties.

2. On the Connection tab, choose how you want Microsoft Mail to connect (see fig. 27.11). If you carry a notebook computer between the office and home, you can choose Automatically Sense LAN or Remote to have Exchange decide how you

27

should connect on each session. Or, if this is a separate profile for when you travel, choose Remote Using a Modem and Dial-Up Networking.

Fig. 27.11

To access Microsoft Mail remotely, you must choose either Automatically Sense LAN or Remote, or Remote Using a Modem and Dial-Up Networking. Do not choose Local Area Network or Offline.

3. Click the Dial-Up Networking tab and choose Add Entry to launch the Make New Connection Wizard.

4. In the first screen of the wizard, give your new connection a name and choose the modem you want to use (see fig. 27.12). Choose Next to continue.

Fig. 27.12

The first step in establishing a new Dial-Up Networking connection is to give it a name and select a modem.

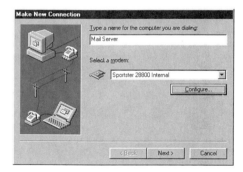

5. In the next screen, enter the Area Code, Telephone Number, and Country Code for your dial-up connection (see fig. 27.13).

6. Choose Next to continue, then choose Finish to complete the Make New Connection Wizard and return to the Dial-Up Networking tab.

7. The default settings for remote access to Microsoft Mail are usually fine, but before leaving the Properties dialog box, you might want to look at the Remote Connection and Remote Session tabs (where you can schedule your mail connections), as well as the other settings on the Dial-Up Networking tab.

8. When you finish working with the Properties for Microsoft Mail, choose OK.

Fig. 27.13

Enter the phone number you will use to access the postoffice.

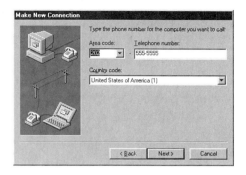

As with CompuServe Mail, you can configure Microsoft Mail to connect automatically at times you specify by following these steps:

1. Choose Tools, Services, and then select Microsoft Mail and choose Properties.

2. Click the Remote Session tab (see fig. 27.14).

3. If you want to dial in and get your mail remote when you run Exchange, select When This Service Is Started.

Fig. 27.14

Configure the remote settings for Microsoft Mail on that service's properties sheet.

4. Choose Schedule Mail Delivery to open the Remote Scheduled Sessions dialog box shown in figure 27.15.

Fig. 27.15

You can schedule several different remote connection sessions.

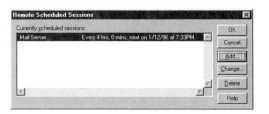

27

5. To add a new remote Microsoft Mail session, choose <u>A</u>dd.

6. In the Add Scheduled Session dialog box, select the Dial-Up Networking connection under <u>U</u>se (see fig. 27.16).

7. Under <u>W</u>hen, select whether to make the connection at regular intervals, on a weekly basis, or as a one-time operation.

8. Depending on your <u>W</u>hen choice, fill in the date, day(s), and time.

9. Choose OK three times to save the scheduled connection settings and return to Exchange.

Fig. 27.16

Select the Dial-Up Networking connection you want to use and when you want to make that connection.

 Tip

If you want to connect remotely to Microsoft Mail on a daily basis at a particular time, select Weekly under <u>W</u>hen, and then click all the days of the week.

As with the Microsoft Network and CompuServe Mail clients, you can choose <u>T</u>ools, <u>D</u>eliver Now Using to send and receive Microsoft Mail remotely at any time, getting all incoming messages and sending everything in your Outbox. But you also have the option of selectively downloading messages, covered in the next section.

Downloading and Marking Headers

The technique you're about to learn has three easy steps:

1. Download a list of pending incoming messages.

2. From that list, select what you want to retrieve.

3. Download the messages marked for retrieval.

When is this more useful than downloading all the incoming messages at once? The users who find this feature valuable include those who get so much mail that they have to prioritize it, and those who have subscribed to a number of Internet list servers and need help sorting the wheat from the chaff.

Remote mail works the same for any service. Here are the steps to follow:

1. Choose Tools, Remote Mail and select the service you want to access. The Remote Mail dialog box appears (see fig. 27.17).

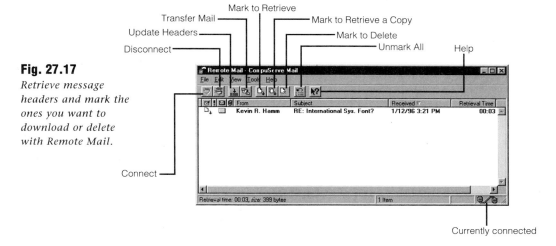

Fig. 27.17

Retrieve message headers and mark the ones you want to download or delete with Remote Mail.

2. Click the Update Headers button, or choose Tools, Connect and Update Headers.

3. Review the list of message headers downloaded in the previous step, and mark them for action. You can use the toolbar buttons or the options on the Edit menu. You don't have to mark all items, only those you want to retrieve or delete.

4. Click the Transfer Mail button, or choose Tools, Connect and Transfer Mail to send any messages in your Outbox, download the messages you marked for retrieval, and delete those you marked for deletion.

5. After the transfer has completed, choose File, Close or press Alt+F4 to close the Remote Mail application.

The messages you marked for retrieval will be in your Inbox.

Sending Mail from Office Applications

All Office applications (and many other Windows applications) allow you to send a document directly from within the application. Choose File, Send. If you're not already logged into Exchange, the login process will start up automatically. After you're logged in, the document will appear as an attached file in a normal message box, where you can select recipients, enter a cover note, and send the message (see fig. 27.18).

27

Fig. 27.18

Mail the current document from within Office or other mail-enabled applications.

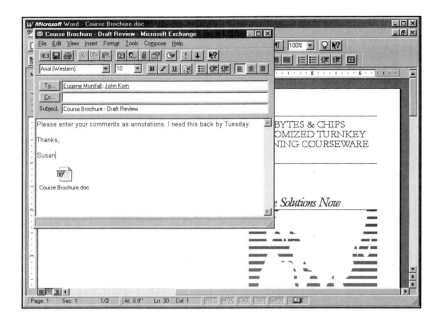

Routing Mail

For a more structured approach to sending documents, you can use a routing slip. This message, which is attached to your document, keeps you updated on a document's progress. In particular, you can route a document to a group of people one-by-one, so you get only one copy of the document back, with all revisions or annotations in one place for your review.

To use a routing slip with an Office document, choose File, Add Routing Slip. You see the Routing Slip dialog box shown in figure 27.19.

Fig. 27.19

A routing slip lets you send a document to users in sequence.

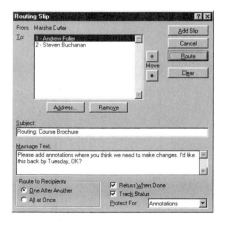

This is one situation in which you can't do any rich formatting with your message. The routing slip allows you to type in only a simple text message.

If your document is complete and you're ready to send it, choose Route in the Routing Slip dialog box; otherwise, choose Add Slip. This will attach the routing slip to your document for later use. Choose File, Send when you're ready to send it on its way.

A document sent to you with a routing slip will look like the message shown in figure 27.20. Double-click the attached file to open it. Make any changes or notations, then choose File, Send in the application to send the document to the next person on the routing list. You see a dialog box similar to the one shown in figure 27.21. Choose to route the document to its next recipient.

Fig. 27.20

An incoming routing slip includes the document, the cover note, and a reminder of how to route the document to its next stop.

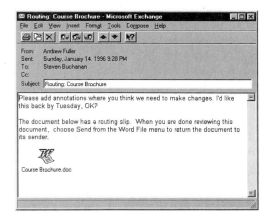

Fig. 27.21

A document with a routing slip attached reminds you that it needs to move on to the next recipient.

 Tip
When you work with a document with a routing slip attached, do not forward the message from Exchange or you'll lose some of the routing information.

27

Using Microsoft Word as Your Mail Editor

Although Exchange's message editor includes many formatting options, you can add even more by using Word as your mail editor. The component of Word that works with Exchange is called WordMail. It adds format tools, macros, AutoText, background spell checking, and most of the other features you enjoy with Word.

 Tip
Microsoft recommends a minimum of 12M of RAM for adequate WordMail performance; 16M is even better.

Enabling WordMail

If you didn't choose WordMail as one of your setup options for Office, run the Office setup again and choose it from the Word options shown in figure 27.22.

Fig. 27.22
WordMail is a separate Word option you install during Office setup.

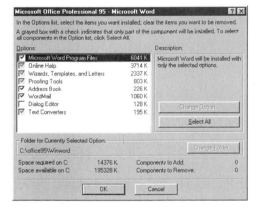

If you installed Exchange first, then Word (with the WordMail option), the choice to activate WordMail appears automatically in Exchange. Choose Compose, WordMail Options to open the WordMail Options dialog shown in figure 27.23. Select Enable Word as Email Editor to put WordMail to work as your mail editor. You can return to this dialog box at any time to deactivate WordMail.

If you installed Word, then Exchange, the procedure to activate WordMail is more complex. You will need your setup disk 1 or CD-ROM. Follow these steps:

1. Insert the Word or Office setup disk 1 or CD-ROM.

Fig. 27.23

*You can have more
than one e-mail
template with
WordMail.*

2. Choose Start, Run and enter the following command:

   <*drive*>:\Setup /Y

   where <*drive*> is the appropriate letter for your floppy or CD-ROM drive. Click OK
   to start Setup.

3. In the Microsoft Office 95 Setup dialog box shown in figure 27.24, choose Reinstall.

Fig. 27.24

*If you installed Word
then Exchange, you
need to run Setup and
choose Reinstall to
activate WordMail.*

Setup will take a moment or two to re-register your application(s), making WordMail
available to Exchange. After this procedure, WordMail Options will be available on the
Compose menu.

Exploring WordMail's Features

As figure 27.25 shows, when you read or compose a message with WordMail activated,
you'll see all the familiar Word toolbar buttons, plus the messaging buttons from Exchange. As you type, the background spell checker, AutoFormat, and AutoCorrect will go
to work for you.

27

For example, if you type **>** at the beginning of a line of incoming text, WordMail uses AutoFormat to turn that into an attractive arrow bullet and treats that line as bulleted text. If you type **:-)**, WordMail turns it into a smiley face symbol.

You can also use most of the shortcut keystrokes from the Exchange New Message dialog box, such as Ctrl+Shift+B to view the Address Book or Ctrl+R to reply to a message.

Fig. 27.25

WordMail combines the word-processing features of Word with the messaging tools of Exchange, all in one window.

Message function buttons

Template styles for message header elements

AutoFormat bullets

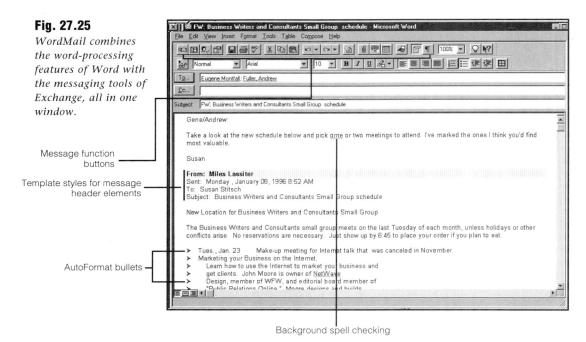

Background spell checking

Adding an Automatic Signature

The first thing you might want to do to customize WordMail is to add an automatic signature, displaying not just your name, but your e-mail address(es), and perhaps a catchy quote or tip of the day. Follow these steps:

1. In any Word document or WordMail message, type the signature you want to use and format it as you like. It can be a single line or many lines.

2. Highlight the signature, including the paragraph mark from the previous line (so the signature will always begin on a new line).

3. Choose Edit, AutoText.

4. Type **signature** in the Name text box. You must use this name for the AutoText entry in order for WordMail to append it to all your messages.

5. Choose Add to put your new signature on the list of AutoText entries.

> **Tip**
>
> If you send a lot of mail via the Internet, make sure you include your Internet address in your signature. Some systems strip off the incoming message headers. Without a return address somewhere in the body of your message, your recipients won't know where to send their replies.

Using E-Mail Templates

WordMail comes with four built-in templates for e-mail. You can make one the default, but still use the others—and any new ones you create—at any time.

To make a particular template the default, follow these steps:

1. Choose Compose, WordMail Options to open the WordMail Options dialog box (refer to fig. 27.23).

2. Select the template you want to use.

3. Choose Set as Default Template.

4. Choose OK to close the dialog box.

To edit one of the templates, select it from the WordMail Options dialog box, and then choose Edit.

To create a new e-mail template of your own, it's important to use the Email template as a starting point. This will copy the special styles for message headers and all the shortcut keys for message functions. Follow these steps:

1. Choose Compose, WordMail Options to open the WordMail Options dialog box (refer to fig. 27.23).

2. In the WordMail Options dialog box, select the Email template, then choose Edit to open it in Word.

3. Choose File, Save As and provide a file name and location for your new e-mail template.

4. Edit the template's styles, macros, and so on.

5. After you've made the changes, choose File, Close and respond Yes when you're asked if you want to save the changes.

6. Return to Exchange and choose Compose, WordMail Options to open the WordMail Options dialog box again.

7. Choose Add, and then select the template you want to add to WordMail and choose OK.

27

8. If you want your new template to be the default, select it, and then choose <u>S</u>et as Default Template.

9. Choose C<u>l</u>ose to exit the WordMail Options dialog box.

If you want to use the Email template for most messages, but occasionally use one of the other templates, make the Email template the default. When you want to create a message using a different template, choose Co<u>m</u>pose, <u>W</u>ordMail Options, and then select the template and choose <u>C</u>ompose.

How WordMail Looks to Recipients

The most amazing thing about WordMail is that you can use it to compose messages to any kind of recipient—even those who receive text-only messages. Messages created with WordMail are stored in plain-text and richly formatted versions. For the plain-text version, tables are converted to a columnar text format. Even special AutoCorrect characters like smiley faces and copyright symbols are converted to the nearest text equivalent.

As you might guess, this occurs at some cost in size. A typical WordMail message is larger than the same message created in Exchange's own message editor. But it is smaller than the equivalent Word file sent as an attachment to an Exchange message.

Working with the Address Book

One of the services installed when you first set up Exchange was the Personal Address Book. This data store holds all the addresses you add for your own use.

But it's only one of several lists of addresses to which you might have access. You might see a list corresponding to each of the mail services you use (see fig. 27.26).

Fig. 27.26

In the Address Book, you can choose from a number of sources of addresses, including your Personal Address Book.

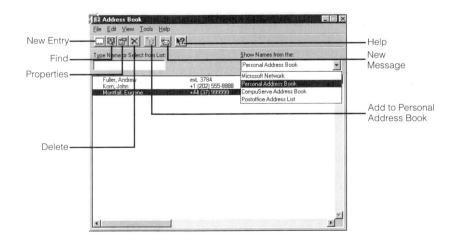

To access the Address Book, click the Address Book button, choose <u>T</u>ools, <u>A</u>ddress Book, or press Ctrl+Shift+B. From the Address book, you can perform several message and maintenance functions:

▶ Start a new message to one or more addresses

▶ Copy addresses to your Personal Address Book from the other lists in the Address Book

▶ Maintain phone numbers and other information about your recipients

Using the Address Book to Send Mail

To pick your recipients and start a message right from the Address Book, use these steps:

1. If the address list you want to use is not the active one, choose <u>S</u>how Names and pick the list you want to use.

2. From the active address list, select one or more recipients. To select more than one, hold down the Ctrl key as you click each name.

3. Click the New Message button, choose <u>F</u>ile, <u>N</u>ew Message, or press Ctrl+N to open a new message addressed to the people you've chosen.

Adding an Entry to Your Personal Address Book

There are three ways to add an entry to your Personal Address Book:

▶ Copy it from another address list

▶ Copy it from an incoming message

▶ Type it in

Each entry has a particular service associated with it. For example, if someone is listed in your Personal Address Book with a Microsoft Mail address, you cannot use that address to send them a fax. You will need to create an additional entry for that person, associated with the Microsoft Fax service.

 Tip

Exchange lets you enter a fax number for each person in the Address Book, but these numbers are not used for sending faxes with Microsoft Fax. You must set up a fax recipient with the entry type Microsoft Fax, even if you already have that person in the Address Book with an e-mail address.

27

The service type for each entry is determined when you create that entry. If you have a CompuServe address for a customer and they later switch to Microsoft Network, you should add a new entry to reach them via MSN.

Copying a Name from Another Address List

Adding a name from another list lets you address mail to that person even when you aren't connected to that particular mail service. It also helps you maintain a more manageable list.

For example, if you work for a company of 500 people, but send mail to only 40–50 of those, then add them to your Personal Address Book for easier reference. You'll also want to set up Exchange so it checks your Personal Address Book first when it's time to resolve names before sending a message.

 Tip
If you choose Show Names, Microsoft Network, you will be prompted to dial into the MSN. Definitely add MSN recipients to your Personal Address Book unless you want to have to dial in every time you need an MSN address.

To add an entry from another address list, switch to that list by choosing Show Names. Select one or more names to add. (You can add several addresses at a time. Hold down the Ctrl key as you click each name.) Then click the Add to Personal Address Book button or choose File, Add to Personal Address Book.

Copying a Name from an Incoming Message

Perhaps the best source of addresses for your Personal Address Book is from incoming messages. Any time you receive a message, you can add the address of the sender to your Personal Address Book. The procedures are a little different, depending on whether you're using WordMail.

If you are using Exchange's normal message form and not WordMail, open the message whose sender you want to add. Then, right-click the sender's name and choose Add to Personal Address Book from the shortcut menu.

Or, you can double-click the sender's name to open the properties of his or her address, as shown in figure 27.27. Choose Add to Personal Address Book.

Fig. 27.27

While viewing the details of the sender's address, you can add that person to your Personal Address Book.

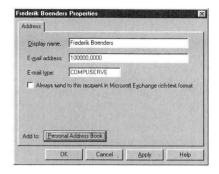

If you are using WordMail, you cannot use the second option (calling up the properties). You must right-click the sender's name to add it to the Personal Address Book.

 Tip

These same methods work when you are replying to a message. Either right-click or double-click the sender's name, which will appear in the To box.

Adding a Name from Scratch

The third way to add an entry to your Personal Address Book is by hand. This is probably the method you'll use for most fax addresses and quite a few others.

To add an address from scratch, follow these steps:

1. Click the New Entry button or choose File, New Entry.

2. In the New Entry dialog box, choose the type of entry you want to create (see fig. 27.28). Choose OK to continue.

Fig. 27.28

To create a new Personal Address Book entry, you must specify what kind of address to use.

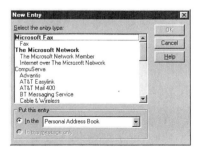

27

3. The Properties dialog box appears, where you enter the details of the new address (see fig. 27.29). The exact fields will vary depending on the type of address you've chosen.

4. If you want, switch to the Business, Phone Numbers, and Notes tabs to enter more than just the e-mail address for this recipient.

5. When you've completed the new entry, choose OK to add it to the Personal Address Book.

Fig. 27.29

The details needed to create a new address entry will vary, depending on the type of address—whether it's Microsoft Mail, fax, and so on.

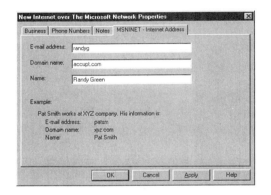

Reaching the Internet If You Don't Have Internet Mail

As you might have noticed, figure 27.29 shows an Internet address, in particular Internet via Microsoft Network. Exchange includes two ways to reach the Internet, even if you don't have the separate Internet Mail service that comes with Microsoft Plus! or Internet Explorer.

Internet via Microsoft Network is one method. The other is via CompuServe. Both entry types require you to know the name and domain for the recipient. In the example in figure 27.29, the Internet address for Randy Green is actually **randyg@accupt.com**; the name is to the left of the @ sign, the domain is to the right.

What to Use for Your Own Internet Address

What if you have a CompuServe or Microsoft Network address? Can other people reach you via the Internet? Yes, they can. Just tell your friends, customers, and colleagues to address you with these formats:

| CompuServe | <XXXXXX.XXXX>@compuserve.com |
| Microsoft Network | <member ID>@msn.com |

If you're on CompuServe and your ID is 77777,6666, then your Internet address is **77777.6666@compuserve.com**. Notice how the comma turns into a period.

As for Microsoft Network, if your ID is FastLane, you can be reached from the Internet at **FastLane@msn.com**.

Creating Distribution Lists

If you often send messages to the same group of people, take the time to create a distribution list that contains all of their addresses. Here's how:

1. Click the New Entry button or choose File, New Entry.
2. In the New Entry dialog box, choose Personal Distribution List from the list labeled Select the Entry Type (refer to fig. 27.28). Choose OK to continue.
3. The New Personal Distribution List Properties dialog box appears (see fig. 27.30). Give the list a name.

Fig. 27.30

A distribution list is a collection of recipients you can address as a group.

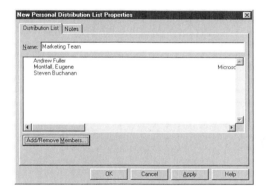

4. Choose Add/Remove Members to open the Edit New Personal Distribution List Members dialog box, shown in figure 27.31.
5. Select a name or names to add from the left-hand list, then choose Members to add them to the Personal Distribution List names on the right side.
6. If you add a name by mistake, select it under Personal Distribution List and press Delete.
7. To use names from more than one address list, select the list from the Show Names list box. You can mix different types of recipients in a distribution list.
8. When you've built your distribution list on the right-hand side, choose OK to save it in your Personal Address book.

27

To use a distribution list, enter its name in the To or Cc text box of any message.

Fig. 27.31

To build a distribution list, select as many names as you want from as many address lists. You can mix fax and e-mail recipients.

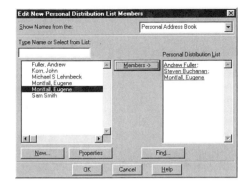

 Tip

If you have two types of addresses for a person, that name might appear twice in your Personal Address Book. You can choose Properties to view the details of an address so you can decide which one to add to the distribution list.

Editing Address Book Information

The Personal Address Book holds more than just e-mail and fax addresses. You can also use it to store phone numbers and addresses for contacts—information you can use in a Word mail merge. To edit an address book entry, open the address book and click the Properties button, double-click the entry, or choose File, Properties. You see a Properties dialog box similar to the one shown in figure 27.32, except the entry's name will be in the title bar.

 Caution

You can open a Personal Address Book directly into Word; it will appear as a table. However, you cannot add new items to the Personal Address Book by adding them to this table. Also, you will render your Personal Address Book incompatible with Exchange if you save it. You should turn off Automatic Save before opening a Personal Address Book or, after you open it, immediately choose File, Save As to save a copy under a new file name.

Enter additional information on the Business, Phone Numbers, and Notes tabs. The Address Book does display these different fields; however, it does not allow you to rearrange the columns or set their width. Consequently, the only information you'll normally see in the Address Book is the First Name, Last Name, Phone Number, and Title from the Business tab (see fig. 27.32).

Fig. 27.32

You can use additional information entered in your Personal Address Book for mail merges and to dial telephone numbers.

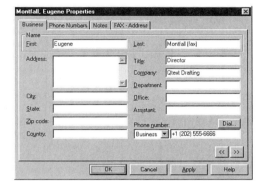

 Tip

If you have a person in your Personal Address Book twice with, say, both a fax and an e-mail address, use the First Name or Last Name text box on the Business tab to specify what type of address is used for this particular entry.

Notice the Dial button on the Business tab. You can click it to dial the number in the Phone Number text box, using Windows 95's Phone Dialer application, which maintains a call log for you.

Using Address Books from Other Sources

Exchange allows you to maintain only one Personal Address Book in each profile, but as you've seen, you can look at other address books tied to particular mail services.

 Tip

Although you can have only one Personal Address Book in your profile, you could have multiple profiles, each using a different Personal Address Book. For example, you might have one for office work and another for personal correspondence.

What about company or department-wide address books? The best way to handle those is to create a profile containing a Personal Address Book that resides on a network server everyone can reach. Then, each user can import the entries from that address book into their own Personal Address Book. Simply choose File, Import, and specify the location of the common address book.

If you are using Schedule+, you might wonder how its Contacts list interacts with Exchange's Personal Address Book. Basically, it doesn't. While the two are very similar, entries cannot be directly imported or exported from one to the other.

However, at least one macro is available on various online services for exporting fax addresses from the Schedule+ Contact list to Exchange, using an AddAddress function in Word Basic. AddAddress also works to insert new addresses into the Personal Address Book.

Another possible method is to open a Personal Address Book in Word (saving it immediately with a new file name), then export the address information as a comma-delimited file, which Schedule+ can import (see Chapter 22, " Exchanging Information Using Schedule+").

Using Personal Folders

You can get by with just the folders that Exchange normally places in your Personal Folders: Inbox, Sent Items, Outbox, and Delete Items. But that's just the beginning of the tools that Exchange offers for organizing your work, and by that I mean more than just messages.

In Chapter 25, you learned how to create new folders in Exchange. Now you're going to look at how to change the way they look, add documents to turn them into information databases, and find a new way of archiving projects and sharing information.

Storing Messages and Other Files

First, throw away the concept that Exchange is a universal inbox and start thinking about it as a universal storage system. An example should help. Figure 27.33 shows a custom folder called Internet. Imagine you've decided to finally start collecting all those interesting messages about great Web sites and new authoring techniques into one place. You could create a new folder in Explorer, but instead you create it in Exchange.

Fig. 27.33

Exchange's Personal Folders can be a comprehensive document database, not just a universal inbox.

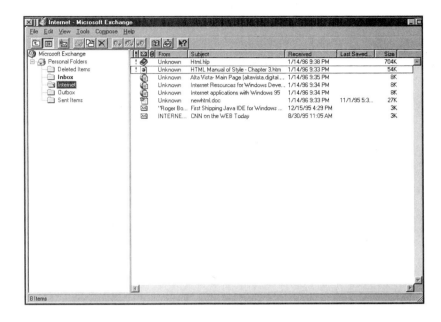

To move a document or message into an Exchange folder, just drag it from Explorer or from another folder in Exchange. For Exchange messages, you can also choose File, Copy or File, Move to view the folder hierarchy and choose a destination folder.

To view a document, just double-click it (or select it and press Enter). It opens in its own application (assuming it's a registered file type). Make changes there, and then close the document to save it back in the Personal Folders.

Viewing, Sorting, and Filtering

You might have noticed that the fields in figure 27.33 are a little different from those you saw in figure 27.1. Each folder in Exchange can display a distinctive array of columns, in the order and widths you choose.

To change the columns display, follow these steps:

1. Select the folder you want to work with.

2. Choose View, Columns to open the Columns dialog box (see fig. 27.34).

27

Fig. 27.34

You can give each folder an individual view, changing the columns displayed and their width and order.

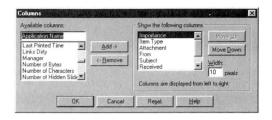

3. From the A̲vailable Columns list, select each column you want to use, then choose A̲dd.

4. Remove unwanted columns by selecting them in the Sho̲w the Following Columns list, then choosing R̲emove.

5. Use the Move U̲p and Move D̲own buttons to adjust the position of your columns.

6. Set the width of each column in the W̲idth box. (You can also adjust the size on-screen by dragging the boundary between two columns.)

7. When you finish rearranging the columns, choose OK.

 Tip

Some of the columns in the Available Columns list should look familiar if you've done any work with the Properties dialog box for Office documents. You can include those same fields, like Last Saved Time, in an Exchange folder view.

Another way to change the folder view is to alter the sorting of items. The easiest way is to click the column head of the column you want to sort by. You can also choose V̲iew, S̲ort. In figure 27.33, I sorted by Importance.

 Tip

To change an item's importance, choose F̲ile, P̲roperties or right-click the item and choose P̲roperties.

Adding Another Set of Personal Folders

Imagine that you like the way this Internet folder is shaping up, but other projects take precedence, so you're going to work on your Internet research only once every two weeks. There's no need to have that folder take up space in your main Personal Folders—not when you can move it to its own new set of Personal Folders.

You can add new Personal Folders to your Exchange profile at any time. These can be new folders created on the spot, or existing folders containing information you filed away previously.

You can also share them with other users. For example, you can move all your Internet research to a separate folder, which has its own PST extension, then place that folder on a network server for common use or e-mail it to everyone who needs a copy. They can then add it to their Exchange profiles using the following procedure.

> **Tip**
>
> Only one person at a time can use a particular Personal Folders file, so sending a copy of the file might work better than putting it on a server.

To create a new set of Personal Folders, follow these steps:

1. Choose Tools, Services.

2. Choose Add, then select Personal Folders from the Add Service to Profile dialog box (see fig. 27.35). Choose OK.

Fig. 27.35

Exchange allows you to include more than one message store in your profile. Extra sets of Personal Folders are useful for archives and projects.

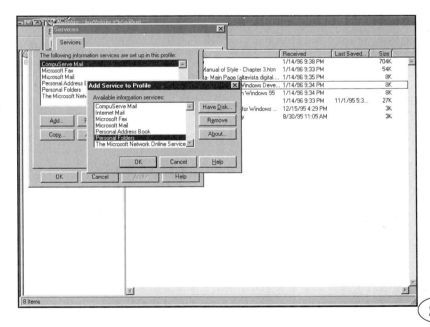

3. In the Create Microsoft Personal Folders dialog box, give your new set of folders a Name (see fig. 27.36).

4. Choose OK to complete the addition of the new Personal Folders.

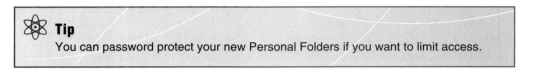

Tip

You can password protect your new Personal Folders if you want to limit access.

Fig. 27.36

You need to name the new Personal Folders file. You can also give it a password.

To move items to the new Internet Research folders, shown in figure 27.37, select and drag them to the new location or select them and choose File, Move. Pick a destination folder from the Move dialog box.

Fig. 27.37

Added Personal Folders, such as Internet Research in this example, have their own hierarchy of folders and messages.

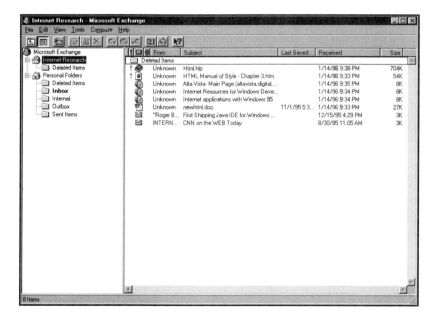

Use this same technique of creating new Personal Folders storage files to archive your messages. After you create the new Personal Folders file and move the old messages to it, return to the Services dialog box (choose Tools, Services), select the archive Personal Folders file, and choose Remove to exclude it from your current profile. You can add it again at any time if you want to review your old messages.

 Tip

Choose Tools, Find and use an Advanced date filter to find all your messages for a particular month so you can archive them efficiently.

Finding Messages

With the virtually unlimited capability to create new folders and new Personal Folders files, you can imagine that you'll need a way of locating specific items. Exchange does have such a function. Choose Tools, Find to display the Find dialog box (see fig. 27.38).

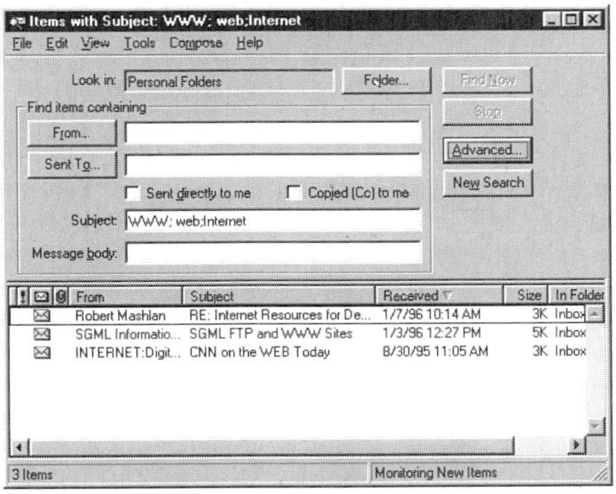

Fig. 27.38

A sophisticated Find utility helps you keep track of all those incoming and outgoing messages and other items in your Exchange folders.

Choose Folder to set the scope of your search, either a whole set of Personal Folders or any folder in it.

In the From, Sent To, Subject, and Message Body text boxes, you can enter more than one word or phrase to search for (separate them with semicolons). Exchange will find all items that match at least one of your search terms.

Choose Advanced for additional search filters, including size and date.

When you've chosen all the elements of your search, choose Find Now. The list of matching items will appear at the bottom of the dialog box.

27

Notice the message `Monitoring New Items` in the lower-right corner of the dialog box. You can create a search, then minimize it and have it examine all incoming messages. This could be a big help, for example, if you're a human resources manager responsible for responding to all vacation requests. Just set up a search for "Vacation" in the Subject and/or Message Body and you'll quickly be able to sift those requests from the rest of your incoming messages.

Maintaining Files

Like most applications, Exchange requires some housekeeping. Because it does not purge old messages automatically, you must do this yourself or you'll find that your Personal Folders file quickly reaches an enormous size.

Deleting Messages

To delete a message you don't want to archive or keep, simply select it and press Delete or click the Delete button.

Deleted messages are copied to the Deleted Items folder. If you've set up Exchange with the option to empty Deleted Items when you exit Exchange, this folder will be purged when you exit. However, if you shut down Windows 95 without first closing Exchange, the Deleted Items folder will not be emptied.

If you have more than one Personal Folders file in your profile, only the one that is your primary delivery location will have its Deleted Items folder emptied when you exit.

 Note

New messages are placed in the Inbox folder of the Personal Folders file that's designated as your delivery location. To select which Personal Folders file gets the new messages, choose File, Options. In the Options dialog box, choose the Delivery tab. Make your choice from the Personal Folders files listed under Deliver New Mail to the Following Location.

 Tip

You can delete items permanently by deleting the items in the Deleted Items folder.

Compression

If you have deleted a large number of items recently, you might want to compact your Personal Folders file to reduce its size. Follow these steps:

1. Choose Tools, Services.
2. Select the Personal Folders you want to compact, then choose Properties.
3. In the Personal Folders dialog box, choose Compact Now.

Backup

If you are working in Exchange, your system backup utility cannot back up any Personal Folders files in your profile that are open in Exchange.

One solution is to close Exchange before backing up. Another technique is to copy any essential messages to a separate Personal Folders file, then remove that from your profile before running the backup. This is also a good way to move in-progress work between your office system and your laptop or home system.

Inbox Repair Tool

On occasion, you might have problems receiving or sending messages. Microsoft included a tool to repair damage to any Personal Folders file. To use the Inbox Repair Tool follow these steps:

1. Close Exchange.
2. Click the Start menu, then choose Programs, Accessories, System Tools, Inbox Repair Tool.
3. Enter the name and path to the Personal Folders (PST) file you want to repair or choose Browse to locate it on your system.
4. Choose Start.

When it finishes, the Inbox Repair Tool will display a report similar to the one shown in figure 27.39. You can then choose whether to correct any errors it found. Choose Repair to make the repairs.

Fig. 27.39

The Inbox Repair Tool can fix problems in your Personal Folders files.

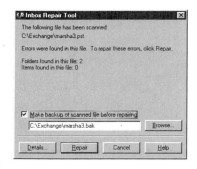

Summary

E-mail via Exchange opens the door to revolutionary changes in the way you communicate. You can transmit short messages or long documents and send to one person or a whole group. You can reach people down the street or around the world, all from your desktop, usually at less cost than sending the printed material.

You should now be able to use all the e-mail services that come with Windows 95, organize the messages you send and receive into Personal Folders along with other files, and manage a Personal Address Book containing your most frequently used recipients.

This chapter briefly mentioned Internet Mail as one of the additional Exchange services available apart from the Windows 95 package. Expect more such Exchange clients to emerge at a steady pace to help you connect efficiently to even more services.

Integration

VII

chapter 28

Critical Skills for Integrating Applications

by Donna Payne

In this chapter

◆ **What MS Office integration can mean to your custom application**
Learn how Office integration can be used to build customized documents that combine features of one application with another without the need to write macro code. When coding is necessary, learn how to use Microsoft Office's Visual Basic for Applications, a common macro language.

◆ **About OLE and OLE Automation**
Learn to use and understand OLE terminology and its function.

◆ **About Dynamic Data Exchange**
Learn how DDE works and how to use DDE commands.

◆ **How to manage links**
When you create compound documents, you may create links that are hard to find, edit, and delete. Learn to manage and remove links that are created when inserting objects between applications.

◆ **How to use Microsoft Binder**
Learn to use the Binder application that is new to Office 95.

The Microsoft Office copy advertisement reads:

Office 95, Next Generation Integration Tools for Windows 95...integration that makes it easy to focus on your job instead of your software.

With promises like these, it's not hard to understand how Office has become the best selling suite of software applications today.

By combining some of the best features from individual applications—such as relational databases, PivotTables, mail merge, and slide show presentations—you are equipped to pack more power in your punch and get better results faster than you ever thought possible while writing less code.

This chapter provides an overview of techniques, concepts, and critical skills that are necessary in understanding the remaining chapters in this book.

Integration—The Future of Applications?

Although each application provides a tremendous amount of functionality, no single application can do it all. And even if the functionality is available in the application, it might be accomplished better in another application within the Office suite. For example, Excel used to have the capability to create a slide show. The process of creating the Excel slide show was much more difficult than creating a slide in PowerPoint, an application designed to create presentations. Likewise, there is no reason to create a database in Word or PowerPoint. A database should be created and maintained in Access or Excel.

So what is Office integration? It's the process of sharing information between two or more applications found in the Microsoft Office suite of applications. For the Standard edition, this means Word, Excel, PowerPoint, and Schedule+. The Professional version adds Access.

Although each application within Office has many features that overlap in functionality, it's important to understand the primary function of each of the applications. Table 28.1 shows the primary function of each application that is a part of the Office suite.

Table 28.1   Office 95 Applications

Application	Description
Access 95	Database, data entry, forms, and reports
Excel 95	Data analysis, data viewing, and presentation
Office Binder	Electronic notebook that stores files
PowerPoint 95	Presentation
Schedule+ 95	Time management
Word 95	Word processing, report generation

Microsoft's corporate strategy is to build a set of tools that can be easily used to integrate and develop custom business solutions. The tools include the following elements:

▶ Exposing the functionality in applications through an object-like interface. Office provides more than 300 programmable OLE objects. Objects that are exposed in an application have properties and methods that can be manipulated by the developer.

▶ Supported by OLE Automation for messaging transport within and between applications.

▶ Providing access to many database and messaging sources through support of messaging application programming interface (MAPI) and open database connectivity (ODBC) technology.

▶ A single programming environment for Microsoft Applications, Visual Basic for Applications. Word does not yet support VBA.

You don't even have to be a developer to use and integrate Office and reap the rewards. It's hard to find anyone who hasn't copied an object from one application and pasted it into another.

Visual Basic for Applications

Microsoft has implemented a strategy for using a common programming language in all of its Office applications. This language is Visual Basic for Applications (VBA). VBA was first shipped with Excel 5 and has since been added to Project, PowerPoint, Access, and FoxPro. Microsoft has announced its intention to include VBA in future versions of Word (which currently uses WordBasic).

VBA is an object-oriented version of Visual Basic, and it is hosted in another application. Developer tools in VBA include debugger (Debug Window), editor, Object Browser, and online reference and help from the application's help menu.

Visual Basic can be summarized as follows:

▶ Code written or recorded that is stored on a module sheet that can be edited.

▶ Objects that are arranged in a hierarchy, have properties and methods associated with them, and can be manipulated by VBA.

▶ Modules that contain VBA subroutines and function procedures.

▶ Similar objects that can form a collection and can be manipulated together.

▶ Dot operators that are used to separate objects, objects and their properties, and objects and their methods.

The best way to learn VBA is to dig in and get your hands dirty. Learning the objects, properties, and methods can be a little daunting, but once you've seen it for a while, it starts to make sense.

28

Shared Resources of Office 95

Office uses shared resources between applications. These resources are tools that, once implemented, are available in all Office 95 applications. The shared resources included are as follows:

- ▶ AutoCorrect list storage
- ▶ File Open
- ▶ Find Fast
- ▶ File Save
- ▶ File New
- ▶ File Properties
- ▶ Answer Wizard
- ▶ MSN Integration
- ▶ Notes/FX thunking layer
- ▶ Print dialog (Consistent, not shared)
- ▶ Spell checking
- ▶ OLE Servers (Graph, WordArt, Equation Editor, Data Map, Clipart Gallery, Imager)
- ▶ Text Converters
- ▶ Graphic Filters
- ▶ MSInfo

OLE and OLE Automation

You don't need to be a developer to appreciate the things that can be done with Object Linking and Embedding (OLE). In fact, most novice Office users can figure out how to insert an object into an application. The purpose of OLE (pronounced *o-lay*) is to make sharing components of other applications as easy as possible.

As a developer, you can tap into the capabilities of OLE with OLE Automation. With OLE Automation, through VBA, you can control objects from other applications by exposing their object model and manipulating the application's objects.

OLE Automation servers are applications that are controlled by OLE Automation controllers, and OLE Automation controllers are applications that can control OLE Automation servers. Table 28.2 lists OLE controllers and servers for Office 95.

Table 28.2   OLE Automation, Controllers, and Servers

OLE Controllers	OLE Servers
Access	Access
Excel	Excel
Project	Office Binder
	Word
	PowerPoint
	Project
	Schedule+
	Office Document Property Object Library

To support OLE, an application must be OLE-compatible (written to the OLE specification), and the application must have been installed and registered in the system's OLE Registry. The entry has a unique identification for each object and includes an application identifier. Windows applications can be OLE servers, OLE clients, or both.

You can see all of the OLE Registry information by choosing Start, Find, Files or Folders, and then type **MSInfo** in the Name Edit box and click Find Now. You can also use EXPLORER.EXE and navigate to Program Files, Common Files, Microsoft Shared, MS Info, MSINFO32.EXE, and OLE Registration. There is an entry called OLE Registration, Registry Settings and INI Settings. Figure 28.1 shows the expanded Registry Settings folder and the files the folder contains.

Fig. 28.1

The OLE Registry shows all of the OLE applications and objects on your system.

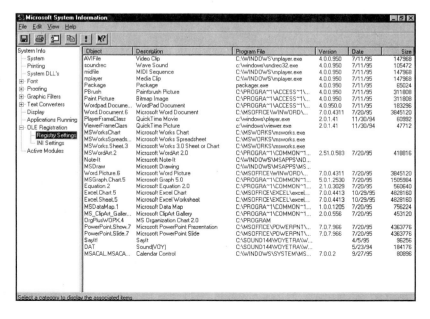

Figure 28.2 shows the OLE INI Settings folder.

Fig. 28.2

The INI Settings are for OLE applications and objects.

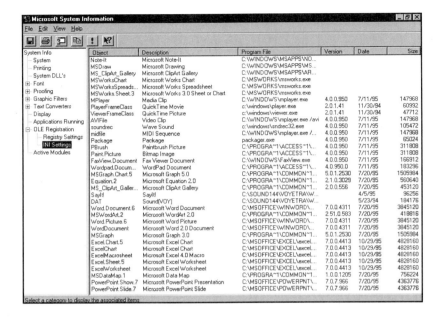

All Office applications support OLE to some extent. Most support the new breed of OLE technology, OLE 2.0, with the exception of Windows Paint that ships with Windows 95. Windows Paint supports OLE technology, but not OLE 2.0.

Problems still need to be ironed out with OLE, and Microsoft is quick to acknowledge this. However, if you use OLE, and especially OLE Automation, you will find the possibilities of what can be done in developing a custom application impressive.

Defining OLE

If you've ever inserted an Excel chart into Word or PowerPoint, added Word Art to your document, or inserted a sound clip or Quick-Time movie, you've used OLE technology.

With OLE, there is a container application and an object application. Just as the name indicates, the *container application* "contains" or maintains OLE documents. The *object application* provides data objects to be included in the container document.

OLE is a protocol that enables objects created in one application to be stored, linked, or embedded in other Windows applications that are OLE compliant. The current version of OLE, OLE 2.0, supports in-place or visual editing and OLE Automation—the capability to control another application's objects through the use of programming code.

Creating OLE Documents

By choosing Insert, Object, you can quickly insert an object with OLE technology into a host application. Because most Office applications have similar dialog interfaces, it is a fairly simple procedure to complete. Figure 28.3 shows the Insert Object dialog box called from inside of PowerPoint.

Fig. 28.3

Accessing OLE technology is as easy as choosing Insert, Object from the within the container application.

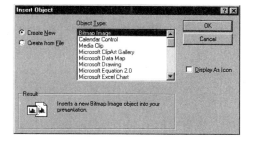

You can choose to create a new object with OLE, or you can select a file that has already been created by choosing the Create From File option button in the Insert Object dialog box. From this tab, you can choose an existing file, create a Link to File between the source file and the container file, and Display the information as an icon. Figure 28.4 shows these options from the Insert Object dialog box.

Fig. 28.4

By clicking the Browse button, you can search for the existing file that you want to insert an object from.

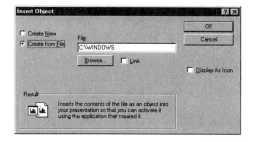

Visual Editing

Thanks to OLE 2.0, an object can be edited within the context of its container application without having to launch the application that created the object. For instance, if an Excel table has been inserted into Word, you can edit the Excel table in Word by double-clicking the table. Upon double-clicking the table, Word's menu bars temporarily change to display the menu bars that are a part of Excel. When the object is no longer active, Word's menu bars return.

Visual editing gives you access to all of the functionality in the embedded object's application without having to open the application. Previous versions of OLE did not offer visual editing. When the object was activated, the application that created the object was opened, and the edit would take place in the native application. Excel, PowerPoint, Word, and Access support visual editing.

Drag and Drop

Another feature of OLE 2.0 is the capability to select a range of cells or an object, drag it over to another application's window, and drop it by releasing the mouse button. To see how this works, resize your windows so you have Word and Excel showing at the same time. Select an Excel object or range and drag it over to the Word document. Now release the mouse and watch the object drop into Word. An example of this is shown in figure 28.5.

Fig. 28.5

With two applications showing, an object—in this case a map of Australia—can be dragged and dropped from one application to another with OLE.

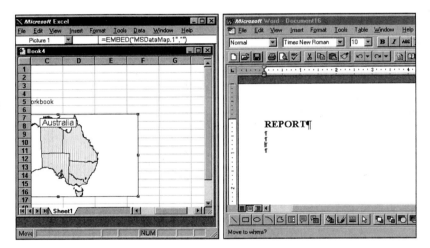

Paste Special

A link can be created by copying an object. Choose Edit, Copy, switch to the container application and choose Edit, Paste Special, and then select the option to Paste Link. By creating a link between the source and the container data, each time the information is updated, it is updated in both places. By linking an object that is stored in one application into another application, you create what is called a *compound document*. A compound document takes advantage of features that are available in multiple applications without changing the source of the data.

If you choose Edit, Copy, switch to the container application, and choose Edit, Paste, a static or unchanging object is inserted that will not contain an OLE link.

Object Conversions

If you exchange files with different people, you sometimes find that an embedded object has been created in an application that you don't have access to. Through OLE, it's possible to convert objects to a format that can be edited by performing the following steps:

1. Select the object that was created in another application.

2. Choose <u>E</u>dit and select the last option on the <u>E</u>dit menu. This will vary between applications and will depend on what type of object you are attempting to convert. A submenu appears.

3. Select Con<u>v</u>ert.

4. Select the <u>C</u>onvert To option in the Convert dialog box and choose the file format that allows you to edit the object in your application. Click OK.

Now you can edit the embedded object by double-clicking it. An example of the Convert dialog box is shown in figure 28.6.

Fig. 28.6
You can convert an object that was created in another application to one that can be edited from within your current application.

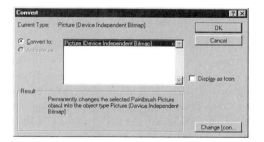

Jazzing Up Your Documents with OLE Sound and Video

If you have the right equipment, sound cards, and video drivers, you can jazz up your presentation or custom application by inserting sound or video clips. This is accomplished by choosing <u>I</u>nsert, <u>O</u>bject and selecting the correct object just as you would any other object. In figure 28.7, you see the options available from PowerPoint to insert a sound or video clip.

Fig. 28.7
With OLE, you can include professional quality video and sound with relatively little effort.

28

To add or edit an existing sound or video file, choose Insert, Object, click the Create from File tab in the Object dialog box and select the file that you want to insert. To play the embedded sound or video, select the object, choose the last item on the Edit menu, and then choose Play from that item's submenu. The sound or video file then plays.

OLE Automation

OLE Automation is used to control one application and its objects from a second application through macro code. OLE Automation can be used to create new objects (`CreateObject`); get existing ones (`GetObject`); access an object's properties and methods; close, insert, and delete objects; and even start and close an application.

By exposing each application's object model, the application's objects, properties, and methods can be manipulated with VBA. In Excel, the objects that are created through OLE Automation do not necessarily become a part of your worksheet. Usually, they are displayed by the application where they were created and can run in the background of the application.

A practical example of the need to use OLE Automation is when a user has an Open Database Connectivity (ODBC) source that ports information into an Excel PivotTable. The user needs to refresh the data and copy the data into Word to prepare a report. Figure 28.8 shows a simple Excel PivotTable that receives updated information from an ODBC source.

Fig. 28.8

A simple PivotTable from an external database is a great way to show data; the information is presented in a clear, effective way.

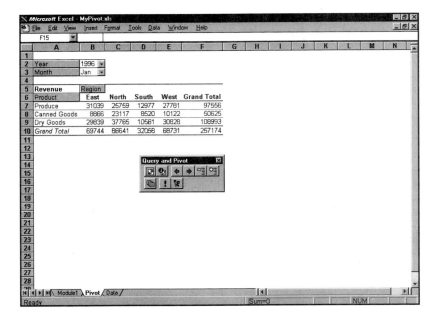

The subroutine, `GetNewDataIntoWordFromExcel()`, takes the PivotTable data and copies it into Word. A breakdown and explanation of each procedure in the subroutine follows the macro.

```
Sub GetNewDataIntoWordFromExcel()
    Dim oPivot As PivotTable
    Dim oWord As Object

    Set oPivot = ThisWorkbook.Worksheets("Pivot") _
        .PivotTables("Revenue PivotTable")
    With oPivot
        .RefreshTable
        .PageFields("Year").CurrentPage = Format(Now, "YYYY")
        .PageFields("Month").CurrentPage = Format(Now, "MMM")
    End With

    Set oWord = CreateObject("Word.Basic")
    oWord.FileNew "C:\MSOffice\Templates\Normal.dot", 0

    oWord.Insert "Current Revenue data for " & Format(Now, "MMM YYYY")

    oPivot.TableRange1.Copy
    oWord.editpaste

    On Error Resume Next
    Kill "C:\" & Format(Now, "YYYYMMM") & ".DOC"
    On Error GoTo 0

    oWord.filesaveas "C:\" & Format(Now, "YYYYMMM") & ".DOC"
    oWord.fileclose
End Sub
```

The variable `oPivot` is set, and then the `PageField` is set accordingly. The PivotTable is refreshed.

```
    Set oPivot = ThisWorkbook.Worksheets("Pivot") _
        .PivotTables("Revenue PivotTable")
    With oPivot
        .RefreshTable
        .PageFields("Year").CurrentPage = Format(Now, "YYYY")
        .PageFields("Month").CurrentPage = Format(Now, "MMM")
    End With
```

A Word Object is created and a new Word file is opened.

```
    Set oWord = CreateObject("Word.Basic")
    oWord.FileNew "C:\MSOffice\Templates\Normal.dot", 0
```

Descriptive text is added—in this example, `Current Revenue data for` and today's date formatted with an abbreviated month and the year (for example, Mar 1996).

```
    oWord.Insert "Current Revenue data for " & Format(Now, "MMM YYYY")
```

Copy `TableRange1` of the PivotTable and Paste it into the Word document.

```
oPivot.TableRange1.Copy
oWord.editpaste
```

Make sure no other document exists by the proposed name.

```
On Error Resume Next
Kill "C:\" & Format(Now, "YYYYMMM") & ".DOC"
On Error GoTo 0
```

Save the document using YYYYMMM.DOC as the naming convention, and close the Word file. If you want the Word file to remain open, remove the procedure `oWord.fileclose`.

```
    oWord.filesaveas "C:\" & Format(Now, "YYYYMMM") & ".DOC"
    oWord.fileclose
End Sub
```

Figure 28.9 shows how by using OLE Automation, data that was maintained in an Excel PivotTable was transferred to a Word document.

Fig. 28.9

The finished product is ready to be included in a monthly report.

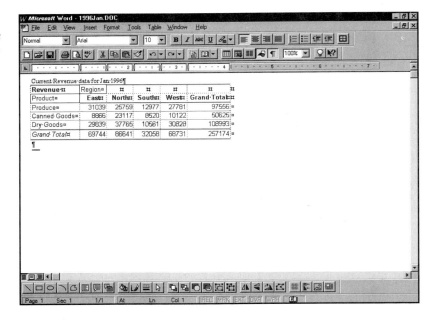

Note

Knowing when to link and when to embed confuses many users. Although knowing how to use them is good, understanding in which circumstance to use one over the other is vital. When you link an object, you create a communication to the source data. When you insert an embedded object, you embed a copy of the object in the document.

A good time to use linking might be when you use monthly sales figures that are stored in Excel and you prepare a report in Word. If you create a link to the Excel file from Word, your figures automatically update when the figures in the source document are changed.

If you want to insert an object that you want to stay static (unchanged), you would choose to embed the object. Embedding is also a good idea if you are transferring files to different users who may not have access to the same files in the same locations that you may access.

Dynamic Data Exchange

Dynamic Data Exchange is a protocol to exchange data between two or more applications by way of a DDE conversation. The DDE conversation is channeled between the client and server application. The client application is the application that initiates the conversation. The application that responds is called the server. An application can engage in several DDE conversations at the same time, as a client in some, and as a server in others.

The client application initiates conversations, sends commands, requests information, sends information, and ends the conversation.

The server application carries out commands from the client application, and supplies and accepts information.

You can create DDE links manually by copying data from one application and choosing Edit, Paste Special into another application. This takes advantage of the Clipboard where the data is stored between the Copy and the Paste Special commands. Most developers use DDE commands to automate requests between applications. One use of DDE commands is when you need to grab current data from a stock portfolio, a financial software package such as Quicken, or other applications that you need to get information from.

Tip

There is a file in the Excel library on CompuServe (type **GO MSEXCEL**) that takes information from Quicken and puts it into Office applications (and non-Office applications) using DDE commands. The file name is QW-DDEDK.ZIP.

OLE 2.0 is thought of by many as a replacement for DDE because it is faster and less awkward. However, because OLE Automation is not yet supported by all applications, it may still be necessary to use DDE.

 Note

With DDE the terms *client* and *server* are often used. A client is the application that initiates and controls the other application through DDE. The server receives commands from the client and responds to the commands and inquiries from the client application.

Macros can perform many tasks automatically for you in other applications. In order to control another application's behavior with DDE, you must write code in an application's macro language. Although DDE commands vary between macro languages, there are some similarities. A table of tasks and the methods they perform are shown in the following table.

Method	Task
DDEInitiate	Initiating DDE
DDERequest	Getting text from other applications
DDEPoke	Sending text to other applications
DDEExecute	Executing a command in other applications
DDETerminate	Terminating DDE
DDETerminateAll	Terminates all conversations with other apps

 Caution

If you develop multilingual applications using DDE commands, the commands may not be recognized. For example, the Spanish and German versions of Excel do not recognize English DDE commands from another application. These DDE commands are sent into Excel as text strings that would need to be in the native language.

Managing Links

A frequently asked question on the MS Excel forum on CompuServe is how to find links. Sometimes links are obvious, and sometimes they're not. Most links can be found by choosing Edit, Links. There you can view, edit, update, and delete links. Word creates a bookmark for links and makes it easy to go to and find links that exist in your document. Word creates a bookmark for each server link and names them OLE_LINK with an incremental number following.

Editing and Deleting Links

Fortunately, dialog boxes are pretty standard between applications for managing links. Access, PowerPoint, and Word have similar dialog boxes. Figure 28.10 shows the Links dialog box in Access.

Fig. 28.10

An advantage to the Office suite of applications is the similar user interface, including this Links dialog box.

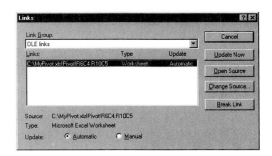

An option that is included on the Links dialog box in all applications except for Excel is Break Links. The dialog box displays information about the link including the source of the link, the type of document that created the link, and whether or not the link is updated manually or automatically.

 Note

In Excel, you can create a link to an external worksheet by choosing Edit, Copy, Edit, Paste Special and then selecting the Paste Link option. The link automatically updates the data that is linked. It is not possible to change the update option to manual updating.

The Links dialog box also provides options to update the link (Update Now), open the source of the link (Open Source), change the source of the link (Change Source), and to break the link altogether (Break Link).

 Note

Usually, the best way to edit a link is to use the Change Source option.

The Links dialog box for Excel, as shown in figure 28.11, does not provide a Break Links option.

Fig. 28.11

It's expected that future versions of Excel will have the Break Links option that the other Office applications offer.

A link in Excel displays an exclamation point in the formula bar, where you can edit it directly. However, you must remember to enter the revised formula as an array formula by pressing Ctrl+Shift+Enter.

 Note

Many Excel users complain of links in documents that do not show up in the Edit Links dialog box. These links can reside in several places within the workbook:

▶ A spreadsheet formula that is linked to another cell

▶ A defined name (including Print Area)

▶ A hidden name

▶ An object, especially with a macro assigned to it

▶ A chart

▶ External Query Definition (choose Data, Get External Data)

In Excel, you can choose Edit, Find and type an exclamation point in the Find What edit box to find links within your worksheet. To find links in your print area definition or within other defined names, choose Insert, Name, Define and look for defined names that have square brackets and an exclamation point. This is considered a link.

To find a hidden name in Excel that may contain a link, you need to do a bit more sleuthing. Two macros that look for and delete hidden names are shown here. The subroutine `DeleteHiddenNames()` deletes all names that are hidden without any interaction. The subroutine `DisplayHiddenNamesAndInteractDelete()` asks to confirm that the hidden name should be deleted.

```
Sub DeleteHiddenNames()
'''Deletes All Hidden Names Without Any Interaction
  Dim oName As Object
  For Each oName In ActiveWorkbook.Names
    If oName.Visible = False Then oName.Delete
  Next oName
End Sub

Sub DisplayHiddenNamesAndInteractDelete()
''' Delete All Hidden Names Interactively
  Dim oName As Object
  Dim iCount As Integer
  For Each oName In ActiveWorkbook.Names
    If oName.Visible = False Then
      iCount = iCount + 1
      If MsgBox("Hidden Name: " & oName.Name & " = " & _
        oName.RefersTo & Chr(10) & "Delete?", vbYesNo) = vbYes Then
        oName.Delete
      End If
    End If
  Next oName
  If iCount = 0 Then MsgBox ("No Hidden Names in " & ActiveWorkbook.Name)
End Sub
```

Another place where links can occur is in drawing objects that have macros attached to them. A macro to set all drawing objects to visible is the VBA subroutine

```
SetVisibletoTrueAllDrawingObjectsInActiveSheet
```

which calls a function procedure to loop through the Objects Collection and change the visible property of each object to True.

```
Function SetVisiblePropertyAllObjectsInCollection _
   (oCollection As Object, Optional viSetting) As Boolean
  Dim oObject As Object
  If IsMissing(viSetting) Then viSetting = xlVisible
  For Each oObject In oCollection
     If oObject.Visible <> viSetting Then oObject.Visible = viSetting
  Next oObject
SetVisiblePropertyAllObjectsInCollection = True
End Function
Sub SetVisibletoTrueAllDrawingObjectsinActiveSheet()
''' Make all objects in Sheet Visible
If SetVisiblePropertyAllObjectsInCollection _
   (ActiveSheet.DrawingObjects, True) = False Then
    MsgBox "Error Making All object Visible"
End If
End Sub
```

Links can exist in charts. Select the chart, activate ChartWizard, and then select the data series, data labels, and titles to find links to other workbooks. Finally, if you choose <u>D</u>ata, Get E<u>x</u>ternal Data, remove the check in the option to <u>K</u>eep Query Definition.

Tip

Before you create a link, it's a good idea to check the <u>T</u>ools, <u>O</u>ptions settings in your workbook. Settings there can affect how links are handled.

Choose <u>T</u>ools, <u>O</u>ptions, select the Edit tab and check the option setting to Ask to <u>U</u>pdate Automatic Links. Choose the General tab and uncheck the option to <u>I</u>gnore other Applications. The Calculation tab has two options that should have a check in the check box next to them: Update <u>R</u>emote References and Save External <u>L</u>ink Values.

Caution

A bug occurs in Excel 95 when certain cells from one worksheet are linked to the same cell in another sheet in the same workbook. When you change the data after these cells have been linked, the data will not update on the second sheet.

A fix for this bug is available on CompuServe in the MSExcel library. This file, which is called EXCEL95.EXE, actually includes three patches for bugs in Excel 95.

Breaking and Restoring Links

By clicking the <u>B</u>reak Links button in Word's, Access', or PowerPoint's Links dialog box, you can quickly break a link that exists in your document.

By default, links are automatically updated. If you want to change the links to be manual only when you want to update the links, choose <u>E</u>dit, Lin<u>k</u>s and change the Links Update option to <u>M</u>anual. The links no longer update automatically. You need to choose <u>E</u>dit, Lin<u>k</u>s, <u>U</u>pdate Now to update the data associated with the links, and click OK.

To break or delete a link, choose <u>E</u>dit, Lin<u>k</u>s, <u>B</u>reak Link (in Excel, select the linked object and press the Delete key) followed by OK, so the link will break. To restore a broken link, choose <u>E</u>dit, Lin<u>k</u>s and select the broken link. Click the <u>C</u>hange Source button, locate the source where the link should be, and click OK.

Using Microsoft Binder

The Microsoft Binder is a new tool available in Office 95 and may be thought of as an electronic notebook that is an OLE container. Binders aid in assembling and distributing documents. The Binder application allows you to store documents from Excel, Word, and PowerPoint into one file. The Binder document uses the OBD extension, the Binder template uses the OBT extension, and OBZ for a Binder Wizard template that includes macros.

Because a binder is treated as one file, you are able to treat all or selected documents that are a part of a binder as one file, and are able to print consecutive page numbering, reorder and rename documents, store all documents in one location, and use OLE in-place editing technology to view and change the sections of the binder.

 Note

Some third-party products support the Binder. These include TriSpectives by 3D/Eye, Designer, and Picture Publisher by MicroGrafx, and Visio by Visio Corporation.

Starting Binder

There are several ways to launch the Binder application. You can find Binder in the MSOFFICE\OFFICE folder.

▶ Double-click the BINDER.EXE file. When you open a binder in this manner, a blank Binder window appears.

▶ Using the Office Shortcut Bar, click the MS Binder button.

▶ Double-click an existing binder that you have created.

A lone toolbar button appears that toggles the Hide Section pane. The *section pane* is the area that shows the documents in the binder. In figure 28.12, the Office Binder application has been launched, and a new or existing binder can be opened.

To open an existing Binder, choose File, Open, select the appropriate binder file, and choose OK.

By choosing File, New, the New Binder dialog box appears, presenting a two-tabbed option either to create a new blank binder, or to use one of four pre-built binder templates. You can create your own custom binder templates as you can with Word and Excel. If you select a built-in template, a wizard or a pre-built form appears and walks you

28

through the steps of creating documents. When you use a wizard, you create documents that have the same professional appearance and that will all be stored in an electronic binder.

Fig. 28.12
When you launch Binder, this window appears. Notice the menu and toolbar button.

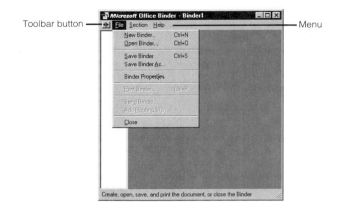

Toolbar button

Menu

The built-in binder templates are the following:

▶ *Client Billing Binder.* Helps you create and organize a binder of documents to bill a client.

▶ *Meeting Organizer.* Contains a series of pre-built documents that you can customize for your use. These include an invitation, address list, agenda, slide show, minutes, and a memo.

▶ *Proposal and Marketing Plan.* Contains a series of documents that include a cover letter, quote, slide show, referrals, detail, and follow-up.

▶ *Report.* Contains a cover letter, executive summary, slide show, analysis, and data.

Adding Documents to the Binder

You can add existing documents to a binder in one of two ways. As with most Office applications, you are able to drag and drop the document onto the Binder section pane, or you can choose Section, Add From File, which opens a Browse dialog box.

To use the drag-and-drop method, open the EXPLORER.EXE window from the Start menu and drag the desired file over to the left pane of the Binder window and release (or drop) the file into the Binder.

> ## α Note
>
> When you use the drag-and-drop method, the original file is preserved and a copy of the file is created and added to the Binder.

To add a new section to the Binder, choose Section, Add. A dialog box appears and prompts you to choose which type of document the new section should be: an Excel chart, Excel worksheet, PowerPoint presentation, or Word document. Figure 28.13 shows a binder with a Word documents and an Excel file. The icons in the left pane of the Binder show which files are in the current binder. The active file icon is highlighted, and an arrow pointing toward the large section pane is next to the icon. The active file appears in the right second pane—in this case, a Word document.

Fig. 28.13

Place all files that belong to the same report in one binder, as long as the files are Word, Excel, or PowerPoint documents.

Active Word file icon

Excel file

Active Word file

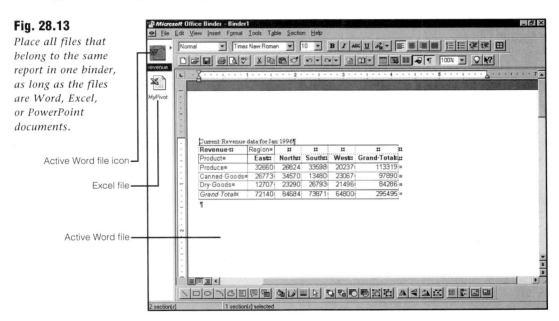

To add an existing document to the Binder, choose Section, Add From File, and select the file in the Add From File dialog box.

Deleting a file or files from a binder is done in much the same way. Choose Section, Delete, and the selected or active section is deleted.

28

Working with Documents in the Binder

One reason to use the Binder is if you want to create a report that uses different files created from multiple applications. You can create a document that keeps all files in one place, and you can treat all or specified documents in the Binder as one file. The following are ways to operate a binder as one file:

▶ A binder can be printed all at once or by individual section

▶ By Ctrl+clicking each icon in the binder, you can print only the documents you need.

▶ Page numbering can be consecutive throughout the report, no matter what type of application is being printed.

The File and Section menus are specific to the Binder, while the other menus are specific to the active application of the document that is being shown in the right pane of the Binder window.

The section panes of the binder are divided into two parts. The left section displays the icons for the individual documents in the binder. The right section pane displays the active document and its native menu and toolbars.

Note

When saving a binder, the default file location that it's saved in is \WINDOWS\MY DOCUMENTS.

Note

Currently, it is not possible to save a binder with password protection. When a password-protected document is added to a binder, the binder prompts for the password. But when the document is added to a binder, the password protection is lost. To protect a binder from changes, place it on a read-only shared network.

Troubleshooting the Binder

Because the Binder is a feature new to Office 95, the following is a list of potential problems and a way to resolve each problem:

▶ *The binder is too large to print.* Binders are printed as one file and can become very large. If a problem occurs while printing the entire binder, try printing sections instead.

▶ *Page numbers do not print.* The page numbers must be in place in the header or footers. Make sure that page numbers are enabled in the application that created the document.

▶ *Wrong page numbers print.* If the user changes the page number in the application that created it, the binder does not override this setting.

▶ *E-mailing binders.* Because binder files can become very large, problems may be experienced when you try to e-mail them. Consider placing the files instead in a shared folder that users may access.

▶ *Binder file is too large.* You may need to defragment the binder file and reduce its size by choosing File, Save As, and save the file as a new file and delete the old one.

▶ *Embedding and linking objects.* You cannot link an object to a document that is not a part of the binder, you must embed the object.

▶ *Loading the Binder.* If you experience a problem loading a binder or a binder section, load the binder and unbind it into separate files using the Unbind command on the shortcut menu.

▶ *Macros.* A macro cannot be edited while it is stored in a binder.

The Binder Object Model

A binder, as an OLE object, can be controlled programmatically using OLE Automation. The Binder object corresponds to a binder file and can be created using `CreateObject()`. `GetObject()` is used to access existing binders.

The default property of the Binder object is the `Name` property. Other properties include `Path`, `Sections`, `ActiveSections`, and `Visible`. Some methods are `PrintOut`, `Save`, and `Save As`.

The Binder Object model is made up of three classes of objects:

▶ *Binder.* References a binder file. Binders can be opened, a section can be added to the binder, and the binder can be printed and saved.

▶ *Section.* Refers to an embedded file that is a section of the binder. A section may be added, created, activated, deleted, printed, or moved.

▶ *Sections.* Enables access to the object models of embedded files within the Binder.

An example of using Excel VBA and OLE Automation to control a binder is shown in the following subroutine, `CreateABinder()`.

28

```
Sub CreateABinder()
    Dim ThisBinder As Object
    Set ThisBinder = CreateObject("Office.Binder")
        ThisBinder.Sections.Add Type:="excel.chart"
        ThisBinder.Sections.Add Type:="word.document"
        ThisBinder.Sections.Add Type:="excel.sheet"
        ThisBinder.Visible = True
End Sub
```

This simple subroutine creates a new binder; adds an Excel chart, Word document, and Excel worksheet; and then makes the binder visible.

 Note

If you want to see the binder, you must use the `Visible` property in your subroutine. For this reason, the procedure `ThisBinder.Visible = True` was added to the subroutine.

Summary

In this chapter, you have examined how Office integration can aid you in your custom application development process, and you have covered the critical skills necessary to use the remaining chapters in this book. This includes an overview of the common macro language included in Office applications, VBA, OLE technology, and DDE.

By breaking down some of the barriers that previously existed between applications, Office integration can be instrumental in helping you access the functionality of multiple applications and take advantage of new features such as the Binder application.

chapter 29

Integrating Excel and Word

29

by John Lacher

In this chapter

◆ **Combining the strengths of Word and Excel in an integrated application**
By combining Excel's data analysis features with Word's text processing capabilities, you can build a powerful report generator.

◆ **Using Excel worksheet data in Word documents**
Worksheet data can be embedded, linked, or pasted into a Word document.

◆ **Integrating Excel charts with Word documents**
You can develop convincing reports using Excel charts in a Word document.

◆ **Using Word documents in Excel workbooks**
Word can add bulleted lists and outlining to an Excel workbook.

◆ **Importing Excel data with Word's mail merge**
The mail merge catalog provides an easy way to organize and print Excel data in a Word document.

◆ **Creating Word form letters from Excel**
With OLE automation, you can print letters in Word with the click of a button.

◆ **Printing a PivotTable report in Word**
Learn how to use OLE automation and VBA to prepare a more sophisticated report.

Excel and Word combine to create a powerful *report generator* you can use to make your reports, proposals, letters, memos, and e-mail messages more effective. By linking Excel's data analysis features to Word's text processing capabilities, you can produce professional combinations of charts, tables, and text. You can make your proposals and reports more convincing and eye-catching.

Combining data from Excel and Word calls for skills beyond the basic "cut-and-paste" technique. In this chapter, you learn to use the methods and techniques that Excel and Word provide for integrating features.

Combining the Strengths of Excel and Word

An understanding of the strengths of Excel and Word help you recognize opportunities to combine those strengths in a workbook or document. Excel provides data analysis, charting, and reporting features. Word provides text processing and document layout features not available in Excel.

You can develop an integrated solution that contains the strengths of both packages. By using the integration techniques explained in this chapter, you'll be able to implement solutions like these:

▶ Make your reports more convincing by providing background text next to the numbers in your Excel workbook. You can store the background text in Word documents that are built in to your Excel workbook.

▶ Save time when publishing your weekly report by linking Excel tables and charts with a Word document. Excel's linking ability updates your data automatically.

▶ Create a condensed executive overview in your report. You can display an embedded Word outline in your Excel workbook.

▶ Catch the reader's eye by wrapping columns of text around an Excel chart or table. Excel data can be embedded in a Word document with column formatting.

▶ Organize your Excel data with a table of contents. If you include Excel data in Word and add headings, you can use Word's Insert, Index and Tables command to create a table of contents with multiple levels of detail and automatically added page numbers.

▶ Publish Excel data in directory format. You can print lists of selected data from Excel with Word's mail merge catalog feature.

▶ Complicated report preparation processes can be reduced to the click of a button. By including modified Word Basic statements in your Visual Basic for Applications code, you can control Word from Excel. Visual Basic for Applications can automatically copy data from Excel to Word, insert text and headings, and print a report.

▶ Customize an Excel chart. You can use Word's picture editing capabilities, drawing objects, captions, and callouts to fine-tune the look of your Excel chart.

The following sections show you how to select from the many options used to integrate Word and Excel. Understanding the differences between options such as linking and embedding help you select the most effective method to combine the strengths of Excel and Word in your reports.

Using Excel Worksheets in Word Reports

You can transform an ordinary Excel worksheet into an eye-catching report by using Worksheet data in a Word document. Once you have moved the data to Word, you can add text, formatting, and layout features that focus your reader's attention on the message in your report.

Understanding Methods of Sharing Data

You can choose from the options in table 29.1 to copy Excel data to Word. Each of the options provides you with a tool to use in constructing a report. You can use a different option for each range of worksheet data you insert in a Word document.

Table 29.1 describes when and why each of the options are used. The table contains a row for each data presentation type. The *Linked Version* column describes when and why you would link the data in Word to an Excel worksheet. The *Copied Data or Embedded Worksheet* column describes the advantages of embedding or copying the data. The data presentation types listed in the rows of the table are pictured in figure 29.1.

Table 29.1   Methods of Inserting Excel Worksheet Data in a Word Document

Presentation Type	Linked Version	Copied Data or Embedded Worksheet
Bitmap	Display a worksheet range exactly as it appears in the linked Excel worksheet.	Convert an exact image of worksheet range to a bitmap that is stored in the Word document.
Unformatted Text	Insert worksheet data in a paragraph. The data is updated automatically when the worksheet is modified.	Insert a copy of worksheet data in a Word paragraph.
Formatted Table (RTF)	Display data from an Excel workbook in standard Word table format. You can break the link to convert data to a Word table.	Copy a range of Excel worksheet data to cells in a Word table. You can add formulas and other Word features to the table.

continues

Table 29.1   Continued

Presentation Type	Linked Version	Copied Data or Embedded Worksheet
Icon	Use icons to provide easy-to-use links to several Excel files.	Use icons as an index to multiple embedded Excel workbooks.
	Open a linked Excel workbook with a double-click of the mouse.	When you double-click an icon, the embedded workbook opens in an Excel window.
Worksheet	Update a periodic report automatically with data from an Excel workbook.	Add Excel data analysis features to Word.
	Double-click the worksheet to open and modify the Excel workbook.	Double-click the worksheet to display the Excel menu and allow editing in place.
	Data is not stored as part of a Word document.	Workbook data can be distributed with the document because all data is contained in Word.
Picture	Same as linked worksheet option.	You can double-click the picture and use Word's picture editing to modify elements of the picture.

In figure 29.1, the bitmap image shows the shading of the field names exactly as it appears in the PivotTable on the Excel worksheet. The Picture and Worksheet presentation methods produce identical images in the Word document, but give different results as described in table 29.1. The Formatted Table (RTF) is displayed with the grid lines of a standard Word table.

Fig. 29.1

Six methods are available for displaying Excel worksheet data in a Word document.

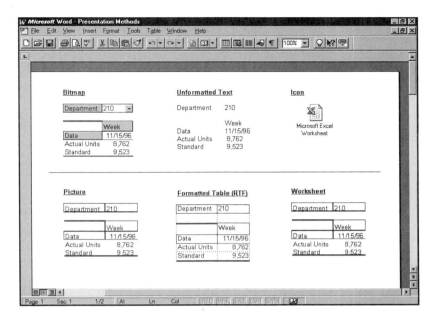

29

Word Field Codes

As you become skilled in integrating Word and Excel, the options described in table 29.1 will become part of your report-building tool set. Word field codes can help you understand this tool set more thoroughly.

A Word field code is created for you every time you *link* or *embed* data in a Word document. If you *copy* data, no field code is created. The LINK field code includes all of the parameters Word needs to find the linked Excel file. The EMBED field code contains the class code which defines the type of object.

Field codes are normally hidden. You can display them by pressing Shift+F9. They appear in place of the linked and embedded images they represent. Pressing Shift+F9 to turn field codes off again returns the images to their original place.

If you turn on field codes with a screen display of *linked* data identical to figure 29.1, the screen changes to display what is shown in figure 29.2. If the images are copied and embedded, the screen displays what is shown in figure 29.3. The images of copied data remain unchanged because only the linked and embedded images have field codes.

Fig. 29.2
To understand how Excel data is linked in Word, you can view the Word field codes.

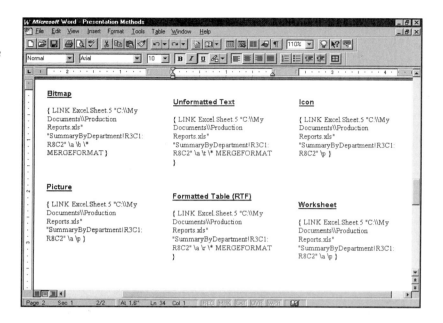

Fig. 29.3
Word creates field codes for embedded data. Copied data does not display a field code.

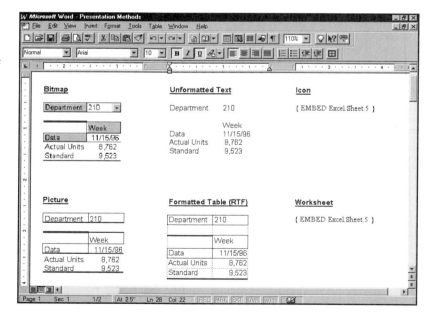

By turning on field codes, you can see if data is linked or embedded. You can view the path Word uses to find the linked Excel workbook. The LINK and EMBED field codes also contain parameters that control sizing and formatting.

Using Excel Worksheet Data in Word

In the following examples, you learn the steps involved in using Excel worksheet data in Word. You can use copy and paste, drag and drop, or the Insert, Object command to insert Excel data in your Word document.

Using Copy and Paste

When you want to copy Excel worksheet data to cells in a Word table, you can use copy and paste. Select a range of cells in Excel and choose Edit, Copy. When you switch to Word and choose Edit, Paste, the Excel range is copied as a formatted table without linking.

Figure 29.4 shows Excel data that has been copied to Word. The comment and arrow was added in Word using the Callout button on Word's Drawing toolbar.

Fig. 29.4

You can copy and paste Excel data into Word.

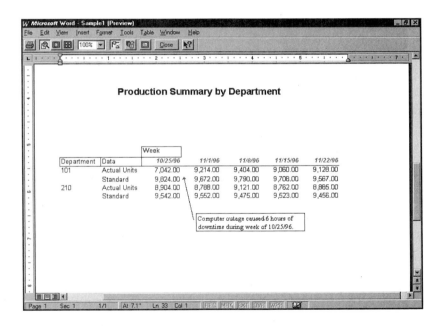

Once the data is copied into a Word table, you can use all of Word's table formatting and formula options to modify the data. If you need to work with the data in Excel after you have modified it in Word, you can copy a Word table to a range of cells in an Excel worksheet.

Figure 29.5 shows the Word table after reformatting with Word's Table, Table AutoFormat command.

Fig. 29.5

*You can apply an
AutoFormat to a
Word table.*

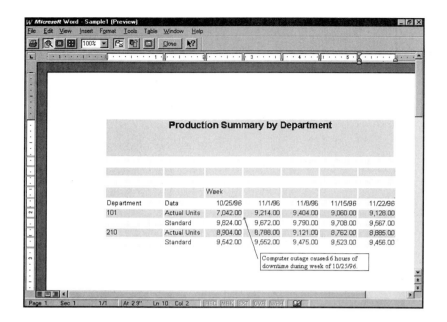

Using a Linked Worksheet in Word

If you want the data in Word updated automatically when the Excel workbook is modified, you must link the Worksheet data. In the next example, an Excel worksheet range is copied and pasted into·Word as a linked worksheet, using the Edit, Paste Special command. The Paste Special dialog box, shown in figure 29.6, contains all of the options described in table 29.1. When you click Paste Link and choose Microsoft Excel Worksheet Object, the data is inserted in Word as a linked worksheet.

To position the worksheet in Word, select the worksheet by clicking it and choose Insert, Frame. Word encloses the worksheet in a frame that you can move anywhere in the Word document. Figure 29.7 shows a framed worksheet that is positioned in the center of a two-column Word document.

You can convert a linked worksheet into a picture by choosing Edit, Links. Figure 29.8 shows the Links dialog box with the cursor positioned over the Break Link button. Once the link is broken, the picture in the document remains constant and does not reflect changes in the Excel workbook. This feature is useful when you need to distribute the Word document to users who do not have access to the Excel workbook.

Fig. 29.6

You can use Paste Special options to paste an Excel worksheet range into Word.

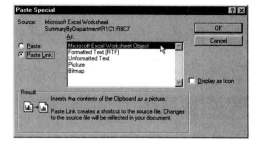

Fig. 29.7

You can use a frame to position an Excel chart in a Word document.

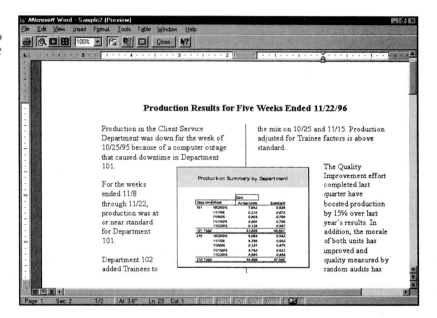

Fig. 29.8

You can use the Break Link option to freeze Excel worksheet data.

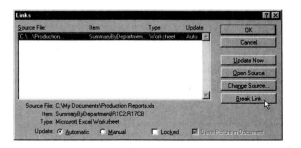

Note

You can choose when you want linked data to be updated. Choose one of the Update options in the Links dialog box (refer to fig. 29.8). Automatic update occurs when the document is opened and when the Excel workbook is modified after the document is opened. To update the data manually, press F9 or click the Update Now button. The Locked option prevents an update.

Embedding an Excel Worksheet in Word

When you need to distribute the data in a worksheet with your Word document, you can embed the worksheet in Word. A copy of all of the data in the workbook is copied into the Word document file.

To embed a worksheet in a Word document, follow these steps:

1. In Word, choose Insert, Object.
2. Choose the Create From File tab.
3. Choose the Excel file you want to embed in Word (see fig. 29.9).

Fig. 29.9

The Create From File tab enables you to embed an existing Excel workbook in Word.

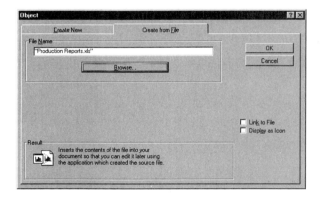

4. Leave the Link to File option blank.
5. Click OK, and the embedded workbook appears in your Word document.

When you embed a workbook in Word, the selected worksheet (top sheet) displays in the Word document. To display another worksheet, double-click the embedded workbook and select another worksheet using the sheet tabs.

When you double-click an embedded Excel workbook, it opens for *in-place editing*, as shown in figure 29.10. With in-place editing, the Excel menu options replace Word's menu options and the workbook is displayed in an editing window. When you are finished editing the Excel workbook, you can click anywhere in the document outside the editing window and return to Word.

Fig. 29.10

In-place editing enables you to edit Excel workbooks in Word.

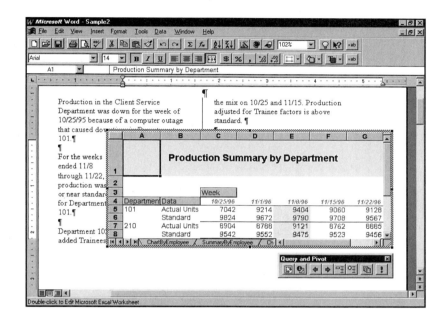

When the workbook is opened for in-place editing, you can scroll the window and use the fill handles on the frame of the worksheet to select the range of cells you want to display in Word. If you want to change the size of the picture displayed in the document, close the workbook and drag the handles on the border of the picture.

 Note

When you link an Excel workbook to a Word document, you can use the Edit, Copy option in Excel and then switch to Word and choose Edit, Paste Special with the Paste Link option.

Another way to perform the link is to choose the Insert, Object command from Word and select the Excel file name in the Create from File tab of the Object dialog box.

If you create the link using the Paste Special method, Word creates a link to the *worksheet* and *range* of data that was selected when you chose Edit, Copy in Excel. With the Insert, Object method, Word creates a link to the top or *active sheet* in

> the workbook. If another sheet is selected as the active sheet in the Excel workbook, Word displays that sheet.
>
> Use the Paste Special method to display a specific range of data from a linked Excel workbook. Use the Insert, Object method to display whichever sheet was made active when the Excel workbook was last updated.

Using Excel Charts in Word Reports

The combination of Excel charts with the features of Word can communicate a message in new and exciting ways. You can embed, link, or copy a chart to a Word document. With Word's layout features, you can integrate the chart with bulleted lists, outlines, and columns of text.

Understanding Methods of Sharing Data

To effectively use charts in your Word documents, you must first understand the options Word provides for inserting a chart in a document. Table 29.2 describes each option and how it can be used.

Table 29.2   Methods of Inserting Excel Charts in a Word Document

Presentation Type	Linked Version Chart	Copied or Embedded
Bitmap	Display a chart exactly as it appears in the linked Excel workbook.	Convert exact image of chart to bitmap stored in Word.
Excel Chart	Update periodic reports automatically with a chart from an Excel workbook.	Add chart features to Word.
	Double-click the chart to open and modify the Excel chart.	Double-click the chart to display the Excel menu and allow in-place editing.

Presentation Type	Linked Version Chart	Copied or Embedded
Excel Chart (continued)	Excel workbook data is not stored as part of the Word document.	Chart data can be distributed with the document because all data is contained in Word.
Picture	Same as linked Excel chart option above.	You can double-click the picture and use Word's picture editing to modify each element of the chart.

When you insert a linked or embedded chart, Word creates field codes automatically, as described in the earlier section "Using Excel Worksheets in Word Reports."

In the examples that follow, you learn how to insert a chart using the options listed in table 29.2.

Using Excel Chart Data in Word

You can use drag and drop, copy and paste, or the Insert, Object command to insert an Excel chart in a Word document. Once you have inserted the chart, you can enclose it in a frame and position it anywhere in the Word document. The sizing handles on the picture of the chart in the Word document can be used to change the size and shape of the chart.

Using Copy and Paste

Copy and paste is the simplest way to embed a chart in Word. Select a chart in Excel, copy the chart using the Excel Copy command, and then paste it into your Word document. The chart is inserted as an embedded chart. All of the data in the workbook containing the chart is copied into the Word document. You can make changes to an embedded chart without affecting the original Excel workbook file.

 Note

Word's copy-and-paste behavior for worksheet ranges is different than it is for charts. If you copy a worksheet range and paste it into Word, the result is a Word table that contains the worksheet data. To embed a worksheet range into a Word document, you must use the Edit, Paste Special command.

Once you have copied a chart into your Word document, you can activate it for in-place editing by double-clicking it. Word's menu is replaced by Excel menu items. You can use worksheet tabs and scroll bars to navigate through the embedded workbook. Figure 29.11 shows an embedded chart open for in-place editing.

Fig. 29.11

You can open an Excel chart in Word for in-place editing.

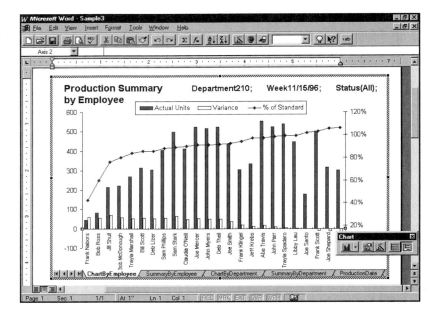

To open the embedded chart in Excel, right-click the embedded chart and choose the option Open Chart from the menu.

Using Copy and Paste Special

To insert the chart as a linked chart or picture, you can use the Copy and Paste Special menu commands. Figure 29.12 shows the Paste Special options for inserting a chart.

Fig. 29.12

The Paste Special options for inserting a chart include Chart Object and Picture.

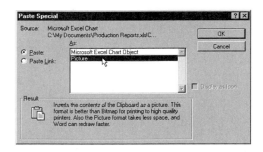

The Paste Link option in the Paste Special dialog box creates a linked chart or picture. When the original chart in the Excel workbook is modified, those changes are displayed in the chart.

When you insert a chart as a picture, you can use Word's picture editing features to customize the appearance of the chart. Each line, shape, symbol, and text entry on the chart is a separate drawing object in the Word picture. You can delete, move, rotate, and change the color of objects. You can use all the buttons on Word's Drawing toolbar with the picture.

Another option you can use to insert a linked or embedded chart is the Insert, Object command, as described earlier. (Refer to fig. 29.9 for the Object dialog box.)

Using Word Documents in Excel Workbooks

You now know how to insert Excel data in a Word document. This section explains the methods of inserting text from Word in an Excel workbook.

When you include Word text in an Excel workbook, you can create workbooks with bulleted lists, outlines, and other text features that are not available in Excel. By adding these text features to your workbooks, you can add focus to the data displayed in the Excel tables and charts.

Integrating Word text in an Excel workbook lets you store written reports and memos that provide background on the numbers in the workbook. With a double-click of the mouse, you can open a Word document that provides an explanation of the numbers on your Excel worksheet.

You can use Word's outlining feature to create a short list of text topics and click the topic you want to explore. When you link the Excel workbook to the Word document, updates in the Word document appear as new information in the Excel workbook as well.

Understanding Methods for Inserting Text

To put the power of Word to work in your Excel workbooks, you first need to understand the methods you can use to link, copy, and embed the text in Excel. These methods, described in table 29.3, can be used to enhance your workbooks. The examples that follow provide step-by-step instructions for inserting Word text into Excel workbooks.

Table 29.3   Methods of Inserting Word Text in an Excel Workbook

Presentation Type	Linked Version Embedded Word	Copied Text or Document
Text	This method inserts text in worksheet cells. If you are linking to a Word table, the data in the cells of the Word table will display in cells of the worksheet.	This method copies text or a Word table to worksheet cells when you do not want the data to be linked to the Word document.
Picture	The data is displayed as in Word, including any formatting or added drawing objects. The picture is linked to the Word document and automatically updates when you open the Excel workbook.	The text or Word table is displayed as it appears in Word, but the picture is not updated when the Word document changes.
Icon	Icons provide links to several Word documents. When the linked Word document is open, you can use Word's outlining feature to find text descriptions for numbers in the Excel workbook.	An icon can open an embedded Word document. When you click the icon, the document opens in a Word window. All of the features of Word, including outlining, are available for use.
Word Document	Automatically updates text information that accompanies a periodic report. Double-click the Word document to open and edit the document inplace. Word's menu items will replace the Excel menu options. The Word document is not stored as part of the Excel workbook.	Adds Word text features (such as bulleted list or style) to the Excel worksheet. The Word document is stored as part of the Excel workbook.

Using Word Documents in Excel

Word is an ideal tool to use in developing convincing reports. You can use Word's outlining, heading styles, and formatting to add emphasis to your message. The following section shows how to add Word features to your Excel worksheet.

The Excel worksheet in figure 29.13 contains two features from Word that are not available in Excel. You can insert a picture of a bulleted list like the one below the PivotTable by copying and pasting the data from Word. The Production Memo icon accesses a linked Word document, providing descriptive information to back up the numbers in the Excel PivotTable.

Fig. 29.13

Word can provide bulleted lists and icons that you can insert in an Excel worksheet.

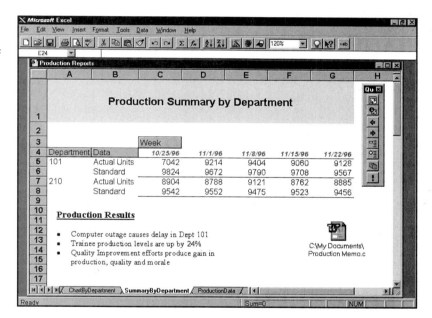

Inserting a Picture of a Bulleted List

To insert a bulleted list in an Excel worksheet, follow these steps:

1. Create the list in a Word document. Use the Bullets button on Word's Formatting toolbar to add bullet symbols to your list.

2. In Word, choose Edit, Copy.

3. Switch to Excel. You can use the Win95 task bar or the shortcut keys Alt+Tab to switch back and forth between applications.

4. In Excel, select the worksheet cell where you want to insert the bulleted list and choose Edit, Paste Special.

5. In the Paste Special dialog box (refer to fig. 29.6), choose `Picture`. If you want the list to update automatically when you change the Word document, click Paste Link.

   The bulleted list appears, as shown in figure 29.13.

Linking a Word Document with an Icon

When you want to add descriptive information to your worksheet, you can add an icon that opens a Word document with the click of a mouse. When the document opens, you can use the outlining feature to find information that relates to the numbers on the worksheet.

To insert a Word document in the form of an icon, you can use the Copy, Paste Special, or Insert, Object command. The following procedure uses the Insert, Object command:

1. In Excel, choose Insert, Object.

2. In the Object dialog box (refer to fig. 29.9), choose the Create from File tab.

3. Use Browse to locate the Word document, and choose the Link to File and Display as Icon options. An icon appears on your worksheet (refer to fig. 29.13).

4. Double-click the icon; the Word document opens in a separate Word window. In Word, choose View, Outline to collapse and expand information, as shown in figure 29.14.

Fig. 29.14

Linked Word documents can be opened and shown in outline view.

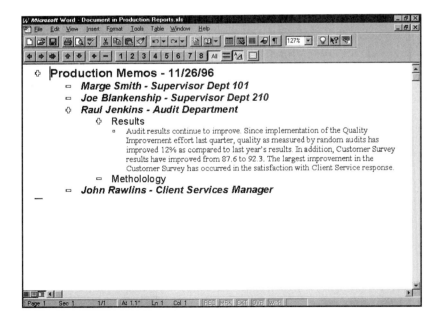

5. To switch back and forth between the Word document and the worksheet, use the Win95 task bar or the shortcut keys Alt+Tab. When you are finished using the Word document, choose <u>F</u>ile, <u>C</u>lose in Word to return to the Excel workbook.

Inserting Data from a Word Table into a Worksheet Range

You can develop an exhibit of numbers in a Word document and then copy the data to Excel for analysis. After you have worked with the numbers in Excel, you can transfer them back to the Word document.

To transfer numbers from Word to Excel, follow these steps:

1. Create a table of numbers in the Word document. In Word, choose T<u>a</u>ble, <u>I</u>nsert Table to create the table. Enter the numbers into the table using the number keys. Press the Tab key to move from cell to cell in the Word table.

2. Select the Word table and choose <u>E</u>dit, <u>C</u>opy. The T<u>a</u>ble, Select T<u>a</u>ble command on the Word menu bar can be used to select all the cells in a large table.

3. Switch to Excel and select the worksheet cell where you want to copy the data.

4. In Excel, choose <u>E</u>dit, <u>P</u>aste. The data in the cells of the Word table is copied into the worksheet, beginning with the selected worksheet cell.

5. After you modify the data in Excel, you can paste it back into the Word document by choosing <u>E</u>dit, <u>P</u>aste. All of the formulas in Excel are changed automatically to constant values in Word.

Importing Excel Data with Word's Mail Merge

One way to import Excel data to Word is to code a VBA procedure in Excel that uses templates and WordBasic statements to create the report. Later in this chapter, you will learn how to use this technique to create a complex report based on Excel PivotTables.

Another way to print Excel data in a Word report is to use Word's mail merge feature. Mail merge may sound like a simple tool you use to print form letters, but Word's mail merge includes many other features, such as sorting and query capability and the catalog format.

Exploring Uses of Mail Merge

When you choose <u>T</u>ools, Mail Me<u>r</u>ge in the Word menu, Word presents these mail merge options:

▶ *Form Letters.* This is the traditional use of mail merge. Each selected row in an Excel list can be used to fill in the blanks of a form letter. One letter is printed for each row in the list.

▶ *Mailing Labels.* Word provides excellent tools you can use in formatting data to print on standard sizes of labels. One row of data prints on each mailing label.

▶ *Envelopes.* If you need to print envelopes, Word provides easy-to-use help for positioning addresses and feeding envelope documents.

▶ *Catalog.* You can use the Catalog feature to print an employee directory, sales catalog, or other list.

In the example that follows, you learn how to import Excel data in catalog format. Word's mail merge provides a Data Source option to select from a variety of databases. Figure 29.15 shows the different options you can use to access data in an Excel database.

Fig. 29.15
Word's mail merge options enable you to import Excel data into a Word document.

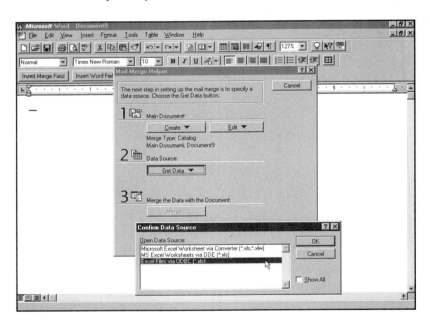

In this example, Excel File via ODBC is selected to obtain data from an Excel workbook named BOOK2.XLS. As shown in figure 29.16, the Excel workbook contains a named range EmployeeList.

After the named range EmployeeList is selected, Word provides an Insert Merge Field button that can be used to add fields from the Excel list to the Word mail merge document.

Figure 29.17 shows the fields you can select from when you click the Insert Merge Field button.

Fig. 29.16

You can select an Excel named range as a Word mail merge data source.

Fig. 29.17

The mail merge toolbar provides a drop-down menu you can use to add Excel fields to a Word document.

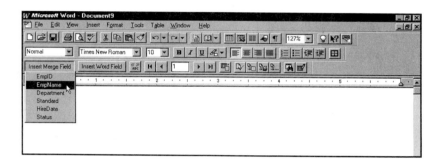

After the fields are added to the Word document, they display as merge fields, as shown in figure 29.18.

Fig. 29.18

Merge fields are displayed with field names in a Word document.

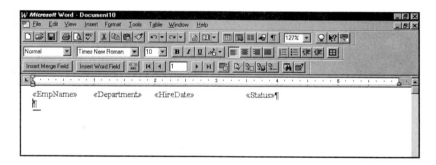

You can control how data in merge fields is formatted. Without formatting the example merge fields shown in figure 29.18, the department field displays in Word with one decimal place and the hire date field displays with the date and time. In the Excel worksheet, department does not contain a decimal and time is not a part of hire date. To change the formatting of the merge fields to match the way they are displayed in Excel, follow these steps:

1. Select the merge field in Word.

2. Right-click the field and choose the menu option Toggle Field Codes.

3. Add a formatting switch to the field code, as shown in figure 29.19.

Fig. 29.19

You can add switches to Word field codes.

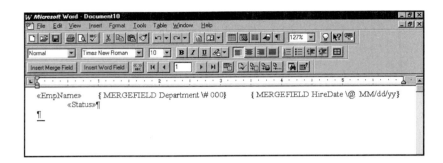

The \# switch changes the format of a number. In the department field shown in figure 29.19, the format is changed to three numbers with leading zeroes and no decimal places.

To format a date, use the \@ switch. In figure 29.19, the hire date is formatted to display as month/day/year. With date formatting, you must use an uppercase M to represent month. Lowercase m is used in Word to represent minutes.

Use the Merge to New Document button on the Mail Merge toolbar to create the merged document. Figure 29.20 shows the merged catalog. The headings at the top of figure 29.20 were added after the merge.

Fig. 29.20

The catalog format in mail merge prints multiple rows of the Excel data as a list in the Word document.

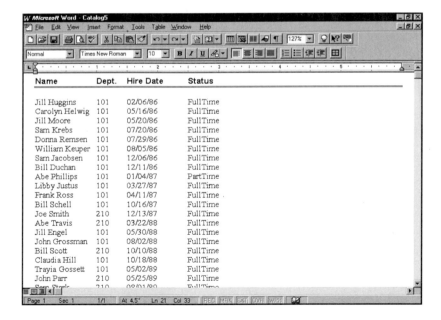

Using Mail Merge Query and Sort

Mail merge provides a query option. With query, you can filter and sort the data from Excel before Word inserts it into the merged document. Choose Tools, Mail Merge and click the Query button in the Mail Merge Helper dialog box. Figure 29.21 shows the Query Options dialog box with Department Equal to 210.

Fig. 29.21

Mail merge provides built-in query filter capabilities.

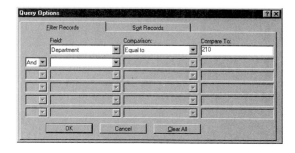

Mail merge can also sort the merged data. You can set the sort parameters by clicking the Query button on the Mail Merge Helper dialog box. As shown in figure 29.22, the merged data can be sorted by three fields, in ascending or descending order.

Fig. 29.22

Mail merge can sort source data before merging it with the Word document.

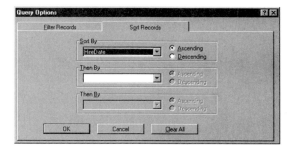

After the data is filtered to show only department 210 and sorted in ascending order by hire date, the merged document appears as shown in figure 29.23.

Fig. 29.23

Mail merge can print Excel data in catalog format.

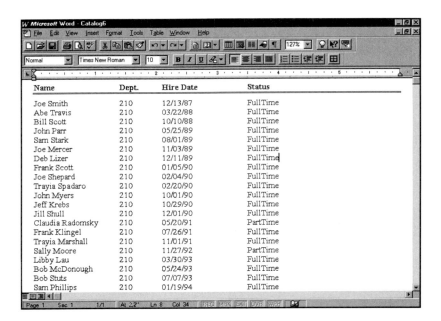

Inserting a Table of Contents in the Merged Document

Word's automatic table of contents can also be used with a mail merge catalog. After your Excel data has been merged into the Word catalog, you can add headings in Word.

In order to be used with a table of contents, the headings must use the standard Word heading styles Heading 1, Heading 2, and so on. After you add headings, you can use the Insert, Index and Tables command to add a table of contents at the beginning of your document. Figure 29.24 shows the table of contents for the catalog created in figure 29.23.

The flexibility of Word's mail merge creates many opportunities for you to develop reports from data in Excel. You can create catalogs with multiple lines of data for each row in an Excel list. Word provides the capability to prompt for user input at each line of the merged document. An If…Then option can be used to print merged data selectively, based on complex criteria that compares the values of two or more merge fields.

Fig. 29.24

Automatic table of contents can be added to a mail merge catalog.

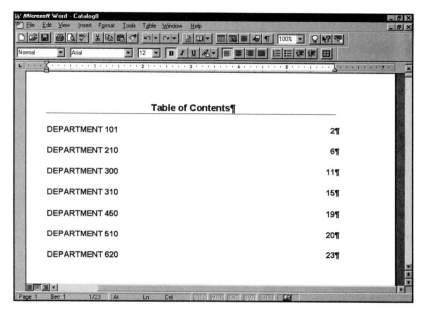

Automatically Creating a Word Document from Excel

You can save time and simplify a repetitive task by automating the interface between Excel and Word. You can design a Visual Basic for Applications procedure that can be run from a button on your Excel worksheet. When you click the button, Word creates a new document and Excel inserts data, charts, and PivotTables in the document. You won't need to remember each of the steps in creating the new document because all of the parameters and logic are stored in the Visual Basic for Applications procedure.

Controlling Word from Excel with OLE Automation

Object Linking and Embedding (OLE) automation is a tool you can use to control one application while you're in another application. OLE allows Excel to control Word with a Visual Basic for Applications procedure.

You can use the macro recorders in Excel and Word to help develop the Visual Basic for Applications code. The Excel macro recorder creates ready-to-run Visual Basic procedures. Word's macro recorder creates macros in WordBasic.

The other source of intelligence in an integrated Excel and Word application is a Word document template. The template can contain all of the formatting and positioning you need to create the new document. Templates make it easy to adjust the format and layout of the documents produced by the Visual Basic for Applications procedure. Visual Basic for Applications tells Word to insert certain data at marked positions in the template. The marks are called *bookmarks* and can be rearranged in the template with a few clicks of the mouse.

 Note

To create a bookmark in a Word template, choose Edit, Bookmark. Type a new bookmark name and click Add. Word adds a new bookmark.

You can test a bookmark by choosing Edit, Bookmark and selecting the bookmark name. When you click Go To in the Bookmark dialog box, Word moves the cursor to the bookmark you selected.

Creating a Report Template

The first step in building an application that prints a Word document from Excel is to create a document template in Word.

Figure 29.25 shows a template. The bookmark, named "Department," appears after the word Department in the second line of the template. The other bookmark on the document is named "ProductionTable." It is located below the word Table. In Word, you can choose Tools, Options, View to display bookmarks on the document as "I" shapes.

Creating a Pivot Table for the Word Report

Figure 29.26 shows a pivot table created in Excel. The Visual Basic for Applications procedure copies the Department number from cell B3 to the bookmark "Department" in the Word document. The pivot table range A5:F8 is copied to the bookmark named "ProductionTable." After the department number and pivot table are copied to Word, you can add text to the Word document and apply formatting such as frames and multiple columns.

Fig. 29.25

Bookmarks in a Word template mark the insertion point for Excel data.

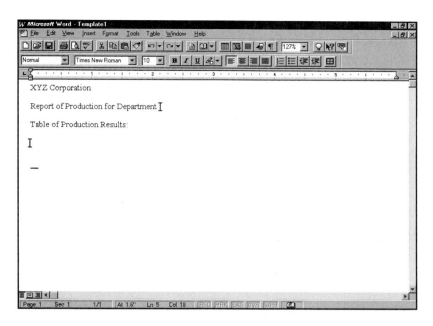

Fig. 29.26

An Excel pivot table can be used as a source of data for a Word report.

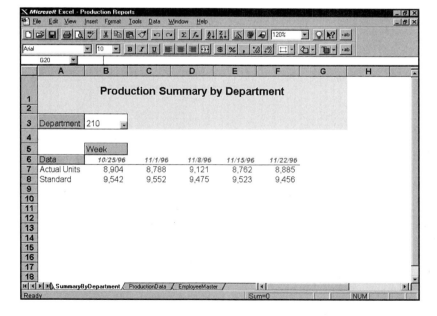

Writing the Visual Basic for Applications Procedure

The Word and Excel macro recorders can be your personal code writing assistants. Use Word's macro recorder as you copy data from Excel to the Word document. You can then use Excel's macro recorder as you perform the same procedures.

Figure 29.27 shows the code recorded by the Word macro recorder. The macro starts with the Sub statement. The first action in the macro is to move to the beginning of the document with the StartOfDocument command. Then the EditGoTo command moves to the first bookmark. The Excel department number is pasted into the document with the EditPasteSpecial command. The process repeats for the next bookmark to paste the pivot table range at the bookmark named "ProductionTable." The last action in the macro is to print the document with FilePrint command.

Fig. 29.27

Word's macro recorder can produce the WordBasic code needed to insert data into a Word template.

```
Sub MAIN
StartOfDocument

EditGoTo .Destination = "Department"

EditPasteSpecial .IconNumber = 1, .Link = 0, .DisplayIcon = 0, .Class =
"Excel.Sheet.5", .DataType = "Text", .IconFilename =
"C:\MSOffice\Excel\excel.exe", .Caption = "Microsoft Excel Worksheet"

EditGoTo .Destination = "ProductionTable"

EditPasteSpecial .IconNumber = 1, .Link = 0, .DisplayIcon = 0, .Class =
"Excel.Sheet.5", .DataType = "RTF", .IconFilename =
"C:\MSOffice\Excel\excel.exe", .Caption = "Microsoft Excel Worksheet"

FilePrint .AppendPrFile = 0, .Range = "0", .PrToFileName = "", .From =
"", .To = "", .Type = 0, .NumCopies = "1", .Pages = "", .Order = 0,
.PrintToFile = 0, .Collate = 1, .FileName = ""

End Sub
```

Figure 29.28 shows the code recorded by Excel's macro recorder. The Excel macro recorder captures the action of selecting the department number and copying it to the Clipboard. Excel does not record the paste action because it happens in Word. The next action that the Excel macro recorder sees is selecting the range of pivot table cells and copying that data to the Clipboard.

Listing 29.1 combines the code from Excel and Word to produce an Excel Visual Basic procedure that will create the Word document. The procedure inserts the department number and pivot table data at the bookmarks in the Word document and then prints the document.

Fig. 29.28

Excel's macro recorder can create VBA code for copying the pivot table page field and data values.

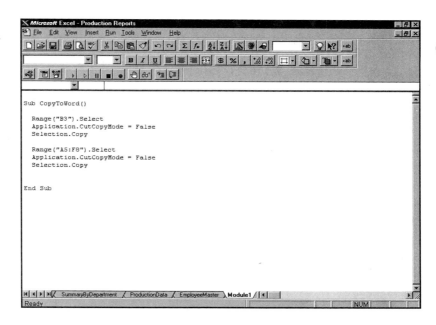

Listing 29.1 - Excel Visual Basic for Applications Procedure to Print PivotTable in Word Document

```
Sub CopyToWord()
  Dim wrdbas As Object
  Application.ActivateMicrosoftApp xlMicrosoftWord
  Set wrdbas = CreateObject("Word.Basic")
  wrdbas.filenew ThisWorkbook.Path & "\PrintPivot.dot", 0

  Range("B3").Select
  Application.CutCopyMode = False
  Selection.Copy

  wrdbas.StartOfDocument
  wrdbas.EditGoTo Destination:="Department"
  wrdbas.EditPaste

  Range("A5:F8").Select
  Application.CutCopyMode = False
  Selection.Copy

  wrdbas.EditGoTo Destination:="ProductionTable"
  wrdbas.EditPaste

  wrdbas.FilePrint

  Set wrdbas = Nothing

End Sub
```

The first four lines of the procedure in listing 29.1 create the connection to Word and open a new file based on the template named PrintPivot.dot. The `Application.ActivateMicrosoftApp xlMicrosoftWord` statement opens Word if it is not already open and makes it the active window. This step makes Word visible to you as the new document is being built. After the document is complete, you can choose to save or discard it. When you close Word, the Excel window once again becomes active.

`Set wrdbas = CreateObject("Word.Basic")` creates a reference to Word. Each of the Word actions in the procedure is prefixed by `wrdbas`. The next statement starts with `wrdbas.filenew` and uses the Word `filenew` statement to create a new document based on the template.

The next statements in listing 29.1 are combinations of the Word macro and Excel macro code. Notice that the `.Destination =` WordBasic code in Word must be modified to `Destination :=` in the Visual Basic for Applications procedure. The process of combining Excel and Word features will become less complicated when future versions of Word use the Visual Basic for Applications language.

The last statement in the procedure is `Set wrdbas = Nothing`. This statement breaks the connection between Excel and Word.

Figure 29.29 shows the completed Word document with department and pivot table data inserted at the bookmark locations.

Fig. 29.29

The Word report contains headings and a copy of the Excel pivot table.

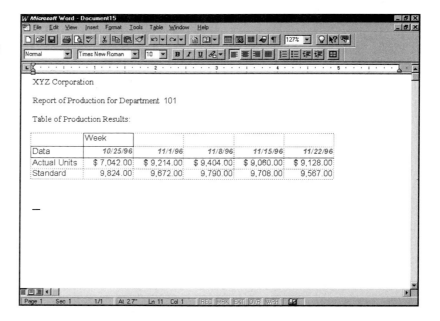

If you assign the Excel Visual Basic for Applications procedure to a button on the PivotTable worksheet, printing the PivotTable in Word can be as easy as clicking the mouse. This replaces the complex procedure of selecting data in Excel and copying it to Word. If you need to print Word reports for many department numbers, the Visual Basic for Applications procedure can save you a substantial amount of time.

Printing a Pivot Table Report in Word

The previous section describes how to create a simple report in Word with OLE automation and VBA. This section demonstrates how you can put these tools to use to prepare a more sophisticated report.

The report prepared in this section prints a copy of an Excel pivot table for each combination of page field values. You can create a similar report in Excel by right-clicking a cell in a pivot table and choosing the ShowPages menu option. The Word report described below includes these enhancements to the Excel version:

▶ Support for multiple page fields. The Excel version is limited to one page field.

▶ Automatic creation of title page and table of contents.

▶ Subtotal pivot tables for each combination of page fields. The subtotal pivot tables are shown as subheadings in the table of contents.

▶ Ability to select a pivot table before running the report. This feature is useful if you have more than one pivot table on a worksheet.

▶ User input of report title and subtitle using the InputBox method.

▶ Error checking with error messages displayed in a message box.

Creating a Pivot Table in Excel

Figure 29.30 shows a pivot table of sales results by Location, Unit, and Division. The Excel workbook that contains the pivot table is included as file PIVOTPRINT_8.XLS on the CD-ROM that accompanies this book. This file also contains the complete VBA code listing for the example report. To experiment with the example file, copy the workbook file and the Word template file TABLEDOC.DOT to a folder on your system. You can run the example with the sample data that is provided or you can copy the module page in the example workbook to one of your workbooks and run the report using your pivot table data. The VBA procedures and Word template will work with any pivot table.

Fig. 29.30

An Excel pivot table with two page fields is used to produce a report in Word.

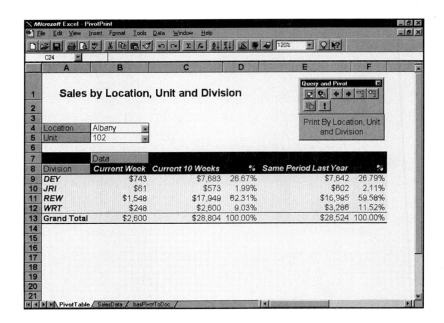

The button labeled Print By Location, Unit and Division beneath the toolbar in figure 29.30 calls the Visual Basic for Application procedures described below.

Checking to See If a Pivot Table Is Selected

When you click the button shown in figure 29.30, a VBA procedure checks to see that a pivot table has been selected. If the active cell is not in a pivot table, the error message shown in figure 29.31 appears.

Fig. 29.31

An error message appears if a pivot table has not been selected.

The VBA procedure that displays the error message is shown in the following code. In the procedure, a For Each loop cycles through each pivot table on the ActiveWorksheet. If the active cell on the worksheet is contained within a pivot table, pvtSelected is assigned to that pivot table.

```
'Check to see if pivot table is selected
  Set pvtSelected = Nothing
  Set wksSelected = ActiveSheet
  For Each pvtWork In wksSelected.PivotTables
    If Intersect(ActiveCell, pvtWork.TableRange2) Is Nothing Then
      ' next statement
```

```
      Else
        Set pvtSelected = pvtWork
        Exit For
      End If
  Next pvtWork
```

The `Intersect` function tests to see if the `ActiveCell` is in the `TableRange2` of the pivot table. `TableRange2` is the range of cells that contains both the data and page fields of the pivot table. If a pivot table is not selected, the following statements display an error message and exit the procedure.

```
  If pvtSelected Is Nothing Then
    MsgBox "You must select a cell in a pivot table before starting this Macro.", _
      vbInformation
    GoTo PivotToDoc_Exit
  End If
```

Using *InputBox* to Capture Report Titles

In the next section of code, the `InputBox` method is used to prompt for titles for the Word report. Figures 29.32 and 29.33 show the `InputBox` prompts as they appear on-screen.

Fig. 29.32

InputBox *prompts user for report title.*

Fig. 29.33

InputBox *prompts user for report subtitle.*

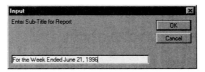

The VBA procedure used to prompt for the titles is shown next. If the Cancel button is selected in either of the dialog boxes, the `InputBox` statement returns a value of false and the `MsgBox` statement displays a message before exiting the procedure. `srtTitle` and `strSubTitle` are string variables used to store user input.

```
    'prompt user for report titles
    strTitle = Application.InputBox(prompt:="Enter Title for Report",
      default:="Pivot Table Summary Report")
    If strTitle = False Then
      MsgBox "Pivot Table Printing Cancelled"
      Exit Sub
    End If
    strSubTitle = Application.InputBox(prompt:="Enter Sub-Title for Report",
      default:=Date)
```

```
If strSubTitle = False Then
  MsgBox "Pivot Table Printing Cancelled"
  Exit Sub
End If
```

Connecting to Word

The next segment of code connects to Word. In this example, the Word document will be active at the completion of the procedure, and you can use Word to modify and print the finished report.

The following code activates Word so its window is on top of Excel's. As shown in figure 29.34, the window for Word is resized so you can see the Excel application behind it.

```
'create connection to Word
  Application.ActivateMicrosoftApp xlMicrosoftWord
  Set wrdbas = CreateObject("Word.Basic")
  With wrdbas
    .Filenew ThisWorkbook.Path & "\TableDoc.Dot", 0
    .AppRestore
    .AppSize 407, 327
    .AppMove 33, 84
```

The `CreateObject` method is used to start Word, and the variable `wrdBas` becomes the link to all Word features. The `.Filenew` statement opens a new document based on the template `TableDoc.Dot`. This template, which must be stored in the same directory as the Excel file, contains bookmarks used to insert the titles and tables. A copy of the template is included on the CD-ROM that accompanies this book.

Fig. 29.34

The VBA macro positions Word's window on top of Excel's window.

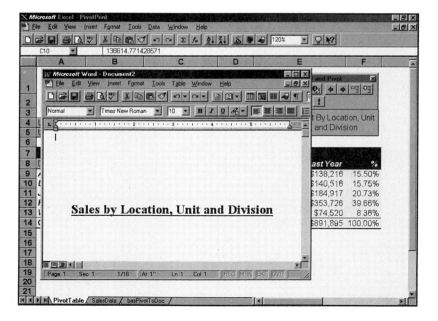

Creating an Array of Page Fields

The report will contain a copy of the pivot table for every combination of the Location and Unit page fields. To control the process of changing values in page fields, this example creates an array that stores page field values. The array also stores a Word heading style used to insert headings for each pivot table in the Word document. Word uses the heading styles to build the table of contents.

The following code segment uses a For Each loop to obtain the name of each page field in the selected pivot table. The variable iintLoop is used to assign the page fields to the array.

```
'Create array of page fields

    ReDim atypPageField(pvtSelected.PageRange.Rows.Count)
    iintLoop = 1
    For Each rngWork In pvtSelected.PageRange.Rows
      Set atypPageField(iintLoop).pvfPageField =
        pvtSelected.PivotFields(rngWork.Cells(1).Value)
      atypPageField(iintLoop).strWordStyle = "Heading " & iintLoop
      iintLoop = iintLoop + 1
    Next rngWork
```

The array atypPageField is an array of user defined type. Each element of the array contains a pvtPageField and a strWordStyle. The array and user defined type are defined at the top of the module page:

```
Type typPageField
    pvfPageField As PivotField
    strWordStyle As String
End Type

Dim atypPageField() As typPageField
```

The array atypPageField is used to control the process of changing page field values and copying the pivot table to Word. The following code calls the FirstPageField procedure, which loops through the page field values in the array and prints the pivot tables. After the pivot tables are printed, the procedure prints the report titles and table of contents.

```
'loop through page fields and print table

    .StartOfDocument
    .editgoto Destination:="StartTables"
    Call FirstPageField
    .StartOfDocument
    .editgoto Destination:="TitleText"
    .Insert strTitle
    .insertpara
    .editgoto Destination:="SubTitleText"
    .Insert strSubTitle
    .insertpara
    .InsertPageBreak
    .Insert "Table of Contents"
```

```
        .inserttableofcontents
        .StartOfDocument
End With
```

The `.StartOfDocument` and `.EditGoTo` commands at the beginning of the code move the insertion point in Word to the bookmark named StartTables. The `FirstPageField` procedure calls the subroutines that print the headings and tables.

The next `.EditGoTo` and `.Insert` statements are used to insert the title and subtitle at the bookmark locations defined in the TABLEDOC.DOT template file.

The `.InsertTableOfContents` statement starts Word's automatic indexing features. Word builds a table of contents that includes all text entries in the standard heading styles.

Sample pages from the completed Word document are shown in figures 29.35, 29.36, and 29.37.

Fig. 29.35

The title page contains the title and subtitle text collected with the InputBox *statements. The text is inserted at bookmarks set in the template document.*

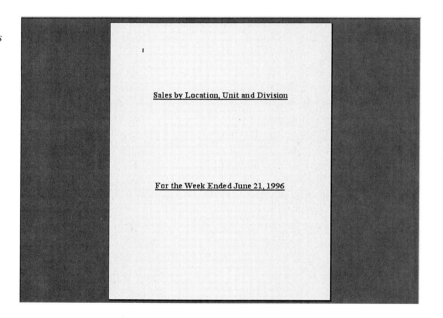

Each pivot table copy in the body of the document is preceded by headings that contain page field values. In the example shown in figure 29.37, the Charlotte Location heading is inserted in Heading style 1. This heading is the major heading used by the table of contents. The heading 101 Unit is inserted as Heading style 2 and appears as a sub item in the table of contents.

This example has demonstrated some advanced techniques using OLE automation and VBA to create a sophisticated report in Word. To apply these techniques to your applications, you can begin by studying the complete VBA code example contained on the CD-ROM.

Fig. 29.36

The table of contents lists each Location and within Location lists each Division. It contains a page number that shows where you can find each table in the body of the document.

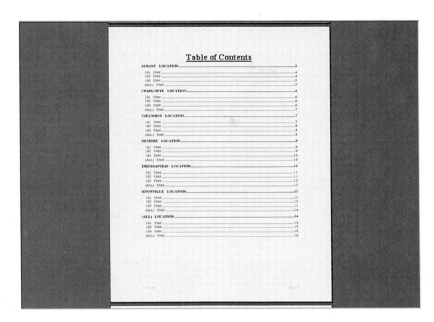

Fig. 29.37

The body of the Word document contains headings and copies of the pivot table.

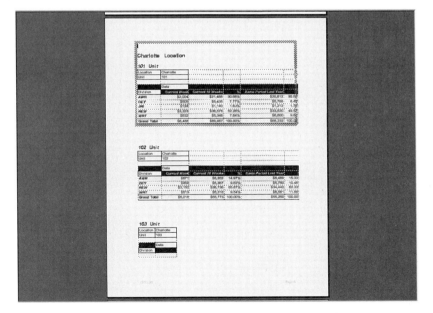

Summary

In this chapter you have learned how to combine Excel and Word features by linking, copying, and embedding data from Excel into Word. The chapter explored methods of inserting text and tables from Word into Excel. You learned how to use Word's powerful mail merge feature to include Excel data in a Word catalog. The last example in the chapter explored the use of OLE automation and Visual Basic for Applications to automate the transfer of data between Excel and Word.

From here, you can learn more about writing Excel Visual Basic for Applications code in Chapter 5, "Customized Applications." Word Basic code is explained in Chapter 8, "Word Macros."

The linking and embedding skills you learned with Word and Excel are applied to other combinations of applications in Chapters 30 through 34. Chapter 28, "Critical Skills for Integrating Applications," provides more background on linking, embedding, and OLE automation with Visual Basic for Applications.

chapter 30

Integrating Excel and Access

30

by Conrad Carlberg

In this chapter

◆ **Analyzing Access Data with Excel**
This section shows you how to automate the creation of a pivot table using data from an Access database.

◆ **Importing data from Access with XLODBC.XLA**
The XLODBC.XLA Add-In retrieves data from Access databases, regardless of whether you are using Excel 5 or Excel 95.

◆ **Importing data from Access with DAO (Data Access Objects)**
DAO is faster than XLODBC.XLA, but you must use Excel 95.

◆ **Creating a new database with DAO**
In this section, you learn how to create a new Access database from within Excel 95.

I f you've ever tried to use Excel as a database manager, you'll appreciate being able to integrate it with Access. Suppose that you have a database of any appreciable size. It's comparatively clumsy to store that database in one Excel location, and to copy records that meet certain criteria for analysis in another Excel location. It's *much* easier to store the entire database in Access, and to retrieve specific records to Excel as needed.

When you take advantage of the integration capabilities of Excel and Access, it's much more common to do your work in the Excel environment. While you frequently need to bring data from Access into Excel for analysis, you rarely need to bring the results of an Excel analysis into Access. Therefore, this chapter focuses on interacting with Access from the Excel context.

Office provides both interactive and automated methods for bringing Access data into Excel. In this chapter, you see how to create a pivot table based on data you retrieve from Access, both interactively and by means of VBA. You also learn how to use VBA to bring Access data into Excel in the familiar list format. Finally, you see how you can use VBA to create a new Access database, and to populate it with data from an Excel worksheet.

Analyzing Access Data with Excel

The entire point of integrating Excel with Access is to take advantage of the analytic tools in Excel and the storage and retrieval tools in Access. The most straightforward way of doing this is to pull data from an Access database into an Excel pivot table.

You can do this interactively and manually without opening any add-ins, or establishing any library references from the PivotTable Wizard.

Alternatively, you can automate the process of retrieving the data and creating the pivot table by means of VBA. This section describes both approaches.

Using Data in Access to Create a Pivot Table in Excel

Suppose that you have an Access database that is updated from time to time. This database contains, among other information, data on a customer name, type of product purchased, equipment parts in each product, your cost for the parts, and the list price paid to you for the parts. The layout of this database, CHAP30.MDB, is shown in figure 30.1. You can find CHAP30.MDB on the companion CD.

Notice that the database is relational, with the joins indicated by the arrows between its tables.

If you have worked your way through this book's section on Access, you are familiar with the concept of queries. CHAP30.MDB has a query defined, named InstalledBase. You can use the PivotTable Wizard to connect to this query and return the data to Excel in a pivot table format. To do so, follow these steps:

1. From an empty Excel worksheet, start the PivotTable Wizard by clicking its toolbar button or choosing <u>D</u>ata, <u>P</u>ivotTable.

2. In Step 1 of the PivotTable Wizard, choose <u>E</u>xternal Data Source. When you click Next, Step 2 appears. This version of Step 2 is different from the Step 2 that's associated with the default data source (<u>M</u>icrosoft Excel List or Database); see figure 30.2.

Fig. 30.1

You can query this Access database and return information directly into an Excel pivot table.

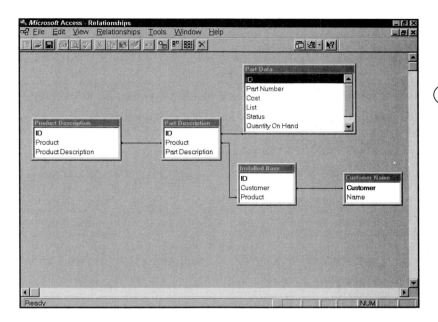

30

Fig. 30.2

When you choose an external data source, the PivotTable Wizard takes you to Microsoft Query.

   3. Click <u>G</u>et Data. Query starts and prompts you to select a data source, as shown in figure 30.3.

Fig. 30.3

The available data sources depend on which ODBC drivers you chose to install from the Office CD or disks.

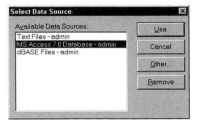

4. Double-click MS Access 7.0 Database—Admin, or highlight it and choose Use. CHAP30.MDB is an Access database.

5. The Select Database dialog box appears. Use it to navigate to the location on your disk where you installed CHAP30.MDB from the companion CD. Select the database, and choose OK.

6. The Add Tables dialog box appears. Its Table list box includes any tables and queries defined for the database. Because the query named InstalledBase contains the desired joins among the tables, select it in the Table list box. Click Add, then choose Close (see fig. 30.4).

Fig. 30.4

The InstalledBase Query box contains fields from different tables in the database.

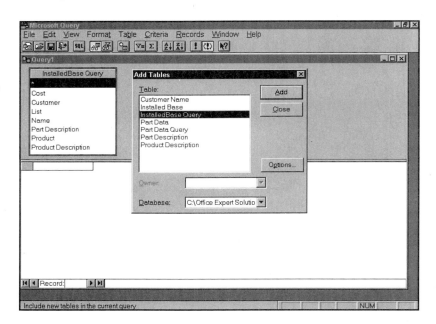

7. Click the drop-down box in the Query window's data pane. The drop-down displays the fields available to the InstalledBase query. Click Name to display in the data pane a column containing the customers' names (see fig. 30.5).

8. A new field column and drop-down appears in the data pane. Continue to choose fields from the query until you have Customer, Product Description, Part Description, Cost, and List.

9. Choose File, Return Data to Microsoft Excel. You are returned to Step 2 of the PivotTable Wizard. Click Next. Query will return the data to Excel, and you can now complete the PivotTable Wizard as usual.

Fig. 30.5
When you choose a field from a table or query, its records appear in the current column drop-down box.

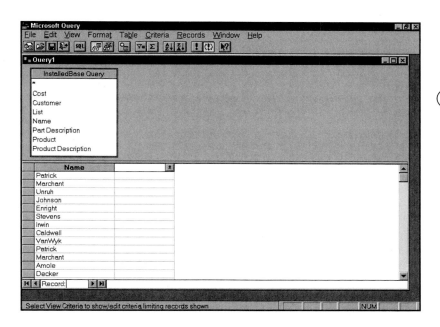

To obtain the pivot table shown in figure 30.6, set Name as the row field, Product Description as the column field, and both Cost and List as data fields.

	A	B	C	D	E	F
1			Product Description			
2	Name	Data	Key System	Modem, External	Modem, Internal	Grand Total
3	Amole	Sum of Cost	0	571.37	288.15	859.52
4		Sum of List	0	697.94	290.59	988.53
5	Beatty	Sum of Cost	122.27	0	288.15	410.42
6		Sum of List	147.27	0	290.59	437.86
7	Caldwell	Sum of Cost	0	571.37	288.15	859.52
8		Sum of List	0	697.94	290.59	988.53
9	Decker	Sum of Cost	0	571.37	288.15	859.52
10		Sum of List	0	697.94	290.59	988.53
11	Enright	Sum of Cost	0	1142.74	0	1142.74
12		Sum of List	0	1395.88	0	1395.88
13	French	Sum of Cost	0	571.37	288.15	859.52
14		Sum of List	0	697.94	290.59	988.53
15	Goddard	Sum of Cost	0	0	576.3	576.3
16		Sum of List	0	0	581.18	581.18
17	Hawthorne	Sum of Cost	0	0	576.3	576.3
18		Sum of List	0	0	581.18	581.18
19	Irwin	Sum of Cost	0	571.37	288.15	859.52
20		Sum of List	0	697.94	290.59	988.53

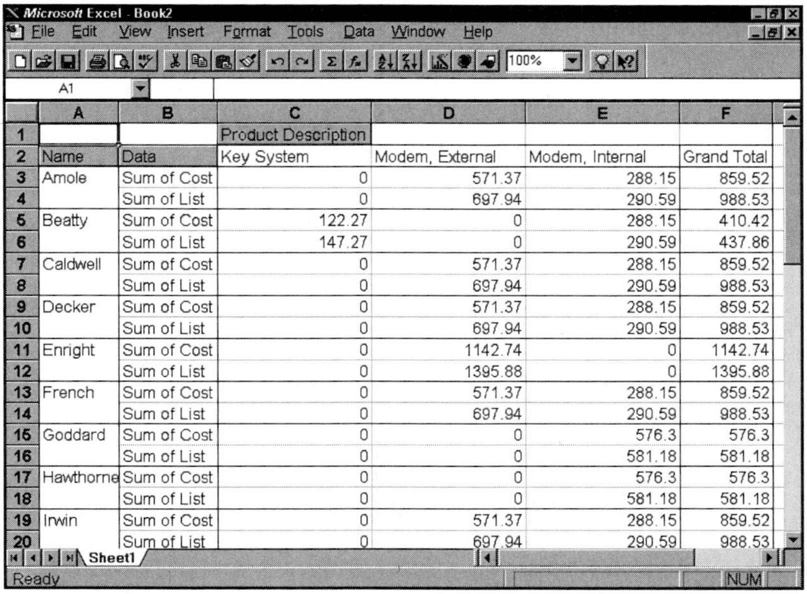

Fig. 30.6
The pivot table automatically analyzes the data that you store in an external data source.

If you were to perform this analysis only once, it would be best to do it interactively and manually as described in this section. But if you wanted to determine your profitability, by customer and by product line on a regular basis, it's much faster to turn the work over to VBA. This process is described in the next section.

Making a Pivot Table from an Access Database with VBA

This chapter describes several methods to move data back and forth between Excel workbooks and Access databases by means of VBA. Placing data into an Excel pivot table is one such method, but it has one direction only: into Excel. You cannot, using VBA (or manually, for that matter), send data directly from an Excel pivot table into an Access database.

If a pivot table is limited in terms of connectivity, it more than makes up for it in terms of flexibility. And, with VBA, you can make the process of pulling data from an external database into a pivot table *much* faster.

Below is the VBA code that replicates the process described in the previous section. You would want to use code such as this if you routinely create a pivot table that is based each time on the same external database fields. The code is found in the module named ImportViaPivotTable in the CHAP30.XLS file on the companion CD.

```
Option Explicit

Sub ImportFromAccessViaPivotTable()
Dim DataSource As String
Dim SQLSelect As String
Dim SQLFrom As String
Dim DatabaseName As String
```

The subroutine begins by declaring a few string variables. These will comprise:

- ▶ Information for the connection string, such as the type of database and the user ID (DataSource).
- ▶ The fields to choose from the query (SQLSelect).
- ▶ The name of the query from which the fields will be obtained (SQLFrom).
- ▶ The name of and path to the external database (DatabaseName).

Placing this information in separate string variables makes it much easier to construct and subsequently edit the command that actually retrieves the data.

The screen is frozen to speed up execution, and the string variable *DatabaseName* is assigned its value in the next two statements:

```
Application.ScreenUpdating = False
DatabaseName = ThisWorkbook.Path & "\Chap30.mdb"
```

Note the value assigned to *DatabaseName*. `ThisWorkbook` is a property of the `Application` object, and it identifies the workbook where the VBA code exists. This is a useful way to specify the workbook when another workbook is active. The `Path` property returns the fully qualified path to `ThisWorkbook`, but does not end in a backslash. Therefore, the final backslash is provided in the string that contains the name of the database. The assumption is that the database is in the same directory as the workbook containing the VBA code.

```
DataSource = "DSN=MS Access 7.0 Database;DBQ=" & DatabaseName & _
     ";DriverId=25;FIL=MS Access;UID=admin; "
```

The *DataSource* string, also called the *connection string*, specifies how to establish the database connection. It can be a little confusing. Its components are:

▶ The DSN keyword identifies the data source: this is not the database, but the driver for the desired database.

▶ The DBQ keyword identifies the path to and name of the database itself, so it is assigned *DatabaseName*—as described earlier, this variable contains both the path and the name.

▶ The FIL keyword specifies the database type. In this case, it is MS Access. If the database were, for example, a dBASE file, then the FIL keyword might be DBASE3, DBASE4, or DBASE5.

▶ The DriverID keyword specifies an integer ID for the driver. The integer ID for the Access driver is 25; for Paradox 4, it would be 282; and for Paradox 5, it would be 538.

Tip

For a full list of DriverIDs, open the file named ODBCJET.HLP and search for the DriverID keyword. It is installed on your computer by the Office Pro Setup routine, and you can then open it directly from the Explorer.

▶ The UID keyword specifies the user login ID to access the database.

Note

If you create a pivot table manually using an external data source, and during the process record a VBA macro, the resulting code will probably contain additional information in the connection string. The macro recorder provides information that is not strictly necessary to establish the connection.

```
SQLSelect = "SELECT 'InstalledBase Query'.Name, " & _
    "'InstalledBase Query'.'Product Description', " & _
    "'InstalledBase Query'.'Part Description', " & _
    "'InstalledBase Query'.Cost, 'InstalledBase Query'.List "
```

The SQLSelect string specifies which fields in a database table or database query are to be accessed.

```
SQLFrom = "FROM '" & DatabaseName & "'.'InstalledBase Query'"
```

The SQLFrom string defines the name of the table or query in the database from which the data is to be returned.

After the strings have been defined, they are provided to the active sheet's PivotTableWizard method:

```
ActiveSheet.PivotTableWizard SourceType:=xlExternal, SourceData:= _
    Array(DataSource, SQLSelect, SQLFrom), _
    TableDestination:="R1C1", TableName:="CostsAndLists"
```

Notice that they are provided as an array, using the Array function in the named argument SourceData. There are several reasons to do it in this fashion, but two of the most important are the length of the strings and the structure of the resulting SQL statement.

You cannot pass a string that contains more than 255 characters to an Excel object. If the SourceData argument is longer than 255 characters, then the PivotTableWizard method will fail.

But if you pass several strings as an array, their combined length can be greater than 255 characters—so long as each individual string is no longer than 255 characters. After they have been passed, as an array, the strings are combined into one SQL statement that might well be longer than 255 characters.

The second reason for passing the strings as an array has to do with delimiting the different parts of the SQL statement. Suppose that you create the pivot table by hand. During that process, in Query, you have chosen the table or query in the database and have selected the fields that you want to return to Excel. At this point, you can click the SQL toolbar button to view the SQL statement that Query has built. When you do so, you see that the Select and From portions of the statement appear on different lines (see fig. 30.7).

And if you use the macro recorder to create the VBA code that will replicate the process, you find that it returns some special characters, embedded in the SQL statement. These are the delimiters that cause the different portions of the full SQL statement to appear on different lines. You will have a very difficult time replicating these characters in your own VBA code.

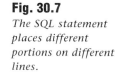

Fig. 30.7

The SQL statement places different portions on different lines.

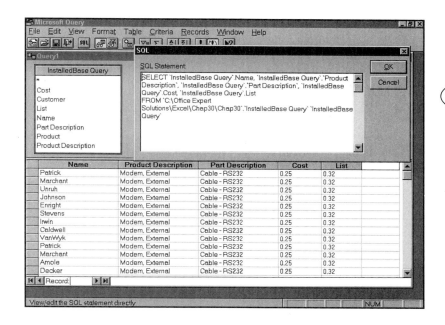

But if you pass the different portions of the full statement as elements in an array (by means of the Array function), the fact that they are in different array elements provides the required delimiters.

The final portion of the VBA code structures the pivot table. This code replicates the actions that you would take in Step 3 of the PivotTable Wizard: assigning fields as rows, columns, or data fields.

```
With ActiveSheet.PivotTables("CostsAndLists")
    .AddFields RowFields:=Array("Name", "Product Description", "Data")
    With .PivotFields("Cost")
        .Orientation = xlDataField
        .Position = 1
    End With
    .PivotFields("List").Orientation = xlDataField
End With

End Sub
```

Using code such as this, you can quickly create a new pivot table. Ordinarily, you would base the pivot table on an Access database that has different information than it did when you last examined its data.

Importing Data from Access with XLODBC.XLA

Both Excel 5 and Excel 95 provide an add-in file named XLODBC.XLA. This add-in defines some ODBC (Open Database Connectivity) objects that you can use to control an ODBC database; examples of these objects include `SQLOpen` to open a channel to the database, `SQLExecQuery` to submit a query to the database, and `SQLRetrieve` to return the data from the database.

Excel 95, but not Excel 5, provides a DAO (Data Access Objects) library containing objects that execute faster than those in XLODBC.XLA. DAO offers all the functionality found in XLODBC.XLA, and more. If you're using Excel 95, and if you can be sure that any users who run your VBA code are using Excel 95, you should use DAO for ODBC database access.

But if you or any of your users run Excel 5, you should use XLODBC.XLA as a means of ODBC database access. For DAO to work, you need to be using Excel 95.

Before you can run code that uses the objects provided by XLODBC.XLA, you need to take two sequential steps:

1. Choose Tools, Add-Ins. In the Add-Ins Available list box, select ODBC Add-In, and then choose OK.
2. Switch to the module that has, or will have, the code that makes use of the objects provided by XLODBC.XLA. Choose Tools, References. In the Available References list box, check XLODBC.XLA and choose OK. This makes the add-in's objects available to the code in the module.

Now you're ready to run the code that returns data to an Excel worksheet by a direct ODBC connection. Here's an example found in the module named `ImportViaXLODBC` in the CHAP30.XLS file on the companion CD. This example code uses the NORTHWIND.MDB file that accompanies Access as its database.

The first few statements in the subroutine declare two string variables, for the reasons described in the prior section:

```
Option Explicit
Sub ImportDataViaXLODBCXLA()

Dim DatabaseName As String
Dim SQLQueryString As String
Dim ConnectionNumber As Integer
Dim OutputRange As Range
Dim StartTime As Variant, StopTime As Variant, ElapsedTime As Variant
```

A variable that will contain a connection number is also declared, as is an object variable that defines the range that will contain the returned data. The *StartTime*, *StopTime*, and *ElapsedTime* variables are used to measure the macro's speed of execution; they can be used as a comparison with the speed of a macro that uses DAO instead of XLODBC.XLA.

```
Application.ScreenUpdating = False
DatabaseName = "C:\MSOffice\Access\Samples\NorthWind.mdb"
SQLQueryString = "SELECT * FROM Products"
StartTime = Timer
```

The screen is frozen to improve execution speed, and the query strings are assigned. The asterisk in *SQLQueryString* means to select all fields in the database's Products table. Then, *StartTime* is assigned the value of the Timer—the time that is current when the statement executes.

```
ConnectionNumber = SQLOpen("DSN=MS Access 7.0 Database; _
    DBQ=" & DatabaseName & ";")
```

The variable *ConnectionNumber* is assigned the result of the SQLOpen object from XLODBC.XLA. The argument to SQLOpen is the DSN for the database desired, and the DBQ for the database. Again, the DSN is simply the type of driver needed, and the DBQ is the path to and name of the database.

SQLOpen, an XLODBC.XLA object, establishes the path to the database via the appropriate driver, and opens a channel to the database. The channel is identified by an integer, which is assigned to *ConnectionNumber*.

Then, the connection number and the query string are passed to SQLExecQuery, another XLODBC.XLA object. The query does not actually retrieve the data to Excel—it just finds the information requested by the Select and From components of the query string:

```
SQLExecQuery ConnectionNumber, SQLQueryString
Set OutputRange = Worksheets("Sheet1").Range("A1")
SQLRetrieve ConnectionNumber, OutputRange, , , True
```

The output range is assigned to the worksheet named Sheet1, in cell A1. When retrieved, the data is written onto Sheet1 starting at cell A1. And the object SQLRetrieve is executed, using the connection number and the output range as arguments. This actually returns the data from the database into the Excel worksheet. Setting the fifth argument of SQLRetrieve to **True** returns the field names as well as their values; the field names are written to the first row of the output range.

```
StopTime = Timer
SQLClose ConnectionNumber
ElapsedTime = StopTime - StartTime
Cells(1, 12) = ElapsedTime
End Sub
```

The current value of the Timer is placed into *StopTime*, and the connection to the database is closed. The elapsed time between opening and closing the connection is calculated and placed in the first row, twelfth cell of the active worksheet. Then, the subroutine is terminated.

After running this code, the worksheet named Sheet1 should appear as shown in figure 30.8.

Fig. 30.8

Results returned from SQLRetrieve *include the field names.*

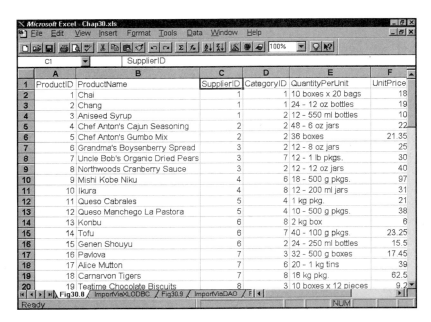

You might find it useful to compare the results in the Excel worksheet with the data in the database by opening it from Access. When you do so, notice that the SupplierId and CategoryID fields show the actual values that are contained in the table.

Because the code queries the Products table, rather than addressing a defined query as was done in the pivot table example, the relationships among the Products table and other tables are not invoked. Therefore, the Supplier name and the Category label are not returned.

Importing Data from Access with DAO

If you and any users of your code are running Excel 95 only, you'll find that it's nearly always faster to connect to Access databases using DAO instead of the objects provided by XLODBC.XLA. The code discussed in this section demonstrates one way to retrieve data from an Access database using DAO.

Before you can use DAO objects in your code, you must first establish a reference to the DAO Object Library. Switch to the module that has, or will have, the code that makes use of the DAO objects. Choose Tools, References. In the Available References list box, check Microsoft DAO 3.0 Object Library, and choose OK. This makes the DAO objects available to the code in the module. Notice that, in contrast to making XLODBC.XLA objects available, you need not load an add-in first before you establish DAO references.

The code that follows performs the same task as did the previous example: it returns the contents of the Products table in the NORTHWIND.MDB sample Access database. Although you will find that it does so faster than by using XLODBC.XLA objects, it does not retrieve the field names along with the records.

Again, to run this code successfully, you need to have the sample NORTHWIND.MDB database installed from the Office CD or disks, and installed in the path indicated in the code. The code can be found on the module named ImportViaDAO in the companion CD's file named CHAP30.XLS.

 Tip

To determine the objects supplied by the DAO library and their methods and properties, use the Object Browser after establishing a module's reference to the Microsoft DAO 3.0 Object Library.

The macro first declares several variables. DatabaseToOpen is declared as a Database, which is an object provided by the DAO library. The name of and the path to the database will be put in the string variable *DatabaseName*. The macro declares another variable, *RecordSetName*, as a Recordset—another DAO object.

```
Option Explicit

Sub ImportDataViaDAO()
Dim DatabaseToOpen As Database
Dim DatabaseName As String
Dim RecordSetName As Recordset
Dim OutputRange As Range
Dim StartTime As Variant, StopTime As Variant, Elapsed As Variant
```

The Recordset object defines how the data in a database is to be accessed. There are three types of Recordset objects:

▶ *Table Recordset.* This type of Recordset can be used to read from, add to, modify, or remove records in a *single* table. When you open a Table Recordset with the OpenRecordset method (see the following section), you set the RecordSet's type to dbOpenTable.

▶ *Dynaset Recordset.* This type of Recordset can be used for the same purposes as a Table Recordset, but you can use it on more than one table. A Dynaset is specified in the OpenRecordset method as dbOpenDynaset.

▶ *Snapshot Recordset.* A Snapshot also works on multiple tables, but you can use it only to read records.

The other variables, that will define the worksheet output range and that will be used to evaluate the macro's speed, are declared as in the prior example.

Note

Notice that the declaration section of the macro declares no SQL strings. Using the DAO objects instead means that you need not write the SQL commands yourself.

Then, the macro assigns the name of the database that will be opened, freezes the screen, and sets the value of *StartTime*:

```
DatabaseName = "C:\MSOffice\Access\Samples\NorthWind.mdb"
Application.ScreenUpdating = False
StartTime = Timer
```

Next, the object variable DatabaseToOpen is assigned by means of the OpenDatabase object. This object returns a reference to the database:

```
Set DatabaseToOpen = OpenDatabase(DatabaseName)
```

The database reference is used to define the RecordSet:

```
Set RecordSetName = DatabaseToOpen.OpenRecordset _
    (Name:="Products", Type:=dbOpenTable)
```

This statement sets the *RecordSetName* object to the Products table in the NORTHWIND.MDB database. Because the macro returns data from one table only, the Recordset Type is set to dbOpenTable.

Then, the output range on an Excel worksheet is assigned, and the records are actually retrieved:

```
Set OutputRange = Worksheets("DataReturnedByDAO").Range("A1")
OutputRange.CopyFromRecordset RecordSetName
```

The *CopyFromRecordset* method is an Excel method of the Range object. It returns the data from the Recordset that's provided as the method's argument. The method places into its Range the data from the Recordset.

Lastly, the macro sets the *StopTime*, calculates the elapsed time and writes it to the worksheet, closes the database, and ends:

```
StopTime = Timer
Elapsed = StopTime - StartTime
Cells(1, 12) = Elapsed

DatabaseToOpen.Close

End Sub
```

The results of the macro are shown in figure 30.9.

Fig. 30.9

Results returned by
`CopyFromRecordset`
do not include the
field names.

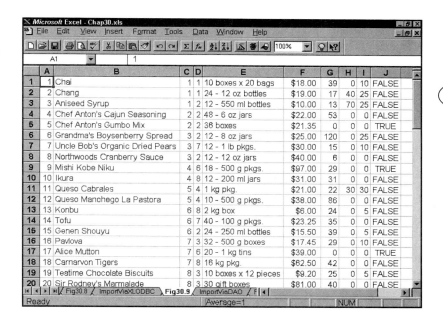

You should find, when you import records using DAO objects, that your code executes much faster than when you use XLODBC.XLA objects.

Creating a New Database with DAO

You can also use DAO to create and populate a new database. Suppose that you have the names and Social Security numbers of a group of employees on an Excel worksheet, and that you want to create an Access database that contains the worksheet data. You can do that without starting Access by means of VBA code that uses DAO.

The worksheet with the employee data is shown in figure 30.10.

If you install the Access Links Add-In, new items appear in the Data menu that enable you to use Access Forms and Reports, and to convert worksheet data to an Access database. However, this must be done interactively, and Access must be opened to create the database.

By using code similar to that discussed in this section, you can create and populate the database in one step. As usual, the code can be found in the module named `CreateDbWithDAO` in the companion disk's CHAP30.XLS file. And again, the module that contains the code must have a reference to the DAO library established.

Fig. 30.10

This data can be moved to a new Access database without choosing Data, Convert to Access.

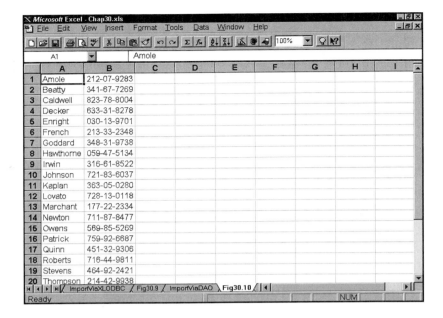

Several variables must be declared:

▶ *EmployeeDatabase* is declared as a `Database`, one of the DAO objects.

▶ *EmployeeTable* is initially declared as a generic object. Subsequently, it will be set to the result of the `CreateTableDef` method—thus representing a database table.

▶ *EmployeeRecordset* is declared as a Recordset, just as in the prior example.

▶ *EmployeeNumber*, *EmployeeName*, and *EmployeeSSN* are declared as generic objects. Subsequently, they will be set to the results of the `CreateField` method—thus representing fields in a table.

▶ *DatabaseName* is declared as a string. It holds the desired path to the database, as well as the database's name. *RecordCount* and *i*, both integers, will be used to control a loop that adds new records to the database.

```
Option Explicit

Sub CreateDbAndAddRecordsWithDAO()
Dim EmployeeDatabase As Database
Dim EmployeeTable As Object
Dim EmployeeRecordset As Recordset
Dim EmployeeNumber As Object
Dim EmployeeName As Object
Dim EmployeeSSN As Object
Dim DatabaseName As String
Dim RecordCount As Integer, i As Integer
```

After declaring the variables, the code assigns a path and name for the new database. It then checks to see whether a database with that name already exists in that path:

```
DatabaseName = ThisWorkbook.Path & "\Employees.mdb"
If FileExists(DatabaseName) Then
  ProcessFile DatabaseName
End If
```

The method that actually creates the database will fail if a file with the database's name already exists in the specified path. To prevent this, the UDF named FileExists is called with the path and file name as its argument. Its code is quite simple:

```
Function FileExists(FileName As String) As Boolean
    FileExists = False
    If Dir(FileName) <> "" Then FileExists = True
End Function
```

This Boolean UDF returns True if the VBA Dir function returns the name of the file that's specified in Dir's argument. The Dir function does so if that file exists in the path. (Remember: the argument *FileName* was assigned both the path and the file name.) If Dir returns anything other than a null string, a file with the specified name already exists in the path, and the function FileExists is set to **True**.

In the main subroutine, if FileExists returns **True**, the subroutine ProcessFile is called, also with *DatabaseName* as its argument:

```
Sub ProcessFile(FileName As String)
If MsgBox(Prompt:="Replace the database named " & FileName & "?", _
      Buttons:=vbYesNo, Title:="Filename found") = vbYes Then
   Kill FileName
Else
   MsgBox "OK, leaving " & FileName & " alone and ending the macro."
   End
End If
End Sub
```

The ProcessFile subroutine displays a message box, alerting the user that a file with the desired name for the database already exists in the path. The user can choose to delete the file (by means of the VBA Kill method), or to stop processing.

After ProcessFile has finished, either the user has opted to end processing or to delete the existing file from the disk. If the file is deleted, the main subroutine can continue. There is now no file on the disk to interfere with the CreateDatabase method.

```
Set EmployeeDatabase = CreateDatabase(Name:=DatabaseName, Locale:=dbLangGeneral)
```

The object variable *EmployeeDatabase* is set to the result of the CreateDatabase method. This method creates a new Database object with the path and name that's specified by its first argument. When the method has completed, the database is saved to the disk, and it returns an open database object to the variable *EmployeeDatabase*.

The CreateDatabase method's second argument is the Locale argument. This argument specifies the collating order that will be used for text comparisons. In this case, Locale is set to dbLangGeneral, which gives the proper collating order for six languages, including English.

 Note

You must supply the Locale argument, or the CreateDatabase method will fail.

Now that the database has been created, the code establishes a new table in the database, named Employee, and sets the object variable *EmployeeTable* to represent that table:

```
Set EmployeeTable = EmployeeDatabase.CreateTableDef("Employee")
```

The CreateTableDef method creates a new database table. However, it does not actually add the table to the database—that is done with the Append method. But appending the table to the database must be deferred until at least one field has been placed in the table. That's accomplished in the next With block:

```
With EmployeeTable
   Set EmployeeNumber = .CreateField("Employee Number", dbLong)
   .Fields.Append EmployeeNumber
   Set EmployeeName = .CreateField("Employee Name", dbText)
   .Fields.Append EmployeeName
   Set EmployeeSSN = .CreateField("Employee SSN", dbText)
   .Fields.Append EmployeeSSN
End With
```

The CreateField method establishes a new field. It's used three times in the With block to create an Employee Number field (that will contain a sequential number, not the Social Security number), the Employee Name field, and the Employee SSN field.

After the three fields are established with a field name and a data type, the code can append the table to the database:

```
EmployeeDatabase.TableDefs.Append EmployeeTable
```

Now that the database, its table, and the table's fields have been established, it's time to begin populating it with data records. The first step is to create a Recordset object:

```
Set EmployeeRecordset = EmployeeTable.OpenRecordset(dbOpenTable)
```

In contrast to the prior example, the OpenRecordset method as used here does not specify a source—just a type. Because the Recordset is based on the table, the source can be omitted. The Recordset applies to a single table, and it will be used to write records to the table, so the type to choose is dbOpenTable.

With the Recordset established, the code can start to move records from the worksheet to the database. This process begins by selecting the current region in the active worksheet and counting its rows. This count is used to terminate the For loop:

```
Selection.CurrentRegion.Select
RecordCount = Selection.Rows.Count
For i = 1 To RecordCount
    With EmployeeRecordset
        .AddNew
        .Fields("Employee Number").Value = i
        .Fields("Employee Name").Value = ActiveSheet.Cells(i, 1)
        .Fields("Employee SSN").Value = ActiveSheet.Cells(i, 2)
        .Update
    End With
Next i
```

Each time through the loop, the following events occur:

▶ The AddNew method clears a location termed the *copy buffer*, where record editing takes place.

▶ The value of the Employee Number field in the copy buffer is set to the counter, i.

▶ The values in columns A and B of the worksheet are copied to the copy buffer.

▶ The database itself is updated—in this case, the new record is written—from the copy buffer.

The loop terminates when the final data row on the worksheet has been written to the database. Then, the database is closed, and the subroutine ends:

```
EmployeeDatabase.Close

End Sub
```

Compared to the other examples in this chapter of exchanging data between Excel and Access, this is a lengthy subroutine. It may help to review the process briefly:

1. The necessary variables, particularly the object variables, are declared.

2. The disk is checked for an existing file with the same path and name as the one that's desired for the new database. If such a file exists, the user is given the choice of deleting it, or ending the macro.

3. The database is established, as is a table within the database. Once the table is established, its fields are created and appended to the table. And once the fields have been appended, the table can be appended to the database.

4. A Recordset is created, with the names and the data types required for each field.

5. The data is read from the worksheet, one row at a time, and written to the copy buffer. When each field in the Recordset has been copied, the Update method writes the information from the copy buffer to the database.

6. When the last record has been written, the database is closed, and the subroutine terminates.

Summary

In this chapter, you learned how to use VBA, the XLODBC.XLA Add-In, and DAO to exchange data between Excel workbooks and Access databases. In particular, you have learned:

▶ How to create VBA code that automates the creation of an Excel pivot table from an Access database.

▶ Two approaches to returning data from an Access database to an Excel worksheet, without invoking the PivotTable method. Using the XLODBC.XLA, you can retrieve the data whether the user is running Excel 5 or Excel 95. However, this approach is slower and more cumbersome than using DAO directly. If you can be sure that any user of your code will be running Excel 95, use the DAO approach.

▶ How to create a new Access database and populate it with worksheet data using DAO.

chapter 31

Integrating Excel and PowerPoint

31

by John Lacher

In this chapter

◆ **Integrating the features of Excel and PowerPoint**
PowerPoint's presentation features can be combined with Excel's data analysis to create compelling presentations that include complex calculations and charts.

◆ **Using Excel worksheets and charts in PowerPoint presentations**
When worksheets and charts are built into a PowerPoint presentation, all of Excel's charting and data analysis features can be used in building presentations.

◆ **Inserting PowerPoint presentations into Excel workbooks**
PowerPoint slides inserted in an Excel workbook add text and images that enhance Excel's number presentation capabilities.

◆ **Creating a PowerPoint presentation from Excel with VBA**
You can create a presentation with the click of a button, saving hours of time you would spend updating or creating the presentation manually.

Before the release of Office 95, users of presentation packages copied charts from spreadsheets to slides for a presentation. But beyond this sharing of chart images, there was little opportunity to integrate the features of a presentation package and spreadsheet. With Office 95, these features can be combined easily to produce enhanced presentations that communicate your information creatively and effectively.

The added processing power of Windows 95 makes it possible—and practical—to include PowerPoint presentations in Excel workbooks. With PowerPoint's new Object Model, you can control the display of the presentation with VBA. These features can be integrated to create an entire PowerPoint presentation automatically from an Excel workbook.

Combining the Strengths of PowerPoint and Excel

PowerPoint is an idea organizer as well as a tool for persuasion. The Office 95 version of PowerPoint includes an AutoContent Wizard to help novice users organize ideas and develop presentations for topics such as:

▶ Recommending a strategy

▶ Selling a product, service, or idea

▶ Training employees or customers

▶ Reporting progress

▶ Communicating bad news

Along with the AutoContent Wizard, PowerPoint provides an Outlining feature that is helpful in organizing a presentation before developing the detail.

Excel adds data analysis strengths to PowerPoint's idea organizing and persuasion power. When you know how to combine the features of Excel and PowerPoint, you can develop presentations with a depth of what-if, charting, forecasting, and data presentation features.

Together, Excel and PowerPoint create a powerful tool for data analysis, organization, and persuasion. When you learn the techniques for integrating Excel and PowerPoint, you will be able to develop applications like these:

▶ Presentations that are automatically updated with the latest sales, production, or other data.

▶ Slide shows that persuade your audience with complex what-if, projection, and data analysis features.

▶ PowerPoint presentations built into Excel workbooks that explain the worksheet data and emphasize your message.

▶ Excel workbooks that are programmed to produce a PowerPoint presentation automatically.

▶ Data-conferencing tools to facilitate meetings between PC users at remote locations. While conferencing, all the integrated features of Excel and PowerPoint are available for use. Meeting participants can review the information on the slides as well as the detailed Excel data integrated into the presentation.

Note

If you have a machine without sufficient memory to run Excel and PowerPoint simultaneously, you can use the Windows 95 desktop as a temporary holding area to transfer data from Excel to PowerPoint. You can drag Excel data to the desktop, then close Excel, open PowerPoint, and drag those "scraps" of data into PowerPoint.

Using Excel Worksheets and Charts in PowerPoint Presentations

In this section, you learn how to build Excel's data analysis and charting features into PowerPoint to create more convincing presentations. The data and chart portions of your presentations will be easier to keep up-to-date when they are linked to Excel workbooks. Excel's automatic calculation features can save you time modifying charts and tables in your presentation.

Understanding Methods of Sharing Data

To use Excel data in PowerPoint, you can copy data from an Excel worksheet and paste the data into a PowerPoint slide. You can use any of the options listed in the Paste Special dialog box shown in figure 31.1.

Fig. 31.1

The Paste Special command in PowerPoint displays options for adding Excel data to PowerPoint.

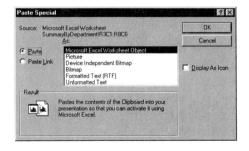

When you paste Excel chart data into PowerPoint, you can select any of the options listed in figure 31.2.

Fig. 31.2

The Paste Special options for adding Excel chart data to a PowerPoint presentation are different from those for adding Excel worksheet data.

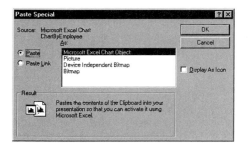

The Paste Link option in the Paste Special dialog box enables you to add a *linked* table or chart to PowerPoint. The linked data is automatically updated in PowerPoint whenever the Excel workbook changes. The Paste option *embeds* a copy of the Excel workbook that is not linked to the original. You can modify the embedded copy in PowerPoint, but modifications do not affect the original workbook. Tables 31.1 and 31.2 summarize the differences between these options.

Table 31.1   Methods of Linking or Embedding Excel Worksheet Data in a PowerPoint Presentation

Presentation Type	Linked Version	Embedded Data
Microsoft Excel Worksheet Object	Updates presentation automatically by linking a picture of a worksheet range.	Displays data in Excel format and adds Excel data analysis capabilities to your PowerPoint slide.
	When you double-click the worksheet, the Excel file will open for editing.	When you double-click the worksheet, Excel's menu options replace PowerPoint's and you can edit the worksheet in-place.
	The Excel workbook data is not stored as part of the PowerPoint presentation file.	All of the worksheet data is stored in the PowerPoint presentation.
Microsoft Excel Chart Object	This option adds a chart to PowerPoint with a link to an Excel workbook.	Use an embedded chart to store Excel data in a PowerPoint presentation.
	When the workbook containing the chart sheet is updated, the PowerPoint slide will show the differences automatically.	This option displays an Excel chart on a PowerPoint slide. By double-clicking the chart, you can update the data stored in the PowerPoint presentation.

Presentation Type	Linked Version	Embedded Data
	As with a linked worksheet, the data is stored in a separate Excel XLS file.	Data for embedded charts is stored as part of the PowerPoint presentation file.

Table 31.2   Methods of Copying Excel Data to a PowerPoint Presentation

Presentation Type	Description of Copied Data
Picture	When a worksheet range or chart is copied as a picture, you can use PowerPoint's drawing tools to change each line, dot, or shape that makes up the picture. Only the drawing shapes and text that make up the picture are copied to PowerPoint. Excel cannot be used to modify the data after it has been copied to PowerPoint.
Bitmap	By copying the image as a bitmap, you can use the six resizing handles that appear as solid boxes on the outline of the image to change the size of the image. You cannot use drawing tools to edit elements of a bitmap.
	Bitmaps are slower to display and require more file space than pictures.
Formatted Text (RTF)	Data will be copied to PowerPoint in Rich Text Format (RTF) as shown on the worksheet.
Unformatted Text	Data copied to PowerPoint is converted to the default text style in PowerPoint.

You learn more about these methods of inserting data in the examples that follow.

Using Excel Data in PowerPoint

Using Excel data in PowerPoint can be as simple as copying and pasting an Excel worksheet or chart. This section describes the steps of a simple copy function and then demonstrates more advanced methods of linking and embedding.

In the second example, a linked worksheet displays Excel data in PowerPoint using formulas that update automatically when new data is added to Excel. As weekly production numbers are added to an Excel worksheet, the linked range always displays the most current six weeks of data.

Excel workbooks can automate the process of updating a presentation. The last example in this section demonstrates an embedded workbook containing a VBA procedure that is used to automate the process of adding new data to a presentation. When you use Excel's automation features, you can automate worksheet tasks so that someone without Excel training can add new data to a presentation.

Using Copy and Paste

Sharing data between Excel and PowerPoint can be as simple as copying and pasting. To copy and paste data from Excel to PowerPoint, follow these steps:

1. Select an Excel Chart sheet or worksheet range.

2. Choose Edit, Copy to copy the data.

3. Switch to PowerPoint. When both Excel and PowerPoint are open, you can use the Windows 95 Taskbar to switch back and forth between them.

4. Select the slide that will receive the Excel data.

5. Choose Edit, Paste to paste a copy of the data on the slide.

This method pastes the data as an embedded Excel worksheet or chart object. If you want to change the data after it is copied, you can double-click the worksheet or chart object and use all of Excel's data analysis features to make your changes. While the object is opened for editing in-place, Excel's menu items replace the PowerPoint menu. When you are finished editing the object, click anywhere on the slide and PowerPoint's menu will return.

Double-clicking an embedded Excel worksheet or chart object produces the same result as right-clicking the object and choosing the option Edit Object. In both methods, the editing window is slightly larger than the picture of the object on the slide. Once in Edit Object mode, you can only modify worksheets and charts. You cannot make changes to modules or dialog sheets while in Edit Object mode.

If you need to have access to all the sheets in the workbook, right-click the Excel object and choose the option Open Object. An Excel window opens and fills the screen. When you have finished modifying the Excel workbook in this window, you can close it by choosing File, Close and returning to the PowerPoint screen.

Embedded objects store all the workbook data in the PowerPoint presentation. You can save file space by eliminating unneeded workbook data before copying from Excel to PowerPoint. If you don't need to modify the data after it is copied to PowerPoint, you can choose <u>E</u>dit, Paste <u>S</u>pecial to insert the data as a picture instead of storing the data as an embedded object. Pictures occupy significantly less file space than embedded objects. To modify data stored as a picture, you can use PowerPoint's drawing tools.

 Note

You can use shortcut keys to speed the process of copying Excel data into a PowerPoint presentation. Ctrl+C copies Excel data to the Clipboard and Ctrl+V pastes the data into PowerPoint. You can use Alt+Tab as a shortcut to quickly switch back and forth between Excel and PowerPoint while performing the copies.

Using a Linked Worksheet or Chart in PowerPoint

Presentations have a tendency to become outdated quickly. When plans change or assumptions are modified, the tables and charts in your presentations may need substantial revision. Making a presentation before you've completed all the necessary changes weakens your message as you take detours explaining outdated information to your audience.

Linking ties your presentation directly to data in your Excel workbooks. When you link your presentations to Excel, you can update your presentations automatically when you update the data in Excel. With your workbooks designed to provide both data analysis and presentation data, finishing your workbook data brings your presentations up-to-date immediately.

In this example, you learn how to structure an Excel worksheet so that when you add new detail, the worksheet immediately updates a summary range and chart linked to a PowerPoint presentation. If you use similar techniques in your Excel workbooks, you can be ready to give a presentation immediately after updating your Excel worksheet. For example, if you need to be ready to make a presentation at a Monday morning staff meeting, you can update Excel with the preceding week's data just a few minutes before the meeting and be ready to show your updated slides.

The presentation in figure 31.3 contains three links to an Excel workbook. The title at the top of the slide and the table in the bottom-right corner are both linked to different worksheet ranges. The chart is linked to an Excel Chart sheet. When new data is added to the Excel workbook, the slide is updated automatically with the current week's information, a revised chart, and a new title at the top of the slide.

Fig. 31.3
A PowerPoint slide can be linked to Excel worksheet ranges and charts so that changes in Excel become immediately visible in the PowerPoint presentation.

Excel chart—

Excel worksheet range—

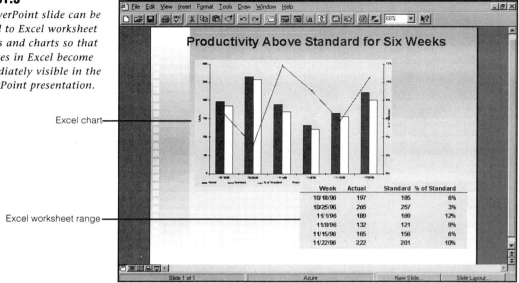

When you double-click the table in the bottom-right corner of the slide, the linked Excel workbook opens for editing as shown in figure 31.4.

Fig. 31.4
Double-clicking a linked Excel table opens a workbook for editing.

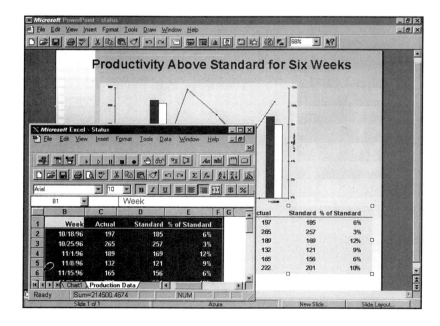

Excel shows the linked worksheet range selected with white text on a black background. You can maximize the Excel window and use the full screen to edit the Excel workbook.

The workbook shown in figure 31.5 is designed to feed data to the PowerPoint presentation. The table in cells B1:F7 is used as the source range for the Chart sheet named Chart1 displayed in the presentation. Below the table is the title for the slide and a list of weekly data.

The values in the table at the top of the screen are lookup formulas. Each formula uses the week ending date in cells B2:B7 to return values from the list of weekly data. In figure 31.5, the formula for cell C7 is displayed in the formula bar.

31

Fig. 31.5

You can design an Excel worksheet to provide data for PowerPoint presentations.

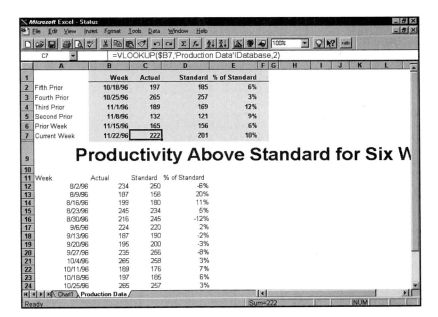

You can save time updating your data by using Excel's automatic calculation techniques. In the example shown in figure 31.5, Excel's Data, Form command is used to add new rows of weekly data to the named range 'Production Data'!Database. By changing the weeks listed in range B2:B7, you can create a new table and chart automatically. Insert your new slide title in cell A9, close Excel, and your PowerPoint presentation is ready to run.

When you link your presentation to an Excel workbook, you can control the frequency of updates. To make changes to your Excel workbook without changing your presentation, choose Edit, Links in PowerPoint to display the Links dialog box shown in figure 31.6.

Fig. 31.6

You can use the Links dialog box options in PowerPoint to manage your links to Excel worksheets and charts.

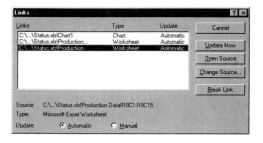

You can use the Update Now option when you want to bring new data from Excel into PowerPoint. Choose Automatic Update so PowerPoint prompts you to update the data each time you open the presentation. The Break Link option can be used to freeze the worksheet and chart data in PowerPoint. When you freeze the data, it no longer reflects changes in the Excel workbook.

Embedding an Excel Worksheet or Chart in PowerPoint

If the numbers you need to present don't yet exist in an Excel workbook, it may be more convenient to enter the data into an Excel workbook embedded in your PowerPoint slide. With embedding, all the workbook data is included in the PowerPoint presentation file. You can edit and modify the workbook while working in PowerPoint.

The following example demonstrates how a VBA procedure in the embedded Excel workbook can make your presentation easy to update. Updating an embedded worksheet can be confusing to someone who does not have Excel experience, but if you automate the process with VBA, you can make the update as easy as clicking a button.

Figure 31.7 shows a worksheet range of an embedded Excel workbook. The worksheet range includes a chart and table of values. In the bottom-right corner of the chart is a button that updates the table and chart automatically with a VBA procedure.

When you double-click an embedded Excel object, PowerPoint's menu choices are replaced with Excel menu items. You can edit the object in-place. Figure 31.8 shows the worksheet range B1:F21 opened for editing in-place.

After you open the workbook for editing in-place, you can click the Update button to run a VBA procedure. The first action taken by the procedure displays the Production Data dialog box shown in figure 31.9. You can use this dialog box to enter data for the current week, or change the data for a week that has already been entered. After the data is entered, the VBA procedure automatically updates the table and chart to show the most current six weeks of data.

Fig. 31.7

You can embed Excel tables and charts in a PowerPoint slide.

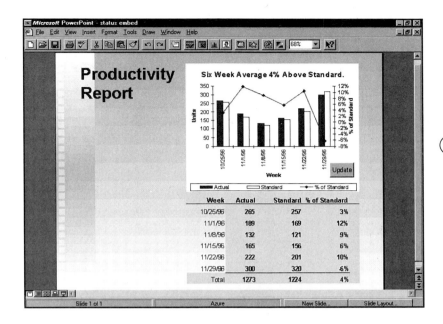

Fig. 31.8

When you double-click an embedded Excel worksheet, you can make changes to it in PowerPoint.

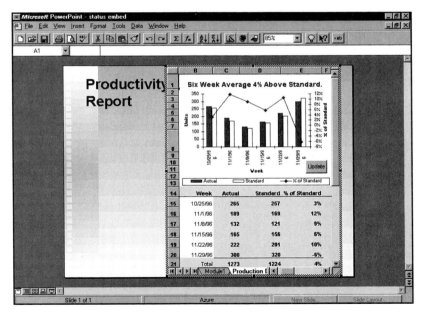

31

Fig. 31.9

You can use an Excel VBA procedure to automate the process of updating information in the presentation.

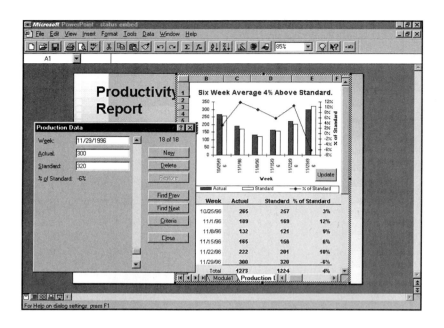

These techniques can save you hours of time spent updating your presentation. By double-clicking the embedded workbook, clicking the Update button, and entering a new week's data, your presentation is brought up-to-date automatically. This eliminates the need to redraw charts or change formulas by hand.

The VBA procedure that performs the automatic update is the following:

```
Sub UpdateData()
  With Worksheets("Production Data")
    Worksheets("Production Data").ShowDataForm
    .Range("Database").Columns(1).Cells(.Range("Database").Rows.Count - 5).Resize _
    (6, 1).Copy destination:=.Range("Weeks")
  End With
End Sub
```

The procedure uses the ShowDataForm method to display Excel's built-in data form. After the new data is entered, the Copy method is used to copy the last six rows of data to the table below the chart. The chart updates automatically when the data in the table is changed.

In figure 31.10, the formula used to create an automatic title appears above the chart. If the value in cell E21 is less than 0, the value of cell I22 appears above the chart.

In figure 31.11, the value of cell I22 is a formula that combines the value of cell E21 and the text strings Six Week Average and Below Standard. When E21 is less than 0, the value of this formula appears above the chart.

Fig. 31.10

You can use a formula to create an automatic title in Excel that is linked to your PowerPoint presentation.

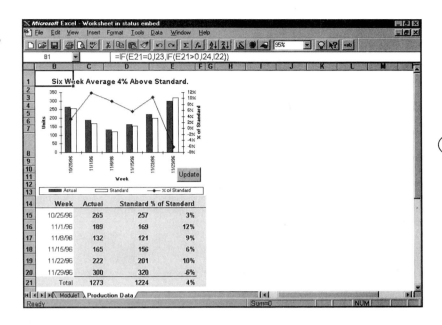

Fig. 31.11

You can use worksheet formulas to automatically update a PowerPoint presentation.

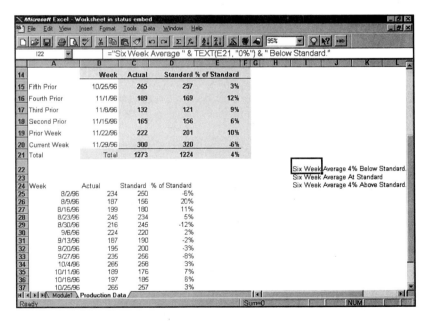

In the example shown in figure 31.10, the value of cell B1 uses the value of cell I24 to return the value Six Week Average 4% Above Standard. If the value of cell E21 had been 0, the formula in cell B1 would select cell I23 to provide the title above the chart.

By using a VBA procedure and worksheet formulas, you can create an embedded Excel worksheet object that updates automatically. By using these techniques to automate the update of slides that require frequent changes, you can save hours of manual revision and always have an updated presentation on hand.

 Note

The PowerPoint presentation examples described here are included on the CD-ROM that accompanies this book. You can use the examples to learn more about linked and embedded objects in PowerPoint presentations.

The Linked Excel Object example can be found in the file LINK.PPT. The Excel workbook file STATUS.XLS contains the linked data.

The Embedded Excel Object example is contained in the PowerPoint file named EMBED.PPT.

Using PowerPoint Presentations in Excel Workbooks

In the days of Windows 3.1, few desktop computers could run Excel and PowerPoint simultaneously. Now with Windows 95 and a powerful desktop processor, the integration of Excel and PowerPoint has become practical. The techniques and examples in this section help you understand the potential of integrating Excel and PowerPoint by building PowerPoint presentations into Excel workbooks. The examples illustrate simple links as well as automated methods of integration.

Understanding Methods for Linking and Embedding PowerPoint Presentations

You can choose Insert, Object or Edit, Paste Special to embed a PowerPoint presentation into an Excel worksheet. To link a PowerPoint presentation to an Excel worksheet, you must choose Insert, Object, Create From File.

An embedded presentation is completely contained within the Excel workbook. Double-clicking the embedded PowerPoint object opens the presentation in Slide Show mode. You can open an embedded presentation for editing by right-clicking the object and selecting Presentation Object, Edit.

When you insert a linked presentation object in an Excel worksheet, double-clicking the object opens the presentation in Editing mode. To run a slide show, open the presentation in Editing mode and click the Slide Show button or choose <u>V</u>iew, Slide Sho<u>w</u>.

 Note

Slide Show mode offers the Meeting Minder feature, which enables you to take notes and record action items related to each slide in the presentation. To choose from a list of all the slides in the presentation, right-click the slide or click the Slide Show menu icon in the bottom-left corner of the slide and choose the Go To option.

To copy a picture of a slide or an object on a slide, use the Paste <u>S</u>pecial Picture option. You can modify the picture with Excel's drawing objects. Pictures take up less file space than embedded objects and are an easy way to include PowerPoint graphics in your Excel workbook.

Using PowerPoint Presentations in Excel

In this section, you learn how to integrate PowerPoint presentations into your Excel workbooks. At first, this combination may seem unlikely. Why would you want to include a PowerPoint presentation in a workbook?

If you consider the capabilities of PowerPoint and Excel, the benefit of integration becomes clear. PowerPoint is an *idea* processor that organizes ideas in presentation form. Excel is like a person who is "good with numbers" but has problems communicating ideas. A PowerPoint presentation can help to improve Excel's communication capabilities.

The first example in this section demonstrates the use of PowerPoint as an idea processor. You learn how to use PowerPoint's AutoContent Wizard to assist in the process of organizing your ideas.

The second example demonstrates how you can link PowerPoint presentations to Excel worksheets. For example, if you use Excel to summarize regional sales budgets, you can link each region's Excel worksheet to a PowerPoint sales plan. When you use the workbook to explain the sales numbers, you can click a picture of a PowerPoint slide and run the appropriate presentation. Switching back and forth between the numbers in Excel and the ideas in PowerPoint becomes an easy and natural process.

The last example in this section takes the integration of PowerPoint and Excel a step further. In the example, selected slides from a presentation are displayed in a workbook based on the topic. For example, if you want to display a slide that explains the reason for a particular budget variance, you can place a button on your worksheet beside that variance and write a VBA procedure to automatically display the appropriate slide when the button is clicked. After displaying the first slide in the series, you can use Power-Point's *interactive buttons* to provide additional navigation choices within the presentation.

 Note

With the arrival of more powerful desktop processors and operating systems, spreadsheets are poised to enter the new world of multimedia. You can use PowerPoint's multimedia presentation capabilities to add animation, video, and sound to an Excel workbook.

Imagine a workbook containing not only the sales forecast, but videos explaining each of the components of the forecast. PowerPoint is becoming the tool of choice to deliver this type of multimedia capability.

Creating a Presentation with the AutoContent Wizard

PowerPoint's AutoContent Wizard can help you organize ideas in an outline form. Figure 31.12 shows the AutoContent Wizard option on the dialog box that appears when you start PowerPoint.

Fig. 31.12

You can use the AutoContent Wizard to help organize ideas for presentation.

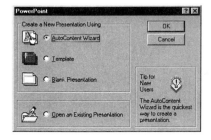

Select the AutoContent Wizard as shown in figure 31.12. In the dialog box that appears, choose the option Reporting on Progress. PowerPoint creates an outline as shown in figure 31.13.

Replace each suggested topic in the AutoWizard outline with facts and ideas about your presentation topic. When you have modified the outline, you can choose View, Slides to view your completed presentation.

Fig. 31.13

PowerPoint creates an automatic outline you can use for developing a presentation to report progress.

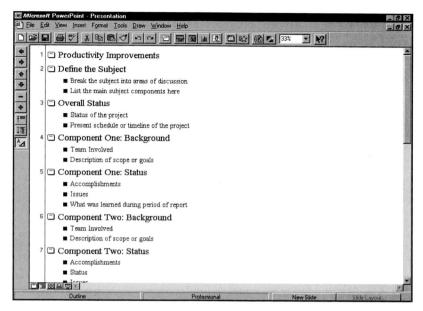

Controlling PowerPoint from the User Interface

You can link your completed presentation to an Excel worksheet by choosing Insert, Object. Select the Create From File tab and choose a presentation as shown in figure 31.14. Excel automatically checks the Link to File option. The presentation is inserted in your worksheet and linked to the PowerPoint presentation file.

Figure 31.15 shows a linked PowerPoint presentation on an Excel worksheet. As you work with data in Excel, you can use the linked presentation to view and edit the PowerPoint slides or outline.

Fig. 31.14

You can use the Create From File option to link an Excel workbook to a PowerPoint presentation.

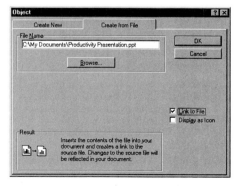

Fig. 31.15
A linked presentation in an Excel workbook is displayed as a picture of the first slide in the presentation.

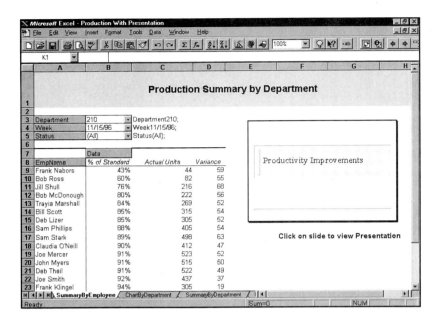

To make changes or run a slide show, double-click the presentation object. A PowerPoint window opens for editing in Slides view. You can choose the View menu to display the presentation in Outline, Slide Sorter, or Slide Show view. When you close the PowerPoint window, you return to the Excel window. Figure 31.16 shows the presentation in Slide Show view.

Fig. 31.16
You can edit or show a presentation from Excel.

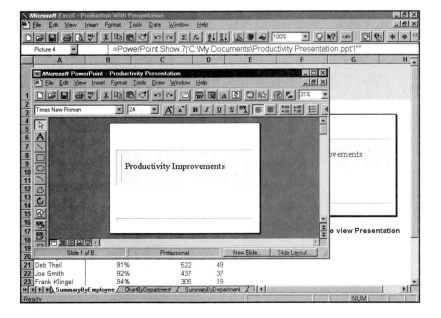

Using Excel and PowerPoint as two separate programs can be effective but is not always efficient. After analyzing your data in Excel, you can begin to create a presentation in PowerPoint and then copy the Excel data into PowerPoint manually. By integrating the features of PowerPoint with your Excel worksheet, you can develop your presentation as you are analyzing data. Notes and explanations that back up your Excel data can be added to the PowerPoint presentation.

Controlling PowerPoint from Buttons on a Worksheet

You can stage a PowerPoint presentation from your Excel worksheet by combining the power of the following:

▶ Object Linking and Embedding (OLE) Automation

▶ Visual Basic for Applications (VBA)

▶ PowerPoint's Interactive Settings feature

Buttons on an Excel worksheet can control the order of your slide presentation based on the audience's interest and questions. You can make modifications to your Excel workbook to analyze data or change assumptions during the presentation and display the results to your audience immediately. The following example shows you how to build an Excel workbook to control a PowerPoint slide show.

In figure 31.17, the Excel workbook shows three buttons in column A. When you click any button, an Excel VBA procedure starts PowerPoint, loads a presentation in Slide Show view, and advances to a designated slide.

Fig. 31.17

You can use a button on an Excel worksheet to display slides in a PowerPoint presentation.

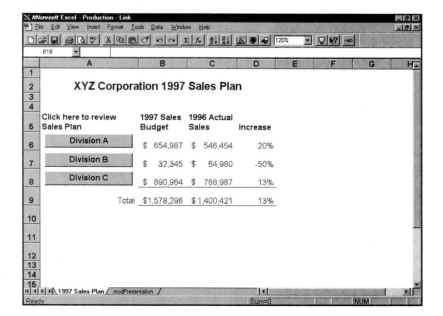

Figure 31.18 shows the Division A Sales Plan slide that appears when you click the Division A button in Excel. To create a PowerPoint button on the slide that will automatically advance to another slide, you can use PowerPoint's Tools, Interactive Settings feature. The Interactive Settings feature allows you to draw a button on a slide and assign an action to that button. In this example, clicking the Click Here for Plan Details button at the bottom of the slide in figure 31.18 advances the presentation to a slide later in the show.

Fig. 31.18

The Click Here for Plan Details button automatically selects and displays another slide in the presentation.

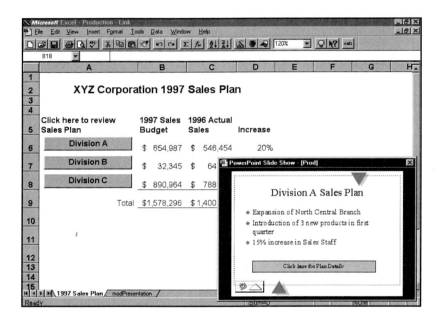

Each button on the Excel worksheet opens the slide show at a designated slide. With this technique, you can provide immediate display of the slides associated with each set of values on your worksheet. The VBA procedure that opens the slide show when a button is clicked is:

```
Sub SlideNumber()
 Dim iSlide As Integer
 Select Case Application.Caller
 Case "Button 1"
 iSlide = 2
 Case "Button 2"
 iSlide = 3
 Case "Button 3"
 iSlide = 4
 End Select
 Call Presentation(iSlide)
End Sub
```

The variable `iSlide` is set to a slide number determined by the name of the button that was clicked.

The Presentation procedure is called with the slide number as an input parameter:

```
Sub Presentation(iSlide)
  Dim pptapp As Object
  Set pptapp = GetObject("c:\prod.ppt")
  pptapp.SlideShow.StartingSlide = iSlide
  pptapp.SlideShow.Run (ppSlideShowWindow)
  Set pptapp = Nothing
End Sub
```

The Presentation procedure uses the `GetObject` method to open the PowerPoint presentation named `prod.ppt`. The starting slide is set to the slide number, and the `Run` method is used to start the show. The object variable `pptapp` is used to change properties and activate methods of the PowerPoint presentation. After the slide show has been started, `pptapp` is set to `Nothing` to conserve system resources.

Creating a PowerPoint Presentation from Excel Automatically

If you need to update a presentation frequently, you can automate the process of creating slides from your Excel data. In the following example, an Excel workbook contains VBA procedures that automatically create a new presentation from selected views of a PivotTable.

You can use similar techniques to automatically create presentations from your workbooks. For example, if you need to present production results on a weekly basis, you can use a workbook similar to the one shown in figure 31.19 and select the PivotTable page field values to include in your presentation. Because the process of creating the presentation and slides is automated, you can delegate the task to a member of your staff who is not trained in PowerPoint. The automated process also helps to reduce the potential for errors that can occur when creating a presentation manually.

Figure 31.19 shows an Excel workbook with a PivotTable and three buttons. The Start New Presentation button creates the title slide for a new PowerPoint presentation. The Add Slide button adds a copy of the PivotTable to the presentation. The View Slides button displays the presentation in a PowerPoint application window.

When you click Start New Presentation, the VBA procedure prompts you for the title and subtitle of the first slide. Figure 31.20 shows the prompt for the title.

After prompting for the title and subtitle, Excel creates the first slide in the presentation as shown in figure 31.21.

Fig. 31.19

Using a VBA procedure, you can click buttons on a worksheet to automatically create a new presentation.

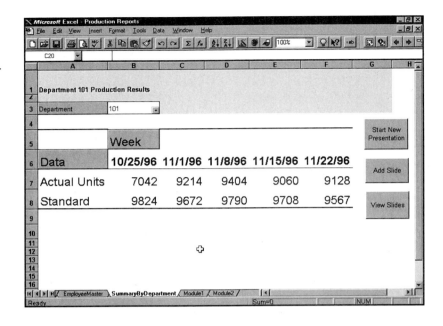

Fig. 31.20

The Input dialog box prompts the user for a title of the slide presentation.

Fig. 31.21

You can create a title slide automatically using the VBA procedure.

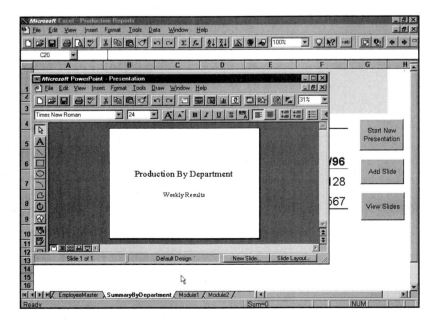

When you click Add Slide, Excel creates a slide from the PivotTable. You can now create a slide for selected departments.

Figure 31.22 shows a slide created from a copy of the PivotTable.

Fig. 31.22

A PowerPoint slide can include a copy of an Excel PivotTable.

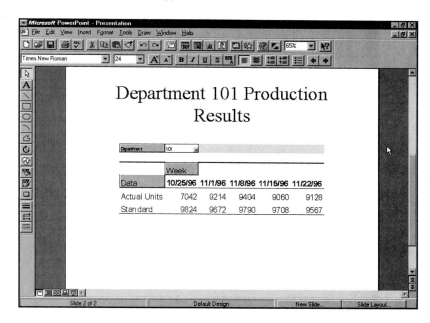

The VBA procedures attached to the buttons share these module level object variables:

```
Dim pptapp As Object
Dim psn As PowerPoint.Presentation
```

The variable pptapp is used to reference the PowerPoint application, and the variable psn is used to reference the presentation.

When you click Start New Presentation, this procedure creates a new presentation title slide:

```
Sub CreateNewPresentation()
 Dim sli As PowerPoint.Slide
 Dim strTitle As String
 Dim strSubTitle As String

 strTitle = Application.InputBox(prompt:= _
    "Enter Title for First Slide", _
 default:="Production By Department")
 strSubTitle = Application.InputBox(prompt:= _
    "Enter Sub-Title for First Slide", _
 default:="Weekly Results")
```

```
Set pptapp = CreateObject("PowerPoint.Application.7")
pptapp.appwindow.Visible = True

Set psn = pptapp.Presentations.Add
Set sli = psn.slides.Add(1, ppLayoutTitle)
sli.objects(1).Text = strTitle
sli.objects(2).Text = strSubTitle
End Sub
```

The InputBox method is used to prompt the user for a title and subtitle. The input values are stored in the variables strTitle and strSubTitle. After the CreateObject method opens PowerPoint, the Presentation.Add method creates a new presentation file. The Slides.Add method adds a slide. The last two lines of the procedure insert the title and subtitle into the new slide.

Clicking Add Slide causes this procedure to execute:

```
Sub CopyToPowerPoint()
Dim sli As PowerPoint.Slide

On Error Resume Next
Set sli = psn.slides.Add(psn.slides.Count + 1, ppLayoutTitleOnly)
If Err <> 0 Then
MsgBox "Warning -- You must start new presentation before adding slides", _
    vbExclamation
Exit Sub
End If

sli.objects(1).Text = _
    ThisWorkbook.Worksheets("SummaryByDepartment").Range("A1").Value

ThisWorkbook.Worksheets( _
    "SummaryByDepartment").PivotTables(1).TableRange2.CopyPicture
pptapp.ActiveWindow.view.GotoSlide psn.slides.Count
pptapp.ActiveWindow.view.Paste

End Sub
```

The procedure references the presentation with the object variable psn that was set by the first procedure. If psn is an invalid reference, it causes an error, and a message box appears, instructing the user to start a new presentation before adding slides.

The title of the new slide is set to the value of worksheet cell A1. This cell, shown in figure 31.20, contains a text formula that includes the value of the PivotTable page field.

The last lines of the procedure copy the PivotTable in the worksheet to the slide.

The View Slides button activates this procedure:

```
Sub ViewPresentation()
 Application.ActivateMicrosoftApp xlMicrosoftPowerPoint
End Sub
```

`ActivateMicrosoftApp` is a method that makes the selected application the top or active window. When this procedure runs, the PowerPoint presentation appears on top of the Excel window (refer to fig. 31.21).

 Note

The Excel presentation examples described in this section are included on the CD-ROM that accompanies this book. You can use the examples to learn more about using PowerPoint presentations from Excel.

The First Excel file that contains a linked presentation is named LINK.XLS. It links to the presentation file named PRESENT.PPT.

The second Excel example can be found in the file SHOW.XLS. The PowerPoint file PROD.PPT contains the PowerPoint presentation shown from the Excel workbook. The VBA code in SHOW.XLS looks in the root directory of the C drive to find the PROD.PPT file. You can modify the `GetObject` statement in SHOW.XLS to find the PowerPoint file in another directory.

The Excel file used to create a new presentation file is named CREATE.XLS.

Summary

In this chapter, you learned how Excel and PowerPoint can be combined to create a powerful data analysis and idea-processing tool. You also learned methods of integrating the two applications to improve your ability to organize your ideas and prepare a more convincing presentation.

Two new technologies may make the integration of Excel and PowerPoint the preferred method of preparing presentations and workbooks. With the new PowerPoint Object Model, you can now control PowerPoint from Excel. Windows 95 provides new capabilities for running multiple applications. The methods and examples in this chapter can help you stay abreast of changes and put these technologies to work for you.

chapter 32

Integrating Word and Access

32

by Shane Devenshire

In this chapter

◆ **Merging Access Data to Word**
You can quickly merge data from Access tables or queries into Word documents, such as envelopes, form letters, or mailing labels.

◆ **Publishing Access Data in Word**
You can enhance Access reports, forms, tables, and queries by publishing them in Word

◆ **Bringing Word Tables into Access**
Bring Word tables into Access so you can analyze and report on them using the query and report features in Access

◆ **Embedding Word Documents in Access**
You can copy or link large Word documents to Access tables and forms using memo fields or OLE fields.

O
n first consideration, it might seem that there are few reasons to move data between Access and Word. After all, isn't each program designed to stand on its own? Either program certainly provides powerful tools to deal with all of the demands of your job without resorting to outside help. In many cases this is true; even when it isn't completely true, you can make do despite any limitations.

Because either program is capable of accomplishing every assignment, the real questions are whether you can save time, money, or create a more attractive result by having the power of both programs at your fingertips. Of course, the answer to these questions is yes. Although you can find workarounds to the limitations of a software package, it might require many hours of fruitless searching, the need to resort to unnecessarily circuitous solutions, or the acceptance of results short of your goals.

Maybe these software limitations would be acceptable if they were imposed equally on you and your competition—but if the tools are available, your rivals will find them. In today's business climate, you can aptly paraphrase Darwin—evolve or perish. You might remember the days when spreadsheet users prepared their memos in their worksheets. It seemed like the best alternative at the time. They have found better ways by now. In those early days of the computer, it was often difficult—if not impossible—to move data from one program to another, and to rekey data (then as now) was an unacceptable nightmare. The tight integration of Microsoft Office programs presents simple and elegant solutions to these problems.

To illustrate the potential for integrating Word and Access, consider the following situations. Suppose you want to produce envelopes with bar codes for a large mailing using data you stored in Access. One way to accomplish this is to merge your Access data with Word. This would be useful because Word has a tool for creating envelopes and generating address bar codes automatically. Another possible problem you might consider addressing with an Access-Word integration solution would be the creation of a form letter to clients letting them know whether you will continue to sell their product in the upcoming year. You might choose to continue a product if the prior year's total sales were above a predetermined amount. If you keep the sales and client information in separate Word tables, there's no easy way to prepare the form letters in Word. If you keep the data in two or more Access tables, you can quickly merge the data into one Word form letter.

Sometimes, you might want to incorporate Word data into an Access table, form, or report. For example, you might prepare performance reviews in Word and want to bring that data into your Access personnel database. Alternatively, you might want to view a copy of a contract prepared in Word when you are in your client database.

The reason for employing software integration is to take advantage of the strengths of each type of program. For example, databases allow you to maintain tables with large numbers of records and fields. Maintaining a table with 40,000 records and 50 fields in Word would be impossible, but it's no problem for Access. If you want to create documents rather than reports, Word's myriad of word processing features is far superior to Access' reports. Therefore, to merge a 50,000 record database with a form letter, the best results would come from using features of both Access and Word.

Merging Access Data into Word

Merging Access data into Word is probably the most common type of data exchange between these two programs. You can do it quickly and easily by using the Merge to Word toolbar button. With one click of this button, you can create a Word document that is ready for you to place merge fields in. In the following section, you see how to merge Access data into Word to create envelopes and form letters. Each of these examples illustrates different capabilities of the two programs.

Why Merge Access Data?

The first reason to merge Access data with Word has already been pointed out: Access can handle much larger tables than Word. To be exact, Word allows a maximum of 31 fields (columns) and 32,767 records (rows); Access allows 255 fields and the number of records is limited only by available memory or the 1G maximum file size. Another reason for using Access is its powerful query capabilities. Although Word does provide a merge criteria option, it is not nearly as powerful as Access' queries. For example, you can put a maximum of six criteria in Word's Query Options dialog box; Access criteria can be far more complicated, the actual limit being dictated by the nature of the query. A third reason to consider maintaining data in Access is its capability to perform relational database queries. Word can work with one data table at a time; Access can work with the data in many tables simultaneously because of its relational database capabilities.

Merging to an Envelope

In this section, you look at the basic process of a mail merge from an Access table to a Word document. If you have already used the mail merge feature in Word, you might want to skip to the following section, "Producing Form Letters from Queries."

Caution
When you run the Word Mail Merge Wizard, Word opens and a second copy of Access opens. This means your computer will need sufficient resources to run Word and two copies of Access simultaneously. The reason for this is that Access is not a fully developed OLE2 server; therefore, Access opens Word and launches a second copy of Access.

Suppose you want to send Christmas cards to all of your customers. To save time, you want to use a mail merge to prepare the envelopes. Your customer data is in an Access table and you want to print the envelopes from Word. For this example, use the Northwind database that comes with Access. To create your envelopes, follow these steps:

1. With your database open in Access, select the Tables category and choose the table containing your merge data. In this example, select the Customers table, as shown in figure 32.1.

Fig. 32.1

When you want to merge data to Word, you don't need to open the table or query; you only need to select it in the database window.

2. Choose Tools, OfficeLinks, Merge It to open the Word Mail Merge Wizard.

3. Choose Create a New Document and then link the data to it. Word opens with an empty document and the Mail Merge toolbar displayed (see fig. 32.2).

Fig. 32.2

When Word opens, the Mail Merge toolbar automatically appears and is ready to go.

Mail Merge toolbar

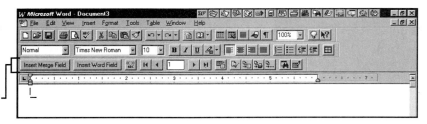

4. Choose Tools, MailMerge to open the Mail Merge Helper dialog box (see fig. 32.3).

5. Choose the Create button, and then choose Envelopes, Change Document Type to change the document type to an envelope and return to the Mail Merge Helper dialog box.

6. Choose Setup and click the Envelope Options tab. Pick an envelope from the Envelope Size list box or create a custom envelope by choosing Custom Size from the list (see fig. 32.4). Then choose OK.

Fig. 32.3

The Mail Merge Helper dialog box steps you through the mail merge process.

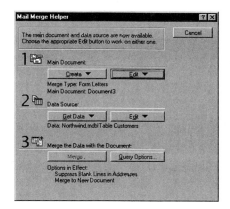

32

Fig. 32.4

From the Envelope Options dialog box, you can select envelope design and printing options.

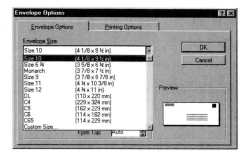

7. In the Envelope Address dialog box, add the fields you want on your envelopes by choosing them from the Insert Merge Field list.

8. If you want a postal bar code, choose the Insert Postal Bar Code button to open the Insert Postal Bar Code dialog box.

9. Select the field that contains your ZIP codes from the Merge Field with ZIP Code list box. Next, indicate the field containing the street address by selecting it from the Merge Field with Street Address list box. Finally, select FIM-A Courtesy Reply Mail if you want a facing identification mark on courtesy reply envelopes. At this point, your screen should look like figure 32.5.

10. Choose OK twice, and then choose Close to return to the document window. Figure 32.6 shows how the document should now look.

11. You can enter the return address manually; however, if you will be using the same return address on other documents, you can let Word know. To establish a semi-permanent return address, choose Tools, Options, click the User Info tab, and enter your address in the Mailing Address text box.

Fig. 32.5
Click the Insert Postal Bar Code button in the Envelope Address dialog box in order indicate the ZIP code and street address fields.

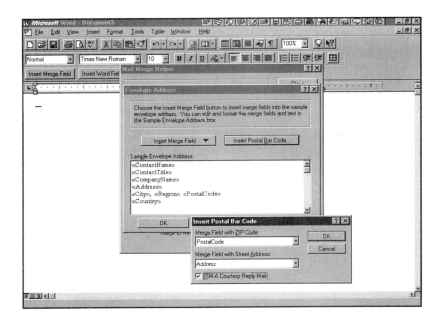

Fig. 32.6
You may need to add a return address to the envelope, or it may appear automatically as shown here.

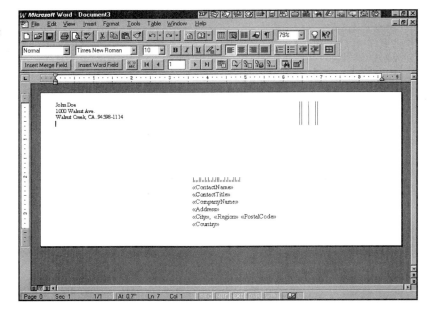

12. After you enter a return address in the Options dialog box, if the return address does not display on your envelope, choose Insert, Field, User Information from the Categories list, and choose UserAddress from the Field Names list.

Your envelope is ready to go. Click the Merge to New Document button on the Mail Merge toolbar and you will generate a document containing one envelope for each customer, as shown in figure 32.7. You can also print the envelopes directly by choosing the Merge to Printer button. Word automatically designed an envelope of the correct size and positioned all the elements. Creating a report in Access to include all of these features would be more challenging. With this example, you see some of the reasons to integrate Access data into Word. The next section describes more reasons for merging data.

Fig. 32.7

An envelope generated using mail merge can look as good as one produced by a professional print shop.

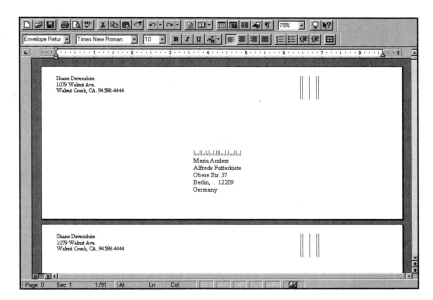

Producing Form Letters from Queries

One of the most common reasons to integrate Access data with Word is to create a mail merge form letter. You can merge either Access table or query data into a new or preexisting form letter. The following example illustrates a number of techniques you might consider for merging form letter data.

Suppose you manage a large chain of specialty food stores. Each year you review the success or failure of the products you carry to decide if you will continue stocking them in the upcoming year. You maintain all the order information in an Access database, but you want to produce a Word form letter to advise each supplier whether you will be continuing with their product or not. For clarity, assume that the decision will be made strictly on total sales. To increase the efficiency of the mail merge process, you want to design one form letter that will notify the suppliers whether their product will be continued or discontinued in the upcoming year.

To make the process easy to follow, this example uses the Northwind database that comes with Access. All the tables and data for the following discussion are already available in Northwind.

The Access database must supply Word with the name of each product and the sum of the sales for that product for any given year. You also need to supply Word with supplier-related information, such as contact name and company address. This information is retained in a number of Access tables. To prepare the information for the mail merge process, you need to design a number of multi-table queries to bring all the data together in one dynaset.

Designing Multi-Table Queries

After looking over your Access tables, you determine that the data you need is located in four tables. For this example, the data is in the Products, Orders, Order Details, and Suppliers tables in the Northwind database. The Products table provides the name of each product and the supplier, but it does not contain other supplier-related information that you need. That information, the contact name and company address, is located in the Suppliers table. To determine the total value of all sales of a particular product, you need to use the unit price and quantity information, which is located in the Order Details table. To determine when the sale was made, you need the order date information, which is retained in the Orders table. You also need to make some calculations before you merge the data with Word. For example, the Order Details table shown in figure 32.8 retains the unit price and quantity for each order, but not the total charge.

In the Query Design window, the bottom half of the window is the query-by-example grid (QBE grid). This is where you specify which fields and records you want to see. Fields are the database equivalent of spreadsheet columns, and records are the equivalent of rows.

You need Access to calculate the extended price, which is the unit price times the quantity less any discounts. You need to design a query to calculate the extended price for each product ordered. Figure 32.9 shows the necessary query, Order Charges.

Fig. 32.8

The Order Details table does not contain the actual cost of an order, so you will need to calculate using the data in the unit price and quantity fields.

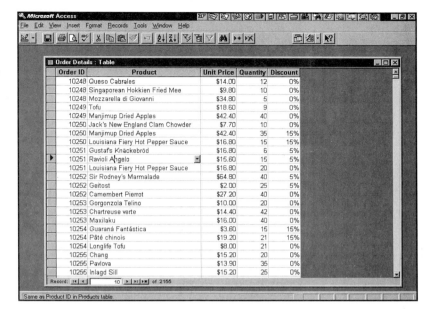

Fig. 32.9

The Order Charges query calculates the price you actually charged for each order.

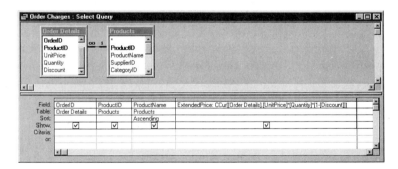

To create the Order Charges query, follow these steps:

1. With the Queries category selected, choose the <u>N</u>ew button and select Design View in the New Query dialog box. When you click OK, the Show Table dialog box appears.

2. Add the Order Details and Products tables to the query, and then choose <u>C</u>lose.

3. The two tables will automatically link on the primary key fields ProductID. Double-click the OrderID field in the Order Detail table to send it to the first cell of the Field row. Do the same to add the ProductID and ProductName field from the Products table.

4. Enter the following formula in the fourth field cell of the QBE grid to calculate the extended price:

```
Extended Price:CCur([Order Details].[UnitPrice]*[Quantity]*(1-[Discount]))
```

5. Save the query as Order Charges.

How does the preceding formula work? The text to the left of the colon names the new field. The CCur function converts the results of the expression to Currency. In the example, this function is optional, but if you remove it you might want to change the format property of the ExtendedPrice field to Currency and the decimal place property to 2. Normally, you don't need to include the table name in your calculations, but in this case both the Products and Order Details tables contain a UnitPrice field, so you need to eliminate the ambiguity.

The second query you need to create calculates the sum of sales by product for any given date range. Information for this query comes from the Products, Order Charges, and Orders tables. To construct the Sum of Sales by Product by Period query, follow these steps:

1. With the Queries category selected, choose the New button and select Design View in the New Query dialog box. In the Show Table dialog box, click the Both tab and add the Products table, the Order Charges query, and the Orders table to the new query.

2. Double-click the ProductName field from the Products table to send it to the first cell of the Field row. Do the same to add the ExtendedPrice from the Order Charges query and Order date field from the Orders table.

3. When you run a query, the table-like result is called a *dynaset*. You may not want to keep the same field names in the dynaset as you used in the original tables. It is a simple matter to change the field names in the Query Design window. For example, to change the name of the ExtendedPrice field, you could type **Sum of Sales:** in front of the ExtendedPrice field name in the QBE grid.

4. Choose View, Totals to add a Total row below the Field row. Click the Total row under Sum of Sales and choose the Sum function. Click the Total row under the OrderDate column and choose Where. These changes will cause the query to sum the ExtendedPrice field for each ProductName when the order date meets a condition. Make sure the Show check box under the OrderDate field is deselected.

5. To make the query more flexible, make it a parameter query. To do this, enter the following on the criteria row under OrderDate column:

```
Between [Earliest Order Date of:] and [Latest Order Date of:]
```

6. Save the query. Name it Sum of Sales by Product by Period.

A *parameter query* prompts the user to enter values that will be used as the criteria for the query. By using this type of query, you are creating a *dynamic query*—one query that can address many criteria. Figure 32.10 shows the final Sum of Sales by Product by Period.

Fig. 32.10

The Sum of Sales by Product by Period is a multi-table parameter query that totals the sales for each product.

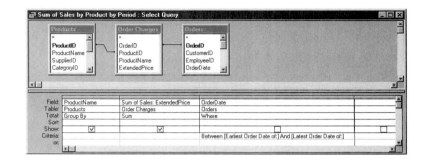

Finally, you need a query to combine the sum of sales figures with the product supplier information. The data you want is in the Suppliers table and the Sum of Sales by Product by Period query. However, there is no common element in both tables, so you must use the Products table as an intermediate link. To create a query that links two tables through a third table, follow these steps:

1. Create a new query as you did for the two prior queries, adding the Supplies and Products tables and the Sum of Sales by Product by Period query.

2. The Products and Suppliers tables automatically link. However, you need to link the Sum of Sales by Product by Period query to the Products table manually. Drag the ProductName field from the table to the same field in the query.

3. Add the fields you want to merge into Word. Add the CompanyName, ContactName, ContactTitle, Address, City, Region, PostalCode, and Country fields from the Suppliers table and the Sum of Sales and ProductName fields from the Sum of Sales by Product by Period query. Notice that no fields were added from the Products table—it's being used as the intermediate link. In this example, the Sort cell under PostalCode was set to Ascending so you can easily sort the Word form letters by ZIP code, which might reduce your postal expenses because of the lower presort rates.

4. Save the query as Merge Data. Figure 32.11 shows the completed query.

Notice that the final query queried two tables and a query, Sum of Sales by Product by Period. This last query also queried some tables and a query, Order Charges.

Fig. 32.11

The Merge Data query combines data from a table and a query that are joined through another table. The result of this final query will be merged into Word.

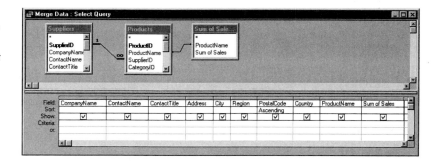

Creating a Macro to Run the Query and Start the Mail Merge

When you create your own databases, you will want to add all the features that can simplify your work, such as macro or VBA code to automatically run common tasks. To demonstrate that process, create a macro and attach it to a custom button on the Database toolbar. Remember that the current task only involves a few steps, so the macro isn't very long. To create a Merge Order Data macro, follow these steps:

1. Select the Macros category in the Database window. Click the New button to open a new, blank macro sheet.

2. On the first Action row, select the SelectObject command. In the Action Arguments area, choose Query for Object Type, Merge Data for the Object Name, and Yes for In Database Window.

3. On the second Action row, select the SendKeys command. Enter **{Enter}** as the Keystrokes action argument and **No** as the Wait argument.

4. On the third Action row, select the SendKeys command and enter the complete path to your predesigned master document as the Keystrokes action argument and **No** as the Wait argument. For example, the keystrokes line might read: D:\ MSOffice\Access\Data\Supplier Notification.doc.

5. On the fourth Action row, select the SendKeys command and enter **%O** as the Keystrokes Action Argument and **No** as the Wait argument.

6. On the fifth Action row, select the DoMenuItem command, select Query as the Menu Bar argument, Tools as the Menu Name argument, OfficeLinks as the Command argument, and Merge It as the Subcommand argument.

7. It's a good idea (but not required) to add documentation in the Comment column. Also, you can add a name for the macro if you intend to have more than one macro on a macro sheet. To add a name for individual macros, choose View, Macro Names, and then enter a name on the first line of the Macro Name column. Here the macro has been named WordMerge.

8. Save the macro sheet as Merge Order Data. Figure 32.12 shows the completed macro.

Fig. 32.12

The WordMerge macro on the Merge Order Data macro sheet runs the Merge Data query then begins the Microsoft Word Mail Merge Wizard.

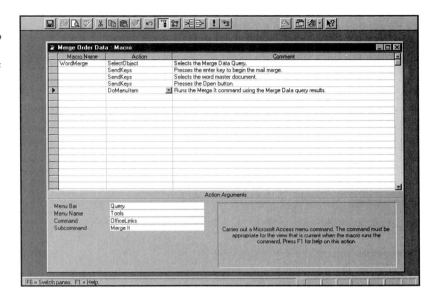

Here is what this macro does. The first command selects the Merge Data Query in preparation for running the Microsoft Word Mail Merge Wizard. Then the SendKeys commands send the Enter key, the path and file name of the master document, and the keystrokes to press the Open button to the keystroke buffer for execution during the running of the Wizard. Finally, the Wizard is started. Because SendKeys commands cannot be executed during the running of the Wizard, they must be executed prior to running the Wizard. They are not processed until the macro is complete—in other words, after the Wizard has begun. The last macro action finishes at the opening screen of the Microsoft Word Mail Merge Wizard. At that point, the SendKeys commands take effect. The {Enter} command presses the OK button, which takes the Wizard to the Select Microsoft Word Document dialog box with the focus in the File Name text box. The second SendKeys command enters the path and file name into this box. The last SendKeys command, %O, sends the keystrokes Alt+O to press the Open button. You could also choose to create a VBA module to accomplish the same tasks as this macro, but it's not as easy.

The syntax of the SendKeys command has changed between Access 2 and Access 7. In Access 2, the Keystrokes arguments needed to be enclosed in quotes; in Access 7, you cannot use quotes. For example, the Access 2 command "{Enter}" is now {Enter}.

Caution

If you use incorrect syntax with the SendKeys command, Access displays an error message stating `The SendKeys action requires the Microsoft Access Utility Add-in to be loaded. Solution. Run Setup to reinstall Microsoft Access and the Microsoft Access Utility Add-in.` You will get this error message even if the Utility Add-in is loaded, which means you might be tempted to try reinstalling Access. Chances are the add-in is installed. Don't worry if you don't remember doing it; they were added automatically when you installed Access.

Attaching a Macro to a Custom Toolbar Button

To make any macro easy to run, you can attach it to a button on a form, attach it to a custom toolbar button, or customize the Access menu system. For a macro you run only once a year, you probably should only consider a button on a form if you choose to attach it to anything. To add a custom toolbar button and attach a macro to it, follow these steps:

1. If you want to add the custom button to the Database toolbar, activate the Database window and choose <u>V</u>iew, <u>T</u>oolbars, <u>C</u>ustomize to open the Customize Toolbars dialog box (see fig. 32.13). Select All Macros from the <u>C</u>ategories list and drag the Merge Order Data macro from the <u>O</u>bjects list to the toolbar.

Fig. 32.13

The <u>O</u>bjects list shows the options available when you choose All Macros from the <u>C</u>ategories list.

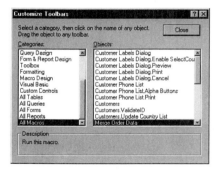

2. With the Customize Toolbars dialog box open, right-click the new toolbar button and select Choose Button Image from the shortcut menu. The Choose Button Image dialog box appears (see fig. 32.14).

Fig. 32.14

The Choose Button Image dialog box allows you to choose a predesigned button or to create a text button. You can also add or modify a ToolTip by changing the Description.

3. If you want to use one of Access' button images, click it and click OK. If you want a text button, select the <u>T</u>ext check box and type the text you want on your button. For this example, type **Merge Order Data** in the <u>T</u>ext text box. Modify the <u>De</u>scription text box if you want, and then choose OK and Close.

Figure 32.15 shows the customized toolbar button. With one click you will find yourself choosing between merging to an existing Word document or creating a new one. Now take a look at the Microsoft Word end of the integration.

Fig. 32.15

Here you see the Database toolbar displaying your custom toolbar button. The Merge Order Data button runs the Merge Order Data macro.

Custom toolbar button ——

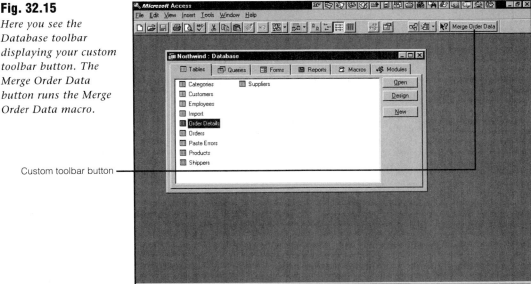

32

Preparing Word Documents for a Mail Merge

When you use the Tools, OfficeLinks, Merge It command, you are running Access'
Microsoft Word Mail Merge Wizard, which will allow you to use a previously existing
Word document or begin with a new one. For this example, set up the Microsoft Word
documents in advance. Remember, your goal is to send different letters to suppliers depending on whether their product's yearly sales figures were above or below an acceptable cutoff amount of $3,000.

Suppose the two letters contain substantially different text. To handle this situation and
make this example a little more challenging, the merge document will be set up to contain text from two other files, and the mail merge will automatically decide which file's
text to add for each letter. This means you will need three documents: a document to
inform suppliers that their product has been discontinued, a document to advise suppliers that your company will continue to sell their product in the upcoming year, and a
master letter to receive the mail merge data and the text of the rejection or acceptance
documents. To create your mail merge documents, follow these steps:

1. In Microsoft Word, create the rejection and acceptance letters. Save and close each
   document. For this example, name the documents RETAINING.DOC and
   CLOSEOUT.DOC.

2. Switch to Access and, if necessary, open the appropriate database. Click the Merge
   Order Data custom toolbar button. Depending on the speed of your computer, this
   stage can take a minute or two. Eventually, the Enter Parameter Value dialog box
   appears in front of Word (see fig. 32.16).

Fig. 32.16

*When you run this
macro, Word opens
in front of Access and
the Enter Parameter
Value dialog box also
displays.*

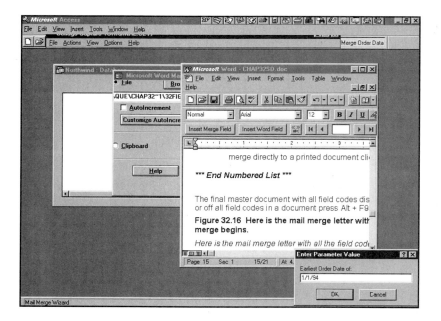

3. When it appears, the Enter Parameter Value dialog box will not be the active window, so you should click it to bring it to the front and enter the appropriate criteria.

4. Enter the appropriate parameters in the Enter Parameter Value dialog box. Shortly, Microsoft Word will be on-screen with the Mail Merge toolbar visible and ready for you to create the master document for the mail merge. For example, with the Northwind data, you could enter **1/1/93** as the earliest order date and **12/31/93** as the latest order date.

5. In Word, create your master document. To enter the fields from Access, position the cursor where you want the field, click the Insert Merge Field button on the Mail Merge toolbar, and select the field you want. Repeat this process for each field you want inserted into your documents.

6. To add a date field to your document that will automatically update, position the cursor where you want the date and choose Insert, Field. Choose Date and Time from the Categories list, Date from the Field Names list, and select the Preserve Formatting During Updates check box.

7. To enter the Word field that will embed text from either the RETAINING.DOC or CLOSEOUT.DOC, choose the Insert Word Field button on the Mail Merge toolbar and choose If...Then...Else. This opens the Insert Word Field: IF dialog box shown in figure 32.17.

Fig. 32.17

The Insert Word Field: IF dialog box simplifies the process of adding complex fields to your document.

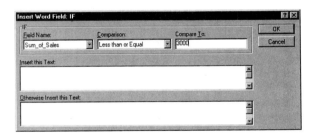

8. Choose the field you want to test from the Field Name drop-down list, choose the type of test you want from the Comparison drop-down list, and enter the desired value in the Compare To text box. For this example, choose Sum_of_Sales for the field name, Less than or Equal for the comparison operator, and 3000 as the value to compare to. You could enter the text you want displayed by the IF field directly into this dialog box by entering the True text into the Insert this Text box and the False text into the Otherwise Insert this Text box. Close the dialog box without entering any text in these last two boxes.

9. To display the inserted field codes, select the location where the field was inserted and press Shift+F9. For this example, you will see this:

```
{IF {MERGEFIELD Sum_of_Sales} <= 3000 "" ""}
```

10. To add text from another file depending on the results of the IF test, place the insertion point between the next-to-last pair of double quotes and choose Insert, Field. From the Categories list, choose Links and References. From the Field Names list, choose IncludeText. In Field Codes, leave a space after the field name and enter the path and file name of the document you want inserted. Repeat the process for the False portion of the IF test by entering the path and file name between the last set of double quotes. The result in the current case would be:

```
{IF {MERGEFIELD Sum_of_Sales} <= 3000 "{INCLUDETEXT "D:\\QUE\\Chap 32
   MSOffice\\CloseOut.Doc"}"
"{INCLUDETEXT "D:\\QUE\\Chap 32 MSOffice\\Retaining.Doc"}"}
```

11. After adding all finishing touches, save the master document. Name it SUPPLIER NOTIFICATION.DOC.

12. You can merge to a new document or print the merged results. To merge to a new document, click the Merge to New Document button on the Mail Merge toolbar. To merge directly to a printed document, click the Merge to Printer button.

Figure 32.18 shows the final master document with all field codes displayed. To turn on or off all field codes in a document, press Alt+F9.

Fig. 32.18

Here is the mail merge letter with all the field codes displayed before the merge begins.

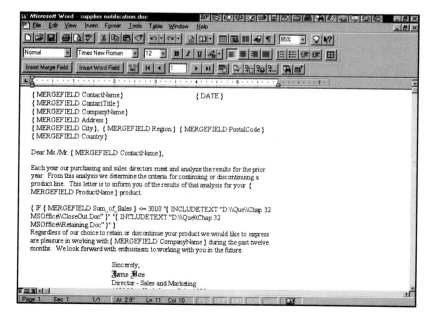

When you use the INCLUDETEXT function, take care with the syntax. The entire path and file name should be surrounded by double quotes, and each single backslash in the path should be replaced by two backslashes.

The next time you want to run the mail merge, you can do so in Access or Word. If you open the Supplier Notification document in Word, Access will be launched with the appropriate database. Because the query that merges with Word is a parameter query, you need to activate Access to display the Enter Parameter Value dialog box to enter the appropriate date range. If you run the mail merge from Access, when the Enter Parameter Value dialog box appears, activate it and enter the desired dates. When the process is complete, the master document will be open and ready to go. Figure 32.19 shows a sample of the results.

Fig. 32.19

This is one of the letters generated by the mail merge. In this example, the IF test returned true so the RETAINING.DOC text was embedded in the master document.

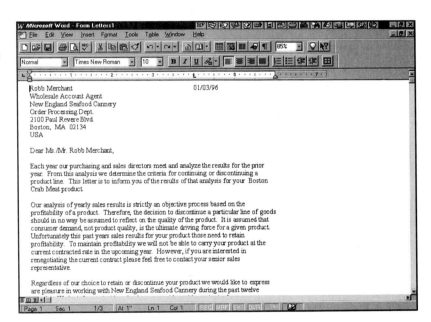

Publishing Access Data in Word

Although you can only merge tables and queries into Microsoft Word, you can publish tables, queries, forms, or reports. You might consider doing this if your Access data will become part of a larger Word document. Also, if you intend to add a lot of text to your report, Word has superior tools for managing text. When you publish Access data in Word, no link is created so the data is static. Also, not all data types or formatting will be transferred to Word. For example, OLE field data will not transfer to Word and Memo fields will truncate to what is displayed on-screen in Access. All formatting other than font formats will be lost. For example, Access lines, rectangles, charts, and graphics will not publish. For all practical purposes, the results of publishing a form look very much like the results of publishing a table. So, if published forms and reports don't allow the graphical enhancements of Access to be transferred to Word, why bother publishing?

First, published documents are not mail merge documents; they are basically copies of the Access objects minus some graphical information. So when you're not interested in producing a separate document for each database record, but want to put all the information into one document, publishing is the perfect solution. Second, to design queries that display results in a fashion similar to a report can sometimes be difficult if not impossible. For example, suppose you want to create a query that displays sales by quarter and subtotals those results by year. You might find it rather challenging. But you can create a report to accomplish this in a flash. If this is the result you want to enter in a Word document, publishing the report is the technique of choice.

Although the process is straightforward, an example will illustrate the differences between the Access report results and the published Word document. To demonstrate the method and benefits of publishing a report, you can step through the following example. Suppose you want to incorporate the Summary of Sales by Year report, shown in figure 32.20, into a lengthy Microsoft Word document.

Fig. 32.20

This is part of an Access report summarizing sales results by quarter and rolling them up by the year. Notice the graphical enhancement.

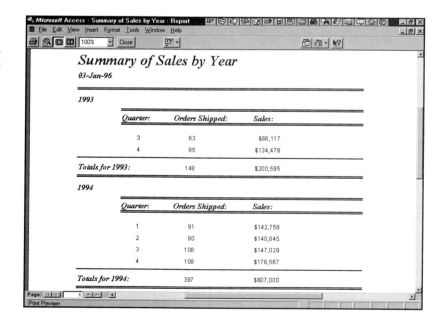

To publish this report in Word, follow these steps:

1. With Access open and the Northwind database displayed, select the Reports category and select the Summary of Sales by Year report.

2. Choose <u>T</u>ools, Office<u>L</u>inks, <u>P</u>ublish it With MS Word.

Access will create a Microsoft Word document with the same name as the Access report, and then it will open the new document in Word. Figure 32.21 shows the result of this process.

Fig. 32.21

Here are the results of publishing the Summary of Sales by Year report into Word. Notice that most of the graphical enhancement from figure 32.20 has not been published.

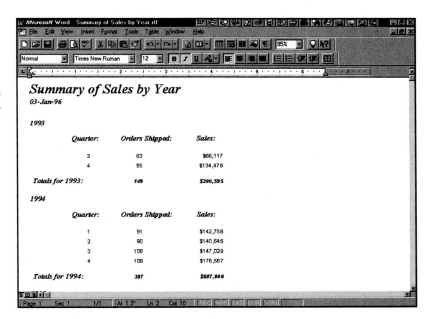

α **Note**

After the published document is opened, Word displays the message `D:\...\Summary of Sales by Ye...` is being used by John Doe. Do you want to make a copy? There is no good reason for this message. If you choose OK, you get a copy you can close; if you choose Cancel, you get a WordBasic Err=102 dialog box stating `Command Failed`. By choosing OK, you're done. This problem might originate if you install Access 7 over a Beta version. If this is your only problem, you might want to just ignore it. Alternatively, you can search your Access95 directory and subdirectories for the file SOA300.DLL. If you find two versions of the file, rename the earlier version by changing the extension. Another solution for problems related to installing Access 7 over Beta versions is to rerun Access setup using the /Y switch.

By comparing the Access report with the Word document, you can see that almost the only difference is the loss of the graphical lines. On careful inspection, you might notice that in the Word document all the figures on the Totals lines are bold, while in the original Access report only the titles are bold. Unlike the Merge It command, Access does not allow you to publish the report in a document of your choosing. Therefore, you will need to copy and paste the published data into the appropriate file. Also, notice that the data is actually not published in a Word document but is created as a RTF file, so you might want to save it as a DOC file.

Moving Word Data into Access Tables

There are a number of situations in which you might want to bring Word data into Access. You might be working with data that you want to analyze or report on using Access tools. For example, if you want to work with data from two Word tables, Access—not Word—is the perfect place to deal with this related data. A second possibility arises when there is too much data for Word to handle. You might also want to store Word documents with related information in an Access database. For example, a copy of a contract prepared in Word, but stored with a customer database, might prove more efficient than keeping the data in two separate programs.

When you want to copy a Word table into Access, it is a simple matter of using the copy and paste commands. There are a few things to remember when doing a copy and paste between a Word table and an Access table:

- ▶ If you have field names in your Word table, don't copy them.
- ▶ You must have a table to copy the Word data to. Access will not create a table on-the-fly.
- ▶ The Access table should have the same number of fields as the copied data.
- ▶ The Access fields should be in the same order as in the Word table or you might have data type conflicts.
- ▶ The Access fields should be of a compatible data type. For example, don't try to bring non-numerical data into a number field.
- ▶ The Access table you want to copy into must be open.

When you bring data from Word to Access using the copy and paste commands, you will find that there is no way to create a link—your data is static. If you make changes to the Word table, Access will be unaware of it.

When your data is in Access, you can use all of Access' tools to analyze and report on it.

Using Memo Fields for Word Documents

If you want to enter large amounts of Word data (such as entire documents), you can copy and paste them into Access memo fields. Suppose you prepare performance reviews using Word but you want to retain a copy of the reviews in an Access personnel database. If the Word document contains up to 64,000 bytes of information, you can store it in an Access memo field. A possible drawback is that all Word formatting will be lost when the data is pasted into a memo field, but this also means that you can save up to 64,000 bytes of text, wasting none of the memo field for formatting. If you need to include the formatting with the text, you can use an OLE field type, as discussed in the next section.

After you paste your Word document into an Access memo field, you can view the data in a table or form. In either case, you can select the memo field and press Shift+F2 to open the Zoom dialog box. Suppose you add a memo field called Notes to the Employees table in the Northwind database. Then you copy the performance review for each employee from a Word document into Notes field for that employee. For example, the first employee in the Employees database is Nancy Davolio. Her performance review, which has been copied from Word and stored in an Access memo field, is displayed in the Zoom box shown in figure 32.22. The text shown in figure 32.22 is not in the Northwind database supplied with Access; it has been copied from Word to illustrate the technique. In a form, you don't need to use the Zoom dialog box, because you can make the text box as large as necessary or you can add scroll bars to simplify moving around (see fig. 32.23).

Fig. 32.22

You can store up to 64K of unformatted text in a memo field and view it quickly by pressing Shift+F2.

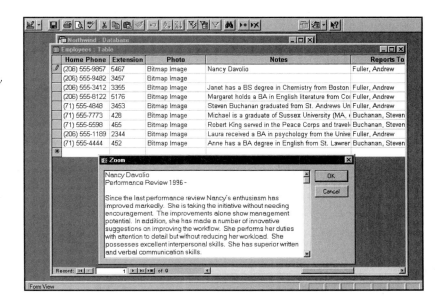

Fig. 32.23

In a form, you can view the contents of a memo field using the Zoom dialog box or by creating a large text box such as the one shown here.

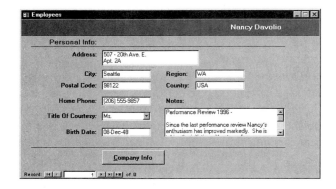

In a report, you should consider setting a memo field's Can Grow and Can Shrink properties to Yes. This allows the entire memo field to be printed regardless of the amount of data in the field. The Can Grow and Can Shrink properties are set by selecting the appropriate field in the Form Design view and choosing the View, Properties command. The Format tab is selected, and the Can Grow and Can Shrink properties are set to Yes. Figure 32.24 shows the print preview of a report containing a memo field that has grown to accommodate all the text stored in the Notes memo field for Nancy Davolio, the first employee in the Employees table.

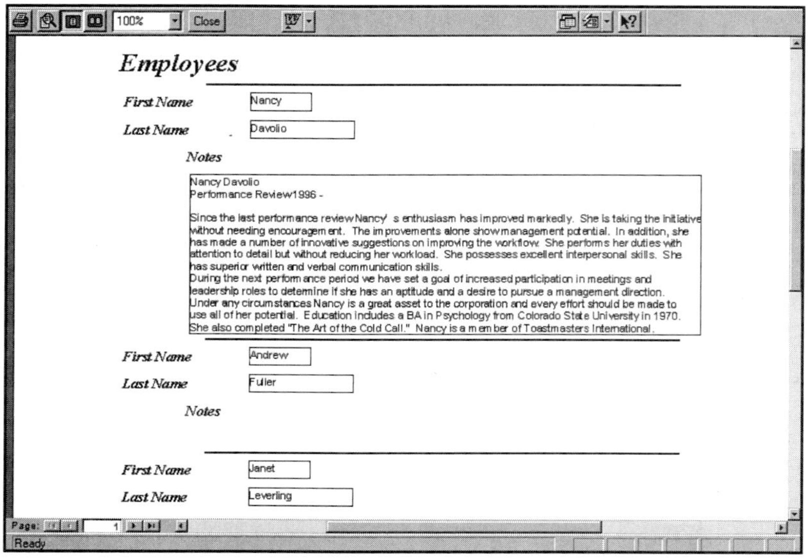

Fig. 32.24

The first employee's memo field expands to display a number of paragraphs of text while the second employee's memo field is empty.

Using OLE Fields for Word Documents

The last type of integration to be discussed involves bringing Word data into an Access OLE field. By doing this, you can retain all the formatting from your Word document. Suppose you want to keep a copy of your employee performance reviews—with all their formatting—in your personnel database. For this example, assume that all the performance review documents have been created and saved. To insert a Word document into an Access OLE field, follow these steps:

1. In Access, open a table that has the OLE field in which you want to keep your Word documents, and place your cursor in the OLE field.

2. Choose Insert, Object, and then choose Create from File. The Insert Object dialog box appears (see fig. 32.25).

Fig. 32.25

In the Insert Object dialog box, you can specify where the file you want is located.

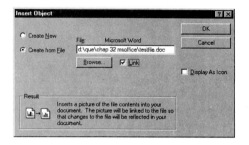

3. Type the path and file name of the Word document or choose Browse to locate it. If you want the OLE field to be linked to the original document, select the Link check box.

You can't view the OLE field contents directly in the table, although you can double-click the field to open the embedded document in Word. If you want to see the OLE field in Access, you can create a form. Figure 32.26 shows a form containing an OLE field and a Memo field. Both of the fields contain the same text. As you can see, the Memo field is easier to read but contains none of the formatting of the original Word document. To make the OLE field legible, its Size Mode property was set to Zoom. Also, remember that you can edit the Memo field in Access, whereas the OLE field must be edited in Word.

The Zoom property causes the OLE object to fit inside its control without distorting the object. Two other size modes are possible: Stretch and Clip. In Stretch mode, the OLE object stretches to fit the control but allows distortion to occur—distorted text can be virtually unreadable. Clip mode maintains the object in its original size, while only displaying the portion that fits in the control. With the size mode property set to Clip, you might see nothing of your OLE object.

Fig. 32.26

Some of the differences between an OLE and Memo field are apparent in this form.

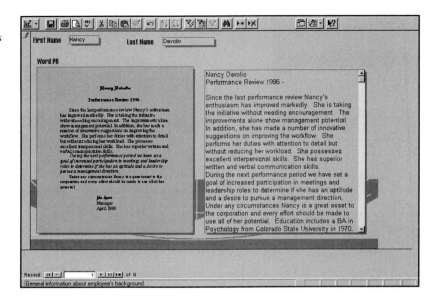

You can display Word data in a report using the same approach as with forms; you add a text box or a bound object frame to your report for the Memo and OLE fields, respectively. Figure 32.27 show an OLE field and a memo field displaying the same data, but this time in a report.

No unusual techniques were used to create the form or the report. As you can see, it's easy to transfer Word data into Access if you have the need.

Fig. 32.27

The Memo field is shown at the top of this report with an OLE field below it. Your needs will dictate which field type you employ.

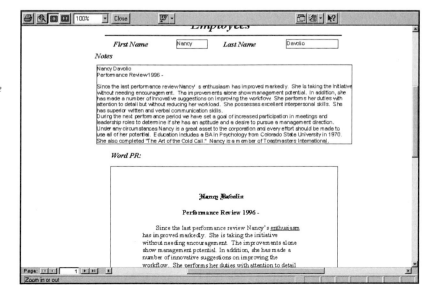

Summary

This chapter dealt with merging Access data into Word—this is the most common type of integration between these two software packages. You saw that most of the process is automated through wizards; however, you can automate even more of the process with buttons and macros if you want.

If you have large amounts of data or you need to analyze it with database tools such as sophisticated queries and calculations, Access is the place to work with it. If you are doing a lot of writing about your data or you need powerful word processing tools, Word is the first choice. Integration allows you to take advantage of the best of both worlds.

chapter 33

Integrating Word and PowerPoint

33

by Donna Payne

In this chapter

◆ **Object transfer methods**
Learn how to use different commands and methods to copy, paste, and insert objects between Word and PowerPoint.

◆ **How to work with links**
Use the Links dialog box to edit, break, change, or update a link between documents.

◆ **Built-in tools to integrate Word and PowerPoint**
Learn how to access built-in integration tools as well as tools that will enhance your reporting and presentation capability.

◆ **About automation in Word and PowerPoint**
Learn to insert objects, embed presentations, and view the objects, properties, and methods of PowerPoint.

Inter-application integration is one of the hottest trends in improvements appearing in personal computing software. With almost every upgrade release, you see new functionality enabling applications to work in synergistic ways that are greater than the sum of the individual applications. Integrating Word and PowerPoint combines Word's word processing or reporting features with PowerPoint's presentation capability. Word and PowerPoint work beautifully together for these tasks.

Of course, Microsoft's mandate to make these applications seamlessly work in tandem helps their bottom line. It is one of the strongest arguments for buying both tools from Microsoft versus buying one from another vendor. This chapter demonstrates Microsoft's strong commitment to making the use of both applications in the same document as easy as working with either application alone.

Integrating Applications

Integration sounds like a good idea, but what does it really mean in terms of your everyday work running Word and PowerPoint? On a fundamental level, it makes the process of transferring text and objects from one application to the other about as easy as moving it in the same application. Because it's easy to transport objects, you don't have to worry about losing the integrity of formatting of objects, whether you're moving, pasting, embedding, or linking them. It also streamlines the editing process, enabling you to use one application's tools in another application rather than having to switch back and forth, copying and pasting text and objects as you go. Finally, it facilitates file integrity and version control, allowing you to update more than one document simultaneously and save disk space if you need to.

Translated into Microsoft application-speak, you can do the following:

▶ Embed an entire file created in one application into another application.

▶ Use the Clipboard or OLE and DDE to transfer or insert objects.

▶ Create links from the source document (also called the *server document*) to the container (also called the *destination*) document.

▶ Use built-in features included in the application—all without writing a single line of code.

Much of the credit for the ease and successfulness of Office integration goes to a technology called Object Linking and Embedding, or OLE (pronounced o-lay), which allows applications to talk to and appear to coexist inside each other's documents.

Creating Compound Documents

When you insert an object that was created in another software application (or the same application if you are linking the documents) into your current document, you create a *compound document*. Think of a compound document as a "document within a document." It allows you to edit material created in one application while working in another application's document. A good example of this is when you create a letterhead for a Word document.

Figure 33.1 shows an object that was created using the WordArt 2.0 mini-application and then inserted into the header of a Word document.

Fig. 33.1

WordArt 2.0 is a Word applet that is OLE 2.0-compatible.

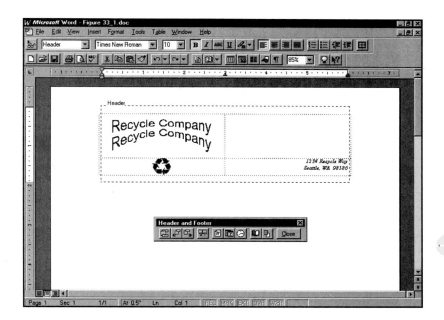

Understanding Static versus Linked Object Insertion

You have decided that you want to insert an object you created in Word into PowerPoint. You can either insert a *static object*—one that will not change, no matter how the original source document changes—or you can create a link to the original file that will update dynamically when the source file changes.

To help you decide whether to use static or linked objects, evaluate whether

▶ The object will change in the future and, if so, will you want to include the changes.

▶ The source file will be available to other users that might access this file.

▶ You need to minimize the size of the file.

If the source file changes and you want the file to change, you will want a link. Also, if it is necessary to keep the file size at a minimum, you will want to create a link. However, if the source file may not be available to others who might have access to the file, you should consider inserting a static object from the source document so—no matter what the location of the server—users will have full access to the contents of the container document.

Embedding versus Moving or Copying Static Objects into PowerPoint

What happens after you choose to include a static copy of an object you created in Word within a PowerPoint presentation? First, think about whether simply moving or copying from Word using Edit, Cut or Edit, Copy and Edit, Paste would do the job adequately. Use embedding for static objects instead of moving or copying when the following are true:

▶ You want the convenience of using Word editing tools while working in PowerPoint, eliminating switching back and forth between the applications.

▶ You are not overly concerned about file size. Embedding objects in PowerPoint increases the size of the PowerPoint file by about as much as the size of a separate Word file containing the object.

▶ You want the option of saving the object as a Word file (independent of the PowerPoint file it is embedded in).

Moving or copying is the fastest method if you do not have any of the preceding concerns. However, there are a few things to keep in mind about pasting between Word and PowerPoint (which are mostly true for moving or copying from any other application as well):

▶ Pasting a Word graphic into PowerPoint automatically embeds it as a Word object. You cannot convert it to a PowerPoint object (to make it editable with PowerPoint tools) by double-clicking, as you can for objects pasted from other non-OLE applications.

▶ Paste as a picture by choosing Edit, Paste Special, and then double-clicking to convert it to a PowerPoint object. Figure 33.2 shows the Microsoft PowerPoint dialog box that appears when you double-click to convert an object that was pasted from Word into PowerPoint as a picture.

Fig. 33.2

You must convert a pasted object to the container application's format when you want to edit it.

Most of the time you should convert non-embedded pictures to PowerPoint objects to give you the greatest flexibility in editing. Pictures appear as bitmaps, so you cannot use PowerPoint vector (draw) editing tools.

Note

You cannot properly convert Postscript (EPS) drawings, 24-bit color drawings, or bitmaps to PowerPoint objects from Word or any other application.

There might be times when you want to retain the picture status of a graphic in PowerPoint: for instance, to allow you to recolor the background of the picture inside the bounding box or the border of the bounding box.

Keep in mind the following tips and techniques when you want to transfer text or objects between PowerPoint and Word and you need to retain native or picture status of the transferred object:

▶ You must activate the Text tool in PowerPoint before pasting text from Word if you want to retain the text's property as editable characters. Otherwise, it will be pasted as a picture.

▶ You can use Microsoft's drag-and-drop editing between applications to move text or objects quickly. Both applications must be configured to support OLE 2.0. Also, make sure drag-and-drop editing is enabled in Word's Edit dialog box, accessed by choosing Tools, Options, Edit. Select the text or object and drag between documents just as you would in the same document.

Editing Embedded Objects in PowerPoint

Objects that are embedded by choosing Edit, Paste Special, MS Word Document or by using normal pasting from Word remain objects in their native format and can be edited in Word. Using in-place, or visual, editing—a feature of OLE 2.0—double-clicking the object to edit it activates the object's native menu and toolbars without fully launching the native application (but you do need to have Word installed on your disk or on a network server that you can access for this to work).

Figure 33.3 shows that Edit mode has been activated for an embedded object by double-clicking it.

Fig. 33.3

When the embedded object is activated, the object's native menu bar and toolbars appear in the container application's window.

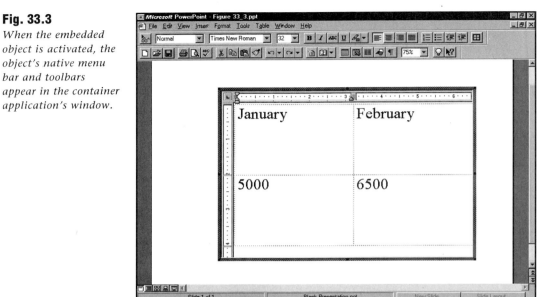

 Note

Others can view and print documents that contain embedded objects even if they don't have access to the applications that created the objects. They can convert an embedded object to a PowerPoint object by selecting it, choosing Edit, choosing the last item on the menu, and then choosing Convert. (The menu item will vary, depending on the application from which the object was created.)

 Note

When you double-click sound, video, and other multimedia objects in PowerPoint, they play rather than activate Edit mode in the source application. You cannot activate Edit mode in the source application for these objects.

Editing Embedded Objects in Word

To embed an object from PowerPoint into Word, you follow the same steps as embedding from Word to PowerPoint. The difference between how the application handles objects becomes apparent when you try to edit them. When you double-click an object that was copied from PowerPoint and embedded into Word, you see the toolbars that are shown in figure 33.4.

Fig. 33.4

*The container
document is Word.
Word handles the edit
process of a picture
differently than
PowerPoint.*

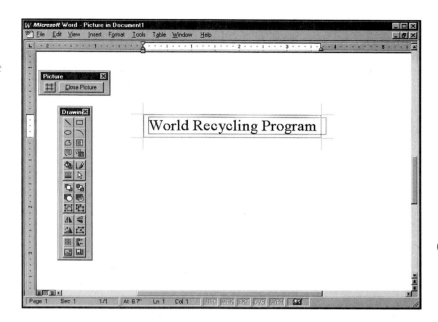

Notice how the title of the window has changed to `Picture in Document1` and the new
toolbar with the tools to reset the picture boundary and to close the picture window
becomes active.

 Note

As with PowerPoint, when you double-click sound, video, and certain other multimedia objects in Word, they play rather than activate Edit mode in the source application. You cannot activate Edit mode in the source application for these objects by
double-clicking. In Word, however, you can edit some of these objects as embedded objects by choosing Edit, Object.

In this section, you learned how to create the most basic embedded objects and you
learned about the differences between doing so in Word and in PowerPoint. In the next
section, you learn how to link and embed objects using the Insert menu.

Linking or Embedding Using the Insert Menu

All Office applications have an Insert menu, and all except Schedule+ allow you to insert
an object into your document. You have the choice of linking or embedding for most

objects. Linking can be more difficult to manage because you are dealing with two files—a server and a container—instead of one. In spite of this, it definitely wins out over embedding when the following are true:

▶ You are dealing with disk space limitations and/or large file sizes. The file size will increase by the size of the image of the file displayed in the application, but not by the actual file itself. This consideration can be especially critical with video and other multimedia documents.

▶ You are working in a networked workgroup environment and there is material (especially material that undergoes periodic revisions) that group members need to have access to. Linking updates documents for all members in one editing swoop.

▶ You want a foolproof way to ensure that information in a document is current: for example, a PowerPoint presentation based on information that gets updated in a Word table. Without a link between the Word table and the PowerPoint presentation, you cannot be sure that you have the most current data from the Word table.

 Note
For linking to work, the source file must be accessible to all users.

Using the Word Insert Menu

Word offers several types of items that can be inserted into a container document. This chapter discusses the objects that can be linked to the source document. The Word Insert menu options related to these objects are the following:

▶ *File.* The Insert File dialog box allows you to select the desired file and choose whether you want to create a link.

▶ *Frame.* When you select an object and choose Insert, Frame, a frame appears around the selected object. The frame allows you to precisely position the object on the page and have text flow around it.

▶ *Picture.* Choose Insert, Picture to open the Insert Picture dialog box (see fig. 33.5).

▶ *Object.* Inserting an object into a container document creates an OLE object that can be edited in place and is available to drag and drop into another application. In the Object dialog box, the Create From File tab allows you to insert an object that already exists in a saved file you have access to (see fig. 33.6). To select the file, click the Browse button. You can also select Link To File and Display As Icon.

Fig. 33.5
You can choose to display the inserted object as an icon to save room in your container document— it will only appear when the icon is double-clicked.

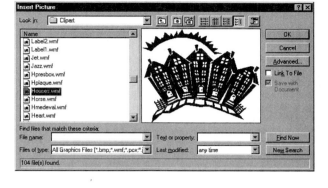

Fig. 33.6
By choosing to insert a file that has already been created, you can edit the file later using the application that created the source file.

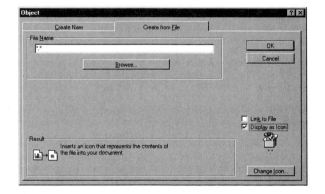

You can insert a database into a Word document by simply choosing Insert, Database. This opens the Database dialog box (see fig. 33.7).

Fig. 33.7
Even though Word is considered a word processing and desktop publishing package, you can access external databases that are created in other applications.

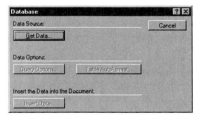

The Data Source option Get Data allows you to choose the source where your data is saved. Other options from the database include Query Options, Table AutoFormat, and Insert Data. When you click the Get Data button, you are prompted to select the source of your external data that you want to return to Word. After you return the data, you are asked if you want to use Query to specify what parts of the database you want to retrieve. After you select the data source and have the data as you want it to appear in Word, click the Insert Data button.

Using the PowerPoint Insert Menu

PowerPoint offers slightly different Insert menu items than the ones offered by Word. In PowerPoint, you can insert the following objects:

- Clip Art
- Picture
- Movie
- Sound
- Microsoft Graph
- Microsoft Word Table
- Object

This section addresses the Microsoft Word Table and Object options.

 Note

For information on the other objects that do not have to do with Word/PowerPoint integration, see Part III, "PowerPoint," or refer to the online help.

When you choose Insert, Microsoft Word Table, the Insert Word Table dialog box appears (see fig. 33.8). Specify the Number of Columns and Number of Rows for the layout of the table you are inserting in the PowerPoint document.

Fig. 33.8

This dialog box is very similar to the Insert Table dialog box in Word.

 Note

The maximum number of columns is 26. The maximum number of rows is 6. The minimum number for each setting is 1.

There are three Word object types that appear in the list Object Type in the Insert Object dialog box when you choose Insert, Object in PowerPoint: Microsoft Word Document, Word Picture, and WordArt 2.0. When you choose to insert an object into PowerPoint, the dialog box functions in the same manner and offers the same options as Word.

Using OLE Commands

A common way to create a link in Word and PowerPoint is to create an object, choose Edit, Copy, switch to the other application, choose Edit, Paste Special, choose the format, and create a link. Figure 33.9 shows the Paste Special dialog box.

Tip

If you want to create a link, you must have enough memory to run both applications at the same time. To run two applications on Windows 95, it takes approximately 8M of memory. You need 16M to run two applications simultaneously on Windows NT Workstation.

Fig. 33.9

You have different options you can choose when pasting an object.

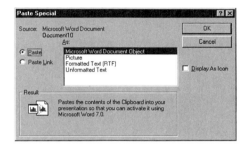

Note

When you are copying and using the Paste Special command from an OLE application, the Paste Special dialog box lists several options for selecting a data type. These options include Object, Picture, and Bitmap. If you select Object, Word embeds the object and you can edit the object by double-clicking it. However, if you select Bitmap or Picture, Word inserts the information as a Picture and, when you double-click the picture, you have to edit it using Word's tools. Copied text provides two additional data types: Formatted Text (RTF) and Unformatted Text.

If the program used to create the embedded object is no longer available, consider converting it to a format that can be read and edited by the program you're using. You can edit or convert an object by selecting it and choosing Edit, choosing the last option on the submenu (this changes depending on the type of object), choosing Object in the source application and choosing either Edit, Open or Edit, Convert. By choosing Edit, the source application will launch and the object will be sent to the source application. Choosing the Convert command displays the Convert dialog box (see fig. 33.10).

Fig. 33.10
*Convert an object to
the current application
type to be able to edit
the object.*

 Tip
You can convert a drawing object created in Word to a picture by clicking the
Create Picture button on the Drawing toolbar.

Table 33.1 summarizes the differences between working with and inserting objects by
various methods. To understand the following table, look closer at the Object Type option to drag and drop. When you create an object by dragging an object from one application to another, you are not able to link the object to the source file and instead must
embed the object with the object's native application format.

Table 33.1   Inserting Objects

Object Type	Link	Embed	Format
Existing Object	Yes	Yes	Object's native application
New Object	No	Yes	Object's native application
Picture	Yes	Yes	Picture Editor
Paste Special	Yes	Yes	List, type chosen by user
Clipboard and native Drag-and-Drop	No	Yes	Object's application

Managing Links

A *link* is simply a connection existing between two documents that allows the container
document to connect to the source document as long as both applications are OLE compliant. The object or linked file is stored in the source document, while the container (or
receiving) document only stores information necessary for locating the source data.

By default, a link updates automatically; however, you can change this option to manual. Select the object and choose Edit, Links to open the Links dialog box (see fig. 33.11). Select the Manual option. An automatic link keeps the object updated when the source data is modified; a manual link will not update until you tell it to.

Fig. 33.11

If your document contains links, they'll probably appear in the Links dialog box.

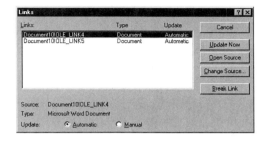

The Links dialog box shows what links exist, the source of the link (including the full path of the file), the type of object the link represents, and whether the link is updated automatically or manually. Four buttons allow you to update the link (Update Now), open the source document (Open Source), change the source document (Change Source), and to break the link (Break Link).

 Note

You can select multiple links in the Links dialog box; however, only two buttons are active when more than one link is selected: Update Now and Break Link.

 Tip

There are keyboard shortcuts for updating the linked object. By pressing F9 when the linked object is selected, you are in effect clicking the Update Now button. Pressing Ctrl+Shift+F9 while the linked object is selected will simulate clicking the Break Link button.

The Change Source button will allow you to change the source of the link. This button becomes important if you change the name of the source file or the source file's location. Many users find that it's easier to delete the link in the container document and create a new link after they rename the source file.

With a link selected in the Links dialog box, click the Break Links button to leave the data or object in your container document and to break the link between the two files.

Built-In Integration Tools

It's very easy to integrate Word and PowerPoint; there are several built-in toolbar buttons and menu items to facilitate this process. Additionally, there are option settings that will affect how object links are handled.

In Word, there is a toolbar button on the Tools toolbar that launches or switches to PowerPoint. The name of the button, Microsoft PowerPoint, appears when the mouse pointer arrow is over the toolbar button. The button itself resembles a PowerPoint presentation icon.

In Word, there are several settings you should be aware of. You can find these settings in the Options dialog box by choosing Tools, Options and looking at the General and Print tabs. The following options are available for each tab that pertains to linking:

Tab	Option
General	Update Automatic Links at Open
Print	Update Links

PowerPoint provides multiple buttons for integrating the application with Word. On the Insert toolbar is a button that will expedite the insertion of a Word table. The Report It button on the Tools toolbar takes textual information and places it in a Word document. Figure 33.12 shows a PowerPoint slide with the Report It button as part of its own toolbar located on the actual slide.

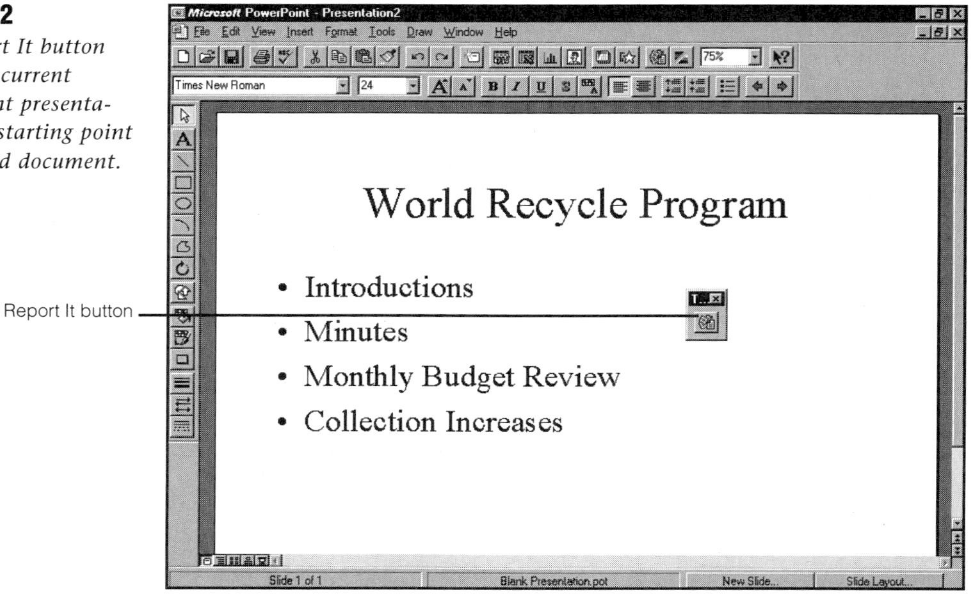

Fig. 33.12
The Report It button uses your current PowerPoint presentation as a starting point for a Word document.

Report It button

After you click the Report It button, your presentation is placed in a newly created Word document. Figure 33.13 shows the results of using the Report It button.

Fig. 33.13

The Word document is named with a PPT(number).RTF file format.

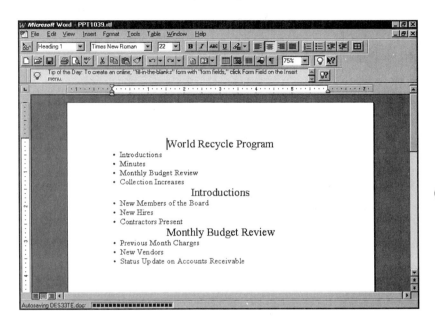

You can quickly convert a PowerPoint presentation into a Word document that includes your slide formatting and can contain a link to the source file. Choose Tools, Write-Up to open the Write-Up dialog box (see fig. 33.14). The Write-Up feature is valuable if you want to quickly take a presentation that you have created in PowerPoint and place it into a report or with other data in Word.

Because you can choose different options in the Write-Up dialog box, you can specify how you want the data presented in Word. The option that you choose depends on how you want to use the data and how you want the data presented. For instance, the Notes Next to Slides option will present three columns in a table layout: column one contains the slide number, column two contains the actual slide, and the third column is an area to write notes. The Blank Lines Next to Slides creates lines in the third column that notes can be written in. The option descriptions are a good representation of what each option does.

After you have selected the preferred option to write up the presentation and you have clicked the OK button, the information is placed in a table format in the Word document.

Fig. 33.14

A diagram of how each option is placed into Word is shown next to each option in the dialog box.

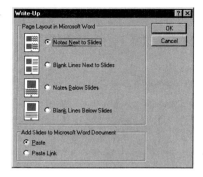

Automation

Currently, there is no way to control OLE Automation services in Word. This means that from Word, you cannot control objects in PowerPoint, Excel, or Project. Because OLE Automation is an integral part of the Microsoft strategy, it shouldn't be long before you can use OLE Automation in all Microsoft applications, including Word.

You can insert a PowerPoint slide or presentation into a Word document by creating a simple WordBasic macro, similar to the following code. This macro inserts a PowerPoint presentation in a Word document and displays the presentation as an icon.

```
Sub MAIN
InsertObject .IconNumber = 2, .FileName = "", .Link = 0, .DisplayIcon = 1, .Tab = "0",_
.Class = "PowerPoint.Show.7", .IconFilename = "C:\MSOFFICE\POWERPNT\powerpnt.exe", _
.Caption = "Microsoft PowerPoint Presentation"
End Sub
```

InsertObject starts an OLE application or switches to the application in which the object was created and embeds the object at the insertion point in Word. There are eight arguments to InsertObject. These arguments appear in the table following this macro:

```
InsertObject[.IconNumber = number][, .FileName = text][, .Link = number]
  [, .DisplayIcon = number][, .Tab = number][, .Class = text][, .IconFileName =number]
  [, .Caption = text]
```

Argument	Description
.IconNumber	If the argument .DisplayIcon is 1 (as shown in the preceding macro), the argument .IconNumber indicates which icons the user wants to display. If the argument is omitted, the default icon is used.
.FileName	This is the full path and file name of the file you are storing as an embedded object.

Argument	Description
.Link	If .Link is set to 1, links are embedded to the file specified in the argument .FileName.
.DisplayIcon	If .DisplayIcon is 1, the link is displayed as an icon. If 0, the link is not displayed as an icon.
.Tab	A 0 value indicates that the user selected the Create New tab on the Insert Object dialog box. A value of 1 indicates that the user selected the Create From File tab.
.Class	The class name of a new object to insert.
.IconFilename	If 1, the full path of the file name is stored.
.Caption	If 1, the caption on the icon is displayed. If omitted, Word inserts the name of the object.

Fig. 33.15

Double-click the icon to display the PowerPoint presentation.

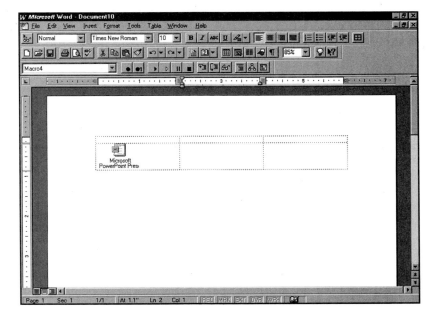

Figure 33.15 shows the result of running the preceding macro.

Because Word cannot yet control PowerPoint objects or the PowerPoint Object Model and there is no way to access the Object Model from PowerPoint, you have to go to Excel to see what the PowerPoint Object Model looks like.

Create a module sheet in Excel and choose Tools, References. In the References dialog box, select the option to access the PowerPoint 7.0 Object Library and click OK. Now choose View, Object Browser to open the Object Browser dialog box. Choose PowerPoint from the Libraries/Workbooks drop-down list (see fig. 33.16).

Fig. 33.16

No help is provided for the PowerPoint Object Model from this dialog box. In fact, not much documentation exists on the PowerPoint Object Model.

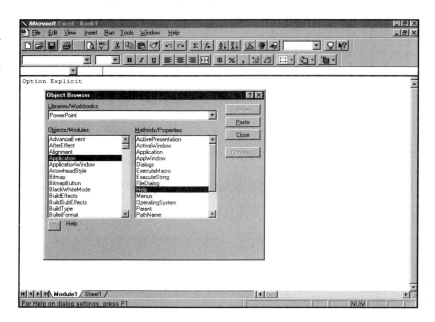

Not all of the objects listed in the Object Browser dialog box are available in this PowerPoint version release. Some are scheduled to be accessible in the next major release of PowerPoint.

Summary

In this chapter, you looked at how well PowerPoint and Word work together. By creating compound documents, you can insert an object into one document and use the features and functionality of another application without having to open the other application.

Word and PowerPoint are a good match for creating integrated applications. By taking the desktop publishing and reporting capability of Word and combining it with the presentation capability of PowerPoint, you are able to create effective presentations without spending a lot of time and energy by using the built-in application tools.

chapter 34

Integrating Schedule+ and Exchange

34

by Heidi Sullivan-Liscomb

In this chapter

◆ **Log into Schedule+ in Group-Enabled mode**
This section provides you with the steps to get you up and running using Schedule+ on your network.

◆ **Use the Options dialog box**
Use the information in this section to set up your Schedule+ account.

◆ **Use the Set Access Permissions dialog box**
Determine which network users will have access to your schedule, and to what extent users can modify your account information.

◆ **Use the Planner tab and the Invite button**
Learn to use these functions to check on the schedules of other users and invite them to meetings or appointments.

◆ **Schedule, reschedule, and cancel meetings**
This section covers the myriad ways to schedule, reschedule, or cancel a meeting over the network.

E arlier in this book, you learned how to use Microsoft's scheduling tool to manage your appointments and meetings. Using Schedule+ in Stand-Alone mode provides you with a place to manage your personal scheduling information, maintain a Rolodex-style file of your personal and business contacts, and track your projects. In this chapter, you learn how to use the power of group-enabled software by using Schedule+ with Microsoft's mail system, Exchange. Please note that no changes need to be made to Exchange when using Schedule+ in Group-Enabled mode. This chapter will cover what it is like to use Schedule+ in Group mode and will not delve into Exchange. See the chapters on Exchange for any questions involving Exchange.

Using Schedule+ in Group mode provides you with access to the schedules of other users on your network. When you are working on a network and all users have Schedule+ and Exchange, you can use these tools to schedule, reschedule, and cancel appointments with an unlimited number of people. You can instantly determine if the time you have chosen for a meeting is convenient for all attendees, decide which room and what equipment to use, and send meeting invitations to your colleagues. This procedure can save you some footwork and potential aggravation when trying to schedule a meeting for a group of people.

Schedule+ is the scheduling tool; Exchange is the communication tool. You bring them together.

Getting Started

Earlier in this book, you learned how to use Schedule+ as a single user. This chapter concentrates on using Schedule+ in Group mode, enabling you to send and receive schedules, meetings, and appointment requests via Exchange.

When you are working as a member of a group of users on a network, accessing Schedule+ is a little different from using it as a single user. Your network administrators must provide you with an account and a password for Exchange. Be sure the account is set up prior to attempting any of the group scheduling tasks included in this chapter.

After your account with Exchange is established on the network, it automatically opens when you log in. Schedule+ asks if you want to work alone or in Group mode. Choose Yes, Work in Group-Enabled Mode. To set up Schedule+ to run in Group mode each time you log in, choose Don't Ask Me This Question Again. Schedule+ automatically logs you in to Group mode.

To log into Schedule+ in Group-Enabled mode, follow these steps:

1. Select Start, Programs, Microsoft Schedule+. The Profile Name box appears.
2. Select your name from the drop-down list. If your name does not appear, type it in the box.
3. Enter your password. Schedule+ displays the Daily tab screen.

Caution
Choosing Remember Password enables anyone with access to your computer to start and view your schedule.

Note

If you are logging in for the first time and are unsure of your password, ask your system administrator for it. You can change your password by choosing <u>T</u>ools, Change <u>P</u>assword.

The first default view in Schedule+ is the D<u>a</u>ily tab, which shows time slots running down the left of the screen and any scheduled events on the right. This view looks like a legal pad and is called your Appointment Book. If you have already worked in Schedule+ as a single user, your scheduled events for the day appear in the D<u>a</u>ily screen.

You can switch to a view of your monthly or weekly schedule to see any events, tasks, or projects you have. To change the view of your schedule, click the <u>M</u>onthly, <u>W</u>eekly, or D<u>a</u>ily tabs running down the left side of the Schedule+ window. Clicking the To <u>D</u>o tab gives you a list of all the current tasks and projects you are involved in. Figure 34.1 shows the Appointment Book with the D<u>a</u>ily tab displayed.

Fig. 34.1

This is the default view of the Appointment Book; the Daily tab is displayed.

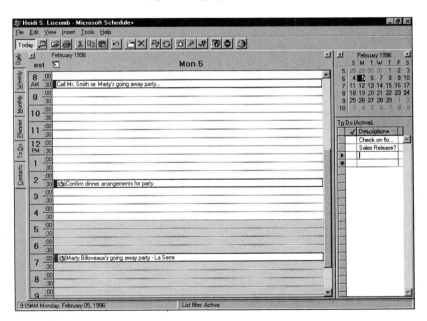

Schedule+ enables you to add, remove, mail, or change appointments and resources in your schedule as needed. But first you must set yourself up to use Schedule+ in Group mode. The first step is to set up your account so it works best for you. You begin with the Options dialog box, as described next.

Setting Up Scheduling Options

The most important part of managing your schedule begins with an accurate representation of your business day. Setting up your calendar so that it manages your schedule is easy; you first do it during the initial setup, and then any time you have major changes in how you structure your day. To set up your file, you choose Tools, Options. Take some time to familiarize yourself with the different sections of the dialog box—you need them all for effectively maintaining your schedule.

The Options dialog box is where you set up the basic information for your Schedule+ account. You will define your defaults, determine how your calendar is displayed, archive older data, and set up a resource account. Also in this dialog box are the functions for setting daily reminders for appointments, automatically accepting meeting requests as they arrive from the network, and removing appointments from your schedule. Finally, you can coordinate the schedules in different time zones and synchronize your schedule file with the network schedule file.

Selecting from a series of tabs that run across the top of the Options dialog box allows you to access these functions. Figure 34.2 shows the Options dialog box open to the General tab. By clicking any of the tabs, you can switch to that screen and make changes to your Schedule+ setup.

Fig. 34.2

Use the Options dialog box to set up your Schedule+ files.

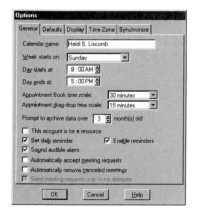

Using the General Tab

Choose Tools, Options to open the Options dialog box. The first time you do this, the General tab appears (see fig. 34.3). If you switch to one of the other tabs, perhaps the Display tab, and you close the Options dialog box, the next time you open this dialog box, it will open to the Display tab.

Fig. 34.3

*The General tab in the
Options dialog box
allows you to define
your Schedule+
account setup.*

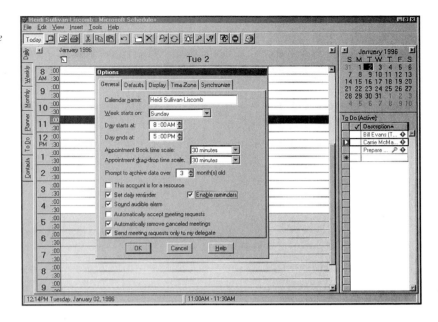

The Calendar Name box refers to the name of the user that owns the calendar at which
you are looking. Your name should appear, or if you are a delegate or are accessing someone else's schedule, the owner's name appears in the box. You learn about assigning a
delegate to handle your schedule later in this chapter.

A series of check boxes define how your calendar appears. On what day and at what time
does your week begin? At what time does it end? At what time intervals do you want
your appointments to appear in your calendar? Click the arrows in each of the boxes to
open the drop-down lists. Select the information that best describes your day, and your
calendar will appear accordingly.

To set the day and time for your calendar, follow these steps:

1. Click the down arrow next to the Week Starts On box.

2. Select the day on which your week begins.

3. Click the hour or minute in the Day Starts At box to select it and use the up/down
   arrows to change the time. Do the same for the Day Ends At box.

4. The Appointment Book Time Scale box refers to the time intervals that display in
   your calendar. Select the time by clicking the down arrow next to the box. You can
   choose 5, 6, 10, 15, or 30 minute intervals.

5. The Appointment Drag-Drop Time Scale box enables you to determine the time
   intervals that are available if you need to move or extend an appointment. You
   have the option of extending your appointments by 10, 15, or 30 minutes.

For example, if you have a 9:30 am appointment that you initially set up for 30 minutes, and you realize that it's going to run longer, you can grab the handles of the appointment box in your Appointment Book and drag. The appointment drags in whatever time increments you have set. If you need to extend an appointment an extra 30 minutes, you can grab the appointment handles in your calendar and drag it for 30 minutes. If you have set the time scale in your calendar to be 15 minutes, you can drag the appointment in 15-minute intervals. If you have set up the time scale to be 10 minutes, you can drag the calendar for a 10-minute interval.

 Note

If the time scale differs from the drag-drop scale, Schedule+ shows the difference in the far-left handle of the appointment bar.

After you use Schedule+ for some time, your calendar fills up. Use the archive function in the General tab to store older information. In the Prompt to Archive Data Over box, use the up/down arrows to select the age of the information in number of months. You can select up to 99 months. Schedule+ automatically takes any information in your calendar that meets the specified age and puts it in an archive file. You can access your archived files any time by choosing File, Open, Archive or Project Schedule.

If your company has specific rooms set aside for meetings, you can set up a file in Schedule+ to sign out the rooms or equipment. Assign the account a Calendar Name that reflects the resource: Conference Room 6 or Overhead Projector #1. Check the This Account Is for a Resource box to establish the account as a room or equipment. You can then refer to this account when you need to confirm a specific room or piece of equipment for a meeting.

 Note

A *resource* can be a room or piece of equipment. By assigning a mailbox to a resource, you can sign out the resource for use. The item shows up as busy on the calendar.

Check Automatically Accept Meeting Requests to accept all meeting requests that arrive from other users on the network. Any time users on your network want to schedule a meeting with you, they can—provided you are not already engaged. If you have disallowed overlapping appointments, you don't need to worry about conflicting appointments; Schedule+ will not accept two appointments for the same time slot. To prevent appointments from overlapping or being scheduled repeatedly, follow these steps:

1. Choose Tools, Set Access Permissions.
2. Click the Global tab.
3. Choose Disallow Overlapping Appointments.

There is an option in the General tab that allows you to set daily reminders with audible alarms for any appointments you have. Simply check the Sound Audible alarm box by clicking it. Schedule+ will remove canceled meetings and send meeting requests from other network users only to your delegate or assistant if you check these boxes. Whatever format you assign your Appointment Book today can be changed at any time simply by returning to the General tab and making the desired changes.

 Note

When setting Schedule+ up to sound an audible alarm and display daily reminders, be sure to check the Enable Reminders box. If you don't, the reminders do not appear, and the alarm doesn't sound.

34

Using the Defaults Tab

Click the Defaults tab to work with specific details regarding your calendar (see fig. 34.4). Perhaps you want to set a reminder to go off 15 minutes before your appointments. Click the Set Reminders for Appointments Automatically box and scroll to the time you want. You can set the alarm to go off up to 99 minutes before the appointment.

Fig. 34.4

Use the Defaults tab to set reminders and prioritize your tasks.

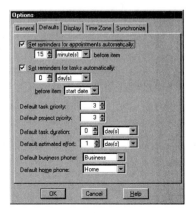

The Defaults tab is particularly useful if you are working on a task or project that you want to track to completion. You can set reminders regarding an action you must take by clicking Set Reminders for Tasks Automatically. Then before each task is due, Schedule+ reminds you. Select days, minutes, hours, weeks, or months from the drop-down list, and use either the start or end date for the task as your reference point.

You can prioritize your projects by assigning them a priority number up to nine or a letter from A to Z. You can use numbers or letters alone or in combination. Numbers are higher in priority than letters, meaning that nine is a higher priority than A.

To track the length of time it takes you to complete a task or set of tasks and the effort you estimate it will take, follow these steps:

1. Select the Default Task Duration box.
2. Use the up/down arrows to select the number of days, weeks, or months.
3. Select the Day(s) box and use the drop-down list to determine whether your project or task will take days, weeks, or months.

The Default Estimated Effort box allows you to estimate the effort that will go into a specific project. This would be useful when you are attempting to assign the same person to a series of projects. You can then estimate when a person will have one project completed and might be ready to begin another. You can repeat these same steps for the Default Estimated Effort box. Set the task duration and estimated effort by selecting days, hours, minutes, weeks, or months from the drop-down lists in each box.

Finally, if you want to be available by telephone to the other network users, you can put your business or home telephone numbers in the appropriate boxes. These numbers are the ones your contacts will see when they access your account.

Using the Display Tab

The Display tab is the place to custom format the appearance of your Appointment Book (see fig. 34.5).

You can select background colors for the different aspects of the Appointment Book and choose different color bars for the required and optional meeting attendees. Whatever selections you make for your calendar will appear even when someone else accesses your schedule.

To select a color for the backgrounds of your Appointment Book, Planner, Grid, and Page, follow these steps:

1. Choose Tools, Options, then click the Display tab.

2. Choose the Appointment Book, Grid, or Page bar. Click the down arrow to display the colors that are available to you.

3. Use the up/down arrows to scroll through the colors that are available. Select the color that you want for each background.

4. Click OK.

Fig. 34.5

Use the Display tab to set different colors for yourself and the required and optional attendees.

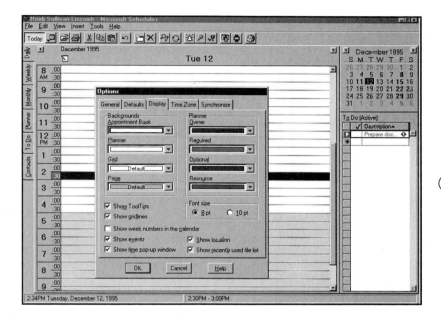

The next step is to assign colors to the different users. Then when you check the schedule for someone, you can simply glance at the grid, and the user's busy times appear in colored bars.

Assigning colors to yourself, required and optional meeting attendees, and a designated resource for the meeting is similar to the preceding steps. After clicking the Display tab, choose the Owner, Required, Optional, or Resource box. Then select the color you want.

α Note

Select the Show Gridlines box if you want gridlines to appear in your Contacts list, To Do list, or Projects list.

The Show Week Numbers Option

Another option in the Display tab is Show Week Numbers in the <u>C</u>alendar. In the top-right corner of your Appointment Book is a mini-calendar called the Navigator, which shows the entire month with today's date highlighted. Selecting this option puts week numbers before each week in the Navigator. The first week will have a 1 next to it, the second week a 2, and so on.

The Show Events Option

In the upper-left corner of the Appointment Book is a tiny white box with a pen icon in it. If you have any events scheduled (all-day meetings, conferences, seminars), the little box appears to have writing in it. To display your events, click the box.

To display your events all the time, select Show E<u>v</u>ents in the Display tab; the events appear above your calendar. To insert new events, click the box. If you right-click, Schedule+ asks you if the new event is an annual event. If you left-click, you can schedule an event for the current day.

 Tip

You can set reminders for events days, weeks, or months ahead of the event, but not hours or minutes. The reason is that an event is generally an activity that takes all day.

Pop-Up Windows and Appointment Locations

Select the Show Ti<u>m</u>e Pop-Up Window if you want a pop-up window to display the date and time of a selected time slot in your Appointment Book.

One very important aspect of the Display tab is the <u>S</u>how Location box. If you want to display the location and a brief description of your appointment in the Appointment Book, you must select this check box. If you don't select this option, you can enter the information but it doesn't appear in your Appointment Book. You need to go to the Appointment dialog box to see the information.

Using the Time Zone Tab

If you work in an organization that has employees or offices scattered throughout the world, or even the country, you know how difficult it can be to schedule appointments with everyone. This situation is particularly true for those who are working in different

time zones. Getting in touch with someone who is 12 hours ahead or behind your schedule can be frustrating. Schedule+ and Exchange handle these situations easily with the
Time Zone tab (see fig. 34.6).

Fig. 34.6

*Use the Time Zone
tab to work with your
colleagues in another
time zone.*

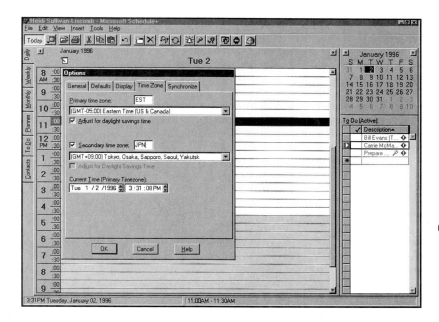

To set up time zones for you and a colleague, follow these steps:

1. Choose Tools, Options, then click the Time Zone tab.

2. Put your time in the Primary Time Zone box. Type three characters to name the
   time zone. For instance, if you are working in Eastern Standard Time, put **EST**.

3. Enter your colleague's time zone in the Secondary Time Zone box. Type three
   characters to name the time zone.

4. Click OK. You and your colleague's time zones appear in your calendar.

Adjust for daylight savings time for the countries that subscribe to that method by
checking Adjust for Daylight Savings Time box. When you select a country that does
not use daylight savings time, the option grays out.

> **α Note**
>
> Schedule+ enables you to display only two different time zones at one time in your
> calendar.

Using the Synchronize Tab

After you begin using Schedule+ and Exchange to schedule appointments, you want to be sure that the network shows the same version of your schedule that you have. If you give other people access to your schedule—to view your free and busy times or to schedule something for you—your schedule needs to be updated frequently on your network to avoid conflicts. Users should be aware of the time period between synchronizations. For instance, if you decide to synchronize your schedule file with the network's schedule file every 30 minutes, and coworkers don't know this, they may try to schedule something for you during a time you've just filled. Figure 34.7 shows the Synchronize tab.

Fig. 34.7

Use the Synchronize tab to update your schedule on the network.

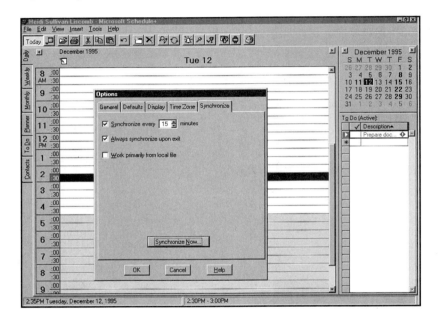

To synchronize your schedule file with the network schedule, follow these steps:

1. Choose Tools, Options, then click the Synchronize tab.

2. Check the Synchronize box. The Minutes box appears to the right of the Synchronize box.

3. Using the up/down arrows, select the time, in minutes, that you want your schedule updated on the network.

4. Check Always Synchronize Upon Exit if you want your schedule updated on the network each time you exit Schedule+.

5. Check Work Primarily from Local File if you don't want to keep your schedule updated on the network. You can always choose the Synchronize Now button when you want your schedule updated.

6. Click OK.

Tip

You can set up Schedule+ to synchronize at whatever time period you prefer, up to 99 minutes, but you probably should update frequently, especially if you have given people permission to use your schedule. You can avoid conflicts this way. Even if you selected to disallow overlapping appointments, this feature doesn't work if the network schedule is not updated.

Congratulations! You have set yourself up to use Schedule+.

Giving Colleagues Permission to See Your Schedule

Using Schedule+ and Exchange together provides all the users on your network with access to your schedule, if you give them permission. You may want certain users to be able to view your schedule so they can set up appointments or meetings that involve you and not create a conflict. You can allow coworkers and team members to have access to your schedule, projects, tasks, and events to modify the information or simply view it. You can track your projects and tasks and give your team members permission to view them using Schedule+.

To set up the permissions for different users, choose Tools, Set Access Permissions. Using the Set Access Permissions dialog box, you can tell Schedule+ who can and cannot gain access to your schedule and what they can do to it. In addition, other users may have access to your list of business and personal contacts and resource lists. You can assign different levels of permissions to different people on your network. You may want to allow some people to modify your schedule and others to only read it.

Using the Users Tab

From the Set Access Permissions dialog box, you can choose from two tabs. The dialog box opens with the Users tab displayed (see fig. 34.8). You see a list of the users on your network who could have access to your schedule. Click each name to select it and set up the type of access he or she will have to your schedule. If you have an assistant who handles most of your scheduling, it may be convenient to give that person numerous permissions. Schedule+ refers to that person as a *delegate*, and the permissions provided for that user enable him or her to effectively manage your schedule. Select that person's name, or if he or she is not listed, choose Add to add the name to the list (as described in the next section).

34

Fig. 34.8

Use the Users tab to set permissions for different users on your network.

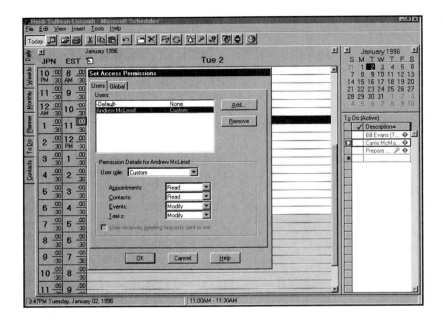

Adding Users

If you are trying to assign certain permissions to a user and his or her name does not appear in the Users box, follow these steps:

1. Choose <u>A</u>dd. The Add Users dialog box opens (see fig. 34.9).

2. Select the Personal Address Book or Postoffice Address List from the upper-right corner.

3. Select the name of the user you want to add, or type the name.

4. Choose <u>U</u>sers to add the name to the list. The name of the user moves to the right dialog box.

5. Choose P<u>r</u>operties to see the user's account information or <u>N</u>ew to set up the user's account information (see fig. 34.10).

Fig. 34.9

To assign permissions to a person not listed in the Users box, open the Add Users dialog box.

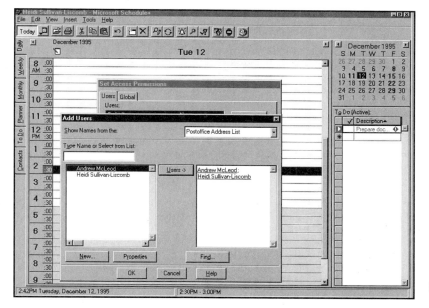

Fig. 34.10

View the user's account information in the Properties dialog box.

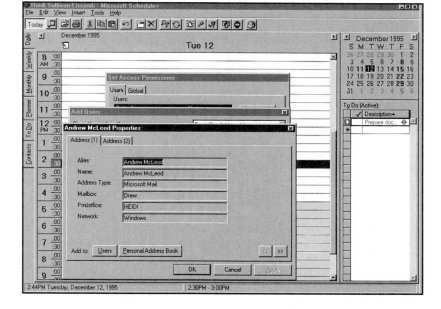

6. If you choose <u>N</u>ew, the New Entry dialog box appears. <u>S</u>elect the entry type; for example, Internet Mail Address, Other Address, or Personal Distribution List. Enter the information in the Address (1) tab. If you are unsure of certain details such as the Postoffice, Mailbox, or Network address for this particular user, ask your system administrator for that information.

7. Select the Address (2) tab. Enter the information and click OK (see fig. 34.11).

Fig. 34.11

Filling in the Address (2) tab in the Properties dialog box is part of setting up the user's account.

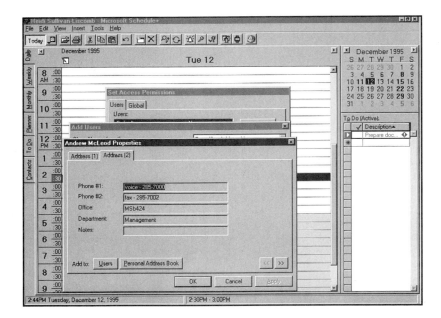

Selecting Permissions

Now that you have set up the accounts for certain users, you can begin selecting permissions for them. Go back to the Users tab shown in figure 34.8 and follow these steps:

1. Select the user's name from the list in the Users dialog box.

2. In the User R<u>o</u>le box, use the down arrow to select the permission (such as Delegate or Custom).

3. Click OK.

In the bottom half of the screen is a User R<u>o</u>le box. Your delegate's name should be listed above that box. Using the drop-down list, scroll until you can select Delegate.

At the bottom of the screen is a box labeled User Receives <u>M</u>eeting Requests Sent to Me. This box is enabled only when you assign someone the role of delegate. You will not receive any of the meeting requests, changes, or cancellations sent to you—your delegate will. This setup does not mean, however, that you don't have access to your schedule. As the owner of the schedule, you can log in at any time and check your schedule. If you decide that you don't want to use a delegate any longer or you want to receive all of your meeting requests, simply change the role of the user, and the Meeting Requests box becomes unchecked.

 Tip

Your delegate does not need to know your password to access your schedule. Schedule+ automatically allows that person access to your schedule.

Whenever your delegate sets up a meeting or responds to a request for a meeting, your schedule automatically updates with the new information.

In the bottom half of the Permissions screen is a series of grayed-out boxes labeled Appointments, Contacts, Events, and Tasks. To assign very specific permissions to certain users for these options, select Custom in the User Role box. You then can edit the permissions for each of these categories for that specific user. You may want to give some users read-only access to your schedule and let other users read and make changes to your schedule.

Giving Customized Permissions

To customize the permissions for specific users, follow these steps:

1. In the Users box of the Users tab, select the name of the user for whom you want to customize permissions. If the name does not appear, choose the Add button and select the name from the list. If the name of the user *still* does not appear, type it in and create a new postoffice address for that user.

2. Click Custom in the User Role box. The Appointments, Contacts, Events, and Tasks bars are enabled.

3. Use the down arrows to the right of each box to select the permissions for the user. See table 34.1 for the definition of each permission.

4. Click OK.

By customizing a user profile, you are assigning a role to your user. You can apply each of these functions to a certain section of your schedule. Some people can only read your schedule; others can make changes to it. Customizing the roles of your users overrides the defaults in Schedule+.

Table 34.1   Permissions List

Permission	Description
Read	Gives users read-only access to items, except items marked Private.
Create	Gives users permission to read and create items except items marked Private.
Modify	Gives users permission to read and modify existing items, except items marked Private.
Delegate	Gives users permission to read and modify existing items, including items marked Private.
Delegate Owner	Gives users permission to read and modify existing items, including items marked Private. Enables users to access permissions and send and accept meeting requests on owner's behalf.
Custom	Gives users specific kinds of access to specific items.
Owner	Gives users permission to read and modify all items in the schedule including items marked Private. Enables users to set permissions for other users.
None	Gives users no permissions.

 Tip

You can change users' roles at any time. Choose Tools, Set Access Permissions, select the user's name, and change the role in the User Role box.

For example, suppose that you want some of your users to be able to view your appointment schedule. You must give them permission to Read in the Appointments box. If you want to let some users make changes to your To Do lists, give them permission to Modify in the Tasks box.

 Note

No one can access items marked private unless they are *owners* or *delegate owners*.

Setting Global Permissions

Setting global permissions provides you with a way to ensure that you don't ever have overlapping or recurring appointments. Using this feature is a great way to avoid conflicts—especially if you are not directly overseeing your own schedule. To set global permissions, follow these steps:

1. Choose Tools, Set Access Permissions. Click the Global tab (see fig. 34.12).
2. Select Disallow Overlapping Appointments.
3. Select Disallow Recurring Appointments.
4. Click OK.

Fig. 34.12

Use the Global tab to disallow overlapping appointments.

Any time someone on your network tries to make an appointment with you, and you already have something scheduled, Schedule+ alerts the user that you are unavailable and does not make an appointment for that time. Also, by checking Disallow Recurring Appointments, you prevent the same appointment from being scheduled more than once.

Making Appointments Private

You may have information that you need or want to keep private. Schedule+ enables you to determine which items should be unreadable to anyone but you and your delegate. To make something in your schedule private, follow these steps:

1. Choose Insert, Appointment, then click the General tab.
2. Set up the time and date for your appointment.
3. Check the box next to the key marked Private. Now only you can see your appointment, and a key appears next to that appointment in the calendar (see fig. 34.13).

Fig. 34.13

Using the Private function prevents users from seeing an item in your schedule.

Private key

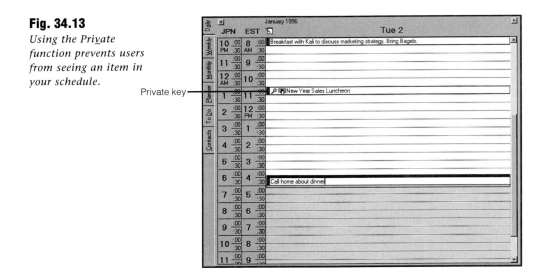

> α **Note**
>
> Remember that users with owner or delegate owner permissions can read your private information.

Another way to mark a meeting private is to select the appointment in your daily calendar and click the key on the toolbar. This method works for privatizing your tasks and events as well as any appointments you have. To make the appointment information available to other users on your network, uncheck the box next to the key in the Appointment dialog box or click the key on the toolbar.

Inviting People to a Meeting

No doubt you turned to this chapter to learn how to schedule a meeting with someone on the same network. Instead of spending time trying to figure out who is doing what, where, and at what time, you can access the schedules of anyone on your network. You can invite other users to a meeting, cancel or reschedule an appointment, and even let someone else handle all these details for you.

Using the Invite Button

You use the Invite button in Schedule+ to set up meetings. After you have decided on a date and time for the meeting (using Schedule+ to verify your own availability), you can check the availability of others then send them an electronic message about the meeting.

You can access the Invite button from anywhere in Schedule+. Each tab in the Appointment Book (Planner, Weekly, Monthly, Daily, To Do, and Contacts) has access to an invitation. Follow these steps to access the Invite button:

1. Choose Insert, Appointment.

2. The Appointment dialog box appears with the default General tab open.

3. Fill in the logistical information regarding your meeting (see fig. 34.14).

Fig. 34.14

Use the Appointment dialog box to fill in the basic details of your meeting.

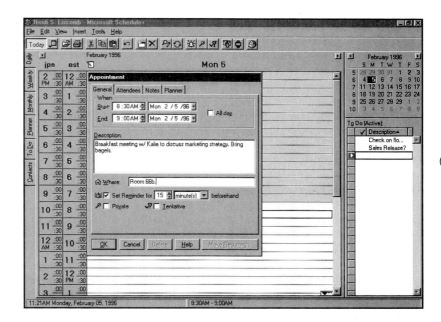

4. Open the Attendees tab by clicking it. Figure 34.15 shows the Attendees tab.

Fig. 34.15

The Attendees tab of the Appointment dialog box lists users on your network.

5. Choose Invite Others to open the Meeting Attendees dialog box. A list of the users on your network and their addresses is available in this screen.

6. Select the Personal Address Book or the Postoffice Address List by clicking the down arrow in the upper-right corner of the screen. This arrow controls the Show Names From The List box.

7. Enter the names of the people you want to invite to this meeting by typing them in the Type Name or Select from List list box.

8. Be sure to identify whose attendance is required, whose attendance is optional, and which resources are required for the meeting. Select the user's name and click the appropriate box to the right.

 Note

If you need to add people or resources to your address book, choose New to open the New Entry dialog box.

---

9. Click OK to return to the Appointment dialog box.

10. Click OK. The Meeting Request dialog box opens (see fig. 34.16).

Fig. 34.16

Exchange uses the information in the Meeting Request dialog box as an e-mail to invite others to your meeting.

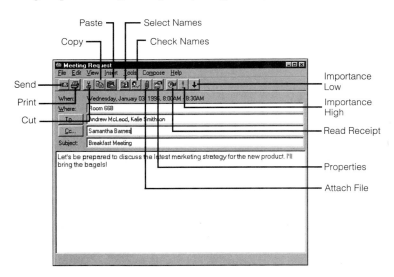

In figure 34.16, note the toolbar that appears at the top of the Meeting Request window. Table 34.2 defines each toolbar function.

Table 34.2   The Meeting Request Toolbar Functions

Button	Description
Send	Sends message to all users addressed.
Print	Prints the message.
Copy	Copies the selection to the Clipboard.
Cut	Cuts the selection and puts it on the Clipboard.
Paste	Inserts the contents of the Clipboard at the insertion point.
Select Names	Selects recipient names.
Check Names	Checks the recipient names.
Attach File	Attaches a file to this message.
Properties	Changes or displays properties of item.
Read Receipt	Set or clear the Read Receipt function.
Importance High	Message is of high importance.
Importance Low	Message is of low importance.

34

The Meeting Request screen looks like a note card. All your meeting information appears on the card, which is addressed to the people you want to invite to the meeting. Those attendees whose attendance is optional receive a Cc of the message. In the body of the message, fill in any additional information you want the attendees to have. Send the message by clicking the envelope button at the top left, or choose File, Send.

Using the New Appointment Button

Another way to invite people to a meeting is to click the Insert New Appointment button on the toolbar of the Appointment Book (see fig. 34.17).

Fig. 34.17

Click the Insert New Appointment button to open the Appointment dialog box.

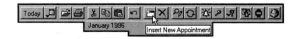

You also can set up a meeting by clicking the desired time slot on your calendar and right-clicking your mouse. Select New Appointment from the drop-down list to fill in the Appointment dialog box, as described in the preceding section.

Acting as a Delegate

When someone assigns you the permissions of a delegate and your position requires that you be responsible for the schedule of another, Schedule+ offers you an easy way to manage all that information. As a delegate, you are allowed to schedule a meeting for another user or resource as well as modify the schedule of another user.

Follow these steps to schedule a meeting for another user:

1. Open the schedule of another user by choosing File, Open.
2. Select Other's Appointment Book.
3. Select the name of the user.
4. Click OK. The schedule appears.
5. Add the appointment using the Appointment dialog box as described in the preceding sections. Click OK.

As a delegate, you always have the updated schedule of the owner, and so does the owner. Any time you send messages, meeting requests, changes or cancellations, Schedule+ identifies you as the sender.

Another way to schedule a meeting for a user is to open that person's schedule and select the Meeting Wizard button from the toolbar or the Planner. You learn how to use the Meeting Wizard a bit later.

Meetings rarely happen without the need for a piece of equipment or an outside office or conference room. To sign out a room or piece of equipment, you must first assign the item an account. Refer to the earlier section, "Using the Options Dialog Box," for those steps.

If you need to sign out a resource for a meeting, follow these steps:

1. Choose File, Open, Other's Appointment Book.
2. Select the name of the resource.
3. Click OK. The schedule appears.
4. Add the appointment using the Appointment dialog box as previously described. Click OK.

You can reply to a meeting request for a resource by selecting Accept, Decline, or Tentative when you receive the meeting request. Accept and Tentative automatically enter the appointment in the resource schedule. After you have confirmed the availability of the schedule owner, click Accept to make the appointment firm.

Using the Meeting Wizard

The Meeting Wizard makes scheduling a meeting very easy. If you don't have the time or inclination to memorize the steps for scheduling a meeting, choose <u>T</u>ools, <u>M</u>ake Meeting, or click the Wizard button (see fig. 34.18).

Fig. 34.18

Using the Meeting Wizard button, open the Meeting Wizard and respond to the questions to schedule your meeting.

After you open the Meeting Wizard, you see a series of screens with check boxes and questions. The Wizard asks you for the basic information regarding your meeting: when, where, what time, and who must attend. After you have entered all the pertinent information, the Wizard opens the standard Meeting Request dialog box. You learned about the Meeting Request function earlier in the section "Using the Invite Button." Follow those steps to send your message to all the meeting attendees.

34

Scheduling a Meeting Using the Planner Tab

The <u>P</u>lanner tab provides you with an area to view your schedule and the schedules of your colleagues. You can see the schedules over a period of days, which gives you more freedom in scheduling meetings for a group of people. To schedule a meeting using the <u>P</u>lanner tab, follow these steps:

1. In the main Schedule+ screen, click the <u>P</u>lanner tab.

   An attendee list appears to the right of the calendar. Users who have their busy times displayed have checks next to their names. Users whose schedules are not available have question marks next to their names. Figure 34.19 shows the Appointment Book open to the Planner tab.

Fig. 34.19

You can check other users' schedules by using the Planner tab of the Appointment Book.

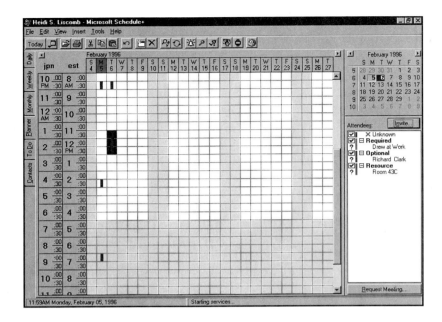

2. Choose <u>I</u>nvite. The Select Attendees dialog box appears.

3. Select the names of the people you want to receive notification of this meeting. Click whether that individual's presence is required or optional.

4. Select a resource if necessary.

5. Click OK.

6. Choose <u>R</u>equest Meeting to open the Meeting Request dialog box. Enter any information you want the recipients to have, and click the Send button to send the meeting invitation.

Rescheduling and Canceling Meetings

You may find that you reschedule and cancel your appointments more often than you actually attend them! Schedule+ allows for this occurrence by offering you a couple different ways to reschedule or cancel your meeting.

Rescheduling a Meeting

If you need to reschedule a meeting, follow these steps:

1. Select the meeting that you want to reschedule by clicking it. Choose <u>T</u>ools, <u>R</u>eschedule Meeting to open the Appointment dialog box.

2. Click the General tab and change the date or time.

3. Click OK.

4. Your Appointment Book is updated, and Schedule+ asks if you want to notify the other attendees of the change. Click Yes.

5. The Meeting Request dialog box appears, addressed to the attendees with a note indicating the cancellation. Click Send.

If you have selected a time that's good for you or the owner of the schedule, and Schedule+ detects that one or more attendees is not available, you can use the Auto Pick function. Instead of trying to find a free time for everyone, let Schedule+ handle it. To reschedule a meeting, choose Tools, Auto Pick. The next available time slot for all attendees is selected in your Planner.

Canceling a Meeting

If you need to cancel a meeting, follow these steps:

1. Select the meeting in your Planner or Appointment Book.

2. Choose the Delete button on the toolbar or choose Edit, Delete Item.

3. Your schedule is updated, and Schedule+ asks if you want to notify the other attendees of the cancellation. Click Yes.

4. The Meeting Request dialog box appears, addressed to the attendees with a note indicating the cancellation. Click Send.

Establishing a Contacts List

Schedule+ provides you with a section to keep the names, telephone numbers, and pertinent personal information of your business and personal contacts. Think of this feature as a giant electronic rolodex. The format is even designed to look like a business card.

You can open your electronic Rolodex of contacts by clicking the Contacts tab in the Schedule+ main screen. The screen changes to look like a business card with tabs for business, phone, address, personal, and other information about that person (see fig. 34.20). In the Contacts list, you can use the Go To function to automatically go to a contact's name.

Fig. 34.20

The Contacts list is similar to a Rolodex of contacts.

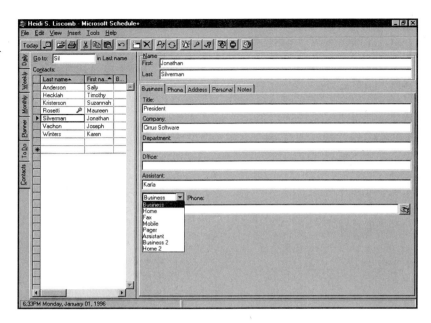

You can enter the contact's name and business information using the Contacts tab, or you can choose Insert, Contact to open the Contact dialog box (see fig. 34.21). The information you enter becomes a permanent part of your contact's file.

Fig. 34.21

You can insert contacts using the Contact dialog box.

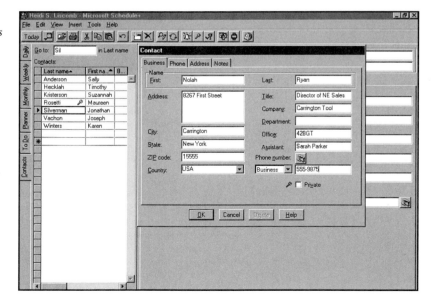

The Appointment dialog box contains a series of tabs that enable you to enter information regarding the appointment you are trying to schedule. Click each tab to open it. The General tab holds the basic information such as date, time, location, and a description of the appointment's purpose. The Attendees tab is where you enter the names of the people to invite to this appointment.

Making Your Contact List Available to Other Users

From time to time, you may want to make your business contacts file available to other users on your network. If you are working on a lengthy task or project with a group of people, convenience may dictate that they have access to business or personal information.

To make your Contacts list available to another user, follow these steps:

1. Choose Tools, Set Access Permissions.
2. Click the Users tab. Select the name of the network user you want to have access to your Contacts list.
3. In the User Role drop-down box, click Custom.
4. In the Contacts drop-down box, select the access that you want the user to have to your Contacts list. Do you want the user to be able to modify your list or just read it?
5. Click OK.

The user can now view your Contacts list and, depending on the permissions that you gave them, make changes to it.

Scheduling Recurring Appointments

Recurring appointments are often the result of tasks and projects that take place over a period of months. In Schedule+, you can schedule an appointment and make sure that it appears every day (or week, or month) at that time for the specified duration. This technique may be helpful in securing specific resources such as equipment or rooms for that meeting.

Using the Make Recurring Button

To make your appointment recurring, follow these steps:

1. On the Appointment Book toolbar, click the Insert New Appointment button.

2. Enter the information regarding the meeting, including a description of the meeting and its location.

3. Choose Make Recurring.

4. Click the When tab and specify the date, time, and duration for the recurring meeting to appear in the schedules of the required attendees. Figure 34.22 shows the When tab as it appears.

5. Click OK.

Fig. 34.22

*Use the When tab
in the Appointment
Series dialog box to
set meeting times
and dates.*

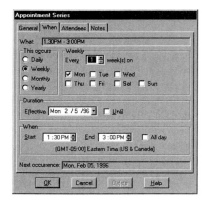

The appointment now appears throughout your calendar.

 Tip

Don't forget to set reminders. Recurring appointments are often forgotten.

Making an Existing Appointment Recurring

If you have an appointment in your schedule that you know is going to become a recurring one, follow these steps:

1. Select the meeting or appointment by clicking it in your Appointment Book.

2. Click the Recurring button on the toolbar (see fig. 34.23).

Fig. 34.23
Select an existing appointment and click the Recurring button to make the appointment recurring.

Recurring button

3. Enter the date, time, and duration information in the When tab. This information appears in the schedules of all the required attendees.

4. Click OK.

 Tip

You can make an existing appointment recurring by right-clicking it and selecting the Make Recurring option from the list.

34

Reviewing Free and Busy Times

When you are trying to set up a meeting, you can avoid frustration by utilizing the Free/Busy times function of Schedule+ and Exchange. You can use this feature if you are part of a network of Schedule+ and Exchange users and have given each other permission to at least view one another's schedules.

Using the Planner to See Who's Busy

If you are in the process of scheduling a meeting and you need to know who is available and who isn't, follow these steps:

1. In the Appointment Book, click the Planner tab.

2. Click a busy time slot in the calendar. A list of users appears to the right.

 Tip

If you click and hold a busy time slot, a window with the date and time of that slot appears.

3. Each user is identified as a required or optional attendee, and resources are designated as such.

4. If you have been given permission, you can click the user's name to see the times, location, and first line of the description of that user's appointment.

 Tip

The busy time slots in the calendar appear as blue bars.

Viewing Another User's Schedule

You can view a user's busy times by double-clicking that user's name in the Attendees box at the far right of the Planner dialog box. The calendar appears with black borders to indicate busy times for that user.

 Tip

An x appears next to the user's name in the Attendees box if that user is busy at the time you have selected. A question mark appears when that user's schedule is not available for viewing.

Viewing the Schedules for a Group of Users

When you need to display the schedules for a group of users, follow these steps:

1. Inside the Planner tab, double-click the Required, Optional, or Resource headings in the Attendees box.

2. The schedules for all selected users appear in the calendar, with black borders indicating busy times.

3. Exit this window by clicking anywhere in the Attendees box.

 Note

Remember, you must have permission from the user to view his or her schedule.

Summary

In this chapter, we have discussed the various methods by which you can manage your schedule using Schedule+ in conjunction with Microsoft's mail program, Exchange. Using the two programs allows you to free up the time that might have previously been consumed attempting to reschedule meetings and appointments.

Each section of this chapter reviews the functionality of Schedule+ and prompts you to think about the possibilities that exist when you use it together with Exchange. The idea that you can check on the schedules of your coworkers all over the globe is a progressive one that you will find irreplaceable once you begin using it regularly. Imagine, you can now schedule a meeting with someone from your Japan, Australia, California, or Maine office without the telephone tag of the past.

The different pieces of Schedule+ and how they operate when you are attached to a network were covered here and if you carefully review this section and Chapters 21 and 24, you will have no problem using Schedule+ to schedule your meetings and appointments over the network.

34

What's on the CD?

by Lisa A. Bucki

This book has provided an in-depth look at techniques you can use to maximize Microsoft Office operating efficiency. To help even further, the CD that comes with this book offers shareware and freeware programs and other add-ons, in addition to data files and source code for the examples shown in this book. This appendix explains how to install the free software available on the CD and provides a brief description of the products included on the CD.

Installing the Software

The CD provides a convenient Installer program that you can use to install the various software programs on the disc as you need them. The Installer launches automatically the first time you insert the CD in your disk drive. The following sections describe how to run the Installer the first time you use it, and for subsequent installs.

> **CAUTION**
> The first time you run the Installer from the CD, it may copy some new and updated system files to your hard disk. If it does, the Installer then asks you to restart your system. Therefore, you should always save your work and close open applications before inserting the CD to ensure that you don't lose any in-progress work.

Installing the First Time

The steps detailed here walk you through the process of using the book CD for the first time. The CD takes advantage of Windows 95 autorun capabilities, meaning that it launches automatically when you insert it in the drive. Thus, be sure to save any work you have
in progress, close any open applications, and then use the following steps:

1. Insert the CD in your CD-ROM drive. The Installer launches automatically, if you haven't installed the CD previously.

2. At the Welcome! dialog box, click OK to continue. (Or click Cancel if you don't want to copy the system files and possibly reboot your system.)

3. The Installer informs you as it's copying files to your system. When it finishes, it may display a message asking whether you want to restart your system. Click OK to do so. (You must click OK to be able to use the Installer to install software from the CD.)

4. If restarting was required by the Installer and if you clicked OK in step 3, the system reboots. If the Installer doesn't restart automatically after rebooting or it doesn't appear automatically after steps 1-3, double-click the icon for the CD drive in the My Computer window. After a brief opening screen, the application installation screen appears. It offers six tabs, which organize the shareware on the disk into six categories:

Office Utilities	VB Custom Controls
Windows 95 Utilities	Miscellaneous
Graphics	Example Files

5. Click a tab to display the software you can install from that category.

6. Scroll through the list that appears on the tab, if needed, to display the name of the software you want to install. Click to select the software to install.

7. (Optional) Click the View Application Information button to take a look at the Readme information included with the application's install files created by the software's author(s). After reading the information, click OK to close the Program Information screen.

8. Click Install Application to tell the installer to install the selected application.

9. Click OK at the Welcome! screen to proceed with the installation. The README information appears on-screen.

10. Click OK to close the Read Me window and continue with the installation.

11. In the Select Destination Directory window that appears, select the appropriate install drive and directory, and then click OK.

12. At the Make Backups? dialog box, click Yes to have the installer create backup copies of any files that may be changed by the program being installed. If you selected Yes at the Make Backups? dialog box, select the backup directory in the dialog box that appears, and then click OK.

13. The application installs. Repeat steps 5-12 to install other applications from the CD.

14. Click Exit to close the Installer window and complete the installation.

Using the Installer Again

After you've used the CD installer the first time, the system files necessary for it to run exist on your system. If, however, you want to use the CD again to install additional applications, there are two methods available:

▶ If the CD isn't already in your CD-ROM drive, insert the CD. The autorun application on the CD will start, and the installer will load, presenting you with the tabs categorizing the software available on the CD. You then can repeat steps 5-14 in the preceding section.

▶ If you've already run the installer and the CD is still in your CD-ROM drive, you can restart the installer by double-clicking its icon in the My Computer window, or by clicking the Start menu, choosing Programs, Que, Microsoft Office Expert Solutions, and choosing Microsoft Office Expert Solutions again.

 TIP
You can uninstall the Office Expert Solutions installer files or run installed shareware from the CD by choosing Start, pointing to Programs, choosing Que, choosing Microsoft Office Expert Solutions, and then choosing the option that you want. Some of the shareware programs also offer uninstall options via this method.

Examples and Source Code from the Book

Throughout this book, you've seen numerous examples to customize Office and build solutions to streamline Office operations. The CD offers the example and source code files used in creating the applications and other solutions discussed in this book. You can install the example and source code files using the Data Files tab in the CD Installer application. Simply click that tab, click to select the chapter for which you want to view the example/source code files, and then click the Install Application button.

Shareware and Add-Ons

The CD that accompanies this book offers a variety of shareware and freeware programs, VB controls, and add-ons that can help you further customize Office and applications. To make it easier to find what you're looking for, the list is broken up into categories that correspond with the category tabs in the CD Installer application.

 NOTE

Most of the applications included on the CD are shareware products. Don't forget to register any products you plan to use regularly. See the Help or README information that accompanies each application for registration information.

Office Utilities

On the Office Utilities tab of the CD Installer, you'll find these choices listed:

▶ **Access ELF**. This shareware places Analyze and Query buttons on the Access Database toolbar. The Analyze button generates a natural language interface for the current database. Clicking the Query button enables you to create plain English queries.

▶ **Formtool**. Formtool offers a palette of special tools for moving, widening, or deepening Access form controls in pixel increments.

▶ **Internet Assistant for Microsoft Word**. This enables you to use Word for Windows to create hypertext markup language (HTML) documents to be published on the World Wide Web. Internet Assistant can convert document files to HTML; it also provides a template for creating new HTML files.

▶ **OfficeCab 1.1**. Somar's OfficeCab provides a substitute for the Find File dialog box in Word, Excel, and PowerPoint. It lists all files by name and title in a folder, and enables you to search and filter by title or file name.

▶ **PowerPoint Backgrounds by Stuart Kippelman**. The BMP images in this collection, which were created by Stuart Kippelman using Corel Photo-Paint 6.0 and Adobe Photoshop 3.0, can be used with any software that supports the BMP format. You need to make sure that these files are copied to the Templates folder used by your Office installation. To use an image as a custom presentation background in PowerPoint, open the Format menu, choose Custom Background, and then choose the desired image.

▶ **Units & Volumes Excel Add-In v1.1**. Load this Excel 5.0 add-in module with the Add-In Manager. The Units & Volumes add-in offers specialized functions for converting measurements. For example, convert a value in a cell from grams to pounds. Units & Volumes provides 17 unit-conversion functions that cover everything from Acceleration to Volumetric Flow (more than 240 common units supported). The six volume functions calculate partial volumes for different tank geometries. Engineers in particular will find this add-in useful.

▶ **Microsoft Word Macro Virus Protection Tool**. The free Macro Virus Protection Tool is designed to detect macro viruses, such as the Concept virus, that infect Word documents. The Tool installs in the NORMAL.DOT template a set of protective macros that detect suspicious Word files and alerts you to the potential risk of opening files with macros. It gives you the option of opening a file without executing any macros the file contains, thereby ensuring that no viruses are transmitted. The Tool also can be used to scan your hard disk for Word files that contain the Concept virus.

Windows 95 Utilities

If you're looking for tools that enable you to work more effectively in Windows 95, consider these items on the Windows 95 Utilities tab of the CD Installer:

▶ **CabWiz v2.00**. This freeware can list the compressed contents of a Microsoft installation cabinet file(s) from a folder on any drive. You can save the list—which shows file names, registered file types, size in bytes, and location in the cabinet—to a text file.

▶ **DumpReg v1.0**. DumpReg places the Windows 95 Registry contents in a list box so that you can sort, find, and print entries. You can find keys and values containing a string, as well as filter the list to display only matching entries.

▶ **Hex Workshop v2.10**. Eliminate some of the pain of editing files and disks in hex with this program. Insert, delete, cut, copy, and paste hex. With Hex Workshop, you can go to, find, and replace hex characters, compare files, and perform checksum calculations. This latest version offers a Base Converter (convert between hex, decimal, and binary) and a Hex Calculator.

▶ **MultiVu v2.0**. MultiVu enables you to scan a disk's text files or scan for text within files. With MultiVu, you can browse the contents of compressed files in the ZIP, ARJ, and LZH formats. This utility can handle files up to 2GB in size. MultiVu enables you to open multiple files at once and create bookmarks in any open file, and supports drag and drop. MultiVu also offers some convenience features. For example, files *preload* for smooth scrolling, and MultiVu will load, search, or print in the background while you're browsing or using other programs. This product supports multiple users on a LAN and works with Windows 3.1, Windows 95, and Windows NT.

▶ **Windows Printer Control Utility**. This add-on offers printer control functions you can access via icons or hot keys. With WinPtr, capture all or part of the screen and send the image to the printer, fax, Clipboard, or file. Print a picture or text file. Print the Clipboard contents (whether picture or text) and store those contents in a file. Also gain control to trigger a page ejection, clear or view the Clipboard, change the default printer, identify the fax driver, and access the Windows printer setup dialog box or the Control Panel printer applet. To inform and entertain you, a pelican icon (pel-icon) shows the default printer orientation (P=portrait, L=landscape) on its body and the current default printer's name in its title.

▶ **WinZip 95**. Zip and unzip compressed ZIP archive files on the Windows 95 Desktop with the latest version of this well-known utility. WinZip enables you to handle several common Internet file formats (TAR, gzip, and UNIX compress) in addition to ZIP files. It supports Windows 95 long file names and more. WinZip 95's point-and-click, drag-and-drop interface provides for painless viewing, running, extracting, adding, deleting, and testing files in archives. It interfaces with other programs to handle ARJ, LZH, and ARC files, and interfaces to most virus scanners.

Graphics

If you work extensively with graphics files in Windows 95, the following applications listed on the Graphics tab of the CD Installer could save you time:

▶ **PolyView Version 2.21 by Polybytes**. Use this shareware to view, convert, and print BMP, GIF, JPEG, Kodak Photo CD, PNG, and TIFF graphics files.

▶ **SnapShot/32**. SnapShot/32 enables you to capture your screen display under Windows 95 and NT. SnapShot/32 allows you to save captured screen images in the BMP, GIF, and JPEG formats (even progressive JPEGs for use on the World Wide Web). You can set up hot keys to automatically capture parts of the screen. SnapShot/32 can automatically save files and increment file names, and offers other features including easy printing and drag-and-drop file opening.

Visual Basic Custom Controls

Shared resources and examples can make any programmer more effective and efficient. The VB Custom Controls tab of the CD Installer offers these resources for programmers developing for Windows 95 and Office:

 Note

Some of the VB control installers enable you to choose between VBX, OCX-16, and OCX-32 formats.

▶ **Alarm Custom Control**. The ALARM1.VBX Visual Basic custom control lets you set multiple alarms (events) at the time(s) you specify or at specified intervals. This control can be useful when you're writing a PIM and enables you to schedule events to happen at various times. ALARM1.VBX can tell you when the date has changed or can be used to remove all current alarms and set new ones. ALARM1.VBX is compatible with VB 2.0 and above.

▶ **Bar Code Custom Control**. BarCod enables you to create an application that generates and prints bar codes in the Code 3 of 9, Code 2 of 5, UPC, Codabar, Code 93 formats, and others. After placing and sizing the bar code on your form, set the Caption property to control the displayed bars. You can control the bar and background colors, printing, and more using other properties, and even bind to a data control under VB 3.0 and VB 4.0. Use BarCod to develop highly automated inventory applications, identification systems, and any other programs that require printed computer-readable data.

▶ **BmpLst Custom Control**. This Visual Basic custom control lets you create a list box displaying bitmap pictures. The bitmaps can be placed above, below, to the right, or to the left of the list text.

▶ **DDD FX '95 Professional Toolkit**. DDD FX '95 Professional Toolkit allows you to add special design effects to your Visual Basic applications via easy-to-use BAS modules holding VBA source code, which means no VBX, OCX, or external DLL files are required. Improve your application's look by adding faded forms with gradient colors; 3D appearance on meters, spin buttons, frames, and more; enhanced check boxes and options buttons; and exploding forms.

▶ **DFInfo Custom Control**. This custom control, DBINFO2.VBX, lets your VB applications read and modify file information, including date, time, size, and so on. You can access information about the computer's drives through another set of properties. It's compatible with VB 2.0 and above.

▶ **FM Drop Custom Control**. Use this custom control, FMDROP1.VBX, to display notification when a file has been dragged and dropped from the Windows File Manager.

▸ **Formatted Label Custom Control**. FLABEL1.VBX is a bound label control that lets you format the text within it using different fonts and colors, multiple paragraphs, paragraph formatting, and so on.

▸ **HiTime Custom Control**. The HiTime high-resolution timer custom control for Visual Basic can fire timer events nearly every millisecond, as opposed to every 55 milliseconds (18.2 times per second) with the normal Visual Basic Timer control. Use this control just like the default Timer control that comes with Visual Basic. The rate at which HiTime can trigger timer events depends on the speed of your machine: 500 ticks per second for a 486DX2/66s and 1,000 ticks per second for 66MHz Pentiums.

▸ **JoyStk Custom Control**. The joystick custom control (JOYSTK1.VBX) provides joystick information and events (movement, buttons) for your programs. It supports two joysticks, one four-button joystick (such as the Gravis PC GamePad), or one 3D joystick. JoyStk comes with a required joystick driver for Windows.

▸ **LED Custom Control**. If you need an LED-like display (such as when you need an on/off indicator for items such as modem lights), use the LED custom control. It allows you to define 3D effects and colors.

▸ **MsStat Custom Control**. MSSTAT1.VBX displays a multi-element status bar on the bottom of your form, and it automatically handles the Num Lock, Caps Lock, Scroll Lock, and Insert key indicators. With MsStat, you can include times/dates in International and programmer-defined formats on the status bar. Use the Item properties to define the elements in the control.

▸ **NED 32-bit Image OCX 1.21 Custom Control**. This 32-bit Windows OLE custom control enables display and printing of various types of image files, including those in the TIFF, BMP, DIB, GIF, JPEG, and Kodak Photo CD formats. Use this control with any host programming environment or application that supports 32-bit OCX controls. OLE version 2.02 or higher is required.

▸ **NED 16-bit VUMeter OCX 1.1 Custom Control**. This 16-bit OLE 2.0 OCX control presents a needle gauge control similar to ones on stereo equipment. When you use the VUMeter control in a finished application, the VUMeter Control DLL (VUMeter.OCX) must be installed with the application. There are properties to adjust the behavior and appearance of the control, such as choosing horizontal or vertical orientation, setting the colors for various parts of the control, and adding 3D effects like bevels. Setting low and high limits (with values from 0–32,767) causes an event to be sent to your application when either the high or low occurs.

▸ **NED 16-bit VUGauge OCX 1.1 Custom Control**. Similar to VUMeter, VUGauge is a 16-bit OLE 2.0 OCX control that presents a needle gauge control like one found on the dashboard of a car. When you use VUGauge in an application, VUGAUGE.OCX must be installed on the user's computer. Use VUGauge's properties to specify one of four orientations, set colors, and add 3D borders and the like. Setting low and high limits (with values from 0–32,767) will cause an event to be sent to your application when either limit is reached.

▶ **NED 16-bit Gauge OCX 1.1 Custom Control**. Add a gauge similar to ones on industrial process control equipment using NEDGUAGE.OCX. It's a 16-bit OLE 2.0 custom control. Make sure NEDGUAGE.OCX is installed on the user's system if you use this control in an application. Properties let you specify one of four orientations, set control colors, and add 3D borders and bevels. Low and high limits with values from 0–32,767 can be set.

▶ **NED 16-bit Knob OCX 1.1 Custom Control**. Add a needle gauge control to your application using KNOB.OCX, a 16-bit OLE 2.0 custom control. Properties let you specify one of four orientations, set control colors, and add 3D borders and bevels. Low and high limits with values from 0–32,767 can be set.

▶ **No Boot Custom Control**. Use NOBOOT1.VBX, a free control, along with VRBTD.386 to enable and disable Ctrl+Alt+Delete. (Make sure you copy NOBOOT1.VBX to the user's Windows SYSTEM folder and install VRBTD.386 in the [386Enh] section of SYSTEM.INI.) Use this control when your application needs to ensure that the computer stays running. At run-time, this control's `Enabled` property determines whether or not Ctrl+Alt+Delete works. Set `Enabled` to False to suspend Ctrl+Alt+Delete does not work.

▶ **PicBtn Custom Control**. The PICBTN1.VBX custom control creates a command button that has both text and a picture on it. You control the picture scaling and placement with regard to the text, which may be multi-line.

▶ **Probe Custom Control**. The PROBE1.VBX enables you to examine and modify other controls' properties at run-time. Probe lists the properties of a specified control so that you can adjust the properties available only at run-time using an easy interface. Use Probe as a debugging tool or include it with your project during beta tests. In a final product, Probe can be a useful diagnostic tool.

▶ **RoText Custom Control**. Use RoText to place a label on a form at any angle or degree of rotation. This control can be bound to a data control.

▶ **Tips Custom Control**. Tips enables users to display a Microsoft-style ToolTip by pausing the mouse pointer over a control. No extra code is required; adjust Tips by setting the `Tag` properties.

▶ **Tip of the Day version 2.0**. This Visual Basic "plug-in" form and code module enables you to add a Tip of the Day screen to your application. This module contains 100 percent source code and does not require any VBXs. To use Tip of the Day, just add its files to your project. Also included is TipEdit, which enables you to create and edit the TOD file that adds tips to your application.

▶ **ToolTips 95 Pro version 3.0**. The ToolTips "plug-in" code module for Visual Basic enables you to add yellow pop-up tips to describe toolbar buttons you add into your applications. To display the tip, the user simply needs to move the mouse pointer over the button. This version of ToolTips eliminates the need for any VBX or DLL that adds ToolTips, and is pure VB source code—it takes up less than 7K.

▶ **Ver Custom Control**. VER1.VBX enables your application to use the functionality of VER.DLL through properties. It simplifies getting version information from a file (EXE, DLL, VBX, and so on), and gives you file installation functionality. Included, find a sample installation/setup utility, which is designed to make it easier for you to write your own installation utilities without the Setup Wizard.

▶ **Wave Custom Control**. You can use WAVE1.VBX to have an application play and get information about WAV files. Use the `Filename` property to select the file. For example, with WAVE1.VBX, an application can play a WAV file in the background, play back recorded speech, or add beeps or other sound effects.

Miscellaneous

If nothing you've read about so far fills your needs of the moment, check out these packages on the Miscellaneous tab of the CD Installer application:

▶ **Visual Help Pro 3.1**. Visual Help offers an intuitive drag-and-drop interface for creating online help systems in Windows. In addition to creating help files for applications, you can use Visual Help to present other documents online, such as procedures manuals, company databases, multimedia presentations, information guides, README files, shared network information, electronic books, and online tests.

▶ **Windows HLP to RTF/HPJ Converter**. Use this application to convert Windows HLP files from Windows 3.1x, Windows 95, and Windows NT 3.51 to RTF (Rich Text Format) for use in other documents.

▶ **Wordware 95**. This popular shareware collection of macros and templates for Word for Windows offers toolbars to place dozens of macros for Word enhancements and other cool add-ons right at your fingertips. Wordware provides shortcuts for printing file summary information, deleting files, toggling Word features like AutoCorrect on and off, and more. It offers unique utilities like one that compiles a list of the contents of a floppy disk, as well project and schedule managers, games, and an audio CD player.

Index

A VIACOM SERVICE
The Information SuperLibrary™

Bookstore	**Search**	**What's New**	**Reference Desk**	**Software Library**	**Newsletter**	**Company Overviews**
Yellow Pages	**Internet Starter Kit**	**HTML Workshop**	**Win a Free T-Shirt!**	**Macmillan Computer Publishing**	**Site Map**	**Talk to Us**

CHECK OUT THE BOOKS IN THIS LIBRARY.

You'll find thousands of shareware files and over 1600 computer books designed for both technowizards and technophobes. You can browse through 700 sample chapters, get the latest news on the Net, and find just about anything using our massive search directories.

All Macmillan Computer Publishing books are available at your local bookstore.

We're open 24-hours a day, 365 days a year.

You don't need a card.

We don't charge fines.

And you can be as **LOUD** as you want.

The Information SuperLibrary
http://www.mcp.com/mcp/   ftp.mcp.com

Complete and Return this Card
for a *FREE* Computer Book Catalog

Thank you for purchasing this book! You have purchased a superior computer book written expressly for your needs. To continue to provide the kind of up-to-date, pertinent coverage you've come to expect from us, we need to hear from you. Please take a minute to complete and return this self-addressed, postage-paid form. In return, we'll send you a free catalog of all our computer books on topics ranging from word processing to programming and the internet.

Mr. ☐ Mrs. ☐ Ms. ☐ Dr. ☐

Name (first) ⬚⬚⬚⬚⬚⬚⬚⬚⬚⬚⬚⬚⬚⬚ (M.I.) ☐ (last) ⬚⬚⬚⬚⬚⬚⬚⬚⬚⬚⬚⬚⬚⬚⬚⬚⬚

Address ⬚⬚⬚⬚⬚⬚⬚⬚⬚⬚⬚⬚⬚⬚⬚⬚⬚⬚⬚⬚⬚⬚⬚⬚⬚⬚⬚⬚⬚⬚⬚⬚

City ⬚⬚⬚⬚⬚⬚⬚⬚⬚⬚⬚⬚⬚ State ⬚⬚ Zip ⬚⬚⬚⬚⬚ ⬚⬚⬚⬚

Phone ⬚⬚⬚ ⬚⬚⬚ ⬚⬚⬚⬚ Fax ⬚⬚⬚ ⬚⬚⬚ ⬚⬚⬚⬚

Company Name ⬚⬚⬚⬚⬚⬚⬚⬚⬚⬚⬚⬚⬚⬚⬚⬚⬚⬚⬚⬚⬚⬚⬚⬚⬚

E-mail address ⬚⬚⬚⬚⬚⬚⬚⬚⬚⬚⬚⬚⬚⬚⬚⬚⬚⬚⬚⬚⬚⬚⬚⬚⬚

1. Please check at least (3) influencing factors for purchasing this book.

Front or back cover information on book .... ☐
Special approach to the content .... ☐
Completeness of content .... ☐
Author's reputation .... ☐
Publisher's reputation .... ☐
Book cover design or layout .... ☐
Index or table of contents of book .... ☐
Price of book .... ☐
Special effects, graphics, illustrations .... ☐
Other (Please specify): _____ ☐

2. How did you first learn about this book?

Saw in Macmillan Computer Publishing catalog .... ☐
Recommended by store personnel .... ☐
Saw the book on bookshelf at store .... ☐
Recommended by a friend .... ☐
Received advertisement in the mail .... ☐
Saw an advertisement in: _____ ☐
Read book review in: _____ ☐
Other (Please specify): _____ ☐

3. How many computer books have you purchased in the last six months?

This book only .... ☐   3 to 5 books .... ☐
2 books .... ☐   More than 5 .... ☐

4. Where did you purchase this book?

Bookstore .... ☐
Computer Store .... ☐
Consumer Electronics Store .... ☐
Department Store .... ☐
Office Club .... ☐
Warehouse Club .... ☐
Mail Order .... ☐
Direct from Publisher .... ☐
Internet site .... ☐
Other (Please specify): _____ ☐

5. How long have you been using a computer?

☐ Less than 6 months   ☐ 6 months to a year
☐ 1 to 3 years   ☐ More than 3 years

6. What is your level of experience with personal computers and with the subject of this book?

	With PCs	With subject of book
New	☐	☐
Casual	☐	☐
Accomplished	☐	☐
Expert	☐	☐

Source Code ISBN: 0-7897-0391-2

7. Which of the following best describes your job title?

Administrative Assistant .... ☐
Coordinator .... ☐
Manager/Supervisor .... ☐
Director .... ☐
Vice President .... ☐
President/CEO/COO .... ☐
Lawyer/Doctor/Medical Professional .... ☐
Teacher/Educator/Trainer .... ☐
Engineer/Technician .... ☐
Consultant .... ☐
Not employed/Student/Retired .... ☐
Other (Please specify): _____ ☐

8. Which of the following best describes the area of the company your job title falls under?

Accounting .... ☐
Engineering .... ☐
Manufacturing .... ☐
Operations .... ☐
Marketing .... ☐
Sales .... ☐
Other (Please specify): _____ ☐

9. What is your age?

Under 20 .... ☐
21-29 .... ☐
30-39 .... ☐
40-49 .... ☐
50-59 .... ☐
60-over .... ☐

10. Are you:

Male .... ☐
Female .... ☐

11. Which computer publications do you read regularly? (Please list)

_____
_____
_____
_____
_____
_____
_____
_____
_____

Comments: _____
_____
_____

Fold here and scotch-tape to mail.

Microsoft Office Expert Solutions CD-ROM

In addition to all the source code and examples from the book, the *Microsoft Office Expert Solutions* CD-ROM contains a number of Que's recommended shareware and freeware programs, utilities, and add-ons to help you further customize your Office applications:

- ▶ **Office utilities** that enhance the power and performance of your applications
- ▶ **Windows 95 utilities** for optimizing the operating system
- ▶ **Graphics tools** that put expanded graphics capabilities at your fingertips
- ▶ **VB custom controls** that simplify procedures and provide preprogrammed, drop-in Visual Basic Objects
- ▶ **Additional shareware packages** that further enhance your Office application environment

See Appendix A, "What's on the CD," for a complete listing and description of the CD-ROM contents. For installation instructions, see "Installing the Software," also in Appendix A.

Licensing Agreement